AUTIS

RECOGNITION, REFERRAL, DIAGNOSIS AND MANAGEMENT OF ADULTS ON THE AUTISM SPECTRUM

National Clinical Guideline Number 142

National Collaborating Centre for Mental Health
commissioned by the

National Institute for Health & Clinical Excellence

published by
The British Psychological Society and The Royal College of Psychiatrists

British Library Cataloguing-in-Publication Data

A catalogue record for this book is available from
the British Library.

ISBN-: 978-1-908020-51-2

Printed in Great Britain by Stanley L. Hunt (Printers) Ltd.

Additional material: data CD-Rom created by Pix18
(www.pix18.co.uk)

developed by   National Collaborating Centre for Mental Health
                                  The Royal College of Psychiatrists
                                         4th Floor, Standon House
                                                21 Mansell Street
                                                         London
                                                         E1 8AA
                                               www.nccmh.org.uk

commissioned by   National Institute for Health and Clinical Excellence
                                              Level 1, City Tower
                                                Piccadilly Plaza
                                                     Manchester
                                                        M1 4BT
                                                www.nice.org.uk

published by   The British Psychological Society
                                             St Andrews House
                                       48 Princess Road East
                                                     Leicester
                                                      LE1 7DR
                                              www.bps.org.uk

                                                            and

                                   The Royal College of Psychiatrists
                                              17 Belgrave Square
                                                         London
                                                    SW1X 8PG
                                           www.rcpsych.ac.uk

The British
Psychological Society
Promoting excellence in psychology

RC
PSYCH
ROYAL COLLEGE OF
PSYCHIATRISTS

CONTENTS

Contents

GUIDELINE DEVELOPMENT GROUP MEMBERS

Professor Simon Baron-Cohen (Chair, Guideline Development Group)
Director, Autism Research Centre, Psychiatry Department, University of Cambridge
Theme Lead, National Institute for Health Research (NIHR) Collaboration for
Leadership in Applied Health Research and Care (CLAHRC) for Cambridgeshire and
Peterborough NHS Foundation Trust

Professor Stephen Pilling (Facilitator, Guideline Development Group)
Director, National Collaborating Centre for Mental Health (NCCMH)
Director, Centre for Outcomes Research and Effectiveness, University College
London

Professor Gillian Baird
Consultant Paediatrician and Professor of Paediatric Neurodisability, Guy's and
St Thomas' NHS Foundation Trust and King's Health Partners

Dr Carole Buckley
General Practitioner, The Old School Surgery, Bristol

Dr Peter Carpenter
Consultant Psychiatrist (Learning Disabilities), Associate Medical Lead, Learning
Disabilities and Specialist Adult Services, Avon and Wiltshire Partnership NHS Trust

Mr Nadir Cheema
Health Economist, NCCMH

Dr Juli Crocombe
Consultant Psychiatrist, St George's Hospital, Stafford

Ms Jackie Dziewanowska
Autism Spectrum Disorder Nurse Consultant, Nottinghamshire Healthcare
NHS Trust
Clinical Lead, Nottingham City Asperger Service

Ms Annie Foster-Jones
Autism Specialist Nurse, Cheshire and Wirral Partnership NHS Foundation Trust,
Learning Disabilities Clinical Service Unit

Ms Naomi Glover
Research Assistant, NCCMH (until August 2011)

Dr Marga Hogenboom
General Practitioner, Camphill Medical Practice Bieldside, Scotland

Professor Patricia Howlin
Professor of Clinical Child Psychology, King's College London
Consultant Clinical Psychologist

Ms Flora Kaminski
Research Assistant, NCCMH (until August 2011)

Ms Rachael Lee
Research Assistant, NCCMH (from September 2011)

Ms Katherine Leggett
Project Manager, NCCMH

Mr Campbell Main
Lay member (representing service user and carer concerns)

Dr Ifigeneia Mavranezouli
Senior Health Economist, NCCMH

Ms Melissa McAuliffe
Asperger Specialist, Social Care, Rehabilitation and Recovery Team, East London
NHS Foundation Trust

Dr Odette Megnin-Viggars
Systematic Reviewer, NCCMH (from March 2011)

Mr Richard Mills
Director of Research, The National Autistic Society (NAS)
Honorary Secretary and Research Director, Research Autism, London

Ms Joan Panton
Lay member (representing service user and carer concerns)

Ms Maggi Rigg
Advisory Board Member, Cambian Group, London
Head, Southlands School (until 2011)

Ms Sarah Stockton
Senior Information Scientist, NCCMH

Dr Clare Taylor
Senior Editor, NCCMH

Guideline development group members

Dr Amina Udechuku
Systematic Reviewer, NCCMH (March 2010 to June 2011)

Ms Anya Ustaszewski
Autism and Disability Awareness Trainer and Rights Advocate
Musician and composer (freelance)
Representing service user and carer concerns

ACKNOWLEDGEMENTS

Editorial assistance

Ms Nuala Ernest, Assistant Editor, NCCMH

1   PREFACE

This guideline has been developed to advise on interventions and support for adults with autism (aged 18 years or older). The National Institute for Health and Clinical Excellence (NICE) has also developed a guideline for the recognition, referral and diagnosis of children and young people with autism (NICE, 2011a) and is currently developing a guideline for the management and support of children and young people with autism, which will address the issues relating to transition between child and adult services.

The guideline recommendations have been developed by a multidisciplinary team of healthcare professionals, people with autism, their carers and guideline methodologists after careful consideration of the best available evidence. It is intended that the guideline will be useful to professionals and service commissioners in providing and planning high-quality care for people with autism while also emphasising the importance of the experience of care for people with autism and their families, partners and carers (see Appendix 1 for more details on the scope of the guideline).

Although the evidence base is rapidly expanding, there are a number of major gaps, and future revisions of this guideline will incorporate new scientific evidence as it develops. The guideline makes a number of research recommendations specifically to address gaps in the evidence base (see Appendix 13). In the meantime, it is hoped that the guideline will assist healthcare professionals, people with autism and their families, partners and carers by identifying the merits of particular support and intervention approaches where the evidence from research and clinical experience exists.

1.1   NATIONAL CLINICAL GUIDELINES

1.1.1   What are clinical guidelines?

Clinical guidelines are 'systematically developed statements that assist clinicians and service users in making decisions about appropriate treatment for specific conditions' (Mann, 1996). They are derived from the best available research evidence, using predetermined and systematic methods to identify and evaluate the evidence relating to the specific condition in question. Where evidence is lacking, the guidelines incorporate statements and recommendations based upon the consensus statements developed by the Guideline Development Group (GDG).

Clinical guidelines are intended to improve the process and outcomes of healthcare in a number of different ways. They can:
● provide up-to-date evidence-based recommendations for the management of conditions and disorders by healthcare professionals

- be used as the basis to set standards to assess the practice of healthcare professionals
- form the basis for education and training of healthcare professionals
- assist service users and their carers in making informed decisions about their treatment and care
- improve communication between healthcare professionals, service users and their carers
- help identify priority areas for further research.

1.1.2 Uses and limitation of clinical guidelines

Guidelines are not a substitute for professional knowledge and clinical judgement. They can be limited in their usefulness and applicability by a number of different factors: the availability of high-quality research evidence, the quality of the methodology used in the development of the guideline, the generalisability of research findings and the uniqueness of individuals.

Although the quality of research in this field is variable, the methodology used here reflects current international understanding on the appropriate practice for guideline development (Appraisal of Guidelines for Research and Evaluation Instrument [AGREE]; www.agreetrust.org; AGREE Collaboration, 2003), ensuring the collection and selection of the best research evidence available and the systematic generation of recommendations applicable to the majority of people with autism. However, there will always be some people and situations for which clinical guideline recommendations are not readily applicable. This guideline does not, therefore, override the individual responsibility of healthcare professionals to make appropriate decisions in the circumstances of the individual, in consultation with the person with autism or their family, partner or carer.

In addition to the clinical evidence, cost-effectiveness information, where available, is taken into account in the generation of statements and recommendations of the clinical guidelines. While national guidelines are concerned with clinical and cost effectiveness, issues of affordability and implementation costs are independent of national guidelines, to be determined by the National Health Service (NHS).

In using guidelines, it is important to remember that the absence of empirical evidence for the effectiveness of a particular intervention is not the same as evidence for ineffectiveness. In addition, and of particular relevance in mental health, evidence-based treatments are often delivered within the context of an overall treatment programme. A treatment may involve a range of activities, the purpose of which is to help engage the person and provide an appropriate context for the delivery of specific interventions. It is important to maintain and enhance the service context in which interventions are delivered otherwise the specific benefits of effective interventions will be lost. Indeed, the importance of organising care in order to support and encourage a good therapeutic relationship is as important as the specific treatments offered.

1.1.3   Why develop national guidelines?

The National Institute for Health and Clinical Excellence (NICE) was established as a Special Health Authority for England and Wales in 1999, with a remit to provide a single source of authoritative and reliable guidance for service users, professionals and the public. NICE guidance aims to improve standards of care, diminish unacceptable variations in the provision and quality of care across the NHS, and ensure that the health service is person-centred. All guidance is developed in a transparent and collaborative manner, using the best available evidence and involving all relevant stakeholders.

NICE generates guidance in a number of different ways, three of which are relevant here. First, national guidance is produced by the Technology Appraisal Committee to give robust advice about a particular treatment, intervention, procedure or other health technology. Second, NICE commissions public health intervention guidance focused on types of activity (interventions) that help to reduce people's risk of developing a disease or condition or help to promote or maintain a healthy lifestyle. Third, NICE commissions the production of national clinical guidelines focused upon the overall treatment and management of a specific condition. To enable this latter development, NICE has established four National Collaborating Centres in conjunction with a range of professional organisations involved in healthcare.

1.1.4   From national clinical guidelines to local protocols

Once a national guideline has been published and disseminated, local healthcare groups will be expected to produce a plan and identify resources for implementation, along with appropriate timetables. Subsequently, a multidisciplinary group involving commissioners of healthcare, primary care and specialist mental health professionals, service users and carers should undertake the translation of the implementation plan into local protocols taking into account both the recommendations set out in this guideline and the priorities set in the National Service Framework for Mental Health (Department of Health, 1999) and related documentation. The nature and pace of the local plan will reflect local healthcare needs and the nature of existing services; full implementation may take a considerable time, especially where substantial training needs are identified.

1.1.5   Auditing the implementation of clinical guidelines

This guideline identifies key areas of clinical practice and service delivery for local and national audit. Although the generation of audit standards is an important and necessary step in the implementation of this guidance, a more broadly based implementation strategy will be developed. Nevertheless, it should be noted that the Care

Quality Commission in England, and the Healthcare Inspectorate Wales, will monitor the extent to which commissioners and providers of health and social care have implemented these guidelines.

1.2   THE NATIONAL *AUTISM* GUIDELINE

1.2.1   Who has developed this guideline?

This guideline has been commissioned by NICE and developed within the National Collaborating Centre for Mental Health (NCCMH). The NCCMH is a collaboration of the professional organisations involved in the field of mental health, national service user and carer organisations, a number of academic institutions and NICE. The NCCMH is funded by NICE and is led by a partnership between the Royal College of Psychiatrists and the British Psychological Society's Centre for Outcomes Research and Effectiveness, based at University College London.

The GDG was convened by the NCCMH and supported by funding from NICE. The GDG included people with autism and carers, and professionals from psychiatry, clinical psychology, general practice, nursing, paediatrics, social care, education and the private and third sectors, including voluntary organisations.

Staff from the NCCMH provided leadership and support throughout the process of guideline development, undertaking systematic searches, information retrieval, appraisal and systematic review of the evidence. Members of the GDG received training in the process of guideline development from NCCMH staff, and the service users and carers received training and support from the NICE Patient and Public Involvement Programme. The NICE Guidelines Technical Adviser provided advice and assistance regarding aspects of the guideline development process.

All GDG members made formal declarations of interest at the outset, which were updated at every GDG meeting. The GDG met a total of 12 times throughout the process of guideline development. It met as a whole, but key topics were led by a national expert in the relevant topic. The GDG was supported by the NCCMH technical team, with additional expert advice from special advisers where needed. The group oversaw the production and synthesis of research evidence before presentation. All statements and recommendations in this guideline have been generated and agreed by the whole GDG.

1.2.2   For whom is this guideline intended?

This guideline will be relevant for adults with autism and covers the care provided by primary, community, secondary, tertiary and other healthcare professionals who have direct contact with, and make decisions concerning the care of, adults with autism.

The guideline will also be relevant to the work, but will not cover the practice, of those in:
● occupational health services
● social services
● the independent sector.

1.2.3 Specific aims of this guideline

The guideline makes recommendations for the support and management of adults with autism. It aims to:
● improve access and engagement with interventions and services for adults with autism
● evaluate the role of specific psychological, psychosocial and pharmacological interventions in the management of autism
● evaluate the role of psychological and psychosocial interventions in combination with pharmacological interventions in the management of autism in adults
● evaluate the role of specific service-level interventions for adults with autism
● integrate the above to provide best practice advice on the care of adults with autism
● promote the implementation of best clinical practice through the development of recommendations tailored to the requirements of the NHS in England and Wales.

1.2.4 The structure of this guideline

The guideline is divided into chapters, each covering a set of related topics. The first three chapters provide a general introduction to guidelines, to the topic and to the methods used to develop the guideline. Chapters 4 to 8 provide the evidence that underpins the recommendations about the management of autism in adults.

Each evidence chapter begins with a general introduction to the topic that sets the recommendations in context. Depending on the nature of the evidence, narrative syntheses and reviews or meta-analyses were conducted, and the structure of the chapters varies accordingly. Where appropriate, details about current practice, the evidence base and any research limitations are provided. Where meta-analyses were conducted, information is given about both the interventions included and the studies considered for review. Clinical summaries are then used to summarise the evidence presented. Finally, recommendations are presented at the end of each evidence review. On the CD-ROM, full details about the included studies can be found in Appendix 14. Where meta-analyses were conducted, the data are presented using forest plots in Appendix 15 and GRADE evidence profiles in Appendix 19 (see Text Box 1 for details of all appendices on the CD-ROM).

Text Box 1: Appendices on CD-ROM

Search strategies for the identification of clinical studies	Appendix 9
Search strategies for the identification of health economic evidence	Appendix 11
Clinical evidence – study characteristics tables	Appendix 14
Clinical evidence – forest plots	Appendix 15
Clinical evidence – completed methodology checklists	Appendix 16
Health economic evidence – completed methodology checklists	Appendix 17
Health economic evidence – evidence tables of published studies	Appendix 18
GRADE evidence profiles	Appendix 19

In the event that amendments or minor updates need to be made to the guideline, please check the NCCMH website (nccmh.org.uk), where these will be listed and a corrected PDF file available to download.

2. INTRODUCTION TO AUTISM IN ADULTS

2.1 THE AUTISM SPECTRUM

2.1.1 History

Autism was first described in 1943 by Leo Kanner in Baltimore (Kanner, 1943) and was independently described in 1944 by Hans Asperger in Vienna (Asperger, 1944). Both of these clinical descriptions described an overlapping core set of features (social difficulties alongside highly repetitive behaviour), but in Asperger's account the children had good intelligence and language skills, whereas in Kanner's there was greater variability in intelligence quotient (IQ) and language development. The children described by Asperger at first received little attention because his account was written in German, and it was not until the 1980s and 1990s that two seminal works brought this account to the English speaking medical world: an article by Lorna Wing in *Psychological Medicine* (Wing, 1981) and a book by Uta Frith entitled *Autism and Asperger's Syndrome* (Frith, 1991). While autism was listed in the *Diagnostic and Statistical Manual of Mental Disorders* – 3rd edition (DSM-III; American Psychological Association, 1980), Asperger's syndrome was not, although it was finally included in the *International Classification of Diseases* – 10th revision (ICD-10; World Health Organization, 1992) in 1992 and in DSM-IV in 1994.

In the 1950s and 1960s autism was often attributed to purely environmental factors, such as unemotional parenting (Bettelheim, 1967). But this theory was overturned in the 1970s by Michael Rutter (Rutter, 1978) who argued that associated phenomena such as epilepsy could not be attributed to environmental factors such as parenting style and instead indicated abnormalities of brain function (which thus meant that the parents themselves were not 'bad' parents) and that the higher concordance of autism in identical as opposed to non-identical twins indicated a genetic cause (Folstein & Rutter, 1977). The idea that autism involves atypical brain development is now firmly established (Courchesne *et al.*, 2001) and that it involves many genes is also no longer in doubt (Geschwind, 2008).

From the 1950s to the 1980s autism was mostly considered to be categorical (either present or absent) and quite rare (four in 10,000 children) (Rutter, 1978). These two views were contested by Wing who found in her epidemiological study that, when partial syndromes were included, autism was much more common than had previously been realised and that autism could come by degrees, warranting the term 'the autistic spectrum' (Wing, 1988). Today we recognise that at least 1% of the population has autism (Baird *et al.,* 2006; Baron-Cohen *et al.*, 2009) rendering it as relatively common.

In the 1970s the symptoms were described as a 'triad of impairments' (Wing, 1976) that included social difficulties, communication difficulties and social imagination difficulties (together with strongly repetitive behaviour). In the planned DSM-5

(American Psychological Association, forthcoming in 2013), the triad will be reduced to two core dimensions. Social and communication difficulties will be collapsed into a single dimension called 'social-communication difficulties', to reflect that these are so intertwined that they cannot be easily disentangled. The dimension 'social imagination difficulties' will be discarded because some people on the autism spectrum demonstrate great imagination in relation to the arts (drawing, in particular) and imagination is not easily operationalised. Strongly repetitive behaviour (incorporating difficulties in adapting to change and unusually narrow interests) will become the second major dimension.

People with autism lie in the intersection of these two dimensions, meaning they show both features, as shown in Figure 1. Exhibiting just one of these features does not warrant a diagnosis on the autism spectrum, and the co-occurrence of the two dimensions means the autism spectrum can still be viewed as a syndrome.

ICD-11 is due to be published in 2015 and the changes made to the DSM-5 will be considered, however, it is not clear if the changes described above will be replicated.

2.1.2   Terminology

A variety of terms are used in the field, which can lead to some confusion. These include subgroup diagnostic categories such as autism, Asperger's syndrome, pervasive developmental disorders and atypical autism. In the planned DSM-5 (2013) these will all be subsumed under a single overarching diagnostic term: autism spectrum disorder (ASD). Intellectual disorder (or what is termed 'learning disability' in the UK) and language disorder will be separately coded, to reflect that these can coexist with ASD (again, it is not yet clear whether similar changes will be made to ICD-11). In the UK some authors prefer to use the term 'autism spectrum condition' because some people with autism see themselves as neurologically different (and in need of a

Figure 1: The two main dimensions in the diagnosis of the autism spectrum (reproduced with permission [Baron-Cohen, 2008]).

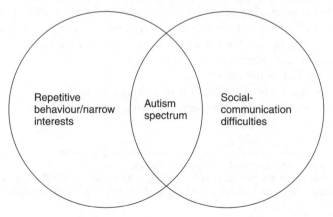

diagnosis to access support) but not necessarily 'disordered'. In the US many authors are keen to retain the term 'disorder' to reflect severity and how the symptoms interfere with everyday functioning. In this guideline, the GDG opted to circumvent the debate over whether to use ASD or autism spectrum condition by using simply 'autism' to cover the whole autism spectrum.

2.1.3   Features and presentation

Autism is a lifelong condition characterised by difficulties in two domains: (a) social-communication, and (b) strongly repetitive behaviour/ difficulties adjusting to rapid and unexpected change/unusually narrow interests, as described below.

Historically, classic autism[1] and Asperger's syndrome have shared the same two diagnostic difficulties above, but in classic autism the child was seen to be late to develop language (no single words by 2 years old, no phrase speech by 3 years old), and there might have been additional learning disabilities (that is, IQ might have been in the below average range[2]). In contrast, in Asperger's syndrome language was seen to develop on time (when a history was taken) and IQ was always above 70, if not above average (that is, no sign of a learning disability). While these two subgroups are delineated in DSM-IV (1994), the plan in DSM-5 (2013), as mentioned earlier, is to collapse these into a single category called ASD (while highlighting levels of severity and associated disabilities such as learning disabilities or language delay).

Social-communication difficulties
These difficulties can manifest in many different ways, including the following (note that none of these is necessarily or inevitably a part of autism and that different features may be evident in different individuals with autism):
- atypical eye contact (staring at people for too long or not maintaining eye contact)
- intrusion into others' personal space (standing too close to someone else, talking too loud or touching people inappropriately)
- reduced interest in socialising
- difficulties understanding others' behaviour, motives and intentions
- difficulties reading other people's facial expressions or vocal intonation
- difficulties taking turns in conversation or tendency towards monologue
- difficulties making small talk or maintaining a conversation
- social naïveté and vulnerability to exploitation
- bluntness or lack of diplomacy
- difficulties reading between the lines or picking up hints
- difficulties seeing things from another person's perspective

---

[1]Also called Kanner's autism, or infantile autism or autistic disorder.
[2]Learning disabilities are classified into bands according to IQ as follows: IQ <20 constitutes profound learning disabilities, IQ 20 to 34 severe, IQ 35 to 49 moderate and IQ 50 to 69 mild learning disabilities (ICD-10).

- difficulties resolving conflict
- difficulties anticipating what might offend others (faux pas)
- lack of social awareness
- difficulties keeping track of what the listener or reader needs to know
- difficulties making or keeping friends
- difficulties understanding other people's expectations
- difficulties conforming
- difficulties judging what might be relevant or irrelevant to others
- difficulties coping with or interacting in social groups
- unable to tell white lies
- difficulties coping with ambiguity in language
- becoming obsessed with a person to an intrusive extent
- social anxiety
- loneliness (and risk of depression)
- reduced empathy.

Strongly repetitive behaviour/ difficulties adjusting to rapid and unexpected change/unusually narrow interests

These difficulties can manifest in many different ways, including the following:
- avoiding crowded places
- difficulties multi-tasking
- doing one thing at a time
- narrow deep interests, rather than broad superficial interests
- preference for repetition and routine
- anxiety in face of change
- need for sameness (eating the same foods, wearing the same clothes, taking the same routes, going to the same places) and avoidance of novelty
- preference for predictability and predictable events (watching washing machines spinning or trains going down tracks)
- being extremely passive if an activity of interest is not available or initiated by someone else
- need for clarity and expressing a pedantic request for precision and avoiding ambiguity
- attention to small details
- development of 'fixated interests'
- need for strict order and precision.

2.1.4   Development, course and prognosis

Difficulties related to autism start early in life: if a developmental history is taken it is usually evident that there have been social difficulties since as early as the second year (from 18 months old) in terms of mixing with other children and adjusting to social groups and change. Average age of diagnosis of autism is in primary school (by 6 years old) (Frith, 1989) whereas Asperger's syndrome is often not diagnosed until secondary school (by 14 years old) or even older (early adulthood or later) (Attwood, 1997). This is often because autism entails some developmental delays and so is noticeable even to an untrained observer. In Asperger's syndrome, however, good language and cognitive skills may mean the child or young person can cope academically and in primary school, which is a fairly small community (typically around 200 children), the social demands may be less challenging (the peer group may be more tolerant of a child who does not conform), whereas secondary schools are usually much bigger (from 600 to 2,000) thereby significantly increasing social demands.

Teenagers with Asperger's syndrome may be difficult for teachers to cope with because they typically demonstrate a lack of social conformity, doing what *they* are interested in rather than what the teacher expects them to do. The student can appear disruptive in a class setting, and their refusal to accept instructions without logical reasons ('do it because I told you to') may mean the student is seen as challenging. Students with Asperger's syndrome can lose motivation educationally and underperform in terms of school leaving qualifications or drop out of school entirely. They are also at risk of being bullied, verbally or physically, because of being 'loners' and not fitting in; some teenagers with Asperger's syndrome retaliate, turning from being the victim to being the bully. Some young people with Asperger's syndrome develop secondary depression and may feel suicidal, as well as showing social anxiety if expected to do group presentations (Tantam, 2000).

Some people manage to proceed through adolescence without receiving a diagnosis because their families 'cushion' them by doing everything for them or tolerating their idiosyncrasies, and the person only starts to experience difficulties at the transition to independence (for example, going to university or moving away from their family) where they may not be able to make friends, becoming depressed and isolated. They may, therefore, only seek a diagnosis in their late teens or early twenties. Others may not seek a diagnosis until mid life following a series of failed relationships, including marriage(s), and failed jobs (they might have been disciplined for having a difficult attitude towards co-workers, not been a 'team player' or simply not been promoted). A study by the UK National Autistic Society (NAS) found that 88% of adults without a learning disability on the autism spectrum are unemployed despite having skills that mean they could be working, although many might require supported or sheltered employment (Barnard *et al.,* 2001). Specific autism traits such as black-and-white thinking or empathy difficulties can also have a significant impact on interpersonal relationships and may complicate assessments, for example rigid thoughts (such as 'my family will be better off without me') can present significant challenges in risk assessment. However, it should not be forgotten that some people with autism go on to lead rich and fulfilling lives.

2.1.5 Impairment, disability and secondary problems

The autism spectrum is very wide, ranging from people with limited self-help, independence, academic or verbal skills through to individuals who are in the gifted range of intelligence and fully independent but who have significant social difficulties. This wide spectrum means that how 'symptoms' present in individuals may be very different, which is in part a function of the extent to which the individual can fall back on general cognitive ability to devise coping strategies and the degree to which they are motivated to try to mask their disability in order to try to fit in.

Autism can coexist with many other diagnoses, including depression, social anxiety, obsessive–compulsive disorder (OCD), attention deficit hyperactivity disorder (ADHD), Tourette's syndrome/tic disorder, dysexecutive syndrome, developmental coordination disorder, catatonia, eating disorders, gender identity disorder, personality disorder and psychosis. A number of genetic syndromes are also associated with autism such as tuberous sclerosis, Fragile X, Angelman syndrome, Rett syndrome and Turner syndrome.

2.1.6   Issues of particular importance

Whereas detection and diagnosis of childhood autism now largely occurs by early childhood (age 3 to 6 years old), diagnosis of Asperger's syndrome is often overlooked until as late as adulthood and can easily be misdiagnosed as simple depression, as a personality disorder or sometimes as psychosis or schizophrenia. A developmental history is the key to making this differentiation. This guideline is, in part, a response to the under-diagnosis in adults.

Sensory and gastrointestinal issues are also very common, the former possibly seen in as many as 90% of adults with autism without a learning disability (Crane *et al.,* 2009) and the latter in almost half of adults with autism and a learning disability (Galli-Carminetti *et al.,* 2006). These should be assessed because they have major implications for management.

It is important that autism is seen not only as a medical diagnosis for which the NHS has responsibilities, but also as a social care responsibility (in the areas of education, housing and employment) because people with autism often fall through the gaps between health and social care, especially if they do not present with an accompanying mental health problem or learning disability. This presents challenges for both health and social care services in developing services that facilitate the engagement of people with autism. The rights of people with autism has become an important social issue and professionals need to be sensitive to the view that many individuals on the autism spectrum regard themselves as an excluded minority whose rights have been overlooked by a 'neurotypical' majority (see Chapter 4). Alongside using medical diagnostic terminology to define themselves, they also use the key concept of 'neurodiversity' to remind society that there are many different routes along which the brain can develop, that one is not necessarily better or worse than another, and that society has to adapt to make space for this diversity. The analogy is with left-handedness, which used to not be tolerated, but which is now seen as a natural minority subgroup in the population. Other recognised subgroups defined by atypical neurological development are those who show a significant discrepancy between their verbal and non-verbal IQ or those with specific developmental disorders such as dyslexia or dyspraxia. Unlike left-handedness, where the individual is simply different but may not need any special support, autism involves both difference and disability, in that the diagnosis of autism is only made when the person is experiencing difficulties arising from their difference.

2.2   INCIDENCE AND PREVALENCE

Childhood prevalence studies suggest that autism occurs in approximately 1% of the population and that for every three known cases, there are two undiagnosed individuals who might need a diagnosis at some point in their lives (Baron-Cohen *et al.,* 2009). Prevalence in adulthood has been found to be similar at 1.1% (Brugha *et al.,* 2012). This suggests that autism is now much more common than was previously thought—in 1978 prevalence of autism was reported to be 4 per 10,000 (Rutter, 1978). This dramatic change is thought to largely reflect greater awareness, growth of services and a widening of diagnostic criteria to include Asperger's syndrome, atypical autism and pervasive developmental disorders (not otherwise specified), which was only brought into the international classification system in 1994. See Figure 2 for a schematic representation of this increase in diagnosis.

However, despite this greater awareness, studies in adulthood have shown that four out of five adults with autism find obtaining a diagnosis in adulthood difficult or not possible (Taylor & Marrable, 2011) and many will not have received a formal diagnosis (Brugha *et al.,* 2011).

Figure 2: The rising prevalence of cases on the autism spectrum. Along the Y (vertical) axis are number of cases on the autism spectrum per 10,000 in the population (reproduced with permission [Baron-Cohen, 2008])

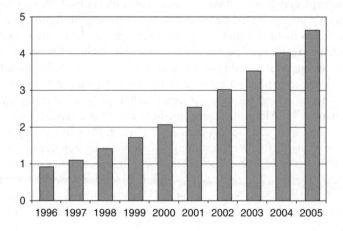

2.3   DIFFERENTIAL DIAGNOSIS

Because OCD also involves unusually repetitive behaviour it is important to highlight some key differences between OCD and people on the autism spectrum:

- social development is not necessarily atypical in childhood in people with OCD
- repetitive behaviours result in anxiety in people with OCD, so the absence of an anxiety response precludes OCD (but the presence of anxiety does not necessarily mean that someone must have OCD and not autism).

Other possible distinguishing features of OCD are outlined in the NICE *Obsessive-compulsive Disorder* guideline (NCCMH, 2006). A person can be comorbidly diagnosed with autism and OCD.

Because personality disorders also involve social relationship difficulties it is important to highlight the key difference between people with autism and those with personality disorders (and so help avoid misdiagnosis). Personality disorders do not typically involve the 'obsessive' narrow interests or resistance to change. In addition, although empathy deficits are present in both autism and psychopathy (or antisocial personality disorder), in people with autism it is the *cognitive* component of empathy that is impaired ('theory of mind' or recognising what others may be thinking or feeling) while *affective* empathy (having an appropriate emotional reaction to/caring about other's feelings) may be intact. In contrast, whereas in psychopathy the cognitive component of empathy is intact (enabling them to deceive and manipulate others) affective empathy is impaired (they do not care about others' suffering, for example).

Autism can coexist with other conditions involving 'rigid' behaviour and cognition such as eating disorders or gender identity disorder, and a dual diagnosis might be appropriate if the difficulties related to autism predate the second diagnosis. Emotional difficulties such as social anxiety disorder or depression are also common in people with autism and are usually seen as secondary to the autism. This is because autism often develops first and can cause social difficulties including social isolation, which can then give rise to anxiety and depression. Individuals can also be diagnosed in childhood as having a language disorder, only later in life receiving a diagnosis of autism (Bishop *et al.*, 2008)

2.4   AETIOLOGY

As mentioned earlier, there is no longer any doubt that autism is strongly genetic (Geschwind, 2008). This evidence comes from studies of twins, family genetics and molecular genetics. To date hundreds of molecular genetic associations have been reported, and it is not yet clear which genes are necessary and sufficient to cause which type of autism. Autism is not 100% genetic (estimates of heritability are between 40 to 90% (Hallmayer *et al.*, 2011) leaving room for a gene–environment interaction, but the environmental factors are not yet known. The idea that the environmental factor was measles, mumps and rubella (MMR) vaccine damage is no longer tenable (for example, the Editors of *The Lancet*, 2010; Taylor *et al.*, 1999). Potential environmental factors include the foetal sex steroid hormones (themselves under genetic influence) (Auyeung *et al.*, 2009) and social training/experience (Lovaas & Smith, 1988).

Autism is also now clearly understood to be neurodevelopmental, meaning that there are differences in the pattern of brain development from the earliest point. For example, early brain overgrowth has been documented in the first 2 years of life (Courchesne *et al.,* 2001), and in later development there are clear differences in the function and structure of the 'empathy circuit' of the brain (amygdala, ventromedial prefrontal cortex, temporo-parietal junction, orbitofrontal cortex, anterior cingulate cortex and other brain regions) (Lombardo *et al.*, 2011). There are also differences in connectivity between frontal and parietal lobe functions that are thought to relate to cognitive style, in particular an over-reliance on processing details and a relative under-reliance on processing gist or holistic information (Belmonte *et al.*, 2004).

2.5　IDENTIFICATION AND ASSESSMENT

The process of identification and assessment is well understood but is limited by the availability of well-validated tools for case identification and the lack of specialist services to undertake the necessary assessments. The identification and assessment process should include a case identification phase followed by a detailed diagnostic assessment if needed. Screening instruments need to be age-appropriate, severity-appropriate, and brief, but are not themselves diagnostic. A typical diagnostic assessment may take at least 2 hours in carefully documenting the developmental history, in order to ensure that the differential diagnoses outlined in Section 2.3 have been excluded. Diagnostic assessment, which in the UK uses ICD-10, is often within a multidisciplinary team but at a minimum is by a qualified clinician, usually a clinical psychologist, psychiatrist or neurologist. In the case of children this is also often conducted by a paediatrician together with a speech therapist. The considerable variability in the nature of autism, the presence of mental and physical health comorbidities, and the apparent skills learnt through observation and structure (rather than through innate ability) can present particular challenges in assessment.

2.6　CURRENT CARE IN ENGLAND AND WALES

2.6.1　Strategic plans for England and Wales

In 2008 the Welsh Assembly Government developed *The Autistic Spectrum Disorder (ASD) Strategic Action Plan for Wales* (Adult Task and Finish Group, 2009), which set out a number of recommendations and actions, supported by £5.4 million given to the 22 local authorities in Wales to implement them during the period 2008 to 2011. A further £2 million in funding was announced to support autism services in Wales for 2011 to 2012.

As part of *The Autistic Spectrum Disorder (ASD) Strategic Action Plan for Wales* a national clinical network for assessment and diagnosis was established in 2011 and is hosted by Betsi Cadwaladr University Health Board. The network has been involved in developing and implementing a standards-based assessment pathway in all the Welsh Health Boards through the education and training of relevant clinicians, the development of teams with local expertise and the support of experts at a national level.

In England, the Autism Act (Her Majesty's Stationery Office [HMSO], 2009) and the subsequent Autism Strategy (Department of Health, 2010) required all NHS trusts to define an autism care pathway by the end of 2011, particularly for adults with autism, since, in many areas, the childhood pathways are already well established.

In Wales diagnostic and assessment survives were established as part of the Strategic Action Plan but few specialist services for the assessment and diagnosis of adults with autism currently exist in the England, such as the Sheffield Asperger Syndrome Service, and fewer are in a position to provide appropriate interventions. The number of adults with autism in contact with specialist mental health services is not known but probably includes a significant number of people whose autism is unrecognised. Developing these care pathways represents a considerable challenge as there are many parts of the UK where there is insufficient training or knowledge about autism and that it may take some time to put in place a care pathway in all regions.

A key purpose of the guideline is to provide evidence-based recommendations that will support the further implementation of the Autism Strategy in England and *The Autistic Spectrum Disorder (ASD) Strategic Action Plan for Wales.*

2.6.2   The National Health Service

Care pathways in the NHS need to start with identification and diagnosis and culminate in a full package of support to meet the needs of the individual, taking into account that the person might need support across their lifespan. At present the level of training in and knowledge about autism is limited among primary and secondary care professionals (Punshon *et al.*, 2009) and will need specific attention if the recommendations developed in this guideline are to be of real benefit. Access to interventions for adults with autism is also limited and may extend beyond mental healthcare to access to physical healthcare.

2.6.3   Social care

Difficulties related to autism can cross all areas of life. As such, it is important that the NHS works closely with other services. This can produce benefits in how well people access the other services, as well as how they access the NHS. In England the Autism Strategy (Department of Health, 2010) is clear that diagnosis of autism is a sufficient ground for offering an assessment for social care services, so there needs to be a clear pathway after diagnosis (or when entering adult services) from health to social care.

In England, councils with adult social care responsibilities use Fair Access to Care Services (FACS), which is a national eligibility framework (amended in 2010) for allocating social care resources. It uses a grading system with four bands (critical, substantial, moderate and low), which assess eligibility in terms of risk to an individual's independence, wellbeing and the consequences of their needs not being met. The Social Care Institute for Excellence (SCIE) has produced a booklet *Facts about FACS 2010: A Guide to Fair Access to Care Services* (Brand *et al.*, 2010a) that clearly explains the criteria for each part of the grading system (this is to be reviewed in April 2013). They have also produced a leaflet *Facts about FACS 2010: Your Questions Answered* (Brand *et al.*, 2010b) for people using or seeking services and support.

At present, due to local budgetary considerations, most areas in England will only offer services if people have critical or substantial needs. However, this guideline recognises that universal services need to be expanded for the general population and work needs to be done to strengthen communities. In order to access any service, people need good social-communication skills in order to request help, complete assessments and engage with new people. These areas can be very difficult for people with autism and access to services are often dependent on support from families, partners and carers.

2.6.4   Other services

As outlined above, the NHS needs to work closely with social care and education services since autism does not just affect mental health but has an impact on independent living (housing, employment, social networks, leisure, shopping and travel) and education at all levels (school, college and university). Care pathways should therefore include liaison with these other agencies and with disability resource centres in colleges or with human resources departments in the workplace.

2.7   ECONOMIC COST

Autism has lifetime consequences and significant economic impact because of the enormous implications for the individual with the condition and their family, partners and carers. Management and support of people with autism incurs substantial costs to the health and social care services and the wider public sector, through provision of services and lost employment. Baird and colleagues (2006) estimated that 116 in every 10,000 children aged 9 to 10 years have autism, which is substantially higher than previous estimates.

Knapp and colleagues (2009) estimated the costs of supporting children and adults with autism in the UK, using published estimates of the prevalence of autism, prevalence of learning disabilities among people with autism, data on accommodation placements, as well as data on support services and interventions used by this population as a consequence of having autism. Costs covered health and social care services, special education, housing placements outside the parental home (for children) or in staffed or supported settings (for adults), leisure services, and included out-of-pocket payments made for services as well as productivity losses for adults with autism and their family, partners and carers. Benefit payments were also considered.

Using a prevalence of autism in children and in adults of 1%, Knapp and colleagues' (2009) study estimated an annual cost of supporting children with autism of £2.7 billion; for adults this cost amounted to £25 billion (in 2005/06 prices). These cost estimates excluded benefits but included lost employment for individuals and hence lost productivity to society. The total estimated UK cost of approximately £28 billion averages out at £500 each year for every person in the country. Ninety percent of the overall cost of supporting individuals with autism relate to supporting adults. The public sector covers the major component of costs of supporting people with autism. The study estimated that, out of the total cost of £25 billion of supporting adults with autism, 59% is attributed to publicly-funded services, 36% to lost employment for the person with autism and the remaining 5% to family expenses (Knapp *et al.,* 2009).

Sensitivity analysis demonstrated that, using a higher prevalence rate of autism of 1.16%, as reported in Baird and colleagues (2006), the total UK cost for children and adults with autism was £3.15 million and £29.56 million, respectively, reaching a total cost of £32.7 (2005/65 prices). This estimate may be more realistic, given that recent research estimated the prevalence of adults with autism at 1.1% (95% confidence interval [CI], 0.3 to 1.9) (Brugha *et al.,* 2012).

Adults with autism have high needs of support at their place of residence. The proportion of people with autism with a learning disability living in institutional facilities is considerably higher than in people without a learning disability (Knapp *et al.,* 2009). Baird and colleagues (2006) estimate that 56% of people with autism have a learning disability. The major component of the total cost (£25 billion) of supporting adults with autism is attributed to the cost of supporting adults with a learning disability, which is almost two thirds (£17 billion) of the total cost. A large proportion of people with autism with a learning disability live in residential care (52%), supported living accommodation (7%) or hospitals (6%) (Knapp *et al.,* 2009). Residential care constitutes a major component of the total cost associated with supporting people with autism as the annual costs per person are very high, ranging from approximately £87,500 per annum for supported accommodation to £98,000 per annum for living in hospital.

One study found that very few people with autism were in employment, because there was little or no support available to get them into work (Howlin *et al.,* 2005). It is estimated that only 12% of adults with autism without a learning disability have full-time jobs (Barnard *et al.,* 2001), leaving 88% unemployed, which has huge costs to the economy in terms of lost productivity. This productivity loss is conspicuous because adults with autism without a learning disability could be employed through supported employment programmes. Järbrink and Knapp (2001) demonstrated that the lack of supported employment programmes for people with autism has negative resource consequences for the economy.

In the UK, the lifetime costs of an individual with autism without a learning disability is estimated at £3.1 million (discounted cost £0.8 million using a rate of 3.5%) and of an individual with autism and a learning disability £4.6 million (discounted cost £1.23 million) (Knapp *et al.,* 2009). Ganz (2007) estimated the lifetime per capita incremental societal cost of autism at $3.2 million in the US (discounted estimate). The substantial costs are borne by adult care and lost productivity of individuals with autism and their family members and carers. Knapp and colleagues (2009) converted the US estimate equivalent to £2 million using gross domestic product purchasing power parity and explained that the different methodology, availability of data, different support systems and the assumption of a different discount rate in the US contributed to the higher estimate of lifetime cost in the US. Ganz (2007) estimated the total annual cost of autism at $35 billion to US society. The medical costs were estimated at $29,000 per person per year, which included physician and outpatient services, prescription medication, and behavioural therapies; non-medical costs were estimated at $38,000 to $43,000 per person per year, depending on the level of disability, including costs of special education, camps and childcare (Ganz, 2006)

The substantial societal cost of autism in adults requires provision of effective interventions that will improve the quality of life of people with autism and their families, partners and carers and will reduce the costs borne to the health services, people with autism and their families and the wider society.

3   METHODS USED TO DEVELOP THIS GUIDELINE

3.1   OVERVIEW

The development of this guideline drew upon methods outlined by NICE (further information is available in *The Guidelines Manual* [NICE, 2009e]). A team of health and social care professionals, lay representatives and technical experts known as the Guideline Development Group (GDG), with support from the NCCMH staff, undertook the development of a person-centred, evidence-based guideline. There are six basic steps in the process of developing a guideline:
1. Define the scope, which lays out exactly what will be included in the guideline.
2. Define review questions considered important for practitioners and service users.
3. Develop criteria for evidence searching and search for evidence.
4. Design validated protocols for systematic review and apply to evidence recovered by the search.
5. Synthesise and (meta-) analyse data retrieved, guided by the review questions, and produce Grading of Recommendations: Assessment, Development and Evaluation (GRADE) evidence profiles and summaries.
6. Answer review questions with evidence-based recommendations for clinical practice.
  The clinical practice recommendations made by the GDG are therefore derived from the most up-to-date and robust evidence for the clinical and cost effectiveness of the interventions and services used in the support and management of autism in adults. In addition, to ensure a service user and carer focus, the concerns of service users and carers regarding health and social care have been highlighted and addressed by recommendations agreed by the whole GDG.

3.2   THE SCOPE

Topics are referred by the Secretary of State and the letter of referral defines the remit, which defines the main areas to be covered (see *The Guidelines Manual* [NICE, 2009e] for further information). The NCCMH developed a scope for the guideline based on the remit (see Appendix 1). The purpose of the scope is to:
- provide an overview of what the guideline will include and exclude
- identify the key aspects of care that must be included
- set the boundaries of the development work and provide a clear framework to enable work to stay within the priorities agreed by NICE and the National Collaborating Centre, and the remit from the Department of Health/Welsh Assembly Government
- inform the development of the review questions and search strategy

- inform professionals and the public about expected content of the guideline
- keep the guideline to a reasonable size to ensure that its development can be carried out within the allocated period.

An initial draft of the scope was sent to registered stakeholders who had agreed to attend a scoping workshop. The workshop was used to:

- obtain feedback on the selected key clinical issues
- identify which population subgroups should be specified (if any)
- seek views on the composition of the GDG
- encourage applications for GDG membership.

The draft scope was subject to consultation with registered stakeholders over a 4-week period. During the consultation period, the scope was posted on the NICE website (www.nice.org.uk). Comments were invited from stakeholder organisations and the Guideline Review Panel (GRP). Further information about the GRP can also be found on the NICE website. The NCCMH and NICE reviewed the scope in light of comments received, and the revised scope was signed off by the GRP.

3.3   THE GUIDELINE DEVELOPMENT GROUP

The GDG consisted of: professionals in psychiatry, clinical psychology, nursing, social work and general practice; academic experts in psychiatry and psychology; a service user and carers, and a representative from a service user organisation. The guideline development process was supported by staff from the NCCMH, who undertook the clinical and health economic literature searches, reviewed and presented the evidence to the GDG, managed the process and contributed to drafting the guideline.

3.3.1   Guideline Development Group meetings

Twelve GDG meetings were held between 27 July 2010 and 7 September 2011. During each day-long GDG meeting, in a plenary session, review questions and clinical and economic evidence were reviewed and assessed, and recommendations formulated. At each meeting, all GDG members declared any potential conflicts of interest (see Appendix 2), and service user and carer concerns were routinely discussed as part of a standing agenda.

3.3.2   Topic groups

The GDG divided its workload along clinically relevant lines to simplify the guideline development process, and GDG members formed smaller topic groups to undertake guideline work in that area of clinical practice. Topic group 1 covered questions relating to assessment and case identification. Topic group 2 covered psychological/educational/social interventions. Topic groups 3 and 4 covered biomedical interventions and experience of care, respectively. These groups were designed to efficiently manage evidence appraisal prior to presenting it to the GDG as a whole. Each topic group was chaired by a GDG member with expert knowledge of the topic area (one of the healthcare professionals). Topic groups refined the review questions and the clinical definitions of interventions, reviewed and prepared the evidence with the systematic reviewer before presenting it to the GDG as a whole, and helped the GDG to identify further expertise in the topic. Topic group leaders reported the status of the group's work as part of the standing agenda. They also introduced and led the GDG's discussion of the evidence review for that topic and assisted the GDG Chair in drafting the section of the guideline relevant to the work of each topic group.

3.3.3   Service users and carers

Individuals with direct experience of services gave an integral service user focus to the GDG and the guideline. The GDG included a service user and carers, and a representative from a service user organisation. They contributed as full GDG members to writing the review questions, helping to ensure that the evidence addressed their views and preferences, highlighting sensitive issues and terminology relevant to the guideline, and bringing service user research to the attention of the GDG. In drafting the guideline, they met with the NCCMH team to develop the chapter on experience of care, they contributed to writing the guideline's introduction and identified recommendations from the service user and carer perspective.

3.3.4   National and international experts

National and international experts in the area under review were identified through the literature search and through the experience of the GDG members. These experts were contacted to identify unpublished or soon-to-be published studies, to ensure that up-to-date evidence was included in the development of the guideline. They informed the GDG about completed trials at the pre-publication stage, systematic reviews in the process of being published, studies relating to the cost effectiveness of treatment and trial data if the GDG could be provided with full access to the complete trial report. Appendix 6 lists researchers who were contacted.

3.4   REVIEW QUESTIONS

Review (clinical) questions were used to guide the identification and interrogation of the evidence base relevant to the topic of the guideline. Before the first GDG meeting, an analytic framework (see Appendix 7) was prepared by NCCMH staff based on the scope and an overview of existing guidelines, and discussed with the guideline Chair. The framework was used to provide a structure from which the review questions were drafted. Both the analytic framework and the draft review questions were then discussed by the GDG at the first few meetings and amended as necessary.

Where appropriate, the framework and questions were refined once the evidence had been searched and, where necessary, subquestions were generated. Questions submitted by stakeholders were also discussed by the GDG and the rationale for not including any questions was recorded in the minutes. The final list of review questions can be found in Appendix 7.

For questions about interventions, the PICO (population, intervention, comparison and outcome) framework was used (see Table 1).

Questions relating to diagnosis or case identification do not involve an intervention designed to treat a particular condition, therefore the PICO framework was not used. Rather, the questions were designed to pick up key issues specifically relevant to clinical utility, for example their accuracy, reliability, safety and acceptability to the service user.

In some situations, the prognosis of a particular condition is of fundamental importance, over and above its general significance in relation to specific interventions. Areas where this is particularly likely to occur relate to assessment of risk, for example in terms of behaviour modification or screening and early intervention. In addition, review questions related to issues of service delivery are occasionally specified in the remit from the Department of Health/Welsh Assembly Government. In these cases, appropriate review questions were developed to be clear and concise.

Although service user experience is a component of all review questions, specific questions concerning what the experience of care is like for adults with autism, and where appropriate, their families, partners and carers, were developed by the GDG.

To help facilitate the literature review, a note was made of the best study design type to answer each question. There are four main types of review question of relevance to NICE guidelines. These are listed in Table 2. For each type of question, the best primary study design varies, where 'best' is interpreted as 'least likely to give misleading answers to the question'.

Table 1: Features of a well-formulated question on effectiveness intervention – the PICO guide

Population	Which population of service users are we interested in? How can they be best described? Are there subgroups that need to be considered?
Intervention	Which intervention, treatment or approach should be used?
Comparison	What is/are the main alternative/s to compare with the intervention?
Outcome	What is really important for the service user? Which outcomes should be considered: intermediate or short-term measures; mortality; morbidity and treatment complications; rates of relapse; late morbidity and readmission; return to work, physical and social functioning and other measures such as quality of life; general health status?

Table 2: **Best study design to answer each type of question**

Type of question	Best primary study design
Effectiveness or other impact of an intervention	Randomised controlled trial (RCT); other studies that may be considered in the absence of RCTs are the following: internally/externally controlled before-and-after trial, interrupted time-series
Accuracy of information (for example, risk factor, test, prediction rule)	Comparing the information against a valid gold standard in an RCT or inception cohort study
Rates (of disease, service user experience, rare side effects)	Prospective cohort, registry, cross-sectional study
Experience of care	Qualitative research (for example, thematic analysis)

However, in all cases, a well-conducted systematic review (of the appropriate type of study) is likely to always yield a better answer than a single study.

Deciding on the best design type to answer a specific review question does not mean that studies of different design types addressing the same question were discarded.

3.5 SYSTEMATIC CLINICAL LITERATURE REVIEW

The aim of the clinical literature review was to systematically identify and synthesise relevant evidence from the literature in order to answer the specific review questions developed by the GDG. Thus, clinical practice recommendations are evidence-based, where possible, and, if evidence is not available, informal consensus methods are used (see Section 3.5.8) and the need for future research is specified.

3.5.1 Methodology

A stepwise, hierarchical approach was taken to locating and presenting evidence to the GDG. The NCCMH developed this process based on methods set out by NICE (*The Guidelines Manual* [NICE, 2009e]), and after considering recommendations from a range of other sources. These included:
- *British Medical Journal* (*BMJ*) Clinical Evidence
- Clinical Policy and Practice Program of the New South Wales Department of Health (Australia)

- The Cochrane Collaboration
- GRADE Working Group
- New Zealand Guidelines Group
- NHS Centre for Reviews and Dissemination (CRD)
- Oxford Centre for Evidence-Based Medicine
- Oxford Systematic Review Development Programme
- Scottish Intercollegiate Guidelines Network
- United States Agency for Healthcare Research and Quality.

3.5.2   The review process

Scoping searches

A broad preliminary search of the literature was undertaken in January 2010 to obtain an overview of the issues likely to be covered by the scope, and to help define key areas. Searches were restricted to clinical guidelines, Health Technology Assessment (HTA) reports, key systematic reviews and randomised controlled trials (RCTs) and conducted in the following databases and websites:

- *BMJ* Clinical Evidence
- Canadian Medical Association Infobase (Canadian guidelines)
- Clinical Policy and Practice Program of the New South Wales Department of Health (Australia)
- Clinical Practice Guidelines (Australian Guidelines)
- Cochrane Central Register of Controlled Trials (CENTRAL)
- Cochrane Database of Abstracts of Reviews of Effects (DARE)
- Cochrane Database of Systematic Reviews (CDSR)
- Excerpta Medica database (Embase)
- Guidelines International Network
- Health Evidence Bulletin Wales
- Health Management Information Consortium (HMIC)
- HTA database (technology assessments)
- Medical Literature Analysis and Retrieval System Online (MEDLINE)/ MEDLINE In-Process
- National Health and Medical Research Council
- National Library for Health Guidelines Finder
- New Zealand Guidelines Group
- NHS CRD
- Organizing Medical Networked Information Medical Search
- Scottish Intercollegiate Guidelines Network
- Turning Research Into Practice
- United States Agency for Healthcare Research and Quality
- Websites of NICE and the NIHR HTA Programme for guidelines and HTAs in development.

Other relevant guidelines were assessed for quality using the AGREE instrument (AGREE Collaboration, 2003). The evidence base underlying high-quality existing guidelines was utilised and updated as appropriate. Further information about this process can be found in *The Guidelines Manual* (NICE, 2009e).

Systematic literature searches

After the scope was finalised, a systematic search strategy was developed to locate all the relevant evidence. The balance between sensitivity (the power to identify all studies on a particular topic) and specificity (the ability to exclude irrelevant studies from the results) was carefully considered, and a decision made to utilise a broad approach to searching to maximise retrieval of evidence to all parts of the guideline. Searches were restricted to systematic reviews, RCTs, observational studies, case series, quasi-experimental studies, qualitative and survey research, and conducted in the following databases:

- Allied and Complementary Medicine Database (AMED)
- Applied Social Services Index and Abstracts (ASSIA)
- Australian Education Index (AEI)
- British Education Index (BEI)
- CDSR
- CENTRAL
- CINAHL
- DARE
- Education Resources in Curriculum (ERIC)
- Embase
- HMIC
- HTA database
- International Bibliography of the Social Sciences (IBSS)
- MEDLINE/MEDLINE In-Process
- PsycBOOKS
- PsycEXTRA
- Psychological Information Database (PsycINFO)
- Sociological Abstracts
- Social Services Abstracts (SSA).

The search strategies were initially developed for MEDLINE before being translated for use in other databases/interfaces. Strategies were built up through a number of trial searches and discussions of the results of the searches with the review team and GDG to ensure that all possible relevant search terms were covered. In order to assure comprehensive coverage, search terms for autism were kept purposely broad to help counter dissimilarities in database indexing practices and thesaurus terms, and imprecise reporting of study populations by authors in the titles and abstracts of records. In the absence of good-quality evidence on autism, additional searching was conducted for wider literature on learning disabilities. The search terms for each search are set out in full in Appendix 9.

Reference Manager

Citations from each search were downloaded into the reference management software and duplicates removed. Records were then screened against the eligibility criteria of the reviews before being quality appraised (see below). The unfiltered search results were saved and retained for future potential re-analysis to help keep the process both replicable and transparent.

Search filters

To aid retrieval of relevant and sound studies, filters were used to limit a number of searches to systematic reviews, RCTs, observational studies, case series, quasi-experimental studies, qualitative and survey research. The search filters for systematic reviews and RCTs are adaptations of filters designed by the Health Information Research Unit of McMaster University. The remaining filters used were developed in-house. Each filter comprises index terms relating to the study type(s) and associated textwords for the methodological description of the design(s).

Date and language restrictions

Systematic database searches were initially conducted in November 2010 up to the most recent searchable date. Search updates were generated on a 6-monthly basis, with the final re-runs carried out in September 2011 ahead of the guideline consultation. After this point, studies were only included if they were judged by the GDG to be exceptional (for example, if the evidence was likely to change a recommendation).

Although no language restrictions were applied at the searching stage, foreign language papers were not requested or reviewed, unless they were of particular importance to a review question.

Date restrictions were not applied.

Other search methods

Other search methods involved: (a) scanning the reference lists of all eligible publications (systematic reviews, stakeholder evidence and included studies) for more published reports and citations of unpublished research; (b) sending lists of studies meeting the inclusion criteria to subject experts (identified through searches and the GDG) and asking them to check the lists for completeness, and to provide information of any published or unpublished research for consideration (see Appendix 6); (c) checking the tables of contents of key journals for studies that might have been missed by the database and reference list searches; (d) tracking key papers in the Science Citation Index (prospectively) over time for further useful references.

Full details of the search strategies and filters used for the systematic review of clinical evidence are provided in Appendix 9.

Study selection and quality assessment

All primary-level studies included after the first scan of citations were acquired in full and re-evaluated for eligibility at the time they were being entered into the study information database. More specific eligibility criteria were developed for each review question and are described in the relevant clinical evidence chapters. Eligible systematic reviews and primary-level studies were critically appraised for methodological quality (see Appendix 10 for methodology checklists). The eligibility of each study was confirmed by at least one member of the appropriate topic group.

For some review questions, it was necessary to prioritise the evidence with respect to the UK context (that is, external validity). To make this process explicit, the topic groups took into account the following factors when assessing the evidence:

- participant factors (for example, gender, age and ethnicity)
- provider factors (for example, model fidelity, the conditions under which the intervention was performed and the availability of experienced staff to undertake the procedure)
- cultural factors (for example, differences in standard care and differences in the welfare system).

It was the responsibility of each topic group to decide which prioritisation factors were relevant to each review question in light of the UK context and then decide how they should modify their recommendations.

Unpublished evidence

The GDG used a number of criteria when deciding whether or not to accept unpublished data. First, the evidence must have been accompanied by a trial report containing sufficient detail to properly assess the quality of the data. Second, the evidence must have been submitted with the understanding that data from the study and a summary of the study's characteristics would be published in the full guideline. Therefore, the GDG did not accept evidence submitted as commercial in confidence. However, the GDG recognised that unpublished evidence submitted by investigators might later be retracted by those investigators if the inclusion of such data would jeopardise publication of their research.

3.5.3   Data extraction

Quantitative analysis

Study characteristics and outcome data were extracted from all eligible studies that met the minimum quality criteria, using Review Manager 5.1 (Cochrane Collaboration, 2011) (see Appendix 14).

In most circumstances, for a given outcome (continuous and dichotomous), where more than 50% of the number randomised to any group were missing or incomplete, the study results were excluded from the analysis (except for the outcome 'leaving the study early', in which case, the denominator was the number randomised). Where there were limited data for a particular review, the 50% rule was not applied. In these circumstances the evidence was downgraded due to the risk of bias.

Where possible, outcome data from an intention-to-treat (ITT) analysis (that is, a 'once-randomised-always-analyse' basis) were used. For dichotomous efficacy outcomes the effect size was re-calculated if ITT had not been used. When making the calculations if there was good evidence that those participants who ceased to engage in the study were likely to have an unfavourable outcome, early withdrawals were included in both the numerator and denominator. Adverse effects were entered into Review Manager as reported by the study authors because it is usually not possible to determine whether early withdrawals had an unfavourable outcome.

Where some of the studies failed to report standard deviations (for a continuous outcome), and where an estimate of the variance could not be computed from other reported data or obtained from the study author, the following approach was taken.[3]

When the number of studies with missing standard deviations was less than one-third and when the total number of studies was at least ten, the pooled standard deviation was imputed (calculated from all the other studies in the same meta-analysis that used the same version of the outcome measure). In this case, the appropriateness of the imputation was made by comparing the standardised mean differences (SMDs) of those trials that had reported standard deviations against the hypothetical SMDs of the same trials based on the imputed standard deviations. If they converged, the meta-analytical results were considered to be reliable.

When the conditions above could not be met, standard deviations were taken from another related systematic review (if available). In this case, the results were considered to be less reliable.

The meta-analysis of survival data, such as time to any mood episode, was based on log hazard ratios and standard errors. Since individual participant data were not available in included studies, hazard ratios and standard errors calculated from a Cox proportional hazard model were extracted. Where necessary, standard errors were calculated from CIs or p value according to standard formulae (Higgins & Green, 2011). Data were summarised using the generic inverse variance method using Review Manager.

Consultation with another reviewer or members of the GDG was used to overcome difficulties with coding. Data from studies included in existing systematic reviews were extracted independently by one reviewer and cross-checked with the existing data set. Where possible, two independent reviewers extracted data from new studies. Where double data extraction was not possible, data extracted by one reviewer was checked by the second reviewer. Disagreements were resolved through discussion. Where consensus could not be reached, a third reviewer or GDG members resolved the disagreement. Masked assessment (that is, blind to the journal from which the article comes, the authors, the institution and the magnitude of the effect) was not used since it is unclear that doing so reduces bias (Berlin, 2001; Jadad *et al.*, 1996).

Qualitative literature review and thematic analysis
A systematic search for published reviews of qualitative studies relevant to the experience of care review question was conducted. Reviews were sought of qualitative studies that used relevant first-hand experiences of service users and their families, partners or carers. A particular outcome was not specified by the GDG. Instead, the review was concerned with narrative data that highlighted the experience of care. Where the search did not generate an adequate body of literature, a further search for primary qualitative studies was undertaken. Studies were excluded based on the criteria specified in the protocol for the review question (see Section 4.2.1), and if they did not provide a first-hand account of experience.

---

[3]Based on the approach suggested by Furukawa and colleagues (2006).

The purpose of the qualitative search was to identify qualitative evidence sources for which an analysis could be undertaken in order to identify themes relevant to the experience of autism, and the experience of services and treatment from the point of view of the service user and/or their families, partners and carers. The intention was that this thematic analysis would inform the development of recommendations about service users' experience of the condition, of care and interventions, and of the organisation and delivery of services.

For primary studies, a broad thematic analysis of individual patient data was undertaken by one reviewer; this was then discussed and developed with another reviewer. The evidence was then extracted and the themes coded independently by the two reviewers; finally the themes were checked to ensure all of the data were covered.

The results of this thematic analysis were used to develop:

- recommendations about service users' and families', partners' and carers' experience of care
- recommendations that were based on other evidence sources but where the data from the qualitative analysis could be used to provide a context for, or inform the wording or focus of, a recommendation.

3.5.4   Synthesising the evidence from comparative effectiveness studies

Meta-analysis

Where possible, meta-analysis was used to synthesise evidence from comparative effectiveness studies using Review Manager. If necessary, re-analyses of the data or sub-analyses were used to answer review questions not addressed in the original studies or reviews.

Dichotomous outcomes were analysed as relative risks (RRs) with the associated 95% CI (see Figure 3 for an example of a forest plot displaying dichotomous data). An RR (also called a risk ratio) is the ratio of the treatment event rate to the control event rate. An RR of 1 indicates no difference between treatment and control. In Figure 3, the overall RR of 0.73 indicates that the event rate (that is, non-remission rate) associated with intervention A is about three-quarters of that with the control intervention or, in other words, the RR reduction is 27%.

The CI shows a range of values within which it is possible to be 95% confident that the true effect will lie. If the effect size has a CI that does not cross the 'line of no effect', then the effect is commonly interpreted as being statistically significant.

Continuous outcomes were analysed using the mean difference (MD), or SMD when different measures were used in different studies to estimate the same underlying effect (see Figure 4 for an example of a forest plot displaying continuous data). If reported by study authors, ITT data, using a valid method for imputation of missing data, were preferred over data only from people who completed the study.

The number needed to treat for benefit or the number needed to treat for harm was reported for each outcome where the baseline risk (that is, the control group event rate) was similar across studies. In addition, numbers needed to treat calculated at

Figure 3: Example of a forest plot displaying dichotomous data

Review: NCCMH clinical guideline review (Example)
Comparison: 01 Intervention A compared to a control group
Outcome: 01 Number of people who did not show remission

Study or sub-category	Intervention A n/N	Control n/N	RR (fixed) 95% CI	Weight %	RR (fixed) 95% CI
01 Intervention A vs. control					
Griffiths1994	13/23	27/28		38.79	0.59 [0.41, 0.84]
Lee1986	11/15	14/15		22.30	0.79 [0.56, 1.10]
Treasure1994	21/28	24/27		38.92	0.84 [0.66, 1.09]
Subtotal (95% CI)	45/66	65/70		100.00	0.73 [0.61, 0.88]

Test for heterogeneity: Chi² = 2.83, df = 2 (P = 0.24), I² = 29.3%
Test for overall effect: Z = 3.37 (P = 0.0007)

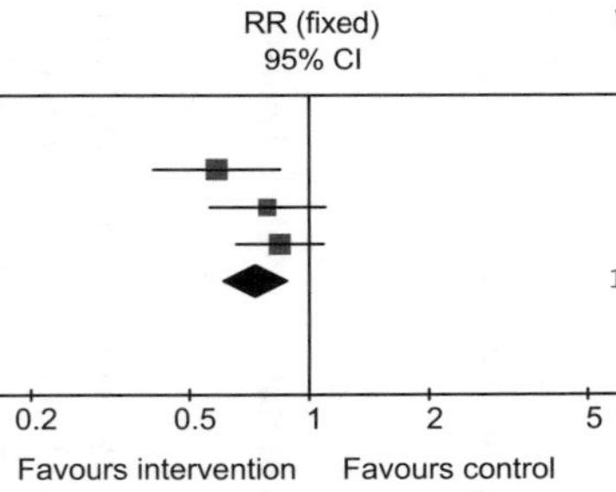

0.2 0.5 1 2 5
Favours intervention   Favours control

Figure 4: Example of a forest plot displaying continuous data

Review: NCCMH clinical guideline review (Example)
Comparison: 01 Intervention A compared to a control group
Outcome: 03 Mean frequency (endpoint)

Study or sub-category	Intervention A N	Mean (SD)	Control N	Mean (SD)	SMD (fixed) 95% CI	Weight %	SMD (fixed) 95% CI
01 Intervention A vs. control							
Freeman1988	32	1.30 (3.40)	20	3.70 (3.60)		25.91	-0.68 [-1.25, -0.10]
Griffiths1994	20	1.25 (1.45)	22	4.14 (2.21)		17.83	-1.50 [-2.20, -0.81]
Lee1986	14	3.70 (4.00)	14	10.10 (17.50)		15.08	-0.49 [-1.24, 0.26]
Treasure1994	28	44.23 (27.04)	24	61.40 (24.97)		27.28	-0.65 [-1.21, -0.09]
Wolf1992	15	5.30 (5.10)	11	7.10 (4.60)		13.90	-0.36 [-1.14, 0.43]
Subtotal (95% CI)	109		91			100.00	-0.74 [-1.04, -0.45]

Test for heterogeneity: Chi² = 6.13, df = 4 (P = 0.19), I² = 34.8%
Test for overall effect: Z = 4.98 (P < 0.00001)

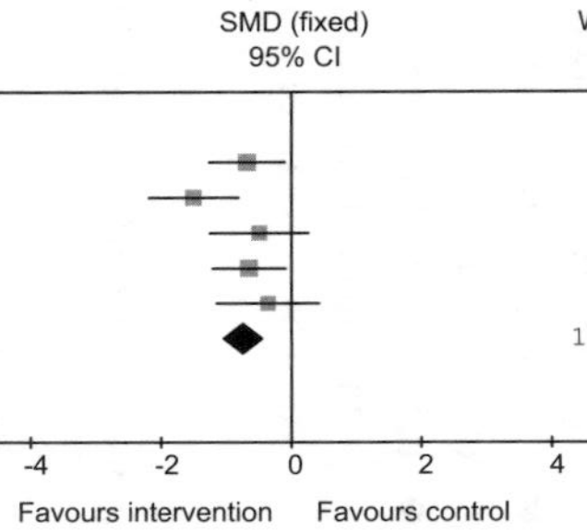

-4 -2 0 2 4
Favours intervention   Favours control

follow-up were only reported where the length of follow-up was similar across studies. When the length of follow-up or baseline risk varies (especially with low risk), the number needed to treat is a poor summary of the treatment effect (Deeks, 2002).

Heterogeneity
To check for consistency of effects among studies, both the I^2 statistic and the chi-squared test of heterogeneity, as well as a visual inspection of the forest plots were used. The I^2 statistic describes the proportion of total variation in study estimates that is due to heterogeneity (Higgins & Thompson, 2002). For a meta-analysis of comparative effectiveness studies, the I^2 statistic was interpreted in the following way based on Higgins and Green (2011):
- 0 to 40%: might not be important
- 30 to 60%: may represent moderate heterogeneity
- 50 to 90%: may represent substantial heterogeneity
- 75 to 100%: considerable heterogeneity.

Two factors were used to make a judgement about the importance of the observed value of I^2: (1) the magnitude and direction of effects, and (2) the strength of evidence for heterogeneity (for example, p value from the chi-squared test, or a CI for I^2).

3.5.5   Synthesising the evidence from diagnostic test accuracy studies

Meta-analysis
Review Manager was used to summarise test accuracy data from each study using forest plots and summary receiver operating characteristic (ROC) plots.

Sensitivity and specificity
The sensitivity of an instrument refers to the probability that it will produce a true positive result when given to a population with the target disorder (as compared to a reference or 'gold standard'). An instrument that detects a low percentage of cases will not be very helpful in determining the numbers of service users who should receive further assessment or a known effective intervention, as many individuals who should receive the treatment will not do so. This would lead to an under-estimation of the prevalence of the disorder, contribute to inadequate care and make for poor planning and costing of the need for treatment. As the sensitivity of an instrument increases, the number of false negatives it detects will decrease.

The specificity of an instrument refers to the probability that a test will produce a true negative result when given to a population without the target disorder (as determined by a reference or 'gold standard'). This is important so that people without the disorder are not offered further assessment or interventions they do not need. As the specificity of an instrument increases, the number of false positives will decrease.

To illustrate this: from a population in which the point prevalence rate of anxiety is 10% (that is, 10% of the population has anxiety at any one time), 1000 people are given a test that has 90% sensitivity and 85% specificity. It is known that 100 people in this population have anxiety, but the test detects only 90 (true positives), leaving ten undetected (false negatives). It is also known that 900 people do not have anxiety, and the test correctly identifies 765 of these (true negatives), but classifies 135 incorrectly as having anxiety (false positives). The positive predictive value of the test (the number correctly identified as having anxiety as a proportion of positive tests) is 40% (90/90 + 135), and the negative predictive value (the number correctly identified as not having anxiety as a proportion of negative tests) is 98% (765/765 +10). Therefore, in this example, a positive test result is correct in only 40% of cases, while a negative result can be relied upon in 98% of cases.

The example above illustrates some of the main differences between positive and negative predictive values in comparison with sensitivity and specificity. For both positive and negative predictive values, prevalence explicitly forms part of their calculation (Altman & Bland, 1994a). When the prevalence of a condition is low in a population this is generally associated with a higher negative predictive value and a lower positive predictive value. Therefore although these statistics are concerned with issues probably more directly applicable to clinical practice (for example, the probability that a person with a positive test result actually has anxiety) they are largely dependent on the characteristics of the population sampled and cannot be universally applied (Altman & Bland, 1994a).

On the other hand, sensitivity and specificity do not necessarily depend on prevalence of anxiety (Altman & Bland, 1994b). For example, sensitivity is concerned with the performance of an identification instrument conditional on a person having anxiety. Therefore the higher false positives often associated with samples of low prevalence will not affect such estimates. The advantage of this approach is that sensitivity and specificity can be applied across populations (Altman & Bland, 1994b). However, the main disadvantage is that clinicians tend to find such estimates more difficult to interpret.

When describing the sensitivity and specificity of the different instruments, the GDG defined values above 0.9 as 'excellent', 0.8 to 0.9 as 'good', 0.5 to 0.7 as 'moderate', 0.3 to 0.4 as 'low', and less than 0.3 as 'poor'.

ROC curves
The qualities of a particular tool are summarised in a ROC curve, which plots sensitivity (expressed as a per cent) against (100-specificity) (see Figure 5).

A test with perfect discrimination would have a ROC curve that passed through the top left-hand corner; that is, it would have 100% specificity and pick up all true positives with no false positives. While this is never achieved in practice, the area under the curve (AUC) measures how close the tool gets to the theoretical ideal. A perfect test would have an AUC of 1, and a test with AUC above 0.5 is better than chance. As discussed above, because these measures are based on sensitivity and 100-specificity, theoretically these estimates are not affected by prevalence.

Negative and positive likelihood ratios
Positive (LR+) and negative (LR-) likelihood ratios are thought not to be dependent on prevalence. LR+ is calculated by sensitivity/(1-specificity) and LR- is (1-sensitivity)/specificity. A value of LR+ >5 and LR- <0.3 suggests the test is relatively accurate (Fischer *et al.*, 2003).

Figure 5: Receiver operator characteristic curve

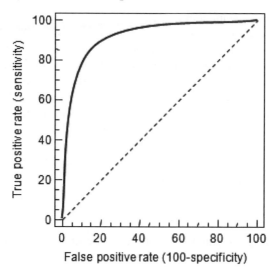

Clinical utility

The assessment instrument should be feasible and implementable in routine clinical care across a variety of assessment settings. The time and skills required to administer, score and interpret the instrument was also considered, as well as the cost and any copyright issues.

3.5.6 Evaluating psychometric data for diagnostic test accuracy studies

In addition to sensitivity and specificity measures, other psychometric properties of case identification and assessment instruments that met inclusion criteria were evaluated according to the following criteria.

Reliability[4]:
- Inter-rater reliability – correlation between two raters ($r \geq 0.70$) = relatively reliable.
- Test-retest reliability – stability of the instrument as shown by the correlation between test scores in the same group of participants across two different times ($r \geq 0.70$) = relatively reliable.
- Internal consistency – the extent to which items measure a single construct ($r \geq 0.70$ or $\alpha \geq 0.50$; $\kappa \geq 0.40$) = relatively reliable.

---

[4]Sattler, J. M. (2001).

Validity:

- Criterion validity – minimum $r = 0.50$[5] (or some suggest 0.30 to 0.40 is more reasonable[6]). Criterion validity refers to the degree to which there is a relationship between the instrument and some other established standard of the measure of interest. There are two subtypes of criterion validity: (1) predictive validity (extent to which instrument scores are correlated with performance on some future criterion) and (2) concurrent validity (extent to which instrument scores are correlated with performance on a related criterion at the same time point).
- Construct validity $r \geq 0.50$ or discrimination index $= 0.3$ to 0.7. Construct validity refers to the degree to which the instrument measures the construct. Construct validity includes two subtypes: (1) discriminant validity (degree to which the instrument differentiates between constructs that are different, such as cases and controls) and (2) convergent validity (correlation between constructs that are similar).

3.5.7   Presenting the data to the Guideline Development Group

Study characteristics tables and, where appropriate, forest plots generated with Review Manager were presented to the GDG. The GRADE approach[7] was used to grade the quality of evidence and strength of recommendations. The technical team produced GRADE evidence profiles (see below) using the GRADE profiler software, and summary of findings tables were presented to the GDG.

Where meta-analysis was not appropriate and/or possible, the reported results from each primary-level study were included in the study characteristics table. The range of effect estimates were included in the GRADE profile, and where appropriate, described narratively.

Evidence profile tables
A GRADE evidence profile was used to summarise both the quality of the evidence and the results of the evidence synthesis (see Table 3 for an example of an evidence profile). The GRADE approach is based on a sequential assessment of the quality of evidence, followed by judgment about the balance between desirable and undesirable effects, and subsequent decision about the strength of a recommendation.

Within the GRADE approach to quality of evidence, the following is used as a starting point:
- RCTs without important limitations provide high-quality evidence
- observational studies without special strengths or important limitations provide low-quality evidence.

---

[5]Andrews and colleagues (1994); Burlingame and colleagues (1995).
[6]Nunnally and Bernstein (1994).
[7]For further information about GRADE, see www.gradeworkinggroup.org.

Table 3: Example of GRADE evidence profile

| | | Quality assessment | | | | | No. of patients | | Summary of findings | | |
| | | | | | | | | | | Effect | |
No. of studies	Design	Limitations	Inconsistency	Indirectness	Imprecision	Other	Intervention	Control	Relative risk (95% CI)	Absolute	Quality
Outcome 1											
6	Randomised trials	No serious limitations	No serious inconsistency	No serious indirectness	Very serious[1,2]	None	8/191	7/150	RR 0.94 (0.39 to 2.23)	0 fewer per 100 (from 3 fewer to 6 more)	⊕⊕○○ LOW
Outcome 2											
3	Randomised trials	No serious limitations	No serious inconsistency	No serious indirectness	No serious imprecision	None	120/600	220/450	RR 0.39 (0.23 to 0.65)	30 fewer per 100 (from 17 fewer to 38 fewer)	⊕⊕⊕⊕ HIGH
Outcome 3											
3	Randomised trials	No serious limitations	Serious inconsistency[3]	No serious indirectness	Very serious[1,2]	None	83	81	–	MD –3.51 (–11.51 to 4.49)	⊕○○○ VERY LOW
Outcome 4											
3	Randomised trials	No serious limitations	No serious inconsistency	No serious indirectness	Serious[1]	None	88	93	–	SMD –0.26 (–0.50 to –0.03)	⊕⊕⊕○ MODERATE
Outcome 5											
4	Randomised trials	No serious limitations	No serious inconsistency	No serious indirectness	Very serious[1,2]	None	109	114	–	SMD –0.13 (–0.6 to 0.34)	⊕⊕○○ LOW

[1] Optimal information size not met.
[2] The CI includes both (1) no effect and (2) appreciable benefit or appreciable harm.
[3] Considerable heterogeneity.

For each outcome, quality may be reduced depending on the following factors:

- **limitations** in study design or execution (risk of bias)
- **inconsistency** (see Section 3.5.4 for how consistency was assessed)
- **indirectness** (that is, how closely the outcome measures, interventions and participants match those of interest)
- **imprecision** (based on the CI around the effect size)
- **publication bias.**

For observational studies, the quality may be upgraded if there is a large effect, all plausible confounding would reduce the demonstrated effect (or increase the effect if no effect was observed), or there is evidence of a dose–response gradient (details would be provided under the 'other' column). Each evidence profile also included a summary of the findings: number of participants included in each group, an estimate of the magnitude of the effect, and the overall quality of the evidence for each outcome.

3.5.8 Method used to answer a review question in the absence of appropriately designed, high-quality research

In the absence of appropriately designed, high-quality research, or where the GDG were of the opinion (on the basis of previous searches or their knowledge of the literature) that there was unlikely to be such evidence, an informal consensus process was adopted.

Informal consensus

The starting point for the process of informal consensus was that a member of the topic group identified, with help from the systematic reviewer, a narrative review that most directly addressed the review question. Where this was not possible, a brief review of the recent literature was initiated.

This existing narrative review or new review was used as a basis for beginning an iterative process to identify lower levels of evidence relevant to the review question and to lead to written statements for the guideline. The process involved a number of steps:

1. A description of what is known about the issues concerning the clinical question was written by one of the topic group members.
2. Evidence from the existing review or new review was then presented in narrative form to the GDG and further comments were sought about the evidence and its perceived relevance to the review question.
3. Based on the feedback from the GDG, additional information was sought and added to the information collected. This might include studies that did not directly address the review question but were thought to contain relevant data.
4. If, during the course of preparing the report, a significant body of primary-level studies (of appropriate design to answer the question) was identified, a full systematic review was done.
5. At this time, subject possibly to further reviews of the evidence, a series of statements that directly addressed the review question were developed.
6. Following this, on occasions and as deemed appropriate by the GDG, the report was then sent to appointed experts outside the GDG for peer review and comment.

The information from this process was then fed back to the GDG for further discussion of the statements.

7. Recommendations were then developed and could also be sent for further external peer review.

8. After this final stage of comment, the statements and recommendations were again reviewed and agreed upon by the GDG.

3.5.9   Extrapolation

In this guideline extrapolation was undertaken where the review question was considered to be important by the GDG but where primary data on adults with autism were not available or were deemed to be insufficient. For the review of organisation and delivery of care the decision was taken to extrapolate from three broad evidence bases. First was the *Common Mental Health Disorders* guideline (NCCMH, 2011), which had recommendations on the organisation and delivery of care for people with depression and anxiety disorders based on an extensive review of: (a) mental health datasets including for local care pathways, and (b) the wider healthcare literature. Second was the evidence base for the *Service User Experience in Adult Mental Health* NICE guidance (NCCMH, 2012), which was used to inform the development of recommendations about the experience of care for both adults with autism and their families and carers. This evidence base supplemented that developed from the review of the qualitative literature in Chapter 4. Third, and in line with other evidence reviews within this guideline, the GDG made a decision to extrapolate from evidence from learning disabilities populations. The GDG was careful to ensure that the extrapolation population shared some common characteristics with the adult autism population, for example age, gender or severity of disorder, and that other aspects of the problem (for example, harms) and outcomes (for example, improved access to services) were similar. The GDG also extrapolated from evidence from populations of children with autism.

Extrapolation was only performed where the quality of the data was equivalent; the same standards were applied for assessing and evaluating the evidence from adults with a learning disability and children with autism as were used for the primary data from adults with autism. In the case of organisation and delivery of care, the focus was not necessarily on common characteristics of the population; as the recommendations from the *Common Mental Health Disorders* guideline provided principles for the organisation of local care pathways, the GDG's concern was whether or not those principles could be applied to people with autism. Extrapolated data were recognised as lower quality forms of evidence than data from adults with autism and this is reflected within the GRADE system with outcomes using extrapolated populations.

3.5.10   The incorporation and adaptation of existing NICE guideline recommendations

The GDG employed the methods developed for incorporation (adoption) and adaptation of existing guideline recommendations in the *Common Mental Health Disorders*

(NCCMH, 2011) guideline. The key principles underpinning this process are twofold: (1) incorporating a recommendation involves a simple transfer of a recommendation from one guideline to another; no changes are made to the wording or structure; (2) adapting a recommendation involves making a number of changes to a recommendation but preserving the meaning and intent of the original recommendation (this is to ensure a clear link to the underpinning evidence base) (NCCMH, 2011). Adaptations can take a number of forms under two broad headings:

- *Changes in terminology*: changing the original wording of a recommendation in order to facilitate understanding, for example using a term such as 'facilitative self-help' to replace 'guided self-help'; this may do nothing more that reflect changes in current usage in the NHS or in the particular services covered by the guideline.
- *Changes in structure and wording in order to best preserve the meaning and intent of the original in a form that is compatible with a recommendation for the new guideline*: this may involve, for example, restructuring and recontextualising a treatment recommendation as a recommendation for referral for that treatment.

In deciding whether to incorporate or adapt existing guideline recommendations, the GDG first considered whether the direct evidence obtained from the autism dataset was of sufficient quality to allow development of recommendations. It was only where such evidence was not available, and drawing on the principles of extrapolation (see Section 3.5.9), that the GDG would move to the 'incorporate or adapt' method.

This process of incorporation and adaptation drew on the knowledge and expertise of the GDG and was guided by a number of considerations. A key concern was that the recommendations in an existing guideline might have been developed for populations not covered by the guideline under development and as such might not be relevant to the experience of those whose care and treatment is covered by this guideline. Nevertheless the principles underpinning the recommendations might have considerable relevance. When incorporating or adapting recommendations from other guidelines the GDG identified those recommendations that might be relevant but might require some adaptation in order to be comprehensible and of value in providing a set of principles underpinning recommendations for the organisation and delivery of care for adults with autism. In identifying those recommendations the GDG was guided by four considerations:

- the recommendation should have real value in improving services
- the inclusion of the recommendation in the guideline should facilitate the understanding, uptake of integration of other recommendations in this guideline
- the inclusion of the recommendation in the guideline should only be necessary where recommendations based on more direct sources of evidence could not be made
- the inclusion of the recommendation in the guideline should not lead to misrepresentation of the original guideline(s) from which it was drawn, or other recommendations developed for this guideline.

The process of identifying the recommendations from an existing guideline followed five stages:

Stage 1 – Identification of any recommendations in an existing guideline(s) that were deemed to be relevant to the care and treatment of the population in the current guideline.

Stage 2 – Identification of any recommendations in an existing guideline(s) that were relevant to the care and treatment of the population in the current guideline but which the GDG considered were of general applicability and would not therefore warrant inclusion in the guideline under development.

Stage 3 – Identification of any recommendations in an existing guideline that were relevant to the care and treatment of the population in the current guideline and which the GDG considered were of such importance in the care and treatment of the population in the current guideline that they needed to be included in this guideline.

Stage 4 – The identification of those recommendations that: (1) could be incorporated in this guideline without adaptation, and (2) required adaptation to be included in this guideline.

Stage 5 – The adaptation of any recommendation is in the line with the methods set out in this guideline and based on the process developed for the *Common Mental Health Disorders* guideline (NCCMH, 2011).

3.6   HEALTH ECONOMICS METHODS

The aim of the health economics was to contribute to the guideline's development by providing evidence on the cost effectiveness of interventions for adults with autism covered in the guideline. This was achieved by:

- systematic literature review of existing economic evidence
- decision-analytic economic modelling.

Systematic reviews of economic literature were conducted in all areas covered in the guideline. Economic modelling was undertaken in areas with likely major resource implications, where the current extent of uncertainty over cost effectiveness was significant and economic analysis was expected to reduce this uncertainty, in accordance with *The Guidelines Manual* (NICE, 2009e). Prioritisation of areas for economic modelling was a joint decision between the health economist and the GDG. The rationale for prioritising review questions for economic modelling was set out in an economic plan agreed between NICE, the GDG, the health economist and the other members of the technical team. An economic model was therefore developed to address the cost effectiveness of an employment support programme versus usual standard service for adults with autism.

In addition, literature on the health-related quality of life of people with autism was systematically searched to identify studies reporting appropriate utility scores that could be utilised in a cost-utility analysis.

The rest of this section describes the methods adopted in the systematic literature review of economic studies. Methods employed in economic modelling are described in the respective sections of the guideline.

3.6.1   Search strategy for economic evidence

Scoping searches
A broad preliminary search of the literature was undertaken in January 2010 to obtain an overview of the issues likely to be covered by the scope, and help define key areas.

Searches were restricted to economic studies and health technology assessment reports, and conducted in the following databases:

- EconLit (the American Economic Association's electronic bibliography)
- Embase
- HTA database
- MEDLINE/MEDLINE In-Process
- NHS Economic Evaluation Database (NHS EED)

Any relevant economic evidence arising from the clinical scoping searches was also made available to the health economist during the same period.

Systematic literature searches

After the scope was finalised, a systematic search strategy was developed to locate all the relevant evidence. The balance between sensitivity (the power to identify all studies on a particular topic) and specificity (the ability to exclude irrelevant studies from the results) was carefully considered, and a decision made to utilise a broad approach to searching to maximise retrieval of evidence to all parts of the guideline. Searches were restricted to economic studies and health technology assessment reports, and conducted in the following databases:

- EconLit
- HTA database
- Embase
- MEDLINE/MEDLINE In-Process
- NHS Economic Evaluation Database (NHS EED)
- PsycINFO.

In addition, Google and Google Scholar were also searched for any research potentially missed by the electronic database searches.

Any relevant economic evidence arising from the clinical searches was also made available to the health economist during the same period.

The search strategies were initially developed for MEDLINE before being translated for use in other databases/interfaces. Strategies were built up through a number of trial searches and discussions of the results of the searches with the review team and GDG to ensure that all possible relevant search terms were covered. In order to assure comprehensive coverage, search terms for autism were kept purposely broad to help counter dissimilarities in database indexing practices and thesaurus terms, and imprecise reporting of study populations by authors in the titles and abstracts of records. In the absence of good-quality evidence on autism, additional searching was conducted for wider literature on learning disabilities.

For standard mainstream bibliographic databases (Embase, MEDLINE and PsycINFO) search terms for autism were combined with a search filter for health economic studies. For searches generated in topic-specific databases (EconLit, HTA, NHS EED) search terms for autism were used without a filter. The sensitivity of this approach was aimed at minimising the risk of overlooking relevant publications, due to potential weaknesses resulting from more focused search strategies. A more focused approach was employed for searches on learning disabilities. The search terms are set out in full in Appendix 11.

Reference Manager

Citations from each search were downloaded into Reference Manager (a software product for managing references and formatting bibliographies) and duplicates removed. Records were then screened against the inclusion criteria of the reviews before being quality appraised. The unfiltered search results were saved and retained for future potential re-analysis to help keep the process both replicable and transparent.

Search filters

The search filter for health economics is an adaptation of a pre-tested strategy designed by the Centre for Reviews and Dissemination at the University of York (2007). The search filter is designed to retrieve records of economic evidence (including full and partial economic evaluations) from the vast amount of literature indexed to major medical databases such as MEDLINE. The filter, which comprises a combination of controlled vocabulary and free-text retrieval methods, maximises sensitivity (or recall) to ensure that as many potentially relevant records as possible are retrieved from a search. A full description of the filter is provided in Appendix 11.

Date and language restrictions

Systematic database searches were initially conducted in November 2010 up to the most recent searchable date. Search updates were generated on a 6-monthly basis, with the final re-runs carried out in September 2011. After this point, studies were included only if they were judged by the GDG to be exceptional (for example, the evidence was likely to change a recommendation).

Although no language restrictions were applied at the searching stage, foreign language papers were not requested or reviewed, unless they were of particular importance to an area under review. All the searches were restricted to research published from 1996 onwards in order to obtain data relevant to current healthcare settings and costs.

Other search methods

Other search methods involved scanning the reference lists of all eligible publications (systematic reviews, stakeholder evidence and included studies from the economic and clinical reviews) to identify further studies for consideration.

Full details of the search strategies and filter used for the systematic review of health economic evidence are provided in Appendix 11.

3.6.2   Inclusion criteria for economic studies

The following inclusion criteria were applied to select studies identified by the economic searches for further consideration:
- Only studies from Organisation for Economic Co-operation and Development countries were included, as the aim of the review was to identify economic information transferable to the UK context.
- Selection criteria based on types of clinical conditions and service users as well as interventions assessed were identical to the clinical literature review.

- Studies were included provided that sufficient details regarding methods and results were available to enable the methodological quality of the study to be assessed, and provided that the study's data and results were extractable. Poster presentations of abstracts were excluded.
- Full economic evaluations that compared two or more relevant options and considered both costs and consequences, as well as simple cost analyses, were included in the review.
- Economic studies were included if they used clinical effectiveness data from an RCT, a cohort study, or a systematic review and meta-analysis of clinical studies.

3.6.3   Applicability and quality criteria for economic studies

All economic papers eligible for inclusion were appraised for their applicability and quality using the methodology checklist for economic evaluations recommended by NICE (NICE, 2009e), which is shown in Appendix 12 of this guideline. The methodology checklist for economic evaluations was also applied to the economic model developed specifically for this guideline. Studies that fully or partially met the applicability and quality criteria described in the methodology checklist were considered during the guideline development process, along with the results of the economic modelling conducted specifically for this guideline. The completed methodology checklists for all economic evaluations considered in the guideline are provided in Appendix 17.

3.6.4   Presentation of economic evidence

The economic evidence considered in the guideline is provided in the respective evidence chapters, following presentation of the relevant clinical evidence. The references to the included studies and tables with the study characteristics and results are provided in Appendix 18. Methods and results of economic modelling undertaken alongside the guideline development process are presented in the relevant evidence chapters. Characteristics and results of all economic studies considered during the guideline development process (including modelling studies conducted for this guideline) are summarised in economic evidence profiles accompanying respective GRADE clinical evidence profiles in Appendix 19.

3.6.5   Results of the systematic search of economic literature

The titles of the studies identified by the systematic search of the literature were screened for their relevance to the topic (that is, economic issues and information on health-related quality of life in adults with autism). References that were clearly not relevant were excluded first. The abstracts of all potentially relevant studies were then assessed against the inclusion criteria for economic evaluations by the health economist.

Full texts of the studies potentially meeting the inclusion criteria (including those for which eligibility was not clear from the abstract) were obtained. Studies that did not meet the inclusion criteria, were duplicates, were secondary publications of one study, or had been updated in more recent publications were subsequently excluded. Economic evaluations eligible for inclusion were then appraised for their applicability and quality using the methodology checklist for economic evaluations. Finally, economic studies that fully or partially met the applicability and quality criteria were considered at formulation of the guideline recommendations.

3.7   FROM EVIDENCE TO RECOMMENDATIONS

Once the clinical and health economic evidence was summarised, the GDG drafted the recommendations. In making recommendations, the GDG took into account the trade-off between the benefits and harms of the intervention/instrument, as well as other important factors, such as economic considerations, values of the development group and society, the requirements to prevent discrimination and to promote equality[8], and the GDG's awareness of practical issues (Eccles *et al.,* 1998; NICE, 2009e).

Finally, to show clearly how the GDG moved from the evidence to the recommendations, each chapter has a section called 'from evidence to recommendations'. Underpinning this section is the concept of the 'strength' of a recommendation (Schunemann *et al.*, 2003). This takes into account the quality of the evidence but is conceptually different. Some recommendations are 'strong' in that the GDG believes that the vast majority of healthcare professionals and service users would choose a particular intervention if they considered the evidence in the same way that the GDG has. This is generally the case if the benefits clearly outweigh the harms for most people and the intervention is likely to be cost effective. However, there is often a closer balance between benefits and harms, and some service users would not choose an intervention whereas others would. This may happen, for example, if some service users are particularly averse to some side effect and others are not. In these circumstances the recommendation is generally weaker, although it may be possible to make stronger recommendations about specific groups of service users. The strength of each recommendation is reflected in the wording of the recommendation, rather than by using ratings, labels or symbols.

Where the GDG identified areas in which there are uncertainties or where robust evidence was lacking, they developed research recommendations. Those that were identified as 'high priority' were developed further in the NICE version of the guideline, and presented in Appendix 13.

---

[8]See NICE's equality scheme: www.nice.org.uk/aboutnice/howwework/NICEEqualityScheme.jsp

3.8   STAKEHOLDER CONTRIBUTIONS

Professionals, service users, and companies have contributed to and commented on the guideline at key stages in its development. Stakeholders for this guideline include:

● service user and carer stakeholders: national service user and carer organisations that represent the interests of people whose care will be covered by the guideline

● local service user and carer organisations: but only if there is no relevant national organisation

● professional stakeholders' national organisations: that represent the healthcare professionals who provide the services described in the guideline

● commercial stakeholders: companies that manufacture drugs or devices used in the treatment of the condition covered by the guideline and whose interests may be significantly affected by the guideline

● providers and commissioners of health services in England and Wales

● statutory organisations: including the Department of Health, the Welsh Assembly Government, NHS Quality Improvement Scotland, the Care Quality Commission and the National Patient Safety Agency

● research organisations: that have carried out nationally recognised research in the area.

NICE clinical guidelines are produced for the NHS in England and Wales, so a 'national' organisation is defined as one that represents England and/or Wales, or has a commercial interest in England and/or Wales.

Stakeholders have been involved in the guideline's development at the following points:

● commenting on the initial scope of the guideline and attending a scoping work-shop held by NICE

● contributing possible review questions and lists of evidence to the GDG

● commenting on the draft of the guideline

● highlighting factual errors in the pre-publication check.

3.9   VALIDATION OF THE GUIDELINE

Registered stakeholders had an opportunity to comment on the draft guideline, which was posted on the NICE website during the consultation period. Following the consultation, all comments from stakeholders and others (see Appendix 5 for a list of stakeholders) were responded to, and the guideline updated as appropriate. The GRP also reviewed the guideline and checked that stakeholders' comments had been addressed.

Following the consultation period, the GDG finalised the recommendations and the NCCMH produced the final documents. These were then submitted to NICE for the pre-publication check where stakeholders were given the opportunity to highlight factual errors. Any errors were corrected by the NCCMH, then the guideline was formally approved by NICE and issued as guidance to the NHS in England and Wales.

4 EXPERIENCE OF CARE

4.1 INTRODUCTION

This chapter provides an overview of the experience of adults with autism, and the experiences of their families, partners and carers. The experience of the care of people with autism has not been well described, with the limited work in the field focusing more on the experience of children and young people and their families and carers (Thomas *et al.*, 2007). However, as the Autism Strategy (Department of Health, 2010) makes clear, adults with autism have considerable problems accessing care, they receive only limited services at best (particularly if they do not have a significant coexisting condition) and there is also considerable concern about the nature of the care provided. Understanding the experience of having autism, of services and of caring for a family member with autism is of central importance in developing this guideline.

This chapter centres on a thematic analysis of the qualitative literature, which was undertaken in order to identify themes relevant to the experience of adults with autism and/or their families, partners and carers. The intention is that this thematic analysis will directly inform the development of recommendations about improving service user experience of care but will also inform the development and content of other recommendations in this guideline, in particular those for the organisation and delivery of services and those that set out the principles of care for adults with autism (see Chapter 6).

4.2 REVIEW OF THE QUALITATIVE LITERATURE

4.2.1 Clinical review protocol (experience of care)

The review protocol, including the review questions, information about the databases searched, and the eligibility criteria used for this section of the guideline, can be found in Table 4 (further information about the search strategy can be found in Appendix 9). A systematic search for published reviews of relevant qualitative studies of adults with autism and their families, partners and carers was undertaken using standard NCCMH procedures as described in Chapter 3. Reviews were sought of qualitative studies that used relevant first-hand experiences of adults with autism and their families, partners and carers. The GDG did not specify a particular outcome. Instead the review was concerned with any narrative data that highlighted the experience of care. Where a significant body of systematic reviews was not identified the GDG looked for primary studies of experiences of adults with autism and their families, partners and carers and adopted the method described in Section 4.3.2 for the analysis of the studies.

Table 4: Databases searched and inclusion/exclusion criteria for clinical evidence

Component	Description
Review question(s)	For adults with autism, what are their experiences of having autism, of access to services, and of treatment? (RQ – F1)
	For families, partners and carers of adults with autism, what are their experiences of caring for people with autism, and what support is available for families, partners and carers? (RQ – F2)
Objectives	To identify the emerging themes for the experiences of adults with autism and their families, partners and carers in terms of the experience of autism, of accessing services and of treatment.
Criteria for considering studies for the review	
• *Population*	Adults and young people aged 18 years and older with suspected autism across the range of diagnostic groups (including atypical autism, Asperger's syndrome and pervasive developmental disorder), and their families, partners and carers.
• *Intervention*	None
• *Comparison*	None
• *Critical outcomes*	None specified – any narrative description of service user or carer experience of autism.
• *Study design*	Systematic reviews of qualitative studies, qualitative studies, surveys.
• *Include unpublished data?*	No
• *Restriction by date?*	No
• *Minimum sample size*	No minimum sample size.
• *Study setting*	Any setting
Electronic databases	ASSIA, CINAHL, Embase, HMIC, IBSS, MEDLINE, PsycBOOKS, PsycEXTRA, PsycINFO, Sociological Abstracts, SSA
Date searched	CINAHL, Embase, HMIC, MEDLINE, PsycBOOKS, PsycEXTRA, PsycINFO: 01.01.1996 to 09.09.2011;
	ASSIA, IBSS, Sociological Abstracts, SSA: 01.01.1996 to 10.10.2011
Searching other resources	Hand reference searching of retrieved literature
The review strategy	Thematic analysis of primary qualitative studies and surveys reporting experiences of adults with autism and/or their families, partners and carers.

4.3   THEMATIC ANALYSIS OF THE QUALITATIVE LITERATURE

4.3.1   Introduction

In line with the method normally adopted for this type of review a search for systematic reviews of the experience of care for individuals with autism and their families, partners and carers was conducted. However, no relevant systematic reviews could be included. Consequently, a second search was conducted to identify relevant primary qualitative studies and survey data for adults with autism and their families and carers. The review question was concerned with exploring the experience of care for adults with autism and their families, partners and carers in terms of the broad topics of receiving a diagnosis, accessing services and treatment, and the experience of autism. The literature review supported a thematic analysis of the qualitative data reported in the primary studies and identified emergent themes relevant to the experience of care.

4.3.2   Method

The method used in this section is set out in Chapter 3. In summary, the included primary qualitative studies and survey data (see Table 4 for details on inclusion criteria) were reviewed using thematic analytic techniques (Boyatzis, 1998; Braun & Clarke, 2006). Each included study was reviewed by members of the review team and broad themes were identified (see Section 4.3.4). Relevant sections of the text were then extracted and categorised under the different headings and themes were checked to ensure all of the data were covered.

4.3.3   Studies considered[9]

Studies were sought that used relevant first-hand experiences of adults with autism and their families, partners and carers. For more information about the databases searched see Table 4.

The search found 27 studies (reported across 28 studies) that met the eligibility criteria and were included (BEMPORAD1979 [Bemporad, 1979], BLACHER2010 [Blacher *et al.,* 2010], CEDERLUND2010 [Cederlund *et al.,* 2010], CESARONI1991 [Cesaroni & Garber, 1991], CLARKE2008 [Clarke & van Amerom, 2008], GRAETZ2010 [Graetz, 2010], HARE2004 [Hare *et al.,* 2004], HURLBUTT2002 [Hurlbutt & Chalmers, 2002], HUWS2008 [Huws & Jones, 2008], JENNESCOUSSENS2006 [Jennes-Coussens *et al.,* 2006], JONES2001 [Jones *et al.,*

---

[9]Here and elsewhere in the guideline, each study considered for review is referred to by a study ID in capital letters (primary author and date of study publication, except where a study is in press or only submitted for publication, then a date is not used).

2001], KRAUSS2005 [Kraus *et al.,* 2005], KRAUSZ2005 [Krausz & Meszaros, 2005], LAU2011 [Lau & Peterson, 2011], MACLEOD2007 [MacLeod & Johnston, 2007], MAGANA2006 [Magana & Smith, 2006], ORSMOND2007A [Orsmond & Seltzer, 2007], ORSMOND2009 [Orsmond *et al.,* 2009], PUNSHON2009 [Punshon *et al.,* 2009], ROBLEDO2008 [Robledo & Donnellan, 2008], RYAN2009 [Ryan & Cole, 2009], RYAN2010 [Ryan, 2010], SELTZER2001 [Seltzer *et al.,* 2001], SHTAYERMMAN2007/2009 [Shtayermman, 2007 and 2009], SHU2006 [Shu *et al.,* 2006], SMITH2010A [Smith *et al.,* 2010], SPERRY2005 [Sperry & Mesibov, 2005]). All of these studies were published in peer-reviewed journals between 1979 and 2011. In addition, 140 studies were considered for the thematic analysis but were excluded as they did not meet the eligibility criteria for inclusion in the review (see Appendix 14a). The most common reason for exclusion was that the people used in the study, or mean age of the sample, were aged under 18 or the studies focused on the predictive value of participant characteristics rather than experience of care. The characteristics of all the studies included in this review have been summarised in Table 5 and Table 6. These have been categorised under two main headings: experience of care of adults with autism and experience of families, partners and carers.

4.3.4   Experience of care of adults with autism

As described in Section 4.3.2, the review team identified broad themes from the primary qualitative studies and survey data. Initially this thematic analysis of the data resulted in seven broad headings:
- impact of autism
- relationships
- awareness of being different
- stigma and judgement by others
- reactions to diagnosis
- interventions and services
- being an expert by experience.

Under these broad headings specific emergent themes were extracted and are discussed below. A summary of the themes identified in each study (marked with a 'Y') can be found in Table 7.

Impact of autism
Participants in the studies expressed a range of different views about the way autism had impacted on their lives. Some participants described feelings of high self-esteem, especially in relation to overcoming difficulties. In addition, autism was viewed by some participants as an advantage, particularly in some areas of cognitive functioning (CLARKE2008, PUNSHON2009). This was, however, coupled with awareness of a negative impact of autism on areas such as quality of life (JENNESCOUSSENS2006), experience of their environment (CESARONI1991, HURLBUTT2002), education (HURLBUTT2002, JENNESCOUSSENS2006) and employment (HURLBUTT2002, JENNESCOUSSENS2006, MACLEOD2007).

Table 5: Study information table for included studies of the experience of care of adults with autism

Experience of care of adults with autism	
Study IDs	(1) BEMPORAD1979 (2) CEDERLUND2010 (3) CESARONI1991 (4) CLARKE2008 (5) HURLBUTT2002 (6) HUWS2008 (7) JENNESCOUSSENS2006 (8) JONES2001 (9) LAU2011 (10) MACLEOD2007 (11) PUNSHON2009 (12) ROBLEDO2008 (13) SHTAYERMMAN2007/2009 (same population used in the two papers) (14) SPERRY2005
Autism population (Axis I/II disorders/ mean age)	(1) 100% autism/31 years (2) 100% Asperger's syndrome/22 years (3) 100% autism (high functioning)/27 years (4) Self-identified Asperger's syndrome/not specified (5) 100% autism (high functioning)/42 years (6) 100% autism/range 16 to 21 years (7) 100% Asperger's syndrome/20 years (8) 60% autism (high functioning), 20% atypical autism/not specified (9)–(10) 100% Asperger's syndrome/not specified (11) 100% Asperger's syndrome/range 22 to 45 years (12) 100% autism/27 years (13) 100% Asperger's syndrome/20 years (14) 100% ASD/34 years
Focus of study	(1) Experience of autism (2) Assessment (3)–(6) Experience of autism (7) Quality of life (8) Experience of autism (9) Relationship satisfaction (10) Experience of support group (11) Experience of autism

Continued

Experience of care of adults with autism	
	(12) Experience of relationships (13) Perception of stigma (14) Perception of social challenges
Data collection method	(1) Interview/case history (2) Interview/questionnaire (3) Interview/content analysis of documents (4) Content analysis of websites (5) Interview/content analysis of documents (6) Interview (7) Interview/questionnaire (8) Content analysis of websites (9) Questionnaire (10) Written interview (11) Interview (12) Interview/content analysis of documents (13) Questionnaire (14) Focus group
Setting	(1)–(2) Not reported (3) Multiple (conference, home, telephone) (4) Online (5) Multiple (conference, telephone, email) (6) Academic institution (7) Home (8) Online (9) Postal questionnaire (10)–(12) Not reported (13) Online and postal questionnaire (14) Social group meeting
Country	(1) US (2) Sweden (3)–(4) Canada (5) US (6) UK (7) Canada (8) UK (9) AUSTRALIA (10)–(11) UK (12)–(14) US

Table 6: Study information table for included studies of the experience of families, partners and carers of adults with autism

Experience of families, partners and carers	
Study IDs	(1) BLACHER2010 (2) GRAETZ2010 (3) HARE2004 (4) KRAUSS2005 (5) KRAUSZ2005 (6) LAU2011 (7) MAGANA2006 (8) ORSMOND2007A (9) ORSMOND2009 (10) RYAN2009 (11) RYAN2010 (12) SELTZER2001 (13) SHU2006 (14) SMITH2010A
Autism population (Axis I/II disorders/ mean age)	(1) 100% autism/23 years (2) 100% ASD/22 years (3) 100% ASD/27 years (4) 100% ASD/32 years (5) 100% autism/19 years (6) 100% Asperger's syndrome/not specified (7) 100% ASD/18 years (8) 100% ASD/35 years (9) 100% ASD/19 and 29 years (10) 100% ASD/range 23 to 53 years (11) 100% ASD/range 18 to 28 years (12) 100% autism/39 years (13) 100% autism/18 years (14) 100% ASD/25 years
Focus of study	(1) Expectations of transition (2) Opportunities in autism (3) Health and social care needs (4) Residential arrangement satisfaction (5) Experience of autism (6) Relationship satisfaction (7) Residential arrangement satisfaction (8)–(9) Sibling relationship

Continued

Table 6: (*Continued*)

	Experience of families, partners and carers
	(10)–(12) Experience of autism (13) Self-identity (14) Experience of autism
Data collection method	(1) Interview (2) Questionnaire (3) Interview (4) Questionnaire (5) Interview (6) Questionnaire (7) Interview/questionnaire (8) Questionnaire (9) Questionnaire/interview (10)–(14) Interview
Setting	(1) Home (2) Online and postal survey (3) Not reported (4) Home (5) Not reported (6) Postal questionnaire (7) Home (8)–(9) Postal questionnaire (10) Not reported (11) Home (N = 2 office settings) (12) Not reported (13) Home (14) Telephone
Country	(1)–(2) US (3) UK (4) US (5) UK (6) Australia (7)–(9) US (10)–(11) UK (12) US (13) Taiwan (14) US

Table 7: Summary of emergent themes for the experience of care of adults with autism

	BEMPORAD1979	CEDERLUND2010	CESARONI1991	CLARKE2008	HURLBUTT2002	HUWS2008	JENNESCOUSSENS2006	JONES2001	LAU2011	MACLEOD2007	PUNSHON2009	ROBLEDO2008	SHTAYERMMAN2007/2009	SPERRY2005
Impact of autism	–	Y	Y	Y	Y	Y	Y	Y	–	Y	Y	–	Y	–
Relationships	Y	Y	Y	–	Y	–	Y	Y	Y	Y	Y	Y	–	Y
Awareness of being different	Y	Y	Y	Y	Y	Y	Y	Y	–	Y	Y	–	–	–
Stigma and judgement by others	–	–	Y	Y	Y	Y	–	Y	–	Y	Y	Y	Y	Y
Reactions to diagnosis	–	–	–	–	Y	Y	–	Y	–	Y	Y	–	–	Y
Interventions and services	Y	–	–	Y	Y	–	Y	Y	–	Y	Y	Y	–	–
Being an expert by experience	–	–	–	Y	Y	–	–	–	–	Y	–	Y	–	–

Difficulties with employment extended beyond finding a job. Participants who were in paid employment also reported difficulties with jobs that were often below their ability and poorly paid (HURLBUTT2002, JENNESCOUSSENS2006):

> *I worked as a caseworker and was asked to leave 5 months later. I could have used support in asking the proper questions. I started in the food industry after that, and the only job I could get was washing pots or doing dishes. I had odd jobs, working in the hospital in the stockroom, and working in department stores in the same capacity. In these jobs, I was fired because either I asked too many questions, or didn't ask enough, or bothered the women, whatever that meant. Since autism was barely heard of, I couldn't figure out why I was having such bad luck. There were no job coaches then. (HURLBUTT2002)*

Experience of care

Increased psychological distress was reported in adults with autism, with anxiety and depression (CEDERLUND2010, HURLBUTT2002, JONES2001, PUNSHON2009, SHTAYERMMAN2007/2009), self-harm and suicidal ideation (MACLEOD2007, PUNSHON2009, SHTAYERMMAN2007/2009) all being experienced. There were also negative emotions around the enduring nature of autism, feelings of frustration and of being 'stuck like this' (HUWS2008, JONES2001, PUNSHON2009), and sadness that their diagnosis threatened their expectations (HUWS2008, PUNSHON2009):

> *There was this dip...I think because I felt like well, you know, I was feeling a bit hopeless, you know that maybe this wasn't something I could overcome...I am never going to be like one of these 'normal' people and you know...and I thought 'I am stuck being like this now'.* (PUNSHON2009)

Relationships

Adults with autism expressed a need for good interpersonal relationships (BEMPORAD1979, CESARONI1991, JONES2001) and intimate relationships (HURLBUTT2002, LAU2011, SPERRY2005) despite an awareness of being different from their peers (CEDERLUND2010, CESARONI1991, HURLBUTT2002, MACLEOD2007, PUNSHON2009) and a self-awareness regarding social difficulties (HURLBUTT2002, JENNESCOUSSENS2006, JONES2001):

> *I've been in dating relationships, so don't tell me autistic people cannot handle marriage relationships or dating relationships. It's a matter of choice. If you really want to make it work, you will go for it. I mean it makes me so angry when people say, 'Well, normal people can get married and autistic people can't.' That's garbage!* (SPERRY2005)

> *I know that every time I try to make a friend or be a part of a group, some autistic trait pops up and seems to sabotage my efforts, no matter how hard I try to hold it back or try to control it. (JONES2001)*

There was an indication that their social needs might not be recognised or might be underestimated by those around them (CEDERLUND2010), and this angered some participants (CESARONI1991, SPERRY2005). There was talk of the difficulties faced by individuals with autism when engaging in social interactions (CESARONI1991), and of the fact that such efforts to socialise were not always successful (BEMPORAD1979, HURLBUTT2002, JONES2001) or sustained (BEMPORAD1979). Misinterpretation of sexual advances could sometimes lead to inappropriate or vulnerable situations (CESARONI1991, HURLBUTT2002):

> *I'm not very good at thinking of people in parts... I could never tell when he was being my boss and when he was being my friend and when he was going to hurt me. (CESARONI1991)*

These difficulties could cause distress and frustration (BEMPORAD1979, HURLBUTT2002, JONES2001, MACLEOD2007). There was also discussion of positive relationships formed (CESARONI1991, HURLBUTT2002, SPERRY2005) and how such support was valued (HURLBUTT2002, JENNESCOUSSENS2006, ROBLEDO2008).

The most appreciated relationships were those formed with other people with autism (HURLBUTT2002, JONES2001, MACLEOD2007, PUNSHON2009), as there could be mutual understanding and a feeling of 'fitting in' (MACLEOD2007, PUNSHON2009), as well as an opportunity to socialise without feeling like 'getting it wrong' (MACLEOD2007, PUNSHON2009). A feeling of relief was discussed upon discovering these relationships (MACLEOD2007), often formed at support groups (HURLBUTT2002, MACLEOD2007, PUNSHON2009):

> *I found it a relief to meet other people who had similar difficulties to myself. For example, I heard people tell anecdotes about times they had 'said the wrong thing' and had accidentally insulted other people. As my mother had described it, in my case, 'Paula tells the awful truth'. When I had been attending the group for some time, I saw one of the members on the bus, and went up to say 'hello'. However, he looked at me blankly and said, 'How do I know you?' which amazed me, as this is an expression I have often used myself. When I meet someone that I deal with quite often, like the doctor's receptionist, but they are in unfamiliar surroundings, like in the street, if they say 'hello', I often can't place who they are, and may have to say, 'How do I know you?' So, to be on the receiving end of this was an uncanny experience.* (MACLEOD2007)

Adults with autism discussed their awareness of their difficulties in social interaction (HURLBUTT2002, JENNESCOUSSENS2006) and with communication (CESARONI1991, HURLBUTT2002, ROBLEDO2008), and their concerns and frustrations about these problems (HURLBUTT2002, JONES2001, MACLEOD2007). They described confusing social environments (BEMPORAD1979, CESARONI1991, JONES2001), sensory overload (BEMPORAD1979, HURLBUTT2002, JONES2001) and having to apologise for their behaviour (JONES2001, PUNSHON2009), which could leave them feeling isolated (BEMPORAD1979, HURLBUTT2002, JONES2001, PUNSHON2009) and envious of 'neurotypicals'[10] (HURLBUTT2002, PUNSHON2009):

> *Many times, I do feel as though I'm buried inside myself (a very comfortable, secure feeling, I might add), sitting in a machine, pushing buttons, playing sound files and pulling levers on programmed cue. Social environments can be so confusing with what is appropriate and inappropriate, and I apologise*

---

[10]A term used by some people with autism to refer to people without autism or another neurodevelopmental condition, the purpose being to emphasise the 'different' rather than the pathological nature of autism.

> *countless times for my speech, best intent, and my efforts to become 'good'*
> *and 'useful'. Truly, the autistic are 'the jailer and captive combined'.*
> (JONES2001)

However awareness was sometimes lacking and some participants spoke of grow-
ing up oblivious to social deficits (HURLBUTT2002, PUNSHON2009) and their
inappropriate behaviour in certain situations (HURLBUTT2002). Participants also
stressed the importance of not using autism as an excuse (SPERRY2005). There was
discussion of strategies for approaching social situations that adults with autism have
developed (PUNSHON2009, SPERRY2005) and interventions to help with learning
social skills (HURLBUTT2002):

> *...I would say you have to figure out about your own personal space and your*
> *comfort. I give people 3 feet of space. With facial expressions you can look at*
> *eyebrows and whether they're smiling. It's experience. If they're staring or*
> *spaced out, that means they're not paying attention.* (SPERRY2005)

Awareness of being different
As mentioned above, adults with autism described an awareness of being different
from their peers (CEDERLUND2010, CESARONI1991, HURLBUTT2002,
JENNESCOUSSENS2006, MACLEOD2007, PUNSHON2009). This was often
associated with feelings of failure, alienation and not belonging (BEMPORAD1979,
HURLBUTT2002, JONES2001, PUNSHON2009). Insight into these differences and
the extent of these difficulties varied, especially when there was a delay in diagnosis
(BEMPORAD1979, CEDERLUND2010, CLARKE2008, HURLBUTT2002,
HUWS2008, PUNSHON2009):

> *I do feel that if people had known then a lot of things could have been different.*
> *And, as well, that's perhaps a difficult thing to think about, just feeling that a lot*
> *of suffering might have been avoided. I wouldn't have blamed myself because I*
> *used to self-harm when I was younger and I don't think I would...if I had known*
> *I had Asperger's earlier. I would have been more aware of my problems...and*
> *better able to cope with them. (PUNSHON2009)*

Adults with autism reported a conflict between the desire and effort expended to
'fit in' and be like others (CESARONI1991, HURLBUTT2002, PUNSHON2009)
and the realisation that they could not or should not have to do so. Participants
described how 'normalising' behaviour would mean they could not be themselves
(BEMPORAD1979, CESARONI1991, HURLBUTT2002, PUNSHON2009).
Attempts to 'fit in' were also linked with negative emotions such as anxiety and stress
(BEMPORAD1979, CESARONI1991, PUNSHON2009). The knowledge that other
people like them existed was a great help for many individuals with autism
(CLARKE2008, HURLBUTT2002, JONES2001, MACLEOD2007, PUNSHON2009).
Following on from this there was much talk of acceptance of their condition and any
difficulties it presented (CLARKE2008, HURLBUTT2002), and frustration at the

view that they should desire to be 'neurotypical' (CLARKE2008, HURLBUTT2002), as they believed that it was society that needed to change:

> *I have been told in the past that certain things I do are weird and unacceptable, but I am not going to change them now. Sometimes, people's reactions would teach me stuff, but not as much now, because I really don't care what other people think of me as much. Now I don't want to be like anyone else, period. I don't necessarily see the idea of NT [neurotypical] as perfection. Hey, regular people do stupid, mean, and often evil things that people with autism would never do. I am supposed to look up to that? I don't think so! I am tired of having to do 100% of the changing, and there is no change with most people without autism.* (HURLBUTT2002)

Stigma and judgement by others

Many adults with autism reported victimisation by peers (especially in the work-place) (CESARONI1991, HURLBUTT2002, HUWS2008, MACLEOD2007, PUNSHON2009, SHTAYERMMAN2007/2009), and those without a learning disability were particularly at risk of this (JONES2001, PUNSHON2009, SHTAYERMMAN2007/2009) because, speculatively, they have more social contact. There were also reports of being stigmatised (CLARKE2008, HURLBUTT2002). Participants described worrying about what others thought of them (HURLBUTT2002, JONES2001) and the desire to be treated like a 'normal' person (ROBLEDO2008, SPERRY2005). However, as mentioned above, this contrasted with feelings of self-esteem about their autism and the view that the problem was the reactions of others, not the condition itself (CLARKE2008, HURLBUTT2002). Participants expressed anger that people with autism were viewed not to have empathy (CESARONI1991, HURLBUTT2002) and it was suggested that 'neurotypicals' may be the ones with-out empathy:

> *Many NTs [neurotypicals] are very narrow in their view. I can look at different points of view. With me, my view is not the only way. Most people with autism get frustrated with NTs because very often, it's the so-called 'normal' people who lack empathy because many of them don't want to listen to any point of view besides their own. Most people with autism I have spoken to are happy being who they are. They find most 'normal' people narrow and biased.* (HURLBUTT2002)

Participants expressed concern about being labelled as autistic as it could lead to people making assumptions about them on the basis of their diagnosis (HUWS2008, PUNSHON2009, ROBLEDO2008, SPERRY2005). The desire for people to get to know them and not the condition was described (ROBLEDO2008, SPERRY2005). However, participants did recognise that such labelling could be helpful in terms of receiving support (PUNSHON2009, SPERRY2005) and could reduce negative treat-ment from others (HUWS2008), although this was not always the case (ROBLEDO2008). Possible reasons for discrimination were perceived to be a lack of understanding of what autism is and how it affects the individual (HURLBUTT2002,

PUNSHON2009), a lack of information available about autism (HURLBUTT2002, PUNSHON2009) and an incorrect portrayal of the condition in the media (CLARKE2008, PUNSHON2009):

> *I have seen...people with Asperger's portrayed in dramas and plays and things and I cringe when I watch [laughs]. I suppose anyone who has got any problem who gets it shown on television goes, 'Oh God, it's not like that in real life'...people get the wrong reaction because someone has stereotyped it. It's quite annoying [laughs], just another one of those things that gets to you.* (PUNSHON2009)

Reactions to diagnosis

Not all of the adults in the studies were diagnosed with autism as children—some received their diagnosis in adulthood (HURLBUTT2002, JONES2001, MACLEOD2007, PUNSHON2009). Mixed reactions to diagnosis were described by adults with autism, with some viewing their diagnosis as a positive thing (HURLBUTT2002, HUWS2008, PUNSHON2009, SPERRY2005), and others as a negative (HUWS2008, MACLEOD2007, PUNSHON2009, SPERRY2005). Positive outcomes of diagnosis discussed were that it could open doors to support, both vocational and autism specific (HUWS2008, PUNSHON2009, SPERRY2005), make the person realise that they were not alone and there were other people like them (HURLBUTT2002, JONES2001), and finally, that they had answers (HURLBUTT2002, HUWS2008, MACLEOD2007, PUNSHON2009), which was especially true in cases of delayed diagnosis or misdiagnosis (HURLBUTT2002, HUWS2008, JONES2001, PUNSHON2009):

> *[It was] the missing piece of the jigsaw, it put everything into place for me and I got the bigger picture then. I knew why this had happened, this was happening and that was happening...it all just came together.* (PUNSHON2009)

Negative reactions in response to a diagnosis included shock, disappointment, loss, anger and suicidal thoughts (HUWS2008, MACLEOD2007, PUNSHON2009, SPERRY2005), sometimes coupled with avoidance (HUWS2008, PUNSHON2009). Other negative feelings around diagnosis included concerns about stigma (HUWS2008, PUNSHON2009, SPERRY2005), negative reactions from others (PUNSHON2009) and mistrust of services after misdiagnoses (PUNSHON2009). However there was also talk among some participants of a gradual acceptance (HUWS2008):

> *At first it was hard for me to accept it and then I sort of learnt to accept it a bit more, when I came here [college for young people with autism] I accepted it even more (...). I really find it annoying to have but it's something that you've got to accept and so, yeah.* (HUWS2008)

Interventions and services

There was relatively little discussion of interventions and services for autism, which perhaps reflects the limited services available for adults (GRAETZ2010, HARE2004).

Interventions that were discussed included group support, which was an important means of help (HURLBUTT2002, MACLEOD2007, PUNSHON2009). Some settings were also talked about, with a dislike of institutionalisation (BEMPORAD1979, HURLBUTT2002), and preference for community living (HURLBUTT2002) being expressed. Those that did discuss services were eager to make suggestions and particE ipate in decisions about their care (HURLBUTT2002, ROBLEDO2008). There was some discussion of feeling let down by services, usually related to misdiagnosis or clinicians' lack of knowledge (PUNSHON2009), and examples of adults with autism being left with no follow-up support following diagnosis (MACLEOD2007, PUNSHON2009, ROBLEDO2008). This led some to seek out support groups (HURLBUTT2002, MACLEOD2007):

> *I was upset about my situation and, even before my diagnosis, I had been trying to get support. Now, at last, I had the opportunity to get some information about my condition and to meet some people who might turn out to be similar to myself. I had always felt so different from other people, which is OK, but I have been at the receiving end of such hostility, for example when I have tried to work. I suppose I was looking for something that might not throw me out!* (MACLEOD2007)

Much discussion focused around the importance of support and how much this support was appreciated (HURLBUTT2002, JENNESCOUSSENS2006, ROBLEDO2008), with family (HURLBUTT2002), other people with autism (CLARKE2008, HURLBUTT2002, JONES2001, MACLEOD2007, PUNSHON2009), religion (HURLBUTT2002) and the internet (CLARKE2008) all being cited as valued sources of support. Supportive relationships were said to help with development of self-worth and social skills (HURLBUTT2002), and were associated with greater quality of life (JENNESCOUSSENS2006). That these relationships were based on trust and an assumption of competence, and allowed independence, was important to individE uals (HURLBUTT2002, ROBLEDO2008):

> *My staff push me to be able to do things with the least amount of support necesE sary. They are constantly teaching me that I must rely on myself first and then ask for aid if I am not able to accomplish something on my own. I find that I am happier being tested to see what my strengths and weaknesses actually are. I am not afraid at all to ask for help from my staff and friends because they are truly there for the purpose of aiding me in my times of need. I feel much more indeE pendent than I could have ever imagined, and that feeling alone is intensely gratE ifying.* (ROBLEDO2008)

Being an expert by experience
Many adults with autism expressed a strong wish to be considered as an 'expert' (HURLBUTT2002) and to have the opportunity to educate others about autism (HURLBUTT2002), and also to be an advocate for other people with autism (CLARKE2008, HURLBUTT2002, MACLEOD2007, ROBLEDO2008). Participants

stressed the importance of being consulted and feeling in control of their life choices (HURLBUTT2002, ROBLEDO2008):

> *I am committed to the cause of autism. I want to see people who are proud to have autism and accept themselves for who they are and all that they are. Too often in the past, people didn't listen to people with autism. Most people do not know about autism, much less what a person deals with. So, educating people about autism is a key.* (HURLBUTT2002)

4.3.5   Summary – experience of care of adults with autism

A number of themes emerged from the literature that captured the experience of adults with autism. One clear theme that was identified and underpins much of what follows was that living with autism represents a considerable burden for most people characterised by limited or lost opportunities to live a fuller life. This was often accompanied by considerable psychological distress that had a further negative impact on people's lives. This distress was further exacerbated by the stigma and exclusion that many people reported as a result of having autism. A strong theme that emerged (and consistent with the core symptoms of autism) was the considerable difficulty people had in developing and sustaining relationships. Often these were best developed with other people with autism and linked to a shared understanding of the problems faced. Intimate relationships were desired, however misinterpretation of social cues could sometimes lead to vulnerable situations or inappropriate sexual advances. There was a shared concern that the nature of autism was simply not understood by others and this added to the difficulties experienced by many people.

Receiving a diagnosis of autism was viewed positively because it offered an explanation and understanding of a person's experience and also increased access to a range of services that otherwise were denied to people. However, it also brought with it concerns about increased stigma and exclusion. There was relatively little qualitative evidence of people's experience of services (perhaps reflecting the limited availability of services for adults) but what was identified emphasised the importance of support and help in developing skills in social interactions with others. On a positive note, the developing voice of people with autism as experts by experience was identified as an increasingly positive aspect of living with autism.

4.3.6   From evidence to recommendations

The GDG carefully reviewed the themes summarised in Section 4.3.4 and considered the implications of these when drafting recommendations in the following areas:

a) Case identification, assessment and diagnosis (see Chapter 5): it was ensured that the recommendations in these areas were drafted in such a way as to reflect the messages that emerged from the themes identified above.

b) Principles of care: the themes identified above were considered in conjunction with the evidence reviewed in the *Service User Experience in Adult Mental Health* NICE guidance (NCCMH, 2012) to identify important areas where a recommendation needed to be developed for this guideline. A particular concern was to ensure that key aspects of the principles of care identified in the evidence review for the *Service User Experience in Adult Mental Health* NICE guidance, and which the GDG viewed as being important in the care of people with autism, were not omitted from this guideline. In both the evidence reviewed in Section 4.3.4 and in the *Service User Experience in Adult Mental Health* NICE guidance the need for working in partnership with people with autism and ensuring that systems are in place that support such processes came through very clearly and this is reflected in the recommendations, specifically in recommendations 4.3.7.1, 4.3.7.2 and 4.3.7.3. In drawing on the evidence base for the *Service User Experience in Adult Mental Health* NICE guidance, the GDG was also mindful of the specific communication problems associated with autism and therefore placed a particular emphasis on the need for any information to be provided in various visual, verbal and aural, easy read, colour and font formats, given the GDG's opinion that this may facilitate the readability, understanding and comprehension of the information for people with autism.

c) Organisation of care (see Chapter 6): the themes identified above were used to inform the selection of recommendations from *Common Mental Health Disorders* (NICE, 2011b) to identify important areas where a recommendation needed to be developed for this guideline.

The GDG developed a number of recommendations for this guideline that drew on evidence from existing guidelines referred to above and which were supported by the review of the qualitative literature conducted for this guideline. The GDG was concerned that some people with autism felt 'let down' by professionals' lack of knowledge of autism, and therefore made a recommendation that all staff working with adults with autism should have a basic understanding of the condition, and that professionals providing care and treatment to adults with autism should have an extensive understanding of its nature, development and course. The GDG also wished to alert all health and social care professionals to the need to make modifications to their assessment procedures (for example, the pacing and duration of assessments) so that adults with autism could receive the most effective care. There was good evidence from the qualitative analysis that talking to other people with autism was felt to be beneficial and therefore the GDG drew on their expert knowledge and experience, along with the evidence in the *Service User Experience in Adult Mental Health* NICE guidance and other NICE guidelines for people with long-term disorders (for example, NCCMH 2010a and 2010c), and made a recommendation for the provision of information about organisations and websites that can provide support and the use of face-to-face self-help and support groups. A desire for interpersonal relationships was also demonstrated in the analysis and it was felt by the GDG that it was important to emphasise that staff need to be sensitive to the need of adults with autism to develop personal and sexual relationships, and to be aware that difficulties with social interaction and communication could lead to misinterpretation of others' behaviours and leave adults with autism open to exploitation. However, it should also be recognised that some adults with autism may be asexual.

The GDG also considered the needs of adults with autism who have caring responsibilities and made a recommendation based on expert opinion that they should have support in their role as parents and also social support, including childcare.

4.3.7   Recommendations

Principles for working with adults with autism and their families, partners and carers
4.3.7.1   All staff working with adults with autism should:
- work in partnership with adults with autism and, where appropriate, with their families, partners and carers
- offer support and care respectfully
- take time to build a trusting, supportive, empathic and non-judgemental relationship as an essential part of care.
4.3.7.2   All staff working with adults with autism should have an understanding of the:
- nature, development and course of autism
- impact on personal, social, educational and occupational functioning
- impact of the social and physical environment.
4.3.7.3   All health and social care professionals providing care and support for adults with autism should have a broad understanding of the:
- nature, development and course of autism
- impact on personal, social, educational and occupational functioning
- impact of and interaction with the social and physical environment
- impact on and interaction with other coexisting mental and physical disorders and their management
- potential discrepancy between intellectual functioning as measured by IQ and adaptive functioning as reflected, for example, by difficulties in planning and performing activities of daily living including education or employment.
4.3.7.4   All health and social care professionals providing care and support for adults with autism should:
- aim to foster the person's autonomy, promote active participation in decisions about care and support self-management
- maintain continuity of individual relationships wherever possible
- ensure that comprehensive information about the nature of, and interventions and services for, their difficulties is available in an appropriate language or format (including various visual, verbal and aural, easy-read, and different colour and font formats)
- consider whether the person may benefit from access to a trained advocate
4.3.7.5   All health and social care professionals providing care and support for adults with autism and their families, partners and carers should ensure that they are:
- familiar with recognised local and national sources (organisations and websites) of information and/or support for people with autism

  ● able to discuss and advise on how to access and engage with these
  resources.

4.3.7.6   Encourage adults with autism to participate in self-help or support groups
           or access one-to-one support, and provide support so that they can attend
           meetings and engage in the activities.

4.3.7.7   All staff working with adults with autism should be sensitive to issues of
           sexuality, including asexuality and the need to develop personal and sexual
           relationships. In particular, be aware that problems in social interaction and
           communication may lead to the person with autism misunderstanding
           another person's behaviour or to their possible exploitation by others.

4.3.7.8   Ensure that adults with autism who have caring responsibilities receive
           support to access the full range of mental and physical health and social
           care services, including:
             ● specific information, advice and support to parents about their parent-
               ing role, including parent training if needed, by professionals experi-
               enced in the care of adults and children with autism
             ● social support, such as childcare, to enable them to attend appointments,
               groups and therapy sessions, and to access education and employment.

Principles for the effective assessment of autism

4.3.7.9   Staff who have responsibility for the identification or assessment of adults
           with autism should adapt these procedures, if necessary, to ensure their
           effective delivery, including modifications to the setting in which assess-
           ment is delivered (see recommendation 6.5.11.5) and the duration and
           pacing of the assessment.

Improving access to care

4.3.7.10   Support access to services and increase the uptake of interventions by:
             ● delivering assessment and interventions in a physical environment that
               is appropriate for people with hyper- and/or hypo-sensory sensitivities
               (see recommendation 6.5.11.5)
             ● changing the professional responsible for the person's care if a
               supportive and caring relationship cannot be established.

4.3.8   Experience of families, partner and carers of adults with autism

As described in Section 4.3.2, the review team identified broad themes from the
primary qualitative studies and survey data. Initially this thematic analysis of the data
resulted in five broad headings, which echo those identified for adults with autism:
● impact of autism
● relationships
● awareness of being different and judgement by others
● interventions and services
● role as advocate.

Under these broad headings specific emergent themes have been extracted and are discussed below. A summary of the themes identified in each study (marked with a 'Y') can be found in Table 8.

Impact of autism
Families, partners and carers of adults with autism discussed the impact of the condition on various areas of their lives. Views were varied, and although difficulties were experienced (BLACHER2010, GRAETZ2010, KRAUSZ2005, MAGANA2006, SHU2006, SMITH2010A), there was a sense of acceptance (HARE2004, MAGANA2006). Parents discussed their own accomplishments (KRAUSZ2005), personal growth (HARE2004, MAGANA2006), happiness (HARE2004) and positive caregiving experiences (KRAUSZ2005):

> *I think when you raise a child like Philip, he teaches me more than I will ever teach him. I'm not a very patient person but I learned how to be patient with Philip. I always wanted everything to happen instantly. But I've learned that some goals are long term and I've settled down and I've become less impatient, less frustrated. That's a good thing to learn. I'm surprised I ever did it. That is not the way I was. I'm just more comfortable and content and satisfied with my life and with the way things go, the speed at which things happen. That's good experience for me. Took a long time (chuckle) to learn. (KRAUSZ2005)*

Table 8: Summary of emergent themes – experience of families, partners and carers of adults with autism

	BLACHER2010	GRAETZ2010	HARE2004	KRAUSS2005	KRAUSZ2005	LAU2011	MAGANA2006	ORSMOND2007A	ORSMOND2009	RYAN2009	RYAN2010	SELTZER2001	SHU2006	SMITH2010A
Impact of autism	Y	Y	Y	Y	Y	–	Y	Y	–	Y	–	Y	Y	Y
Relationships	Y	Y	Y	Y	Y	Y	Y	Y	Y	–	–	Y	Y	Y
Awareness of being different and judgement by others	–	Y	Y	Y	Y	–	Y	–	–	Y	Y	–	Y	Y
Interventions and services	Y	Y	Y	Y	Y	–	Y	–	–	Y	–	Y	Y	–
Role of advocate	–	Y	–	–	Y	–	Y	–	–	Y	–	–	–	–

However families, partners and carers also reported disruption to their work and financial strain (KRAUSS2005, MAGANA2006, SMITH2010A), reduced free time and leisure activities and a limited social life (HARE2004, KRAUSS2005, MAGANA2006, SHU2006, SMITH2010A), restricted choice of living location (HARE2004) and changes to family life (BLACHER2010, GRAETZ2010, HARE2004, KRAUSS2005, MAGANA2006):

> *Life for the parent is like being a prisoner in one's own home.* (KRAUSS2005)

Psychological distress was reported by families, partners and carers of adults with autism (HARE2004, KRAUSZ2005, SMITH2010A), with stress and strain (KRAUSS2005, KRAUSZ2005, MAGANA2006, SELTZER2001, SMITH2010A), worry (BLACHER2010, HARE2004, KRAUSS2005, KRAUSZ2005), frustration (KRAUSZ2005), guilt (KRAUSS2005), fatigue (GRAETZ2010, KRAUSS2005, SELTZER2001, SHU2006, SMITH2010A) and feelings of being overwhelmed (GRAETZ2010, HARE2004) all experienced:

> *You asked me a couple of times; How did I cope with that? How did I get through that? And I didn't even know what to say to you. Because nobody really ever asked me that before. Nobody seemed to care (chuckle) how I was coping as long as Philip was doing okay, you know. I never really thought about that, about how I coped with it. But it's interesting, that just... Everything seemed fine back then, you know, when the kids were little and Philip was going through all those bad things. But now, that Richard's [sibling] living with his dad, and he's like 24 and a half, and Philip's in the group home and I don't have a lot of stress in my life, and some quiet time for myself. And now my nerves are just a wreck. You know, I ended up going to a psychiatrist. And I just said: 'You have to do something because I have to work and I'm a mess! I cannot work you know.' He feels it's delayed stress syndrome. And I, I said: 'But you know, I didn't have any stress. Everything was fine. I had my parents supporting me and the kids are fine. Everything worked out fine. And he said 'You didn't feel it then, you're feeling it now. Because now everything is done and you have time to feel it.' It's seems a little strange to me (chuckle), but that's what he said.* (KRAUSZ2005)

There were also negative emotions about the enduring nature of autism, with parents expressing worry for their sons' and daughters' future (GRAETZ2010, ORSMOND2007A, SELTZER2001) after, they, the parents, had died (GRAETZ2010, HARE2004, KRAUSS2005, SHU2006):

> *After we are gone, he will be hopelessly lost. (KRAUSS2005)*

There were also positive views of the future (BLACHER2010), and reduced worries in some areas of life (HARE2004) compared with families, partners and carers of people with other developmental conditions (BLACHER2010). Some families reported a gradual change in future expectations and acceptance (KRAUSZ2005, MAGANA2006, RYAN2009, SHU2006):

> *I would say that the impact is a total 100% turnaround in my life. Everything I had planned for being a mother has gone because that path, that path I saw around me everywhere just didn't happen and doesn't happen. So as a mother I have had to reassess who I am.* (RYAN2009)

Relationships

Families, partners and carers discussed the supportive relationships they have, and how they valued this support (GRAETZ2010, HARE2004, KRAUSZ2005, SHU2006, SMITH2010A). However, others described a sense of isolation, usually due to reduced social opportunities and freedom (KRAUSS2005, SHU2006). Families reported positive relationships with their family member with autism (HARE2004, KRAUSS2005, LAU2011, MAGANA2006, SHU2006), and when this person had left home, close relationships were still maintained (KRAUSS2005, ORSMOND2009). However, these relationships were not always easy, and difficulties were discussed (KRAUSS2005, ORSMOND2007A, ORSMOND2009, SELTZER2001, SMITH2010A). The person's autism had an inevitable impact on family dynamics, affecting parental relationships with other siblings (HARE2004, ORSMOND2007A), marital relationships (HARE2004, KRAUSS2005, SHU2006) and general family life (BLACHER2010, GRAETZ2010, HARE2004, KRAUSS2005, MAGANA2006):

> *My husband blames me that I over protect him, that he is spoiled.* (SHU2006)

Awareness of being different and judgement by others

Some parents described how they had taken on different roles because of their sons' or daughters' autism, for example mothers felt that they had become 'carers' or 'teachers' (HARE2004, KRAUSS2005, KRAUSZ2005, MAGANA2006, SHU2006, SMITH2010A) and had had to reassess their self-identity (RYAN2009, SHU2006); these self-perceptions changed over time (KRAUSS2005, KRAUSZ2005, SHU2006). Perceptions of others had also changed, and many families expressed concern over how others viewed them and their family member with autism (GRAETZ2010, KRAUSZ2005, RYAN2010):

> *When she is naughty, you look at Mandy when she is like now, when she is walking along, no one would think anything was wrong but all of a sudden in the supermarket she will just have a hissy fit and you get the dirty looks, and you get the 'tch haa' because these people don't know that that is what they are, that is what they do [um] and there is no way that you can stop that because it is just spontaneous, you just don't sort of really know...I sort of see a few signs, you might be able to predict it is going to happen, but not all the time.* (RYAN2010)

Families also reported that their family member with autism was not always accepted in their community (GRAETZ2010):

> *Our son is social. . .but there is a lack of understanding and compassion from the non-disabled. . .for that reason we do not push socialization.* (GRAETZ2010)

Interventions and services

There was some discussion of services for adults with autism, including day centres, respite care and educational settings such as colleges (HARE2004, SELTZER2001) and psychological services (SELTZER2001). Some therapies, such as speech and language therapy (HARE2004) and occupational therapy (SELTZER2001), were also discussed although low numbers of people using these services were reported (HARE2004). However, there was much less discussion of services utilised by families, partners and carers (GRAETZ2010, HARE2004, RYAN2009, SHU2006). In some cases, knowledge of available autism-specific interventions such as social skills training was poor (HARE2004), although, in general, knowledge of services was good (BLACHER2010, GRAETZ2010, HARE2004). Feelings about the family member with autism living at home were contrasted with how the family felt when the person moved to a residential setting, such as a community residential programme or in semi-independent accommodation (KRAUSS2005, KRAUSZ2005, MAGANA2006); positive and negative emotions were associated with both options (BLACHER2010, GRAETZ2010, KRAUSS2005, MAGANA2006, SELTZER2001). For instance, benefits of the person with autism living at home were reported for the parents (their son or daughter '*keeps us company/is fun to be around*' and they have peace of mind) and for the individual with autism (they are getting good care at home and are secure). However, there are also negative aspects including parents finding it difficult to cope with their son or daughter's behaviour, providing constant caregiving and not feeling that they are able to leave their son or daughter alone; there are also problems for the person with autism who may not find living at home very challenging. Similarly, both positive and negative aspects were reported regarding the person with autism living outside the home, with benefits reported for the family (they experienced a calmer, more typical family life), for the parent (they had more free time and freedom and less stress and fatigue) and for the individual with autism (they learned new skills and became more independent and confident). Negative aspects included the parents missing their son or daughter and feeling worried and guilty (KRAUSS2005), the person with autism having concerns about their safety and their grooming or personal appearance and problems with the programme (the staff were not well trained).

Opinions about services were mixed (GRAETZ2010, HARE2004, SELTZER2001), with much discussion of unmet needs (GRAETZ2010, HARE2004, KRAUSS2005, KRAUSZ2005, SELTZER2001). Families, partners and carers expressed the need for more support in planning for the future and transition to adult services (BLACHER2010, GRAETZ2010, HARE2004), more residential, recreation and employment opportunities for the person with autism (GRAETZ2010,

MAGANA2006), and more breaks from caring (GRAETZ2010, HARE2004, KRAUSS2005):

> *Hard to get respite care for a 28-year-old* (KRAUSS2005)
> *[...]*
> *I have no idea where to begin...we want to take a short vacation but there is no one to watch her...she functions at a 36 month level...who will watch her.* (GRAETZ2010)

More services specifically for autism, especially Asperger's syndrome (HARE2004), and improved staff training (GRAETZ2010, HARE2004, KRAUSS2005) were also requested:

> *I feel that staff need more training than is provided to work with people with autism.* (KRAUSS2005)

Role of advocate

Many families, partners and carers of adults with autism found themselves in a new role of being an advocate for their family member and others with autism (GRAETZ2010, KRAUSZ2005, MAGANA2006, RYAN2009) and enjoyed having the opportunity to educate others about the condition (RYAN2009); this role continued as their sons and daughters moved into adulthood (RYAN2009):

> *We [support group] have run Asperger courses at our local community centre. I now go round to talk to mental health teams, schools, colleges, social care departments and give talks about Asperger's raising awareness and, of course, I have got a teaching qualification so I also have a job teaching Asperger youngsters.* (RYAN2009)

4.3.9   Summary – experience of families, partners and carers of adults with autism

A number of themes emerged from the literature that captured the experience of families, partners and carers of adults with autism. Although living with a person with autism could be challenging and could lead to reduced work, accommodation and leisure opportunities, and to financial strain, there was a recognition and sense of pride in their caregiving achievements. Psychological distress was common and often linked to coming to terms with the lifelong impact of autism on their son or daughter as well as their own increasing stress and anxiety. The impact of autism was keenly felt on relationships within the family including the parental relationship, other siblings and spousal relationships. Advice and help from services and from other families, partners and carers of adults with autism was valued highly. Parents also struggled to come to terms with a new identity as a carer and the sense of isolation or ostracism that this could entail.

There was relatively little qualitative evidence of families, partners and carers' experience of services either for themselves or for their son or daughter. No doubt this reflected the limited availability of services for adults. There was considerable concern about the availability of day, residential, employment and support services and the need for support from specialists to access these services. There was little comment on services accessed by families, partners and carers themselves, but there was recognition of the need for increased information about autism (coupled with better trained and informed staff). Some families, partners and carers reported gaining real benefit from involvement in advocating for services for people with autism.

4.3.10   From evidence to recommendations

The summary above identified serious limitations in the services available for families, partners and carers to facilitate and support their active involvement in the care of their child with autism. The GDG considered this, along with the evidence base for the *Service User Experience in Adult Mental Health* NICE guidance (NCCMH, 2012), and their knowledge of, and expertise about, services for families, partners and carers. This led the GDG to identify a number of issues, which in combination with the themes identified above, suggested some key areas for the development of recommendations. These included: the involvement of families, partners and carers in the care of their family member or friend (and how this can be approached if the person with autism does not wish for them to be involved); the assessment of the needs of families, partners and carers; information about and help in accessing care and support for their family member; and a range of family and carer support groups. The GDG carefully considered these issues and the implications of the themes identified in Section 4.3.8 in the drafting of recommendations in the following areas:

a) The involvement of families, partners and carers in the care and treatment of their family member or friend and the information, assessment, care and interventions that families, partners and carers might themselves need: the aim was to ensure that all recommendations in these areas (concerned with the families, partners and carers directly or the care of their family member or friend) were drafted in such a way as to reflect the issues and concerns that emerged from the thematic analysis and the GDG's knowledge and expertise.

b) Principles of care: the GDG's decision was informed by Section 4.3.9 and the evidence base from the *Service User Experience in Adult Mental Health* NICE guidance (NCCMH, 2012) to identify important areas where a new recommendation needed to be developed for this guideline.

4.3.11   Recommendations

Involving families, partners and carers

4.3.11.1   Discuss with adults with autism if and how they want their families, partners or carers to be involved in their care. During discussions, take into account any implications of the Mental Capacity Act (2005) and any communication needs the person may have (see recommendation 6.3.4.1).

4.3.11.2 If the person with autism wants their family, partner or carer(s) to be involved, encourage this involvement and:
- negotiate between the person with autism and their family, partner or carer(s) about confidentiality and sharing of information on an ongoing basis
- explain how families, partners and carers can help support the person with autism and help with care plans
- make sure that no services are withdrawn because of involvement of the family, partner or carer(s), unless this has been clearly agreed with both the person with autism and their family, partner or carer(s).

4.3.11.3 Give all families, partners and carer(s) (whether or not the person wants them to be involved in their care) verbal and written information about:
- autism and its management
- local support groups and services specifically for families, partners and carers
- their right to a formal carer's assessment of their own physical and mental health needs, and how to access this.

4.3.11.4 If a person with autism does not want their family, partners or carer(s) to be involved in their care:
- give the family, partner or carer(s) verbal and written information about who they can contact if they are concerned about the person's care
- bear in mind that people with autism may be ambivalent or negative towards their family or partner. This may be for many different reasons, including a coexisting mental disorder or prior experience of violence or abuse.

5. CASE IDENTIFICATION, ASSESSMENT AND DIAGNOSIS

5.1 INTRODUCTION

The identification, assessment and diagnosis of autism in adults is challenging. Autism can coexist with a number of conditions, including learning disability (an IQ below 70), which may affect up to 60% of people with autism (Baird *et al.*, 2006). In childhood, ADHD is common, affecting 40 to 50% of children with autism (Gadow *et al.*, 2004 and 2005) and the differential diagnosis from a range of other neurodevelopmental conditions can present difficulties (see NICE, 2011a, for a more detailed review of these issues). In adults, particularly those who have not had a diagnosis established in childhood, assessment can be complicated by coexisting mental disorders such as depression and schizophrenia. Finally, the interaction between autism and the person's social and physical environment can further complicate diagnosis.

In the last 30 years effort has been made to improve identification in children and refine the assessment process. This has led to the establishment of multidisciplinary assessment clinics and the development and validation of various screening tools and diagnostic instruments for children. In Wales a network for assessment and diagnosis was established in 2011 following *The Autistic Spectrum Disorder (ASD) Strategic Action Plan for Wales* (Adult Task and Finish Group, 2009). This network has been tasked with developing and implementing a standards-based assessment pathway in all the Welsh Health Boards through the education and training of relevant clinicians, the development of teams of local expertise and the support of experts at a national level. However in England, few equivalent clinics, identification tools, diagnostic instruments or assessment systems have been developed for adults. In the English NHS secondary care health services for children with neurodevelopmental conditions are relatively coherent and have well-established links to the wider health service. In contrast, services provided for adults in England are almost entirely limited to those who have a learning disability. This means that not only is there poor identification of adults with autism who have not been identified as children but there are also very limited specialist services available for people with autism unless they have a physical or learning disability, or become severely mentally or physically ill.

Inadequate identification and assessment of adults with autism not only leads to a lack of adequate provision of care and support for the problems associated with autism but can also lead to inadequate recognition and assessment of coexisting mental and physical health problems with consequent sub-optimal management.

This under-recognition and inadequate care of adults with autism m~ increased health and social care costs. For example, Knapp and collea~ mated that the yearly cost to society for each adult with autism in and with a cost to the economy of around £25.5 billion per year. Of t.

σ

59% is accounted for by services, 36% through lost employment and the remainder by family expenses. There is also an emotional cost not only for adults with autism who have reported a high incidence of depression and attempted suicide (Stewart *et al.,* 2006) but also for their families, partners and carers (Hare *et al.,* 2004).

The GDG recognised the limited provision of specialist assessment and intervention services for adults, particularly in England, but was mindful that some four out of five adults with autism find obtaining a diagnosis in adulthood difficult or not possible (Taylor & Marrable, 2011) and many will not have received a formal diagnosis (Brugha *et al.*, 2011) (see Chapter 2). The GDG also took into account that a number of these people have rewarding and successful lives (Baron-Cohen, 2000), and may require no intervention or would not wish to have a formal diagnosis. This meant that the issue of identification and recognition in non-specialist services such as primary care, social care and general medical settings was of particular importance and this is reflected in the review protocols set out below.

5.2 SIGNS AND SYMPTOMS THAT SHOULD PROMPT ASSESSMENT OF AUTISM IN ADULTS

5.2.1 Introduction

As described in Chapter 2 and Section 5.1, a significant number of adults with autism will have not had a diagnosis (Brugha *et al.*, 2011; Taylor & Marrable, 2011). Those who have previously received a diagnosis during childhood, but have not been in contact with services since childhood, are also unlikely to be recognised as having autism as they do not often present to health or social care services with a complaint directly concerning the core symptoms of autism. Instead, they are much more likely to present with a coexisting mental or physical disorder or with a social problem arising from the autism or the coexisting condition, the course and presentation of which may well have been affected by the autism. In addition, a number of people who have autism and a learning disability may have an existing diagnosis of autism but not disclose it or they or healthcare services might not be aware of it due to the unavailability or inadequacy of the records system. While people with more severe learning disabilities will be recognised as having a significant problem, the autism may go undetected. For individuals with autism who are not learning disabled but who have significant communication problems, an incorrect assumption of learning disability may be made, or diagnostic substitution may occur (Bishop *et al.*, 2008).

In contrast with some common mental health problems such as depression, the core symptoms of autism are often not well understood by health and social care professionals (Heidgerken *et al.*, 2005). However, it should be noted that even in a condition such as depression it is likely that only around 30% of people who present with a depressive disorder are diagnosed and offered treatment (NCCMH, 2010a). The consequences of this under-recognition are not well described (see Chapter 2), but it is likely that they lead to a poor quality of life for the person with autism and inadequate care and support for both the autistic problems and the associated coexisting conditions. A good example of the impact of under-recognition and inadequate treatment is the 88% unemployment rate in non-learning disabled adults with autism (Barnard *et al.,* 2001).

Although the focus of this section of the chapter is on the nature and content of case identification tools it should be noted that consultation skills of health and social care professionals have been shown to be important in determining effective recognition of mental disorders (Gask *et al.,* 1998).

5.2.2   Strategies to improve the recognition of autism

A number of NICE mental health guidelines have considered the case for general population screening for some mental disorders and concluded that general population screening is not appropriate and that approaches to case identification should focus on specific high-risk populations, such as people with a history of depression, with significant physical illnesses causing disability or with other mental health problems, such as dementia, where benefits of early identification outweigh the downsides (see for example, NICE, 2006). The criteria by which the GDGs judged the value of this approach were adapted from those developed for the assessment of screening instruments by the UK NHS National Screening Committee (available from www.screening.nhs.uk/criteria). The GDGs looked for evidence that the instrument in question had appropriate sensitivity and specificity, that interventions for the disorder identified by the instrument were available or could be made available and that the interventions were likely to be of benefit.

An example of this approach can be seen in the updated edition of the *Depression* guideline (NICE, 2009a) and the guideline on *Depression in Adults with a Chronic Physical Health Problem* (NICE, 2009b), both of which reviewed available case identification instruments for depression. These guidelines recommended that healthcare professionals should be alert to possible depression (particularly in people with a past history of depression or a chronic physical health problem with associated functional impairment) and consider asking people who may have depression two questions, known as the 'Whooley questions' (NICE, 2009a):

1. During the last month, have you often been bothered by feeling down, depressed or hopeless?
2. During the last month, have you often been bothered by having little interest or pleasure in doing things?

If a person answers 'yes' to either of these questions, then the guidelines recommend that a practitioner who is competent to perform a mental health assessment should review the person's mental state and associated functional, interpersonal and social difficulties. Furthermore, when assessing a person with suspected depression, the guidelines recommend that practitioners should consider using a validated measure (for example, for symptoms, functions and/or disability) to inform and evaluate treatment.

Compared with depression, case identification of autism has received scant attention despite a demonstrable need for care and intervention. However, the GDG was mindful of the uptake of the case identification questions for depression in the Quality and Outcomes Framework (Department of Health, 2004) and the subsequent adoption of a similar approach to the case identification of anxiety disorders in the *Common Mental Health Disorders* guideline (NICE, 2011b). Following from this the GDG decided to adopt a similar framework when approaching case identification in autism.

5.2.3   Aim of the review

This review aimed to identify the signs and symptoms that may provide an index of suspicion and prompt a healthcare professional to consider referral for or undertake assessment of possible autism.

5.2.4   Clinical review protocol (review of signs and symptoms that should prompt assessment of autism in adults)

A summary of the review protocol, including the review questions, information about the databases searched and the eligibility criteria used for this section of the guideline, can be found in Table 9 (the full protocol can be found in Appendix 8 and further information about the search strategy can be found in Appendix 9).

5.2.5   Methodological approach

The review team conducted a systematic review of the literature (both primary studies and systematic reviews or published guidance) that evaluated the signs and symptoms, and other factors such as personal history, that might raise suspicion about the possible presence of autism. The GDG aimed to critically evaluate the sensitivity and specificity of these signs and symptoms when compared with a DSM-IV (American Psychological Association, 1994) or ICD-10 (World Health Organization, 1992) diagnosis.

5.2.6   Studies considered

The literature search for studies resulted in 9,522 articles overall. Scanning titles or abstracts identified 99 potentially relevant studies that evaluated the recognition and case identification of autism. However, none of these studies met the inclusion criteria as outlined in Table 9. The GDG therefore utilised DSM-IV and ICD-10 criteria for autism, as well as GDG expert knowledge of the epidemiology, aetiology and presentation of autism, to identify the signs and symptoms that may prompt a healthcare professional to seek or conduct assessment. This is summarised below.

Table 9: Clinical review protocol for the review of signs and symptoms that should prompt assessment of autism in adults

Component	Description
Review question (s)	What signs or symptoms should prompt any professional who comes into contact with an adult with possible autism to consider assessment? (RQ – A1)
Objectives	• To identify the signs and symptoms that should prompt referral for diagnostic assessment of autism in adults. • To suggest how recognition of autism can be improved.
Criteria for considering studies for the review	
• *Population*	Adults and young people aged 18 years and older with suspected autism across the range of diagnostic groups (including atypical autism, Asperger's syndrome and pervasive developmental disorder). Consideration should be given to the specific needs of: • people with coexisting conditions • women • older people • people from black and minority ethnic groups • transgender people.
• *Comparison*	People with or without diagnosed autism
• *Critical outcomes*	Sensitivity, specificity, positive predictive value, negative predictive value, AUC
• *Study design*	Cross-sectional, systematic reviews
Electronic databases	AEI, ASSIA, BEI, CDSR, CENTRAL, CINAHL, DARE, Embase, ERIC, HMIC, MEDLINE, PsycINFO, Sociological Abstracts, SSA
Date searched	Systematic reviews: 1995 up to 09/09/2011. RCTs, quasi-experimental studies, observational studies, case series: inception of database up to 09/09/2011.
The review strategy	To provide a GDG consensus-based narrative of signs and symptoms that should prompt assessment as well as identify any amendments that need to be made to take into account individual variation.

5.2.7   Summary of the approach for evaluating signs and symptoms

In the absence of any good-quality evidence regarding the signs and symptoms that should prompt assessment of autism in adults, the GDG used both existing diagnostic systems and the expert knowledge of the group and agreed that the signs and symptoms would need to be identifiable in a range of different care settings and by health and social care professionals with varying knowledge and experience of autism. In a healthcare setting this might include a primary care professional such as a general practitioner (GP), practice nurse, a primary care mental health practitioner with limited experience of working with adults with autism or a doctor or nurse in an acute physical healthcare setting. Others working in social care or the housing sector providing support to people with a range of mental disorders may also have very limited knowledge of autism.

In developing the key criteria that would inform a selection of the signs and symptoms of autism that would need to be identifiable in the settings referred to above, the GDG decided on the following:

- The signs and symptoms[11] should be:
  - based on established and well-validated diagnostic systems
  - those that would provide the best balance between sensitivity and specificity
  - objective and where possible quantifiable against agreed norms
  - understandable by an individual (practitioner or professional) without specialist knowledge of the condition
  - easily observed or inquired about in a brief encounter (of less than 10 minutes)
  - verifiable (where necessary) by an independent informant or review of easily available records.
- The factors[12] concerning personal history should be:
  - based on evidence of an association between the factors and the development of the condition
  - objective and definable against agreed norms
  - understandable to the person with the possible condition or by an individual without specialist knowledge of the condition
  - easily inquired about or extracted from records in a brief encounter (of less than 10 minutes)
  - verifiable (where necessary) by an independent informant or review of easily available records.
- The signs and symptoms and personal factors should be such that they would:
  - be easily assembled in a simple algorithm to support decision-making
  - be understandable to the person with a suspected condition (or their family, partner or carer)
  - facilitate communication about the need for assessment with another professional.

---

[11]In this case these can be taken to refer to an aspect of a person's personal or social functioning.

[12]These can include personal experience of care, diagnoses of other mental and physical disorders and social and occupational performance.

Application of the above criteria led the GDG to identify three key issues for autism, one of which the GDG judged needed to be present:

- persistent difficulties in social interaction
- persistent difficulties in social communication
- stereotypic (rigid and repetitive) behaviours, resistance to change (in, for example, diet, routine or environment) or restricted interests.

The GDG considered the evidence for the association between a number of personal historical factors including service usage and, combined with the epidemiological evidence reviewed in Chapter 2 and their expert opinion, took the view that a number of factors were associated with the presence of autism:

- problems in obtaining or sustaining employment or education
- difficulties in initiating or sustaining social relationships
- previous or current contact with mental health or learning disability services
- history of a neurodevelopmental condition (including learning disabilities and ADHD) or mental disorder.

The GDG also considered that the use of these signs, symptoms and personal historical factors should be part of a carefully constructed protocol for case identification and any subsequent assessment. The recommendations developed from this review and the reasoning behind their development are described in Section 5.3.12 and 5.3.11 respectively where the rationale for their integration into a coherent protocol is set out.

5.3   CASE IDENTIFICATION INSTRUMENTS

5.3.1   Introduction

Autism is under-recognised in adults in the UK (Brugha *et al.*, 2011). There are a number of reasons for this including: healthcare professionals' lack of knowledge and skill in the field of adult autism in non-specialist services; limited teaching about autism in the curricula of many training programmes for health and social care professional; an absence of specialist practitioners to train and support non-specialists; a lack of services to which to refer when problems are identified; and the complexity of identifying autism in people with coexisting conditions that may mask the presence of autism. Given that health and social outcomes are poor for many people with autism, and that the autism may complicate or impair effective treatment of coexisting conditions, effective identification of autism may lead to better outcomes for individuals and more efficient use of healthcare resources.

Current practice
The majority of adults with autism who receive care in the UK are in specialist learning disability services. As at least 40% of adults with autism do not have a learning disability (Baird *et al.*, 2006), and a significant number of people with mild learning disability (IQ in 50 to 69 range) are not in regular contact with learning disability services, this means that the majority of people with autism are not in contact with health

services for care for their autism. A very small number of special assessment and diagnosis teams for adults with autism exist in the country, such as the Autism Assessment Clinic at the Maudsley Hospital in Camberwell, London, and the Cambridge Lifespan Asperger Syndrome Service, which, because of no statutory provision, has been charitably supported for 10 years and which only offers diagnostic opinion. There are also a small number of services providing care and supportive interventions, as well as assessment and diagnosis, such as the Nottingham City Asperger Service, which develops and delivers short-term coordinated packages of support including psychological interventions and specialist group work, for instance, in parenting skills. Of course, an unknown number of adults with autism will be accessing services for mental health problems (often in relation to their autism), but it is probable that for many the problems associated with autism go unrecognised or may be misdiagnosed (Brugha *et al.*, 2011). In this context it is unsurprising that there has been little or no development of case identification tools for routine use, a major issue being the lack of options for referral especially in primary care, but it can also be argued that better identification of autism in other specialist services would lead to improvements in care.

Definition

For the purposes of this review, case identification instruments are defined as validated psychometric measures used to identify people with autism. The review was limited to instruments likely to be used in UK clinical practice, that is, 'ultra-brief instruments' (defined as those with one to three items) or 'longer instruments' (four to 12 items). The identification instruments were ideally assessed in consultation samples (including primary care and general medical services) and community populations. 'Gold standard' diagnoses were defined as a DSM or ICD diagnosis of autism (or their equivalent); studies were sought that compared case identification using an ultra-brief or longer instrument with a gold standard.

5.3.2   Methodological approach

The GDG considered the following criteria when evaluating case identification instruments for inclusion in the review:

Quality of diagnostic test accuracy studies: The QUADAS-2 tool (a quality assessment tool for diagnostic accuracy studies; Whiting *et al.*, 2011) was used to assess the quality of the evidence from diagnostic test accuracy studies. Each study was assessed for risk of bias (in terms of participant selection, the index test, and the reference standard) and for applicability (the extent to which the participant selection, index test and reference standard were applicable with regards to the review question). The GDG considered the quality assessment together with the criteria listed below in making recommendations for case identification and assessment tools.

Primary aim of the instrument: the identification of adults with possible autism but not the formal diagnosis or the assessment of a particular domain.

Clinical utility: this criterion required the use of the case identification instrument to be feasible and implementable in routine clinical care. The instrument may also contribute to the identification of further assessment needs and therefore be useful for care planning.

Tool characteristics and administrative properties: the case identification tool should have well-validated cut-offs in the population of interest. Furthermore, and dependent on the practitioners' skills and the setting, tools were evaluated for the time needed to administer and score them, as well as the nature of the training (if any) required for administration or scoring. A case identification instrument should be brief, easy to administer, score and interpret without extensive and specialist training. Non-experts in a variety of care settings (for example, primary care and general medical services) should be able to complete the instrument with relative ease. The cost of the tool and copyright issues were also considered.

Population: the population being assessed reflects the scope of this guideline (see Table 10). The instrument should have been validated in a population aged over 17 years. Tools that are designed for a child and adolescent population, but were adequately validated in an adult sample, were also considered.

Table 10: Clinical review protocol for the review of case identification tools

Component	Description
Review question(s)	What are the most effective methods/tools for case identification in autism in adults? (RQ – A2)
Subquestion	What amendments, if any, need to be made to the agreed methods for case identification to take into account individual variation (for example, gender, age, intellectual abilities, including cognitive strengths as well as difficulties, communication problems, developmental disorders, coexisting mental disorders and physical health problems including hyper/hyposensitivities, motor impairments, and visual and hearing impairments)? (RQ – A2a)
Objectives	• To identify and evaluate case identification tools used in the recognition of autism. • To suggest how recognition of autism can be improved.
Criteria for considering studies for the review	
• *Population*	Adults and young people aged 18 years and older with suspected autism across the range of diagnostic groups (including atypical autism, Asperger's syndrome and pervasive developmental disorder).

Continued

Table 10: *(Continued)*

Component	Description
	Consideration should be given to the specific needs of: • people with coexisting conditions • women • older people • people from black and minority ethnic groups • transgender people.
• *Intervention*	Case identification instruments (for example, the Autism-spectrum Quotient [AQ]; Social Communication Questionnaire [SCQ]; Autism Behaviour Checklist [ABC])
• *Index test*	Case identification instruments
• *Comparison*	DSM or ICD diagnosis of autism
• *Critical outcomes*	**Sensitivity:** the proportion of true positives of all cases diagnosed with autism in the population. **Specificity:** the proportion of true negatives of all cases not diagnosed with autism in the population.
• *Important, but not critical outcomes*	**Positive predictive value:** the proportion of people with positive test results who are correctly diagnosed. **Negative predictive value:** the proportion of people with negative test results who are correctly diagnosed. **AUC:** constructed by plotting the true positive rate as a function of the false positive rate for each threshold.
• *Other outcomes*	**Reliability** (for example, inter-rater, test-retest) **Validity** (for example, construct, content)
• *Study design*	Cohort and case-control
• *Include unpublished data?*	No
• *Restriction by date?*	No
• *Minimum sample size*	N = 10 per arm

Continued

Table 10: *(Continued)*

Component	Description
• *Study setting*	Exclude studies with >50% attrition from either arm of trial (unless adequate statistical methodology has been applied to account for missing data). • Primary, secondary, tertiary and other health and social care settings (including prisons and forensic services). • Others in which NHS services are funded or provided, or NHS professionals are working in multi-agency teams.
Electronic databases	AEI, ASSIA, BEI, CDSR, CENTRAL, CINAHL, DARE, Embase, ERIC, HMIC, MEDLINE, PsycINFO, Sociological Abstracts, SSA
Date searched	Systematic reviews: 1995 up to 09/09/2011. RCTs, quasi-experimental studies, observational studies, case series: inception of database up to 09/09/2011.
Searching other resources	Hand reference searching of retrieved literature
The review strategy	To conduct diagnostic accuracy meta-analyses on the sensitivity and specificity of case identification tools. This is dependent on available data from the literature. In the absence of this, a narrative review of case identification tools will be conducted and guided by a pre-defined list of consensus-based criteria (for example, the clinical utility of the tool, administrative characteristics, and psychometric data evaluating its sensitivity and specificity).

Diagnostic test accuracy: the instrument (the index test) should ideally have been validated against a gold standard diagnostic instrument (the reference standard) and have evidence of its sensitivity and specificity. Reported findings for sensitivity, specificity, AUC, positive predictive value and negative predictive value were considered. See Chapter 3 for a description of diagnostic test accuracy terms.

Psychometric data: the tool should be applicable to a UK population, for example by being validated in a UK population, or a population that is similar to the UK demographic. Where there were reliability and validity data for the case identification tool these was extracted and reviewed. See Chapter 3 for thresholds for evaluating psychometric data.

5.3.3   Aim of the review

This review aims to identify and evaluate the most appropriate instruments to aid in the identification of adults with possible autism.

5.3.4   Clinical review protocol (case identification instruments)

A summary of the review protocol, including the review questions, information about the databases searched, and the eligibility criteria used for this section of the guideline can be found in Table 10 (the full protocol can be found in Appendix 8 and further information about the search strategy can be found in Appendix 9).

5.3.5   Studies considered[13]

The literature search for observational studies resulted in 9,522 articles. Scanning titles and/or abstracts initially identified 561 studies, which initial screening reduced to 93 potentially relevant studies; a further six studies were identified from hand-searches of relevant articles, giving 99 articles in total. Further inspection of the full citations identified using the criteria outlined in Sections 5.3.1 and 5.3.4, a number of studies did not meet one or more eligibility criteria. The reasons for exclusion were that: the study evaluated children or young people (n = 81); the study was outside the scope for another reason or not relevant to this guideline (n = 1); the study did not have sensitivity and specificity data that could be used in meta-analysis (n = 1); or the study provided a narrative review of issues around case identification (n = 5). As a result of this, a total of nine published studies met the eligibility criteria for this review: ALLISON2012 (Allison *et al.*, 2012), BARONCOHEN2001 (Baron-Cohen *et al.*, 2001a), BERUMENT1999 (Berument *et al.*, 1999), BRUGHA2012 (Brugha *et al.*, 2012), KRAIJER2005 (Kraijer & de Bildt, 2005), KURITA2005 (Kurita *et al.*, 2005), VOLKMAR1988 (Volkmar *et al.*, 1988), WAKABAYASHI2006 (Wakabayashi *et al.*, 2006) and WOODBURYSMITH2005 (Woodbury-Smith *et al.*, 2005). An additional four studies had the full text reviewed but were excluded. The most common reason for exclusion was that no sensitivity and specificity data were available. Further information about both included and excluded studies can be found in Appendix 14b.

Of the nine studies (N = 6,221) included in the review, five were conducted using a sample of adults with high-functioning autism or Asperger's syndrome (ALLISON2012, BARONCOHEN2001, BRUGHA2012, KURITA2005, WAKABAYASHI2006). Three studies included a mixed autism population consisting, for example, of autism, Asperger's syndrome and pervasive developmental disorder (BERUMENT1999, KRAIJER2005,

---

[13]Here and elsewhere in the guideline, each study considered for review is referred to by a study ID in capital letters (primary author and date of study publication, except where a study is in press or only submitted for publication, then a date is not used).

WOODBURYSMITH2005) and three studies included populations with a learning disability (BERUMENT1999, KRAIJER2005, VOLKMAR1988).

5.3.6   Case identification instruments included in the review

The instruments that met the inclusion criteria and are included in the review are the Autism-Spectrum Quotient (AQ; Baron-Cohen *et al.,* 2001a); the Autism Screening Questionnaire (ASQ) now known as the Social Communication Questionnaire (SCQ; Rutter *et al.,* 2003); the ABC (Krug *et al.,* 1979 and 1980); and the Pervasive Developmental Disorder in Mental Retardation Scale (PDD-MRS; Kraijer, 1997a and 1997b). The study characteristics for case identification tools included in the review can be found in Table 11 and the characteristics of the case identification tools them-selves can be found in Table 12. The AQ is the only included case identification tool that has been validated in a number of versions or forms. The standard AQ consists of 50 items, however, more recent studies have assessed the sensitivity and specificity estimates associated with shorter forms (including the 10- and 20-item versions) and with a Japanese-language version in both its full form (AQ-J-50) and shorter forms (10- and 21-item versions, the AQ-J-10 and AQ-J-21, respectively).

5.3.7   Clinical evidence

Review Manager 5 was used to summarise diagnostic accuracy data from each study using forest plots and summary ROC curves. To maximise the available data, the most consistently reported and recommended cut-off points for each of the scales were extracted.

The only instrument evaluated by more than one study was the AQ (six studies). All other instruments were evaluated by single studies. A summary of the evidence for all instruments can be found in Table 13 and a ROC curve displaying the sensitiv-ity and specificity of all instruments is shown in Figure 6. In addition, the AQ was the only instrument to be evaluated for different number of items as well as at different cut-off points. Therefore, these data are extracted and displayed individually in a ROC curve (see Figure 7). Sensitivity and specificity forest plots for included case identification instruments are presented in Appendix 15 (forest plots 1.1.1 and 1.1.2).

5.3.8   Clinical evidence summary

Identification of possible autism
The ASQ/SCQ and the ABC can be used to identify possible autism across a broad range of intellectual, social and personal functioning. The analysis showed that the sensitivity and specificity for both tests were 'good' (see Table 13 for a summary of diagnostic accuracy). The internal consistency for both the ASQ/SCQ and ABC was relatively reliable. The tests were found to have discriminant validity as shown by

Table 11: Study information table for case identification tools included in the review

	Index test						
	ABC	ASQ/SCQ	AQ-50	AQ-21	AQ-20	AQ-10	PDD-MRS
No. of trials (total participants)	1 (157 consisting of 94 cases and 63 controls)	1 (200 consisting of 160 cases and 40 controls)	4 (823, consisting of 140 cases, 583 controls and 100 consecutive referrals)	1 (240, consisting of 25 cases and 215 controls)	1 (617)	2 (1,527, consisting of 474 cases and 1,053 controls)	1 (1,230)
Study IDs	VOLKMAR1988	BERUMENT1999	(1) BARONCOHEN2001 (2) KURITA2005 (3) WAKABAYASHI2006 (4) WOODBURYSMITH2005	KURITA2005	BRUGHA2012	(1) ALLISON2012 (2) KURITA2005	KRAIJER2005
Study design	Case-control	Case-control	(1)–(3) Case-control (4) Cohort	Case-control	Cohort	(1)–(2) Case-control	Cohort
Country	US	UK	(1) UK (2)–(3) Japan (4) UK	Japan	UK	(1) UK (2) Japan	Netherlands
Mean age	19.72 years	Range: 4 to 40 years (means by diagnosis ranged from 7 to 23 years)	(1) 16 to 60 years (means: 31.6 for cases and 37 for controls) (2) Mean ages: 24.2 years for cases and 30.4 years for controls (3) 18 to 57 years (means: 26.9 for cases and 33.6 for controls) (4) 18 to 69 years (median: 32 years)	Mean ages: 24.2 years for cases and 30.4 years for controls	Mean ages not reported but all participants >16 years	(1) Mean ages: 32.9 to 35.6 years across groups (2) Mean ages: 24.2 years for cases and 30.4 years for controls	Range: 2 to 80 years (mean not reported)

N/% female	36/23%	Ratios (male:female): Autism 2.8:1; other PDD 6.7:1	(1) 111/48% (2) 130/54% (3) 104/41% (4) 25/25%	130/54%	Not reported	(1) 718/56% (2) 130/54%	511/42%
IQ	Mean IQ on Stanford Binet (for 147 participants) = 36.80	IQ ranged from 30 to >70 across diagnostic groups	(1)–(4) Not reported but high-functioning autism/ Asperger's syndrome or high-functioning PDD (IQ >70)	Not reported but high-functioning PDD (IQ >70)	Not reported	(1)–(2) Not reported but high-functioning autism/Asperger's syndrome (IQ > 70)	Not reported but mild to profound learning disability
Reference standard	DSM-III clinical diagnosis	ADI (n = 77), Autism Diagnostic Interview – Revised (ADI-R) (n = 123)	(1)–(4) DSM-IV clinical diagnosis	DSM-IV clinical diagnosis	Autism Diagnostic Observation Schedule (ADOS) – Module 4	(1)–(2) DSM-IV clinical diagnosis	DSM-IV-TR clinical diagnosis (using ADOS and ADI-R)
Index cut-off	57 +	Cut-off 15 + (autism versus other diagnosis) 22+ (autism versus other PDDs)	(1) 32 + (2) 26 + (3) 33 + (4) 26 +	12 +	10 +	(1) 6 + (2) 7 +	10 +

Table 12: Characteristics of case identification tools included in the review

Instrument	Disorder evaluated	Intellectual ability	Domains assessed	Number of items/scale/ cut-off	Completed by	Time to administer and score/training required/cost and copyright issues	Notes
ABC	Autism	Across the spectrum	Sensory, relating, body/object use, language, social and self-help	57 yes/no items (weighted from 1 to 4 points each), 54 to 67 = probable autism, >68 = positive case	Teacher or a parent	Estimated 15 minutes. Free and available online	The cut-off suggested is 53. Part of the Autism Screening Instrument for Educational Planning.
ASQ/SCQ	Autism	>2 years mental age	Reciprocal social interaction, language and communication, repetitive and stereotyped patterns of behaviour, self-injurious behaviour, language functioning	40 yes/no items; individuals with language = 0 to 39, without language 0 to 34, one item not included in total score, ≥15 positive case	Parent/primary caregiver	10 minutes, no training required. Not free to use	Two versions – 'Lifetime Form' (covers entire developmental history), 'Current Form' (covers the last 3 months)
AQ-50	High-functioning autism/Asperger's syndrome	IQ in the normal to high range	Social skill, attention switching, attention to detail, communication, imagination	50 items on a Likert scale, 0 to 50, ≥32 positive case	Self-report, 40/50 items can be parent/carer reported (has been found to be reliable – BARONCOHEN2001)	10 minutes. Free and available online	The cut-off suggested is 26 or 32

AQ-21	High-functioning autism/Asperger's syndrome	IQ in the normal to high range	Social skill, attention switching, attention to detail, communication, imagination	21 items on a Likert scale	Self-report	5 minutes AQ-50 is free and available online	The cut-off suggested is 9
AQ-20	High-functioning autism/Asperger's syndrome	IQ in the normal to high range	Social skill, attention switching, attention to detail, communication, imagination	20 items on a Likert scale	Self-report	Not reported but approximately 2 minutes AQ-50 is free and available online	The cut-off suggested is 10
AQ-10	High-functioning autism/Asperger's syndrome	IQ in the normal to high range	Social skill, attention switching, attention to detail, communication, imagination	10 items on a Likert scale	Self-report	2 minutes AQ-50 is free and available online	The cut-off suggested is 6
PDD-MRS	PDD	Mild to profound learning disability	Social interaction with adults, social interaction with peers, language and speech, other behaviours	12 items, 0 to 19: score 0 to 5 = non-PDD; 6 to 9 = doubtful PDD; 10 to 19 = PDD	Practitioner with extensive experience in the field of autism and learning disabilities (observation)	10 to 20 minutes to administer and score, no training required Not free to use	Observation of current behaviour in last 2 to 6 months. Observation can be at home, school day-care centre and so on.

Table 13: Evidence summary table for all case identification instruments included in the review[14]

Instrument	Target condition	Cut-off	Included studies	Sensitivity Specificity	LR+ LR–	Diagnostic OR
ABC	Autism	57	1	0.75 0.81	3.95 0.31	12.74
AQ-10	High-functioning autism/ Asperger's syndrome	6	1	0.88 0.91	9.78 0.13	74.23
AQ-20	High-functioning autism/ Asperger's syndrome	10	1	0.74 0.62	1.95 0.35	5.57
AQ-50	High-functioning autism/ Asperger's syndrome	32/33	3	0.77 to 0.88 0.74 to 0.98	2.96 to 39.5 0.12 to 0.31	9.55 to 244.17
AQ-50 (English and Japanese versions)	High-functioning autism/ Asperger's syndrome	26	2	0.76 to 0.95 0.52 to 0.71	1.98 to 2.62 0.10 to 0.34	7.71 to 19.8
AQ-21 (Japanese version)	High-functioning autism/ Asperger's syndrome	12	1	0.92 0.82	5.11 0.10	51.10
AQ-10 (Japanese version)	High-functioning autism/ Asperger's syndrome	7	1	0.76 0.92	9.50 0.26	36.54
ASQ/SCQ	Autism	15	1	0.85 0.75	3.40 0.20	17.00
PDD-MRS	PDD with intellectual disability	10	1	0.92 0.92	11.5 0.09	127.78

[14]When data for an instrument are available from more than one study, a range of test data across the included studies is provided. See forest plots in Appendix 15 for individual data by study.

Figure 6: Summary ROC curve for the ABC, AQ (10-, 20-, 21- and 50-item versions), ASQ/SCQ and PDD-MRS

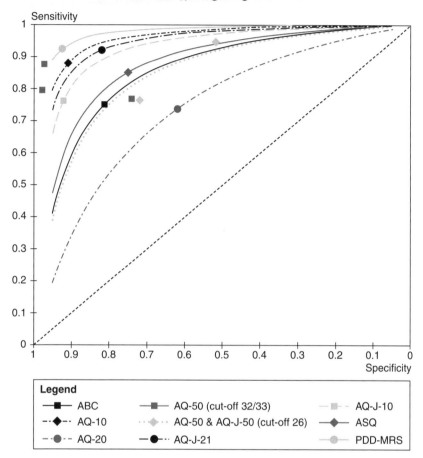

statistically significant t-test differences between participants with autism and those without autism. Concurrent validity was also reasonable for the ABC, which was correlated with the Vineland Adaptive Behaviour Scales (VABS), and was good for the ASQ/SCQ, which was correlated with the ADI (see Table 14 for a summary of psychometric data). However, there was a high risk of bias for both the ABC and the ASQ/SCQ in terms of: participant selection (due to the case-control design in BERUMENT1999 and the lack of consecutive or random enrolment in VOLKMAR1998); the index test (index test results were not interpreted blind to reference standard results and the thresholds were not pre-specified); and flow and timing (the interval between the index test and reference standard was several years or unreported, and for the ABC there were also cases excluded from the analysis). Additionally, for the ASQ/SCQ there was a high risk of bias in the reference standard as the ADI or Autism-Diagnostic Interview – Revised

99

Figure 7: Summary of ROC curve for the AQ alone (10-, 20-, 21- and 50-item versions) at different cut-offs

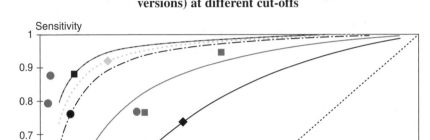

(ADI-R) are not the gold standard for diagnosis. Furthermore, there were applicability concerns with both tests. The ASQ/SCQ and ABC samples combined children and adults. The case-control design of the ASQ/SCQ study also meant that more clinical data were available when the test results were interpreted than would be when the test is used in clinical practice. There were also concerns regarding index test applicability for the ABC because individuals with intermediate ABC scores were classified as 'questionable' and this appears unsatisfactory for a diagnostic test (see Figure 8 for a summary of methodological quality and Appendix 16 for the full methodology checklists). Finally, it should be noted that the GDG had doubts about the clinical utility of the ASQ/SCQ given that it is not freely available and can only be used with permission from the developers.

Table 14: Psychometric data for included case identification instruments

Instrument	Reliability			Validity		
	Inter-rater	Test-retest	Internal consistency	Construct validity (covergent and discriminant validity)	Criterion validity (concurrent and predictive validity)
ABC	X	X	• Correlations between ABC symptom areas and total score correlations, $r = 0.58$ to 0.82 • Split-half reliability for total sample = 0.74	Discriminant validity: significant autistic versus non-autistic group difference ($t = 6.18$, $p = 0.001$)	Concurrent validity: correlation between ABC and Vineland Composite score $r = -0.33$ and Vineland Maladaptive $1 + 2$, $r = 0.36$
AQ-10	X	X	• $\alpha = 0.85$ • AQ-10 and AQ-50 $r = 0.92$	• Discriminant validity: discrimination index 0.37 to 0.62 for most discriminating 10 items (AQ-10) of AQ-50 • Discriminant validity: significant case-control group difference ($t = -31.71$, $p \leq 0.0001$; eta squared = 0.62)	X
AQ-20	X	X	X	X	Predictive validity: correlation between AQ-20 and ADOS-4 $r = 0.24$

Continued

Table 14: *(Continued)*

Instrument	Reliability		Internal consistency	Validity	
	Inter-rater	Test-retest		Construct validity (convergent and discriminant validity)	Criterion validity (concurrent and predictive validity)
AQ-50 item (cut-off 32 to 33)	• Parent versus self-report (N = 22) on AQ-40: MD = 2.8 points (standard deviation = –0.6) with parents scoring more highly (BARON-COHEN2001) • Parent versus self-report (N = 32) on AQ-40, r = 0.71 (WAKABAYASHI2006)	• For subsample of student control group (N = 17): test-retest with 2-week interval, r = 0.7 (BARONCOHEN2001) • For subsample of student control group (N = 54): test-retest with 2- to 3-week interval, r = 0.87 (WAKABAYASHI2006)	• For each of five domains: communication α = 0.65; social α = 0.77; imagination α = 0.65; local details α = 0.63; attention switching α = 0.67 (BARON-COHEN2001) • For student and general population control groups: α = 0.81 for total scale (WAKABAYASHI2006)	• Discriminant validity: significant autistic versus non-autistic group difference (t = -5.59, p <0.0001) (WOODBURY-SMITH2005)	X
AQ-50 (English and Japanese versions) (cut-off 26)	X	For subsample of cases (N = 19 who agreed to participate) test-retest with mean of 7-month interval, r = 0.77	α = 0.73 for cases, α = 0.75 for controls, α = 0.78 for total sample (KURITA2005)	Discriminant validity: significant case-control group difference (t = 5.34, p <0.01) (KURITA2005)	X
AQ-21 (Japanese version)	X	For subsample of cases (N = 19 who agreed to participate) test-retest with mean of 7-month interval, r = 0.61	α = 0.71	Discriminant validity: significant case-control group difference (t = 8.70, p <0.01)	X

AQ-10 (Japanese version)	X	For subsample of cases (N = 19 who agreed to participate) test-retest with mean of 7-month interval, $r = 0.56$	$\alpha = 0.61$	Discriminant validity: significant case-control group difference $t = 10.86$, $p < 0.01$	X
ASQ/SCQ	X	X	• $\alpha = 0.90$ • Individual item to total score correlations, $r = 0.26$ to 0.73 ($23/39 > 0.50$)	Discriminant validity: significant PDD versus non-PDD group difference ($t = 8.73$, $p < 0.0005$)	Concurrent validity: correlation between ASQ and ADI total scores $r = 0.71$
PDD-MRS	• Psychological experts versus medical experts (N = 99 random subsample), $r = 0.83$ • Different psychological experts (two random subsamples of N = 76 and N = 42), $r = 0.85$ and 0.89, respectively	• For random subsample (N = 97) over 6-month period, $r = 0.81$ for medical experts and $r = 0.86$ for psychological experts • For random subsample (N = 42) over 14-year period, $r = 0.70$	• $\alpha = 0.86$ and 0.81 for participants with functional speech and those without speech respectively	X	X

Figure 8: Methodological quality of case identification included instruments

Index Test	Study	RISK OF BIAS				APPLICABILITY CONCERNS		
		PATIENT SELECTION	INDEX TEST	REFERENCE STANDARD	FLOW AND TIMING	PATIENT SELECTION	INDEX TEST	REFERENCE STANDARD
ABC	VOLKMAR1988	⊗	⊗	☺	☺	⊗	⊗	☺
AQ-10 (cut-off 6)	ALLISON2012	⊗	⊗	☺	⊗	⊗	⊗	☺
AQ-20 (cut-off 10)	BRUGHA2012	☺	☺	⊗	☹	⊗	⊗	☺
	BARONCOHEN2001	⊗	⊗	☺	☺	⊗	⊗	☺
AQ-50 (cut-off 32/33)	WAKABAYASHI2006	⊗	⊗	☺	☺	⊗	⊗	☺
	WOODBURYSMITH2005	☺	☺	☺	☺	⊗	⊗	☺
AQ-50 & AQ-J-50 (cut-off 26)	KURITA2005	⊗	⊗	☺	☺	⊗	⊗	☺
	WOODBURYSMITH2005	☺	☺	☹	☺	⊗	⊗	☺
AQ-J-21	KURITA2005	⊗	⊗	☺	☺	⊗	⊗	☺
AQ-J-10	KURITA2005	⊗	⊗	☺	☺	⊗	⊗	☺
ASQ	BERUMENT1999	⊗	⊗	⊗	☺	⊗	☺	☺
PDD-MRS	KRAJJER2005	⊗	☺	⊗	☺	⊗	⊗	☺

☺=Low Risk   ☹=Unclear Risk   ⊗=High Risk

Identification of possible autism when IQ is higher than 70

The AQ (across all versions) was the only instrument that met inclusion criteria for this population and had more than one study that could be included in meta-analysis. The included studies evaluated the original 50-item AQ at the cut-off score of 32 and 26. In addition, a single study also evaluated the sensitivity and specificity of a 20-item version, another single study examined a 21-item version and two studies examined two different 10-item versions of the AQ. At a cut-off of 32, the 50-item AQ had 'good' sensitivity and 'excellent' specificity. However, at a cut-off of 26 points, although the sensitivity was 'good' and 'excellent' in the two included studies, the specificity was very poor ('low' to 'moderate') reflecting the nature of the populations from which the data were collected (see Table 13 for a summary of diagnostic accuracy).

The review of the 20- and 21-item versions of the AQ were based on single studies and the AQ 10-item was based on two studies each evaluating a different set of 10 items of the AQ in two different samples (Japanese and British). The sensitivity and specificity of the AQ-20 item was 'moderate'. The sensitivity of the 21-item version was 'excellent' and the specificity 'good'. The 10-item Japanese version conversely had 'moderate' sensitivity and 'excellent' specificity. The 10-item British version had 'good' sensitivity and 'excellent' specificity (see Table 13 for a summary of diagnostic accuracy summary).

As can be noted from the data, the sensitivity and specify were markedly poorer for the AQ 20-item, and the reason for this disparity probably lies in study design; the questionnaire was used as a general population screen rather than in a clinical sample or where a suspicion of autism had already been raised.

The different versions of the AQ are self-report measures, and thus there may be reliability concerns. However, for the AQ-50 a significant correlation was found between parent- and self-report indicating good inter-rater reliability. Good test-retest reliability was also found for the AQ-50. However, for the AQ-21 and AQ-10 Japanese versions the test-retest reliability failed to meet the 0.70 threshold (see Chapter 3 for methodological details on evaluating psychometric data). Internal consistency was found to be good for all versions of the AQ (where psychometric data were available). Similarly, statistically significant group difference (autism versus non-autism) in AQ scores (as indicated by t-test results) suggested good discriminant validity across all AQ versions (see Table 14 for a summary of psychometric data).

For all AQ studies, except BRUGHA2012 and WOODBURYSMITH2005, there was a high risk of bias in terms of: participant selection (due to case-control design); the index test (index test results were interpreted with knowledge of the reference standard results and the cut-offs were not pre-specified); and the flow and timing (the time interval and any interventions between the index test and reference standard were not reported, only the cases of autism received verification with the reference standard, and clinical diagnosis was performed by different clinicians therefore cases may not have received the same reference standard). In BRUGHA2012 and WOOD-BURYSMITH2005, the risk of bias was lower, largely due to the higher-quality cohort design. However, as with other AQ studies, the index test threshold was not pre-specified and it was not clear that the reference standard results were interpreted blind to the index test results. There was also an additional concern regarding the reference standard in the BRUGHA2012 study, namely, that the Autism Diagnostic Observation Schedule (ADOS-4) rather than a gold standard DSM-IV/ICD-10 clinical diagnosis was used as the comparator. Finally, the concerns regarding applicability were the same across all versions of the AQ and were based on all participants having an IQ higher than 70 and that the index test was not suitable for people with autism who also had a learning disability (see Figure 8 for a summary of methodological quality and Appendix 16 for full methodology checklists). However, the GDG judged the clinical utility of the AQ-10 to be good, given that it is quick to administer and is free and available online.

Identification of possible autism in a learning disabilities population
The PDD-MRS was the only instrument included in the review that was specifically designed for the identification of possible pervasive developmental disorders (including autism) in people with a learning disability. On the basis of a single study, the PDD-MRS was found to have 'good' sensitivity and specificity (see Table 13 for a summary of diagnostic accuracy). The PDD-MRS was also found to have good inter-rater and test-retest reliability and internal consistency (see Table 14 for a summary of psychometric data). However, there was a high risk of bias for: participant selection (enrolment was not consecutive or random); the reference standard (reference standard results were not interpreted blind to the results of the index test); and flow and timing (verification with the reference standard was only performed for a subsample of participants aged 4 to 18 years, and the time interval and any interventions between the index test and reference standard were not reported). There were also no details reported regarding the assessors and/or scoring the index test (see Figure 8 for a summary of methodological quality and Appendix 16 for full methodology checklists). In addition, the GDG had concerns regarding the clinical utility of the PDD-MRS because it has to be administered by a practitioner with considerable experience in the assessment of people with neurodevelopmental conditions, therefore limiting its use in general healthcare settings.

As the review did not identify a tool for routine use for people with possible autism and a learning disability, the GDG reviewed those studies identified in the original literature review that did not report on formal case identification tools as well as the structure and content of the case identification tools identified in this review. Two studies, in particular, provided information that was used by the GDG in developing their recommendations. Bhaumik and colleagues (2010) in a study of carer-reported autistic traits in adults with autism and a learning disability reported that the presence of two or more out of five autistic traits (minimal speech; poor social interaction; lack of empathy; presence of elaborate routines; and presence of stereotypies) gave the best sensitivity (63.2% people with autism with two or more traits) and specificity (78.5% people without autism with fewer than two traits). Those with two or more traits without a diagnosis of autism were likely to be aged over 50 years, have mobility problems, Down's syndrome, cerebral palsy or other significant mental health problems.

The autistic traits referred to above and their description drew on the work of Holmes and colleagues (1982) on the assessment of people with a learning disability. The GDG reviewed this paper in order to inform the structure and content with regards to possible areas for assessment in people with suspected autism and a learning disability. Four areas identified by Holmes and colleagues (1982) were:

1. Poor social interaction:
   - does not interact – mainly aloof, indifferent or bizarre
   - interacts to obtain needs only – otherwise indifferent
   - 'unwarm' – does make social approaches, but these are peculiar, naïve or even bizarre. The person does not modify behaviour in light of these responses, needs or interests of those whom s/he approaches. The interaction is one-sided and dominated by the person being rated.
2. Lack of empathy:
   - no or limited empathy.
3. Elaborate routines:
   - marked repetitive activities (for example, rocking, hand or finger flapping or full body movements), especially when unoccupied, although may be controlled by close supervision or being kept fully occupied—often a constant feature, present each day.
4. Marked stereotypies:
   - has elaborate routines of the kind and intensity found in early childhood autism.

5.3.9   Case identification in populations with specific needs

The GDG had concerns that particular groups, including people with coexisting conditions, women, older people, people from black and minority ethnic groups and transgender people, were less likely to be identified by standard case identification tools. The review of the literature undertaken to address this question failed to find any tools that specifically addressed the needs of these groups. The GDG therefore reviewed the literature identified in the searches undertaken for this guideline where it addressed the needs of the above groups and considered this alongside the expert knowledge of the GDG in developing the brief narrative summaries below.

Women
It has been suggested that there is a significant gender gap in the recognition and diagnosis of Asperger's syndrome and high-functioning autism (Wilkinson, 2008), with women being under-diagnosed (Attwood, 2006a; Ehlers & Gillberg, 1993). Some believe that the manifestation of symptoms may be more subtle in women than in men and hence more difficult to recognise (Attwood, 2006a; Bashe & Kirby, 2005). For example, girls display better superficial social skills, better language and communication, less inappropriate special interests and activities, and less aggressive and hyperactive behaviour than boys (Gillberg & Coleman, 2000). Furthermore, it has

also been suggested that girls who have difficulty maintaining eye contact and seem to be socially withdrawn may be thought to be 'shy' rather than having a symptom of autism (Wagner, 2006). Hence the core symptoms of autism may not be recognised easily in girls. This gender issue may also interact with coexisting mental health conditions and lead to further under-recognition of those disorders (see, for example, Zucker and colleagues [2007] who highlight a particular problem in identifying autism in young women with anorexia nervosa).

Older people

Autism was not included in psychiatric classification systems until DSM-III in 1980 (American Psychological Association, 1980) and the diagnostic criteria for Asperger's syndrome were only established in 1994 with DSM-IV (American Psychological Association, 1994). Therefore those who may meet these criteria and were children prior to this time are unlikely to have been identified and diagnosed with autism and, in particular, Asperger's syndrome. In addition, there is little research evaluating the recognition and diagnosis of autism in adults and even less in older adults.

Therefore, as mentioned in the introduction, some people reach adulthood without ever having received a diagnosis of autism. This could be because they are able to make their way through life with relative success, having finished schooling, married, had children and maintained jobs (James *et al.*, 2006). Such people are also likely to be of average or above average intelligence (see, for example, the case studies described in James *et al.*, 2006). Some may also have a stable social support network, for example still living with parents, and have not had contact with mental health or learning disability services where autism could potentially have been recognised. Conversely, autism might have been missed in people who have severe cognitive impairments (such as Down's syndrome) or mental health problems. Key life events, such as the death of parents, can mean that a diagnosis of autism is made in later life, sometimes as late as retirement or following medical problems (James *et al.*, 2006). Some adults with unrecognised autism may also be identified after contact with the criminal justice system either as offenders or victims (Hare *et al.*, 2000).

Although little is known about the healthcare needs and experiences of older people with autism, what is evident is that there is under-diagnosis in this demographic group (Brugha *et al.*, 2011) and that there are additional barriers to diagnosis such as behavioural or medical problems (Tsakanikos *et al.*, 2007). It is important for healthcare professionals to be aware of the signs and symptoms of autism and that they may be masked by coexisting conditions.

Black and minority ethnic groups

The GDG found no relevant studies of the recognition of autism in adults from black and minority ethnic groups but there is a literature on children and young people that suggests recognition of autism in black and minority ethnic groups is limited. This is briefly summarised below.

Mandell and colleagues (2009) examined racial/ethnic disparities in a community sample of 2,568 children across 14 states of America. Experienced clinicians used clinical and educational records to ascertain previous diagnosis of autism and identify undetected cases of autism. The study reported that black, Hispanic and other ethnic groups had lower odds of being identified than white children. For black children specifically this was still the case across a range of intellectual ability levels. However, for Asian and Hispanic children, this was more likely the case for those with a learning disability. Mandell and colleagues (2009) suggest that health-care professionals screen for autism less often in children from black and minority ethnic groups. Begeer and colleagues (2009) have suggested that this might arise because healthcare professionals are more likely to attribute autistic features and symptoms such as communication and social deficits to culture or language in black and minority ethnic groups, resulting in under-diagnosis of autism. Cuccaro and colleagues (1996), who reported no significant difference in identification between different ethnic groups, suggested any difference may be accounted for by socioeconomic status.

In a study of the prevalence of black and minority ethnic groups in Dutch institutions for people with autism, Begeer and colleagues (2009) reported a significant under-representation of Moroccan and Turkish children and young people. In a linked study they also reported that the ethnic background of the potential patient influenced paediatricians' diagnostic judgements on a series of clinical vignettes, with a diagnosis of autism more likely to be given to white Europeans compared with other ethnic groups.

Transgender people
There are two papers relating to transgender people with autism; one on autistic traits in transsexual people (Jones *et al.*, 2011), reporting elevated autistic traits in female-to-male transsexuals; and one on prevalence of autism in children and young people with gender dysphoria (de Vries *et al.*, 2010). The latter suggests prevalence for autism of around 6% in children and young people with gender dysphoria, a rate significantly higher than in the general population. While this suggests the need for greater vigilance in this population, no specific data on case identification are provided.

5.3.10   Health economic evidence

No studies assessing the cost effectiveness of case identification tools in adults with autism were identified by the systematic search of the economic literature undertaken for this guideline. Details on the methods used for the systematic search of the economic literature are described in Chapter 3.

5.3.11   From evidence to recommendations

The GDG was mindful of the practicalities of developing a measure to improve case identification and recognition of people with autism that would be of value in routine use in primary care and other settings. Initially, as in other NICE mental health guidelines, the GDG attempted to find very brief instruments composed of one to three questions that might have sufficient sensitivity and specificity to be of use for identifying signs and symptoms in routine care. However, the search found no such measures. The GDG therefore used their expert knowledge and judgement, together with the diagnostic criteria and related information contained in existing diagnostic manuals (principally DSM-IV), to identify a number of signs and symptoms that were in their view likely to have sufficient sensitivity and specificity to improve the identification of autism in adults and prompt assessment where necessary. As is appropriate in such circumstances, the GDG favoured sensitivity over specificity.

The review of existing case identification instruments considered the sensitivity and specificity of the five versions of the AQ: the 50-item (AQ-50); the 21-item (AQ-21); the 20-item (AQ-20); and two versions of a 10-item questionnaire (AQ-10 [British] and AQ-10 [Japanese]). The GDG judged that there were no important differences between the AQ-50 (cut-off at 32), AQ-20 and AQ-10 (British) in terms of sensitivity and specificity in populations with normal intellectual ability. The GDG considered the diagnostic test accuracy results together with concerns about the methodological quality. As with all the case identification tools included in this review, all versions of the AQ were associated with a high risk of bias and concerns regarding applicability. A major factor in increasing the risk of bias for AQ studies was the case-control design adopted. A case-control design increases the risk of bias because diagnostic test accuracy may be overestimated—the inclusion of neurotypical controls can be expected to decrease the likelihood of a false positive test (and increase the estimate of specificity) compared with a situation where the test is performed on individuals showing symptoms of autism. However, given that the GDG favoured sensitivity over specificity as appropriate for a case identification tool, and given that the role of the AQ in this context was not as a population-wide screen but in a group where the suspicion of autism had already been raised, the concerns regarding methodological quality were not judged as barriers to making a recommendation. Moreover, the AQ-10 has high clinical utility, in that the test takes only a brief time to administer (2 minutes), and as a self-completion questionnaire requires no particular expertise in its administration or scoring. The GDG therefore decided that the AQ-10 (British) would be appropriate for use in primary care, social care and other non-specialist settings to support the decision to refer for a specialist assessment in people without a learning disability.

However, no such instruments were identified for people with suspected autism and a learning disability. Given that a significant proportion of adults with autism have a learning disability (perhaps 60%), it is important to provide advice in this area. The GDG took the view that a self-completion tool would not be feasible for a significant number of people with a learning disability and that a clinician-completed measure would be unlikely to be used routinely. Therefore, the GDG drew on a review of existing diagnostic manuals and assessment schedules designed specifically for use in people with autism and a learning disability, which enabled the GDG to identify a number of important indicators of autism including: social-interaction problems; lack of responsiveness to others; little or no response to social situations; lack of demonstrable empathy; rigidity of routine; and marked indication of stereotypies. The GDG then formulated them into a list of considerations that should comprise a brief assessment for autism to be performed by health and social care professionals to support them in determining whether or not to refer for a specialist assessment. Again, in developing this recommendation, the GDG adopted an approach that emphasised sensitivity over specificity.

5.3.12   Recommendations

Identification and initial assessment of possible autism

5.3.12.1   Consider assessment for possible autism when a person has:
- one or more of the following:
  - persistent difficulties in social interaction
  - persistent difficulties in social communication
  - stereotypic (rigid and repetitive) behaviours, resistance to change or restricted interests, **and**
- one or more of the following:
  - problems in obtaining or sustaining employment or education
  - difficulties in initiating or sustaining social relationships
  - previous or current contact with mental health or learning disability services
  - a history of a neurodevelopmental condition (including learning disabilities and attention deficit hyperactivity disorder) or mental disorder.

5.3.12.2   For adults with possible autism who do not have a moderate or severe learning disability, consider using the Autism-Spectrum Quotient – 10 items (AQ-10)[15]. (If a person has reading difficulties, read out the AQ-10.) If a person scores above six on the AQ-10, or autism is suspected based on clinical judgement (taking into account any past history provided by an informant), offer a comprehensive assessment for autism.

5.3.12.3   For adults with possible autism who have a moderate or severe learning disability, consider a brief assessment to ascertain whether the following behaviours are present (if necessary using information from a family member, partner or carer):
- difficulties in reciprocal social interaction including:
  - limited interaction with others (for example, being aloof, indifferent or unusual)
  - interaction to fulfil needs only
  - interaction that is naïve or one-sided

---

[15]Allison and colleagues (2012).

- lack of responsiveness to others
- little or no change in behaviour in response to different social situations
- limited social demonstration of empathy
- rigid routines and resistance to change
- marked repetitive activities (for example, rocking and hand or finger flapping), especially when under stress or expressing emotion.

If two or more of the above categories of behaviour are present, offer a comprehensive assessment for autism.

5.4   ASSESSMENT AND DIAGNOSIS OF AUTISM IN ADULTS

5.4.1   Introduction

The purpose of this section is to identify best practice in the diagnosis and assessment of autism in adults across a range of clinical settings. A key aim of the assessment process should be to elicit information regarding the relevant characteristics of autism as outlined in the current diagnostic systems for autism, such as ICD-10 and DSM-IV. Although diagnosis is an important aspect of most assessments, the focus of assessment should not only be on diagnosis but should also consider the person's physical, psychological and social functioning, and any risks that they might face. The range and comprehensiveness of any assessment may vary depending on the setting in which it is undertaken and the particular purpose of the assessment, but in nearly all cases a central aim is to identify any need for intervention and care. The range and depth of the components of assessment should reflect the complexity of tasks to be addressed and the expertise required to carry out the assessment. Crucial to the effective delivery of any assessment is the competence of the staff who are delivering it, including the ability to conduct an assessment, interpret the findings of the assessment and use these findings to support the development of appropriate care plans and, where necessary, risk management plans.

Current practice
As was set out in Section 5.3, there is limited access to services offering assessment for adults with autism outside specialist learning disability services. In services where specialist assessments are available, it will typically consist of a formal assessment of the core symptoms of autism, the nature and extent of any associated problems, the presence of any coexisting physical or mental disorders and an assessment of broader personal, social, educational and employment needs. In many specialist settings this will be undertaken by a multidisciplinary team, who may use structured instruments such as the ADOS (Lord *et al.,* 2001) or the Diagnostic Interview for Social and Communication Disorders (DISCO) (Wing *et al.,* 2002) and involve a family member or carer as an informant.

Definition

For the purposes of this review, assessment and diagnostic instruments were defined as validated psychometric measures used to assess and diagnose people with autism. The review was limited to instruments likely to be used for adults with possible autism in UK clinical practice. 'Gold standard' diagnoses were defined as DSM or ICD (or equivalent) clinical diagnoses of autism.

5.4.2   Aim of the review

First, this section aims to identify and evaluate the diagnostic accuracy and usefulness of assessment instruments (including biological measures) that can aid in diagnosing autism (see Section 5.4.4). The GDG used this review to identify key components of an effective clinical interview to diagnose the presence and severity of autism in adults. Second, this section aims to identify any amendments that may need to be made to take into account the variation in problems experienced by adults with autism including the presence of coexisting conditions (see Section 5.4.5).

5.4.3   Clinical review protocol

A summary of the review protocol, including the review questions, information about the databases searched, and the eligibility criteria used for this section of the guideline, can be found in Table 15 (the full protocol can be found in Appendix 8 and further information about the search strategy can be found in Appendix 9).

5.4.4   Review of autism assessment instruments

Inclusion criteria for autism assessment instruments

Instruments designed to structure and support clinical diagnosis and facilitate and structure direct observation were considered for the review. Instruments were included if they were:

● diagnostic instruments developed for the assessment of autism (but not generic assessment instruments developed to diagnose a range of disorders)
● structured, semi-structured or direct observation instruments validated in a sample aged over 17 years (even if developed for people aged under 17 years).

Biological measures

No studies were identified that provided evidence on the use of biological measures in the routine assessment of autism in adults. A number of recently published studies of brain imaging (Bloeman *et al.*, 2010; Ecker *et al.*, 2010; Lange *et al.*, 2010) suggest that these techniques may have some value in the diagnosis of autism but the authors acknowledge that further development work is required before they could be considered for routine clinical use. The studies were therefore not considered further in this guideline.

Table 15: Clinical review protocol for assessment and diagnosis

Component	Description
Review question(s)	In adults with possible autism, what are the key components of, and the most effective structure for, a diagnostic assessment? To answer this question, consideration should be given to: • the nature and content of the clinical interview and observation (including an early developmental history where possible) • formal diagnostic methods/ psychological instruments (including risk assessment) • biological measures • the setting(s) in which the assessment takes place • who the informant needs to be (to provide a developmental history). (RQ – B1) • What are the most effective methods for assessing an individual's needs (for example, their personal, social, occupational, educational and housing needs) for adults with autism? (RQ – B3)
Subquestion	• When making a differential diagnosis of autism in adults, what amendments, if any, need to be made to the usual methods to make an assessment of autism itself in light of potential coexisting conditions (for example, common mental health disorders, ADHD, personality disorders, gender/identity disorders, eating disorders, Tourette's syndrome, and drug or alcohol misuse)? (RQ – B2)
Objectives	• To identify the key components of an effective clinical interview to diagnose the presence and severity of autism in adults. • To evaluate the diagnostic accuracy of assessment tools that aid the diagnosis of autism in adults. • To identify what amendments, if any, need to be made to take into account individual differences (for example, coexisting conditions). • To identify the most effective methods for assessing an individual's needs. • To evaluate an individual's quality of life. • To suggest how diagnosis of autism in adults can be improved.

continued

Table 15: (*Continued*)

Component	Description
Criteria for considering studies for the review	
• *Population*	Adults and young people aged 18 years and older with suspected autism across the range of diagnostic groups (including atypical autism, Asperger's syndrome and pervasive developmental disorder). Consideration should be given to the specific needs of: • people with coexisting conditions • women • older people • people from black and minority ethnic groups • transgender people.
• *Intervention*	Formal assessments of the nature and severity of autism (including problem specification or diagnosis).
• *Index test*	Formal assessments of the nature and severity of autism (including problem specification or diagnosis).
• *Comparison*	DSM or ICD clinical diagnosis of autism (or equivalent)
• *Critical outcomes*	**Sensitivity**: the proportion of true positives of all cases diagnosed with autism in the population. **Specificity**: the proportion of true negatives of all cases not diagnosed with autism in the population.
• *Important, but not critical outcomes*	**Positive predictive value**: the proportion of people with positive test results who are correctly diagnosed. **Negative predictive value**: the proportion of people with negative test results who are correctly diagnosed. **AUC:** constructed by plotting the true positive rate as a function of the false positive rate for each threshold.
• *Other outcomes*	**Reliability** (for example, inter-rater, test-retest) **Validity** (for example, construct, content)
• *Study design*	Case-control and cohort
• *Include unpublished data?*	No
• *Restriction by date?*	No

continued

Table 15: *(Continued)*

Component	Description
• *Minimum sample size*	N = 10 per arm Exclude studies with >50% attrition from either arm of trial (unless adequate statistical methodology has been applied to account for missing data).
• *Study setting*	• Primary, secondary, tertiary and other health and social care settings (including prisons and forensic services). • Others in which NHS services are funded or provided, or NHS professionals are working in multi-agency teams.
Electronic databases	AEI, BEI, Biosciences Information Service (BIOSIS) previews, CDSR, CINAHL, DARE, Embase, ERIC, HMIC, MEDLINE, PsycINFO, Sociological Abstracts
Date searched	Generic, RCTs, quasi-experimental studies, observational studies: inception of database up to 09/09/2011. Generic, systematic reviews: 1995 up to 09/09/2011.
Searching other resources	Hand reference searching of retrieved literature
The review strategy	• To provide a GDG-consensus based narrative identifying the key components of an effective clinical diagnostic interview (considering possible amendments due to individual variation). • To conduct diagnostic accuracy meta-analyses on the sensitivity, specificity, reliability and validity of assessment tools. This is dependent on available data from the literature. In the absence of this, a narrative review of assessment tools will be conducted and guided by a pre-defined list of consensus-based criteria (for example, the clinical utility of the tool, administrative characteristics, and psychometric data evaluating its sensitivity, specificity, reliability and validity).

Assessment instruments in the review

The GDG identified a list of possible instruments that could be used by clinicians in the diagnostic assessment of adults who are suspected of having autism:

- Adult Asperger Assessment (AAA)[16]
- Autism Spectrum Disorders Diagnosis Scale for Intellectually Disabled Adults (ASD-DA)
- Asperger Syndrome (and high-functioning autism) Diagnostic Interview (ASDI)
- Asperger Syndrome Diagnostic Scale[17]
- Autism-Diagnostic Interview – Revised (ADI-R)
- Autism Diagnostic Observation Schedule (ADOS)
- Behavior Summarized Evaluation – Revised (BSE-R)
- Childhood Autism Rating Scale (CARS)
- Children's Social Behavior Questionnaire[18]
- Developmental, Dimensional and Diagnostic Interview (3di)
- DISCO
- Gilliam Asperger's Disorder Scale[19]
- Gilliam Autistic Rating Scale (GARS)[20]
- Krug Asperger's Disorder Index[21]
- Movie for the Assessment of Social Cognition (MASC)
- Pervasive Developmental Disorders Rating Scale (PDDRS)
- Ritvo Autism and Asperger's Diagnostic Scale (RAADS)
- Ritvo Autism and Asperger's Diagnostic Scale – Revised (RAADS-R)
- Sensory Behavior Schedule (SBS)[22]
- Short-Form Developmental Behaviour Checklist[22]
- Social Responsiveness Scale (SRS)
- Triple C: Checklist of Communicative Competencies[23]

These instruments are for the assessment of autism only and intended to aid diagnosis. The list above informed the development of the search terms and also provided useful markers for the searches. A number were excluded after a preliminary review of their properties. (See footnotes for those that were excluded from further review or for other additional information.)

---

[16]Includes the Autism-Spectrum Quotient (AQ) and the Empathy Quotient (EQ).

[17]Excluded from the review as designed for 5- to 18-year-olds only.

[18]Excluded from the review as designed for 4- to 18-year-olds only.

[19]Excluded from the review as designed for 3- to 22-year-olds only.

[20]Excluded from the review as designed for 3- to 22-year-olds and may also be more appropriate for screening.

[21]Excluded from the review as designed for 6- to 22-year-olds and may also be more appropriate for screening.

[22]Excluded from the review as not autism specific.

[23]Excluded from the review as for learning disabilities (not autism specific)

Studies considered[24]

The literature was then scrutinised and studies considered for inclusion based on:

1. Agreed inclusion and exclusion criteria (see Table 15).
2. The availability of sensitivity and specificity data (see Chapter 3 for a description of the methodological approach for reviewing diagnostic test accuracy studies).

The literature search for observational studies resulted in 22 articles, which were evaluated by reading the full texts. Of these 22 articles, 11 were excluded because the mean age of the sample was too low; only a small proportion of the sample being evaluated had a diagnosis of autism; or no sensitivity and specificity data were provided.

Therefore, 11 articles met the eligibility criteria for inclusion in the review (BARON-COHEN2005 [Baron-Cohen *et al.*, 2005], BRUGHA2012 [Brugha *et al.*, 2012], DZIOBEK2006 [Dziobek *et al.*, 2006], GILLBERG2001 [Gillberg *et al.*, 2001], LORD1997 [Lord *et al.*, 1997], LORD2000 [Lord *et al.*, 2000], MATSON2007A [Matson *et al.*, 2007a], MATSON2007B [Matson *et al.*, 2007b], MATSON2008 [Matson *et al.*, 2008], RITVO2008 [Ritvo *et al.*, 2008], RITVO2011 [Ritvo *et al.*, 2011]).

Of the 11 studies included in the review six were conducted using a sample of people with high-functioning autism or Asperger's syndrome (BARONCOHEN2005, BRUGHA2012, DZIOBEK2006, GILLBERG2001, RITVO2008, RITVO2011), two included participants with an autism diagnosis across the spectrum (LORD1997, LORD2000), and four included participants with an autism diagnosis as well as a learning disability (LORD1997, MATSON2007A, MATSON2007B, MATSON2008).

Further information about both included and excluded studies can be found in Appendix 14c.

A summary of the study characteristics for assessment instruments considered for review can be seen in Table 16 and the characteristics of included assessment instruments can be found in Table 17.

Clinical evidence for autism assessment instruments

No studies that assessed sensitivity and specificity in adults with autism for the CARS, 3di, DISCO, PDDRS, BSE-R or SRS instruments were found. A single study was reviewed for the MASC (DZIOBEK2006). However, this instrument could not be considered any further as sensitivity and specificity data could not be extracted.

All other instruments listed in the section entitled 'Assessment instruments in the review' above met the basic inclusion criteria and did have available sensitivity, specificity and psychometric data. The test accuracy data and clinical utility for each instrument, as well as whether it met the criteria stipulated in Table 15, are described below (see Figure 9 for the ROC curve analysis, Figure 10 for the methodological quality of included assessment instruments and Appendix 15, forest plot 1.2.1, for sensitivity and specificity forest plots). For an evidence summary table for all assessment instruments included in the review, see Table 18. Table 19 shows psychometric data for included assessment instruments.

---

[24]Here and elsewhere in the guideline, each study considered for review is referred to by a study ID in capital letters (primary author and date of study publication, except where a study is in press or only submitted for publication, then a date is not used).

Table 16: Study information table for assessment instruments included in the review

	AAA	ADI and ADI-R	ADOS-G (Module 4)	ASD-DA	ASDI	RAADS and RAADS-R
No. of trials (total participants)	1 (42)	1 (330)	2 (244)	1 (232)	1 (24)	2 (873)
Study IDs	BARONCOHEN2005	LORD1997	(1) BRUGHA2012 (2) LORD2000	MATSON2007A	GILLBERG2001	(1) RITVO2008 (2) RITVO2011
Study design	Cohort	Cohort	(1) Cohort (2) Case-control	Case-control	Cohort	(1)–(2) Case-control
Country	UK	US, UK, France	(1) UK (2) UK and US	US	Sweden	(1) US (2) English-speaking countries
Mean age	Mean 34.1 years	Range 3 to 43 years	(1) Not reported but all participants >16 years (2) Means: 18.7 years for participants with autism; 21.6 years for participants with PDD–not otherwise specified (NOS); 19.1 years for controls	Range 20 to 80 years (mean not reported)	Range 6 to 55 years (mean not reported)	(1) Mean 38 years (2) Mean 30.8 to 42 years across diagnostic groups
N/% female	3/7	Not reported	(1) Not reported (2) 8/18	Not reported	6/25	(1) 47/50 (2) 386/50

Continued

Table 16: *(Continued)*

	AAA	ADI and ADI-R	ADOS-G (Module 4)	ASD-DA	ASDI	RAADS and RAADS-R
IQ	Not reported but Asperger's syndrome/high-functioning autism (IQ >70)	Range: 39 to 144 (means: non-verbal group = 56; verbal group = 94.8)	(1) Not reported, but assumption that IQ >70 as screened using self-report postal questionnaire (AQ-20) (2) Means: verbal IQ (VIQ) = 99.9 for the participants with autism, 105.5 for participants with PDD-NOS, and 99.7 for controls; performance IQ (PIQ) = 94.1 for the participants with autism, 105.2 for participants with PDD-NOS, and 103.8 for controls	Not reported (but mild to profound learning disability)	Not reported	(1) Not reported (2) IQ >80
Reference (2) IQ >80	DSM-IV clinical diagnosis	DSM-III-R clinical diagnosis	(1) Case vignette ratings (2) Clinical diagnosis (including use of ADI-R)	DSM-IV/ICD-10 diagnosis criteria list of symptoms	DSM-IV clinical diagnosis	(1)–(2) DSM-IV-TR clinical diagnosis
Index cut-off	10 +	Communication = 8+ for verbal and 6 + for non-verbal Social reciprocity: 10 + Restricted and repetitive behaviour: 4 +	(1) 7+ and 10 + (2) 13 +	24+ and 28 +	5/6 algorithm criteria	(1) 77 + (2) 65 +

Table 17: Characteristics of assessment instruments

Instrument	Age range	Intellectual ability	Domains assessed	Number of items, scale, cut-off	Completed by	Time to administer/ score, training required, cost/copyright issues	Notes
Adult Asperger Assessment (AAA)	16 years and above	IQ >70	Social interaction, social skills, communication, cognitive empathy	AAA = 23 items; AQ = 50 items; Empathy Quotient (EQ) = 60 items; maximum score 18 Cut-off 10 for autism diagnosis	Two parts (AQ and EQ) are self-administered, diagnostic part is clinician-administered	3 hours (for AAA component), freely available	Three-part instrument consisting of the AQ, EQ and a clinician-conducted diagnostic questionnaire – the AAA. No norms available for the AAA (sample size in BARONCO-HEN-2005 is small). Not been validated by anyone other than primary authors/developers.
Autism Diagnostic Interview –Revised (ADI-R)	18 months to adulthood	Mental age above 2 years	Language and communication; reciprocal social interactions; stereotyped behaviours and interests	93 items, scale and cut-off unclear	Clinician-administered interview of caregivers	1.5 to 2.5 hours, training required, available to buy	Although good for varying levels of severity, it has not been designed to measure change. Can be used for diagnosis.

Continued

Table 17: *(Continued)*

Instrument	Age range	Intellectual ability	Domains assessed	Number of items, scale, cut-off	Completed by	Time to administer/ score, training required, cost/copyright issues	Notes
Autism Diagnostic Observation Schedule – Generic (ADOS-G)	2 years to adulthood Module 4 for high-functioning young people and adults	Across spectrum (verbal adolescents/ adults only)	Social and communicative behaviours	15 items, variable cut-offs suggested	Clinician observation	30 to 40 minutes, training required, available to buy	Originally developed as companion instrument for the ADI.
Asperger Syndrome (and high-functioning autism) Diagnostic Interview (ASDI)	Children (6 years plus) and adults	IQ >70	Social interaction, interests, routine, speech and language peculiarities, non-verbal communication, motor clumsiness	20 items, six sub-scales; two-point scale	Structured interview of person who knows subject well and has knowledge of his/her childhood	10 minutes, no training required, freely available	Instrument still in preliminary stages of validation. Not designed to be used with DSM-IV or ICD-10 criteria but designed to reflect criteria as described by Gillberg and Gillberg (1989), which are much broader and do not include the language delay component. Should not be used as a stand-alone instrument.

Autism Spectrum Disorders Diagnosis Scale for Intellectually Disabled Adults (ASD-DA)	Adults	Intellectual disability	One measure for diagnosing autism and PDD-NOS, one measure for comorbid psychopathology, one measure for challenging behaviour	31 items, 0 to 1 point for each item, cut-off 19 points	Interview of third party informant	10 minutes, unclear about training, unclear about cost	Only validated by developers
Movie for the Assessment of Social Cognition (MASC)	Adults (lower end unclear)	Across spectrum	Social cognition	46 questions, three-point scale, cut-off unknown	Tester	45 minutes, minimal training, available from the author by request (cost unclear)	Validated in an Asperger's syndrome sample because of evidence that social cognition presents with only subtle impairments
Ritvo Autism and Asperger Diagnostic Scale (RAADS)	Adults	IQ >70	Social relatedness, language and communication; sensorimotor and stereotypies	78 items, 4-point scale	Clinician completed interview of individual	1 hour, minimal training, freely available	Superseded by RAADS-R
Ritvo Autism and Asperger Diagnostic Scale – Revised (RAADS-R)	18 to 65 years	IQ >70	Social relatedness, circumscribed interests, language, sensorimotor and stereotypies	80 items, 4-point Likert scale ≥ 65 diagnosis of autism or autistic disorder	Self-rated	45 minutes, unclear about training, unclear about cost	This new version is based on the DSM-IV-TR and ICD-10 criteria. Authors recommend use as part of assessment battery not alone. RAADS-R is still in development and not be validated by anyone other than primary authors/developers.

Figure 9: Summary ROC curve for the AAA, ADI and ADI-R, ADOS-G, ASD-DA, ASDI, RAADS and RAADS-R

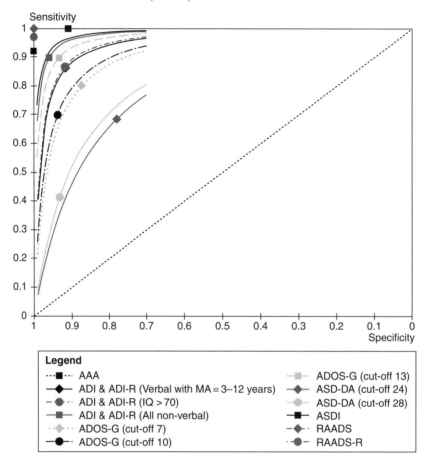

Adult Asperger Assessment (AAA)

The sensitivity and the specificity for the AAA were 'excellent'. However, there was no available evidence evaluating the reliability or the construct and criterion validity of the AAA. There were also methodological concerns regarding the lack of blinding of index test and reference standard results and concerns regarding applicability given that the AAA can only be used with people with an IQ above 70. With regards to clinical utility, the GDG considered that the AA is lengthy to complete. However, it is freely available and does not require extensive training to administer, score or interpret.

Figure 10: Methodological quality of included assessment instruments

Index Test	Study	RISK OF BIAS				APPLICABILITY CONCERNS		
		PATIENT SELECTION	INDEX TEST	REFERENCE STANDARD	FLOW AND TIMING	PATIENT SELECTION	INDEX TEST	REFERENCE STANDARD
AAA	BARONCOHEN2005	☺	☹	☹	⊜	☹	☹	☺
ADI & ADI-R	LORD1997	☹	⊜	☹	☹	☹	⊜	⊜
ADOS-G	BRUGHA2012	⊜	⊜	☹	☹	☹	⊜	☹
ADOS-G	LORD2000	☹	☹	☹	☺	☹	⊜	⊜
ASD-DA	MATSON2007A	☹	☹	☹	⊜	☹	☹	⊜
ASDI	GILLBERG2001	⊜	☹	☺	⊜	☹	☹	⊜
RAADS	RITVO2008	☹	☹	☺	☹	⊜	☹	⊜
RAADS-R	RITVO2011	☹	☹	☺	☹	☹	☹	⊜

☺=Low Risk   ⊜=Unclear Risk   ☹=High Risk

125

Table 18: Evidence summary table for all assessment instruments included in the review

Instrument	Target condition	Cut-off	Included studies	Sensitivity Specificity	LR + LR–	Diagnostic OR
AAA	High-functioning autism; Asperger's syndrome	10 1.00	1	0.92	Cannot calculate	Cannot calculate
ADI and ADI-R	Autism	Original ADI cut-offs: communication = 8 (6 for non-verbal); social reciprocity = 10; restricted and repetitive behaviour = 4	1	0.87 to 0.90 0.91 to 0.96	9.56 to 22.50 0.10 to 0.15	63.73 to 225
ADOS-G (Module 4)	Autism	7	1	0.80 0.87	6.15 0.23	26.74
ADOS-G (Module 4)	Autism	10	1	0.70 0.94	11.67 0.32	36.47
ADOS-G (Module 4)	Autism	13 for ASD	1	0.90 0.93	12.86 0.11	116.91
ASD-DA	Autism	24	1	0.68 0.78	3.09 0.41	7.54
ASD-DA	Autism	28	1	0.41 0.93	5.86 0.63	9.30
ASDI	High-functioning autism; Asperger's syndrome	5/6 algorithm criteria	1	1.00 0.91	Cannot calculate	Cannot calculate
RAADS	Autism	77	1	1.00 1.00	Cannot calculate	Cannot calculate
RAADS-R	Autism	65	1	0.97 1.00	0.97 0.03	32.33

Table 19: Psychometric data for included assessment instruments

| Instrument | Reliability | | | Validity | |
	Inter-rater	Test-retest	Internal consistency	Construct validity (covergent and discriminant validity)	Criterion validity (concurrent and predictive validity)
AAA	X	X	X	X	X
ADI and ADI-R	Criteria set at minimum of 90% agreement on individual items for scoring three consecutive interviews	X	X	X	X
ADOS-G (Module 4)	Social $r = 0.93$; communication $r = 0.84$; social communication $r = 0.92$; restricted repetitive $r = 0.82$ (LORD2000)	Social $r = 0.78$; communication $r = 0.73$; social communication $r = 0.82$; restricted repetitive $r = 0.59$ (LORD2000)	Social $\alpha = 0.86$ to 0.91; communication $\alpha = 0.74$ to 0.84; social communication $\alpha = 0.91$ to 0.94; restricted repetitive $\alpha = 0.47$ (LORD2000)	X	Concurrent validity: ADOS-G and DISCO correlation (N = 56) $\kappa = 0.41$ (at ADOS cut-off of 7) and $\kappa = 0.60$ (at ADOS cut-off of 10) (BRUGHA2012)
ASDI	Inter-rater reliability between two neuropsychiatrists (N = 20 paired ratings): $\kappa = 0.91$	Test-retest reliability with interval of 10 to 15 months (N = 20 paired ratings): $\kappa = 0.92$	X	X	X

Continued

127

Table 19: *(Continued)*

| Instrument | Reliability | | Internal consistency | Validity | |
	Inter-rater	Test-retest		Construct validity (covergent and discriminant validity)	Criterion validity (concurrent and predictive validity)
ASD-DA	169 pairs of raters: average reliability $\kappa = 0.290$	Test-retest reliability over 2-week interval: average reliability $\kappa = 0.306$	Total scale $\alpha = 0.942$	Convergent validity: correlation with DSM-IV-TR/ICD-10 checklist $r = 0.60$; correlation with Matson Evaluation of Social Skills for Individuals with Severe Retardation (MESSIER) total score $r = -0.67$; and correlation with socialisation domain of VABS ($r = -0.42$) Discriminant validity: non-significant correlation with DASH-II ($r = 0.12$)	X
RAADS	X	X	Social relatedness $\alpha = 0.86$; language and communication $\alpha = 0.60$; sensorimotor and stereotypies $\alpha = 0.70$	X	X
RAADS-R	X	Test-retest reliability with mean interval of 1 year (N = 30): $r = 0.987$	Circumscribed interests $\alpha = 0.903$; language $\alpha = 0.789$; sensory motor $\alpha = 0.905$; social relatedness $\alpha = 0.923$	X	X

Autism Diagnostic Interview – Revised (ADI-R)

The sensitivity was 'good' to 'excellent' and the specificity was 'excellent' for the ADI and ADI-R. However, with the exception of a stated minimum criterion for inter-rater reliability, there were no data evaluating the reliability or the construct and criterion validity of the ADI-R in an adult population. The ADI-R can be used with people with a range of IQs. However, it does require training to administer and is not free.

Autism Diagnostic Observation Schedule (ADOS-G) – Module 4 (adults and high-functioning children)

The sensitivity of the ADOS-G (Module 4) ranged from 'moderate' to 'excellent' and the specificity from 'good' to 'excellent'. The ADOS-G was also found to be 'relatively reliable' (inter-rater, test-retest and internal consistency) and have 'moderate' criterion validity. In addition, the ADOS-G is not lengthy to complete. However, training is required to use the ADOS-G. This training is available from a small number of autism clinical academic centres across the UK (and at other training centres outside the UK). Once trained, regular reliability checks are necessary. The ADOS-G is not free and there are resource implications in terms of test equipment, coding the assessment and report writing, and attending regular supervision and reliability meetings to ensure maintenance of high-quality standardised practice between different professionals working in different settings

Asperger Syndrome (and high-functioning autism) Diagnostic Interview (ASDI)

The ASDI was found to have 'excellent' sensitivity and specificity. The ASDI was also found to have 'relatively reliable' inter-rater reliability and internal consistency. No data were available evaluating its test-retest reliability. The ASDI can only be used with individuals with an IQ greater than 70 and it is reliant on an informant. It is quick to administer, with no training available and is free to obtain. However, the developers state it should not be used as a stand-alone instrument for diagnosis but can be used as part of a diagnostic interview.

Autism Spectrum Disorder – Diagnostic for Adults (ASD-DA)

The ASD-DA had 'low' to 'moderate' sensitivity and 'moderate' to 'excellent' specificity. However, the ASD-DA was found to have 'unreliable' inter-rater and test-retest reliability and 'relatively reliable' internal consistency. No evidence evaluating the construct and criterion validity of the ASD-DA was obtained. The ASD-DA was developed for use with an adult learning disabilities population and requires information from an informant. It is quick to administer, however the training and cost properties are unclear.

Ritvo Autism and Asperger's Diagnostic Scale (RAADS and RAADS-R)

The RAADS and RAADS-R were found to have 'excellent' sensitivity and specificity. The RAADS-R was also found to be 'relatively reliable' for test-retest reliability and internal consistency and had some evidence of criterion validity (concurrence with the SRS – Adult). However, there were methodological concerns with regards to a high risk of bias conferred by the case-control design and concerns regarding applicability given that the RAADS and RAADS-R have been developed for use in adults with an IQ greater than 70 as part of an assessment battery and not a stand-alone instrument for diagnosis of autism. The RAADS-R is intended to be completed by clinicians in conjunction with a clinical interview and takes approximately 45 minutes.

Clinical evidence summary

The psychometric evidence evaluating the reliability and validity of diagnostic instruments in adults with autism is limited. For some measures, a number of which are in regular use in the UK, no basic psychometric evidence was available—this includes the CARS, DISCO, 3di, MASC, PDDRS, SRS and BSE-R. In addition the evidence for the reliability and validity of the ASD-DA was poor. Given the quality of the evidence, the GDG did not consider the above measures to have sufficient evidence to support their use as a diagnostic instrument.

The only instruments with adequate reliability and validity data were the AAA, ADI-R, ADOS-G, ASDI and RAADS-R. The AAA, ASDI and the RAADS-R are developed for use with people without a learning disability whereas the ADI-R and ADOS-G (an observational measure) can be used across the whole autism spectrum.

Health economic evidence

No studies assessing the cost effectiveness of autism assessment instruments were identified by the systematic search of the economic literature undertaken for this guideline. Details on the methods used for the systematic search of the economic literature are described in Chapter 3.

From evidence to recommendations

The rationale for the development of recommendations concerning autism assessment instruments is presented in Section 5.4.6, where the assessment of autism is considered by the GDG in an integrated manner. Recommendations regarding autism assessment instruments can be found in Section 5.4.7.

5.4.5 The structure and content of the assessment process (including diagnosis)

Introduction

In the review of the literature the GDG was unable to identify any formal evaluations of the structure and content of the overall clinical assessment process for adults with suspected autism other than the data on the various assessment instruments described in the sections above. In light of this the GDG drew on their expert knowledge and experience regarding the structure and content of a clinical assessment for adults with autism. When considering this, the GDG assumed that any person referred for such an assessment would already have been identified as possibly having autism or there would have been concerns that they did.

Assessment of autism

Given the range of presentations within the autism spectrum and the extent and nature of the common coexisting conditions, the GDG was of the view that any assessment process should be undertaken by professionals who are trained and competent and have specific knowledge of autism and its assessment. The GDG also judged that assessment of adults with autism required such a broad range of skills and knowledge that any assessment should be team based and involve a range of professionals with the requisite skills to contribute to a comprehensive assessment. For people with complex presentations, assessment should be undertaken by professionals with specialist experience in the assessment and diagnosis of autism. In addition, given the lifelong course of autism, a family member or other informant with knowledge of the individual's personal history and development should be involved and where this is not possible, documentary evidence, such as school reports, should be obtained.

In considering the structure and content of a diagnostic assessment of autism the GDG was also mindful of the communication difficulties experienced by many people with autism and therefore thought considerable care and attention should be devoted to informing the person of the structure and content of the specialist assessment and ensuring its outcome is fed back to them in a way in which they would understand. The GDG considered that the involvement of a parent, partner, carer or advocate to support the person during the assessment process and to facilitate the understanding of any feedback would also be very helpful.

The GDG identified a number of key components that should form the basis of any comprehensive assessment of an adult with possible autism, as follows:

- the core symptoms of autism including social-interaction and social-communication difficulties, and stereotypic behaviour
- early developmental history
- behavioural problems
- the impact on current functioning including personal and social functioning, educational attainment and employment
- past and current history of mental and physical disorders
- other neurodevelopmental conditions.

Wherever possible this assessment should be supported by direct observation of the person's behaviour.

Having reviewed the formal assessment instruments, the GDG did not judge that any single instrument had sufficient properties to recommend its routine use in the assessment of adults with autism over any other instrument. The GDG considered that a range of measures, including the AAA, ADI-R, ADOS-G, ASDI and RAADS-R, could be used with adults with average intellectual ability; for those with a learning disability, the use of the ADI-R and ADOS–G should be considered.

The GDG also considered the use of a range of biological and neuroimaging tests for diagnostic purposes. In the review of the literature of diagnostic instruments no good-quality evidence for the use of these tests in routine care was found and therefore no recommendations for their routine use were developed.

The GDG also recognised that for some adults with suspected autism, achieving a correct diagnosis could be difficult even for specialist teams (for example, in the presence of coexisting conditions such as a severe learning disability, hearing or motor problems or severe mental illness). With this in mind, the GDG was of the view that an opportunity for further assessment ought to be considered where there is disagreement within the assessment team about the nature of diagnosis, disagreement from the family, partner or carer about the diagnosis, and also in situations where the team judged themselves not to have the requisite skills and competencies to arrive at an accurate diagnosis. Although the GDG judged that biological tests should not form part of the routine diagnosis of autism, they did accept that in particular circumstances biological tests could be important in the diagnostic process. This might also involve referral to a regional genetic testing centre if there are specific dysmorphic or congenital anomalies or other evidence of a learning disability. Similarly, where epilepsy is suspected an electroencephalogram or a referral to a specialist epilepsy service may be considered. Similarly, specialist testing of hearing and vision may be required.

Autism can have a profound effect on a person's ability to lead a normal life and the GDG's consideration was that a specialist diagnostic assessment must also address individual needs in relation to personal and social functioning and educational, occupational and housing needs. The assessment of these functions and needs may be provided from within a specialist autism team, but where this is not possible it should be the responsibility of the people within the team to obtain and coordinate these specific assessments by other competent individuals.

Assessment of coexisting conditions
The GDG recognised that significant coexisting physical or mental disorders, communication problems or learning disabilities can make the diagnosis of autism complex and challenging. The GDG also considered to what extent an individual assessment might need to be adapted to take these difficulties into account. No evidence was identified that could inform such considerations, for example specific tools for the assessment of autism in people with schizophrenia, except for the tools already reviewed concerning autism and learning disabilities. The GDG therefore took the view that specialist teams should have the skills and knowledge to adapt and develop assessments in relation to specific coexisting mental disorders, for example schizophrenia, depression, OCD and neurodevelopmental conditions such as ADHD and learning disabilities. The GDG considered that the formal assessment of cognitive function may also be necessary.

The GDG was aware that the focus and orientation of many specialist autism teams will be primarily on mental health and neurodevelopmental conditions. It also recognised that in addition to a series of mental disorders, significant physical health problems can also be present in adults with autism. The GDG considered that attention should also be paid to coexisting physical health problems (including those that commonly coexist, such as epilepsy and gastrointestinal problems) that may be unrecognised or not treated, in part because the person with autism had not complained of any such problems or had not been able to communicate their concerns in a way that had been understood. Up to one third of people with autism have a diagnosis of epilepsy, with the highest rates in those with a severe learning disability (Danielsson *et al.*, 2005), and achieving seizure control, for example, may require more specialist knowledge than a specialist autism team or local neurology service may possess. Other important issues relating to physical health problems in adults with autism include compliance with medication and the recognition of side effects.

Clearly a number of the areas referred to above will be outside the expertise of a specialist autism team. Given this, the GDG wished to highlight that an important role of the specialist team is to advise, and to seek advice from, other healthcare professionals on the management of coexisting physical health problems and mental disorders such as anxiety, depression, OCD and generalised anxiety disorder. This responsibility should sit alongside that of those healthcare professionals working in primary care where the adoption of an annual physical health review for all people with autism might be considered.

Risk assessment and management

People with autism are often vulnerable and at risk because of the core symptoms of autism and coexisting mental disorders, and for a significant number, learning disabilities further increase their vulnerability. The GDG considered risk assessment and management to be an important area and in developing their recommendations drew on the advice developed for risk assessment in other relevant NICE guidelines (for example, NICE, 2009a). The GDG judged that any risk assessment of adults with autism should consider the risk of self-harm, in particular, the risk of suicide in people who are also depressed or who have a moderate or severe learning disability. Risk of harm to others also needs to be considered, particularly for family members, partners and carers living at home where there may be significant incidents of challenging behaviour. In addition, many people with autism may be isolated from or have no identified family members or carers. This leaves a number of people at risk from self-neglect, exploitation or abuse (Fyson & Kitson, 2007). The GDG was also mindful that it was important to be aware of the sensitivity of some people with autism to changes in their physical or social environment and the possibility of very rapid escalation of problems, including risk-related problems.

Assessment of challenging behaviour

The GDG also considered the need for an assessment of challenging behaviour, where appropriate, which should be part of the comprehensive assessment outlined above. They were of the mind that this should include not only an assessment of the behaviour itself but any underlying and possible unrecognised physical or mental disorders. The GDG was in agreement that the impact of the physical and social environment would need to be considered in the assessment of challenging behaviour. Finally, a functional analysis of the challenging behaviour should be the basis for the development of any psychological or pharmacological intervention for such behaviour.

Assessing the needs of families, partners and carers

The GDG recognised that given the lifelong nature of autism, and the significant impairment of personal and social functioning experienced by many people across the range of intellectual ability, along with the fact that many adults with autism are not in contact with regular services, there is a considerable burden of care that rests with families, partners and carers (limited evidence for this and the impact on families', partners' and carers' social functioning and mental health is presented in Chapter 4). In light of this it was felt that an assessment of families', partners' and carers' needs should be considered.

Assessment of special populations

The GDG considered special populations in relation to assessment and found no new evidence other than that covered in the section on case identification (see Section 5.3).

Feedback following assessment

The GDG considered how the outcome of a comprehensive assessment should be fed back to the person with suspected autism and their family, partner and carers. The view of the GDG was that there was a need for a comprehensive and informative profile of individual needs and risks and a care plan, which should include specification of:

- the nature and extent of core features of autism
- the nature and extent of any coexisting mental or physical disorders
- the nature and extent of behavioural problems
- current speech, language, and communication skills
- the level of personal, social, occupational and educational functioning
- the risk to self and others including close family members, partners and carers
- the problems faced and their impact on families', partners' and carers' needs
- the impact of the social and physical environment.

The GDG took the view that these should be fed back in a manner adapted to a person's capacity to understand the problem and that also identified any unmet needs and specified the way in which those needs would be addressed. The GDG felt that the offer of a follow-up appointment post-diagnosis was important in order for the person with autism to have the opportunity to discuss the implications of their diagnosis and any concerns they might have, and to discuss needs for future care and support.

Health passports

Finally, the use of a 'health passport' (for example, a laminated card) was viewed by the GDG as providing a useful way of pulling together key aspects of the assessment that could alert staff to the person's care and support needs.

5.4.6   From evidence to recommendations

In developing the recommendations for the assessment instruments and for the structure and content of the assessment process for adults with autism, the GDG was conscious of the limited evidence base identified in the reviews above.

The GDG did not consider that any assessment tool had sufficiently good properties to warrant its recommendation for routine use in the assessment of all adults with autism. However, taking into account the complexity of autism, and recognising that some measures had reasonable reliability and validity, it was the GDG's opinion that some measure may be of value in augmenting a diagnostic assessment, particularly, for more complex diagnoses. The review identified a number of instruments that had reasonable psychometric properties such that it would warrant their use in augmenting an assessment. The AAA, ADI-R, ADOS-G, ASDI and RAADS-R were identified as potentially of value in the diagnosis of autism in adults of normal intellectual ability and the ADI-R and ADOS-G in adults with a learning disability. The GDG also felt that some assessment instruments may be useful as a guide for structuring a more complex assessment of adults with possible autism and in particular identifying their needs for care, even if the absence of good-quality psychometric data precluded their use as a diagnostic tool. The GDG therefore supported the use of the DISCO for this purpose. The ADOS-G and the ADI-R, which were identified as valid tools to aid diagnosis, were also identified by the GDG as valuable in structuring complex assessments.

In addition to the measures described above, the GDG drew on their clinical knowledge and experience and developed recommendations for the structure, content and outcome of an assessment for adults with autism. In addition, the GDG felt that the complexity of autism meant that a team-based approach with a range of skills and, where appropriate, direct observation was required to ensure a comprehensive assessment. The opportunity for further assessment should be available where there were disagreements about the diagnosis.

The GDG also developed recommendations on assessment of coexisting conditions given the problems of diagnostic masking and the difficulties in assessing many of the common coexisting conditions. In addition, drawing on their expert knowledge and experience the GDG raised the issue of potential under-reporting and under-recognition of physical disorders in adults with autism. The GDG felt that assessment of these issues, and advice regarding commonly identified problems such as food intake and exercise, should form part of the assessment and, where necessary, the involvement of the GP or a dietician should be sought.

The GDG recognised that the assessment of risk was important, and was particularly concerned about the risk of abuse and potential exploitation of people with autism. Linked to this is the assessment, where appropriate, of challenging behaviour which should include assessing any underlying physical or mental disorders. The impact of the physical and social environment will also need to be considered in the assessment of challenging behaviour. Finally, the GDG proposed that a functional analysis of the challenging behaviour should be the basis for the development of any psychological or pharmacological intervention for such behaviour.

Given the failure to find any high-quality evidence for routine biological tests such as genetic testing or neuroimaging, the GDG did not make any specific recommendation, although it was recognised that in particular areas, such as dysmorphic facial features, genetic testing would be advised.

The GDG also developed a number of recommendations for the post-diagnostic and post-assessment period such as follow-up meetings and the provision of a 'health passport' to promote better understanding of, and communication about, the needs of the person with autism.

The GDG adapted an existing recommendation from *Autism: Recognition, Referral and Diagnosis of Children and Young People on the Autism Spectrum* (NICE, 2011a) regarding seeking a second opinion if there is uncertainty or disagreement about the diagnosis. Following assessment, the correct treatment and care options for adults with autism should be identified and discussed with the person, and the GDG adapted existing recommendations from *Common Mental Health Disorders* (NICE, 2011b) to cover this. In addition the GDG advised that any discussions should take into account any sensory sensitivities. For the methodology for adapting recommendations, see Chapter 3.

5.4.7   Recommendations

Comprehensive (diagnostic, needs and risks) assessment of suspected autism
5.4.7.1   A comprehensive assessment should:
 - be undertaken by professionals who are trained and competent
 - be team-based and draw on a range of professions and skills
 - where possible involve a family member, partner, carer or other informant or use documentary evidence (such as school reports) of current and past behaviour and early development.
5.4.7.2   At the beginning of a comprehensive assessment, discuss with the person the purpose of the assessment and how the outcome of the assessment will be fed back to them. Feedback should be individualised, and consider involving a family member, partner, carer or advocate, where appropriate, to support the person and help explain the feedback.
5.4.7.3   During a comprehensive assessment, enquire about and assess the following:
 - core autism signs and symptoms (difficulties in social interaction and communication and the presence of stereotypic behaviour, resistance

to change or restricted interests) that have been present in childhood and continuing into adulthood

- early developmental history, where possible
- behavioural problems
- functioning at home, in education or in employment
- past and current physical and mental disorders
- other neurodevelopmental conditions
- hyper- and/or hypo-sensory sensitivities and attention to detail.

Carry out direct observation of core autism signs and symptoms especially in social situations.

5.4.7.4 To aid more complex diagnosis and assessment for adults, consider using a formal assessment tool, such as:

- the following tools for people who do not have a learning disability:
  - the Adult Asperger Assessment (AAA; includes the Autism-Spectrum Quotient [AQ] and the Empathy Quotient [EQ])[25]
  - the Autism Diagnostic Interview – Revised (ADI-R)[26]
  - the Autism Diagnostic Observation Schedule – Generic (ADOS-G)[27]
  - the Asperger Syndrome (and high-functioning autism) Diagnostic Interview (ASDI)[28]
  - the Ritvo Autism Asperger Diagnostic Scale – Revised (RAADS-R)[29]
- the following tools in particular for people with a learning disability:
  - the ADOS-G
  - the ADI-R.

5.4.7.5 To organise and structure the process of a more complex assessment, consider using a formal assessment tool, such as the Diagnostic Interview for Social and Communication Disorders (DISCO)[30], the ADOS-G or the ADI-R.

5.4.7.6 During a comprehensive assessment, take into account and assess for possible differential diagnoses and coexisting disorders or conditions, such as:

- other neurodevelopmental conditions (use formal assessment tools for learning disabilities)
- mental disorders (for example, schizophrenia, depression or other mood disorders, and anxiety disorders, in particular, social anxiety disorder and obsessive–compulsive disorder)

---

[25]Baron-Cohen and colleagues (2005).
[26]Lord and colleagues (1997).
[27]Lord and colleagues (2000).
[28]Gillberg and colleagues (2001).
[29]Ritvo and colleagues (2011).
[30]Wing and colleagues (2002).

- neurological disorders (for example, epilepsy)
- physical disorders
- communication difficulties (for example, speech and language problems, and selective mutism)
- hyper- and/or hypo-sensory sensitivities.

5.4.7.7   Do not use biological tests, genetic tests or neuroimaging for diagnostic purposes routinely as part of a comprehensive assessment.

5.4.7.8   During a comprehensive assessment, assess the following risks:
- self-harm (in particular in people with depression or a moderate or severe learning disability)
- rapid escalation of problems
- harm to others
- self-neglect
- breakdown of family or residential support
- exploitation or abuse by others.

Develop a risk management plan if needed.

5.4.7.9   Develop a care plan based on the comprehensive assessment, incorporating the risk management plan and including any particular needs (such as adaptations to the social or physical environment), and also taking into account the needs of the family, partner or carer(s).

5.4.7.10   As part of a comprehensive assessment consider developing a 24-hour crisis management plan, where necessary in conjunction with specialist mental health services, which should detail:
- the likely trigger(s) for a crisis
- the nature and speed of the reaction to any trigger(s), including details about the way in which autism may impact on a person's behaviour leading up to and during a crisis
- the role of the specialist team and other services (including outreach and out-of-hours services) in responding to a crisis
- advice to primary care professionals and other services on their responsibilities and appropriate management in a crisis
- advice for families, partners and carers about their role in a crisis
- the nature of any changes or adaptations to the social or physical environment (see recommendation 6.5.11.5) needed to manage a crisis.

5.4.7.11   Consider obtaining a second opinion (including referral to another specialist autism team if necessary), if there is uncertainty about the diagnosis or if any of the following apply after diagnostic assessment:
- disagreement about the diagnosis within the autism team
- disagreement with the person, their family, partner, carer(s) or advocate about the diagnosis
- a lack of local expertise in the skills and competencies needed to reach diagnosis in adults with autism

- the person has a complex coexisting condition, such as a severe learning disability, a severe behavioural, visual, hearing or motor problem, or a severe mental disorder[31].

5.4.7.12 On an individual basis, and using information from the comprehensive assessment and physical examination, and clinical judgement, consider further investigations, including:

- genetic tests, as recommended by the regional genetics centre, if there are specific dysmorphic features, congenital anomalies and/or evidence of a learning disability
- electroencephalography if there is suspicion of epilepsy
- hearing or sight tests, if there is suspicion of hearing or visual impairment
- other medical tests depending on individual signs and symptoms (for example, sudden onset of challenging behaviour, change in usual patterns of behaviour, sudden change in weight, or suspicion that the person might be in pain and is unable to communicate this).

5.4.7.13 Offer all adults who have received a diagnosis of autism (irrespective of whether they need or have refused further care and support) a follow-up appointment to discuss the implications of the diagnosis, any concerns they have about the diagnosis, and any future care and support they may require.

Principles for working with adults with autism and their families, partners and carers

5.4.7.14 All health and social care professionals providing care and support for adults with autism should:

- be aware of under-reporting and under-recognition of physical disorders in people with autism
- be vigilant for unusual likes and dislikes about food and/or lack of physical activity
- offer advice about the beneficial effects of a healthy diet and exercise, taking into account any hyper- and/or hypo-sensory sensitivities; if necessary, support referral to a GP or dietician.

Identifying the correct interventions and monitoring their use

5.4.7.15 When discussing and deciding on interventions with adults with autism, consider:

- their experience of, and response to, previous interventions
- the nature and severity of their autism

---

[31] Adapted from *Autism: Recognition, Referral and Diagnosis of Children and Young People on the Autism Spectrum* (NICE, 2011a).

- the extent of any associated functional impairment arising from the autism, a learning disability or a mental or physical disorder
- the presence of any social or personal factors that may have a role in the development or maintenance of any identified problem(s)
- the presence, nature, severity and duration of any coexisting disorders
- the identification of predisposing and possible precipitating factors that could lead to crises if not addressed[32].

5.4.7.16   When discussing and deciding on care and interventions with adults with autism, take into account the:
- increased propensity for elevated anxiety about decision-making in people with autism
- greater risk of altered sensitivity and unpredictable responses to medication
- environment, for example whether it is suitably adapted for people with autism, in particular those with hyper- and/or hypo-sensory sensitivities (see recommendation 6.5.11.5)
- presence and nature of hyper- and/or hypo-sensory sensitivities and how these might impact on the delivery of the intervention
- importance of predictability, clarity, structure and routine for people with autism
- nature of support needed to access interventions.

5.4.7.17   When discussing and deciding on interventions with adults with autism, provide information about:
- the nature, content and duration of any proposed intervention
- the acceptability and tolerability of any proposed intervention
- possible interactions with any current interventions and possible side effects
- the implications for the continuing provision of any current interventions[33].

Comprehensive (diagnostic, needs and risks) assessment of suspected autism

5.4.7.18   Provide a 'health passport' (for example, a laminated card) for adults with autism, which includes information for all staff about the person's care and support needs. Advise the person to carry the health passport at all times.

Assessment of challenging behaviour

5.4.7.19   Assessment of challenging behaviour should be integrated into a comprehensive assessment for adults with autism.

---

[32]Adapted from *Common Mental Health Disorders: Identification and Pathways to Care* (NICE, 2011b).
[33]Adapted from *Common Mental Health Disorders: Identification and Pathways to Care* (NICE, 2011b).

5.4.7.20 When assessing challenging behaviour carry out a functional analysis (see recommendation 5.4.7.21) including identifying and evaluating any factors that may trigger or maintain the behaviour, such as:
- physical disorders
- the social environment (including relationships with family members, partners, carers and friends)
- the physical environment, including sensory factors
- coexisting mental disorders (including depression, anxiety disorders and psychosis)
- communication problems
- changes to routines or personal circumstances.

5.4.7.21 When deciding on the nature and content of a psychosocial intervention to address challenging behaviour, use a functional analysis. The functional analysis should facilitate the targeting of interventions that address the function(s) of problem behaviour(s) by:
- providing information, from a range of environments, on:
  - factors that appear to trigger the behaviour
  - the consequences of the behaviour (that is, the reinforcement received as a result of their behaviour[34]).
- identifying trends in behaviour occurrence, factors that may be evoking that behaviour, and the needs that the person is attempting to meet by performing the behaviour.

5.4.7.22 In addition to the functional analysis, base the choice of intervention(s) on:
- the nature and severity of the behaviour
- the person's physical needs and capabilities
- the physical and social environment
- the capacity of staff and families, partners or carers to provide support
- the preferences of the person with autism and, where appropriate, their family, partner or carer(s)
- past history of care and support.

Interventions for challenging behaviour

5.4.7.23 Before initiating other interventions for challenging behaviour, address any identified factors that may trigger or maintain the behaviour (see recommendation 5.4.7.20) by offering:
- the appropriate care for physical disorders (for example, gastrointestinal problems or chronic pain)
- treatment for any coexisting mental disorders, including psychological and pharmacological interventions (for example, anxiolytic, antidepressant or antipsychotic medication), informed by existing NICE guidance

---

[34]Reinforcement may be by the person with autism or those working with or caring for them.

- interventions aimed at changing the physical or social environment (for example, who the person lives with) when problems are identified, such as:
  - advice to the family, partner or carer(s)
  - changes or accommodations to the physical environment (see recommendation 6.5.11.5).

5.4.7.24 Offer a psychosocial intervention for the challenging behaviour first if no coexisting mental or physical disorder, or problem related to the physical or social environment, has been identified as triggering or maintaining challenging behaviour.

6 PRINCIPLES AND PRACTICE FOR THE EFFECTIVE ORGANISATION AND DELIVERY OF CARE

6.1 INTRODUCTION

In 2008 the Welsh Assembly Government developed *The Autistic Spectrum Disorder (ASD) Strategic Action Plan for Wales* (Adult Task and Finish Group, 2009) setting out a number recommendations and actions to be implemented from 2008 to 2011, including the establishment of a network to develop and implement a standards-based assessment pathway in all the Welsh Health Boards through the education and training of relevant clinicians, the development of teams of local expertise and the support of experts at a national level.

In 2009 the Autism Act (HMSO, 2009), the first ever disability-specific law was passed in England. The impact of the Act was to put a duty on the government to produce a strategy to provide strategic guidance to local authorities and health bodies to implement the strategy by 2010. In response to this the Department of Health's *Fulfilling and Rewarding Lives: the Strategy for Adults with Autism* (Department of Health, 2010) set out a number of aims to promote the development and improvement of services for people with autism. These include: (a) increased understanding among the general population and health and social care professionals about autism; (b) increased access to diagnostic services for autism; (c) increased opportunities for people with autism to choose where they live; (d) increased help for people with autism to find employment; and (e) a requirement for both health services and local authorities to draw up joint plans to ensure people with autism receive the help they need. Implicit in this last aim is that services are organised in a way that facilitates the effective and efficient meeting of the needs of people with autism (the strategy was developed following the recognition that this was not the case for many people with autism).

This guideline and the recommendations for the effective organisation and delivery of care are therefore developed in the context of the Department of Health's (2010) strategy and *The Autistic Spectrum Disorder (ASD) Strategic Action Plan for Wales* (Adult Task and Finish Group, 2009). A key purpose of this chapter is to provide the evidence base to underpin the most effective and efficient means to organise and deliver services for adults with autism.

The effective organisation and delivery of services has to be built on not only an appropriate evidence base but also has to be guided by a number of key principles concerning overall care and treatment, which are informed by a full understanding of the nature of autism and the impact that it has on people's lives. Principles for service organisation and delivery have already been developed in a number of related NICE mental health guidelines. The guideline *Common Mental Health Disorders:*

Identification and Pathways to Care (NICE, 2011b; NCCMH, 2011) not only sets out recommendations for the efficient organisation and delivery of care for people with depression and anxiety disorders, but is based on a set of principles (which are set out in the relevant NICE guidelines from which the *Common Mental Health Disorders* guideline was developed) concerning the manner in which people with mental health problems are understood and treated by health services, which in turn has implications for the organisation and delivery of care. Other NICE guidance, in particular *Service User Experience in Adult Mental Health* (NCCMH, 2012), under development at the time of writing, provides further recommendations on the delivery of care from the perspective of service users of adult mental health services.

While there is no doubt that guidance on the development and organisation of care for people with autism is needed, it is nonetheless very challenging to develop. In significant part this relates to the very limited evidence base on the organisation and delivery of healthcare, a problem not limited to mental health (see NCCMH, 2011 for an overview). In addition the very wide range of problems in adults with autism, the different nature of the presentation of these problems and the needs for care that arise from them, adds considerably to the challenge. Guidance on the organisation and delivery of care has to encompass the needs of people with autism with a moderate or severe learning disability (cared for mainly in learning disability services), those with a milder learning disability (IQ ranging from 50 to 69) and those with normal intellectual ability (IQ of 70 and above). These latter two groups may not have their problems recognised, and even if they are they may find it difficult to access services because no specialist diagnostic or treatment service is available, or because staff in existing mental health and related services have limited knowledge of and expertise in autism.

The approach taken in this chapter is first to identify high-quality evidence drawn from studies of populations with autism, or the families, partners and carers of people with autism, that could inform principles underlying the care and treatment of adults with autism that were not covered in Chapter 4. As can be seen in Sections 6.2, 6.3 and 6.4, very little direct evidence on these issues and on clinical care pathways was identified. However, evidence on the settings for care was available (see Section 6.5). In the absence of evidence to support the development of recommendations on the principles and organisation of care, Section 6.3 reviewed the evidence base for the *Service User Experience of Adult Mental Health* NICE guidance (NCCMH, 2012) and Section 6.4 reviewed the recommendations in the NICE guideline on *Common Mental Health Disorders* (NICE, 2011b). The use of the latter involves the method of incorporation and adaptation developed for that guideline (see Chapter 3 and NCCMH, 2011, for a fuller account).

6.2 REVIEW OF EVIDENCE FOR THE ORGANISATION AND DELIVERY OF CARE

6.2.1 Clinical review protocol (organisation and delivery of care)

A summary of the review protocol, including the review questions, information about the databases searched, and the eligibility criteria used for this section of the guideline, can be found in Table 20 (the full review protocol can be found in Appendix 8 and further information about the search strategy can be found in Appendix 9).

Table 20: Clinical review protocol for the review of organisation and delivery of care

Component	Description
Review question	What are the effective models for the delivery of care to people with autism including: • the structure and design of care pathways • systems for the delivery of care (for example, case management) • advocacy services? (RQ – E1) For adults with autism, what are the essential elements in the effective provision of: • support services for the individual (including accessing and using services) • day care • residential care? (RQ – E2)
Subquestion	None
Objectives	To evaluate the components and effectiveness of different models for the organisation and delivery of care.
Criteria for considering studies for the review	
• *Population*	Adults and young people aged 18 years and older with suspected autism across the range of diagnostic groups (including atypical autism, Asperger's syndrome and pervasive developmental disorder). Consideration should be given to the specific needs of: • people with coexisting conditions • women • older people • people from black and minority ethnic groups • transgender people. Excluded groups include: • children (under 18 years). Where data from adult autism populations were not sufficient, the GDG decided that extrapolating from a learning disabilities population was valid.

Continued

Table 20: (*Continued*)

Component	Description
• *Intervention(s)*	• Case coordination models (for example, case management, collaborative care, key worker systems) • Advocacy and support services • Multidisciplinary team models (for example, specialist assessment teams, specialist community teams, assertive community treatment teams) • Models of care delivery (for example, stepped care, clinical care pathways) • Day care services (including the model and content of services) • Residential care (including the model and content of services).
• *Comparison*	Treatment as usual, standard care or other interventions
• *Critical outcomes*	Outcomes involving core features of autism (social interaction, communication, repetitive interests/activities); overall autistic behaviour; management of challenging behaviour; continuity of care, satisfaction with treatment, engagement, and health-care utilisation (including access to treatment).
• *Study design*	• RCTs The GDG agreed by consensus that where there were no RCTs found in the evidence search, or the results from the RCTs were inconclusive, that the following studies would be included in the review of evidence: • observational • quasi-experimental • case series.
• *Minimum sample size*	• RCT/observational/quasi-experimental studies: N = 10 per arm (ITT) • Case series studies: N = 10 in total Exclude studies with >50% attrition from either arm of trial (unless adequate statistical methodology has been applied to account for missing data).
• *Study setting*	• Primary, secondary, tertiary and other health and social care settings (including prisons and forensic services) • Others in which NHS services are funded or provided, or NHS professionals are working in multi-agency teams
Electronic databases	AEI, AMED, ASSIA, BEI, CDSR, CENTRAL, CINAHL, DARE, Embase, ERIC, MEDLINE, PsycINFO, Sociological Abstracts, SSA

Continued

Table 20: (*Continued*)

Date searched	Systematic reviews: 1995 up to 09/09/2011. RCTs, quasi-experimental studies, observational studies, case series: inception of database up to 09/09/2011.
Searching other resources	Hand reference searching of retrieved literature

The review strategy	• The initial aim is to conduct a meta-analysis evaluating the clinical effectiveness of the interventions. However, in the absence of adequate data, the literature will be presented via a narrative synthesis of the available evidence.
	• Narratively review literature that takes into consideration any amendments due to common mental health disorders.
	• Consider subgroup meta-analyses that take into account the effectiveness of interventions as moderated by:
	    – the nature and severity of the condition
	    – the presence of coexisting conditions
	    – age
	    – the presence of sensory sensitivities (including pain thresholds)
	    – IQ
	    – language level.

6.2.2 Extrapolation

The GDG took the view that with limited primary data of good quality (for example, RCTs and observational studies) for adults with autism, it might be necessary to extrapolate from other populations. Extrapolation was performed in cases where the review question was considered important to the GDG and where primary data for adults with autism were judged to be insufficient. For the organisation and delivery of care, the decision was made to extrapolate from a learning disabilities population. Extrapolation was performed on the basis that the extrapolated population shared common characteristics with the primary adult autism population (for example, age, gender, severity of disorder), where the harms were similar for the extrapolated dataset as for the primary dataset, and where the outcomes were similar across trials. Extrapolation was only performed where the data quality was equivalent and the same standards were applied for assessing and evaluating the evidence from adults with learning disabilities, as for the primary data from adults with autism. Extrapolated data were recognised as lower-quality evidence than data from adults with autism and this is reflected within the GRADE system, with outcomes using extrapolated populations downgraded because of indirectness.

6.3 PRINCIPLES UNDERPINNING EFFECTIVE ORGANISATION AND DELIVERY OF CARE FOR ADULTS WITH AUTISM

6.3.1 Methodological considerations

In reviewing the evidence in this section the GDG followed the methods outlined in Chapter 3 supplemented by the methodological considerations in Sections 6.4.3 and 6.4.4 of this chapter. The GDG drew on two key sources of evidence:

- A review of the methods used and the evidence base in the *Service User Experience in Adult Mental Health* NICE guidance (NCCMH, 2012).
- The experience of adults with autism and their families and carers as reviewed in Chapter 4.

When reviewing the *Service User Experience in Adult Mental Health* NICE guidance, a key concern of the GDG was that the evidence reviewed was for populations with mental disorders and as such was not directly relevant to the experience of many, if not all adults, with autism. In light of this the GDG considered that the evidence was *potentially* relevant to autism and might be of value in providing a set of principles underpinning recommendations for the organisation and delivery of care for adults with autism. In identifying those recommendations the GDG were guided by a further four considerations:

- the evidence should have real value in improving services for adults with autism
- the development of any recommendation based on evidence from *Service User Experience in Adult Mental Health* should facilitate the understanding, uptake and integration of other recommendations in the guideline
- recommendations based on evidence from *Service User Experience in Adult Mental Health* should only be included where recommendations based on more direct sources of evidence could not be made
- the inclusion of recommendations based on evidence from *Service User Experience in Adult Mental Health* should not lead to misrepresentation of the original guideline(s) from which they were drawn, or other recommendations developed for this guideline.

6.3.2 Review and summary of the evidence

As described above, the only direct evidence that related to the principles underpinning effective organisation and delivery of care was the review of the experience of care of adults with autism and their families, partners and carers (see Chapter 4). The GDG also reviewed the evidence base from the *Service User Experience in Adult Mental Health* NICE guidance (NCCMH, 2012). The underlying evidence is described fully in the *Service User Experience in Adult Mental Health* NICE guidance and Chapter 4.

The GDG considered these two evidence sources and identified one area concerning the role and identification of health and social care staff that had been identified in the evidence base of the *Service User Experience in Adult Mental Health* NICE guidance but not in Chapter 4, and which the GDG considered to be of importance.

6.3.3 From evidence to recommendations

In developing the recommendation, the GDG recognised the importance of clarity around the identification of staff and the roles they perform. They were of the view that when considered alongside the nature of the communication problems associated with autism, this required staff to be clear about their role and the nature of any interventions provided because this would help to facilitate the uptake of other recommendations in this guideline.

6.3.4 Recommendations

Principles for working with adults with autism and their families, partners and carers

6.3.4.1 All health and social care professionals providing care and support for adults with autism and their families, partners and carers should:
- ● ensure that they are easily identifiable (for example, by producing or wearing appropriate identification) and approachable
- ● clearly communicate their role and function
- ● address the person using the name and title they prefer
- ● clearly explain any clinical language and check that the person with autism understands what is being said
- ● take into account communication needs, including those arising from a learning disability, sight or hearing problems or language difficulties, and provide communication aids or independent interpreters (someone who does not have a personal relationship with the person with autism) if required.

6.4 CLINICAL CARE PATHWAYS

6.4.1 Introduction

As set out in the introduction, the Department of Health's 2010 autism strategy, which followed the Autism Act (HMSO, 2009), places a requirement on local health services and local authorities to develop systems for the efficient and effective delivery of care for people with autism. The commonly accepted way to do this is to develop a set of services that meet the identified needs of people for autism. These services can be seen as the components of an overall system which, when linked together in an effective manner, provides something more than the sum of the individual parts.

It has long been argued that the effective and efficient organisation of healthcare systems is associated with better outcomes, and much of the effort of managers and funders of healthcare is focused on the reorganisation of healthcare systems. Although there is considerable uncertainty about the best method by which to organise healthcare systems, in recent years a consensus has emerged to support the development of clinical care pathways as one model for doing this (Whittle & Hewison,

2007; Vanhaecht *et al.*, 2007), including in the field of mental health (Evans-Lacko *et al.*, 2008).[35]

Clinical care pathways (also referred to as 'critical pathways', 'integrated care pathways' or, simply, 'care pathways') are defined for the purpose of this guideline as systems that are designed to improve the overall quality of healthcare by standardising the care process. In doing so, they seek to promote organised, efficient care, based on best evidence, which is intended to optimise service user outcomes. Clinical care pathways are usually multidisciplinary in structure, and importantly, are focused on a specific group of service users. These service users have a broadly predictable clinical course in which different interventions provided are defined, optimised and sequenced in a manner appropriate to the needs of the service users and the setting in which they are provided.

Recent changes in the NHS have supported the development of clinical care pathways for the organisation of care, and discussions are currently underway as to whether these may also form the basis for the future funding of mental healthcare (see Health of the Nation Outcome Scales, Payment by Results [HoNOS-PbR][36]). Of particular note is the use of integrated care pathways in NHS Scotland (which has seen the development of locally agreed multidisciplinary and multi-agency practice, including pathways for mental health services[37]). In a recently proposed reorganisation of the NHS by Lord Darzi,[38] considerable emphasis was also placed on care pathways as a means to improve healthcare.

Historically, the development of care pathways has tended to focus more on the provision of specialist services and so uncertainty remains about the best way of structuring mental healthcare in primary or community care and the links between primary and secondary/specialist services. There is also some emerging evidence, for example, in the area of collaborative care for depression (Bower *et al.*, 2006; Gilbody *et al.*, 2006, NCCMH, 2010b) demonstrating that integration (for example, of physical and mental healthcare for people with depression) can bring real benefits.

However, precise methods for the organisation of care across the whole range of mental healthcare have not been well developed.

While there is general agreement about the potential advantages of care pathways for clinical care, there is less evidence for benefits such as changes in professional practice, more efficient care, and more informed and empowered service users (Emmerson *et al.*, 2006; Dy *et al.*, 2005). This may be a particular problem in mental health where coexisting conditions (including mental and physical disorders), and considerable difference in severity and uncertainty about treatment options, mean that specifying interventions for defined service user groups can be challenging and with consequent uncertainty about the benefits (Panella *et al.*, 2006; Wilson *et al.*, 1997).

---

[35]This section draws on the description of the background to care pathways in the *Common Mental Health Disorders* guideline (NCCMH, 2011).

[36]webarchive.nationalarchives.gov.uk/ + /www.dh.gov.uk/en/Managingyourorganisation/ FinanceandplanningNHSFinancialReforms/DH_4137762

[37]www.nhshealthquality.org/mentalhealth/projects/4/Integrated_Care_Pathways.html

[38]www.dh.gov.uk/en/Publicationsandstatistics/Publications/PublicationsPolicyAndGuidance/ DH_085825

With the possible exception of the developments in Scotland (described above) there has been little systematic development of care pathways in the NHS, although it could be argued that the Improving Access to Psychological Therapies[39] (Care Services Improvement Partnership [CSIP] Choice and Access Team, 2007) stepped-care model, with its clear focus on evidence-based psychological interventions, is a form of care pathway, albeit without an explicit claim to such. The work of the National Treatment Agency on models of care for alcohol-use disorders has something in common with the care pathway model (Department of Health, 2006a). More recently, the development of care clusters in mental health, with the intention that such clusters form future funding schemes through Payment by Results, suggest that care pathways will be an increasing aspect of care in the NHS (HoNOS-PbR[40]).

6.4.2   Studies considered

No studies on care pathways for adults with autism were identified; therefore additional sources of evidence were required. The primary source of evidence for this section was the *Common Mental Health Disorders* guideline (NCCMH, 2011), supplemented by the evidence in Chapter 4 of this guideline.

6.4.3   Methodological considerations

In reviewing the evidence in this section the GDG followed the methods outlined in Chapter 3 supplemented by the methodological considerations in Sections 6.4.3, 6.4.4 and 6.3.1 of this chapter, adapted for the review of care pathways for adults with autism.

6.4.4   Review of the evidence

The GDG reviewed recommendations from the *Common Mental Health Disorders* guideline (NICE, 2011b). The GDG first compiled a list of recommendations from that guideline (23 in total) that could potentially be included in this current guideline (see Table 21). After further consideration, and based on a consideration of the principles set out in Section 6.3.1, the GDG decided on eight recommendations from this initial list that would be included in this guideline (see Table 22). The GDG then adapted the recommendations from the *Common Mental Health Disorders* guideline for final inclusion in this guideline (see Table 23). The rationale for why certain elements of the recommendations were adapted is explained in Section 6.4.7.

---

[39]www.iapt.nhs.uk/
[40]webarchive.nationalarchives.gov.uk/+/www.dh.gov.uk/en/Managingyourorganisation/Financeandplanning/NHSFinancialReforms/DH_4137762

Table 21: Initial list of potential recommendations from the *Common Mental Health Disorders* guideline for inclusion

1. Primary and secondary care clinicians, managers and commissioners should collaborate to develop local care pathways that promote access to services for people with common mental health disorders by: • supporting the integrated delivery of services across primary and secondary care • having clear and explicit criteria for entry to the service • focusing on entry and not exclusion criteria • having multiple means (including self-referral) to access the service • providing multiple points of access that facilitate links with the wider healthcare system and community in which the service is located.
2. Provide information about the services and interventions that constitute the local care pathway, including the: • range and nature of the interventions provided • settings in which services are delivered • processes by which a person moves through the pathway • means by which progress and outcomes are assessed • delivery of care in related health and social care services.
3. When providing information about local care pathways to people with common mental health disorders and their families and carers, all healthcare professionals should: • take into account the person's knowledge and understanding of mental health disorders and their treatment • ensure that such information is appropriate to the communities using the pathway.
4. Provide all information about services in a range of languages and formats (visual, verbal and aural) and ensure that it is available from a range of settings throughout the whole community to which the service is responsible.
5. Primary and secondary care clinicians, managers and commissioners should collaborate to develop care pathways that promote access to services for people with common mental health disorders by: • supporting the integrated delivery of services across primary and secondary care • having clear and explicit criteria for entry to the service • focusing on entry and not exclusion criteria • having multiple means (including self-referral) to access the service • providing multiple points of access that facilitate links with the wider healthcare system and community in which the service is located
6. Primary and secondary care clinicians, managers and commissioners should collaborate to develop local care pathways that promote access to services for

Continued

Table 21: (*Continued*)

people with common mental health disorders from a range of socially excluded groups including: • black and minority ethnic groups   • older people   • those in prison or in contact with the criminal justice system   • ex-service personnel.
7. Support access to services and increase the uptake of interventions by: • ensuring systems are in place to provide for the overall coordination and continuity of care of people with common mental health disorders   • designating a healthcare professional to oversee the whole period of care (usually a GP in primary care settings).
8. Support access to services and increase the uptake of interventions by providing services for people with common mental health disorders in a variety of settings. Use an assessment of local needs as a basis for the structure and distribution of services, which should typically include delivery of: • assessment and interventions outside normal working hours   • interventions in the person's home or other residential settings   • specialist assessment and interventions in non-traditional community-based settings (for example, community centres and social centres) and where appropriate, in conjunction with staff from those settings   • both generalist and specialist assessment and intervention services in primary care settings.
9. Primary and secondary care clinicians, managers and commissioners should consider a range of support services to facilitate access and uptake of services. These may include providing: • crèche facilities   • assistance with travel   • advocacy services.
10. When discussing treatment options with a person with a common mental health disorder, consider: • their past experience of the disorder   • their experience of, and response to, previous treatment   • the trajectory of symptoms   • the diagnosis or problem specification, severity and duration of the problem   • the extent of any associated functional impairment arising from the disorder itself or any chronic physical health problem   • the presence of any social or personal factors that may have a role in the development or maintenance of the disorder   • the presence of any comorbid disorders.

Continued

Table 21: (*Continued*)

11. When discussing treatment options with a person with a common mental health disorder, provide information about:
  • the nature, content and duration of any proposed intervention
  • the acceptability and tolerability of any proposed intervention
  • possible interactions with any current interventions
  • the implications for the continuing provision of any current interventions.

12. When making a referral for the treatment of a common mental health disorder, take account of patient preference when choosing from a range of evidence-based treatments.
13. When offering treatment for a common mental health disorder or making a referral, follow the stepped-care approach, usually offering or referring for the least intrusive, most effective intervention first.

14. Local care pathways should be developed to promote implementation of key principles of good care. Pathways should be:
  • negotiable, workable and understandable for people with common mental health disorders, their families and carers, and professionals
  • accessible and acceptable to all people in need of the services served by the pathway
  • responsive to the needs of people with common mental health disorders and their families and carers
  • integrated so that there are no barriers to movement between different levels of the pathway
  • outcomes focused (including measures of quality, service-user experience and harm).

15. Responsibility for the development, management and evaluation of local care pathways should lie with a designated leadership team, which should include primary and secondary care clinicians, managers and commissioners. The leadership team should have particular responsibility for:
  • developing clear policy and protocols for the operation of the pathway
  • providing training and support on the operation of the pathway
  • auditing and reviewing the performance of the pathway.

16. Primary and secondary care clinicians, managers and commissioners should work together to design local care pathways that promote a stepped-care model of service delivery that:
  • provides the least intrusive, most effective intervention first
  • has clear and explicit criteria for the thresholds determining access to and movement between the different levels of the pathway
  • does not use single criteria such as symptom severity to determine movement between steps

Continued

Table 21: (*Continued*)

• monitors progress and outcomes to ensure the most effective interventions are delivered and the person moves to a higher step if needed.
17. Primary and secondary care clinicians, managers and commissioners should work together to design local care pathways that promote a range of evidence-based interventions at each step in the pathway and support people with common mental health disorders in their choice of interventions.
18. All staff should ensure effective engagement with families and carers, where appropriate, to: • inform and improve the care of the person with a common mental health disorder • meet the identified needs of the families and carers.
19. Primary and secondary care clinicians, managers and commissioners should work together to design local care pathways that promote the active engagement of all populations served by the pathway. Pathways should: • offer prompt assessments and interventions that are appropriately adapted to the cultural, gender, age and communication needs of people with common mental health disorders • keep to a minimum the number of assessments needed to access interventions.
20. Primary and secondary care clinicians, managers and commissioners should work together to design local care pathways that respond promptly and effectively to the changing needs of all populations served by the pathways. Pathways should have in place: • clear and agreed goals for the services offered to a person with a common mental health disorder • robust and effective means for measuring and evaluating the outcomes associated with the agreed goals • clear and agreed mechanisms for responding promptly to identified changes to the person's needs.
21. Primary and secondary care clinicians, managers and commissioners should work together to design local care pathways that provide an integrated programme of care across both primary and secondary care services. Pathways should: • minimise the need for transition between different services or providers • allow services to be built around the pathway and not the pathway around the services • establish clear links (including access and entry points) to other care pathways (including those for physical healthcare needs) • have designated staff who are responsible for the coordination of people's engagement with the pathway.

Continued

Table 21: (*Continued*)

22. Primary and secondary care clinicians, managers and commissioners should work together to ensure effective communication about the functioning of the local care pathway. There should be protocols for: • sharing and communicating information with people with common mental health disorders, and where appropriate families and carers, about their care • sharing and communicating information about the care of services users with other professionals (including GPs) • communicating information between the services provided within the pathway • communicating information to services outside the pathway.
23. Primary and secondary care clinicians, managers and commissioners should work together to design local care pathways that have robust systems for outcome measurement in place, which should be used to inform all involved in a pathway about its effectiveness. This should include providing: • individual routine outcome measurement systems • effective electronic systems for the routine reporting and aggregation of outcome measures • effective systems for the audit and review of the overall clinical and cost-effectiveness of the pathway.

Table 22: Revised list of recommendations from the *Common Mental Health Disorders* guideline to be included

3. When providing information about local care pathways to people with common mental health disorders and their families and carers, all healthcare professionals should: • take into account the person's knowledge and understanding of mental health disorders and their treatment • ensure that such information is appropriate to the communities using the pathway.
7. Support access to services and increase the uptake of interventions by: • ensuring systems are in place to provide for the overall coordination and continuity of care of people with common mental health disorders • designating a healthcare professional to oversee the whole period of care (usually a GP in primary care settings).

Continued

Table 22: (*Continued*)

11. When discussing treatment options with a person with a common mental health disorder, provide information about: • the nature, content and duration of any proposed intervention • the acceptability and tolerability of any proposed intervention • possible interactions with any current interventions • the implications for the continuing provision of any current interventions.
14. Local care pathways should be developed to promote implementation of key principles of good care. Pathways should be: • negotiable, workable and understandable for people with common mental health disorders, their families and carers, and professionals • accessible and acceptable to all people in need of the services served by the pathway • responsive to the needs of people with common mental health disorders and their families and carers • integrated so that there are no barriers to movement between different levels of the pathway • outcomes focused (including measures of quality, service-user experience and harm).
15. Responsibility for the development, management and evaluation of local care pathways should lie with a designated leadership team, which should include primary and secondary care clinicians, managers and commissioners. The leadership team should have particular responsibility for: • developing clear policy and protocols for the operation of the pathway • providing training and support on the operation of the pathway • auditing and reviewing the performance of the pathway.
17. Primary and secondary care clinicians, managers and commissioners should work together to design local care pathways that promote a range of evidence-based interventions at each step in the pathway and support people with common mental health disorders in their choice of interventions.
20. Primary and secondary care clinicians, managers and commissioners should work together to design local care pathways that respond promptly and effectively to the changing needs of all populations served by the pathways. Pathways should have in place: • clear and agreed goals for the services offered to a person with a common mental health disorder • robust and effective means for measuring and evaluating the outcomes associated with the agreed goals • clear and agreed mechanisms for responding promptly to identified changes to the person's needs.

Continued

Table 22: (*Continued*)

21. Primary and secondary care clinicians, managers and commissioners should work together to design local care pathways that provide an integrated programme of care across both primary and secondary care services. Pathways should: • minimise the need for transition between different services or providers • allow services to be built around the pathway and not the pathway around the services • establish clear links (including access and entry points) to other care pathways (including those for physical healthcare needs) • have designated staff who are responsible for the coordination of people's engagement with the pathway.

Table 23: Final list of recommendations from the *Common Mental Health Disorders* guideline after adaptation

3. When providing information about local care pathways to adults with autism and their families, partners and carers, all professionals should: • take into account the person's knowledge and understanding of autism and its care and management • ensure that such information is appropriate to the communities using the pathway.
7. Support access to services and increase the uptake of interventions by: • ensuring systems (for example, care coordination or case management) are in place to provide for the overall coordination and continuity of care for adults with autism • designating a professional to oversee the whole period of care (usually a member of the primary healthcare team for those not in the care of a specialist autism team or mental health or learning disability service).
11. When discussing and deciding on interventions with adults with autism, provide information about: • the nature, content and duration of any proposed intervention • the acceptability and tolerability of any proposed intervention • possible interactions with any current interventions and possible side effects • the implications for the continuing provision of any current interventions.
14. Local care pathways should be developed to promote implementation of key principles of good care. Pathways should be: • negotiable, workable and understandable for adults with autism, their families, partners and carers, and professionals • accessible and acceptable to all people in need of the services served by the pathway

Continued

Table 23: (*Continued*)

• responsive to the needs of adults with autism and their families, partners and carers • integrated so that there are no barriers to movement between different levels of the pathway • outcome focused (including measures of quality, service user experience and harm).
15. Autism strategy groups should be responsible for developing, managing and evaluating local care pathways. The group should appoint a lead professional responsible for the local autism care pathway. The aims of the strategy group should include: • developing clear policy and protocols for the operation of the pathway • ensuring the provision of multi-agency training about signs and symptoms of autism, and training and support on the operation of the pathway • making sure the relevant professionals (health, social care, housing, educational and employment services and the third sector) are aware of the local autism pathway and how to access services • supporting the integrated delivery of services across all care settings • supporting the smooth transition to adult services for young people going through the pathway • auditing and reviewing the performance of the pathway.
17. The autism strategy group should design local care pathways that promote a range of evidence-based interventions at each step in the pathway and support adults with autism in their choice of interventions.
20. The autism strategy group should design local care pathways that respond promptly and effectively to the changing needs of all populations served by the pathways. Pathways should have in place: • clear and agreed goals for the services offered to adults with autism • robust and effective means for measuring and evaluating the outcomes associated with the agreed goals • clear and agreed mechanisms for responding promptly to identified changes to people's needs.
21. The autism strategy group should design local care pathways that provide an integrated programme of care across all care settings. Pathways should: • minimise the need for transition between different services or providers • allow services to be built around the pathway and not the pathway around the services • establish clear links (including access and entry points) to other care pathways (including those for physical healthcare needs) • have designated staff who are responsible for the coordination of people's engagement with the pathway.

6.4.5   Clinical summary of evidence

The GDG drew from two evidence sources in developing the recommendations in this section; the *Common Mental Health Disorders* guideline (NCCMH, 2011) and the review of the evidence in Chapter 4 on experience of care for adults with autism and their families, partners and carers. The underlying evidence is described fully in *Common Mental Health Disorders* and Chapter 4. The GDG considered these two evidence sources and identified a number of recommendations from *Common Mental Health Disorders* (see Table 22) that in their view were of importance in improving the care of adults with autism and their families, partners and carers. The GDG then reviewed the recommendations and made a decision on whether to incorporate or adapt the recommendations based on methodological principles as developed in *Common Mental Health Disorders* (see Table 23). The rationale for adapting certain elements of the recommendations is given in Section 6.4.7.

6.4.6   Health economic evidence – systematic literature review

The systematic search of the economic literature undertaken for the guideline identified one eligible study on multidisciplinary support services for organisation and delivery of care for adults with high-functioning autism/Asperger's syndrome (National Audit Office [NAO], 2009). Details on the methods used for the systematic review of the economic literature are described in Chapter 3; details about the study and the results can be found in Appendix 18 and the completed methodology checklist is provided in Appendix 17. The health economic evidence profile is presented in Appendix 19, accompanying the respective GRADE clinical evidence profile.

The NAO (2009) developed a decision-analytic model to assess the economic impact of providing multidisciplinary support services for adults with high-functioning autism/Asperger's syndrome across England. Compared with standard service provision, multidisciplinary support services involved specialist assessment and diagnosis, better intervention in terms of ongoing support, monitoring and counselling by specialists, as well as specialist employment support. In contrast, standard services did not include any specialist input at any stage of identification, intervention or support. The economic analysis adopted the perspective of public sector and individuals, and used a snapshot approach of annual service utilisation at 2007/08 price levels.

Costs considered in the analysis included costs to the NHS (inpatient care, crisis resolution and home treatment teams, other NHS accommodation [separate from hospitals or supported accommodation] and treatment costs); public sector and local authority costs (social services, employment support, housing, adult education and day services); and costs to the individuals and their families (including accommodation, family expenses and productivity losses). The model also took into account the change in benefits claimed and the tax revenue received by the exchequer. Most input parameters of the model were estimated based on data derived from the NAO (2009) survey of Local Authorities and their NHS partners, data supplied by local service providers, other unpublished data and expert opinion. Few data (such as employment rates, some cost figures and unit costs) were based on published literature.

According to the analysis, there were higher rates of identification of high-functioning autism in adults seen by multidisciplinary teams; there were also higher employment rates due to specialised employment support and a higher probability of living in private accommodation. The economic analysis showed that provision of a multidisciplinary team produced overall cost savings compared with standard care. With an identification rate in adults with high-functioning autism of 4% achieved by multidisciplinary teams (versus 1% achieved by standard services), the analysis showed a total saving to the public purse of £200 per 1000 working-age population; although it must be noted that with this identification rate there is a total cost (and not saving) to the NHS of £800 per 1000 working-age population. Using a figure of 31.8 million of the working-age population in England, the estimated total cost saving to the public purse was £6.4 million, whereas the estimated total cost to the NHS was £25.4 million.

Sensitivity analysis showed that the identification rate is the key driver of the cost-saving estimate: at an identification rate of 2% by multidisciplinary teams, the scheme produced an overall total cost to the public purse of £700 per 1000 working-age population, whereas at an identification rate of 14% (achieved by the Liverpool Asperger Team, the longest running specialist Asperger service in England) provision of multidisciplinary teams results in a cost saving to the public purse that reached £5,000 per 1000 working-age population, but the total cost to the NHS rose to £1,100 per 1000 working-age population. Probabilistic sensitivity analysis showed that at an identification rate of 4%, the probability of multidisciplinary teams for adults with high-functioning autism being cost saving to the public purse was 80%, with that probability reaching almost 100% for an identification rate of 8%.

In addition to the identification rate achieved by multidisciplinary teams, other factors driving the findings of the analysis included the proportion of adults with high-functioning autism living in supported housing or residential care who could be cared for in private households following identification, as well as the risk ratio of specialist employment support versus standard service provision.

In summary, the study findings indicated that provision of multidisciplinary teams for identification, management and support of adults with high-functioning autism is likely to be cost saving from a public sector perspective, but may result in a significant cost to the NHS. This does not necessarily mean that provision of multidisciplinary teams for this population is not a cost-effective option, as the study was a cost analysis and did not take into account potential health and non-health benefits to adults with high-functioning autism, such as improvements in health-related quality of life. The results of the study are characterised by rather high uncertainty, attributed to the lack of high-quality data on key input parameters, such as the identification rates of adults with high-functioning autism achieved with and without multidisciplinary teams. Moreover, an important limitation of the study is that the model input parameters (such as the identification rate of autism by multidisciplinary teams) were based on unpublished data (for example, an NAO survey and unpublished data from specialist services), expert opinion and further assumptions, rather than on published literature. The study is only partially applicable to this guideline, as it takes a wider public sector perspective, and not the NHS and PSS, as recommended by NICE.

6.4.7   From evidence to recommendations

The process of moving from evidence to recommendations was in significant part based on a consideration as to whether a recommendation drawn from the *Common Mental Health Disorders* guideline (NICE, 2011b) would add value to the overall guideline in line with the key considerations set out in Section 6.2.1.

Only minor adaptations were made to recommendations 3, 11, 14, 17, 20 and 21 (the numbers refer to Table 22 and Table 23), such as changes to terminology more suitable to the context of this guideline and minor modifications to style.

The GDG made some more extensive adaptations to recommendations 7 and 15.

For recommendation 7, the GDG made adaptations that made the recommendation more suitable to the context of autism, for example by specifying that the professional overseeing the whole period of care should be a member of the primary care team for those not in the care of a specialist autism team or mental health or learning disability service.

For recommendation 15, the GDG wished to make a number of additions that were specific to developing local care pathways for adults with autism, including appointing a lead professional responsible for the pathway, providing training about signs and symptoms of autism, making all professionals aware of the pathway and how to access services, supporting the integrated delivery of services across all care settings, and facilitating a seamless transition for people moving from child and adolescent services to adult services.

In addition, when considering the evidence in Chapter 4 on the experience of care for both adults with autism and their families, partners and carers and the need to provide prompt and efficient access to services, the GDG drew on their expert knowledge and experience to develop two further recommendations to directly address the problems of access to services. This included a recommendation on a single point of referral and one on improving access for a range of groups such as people with a coexisting mental or physical problem (including substance misuse), women, people with a learning disability, older people, people from black and minority ethnic groups, transgender people, homeless people, the traveller community, those in the criminal justice system and parents with autism.

The GDG also made recommendations on the need for a local autism multi-agency strategy group, the structure and function of multidisciplinary teams for the care of adults with autism based on their evaluation of the complexity of the tasks and poor access to specialist assessment services described in Chapter 4 of this guideline, and a recommendation on the development of a specialist multidisciplinary team based on the evidence set out in the report by the NAO (2009), which suggests that the provision of such teams could be cost saving.

6.4.8 Recommendations

Structures for the organisation and delivery of care and interventions

6.4.8.1 In order to effectively provide care and support for adults with autism, the local autism multi-agency strategy group[41] should include representation from managers, commissioners and clinicians from adult services, including mental health, learning disability, primary healthcare, social care, housing, educational and employment services, the criminal justice system and the third sector. There should be meaningful representation from people with autism and their families, partners and carers.

6.4.8.2 In each area a specialist community-based multidisciplinary team for adults with autism (the specialist autism team) should be established. The membership should include:
- clinical psychologists
- nurses
- occupational therapists
- psychiatrists
- social workers
- speech and language therapists
- support staff (for example, staff supporting access to housing, educational and employment services, financial advice, and personal and community safety skills).

6.4.8.3 The specialist autism team should have a key role in the delivery and coordination of:
- specialist diagnostic and assessment services
- specialist care and interventions
- advice and training to other health and social care professionals on the diagnosis, assessment, care and interventions for adults with autism (as not all may be in the care of a specialist team)
- support in accessing, and maintaining contact with, housing, educational and employment services
- support to families, partners and carers where appropriate
- care and interventions for adults with autism living in specialist residential accommodation
- training, support and consultation for staff who care for adults with autism in residential and community settings.

Developing local care pathways

6.4.8.4 Local care pathways should be developed to promote implementation of key principles of good care. Pathways should be:
- negotiable, workable and understandable for adults with autism, their families, partners and carers, and professionals

---

[41]See recommendation 1.1.1 in *Autism: Recognition, Referral and Diagnosis of Children and Young People on the Autism Spectrum* (NICE, 2011a).

- accessible and acceptable to all people in need of the services served by the pathway
- responsive to the needs of adults with autism and their families, partners and carers
- integrated so that there are no barriers to movement between different levels of the pathway
- outcome focused (including measures of quality, service user experience and harm)[42].

6.4.8.5 Autism strategy groups should be responsible for developing, managing and evaluating local care pathways. The group should appoint a lead professional responsible for the local autism care pathway. The aims of the strategy group should include:

- developing clear policy and protocols for the operation of the pathway
- ensuring the provision of multi-agency training about signs and symptoms of autism, and training and support on the operation of the pathway
- making sure the relevant professionals (health, social care, housing, educational and employment services and the third sector) are aware of the local autism pathway and how to access services
- supporting the integrated delivery of services across all care settings
- supporting the smooth transition to adult services for young people going through the pathway
- auditing and reviewing the performance of the pathway[43].

6.4.8.6 The autism strategy group should develop local care pathways that promote access to services for all adults with autism, including:

- people with coexisting physical and mental disorders (including substance misuse)
- women
- people with learning disabilities
- older people
- people from black and minority ethnic groups
- transgender people
- homeless people
- people from the traveller community
- people in the criminal justice system
- parents with autism.

6.4.8.7 There should be a single point of referral (including self-referral) to specialist services for adults with autism.

6.4.8.8 When providing information about local care pathways to adults with autism and their families, partners and carers, all professionals should:

- take into account the person's knowledge and understanding of autism and its care and management

---

[42]Adapted from *Common Mental Health Disorders: Identification and Pathways to Care* (NICE, 2011b).
[43]Adapted from *Common Mental Health Disorders: Identification and Pathways to Care* (NICE, 2011b).

- ensure that such information is appropriate to the communities using the pathway[44].

6.4.8.9   The autism strategy group should design local care pathways that promote a range of evidence-based interventions at each step in the pathway and support adults with autism in their choice of interventions[45].

6.4.8.10   The autism strategy group should design local care pathways that respond promptly and effectively to the changing needs of all populations served by the pathways. Pathways should have in place:

- clear and agreed goals for the services offered to adults with autism
- robust and effective means for measuring and evaluating the outcomes associated with the agreed goals
- clear and agreed mechanisms for responding promptly to identified changes to people's needs[46].

6.4.8.11   The autism strategy group should design local care pathways that provide an integrated programme of care across all care settings. Pathways should:

- minimise the need for transition between different services or providers
- allow services to be built around the pathway and not the pathway around the services
- establish clear links (including access and entry points) to other care pathways (including those for physical healthcare needs)
- have designated staff who are responsible for the coordination of people's engagement with the pathway[47].

6.4.8.12   Support access to services and increase the uptake of interventions by:

- ensuring systems (for example, care coordination or case management) are in place to provide for the overall coordination and continuity of care for adults with autism
- designating a professional to oversee the whole period of care (usually a member of the primary healthcare team for those not in the care of a specialist autism team or mental health or learning disability service)[48].

6.4.9   Research recommendation

6.4.9.1   The structure and organisation of specialist teams
What structure and organisation of specialist autism teams are associated with improvements in care for people with autism?

---

[44]Adapted from *Common Mental Health Disorders: Identification and Pathways to Care* (NICE, 2011b).
[45]Adapted from *Common Mental Health Disorders: Identification and Pathways to Care* (NICE, 2011b).
[46]Adapted from *Common Mental Health Disorders: Identification and Pathways to Care* (NICE, 2011b).
[47]Adapted from *Common Mental Health Disorders: Identification and Pathways to Care* (NICE, 2011b).
[48]Adapted from *Common Mental Health Disorders: Identification and Pathways to Care* (NICE, 2011b).

Why this is important

The Department of Health's autism strategy (2010)[49] proposes the introduction of a range of specialist services for people with autism; these will usually be built around specialist autism teams. However, there is little evidence to guide the establishment and development of these teams. There is uncertainty about the precise nature of the population to be served (all people with autism or only those who have an IQ of 70 or above), the composition of the team, the extent of the team's role (for example, diagnosis and assessment only, a primarily advisory role or a substantial care coordination role), the interventions provided by the team, and the team's role and relationship with regard to non-statutory care providers. Therefore it is likely that in the near future a number of different models will be developed, which are likely to have varying degrees of success in meeting the needs of people with autism. Given the significant expansion of services, this presents an opportunity for a large-scale observational study, which should provide important information on the characteristics of teams associated with positive outcomes for people with autism in terms of access to services and effective coordination of care.

6.5 SETTINGS FOR CARE

6.5.1 Introduction

Care for people with autism in England and Wales is delivered in a number of different settings. For some, particularly those with more severe disabilities, a range of residential services provide 24-hour care, often integrated with services for people with a learning disability. The precise numbers of people in residential care are not known and systems for supporting them vary considerably. For people with a severe disability there has been a move over the last 20 to 30 years away from care in large institutions to smaller community-based settings. Some settings also have an explicit educational function. However, the majority of people with autism live in unsupported residential accommodation either with their family or friends but often alone and potentially socially isolated. This can place a large burden of care on families, partners and carers. A limited range of day facilities and employment services for people with autism are offered, again often integrated with those for people with a learning disability. For people with autism without a learning disability there is often very limited access to specialist services such as diagnostic or community support services. Care pathways, as noted above, are not well developed. This review attempts to address a number of questions about the nature of the settings of care for adults with autism, including the nature of the environment and what support services might be provided to services users, families, partners and carers and staff in order to ensure good outcomes.

---

[49]Department of Health (2010) *Fulfilling and Rewarding Lives: the Strategy for Adults with Autism in England.*

6.5.2   Outcomes

A large number of outcomes were reported by studies of settings for care. Those that reported sufficient data to be extractable and were not excluded (see Appendix 14d) are presented in Table 24.

Table 24: Outcomes extracted from settings for care studies

Category	Sub-category	Scale
Core symptoms of autism	*Communication difficulties*	• VABS
	Social-interaction difficulties	• Staff-rated social skills • VABS
Challenging behaviour	*Total score*	• Part 2 of the American Association on Mental Deficiency (AAMD) Adaptive Behavior Scale (ABS) • Problems Questionnaire
	Irritability	• Aberrant Behaviour Checklist (Community Version) Irritability Subscale
	Aggression	• Modified Overt Aggression Scale (MOAS)
	Hyperactivity	• Aberrant Behaviour Checklist (Community Version) Irritability Subscale
	Lethargy	• Aberrant Behaviour Checklist (Community Version) Irritability Subscale
Adaptive behaviour	-	• ABS • Behaviour Development Survey (modified version) • VABS
Community living skills	-	• Average number of skills gained across community living skills behavioural domains
Access to services	-	• Number of contacts with services
Satisfaction	-	• Lifestyle Satisfaction Scale • Satisfaction Questionnaire of Seltzer and Seltzer's (1978) Community Adjustment Scale
Social inclusion	-	• Diary self-report on the number of trips outside the home • Number of community amenities used in past months
Family contact	-	• Developmental Disabilities Quality Assurance Questionnaire
Quality of life	-	• Behavioural observations of quality of life • Quality of Life Questionnaire (QoL-Q) • The Questionnaire on Quality of Life

6.5.3 Studies considered[50]

No RCTs in adults with autism were found that met the eligibility criteria for this review. However, one observational study (N = 12) was found (SIAPERAS2006 [Siaperas & Beadle-Brown, 2006]).

Based on the expert judgement of the GDG and extrapolation rules, data from a learning disabilities population were therefore considered. Two RCTs (N = 89) were found for adults with a learning disability (HASSIOTIS2009 [Hassiotis *et al.*, 2009], RAGHAVAN2009 [Raghavan *et al.*, 2009]). One quasi-experimental parallel group controlled study (N = 20) (SCHALOCK1984 [Schalock *et al.*, 1984]), ten observational parallel group studies (N = 1,514) (BARLOW1991 [Barlow & Kirby, 1991], CHOU2008 [Chou *et al.*, 2008], CULLEN1995 [Cullen *et al.*, 1995], DAGNAN1994A [Dagnan *et al.*, 1994a], HOLBURN2004 [Holburn *et al.*, 2004], KEARNEY1995 [Kearney *et al.*, 1995], MCCONKEY2007 [McConkey *et al.*, 2007], MOLONY1990 [Molony & Taplin, 1990], SCHWARTZ2003 [Schwartz, 2003], SPREAT1998 [Spreat *et al.*, 1998]), and nine observational before-and-after studies (N = 704) were also found (BHAUMIK2009 [Bhaumik *et al.*, 2009], BOURAS1993 [Bouras *et al.*, 1993], CHOU2011 [Chou *et al.*, 2011], DAGNAN1998 [Dagnan *et al.*, 1998], DONNELLY1996 [Donnelly *et al.*, 1996], GASKELL1995 [Gaskell *et al.*, 1995], HEMMING1983 [Hemming, 1983], SPREAT2002 [Spreat & Conroy, 2002], WEHMEYER2001 [Wehmeyer & Bolding, 2001]). All of these studies were published in peer-reviewed journals between 1984 and 2011. In addition, 61 studies were excluded as they did not meet the eligibility criteria. The most common reasons for exclusion were that the mean age of the sample was below 15 years old, the sample had fewer than ten participants per arm, or data could not be extracted. Further information about included and excluded studies can be found in Appendix 14d.

The observational before-and-after study in adults with autism involved an examination of the Treatment and Education of Autistic and related Communication-Handicapped Children (TEACCH) approach in a residential setting (see Table 25).

Of the two RCTs in a learning disabilities population, one involved a comparison of a specialist behaviour therapy team with treatment as usual and one involved a comparison of a liaison worker in helping to access relevant services with normal service interventions (see Table 26).

The one quasi-experimental study in adults with a learning disability involved a comparison of community living skills training within the participants' current living environment (group home or staffed apartment) with community living skills training within a centre-based training environment (see Table 27).

---

[50]Here and elsewhere in the guideline, each study considered for review is referred to by a study ID in capital letters (primary author and date of study publication, except where a study is in press or only submitted for publication, then a date is not used).

Table 25: Study information table for included observational studies in adults with autism

	TEACCH
No. trials (total participants)	1 (12)
Study ID	SIAPERAS2006
N/% female	4/33
Mean age	21 years
IQ	Not reported (all participants had a learning disability, ranging from mild to severe)
Axis I/II disorders	100% autism; 100% learning disability
Comparator	No comparator
Length of follow-up	6 months

Table 26: Study information table for RCTs in adults with a learning disability

	Specialist behaviour therapy team	Liaison worker
No. trials (total participants)	1 (63)	1 (26)
Study IDs	HASSIOTIS2009*	RAGHAVAN2009*
N/% female	23/37	Not reported
Mean age	40 and 41 years	17 and 19 years
IQ	Not reported (N = 42 with mild/moderate and N = 21 with severe/profound learning disability)	Not reported (N = 10 with mild, N = 8 with moderate, and N = 8 with severe learning disability)
Axis I/II disorders	100% learning disability	4% autism, 8% Down's syndrome, 4% cerebral palsy, 4% Joubert's syndrome and 15% epilepsy; 100% learning disability
Comparator	Treatment as usual	Treatment as usual
Length of follow-up	Mean of 6 months	9 months
Note. *Efficacy data not extractable.		

Table 27: Study information table for quasi-experimental parallel group trials in adults with a learning disability

	Current-living environment for community living skills training
No. trials (total participants)	1 (20)
Study ID	SCHALOCK1984
N/% female	10/50
Mean age	31 years
IQ	Range not reported (mean 51)
Axis I/II disorders	100% learning disability
Comparator	Alternative treatment (centre-based training environment)
Length of follow-up	1 year

Of the ten observational parallel group studies in a learning disabilities population, five compared community housing with residential institutions, one compared small residential homes with an institution, one compared dispersed supported housing with residential homes, one compared semi-independent apartments with group homes, one compared an intermediate care placement between institution and community with direct community placement and one compared person-centred planning with system-centred planning for the move from an institution into the community for adults with a learning disability (see Table 28).

Finally, of the nine observational before-and-after studies, one reported change-from-baseline scores for a specialist assessment and treatment unit for challenging behaviour, six reported change-from-baseline scores for participants moving from an institution into the community, one compared pre-move to post-move scores for individuals placed in small-scale community housing, and one compared change-from-baseline scores for participants who moved from more restrictive to less restrictive work or living environments (see Table 29).

6.5.4   Clinical evidence for community-based teams

The TEACCH approach in a residential setting
The only included study in adults with autism was an observational before-and-after study, which examined the effects of the TEACCH approach in a residential setting (SIAPERAS2006). The TEACCH approach is individualised, but some common features include: strong cooperation between staff and parents; different areas designated

Table 28: Study information table for observational parallel group studies in adults with a learning disability

	Community housing	Small residential homes	Dispersed supported housing	Semi-independent apartments	Intermediate care placement	Person-centred planning
No. trials (total participants)	5 (304)	1 (248)	1 (620)	1 (247)	1 (57)	1 (38)
Study IDs	(1) BARLOW1991 (2) CULLEN1995 (3) DAGNAN1994A (4) MOLONY1990 (5) SPREAT1998	CHOU2008	MCCONKEY2007	SCHWARTZ2003	KEARNEY1995	HOLBURN2004
N/% female	(1) 15/48 (2)–(3) Not reported (4) 26/46 (5) 22/28	71/29	289/47	125/51	27/47	9/23
Mean age	(1) 29 and 33 years (2) Not reported (majority 31 to 50 years) (3) 41 and 42 years (4) 44 and 46 years (5) 40 years	29 to 31 years	Not reported (61% aged under 50 years)	34 years	35 years	39 years
IQ	(1) Not reported (2) Not reported (more than 70% with a moderate of severe learning disability) (3) Not reported (4) Untestable - 80 (medians 45 to 54) (5) Not reported	Not reported (majority with a moderate to severe learning disability)	Not reported	Not reported (N = 131 a mild and N = 116 a moderate or above learning disability)	Not reported (3.5% severe learning disability and 96.5% profound learning disability)	Not reported (68.4% severe/profound learning disability)
Axis I/II disorders	(1)–(5) 100% learning disability	100% learning disability	100% learning disability	100% learning disability	100% learning disability	53% psychiatric diagnosis; 100% learning disability
Comparator	Residential institution	Institution	Residential homes	Group homes	Direct community placement	System-centred planning
Length of follow-up	(1) Mean 1 and 3.5 years (time spent living in relevant setting) (2) 30 months (3) 18 months (4) 1 year (5) 4 years	Not reported	Not reported	1 year	1 year	3 years

Table 29: Study information table for observational before-and-after studies in adults with a learning disability

	Specialist assessment and treatment unit	Move from institution into community	Small scale community housing	Move from more restrictive to less restrictive work or living environment
No. trials (total participants)	1 (34)	6 (590)	1 (49)	1 (31)
Study IDs	GASKELL1995*	(1) BHAUMIK2009* (2) BOURAS1993* (3) DAGNAN1998* (4) DONNELLY1996* (5) HEMMING1983* (6) SPREAT2002*	CHOU2011*	WEHMEYER2001*
N/% female	10/29	(1) 13/27 (2) 25/35 (3)–(5) Not reported (6) 71/40	16/33	14/45
Mean age	29 years	(1) 49 and 51 years (2) 46 years (3) 61 years (4)–(5) Not reported (6) 26 to 27 years	27 years	41 years
IQ	Not reported	(1) Not reported (69% profound, 22% severe, 6% moderate and 2% mild learning disability) (2) Not reported (46% severe, 24% moderate and 30% mild learning disability) (3)–(5) Not reported (6) Not reported (majority have profound learning disability)	Not reported (31 to 33% severe/profound learning disability)	Range not reported (mean 60.25)
Axis I/II disorders	100% learning disability	(1)–(6) 100% learning disability	100% learning disability	100% learning disability
Comparator	No comparator	(1)–(6) No comparator	No comparator	No comparator
Length of follow-up	Not reported	(1) 18 months (2) 1 year (3) 53 months (4) 2 years (5) 5.5 years (6) Over 5 years	2 years	1 year

Note. *Efficacy data not extractable.

for each activity; daily visual schedules; strong work rules, for example, 'first work then play'; a transition area; structured activities; and visual prompts. Efficacy data could not be extracted for this study. However, the authors reported significant change-from-baseline score treatment effects for social ability (z = 3.063; p = 0.002) and functional communication (z = 3.062; p = 0.002) as measured by staff-report questionnaire (based on VABS) and an observation checklist. Thus, the findings from this study are suggestive of significant positive treatment effects for the TEACCH approach (implemented in a residential setting) on core autism symptoms. However, efficacy data could not be extracted for this study and the GRADE quality rating is very low.

Specialist behaviour therapy teams
Based on the very limited evidence for settings of care for adults with autism, the GDG agreed to extrapolate from data for adults with a learning disability. Two RCTs were included from this extrapolation population. One of which, HASSIOTIS2009, compared a specialist behaviour therapy team with treatment as usual for adults with a learning disability and severe challenging behaviour. Unfortunately, median values and interquartile ranges were reported—this does not allow for the extraction of efficacy data and may also imply that the data were skewed. The analysis of the results is therefore by narrative review. The authors reported a significant group difference in mean transformed scores (square root of raw scores) for the Aberrant Behaviour Checklist (Community Version) Hyperactivity and Lethargy Subscales (p = 0.008 for both), with more adaptive scores found for participants in the specialist behaviour therapy team group. However, the Irritability Subscale, which is the more commonly reported outcome measure for challenging behaviour, did not reveal a significant difference between participants who were treated by a specialist behaviour therapy team and participants who received treatment as usual (p = 0.162).

There was also one included observational before-and-after study, which examined the effects of a specialist assessment and treatment unit for adults with a learning disability. GASKELL1995 examined the change-from-baseline adaptive behaviour scores following admission to the Mental Impairment Evaluation and Treatment Service. This was a hospital-based unit that sought to prepare clients with a mild learning disability and challenging behaviour for resettlement in the community. Three broad categories of interventions were used: medication, behavioural techniques (including anger management, graded exposure to stimuli and reinforcement) and skills training (including social skills, sex education and daily living skills). Efficacy data could not be extracted for this study. However, the authors reported statistically significant change-from-baseline scores on the Violent Behaviour Subscale of Part 2 of the AAMD ABS (Z = -3.05; p <0.002).

Current living training environment compared with developmental centre group home training environment
The only included quasi-experimental study in adults with a learning disability examined the impact of the training environment (in the participants' current living environment compared with in a developmental centre-based environment) on the

acquisition of community living skills. Data were extracted from SCHALOCK1984 for the average number of skills gained across community living skills behavioural domains. Significant effects of the training environment on the number of community living skills acquired were observed (test for overall effect: $Z = 20.69$, $p < 0.00001$), with participants who were trained in their current living environment acquiring a greater number of skills than participants who were trained in the developmental centre environment. The evidence from this single trial suggests that community living skills training will be more effective if delivered in the context of the participants' current living environment than if the training environment is centre-based (see Table 30). However, this evidence is indirect as it is an extrapolation from adults with a learning disability and the sample size was very small.

Liaison worker compared with normal service interventions
The second of the two included RCTs in adults with a learning disability, RAGHA-VAN2009, compared the additional help provided by a liaison worker in accessing services with normal service interventions for young people with a learning disability and mental health/challenging behaviour needs and for their families. Unfortunately the data reported in this study did not allow for the extraction of efficacy data. However, the authors reported a significant group difference ($Z = -3.620$; $p = 0.001$), with the group who received the additional help of the liaison worker showing a greater number of contacts with services compared with the treatment as usual group. The group who received the additional help from the liaison worker also showed contact with a greater number of different services ($Z = -3.335$, $p = 0.001$) and more outcomes achieved from such contacts ($Z = -3.579$, $p = 0.001$). This single

Table 30: Evidence summary table for current living training environment compared with centre-based training environment for teaching community living skills to adults with a learning disability

	Community living skills
Study ID	SCHALOCK1984
Effect size	MD = 8.90 (8.06, 9.74)
Quality of evidence (GRADE)	Very low[1,2,3]
Number of studies/participants	K = 1; N = 20
Forest plot	1.3.1, Appendix 15

Note. [1]Downgraded for risk of bias as the non-randomised allocation and non-blind assessment of outcome increases the risk of selection and detection bias. [2]Downgraded for indirectness because of extrapolating from adults with a learning disability. [3]Downgraded for imprecision as the reliability and validity of the outcome measure is unclear and underspecified and the sample size was small.

trial suggests that a liaison worker may help individuals with a learning disability and their families gain greater access to services. This finding is particularly interesting as the participants were all from Pakistani and Bangladeshi communities and people with a learning disability and mental health needs from black and minority ethnic communities face additional problems in accessing services.

6.5.5   Clinical evidence summary for community-based teams

There was limited evidence on the effective operation of specialist community teams, which was predominantly in the area of learning disabilities. The GDG took the view that this evidence was applicable to autism and there was evidence to support a range of functions including assessment, treatment and consultation/liaison roles.

6.5.6   From evidence to recommendations

The GDG did not find evidence to support the development of a particular model for the structure of community-based teams. However, the need for assessment and diagnostic services to provide a focus for the coordination of care, and to advise other professionals, adults with autism and their families, partners and carers, supported the view of the GDG that community-based teams for autism should be developed (see Section 6.4.8). This was also endorsed by the review of experience of care in Chapter 4.

6.5.7   Clinical evidence for residential accommodation and related services

Community housing compared with residential institution
Five of the included observational parallel group studies in adults with a learning disability compared outcomes for participants living in community housing compared with people living in residential institutions.

Three studies compared adults with a learning disability who were living in community housing with participants who were living in residential institutions on adaptive behaviour outcomes (CULLEN1995, MOLONY1990, SPREAT1998). Consistent and statistically significant group differences were found with participants who were living in community housing showing superior scores on measures of adaptive behaviour (test for overall effect: $Z = 3.45$, $p = 0.0006$).

CULLEN1995 also examined the effects of accommodation on social skills and quality of life as measured by staff ratings and behavioural observations. This study failed to find evidence for a statistically significant group difference in social skills (test for overall effect: $Z = 1.09$, $p = 0.28$). However, limited evidence for statistically significant group differences was found on the quality of life outcome (test for overall effect: $Z = 8.02$, $p < 0.00001$), with participants in the community group showing superior scores.

BARLOW1991 examined the impact of accommodation on resident satisfaction as assessed with interview by the investigator, which was based on the Satisfaction Questionnaire of Seltzer and Seltzer's (1978) Community Adjustment Scale. Significant differences between the groups were found for residents' satisfaction with their social life (test for overall effect: $Z = 4.27$, p <0.0001) and total score for resident satisfaction (test for overall effect: $Z = 2.44$, p $= 0.01$), with the individuals living in the residential institution showing superior scores. However, for resident satisfaction with autonomy, significant differences lay in the opposite direction with the residents in community housing showing greater satisfaction than the residents living in the institution (test for overall effect: $Z = 2.18$, p $= 0.03$).

Finally, DAGNAN1994A examined the effects of accommodation on social inclusion as measured by diary self-report on the number and features of trips outside the home. This study failed to find evidence for a statistically significant group difference (test for overall effect: $Z = 1.48$, p $= 0.14$).

To sum up, these observational parallel group studies provide evidence for the superiority of community housing compared with residential institutions for resident satisfaction with autonomy, quality of life and adaptive behaviour outcomes (see Table 31). However, regarding residents' satisfaction with their social life and total satisfaction, scores were higher for participants living in a residential institution compared with participants who had moved into the community. Thus, although community living may offer beneficial effects on some measures it may not be superior in all respects. However, it should be noted that this evidence is of a very low quality (it is indirect and the non-randomised allocation and non-blind assessment of outcome increases the risk of selection and detection bias).

Small residential homes compared with an institution
One of the included observational parallel group studies in adults with a learning disability (CHOU2008) compared people living in small residential homes ($N = 103$) with individuals living in an institution ($N = 76$). Data were also reported for group/community home residents ($N = 69$), however, those data are not extracted here because the authors' statistical analysis (which controlled for group differences in adaptive/maladaptive behaviour) suggested that the largest group differences lay with the groups selected. Limited evidence was found for significant group differences in quality of life (test for overall effect: $Z = 8.57$, p <0.00001), choice making (test for overall effect: $Z = 12.57$, p <0.00001), community inclusion (test for overall effect: $Z = 5.71$, p <0.00001) and family contact (test for overall effect: $Z = 4.96$, p <0.00001) with the residents of the small residential homes showing superior scores for all outcomes relative to the residents living in an institution (see Table 32). It is important to note that significant group differences were found in adaptive/maladaptive behaviour, with the residents of the small residential homes showing more adaptive and less maladaptive behaviour and this may act as a confounding factor. However, the authors controlled for these group differences in their statistical analysis and found that small homes were still shown to provide better subjective and objective quality of life than traditional institutions.

Table 31: Evidence summary table for community housing compared with residential institution for adults with a learning disability

	Adaptive behaviour	Satisfaction (total)	Satisfaction with social life	Satisfaction with autonomy	Social skills	Social inclusion	Quality of life
Study ID	CULLEN1995 MOLONY1990 SPREAT1998	BARLOW1991	BARLOW1991	BARLOW1991	CULLEN1995	DAGNAN1994A	CULLEN1995
Effect size	SMD = -0.48 (-0.75, -0.20)	MD = 5.60 (1.10, 10.10)	MD = 5.80 (3.14, 8.46)	MD = -1.20 (-2.28, -0.12)	MD = -5.10 (-14.31, 4.11)	MD = -3.00 (-6.99, 0.99)	MD = -12.90 (-16.05, -9.75)
Quality of evidence (GRADE)	Very low[1,2]	Very low[1,2,3]	Very low[1,2,3]	Very low[1,2,3]	Very low[1,2]	Very low[1,2,3]	Very low[1,2]
Number of studies/ participants	K = 3; N = 224	K = 1; N = 29	K = 1; N = 29	K = 1; N = 29	K = 1; N = 100	K = 1; N = 36	K = 1; N = 100
Forest plot	1.3.2, Appendix 15	1.3.2, Appendix 15	1.3.2, Appendix 15	1.3.2, Appendix 15	1.3.2, Appendix 15	1.3.2, Appendix 15	1.3.2, Appendix 15

Note. [1]Downgraded for risk of bias as non-randomised allocation and non-blind assessment of outcome increases the risk of selection and detection bias. [2]Downgraded for indirectness as extrapolating from adults with a learning disability. [3]Downgraded for imprecision as the sample size was small.

177

Table 32: Evidence summary table for small residential homes compared with an institution for adults with a learning disability

	Quality of life	Choice making	Community inclusion	Family contact
Study ID	CHOU2008	CHOU2008	CHOU2008	CHOU2008
Effect size	MD = 11.40 (8.79, 14.01)	MD = 36.60 (30.89, 42.31)	MD = 7.40 (4.86, 9.94)	MD = 0.60 (0.36, 0.84)
Quality of evidence (GRADE)	Very low[1,2]	Very low[1,2]	Very low[1,2]	Very low[1,2]
Number of studies/ participants	K = 1; N = 179	K = 1; N = 179	K = 1; N = 179	K = 1; N = 179
Forest plot	1.3.2, Appendix 15	1.3.2, Appendix 15	1.3.2, Appendix 15	1.3.2, Appendix 15

Note. [1]Downgraded for risk of bias due to the non-randomised allocation of participants and significant group differences in adaptive/maladaptive behaviour.
[2]Downgraded for indirectness as extrapolating from adults with a learning disability.

Dispersed supported housing compared with residential homes
One of the included observational parallel group studies in adults with learning disability (MCCONKEY2007) compared participants living in dispersed supported housing (N = 103) with participants living in residential homes (N = 138). Data were also reported for clustered supported living (N = 132), small group homes (N = 152), and campus settings (N = 95), however those data are not extracted here. For the dispersed supported housing group, the participant held the tenancy agreement for an ordinary house or apartment, which is dispersed among other properties, and support staff are provided according to assessed needs and visit on a regular basis. Residential homes were group homes where an average of 19 people lived together. This study found a statistically significant difference between the groups for social inclusion (test for overall effect: Z = 3.75, p = 0.0002), with participants living in dispersed supported housing using significantly more community amenities than participants living in residential group homes (see Table 33).

Semi-independent apartments compared with group homes
One of the included observational parallel group studies in adults with a learning disability, SCHWARTZ2003, compared residents of group homes (N = 147) with residents of semi-independent apartments (N = 57). Data were also reported for an independent apartment (N = 43) group, however those data are not extracted here. This study found evidence for a statistically significant difference between settings (test for overall effect: Z = 4.39, p <0.0001) with participants living in group homes showing significantly higher levels of satisfaction than participants living in semi-independent apartments (see Table 34). However, differences in sample sizes across groups, and

Table 33: Evidence summary table for dispersed supported housing compared with residential homes for adults with a learning disability

	Social inclusion
Study ID	MCCONKEY2007
Effect size	MD = 0.90 (0.43, 1.37)
Quality of evidence (GRADE)	Very low[1,2]
Number of studies/participants	K = 1; N = 241
Forest plot	1.3.2, Appendix 15

Note. [1]Downgraded for risk of bias as limited data could be extracted from the study because a measure of variation (standard deviation) was only reported for one scale item. Non-randomised allocation and non-blind assessment of outcome also increases the risk of selection and detection bias. [2]Downgraded for indirectness because of extrapolating from adults with a learning disability.

Table 34: Evidence summary table for semi-independent apartments compared with group homes for adults with a learning disability

	Resident satisfaction
Study ID	SCHWARTZ2003
Effect size	MD = -8.72 (-12.61, -4.83)
Quality of evidence (GRADE)	Very low[1,2]
Number of studies/participants	K = 1; N = 204
Forest plot	1.3.2, Appendix 15

Note. [1]Downgraded for risk of bias due to differences in sample sizes across groups, and significant difference in demographic factors, which were not controlled for in statistical analysis. Non-randomisation and non-blind assessment of outcome also increases the risk of selection and detection bias. [2]Downgraded due to indirectness because of extrapolating from adults with a learning disability.

significant differences in demographic factors found between groups (for example, participants living in group homes were older) were not controlled for in the statistical analysis. These considerations limit the conclusions that can be drawn from this study.

Intermediate care placement compared with direct community placement
One of the included observational parallel group studies in adults with learning disability compared the effects of placement into a transitional developmental centre before placement into intermediate care facilities with direct placement into an inter-mediate care facility (see Table 35). KEARNEY1995 failed to find evidence for a

Table 35: Evidence summary table for intermediate care placement compared with direct community placement for adults with a learning disability

	Adaptive behaviour
Study ID	KEARNEY1995
Effect size	MD = 5.89 (-12.24, 24.02)
Quality of evidence (GRADE)	Very low[1,2]
Number of studies/participants	K = 1; N = 57
Forest plot	1.3.2, Appendix 15

Note. [1]Downgraded due to risk of bias as there is a discrepancy in sample size between groups. Also non-randomised allocation and non-blind assessment of outcomes increases the risk of selection and detection bias. [2]Downgraded for indirectness because of extrapolating from adults with a learning disability.

significant difference between groups in adaptive behaviour (test for overall effect: Z = 0.64, p = 0.52).

Person-centred planning compared with system-centred planning

One of the included observational parallel group studies in adults with a learning disability (HOLBURN2004) compared the effects of person-centred planning with traditional interdisciplinary service planning (or 'system-centred' planning) on movement into the community for residents at four developmental centres. Person-centred planning involved four phases: (1) introduction; (2) development of a personal profile; (3) creation of a vision of the future; and (4) follow-along. The intervention was a slight modification of Mount's (1992 and 1994) Personal Futures Planning. Person-centred planning meetings were held approximately monthly at the residence of the focus person and team composition varied but often consisted of a facilitator, co-facilitator, service user, family member, behaviour specialist, service coordinator or social worker, bridge-builder, direct-support staff, and unit or house manager. The control group consisted of matched peers who lived in the same developmental centres and received the type of individual habilitation planning typically provided to residents of large intermediate care facilities. The interdisciplinary service planning teams typically met quarterly in the developmental centre and the teams were inter-disciplinary and largely composed of professional staff (for example, client coordinator, nurse, psychologist, speech therapist and teacher). The meetings involved discussion of assessments, review of progress toward service plan goals, and the development of new written habilitative goals and methodologies to be pursued. HOLBURN2004 found evidence for a significant group difference (test for overall effect: Z = 3.20, p = 0.001), with the risk ratio indicating that participants in the person-centred planning group were over three times more likely to move into the community than participants who received traditional interdisciplinary service planning (or 'system-centred' planning) (see Table 36). However, an important potential limitation of this study was that bridge building funds were only available to the person-centred planning participants. Nevertheless, only half of the experimental group who moved into the community used such resources, which might suggest that this fund did not create an advantage favouring the person-centred planning group. The evidence from this study suggests that person-centred planning can produce an improvement (even as an adjunctive process) over more conventional interdisciplinary service planning typical of intermediate care facilities serving people with developmental disabilities, even after potential confounds have been removed.

Observational before-and-after studies for moving from residential institutions into the community
Of the nine included observational before-and-after studies in adults with learning disability, six examined change-from-baseline scores after moving into the community from residential institutions. Three of these studies examined the effects of the move on challenging behaviour (BHAUMIK2009; BOURAS1993; DONNELLY1996). Efficacy data could not be extracted for these studies. However, the authors reported data suggestive of positive effects. BHAUMIK2009 reported a significant change from 6 months' pre-discharge to 6 months' post-discharge in aggression ($p < 0.001$) as measured by the Modified Overt Aggression Scale (MOAS). However, this study reported median scores, which may indicate skewed data. BOURAS1993 reported no significant change from pre- to post-move in total numbers of behavioural problems ($\chi^2 = 0.13$, $p > 0.05$), but significant post-move improvements were observed for frequencies of absconding behavioural problems ($\chi^2 = 8.5$, $p < 0.05$) and disturbance at night ($\chi^2 = 8.2$, $p < 0.05$). DONNELLY1996 also reported positive effects of the move with a statistically significant change from pre-discharge to 12 months' post-discharge in challenging behaviour ($U = -0.502$; $p < 0.05$) as measured by the Problems Questionnaire (Clifford, 1987), which assesses dangerousness, psychological

Table 36: Evidence summary table for person-centred planning compared with system-centred planning for adults with a learning disability

	Movement into the community
Study ID	HOLBURN2004
Effect size	RR = 3.41 (1.61, 7.24)
Quality of evidence (GRADE)	Very low[1,2,3]
Number of studies/participants	K = 1; N = 37
Forest plot	1.3.2, Appendix 15

Note. [1]Downgraded due to risk of bias because the allocation was not randomised and this increases the risk of selection bias. [2]Downgraded due to indirectness because of extrapolating from adults with a learning disability. [3]Downgraded due to imprecision as the sample size was small.

impairment, management problems, socially unacceptable behaviour and problems relating to attitudes and relationships.

The effects of moving from an institution into the community were also examined for quality of life, family contact and adaptive behaviour outcomes. DAGNAN1998 reported a statistically significant change from 5 months pre-move to 30 months post-move on all six subscales of the QoL-Q (Schalock & Keith, 1993): Choice ($t = 6.38$, p <0.001), Dignity ($t = 5.26$, p <0.001), Relationships ($t = 5.72$, p <0.001), Activity ($t = 5.37$, p <0.001), Community ($t = 3.84$, p <0.01) and Individuality ($t = 9.51$, p <0.001). SPREAT2002 reported statistically significant increases in family contact over time for all four of the cohorts ($F = 209.68$, p <0.01 for 24 participants discharged in 1992; $F = 534.98$, p <0.01 for 46 participants discharged in 1993; $F = 338.37$, p <0.01 for 36 participants discharged in 1994; and $F = 334.05$, p <0.01 for 45 participants discharged in 1995). HEMMING1983 reported statistically significant improvements from pre- to post-move (at 5.5 years' follow-up) in adapted behaviour, as reflected by significant changes in total ABS Part I scores (p <0.01), and more specifically for the Independent Functioning (p <0.01), Domestic Activity (p <0.01), Self-Direction (p <0.02), Responsibility (p <0.02) and Socialisation (p <0.01) Subscales.

In summary, these observational studies suggest beneficial effects for resettlement from a residential institution into the community on challenging behaviour, quality of life and family contact. However, this evidence is of very low quality, indirect, and the lack of control groups means that efficacy data cannot be extracted.

Observational before-and-after studies for moving into small-scale group homes
One of the included observational before-and-after studies in adults with a learning disability (CHOU2011) compared change-from-baseline scores for people who moved from their family home or an institution into small-scale residential homes and remained in the same residential home 2 years later. This scheme provided ordinary housing in established residential areas a few minutes' walk from the town or city centre. Each home was limited to six or fewer residents and was staffed by support services 24 hours a day. Efficacy data could not be extracted for this study. However, the authors reported statistically significant change-from-baseline scores for quality of life as measured by the QoL-Q (p <0.01) and family contact (p <0.01).

Observational before-and-after studies for moving from more restrictive to less restrictive work or living environments
The final included observational before-and-after study in adults with a learning disability (WEHMEYER2001) compared change-from-baseline scores for individuals who moved from more restrictive to less restrictive work or living environments. Eight people moved from a more to a less restrictive living environment, for example, an institution or nursing home to a group home or the community, or a group home to community living; 21 moved from a more to a less restrictive work setting, for example, a day programme to a sheltered workshop or competitive employment, or a sheltered workshop to competitive employment. Efficacy data could not be extracted for this study, however, the authors reported statistically significant pre- to post-move differences in self-determination as measured by the Arcs' Self-Determination Scale

(p = 0.017) and autonomous functioning as measured by the Adult Version and the Autonomous Functioning Checklist (p = 0.041).

6.5.8 Clinical evidence summary for residential accommodation and related services

The evidence reviewed for residential accommodation, and related services, was based exclusively on populations with a learning disability. Therefore caution needs to be exercised when using this evidence to develop recommendations for adults with autism, although it should be noted that a significant proportion, if not the majority, of people with autism who live in residential accommodation will have a learning disability. With this caveat in mind the evidence suggests that small group living situations are associated with better outcomes than larger institutional settings and that planning to support transition from residential accommodation is also associated with improved outcomes. Enabling structured environments appear to be linked to better outcomes, as does the provision of support from external agencies.

6.5.9 Health economic evidence for setting for care

No studies assessing the cost effectiveness of settings for care for adults with autism were identified by the systematic search of the economic literature undertaken for this guideline. Details on the methods used for the systematic search of the economic literature are described in Chapter 3.

6.5.10 From evidence to recommendations

The GDG recognised the limitations of the evidence but was of the view that where residential care was needed, small group living situations should be preferred over larger settings, while recognising that for some adults with autism supported individual accommodation may be the preferred option. The GDG also took the view that the presence of specialist community support to enable transition and support people in residential care should be provided. Based on the expert knowledge and judgement of the GDG, and in the absence of evidence pertaining to this issue, the GDG also concluded that certain environments were more conducive to the effective provision of care to adults with autism and that these share common features, such as a structured environment with scheduled activities in and outside the home. Careful consideration to the design of the physical environment should also be considered. This latter point led the GDG to make a further recommendation based on expert opinion regarding adapting the environment in all settings.

6.5.11 Recommendations

6.5.11.1 If residential care is needed for adults with autism it should usually be provided in small, local community-based units (of no more than six people and with well-supported single person accommodation). The environment should be structured to support and maintain a collaborative approach between the person with autism and their family, partner or carer(s) for the development and maintenance of interpersonal and community living skills.

6.5.11.2 Residential care environments should include activities that are:
- structured and purposeful
- designed to promote integration with the local community and use of local amenities
- clearly timetabled with daily, weekly and sequential programmes that promote choice and autonomy.

6.5.11.3 Residential care environments should have:
- designated areas for different activities that provide visual cues about expected behaviour
- adaptations to the physical environment for people with hyper- and/or hypo-sensory sensitivities (see recommendation 6.5.11.5)
- inside and outside spaces where the person with autism can be alone (for example, if they are over-stimulated).

6.5.11.4 Residential care staff should:
- understand the principles and attitudes underpinning the effective delivery of residential care for adults with autism
- work in collaboration with health and community care staff from a range of specialist services to support the delivery of a comprehensive care plan
- be trained in assessing and supporting the needs of adults with autism
- be consistent and predictable, but with some flexibility to allow change and choice
- be committed to involving families, partners and carers.

Principles for working with adults with autism and their families, partners and carers
6.5.11.5 In all settings, take into account the physical environment in which adults with autism are assessed, supported and cared for, including any factors that may trigger challenging behaviour. If necessary make adjustments or adaptations to the:
- amount of personal space given (at least an arm's length)
- setting using visual supports (for example, use labels with words or symbols to provide visual cues about expected behaviour)
- colour of walls and furnishings (avoid patterns and use low-arousal colours such as cream)
- lighting (reduce fluorescent lighting, use blackout curtains or advise use of dark glasses or increase natural light)
- noise levels (reduce external sounds or advise use of earplugs or ear defenders).

Where it is not possible to adjust or adapt the environment, consider varying the duration or nature of any assessment or intervention (including taking regular breaks) to limit the negative impact of the environment.

7   PSYCHOSOCIAL INTERVENTIONS

7.1   INTRODUCTION

Psychosocial interventions, in particular those based on behavioural and educational approaches, have been a mainstay of support for people with autism. Much of the development in this area has focused on interventions in children, in part based on the premise that early diagnosis followed by appropriate support may improve outcomes in later life for most individuals. Over the past 30 years a variety of psychosocial interventions have been developed aimed at improving outcomes for people with autism, including: alternative and augmentative communication interventions (for instance, Picture Exchange Communication System); behavioural therapies; social skills groups; social stories interventions; intensive interaction interventions; sensory integration therapy; facilitated communication; and art, drama and music therapies. A problem in evaluating the efficacy of psychosocial interventions for adults with autism is the availability of evidence given that much of the research comes from children. However, even where an adult with autism has been diagnosed and received interventions in childhood there is a need for ongoing support and intervention as there is no evidence to suggest that long-term outcomes for people with autism are significantly improved following intervention programmes in childhood (Howlin, 1998). This scarcity of evidence is particularly problematic because anecdotal reports and case studies suggest that many individuals with autism may face the greatest challenges during adolescence and adulthood when problems with social relationships can impact significantly upon education, employment, housing and community inclusion (Barnhill, 2007).

The GDG accepted that psychosocial interventions are not discrete or mutually exclusive. For instance, most communication interventions involve behavioural strategies, and most social programmes involve some form of communication skills and behavioural methods. However, the GDG took the view that it was appropriate to classify interventions by the main target or focus of the intervention, rather than its particular components, as this would facilitate the implementation of the recommendations by healthcare professionals. Examples of psychosocial interventions based on the principles of applied behavioural analysis and operant conditioning theory have been used to target core symptoms and to modify challenging or aggresive behaviour or teach adaptive behaviours, such as activities of daily living. Social skills groups attempt to target the core symptoms of autism of social-interaction difficulties through the application of some behavioural therapy techniques within a social learning framework, for instance using video modelling, imitation and reinforcement to teach 'rules' of social engagement.

Many people with autism also experience a number of coexisting mental and physical disorders, the treatment of which may be complicated in people with autism. A number of psychosocial interventions have targeted these conditions, for instance, cognitive behavioural therapies have been used to treat depression or anxiety disorders or the symptoms of OCD in individuals with autism (Russell *et al.*, 2009).

This review will also consider psychosocial interventions that provide support to the families, partners and carers of adults with autism, for instance, through psychoeducation and/or support groups.

During the 1980s and through the 1990s psychosocial interventions for individuals with autism tended to be based on behavioural principles and targeted at learning new skills or increasing adaptive behaviour skills (García-Villamisar *et al.*, 2002). However, there have been recent calls for a different approach that places quality of life at the forefront of all interventions for people with autism (Wehman *et al.*, 2005) and, consequently, it has been regarded as crucial that efficacy studies of therapeutic interventions evaluate potential improvements to the quality of life for individuals with autism, by analysing subjective outcomes including wellbeing, satisfaction with lifestyle, community involvement, personal control and social interpersonal relationships.

Interventions that have a focus more on quality of life rather than explicitly targeting the core symptoms of autism or coexisting behavioural problems include leisure programmes and supported employment programmes (García-Villamisar & Dattilo, 2010; García-Villamisar *et al.*, 2002). Both interventions place an important focus on individual strengths and interests. Leisure programmes provide a structured group recreational context for individuals with autism to engage in leisure activities in an attempt to improve wellbeing, and have an indirect aim of impacting on social skills and community involvement. Supported employment programmes seek to assist adults with autism in finding and retaining jobs in order to increase their independence and improve their self-esteem; evaluation of such schemes has also suggested indirect beneficial effects that extend beyond employment and impact upon core symptoms of autism and quality of life.

7.2 CLINICAL EVIDENCE REVIEW OF PSYCHOSOCIAL INTERVENTIONS

7.2.1 Introduction

This chapter comprises eight reviews: Section 7.3 reviews the evidence for behavioural therapies aimed at communication; Section 7.4 facilitated communication; Section 7.5 behavioural therapies aimed at behaviour management; Section 7.6 cognitive behavioural therapies (anti-victimisation programmes, anger management and CBT for OCD); Section 7.7 leisure programmes; Section 7.8 social learning interventions; Section 7.9 supported employment programmes; and Section 7.10 support for families and carers. Details about included studies can be found in each section.

7.2.2 Clinical review protocol (psychosocial interventions)

The review protocol, including the review questions, information about the databases searched, and the eligibility criteria used for this section of the guideline, can be found in Table 37 (further information about the search strategy can be found in Appendix 9).

Table 37: Clinical review protocol for the review of psychosocial interventions

Component	Description
Review questions	For adults with autism, what are the benefits and/or potential harms associated with different psychosocial interventions (for example, applied behavioural analysis, cognitive behavioural therapy [CBT], mentoring, social groups, and befriending schemes)? (RQ – C1)
	For adults with autism, what is the effectiveness of vocational and supported employment programmes? (RQ – C2)
	For adults with autism, what is the effectiveness of educational interventions (including specialist programmes, or support within mainstream education, or educational software, and so on)? (RQ – C3)
	What information and day-to-day support do families, partners and carers need: • during the initial period of assessment and diagnosis • when interventions and care are provided (for example, telephone helpline, information packs, advocates or respite care, interpreters and other language tools) • during periods of crisis? (RQ – D1)
	What role can families, partners and carers play in supporting the delivery of interventions for adults with autism? (RQ – D2)
Subquestion	For adults with autism, is the effectiveness of interventions moderated by: • the nature and severity of the condition • the presence of coexisting conditions • age • the presence of sensory sensitivities (including pain thresholds) • IQ • language level? (RQ – C5)
	For adults with autism, what amendments, if any, need to be made to the current recommendations for psychosocial and pharmacological treatment (including the nature of drug interactions and side effects) for coexisting common mental health disorders? (RQ – C6)
Objectives	To evaluate the clinical effectiveness of psychosocial interventions for autism.

Continued

Table 37: (*Continued*)

Component	Description
Criteria for considering studies for the review	
• *Population*	Adults and young people aged 18 years and older with suspected autism across the range of diagnostic groups (including atypical autism, Asperger's syndrome and pervasive developmental disorder). Consideration should be given to the specific needs of: • people with coexisting conditions • women • older people • people from black and minority ethnic groups • transgender people. Excluded groups include: • children (under 18 years) However, it was decided, based on GDG consensus, that where primary data from an adult population were absent it might be valid to extrapolate from an autism population with a mean age of 15 years or above. For interventions concerned with the management of behaviour, and where data from adult autism populations were not sufficient, the GDG decided that extrapolating from a learning disabilities population was valid.
• *Intervention(s)*	• Psychosocial interventions aimed at behaviour management (for example, applied behaviour analysis, behavioural therapies, CBT, social learning) • Communication (for example, augmentative and alternative communication, facilitated communication, picture exchange system) • Vocational/employment interventions (for example, vocational rehabilitation programmes, individual supported employment)
• *Comparison*	Treatment as usual, waitlist control, other active interventions
• *Critical outcomes*	Outcomes involving core features of autism (social interaction, social communication, repetitive interests/activities); overall autistic behaviour; management of challenging behaviour; outcomes involving treatment of coexisting conditions

Continued

Table 37: (*Continued*)

Component	Description
• *Study design*	• RCTs The GDG agreed by consensus that where there were no RCTs found in the evidence search, or the results from the RCTs were inconclusive, that the following studies would be included in the review of evidence: • observational • quasi-experimental • case series.
• *Include unpublished data?*	Yes, but only where the evidence was: • accompanied by a trial report containing sufficient detail to properly assess the quality of the data • submitted with the understanding that data from the study and a summary of the study's characteristics will be published in the full guideline.
• *Restriction by date?*	No
• *Minimum sample size*	• RCT/observational/quasi-experimental studies: $N = 10$ per arm (ITT) • Case series studies: $N = 10$ in total Exclude studies with $>50\%$ attrition from either arm of trial (unless adequate statistical methodology has been applied to account for missing data).
• *Study setting*	• Primary, secondary, tertiary and other health and social care settings (including prisons and forensic services) • Others in which NHS services are funded or provided, or NHS professionals are working in multi-agency teams
Electronic databases	AEI, AMED, ASSIA, BEI, CDSR, CENTRAL, CINAHL, DARE, Embase, ERIC, HMIC, MEDLINE, PsycINFO, Sociological Abstracts, SSA
Date searched	Systematic reviews: 1995 to 09.09.2011. RCT, quasi-experimental, observational studies, case series: inception of database to 09.09.2011.
Searching other resources	Hand reference searching of retrieved literature

Continued

Table 37: *(Continued)*

Component	Description

The review strategy	• The initial aim is to conduct a meta-analysis evaluating the clinical effectiveness of the interventions. However, in the absence of adequate data, the literature will be presented via a narrative synthesis of the available evidence.
	• Narratively review literature that takes into consideration any amendments due to common mental health disorders.
	• Consider subgroup meta-analyses that take into account the effectiveness of interventions as moderated by:
	    – the nature and severity of the condition
	    – the presence of coexisting conditions
	    – age
	    – the presence of sensory sensitivities (including pain thresholds)
	    – IQ
	    – language level.

7.2.3 Extrapolation

The GDG took the view that with limited primary data of good quality (RCTs and observational studies) for adults with autism, it might be necessary to extrapolate from other populations (the method for extrapolation was based on the method developed for the *Common Mental Health Disorders* guideline [NCCMH, 2011]; see Section 3.5.8 in Chapter 3 of this guideline for further details on extrapolation). Extrapolation was performed in cases where the review question was considered important to the GDG and where primary data for adults with autism was insufficient. For psychosocial interventions, the GDG made the decision to extrapolate from a learning disabilities population for psychosocial interventions aimed at behaviour management. In addition, where primary data were insufficient for other psychosocial interventions, the GDG considered extrapolation from an autism population with a mean age of 15 years or above on an intervention-by-intervention basis. Extrapolation was performed on the basis that the extrapolated population shared common characteristics with the primary autism adult population (for example, age, gender, severity of disorder), that the harms were similar for the extrapolated dataset as for the primary dataset, and that the outcomes were similar across trials. Extrapolation was only performed where the quality of the data was equivalent; the same standards were applied for assessing and evaluating the evidence from adults with a learning disability and children with autism as were used for the primary data from adults with autism. Extrapolated data were recognised as lower-quality evidence than data from adults with autism and this is reflected within the GRADE system (see Appendix 19), with outcomes using extrapolated populations downgraded on the basis of indirectness.

7.2.4 Outcomes

A large number of outcomes were reported by the psychosocial studies. Those that reported sufficient data to be extractable and were not excluded are in Table 38.

Table 38: Outcomes extracted from psychosocial studies

Category	Sub-category	Scale
Core symptoms of autism	*Social-communication difficulties*	• Number of nouns generalised (designed for Elliott *et al.*, 1991) • VABS (Sparrow *et al.*, 1984) Communication Subscale
	Social-interaction difficulties	• Cambridge Mindreading (CAM) Face-Voice Battery (Golan *et al.*, 2006) • EQ (Baron-Cohen & Wheelwright, 2004) • Facial Discrimination Battery – Spanish version (García-Villamisar *et al.*, 2010) • SRS (Constantino, 2002) • Social Skills Rating System (Gresham & Elliot, 1990) • Test of Adolescent Social Skills Knowledge (TASSK) (Laugeson & Frankel, 2006) • Video recording of social interaction (designed for Herbrecht *et al.*, 2009)
Autistic behaviour	–	• CARS (Schopler & Reichler, 1971; Schopler *et al.*, 1980)
Challenging behaviour	*Total score*	• Part 2 of the AAMD ABS (Nihira *et al.*, 1974)
	Irritability	• Aberrant Behaviour Checklist (Community Version) Irritability Subscale (Aman *et al.*, 1985)

Continued

Table 38: *(Continued)*

Category	Sub-category	Scale
Anger management	-	• Anger Inventory (Benson & Ivins, 1992) • Anger Inventory for Mentally Retarded Adults (Benson *et al.*, 1986) • Dundee Provocation Inventory (DPI) (Lindsay, 2000) • Provocation Inventory (Novaco, 2003) • Videotaped role-play test: aggressive gestures (designed for Benson *et al.*, 1986)
Activities of daily living	*Toileting*	• Behavior Maturity Checklist II-1978 (Soule *et al.*, 1978)
	Showering	• Task-specific checklist (designed for Matson *et al.*, 1981)
Self-care	*Weight management*	• Weight loss (in kg; used in Harris & Bloom, 1984)
Anti-victimisation skills	-	• Bullying Questionnaire (MENCAP, 1999) • Protective Behaviour Skills Evaluation (Mazzucchelli, unpublished) • Self Social Interpersonal Decision Making Scale (Khemka, 1997)
Parenting skills	-	• Child-Care Task Analyses (designed for Feldman *et al.*, 1999)
Cognitive skills	*Executive function*	• Cambridge Neuropsychological Tests: Automated Battery (CANTAB): Stockings of Cambridge (SOC) Planning Task (Cambridge Cognition, 2002)
Quality of life	-	• Quality of Life Survey (Sinnot-Oswald *et al.*, 1991) • QoL-Q – Spanish version (Caballo *et al.*, 2005; Schalock & Keith, 1993)
Employment	-	• Number of job placements (objective measurement used in Howlin *et al.*, 2005)

Continued

Table 38: *(Continued)*

Category	Sub-category	Scale
Coexisting conditions	*OCD*	• Yale-Brown Obsessive Compulsive Scale (Y-BOCS): Severity Scale (Goodman *et al.*, 1989a and 1989b)
Parental outcomes	*Knowledge and awareness of permanency planning*	• Community Resources Scale (Heller & Factor, 1991)
	Social support	• Coping Skills Strategy Indicator (Amirkhan, 1990) Exploring Social Support Subscale
	Parental depression	• Beck Hopelessness Scale (Beck *et al.*, 1974)

7.3   BEHAVIOURAL THERAPIES AIMED AT COMMUNICATION

7.3.1   Introduction

Autism is characterised by a triad of behavioural impairments: impaired social interaction, impaired social communication, and restricted and repetitive interests and activities (American Psychological Association, 1994). Therapies based on behavioural principles have been aimed at communication impairments in autism among other behavioural targets. Behavioural therapies, as defined here, are based on learning theory and the principles of operant conditioning (Skinner, 1953) and can include the application of techniques such as reinforcement, chaining, prompting, shaping, imitation and video modelling in order to modify behaviour. Behavioural therapies have been targeted at communication in autism and have commonly used imitation and backward chaining techniques. Imitation has been associated with the development of language in neurotypical children (Bates *et al.*, 1988) and imitation has been found to be abnormal in autism (Meltzoff & Gopnik, 1994; Rogers, 1999; Rogers & Pennington, 1991; Smith & Bryson, 1994). This association between imitation and social-communicative behaviours in autism has also been corroborated longitudinally with early deficits in imitating body move-ments found to be associated with the development of expressive language 6 months later (Stone *et al.*, 1997). Behavioural interventions aimed at communi-cation have ranged from highly structured discrete trial teaching to more naturalis-tic approaches to language teaching (Ospina *et al.*, 2008). Discrete trial teaching is therapist-controlled and involves a highly structured teaching environment where language is broken down into its constituent parts and taught using intensive teaching sessions. In this way acquisition of language can be facilitated through the use of prompting, fading and contingent reinforcement (Ingersoll & Schreibman, 2006). Conversely more naturalistic behavioural methods have also been aimed at communication in autism (Elliott *et al.*, 1991), for instance, the 'natural language teaching paradigm' (Koegel & Johnson, 1989; Koegel *et al.*, 1987). This approach emphasises the establishment of a normal training environment and teaching language as an incidental part of interactions. Natural language teaching models also involve the therapist taking a modelling rather than a directive role, and reinforcement is directly linked to the meaning of the participants' communications. A number of studies have examined the application of behavioural therapies to communication impairments in children with autism (Ospina *et al.*, 2008). However, less research is available regarding the efficacy of these interventions for adults with autism and this is important given that functional impairments of communication may be expected to differ as people with autism get older.

7.3.2   Studies considered[51]

No RCTs were found that provided relevant clinical evidence in adults with autism and met the eligibility criteria for this review. However, one quasi-experimental crossover study (N = 23) (ELLIOTT1991 [Elliott *et al.*, 1991]) and one observational before-and-after study (N = 18) (POLIRSTOK2003 [Polirstok *et al.*, 2003]) were found and included. Both of these studies were published in peer-reviewed journals. Three studies were excluded as they did not meet eligibility criteria due to mean ages of below 15 years old or failure to meet the sample size criterion of at least ten participants per arm. Further information about included and excluded studies can be found in Appendix 14e.

The quasi-experimental study involved a comparison of analogue language teaching with natural language teaching in adults with autism (see Table 39).

The observational study reported change-from-baseline scores for adults with autism who were receiving a behavioural functional communication intervention (see Table 40).

7.3.3   Clinical evidence for behavioural therapies aimed at communication

Natural language teaching compared with analogue language teaching
There were no RCTs that met the eligibility criteria and could be included for behavioural therapies aimed at communication. The single included cross-over quasi-experimental trial (ELLIOTT1991) compared natural language teaching

---

[51]Here and elsewhere in the guideline, each study considered for review is referred to by a study ID in capital letters (primary author and date of study publication, except where a study is in press or only submitted for publication, then a date is not used).

Table 39: Study information table for quasi-experimental controlled trials in adults with autism

	Natural language teaching
No. trials (total participants)	1 (23)
Study ID	ELLIOTT1991
N/% female	4/17
Mean age	26 years
IQ	Not reported but severe to profound cognitive delays (average estimated mental age equivalent = 3.3 years)
Axis I/II disorders	100% autism
Comparator	Alternative treatment (analogue language teaching)
Length of treatment	1 month per intervention
Length of follow-up	3 months

Table 40: Study information table for observational studies in adults with autism

	Functional communication skills training
No. trials (total participants)	1 (18)
Study ID	POLIRSTOK2003*
N/% female	18/100
Mean age	Not reported (16 to 38 years)
IQ	Not reported but learning disabilities (mental age: 12 to 25 months)
Axis I/II disorders	61% autism; 100% learning disabilities
Comparator	No comparator
Length of treatment	1 year
Length of follow-up	18 months
Note. *Efficacy data not extractable.	

Table 41: Evidence summary table for natural language teaching compared with analogue language teaching in adults with autism

	Communication
Study ID	ELLIOTT1991
Effect size	SMD = −0.71 (−1.55, 0.13)
Quality of evidence (GRADE)	Very low[1,2,3]
Number of studies/participants	K = 1; N = 23
Forest plot	1.4.1, Appendix 15

Note. [1]Downgraded due to risk of bias as the study was non-randomised and non-blind. [2]Downgraded due to imprecision as the study was designed to compare two alternative treatments and not to determine overall treatment efficacy. [3]Downgraded due to imprecision as the sample size was small.

with analogue language teaching in adults with autism (see Table 41). In ELLIOTT1991, analogue language teaching attempted to evoke imitative responses through the use of successive trials, whereas natural language teaching allowed participants to select items, and therefore determine the order of presentation. The primary outcome was language acquisition as measured by the number of nouns generalised. This study failed to find any evidence for a statistically significant difference between these two behavioural techniques as applied to language teaching for adults with autism (test for overall effect: $Z = 1.65$, $p = 0.1$). The authors reported that both techniques increased initial and long-term noun generalisation. However, no statistical analysis was reported enabling this conclusion to be quantified.

Observational study of functional communication skills training

A single observational study of adults with a learning disability and autism (POLIRSTOK2003) examined change-from-baseline communication scores following an intensive habilitation programme that targeted four main areas of functioning: (1) preoccupational skills; (2) occupational skills; (3) psychomotor skills; and (4) functional communication skills. The primary outcome of interest was communication as measured by the VABS. It was not possible to extract efficacy data for this study. However, the authors reported evidence for a statistically significant change-from-baseline score on receptive ($F = 22.33$, $p < 0.001$) and expressive ($F = 15.78$; $p < 0.001$) language after behavioural therapies aimed at functional communication skills. However, this evidence is of very low quality (GRADE) due to the lack of a control group and the inability to extract efficacy data, and also due to imprecision conferred by the small sample size.

7.3.4 Clinical evidence summary for behavioural therapies aimed at communication

The limited evidence identified for behavioural therapies aimed at improving communication in adults with autism did not provide good-quality efficacy data, either because studies were aimed at comparing two alternative treatments rather than determining overall treatment efficacy or because efficacy data could not be extracted.

7.3.5 Health economic evidence for behavioural therapies aimed at communication

No studies assessing the cost effectiveness of behavioural therapies aimed at communication for adults with autism or populations with learning disabilities were identified by the systematic search of the economic literature undertaken for this guideline. Details on the methods used for the systematic search of the economic literature are described in Chapter 3.

7.3.6 From evidence to recommendations

Based on the limited and very low-quality evidence for behavioural therapies aimed at communication in autism the GDG concluded that there was insufficient evidence to make a recommendation about the use of behavioural therapies for the core autistic symptom of social-communication impairment in adults with autism.

7.4 FACILITATED COMMUNICATION

7.4.1 Introduction

Facilitated communication is a form of augmentative communication and describes a therapeutic intervention whereby a facilitator supports the hand or arm of an individual with autism while they are using a keyboard or other devices with the aim of helping the individual to develop pointing skills and to communicate. The application of this intervention to autism is based on the hypothesis that many of the difficulties faced by people with autism are due to a movement disorder rather than social or communication deficits (Research Autism, 2011a). Positive reports of effectiveness have been based almost exclusively on anecdotal evidence such as case studies and informal accounts (Biklen, 1990; Biklen & Schubert, 1991; Biklen *et al.*, 1992; Biklen *et al.*, 1995; Clarkson, 1994; Crossley & Remington-Gurley, 1992; Heckler, 1994; Janzen-Wilde *et al.*, 1995; Olney, 1995; Sabin & Donnellan, 1993; Sheehan & Matuozzi, 1996; Weiss *et al.*, 1996). Proponents of this approach have made bold claims regarding the benefits of facilitated communication for autism, for instance, that individuals with autism communicate that they have normal intelligence and social and affective abilities after as few as a single facilitated communication session (Biklen *et al.*, 1991), or even more extravagantly that facilitated communication represents a cure for autism (Biklen & Schubert, 1991).

However, where scientific studies have attempted to validate facilitated communication there has been no evidence of unexpected communication abilities when the facilitators lack the information needed to answer questions posed to the individuals being facilitated (Bebko *et al.*, 1996; Beck & Pirovano, 1996; Bomba *et al.*, 1996; Braman & Brady, 1995; Crews *et al.*, 1995; Eberlin *et al.*, 1993; Edelson *et al.*, 1998; Hirshoren & Gregory, 1995; Hudson *et al.*, 1993; Klewe, 1993; Konstantareas & Gravelle, 1998; Montee *et al.*, 1995; Myles & Simpson, 1994; Myles *et al.*, 1996b; Oswald, 1994; Regal *et al.*, 1994; Simon *et al.*, 1996; Simpson & Myles, 1995a; Smith & Belcher, 1993; Smith *et al.*, 1994; Szempruch & Jacobson, 1993; Vázquez, 1994; Wheeler *et al.*, 1993). Proponents of facilitated communication have argued against the scientific validation of this intervention (Crossley, 1992; Biklen & Schubert, 1991) on the grounds that systematic attempts to test the efficacy of facilitated communication violate the trust bond between the facilitator and communicator (Biklen & Schubert, 1991).

Even more concerning than the lack of blinded efficacy data, there is evidence that facilitated communication can lead to significant harm; for instance, unsubstantiated claims of sexual abuse against family members have been made while using facilitated communication (Rimland, 1992; Simpson & Myles, 1995b). Reports by the American Association on Intellectual and Developmental Disability[52], the American Psychiatric Association and the American Academy of Child and Adolescent Psychiatry are all highly critical of facilitated communication and strongly recommend that it is not used (Research Autism, 2011a).

7.4.2   Studies considered[53]

No RCTs were found that provided relevant clinical evidence in adults with autism and met the eligibility criteria for this review. One observational study (N = 12) was found and included (MYLES1996A [Myles *et al.*, 1996a]). Three observational studies were excluded; two were excluded because data could not be extracted as no statistical analysis was reported and one because it duplicated data from MYLES1996A. Further information about included and excluded studies can be found in Appendix 14e.

The single included observational study in adults with autism (see Table 42) compared pre- and post-intervention behavioural observations for a group receiving facilitated communication (there was no control group).

---

[52]Formerly the American Association on Mental Deficiency (AAMD) and the American Association on Mental Retardation.

[53]Here and elsewhere in the guideline, each study considered for review is referred to by a study ID in capital letters (primary author and date of study publication, except where a study is in press or only submitted for publication, then a date is not used).

Table 42: Study information table for observational studies of facilitated communication in adults with autism

	Facilitated communication
No. trials (total participants)	1 (12)
Study IDs	MYLES1996A
N/% female	3/25
Mean age	19 years
IQ	Not reported but learning disabilities
Axis I/II disorders	100% autism
Comparator	No comparator
Length of treatment	14 weeks
Length of follow-up	17 weeks (including 3-week pre-intervention baseline observation period)

7.4.3   Clinical evidence for facilitated communication

There was only a single observational before-and-after study (with no control group) that could be included for the review of facilitated communication, and it was not possible to extract efficacy data for this study. This study examined the frequency of seven behaviours and social-interaction outcomes (requesting, getting attention, protesting, giving information, expressing feelings, interacting socially and non-focused response) at baseline, during the facilitated communication intervention, and in the final few weeks of the intervention. The authors reported no evidence for significant improvement in any of the target behaviours over time (all $p > 0.05$).

7.4.4   Clinical evidence summary for facilitated communication

There was very little evidence for facilitated communication in adults with autism and the very low-grade evidence presents results suggestive of no significant treatment effects associated with facilitated communication.

7.4.5   Health economic evidence for facilitated communication

No studies assessing the cost effectiveness of facilitated communication for adults with autism were identified by the systematic search of the economic literature undertaken for this guideline. Details on the methods used for the systematic search of the economic literature are described in Chapter 3.

7.4.6   From evidence to recommendation

No evidence could be found for the efficacy of facilitated communication interventions in adults with autism. Positive reports of effectiveness have been based almost exclusively on anecdotal evidence, and where scientific studies have attempted to validate facilitated communication, there has been no evidence of unexpected communication abilities when the facilitators are blind to the questions posed to the people with autism. The GDG also considered the harms which have been previously reported for facilitated communication, in particular, the reports of unsubstantiated claims of sexual abuse against family members being made via facilitated communication. On the basis of no evidence for significant benefits and concerns regarding potentially significant harms, the GDG took the view that facilitated communication should not be used for adults with autism.

7.4.7   Recommendation

Psychosocial interventions for the core symptoms of autism
7.4.7.1   Do not provide facilitated communication for adults with autism

7.4.8   Research recommendation

7.4.8.1   Augmentative communication devices for adults with autism
What is the clinical and cost effectiveness of augmentative communication devices for adults with autism?

Why this is important
Many people with autism experience significant communication problems (for example, the absence of any spoken language or significant deficits in interpersonal skills), which have a profound effect on their ability to lead a full and rewarding life. It is probable that these problems are related to the core symptoms of autism and are likely to persist for most people given the life-long course of autism and the lack of effective interventions for these core symptoms. A number of communication devices have been developed for autism but few, if any, have been subjected to a proper evaluation in adults. Despite this lack of formal evaluation, individual services have made considerable investments in augmentative communication devices. Research that provides high-quality evidence on the acceptability and the clinical and cost effectiveness of augmentative communication devices could bring about significant improvements in the lives of adults with autism.

The suggested programme of research would need to identify current devices for which there is: (a) some evidence of benefit (for example, case series and small-scale pilot studies); (b) some evidence that it meets a key communication need for people with autism (based on reviews of people's need in this area); and (c) indication that the device is feasible for routine use. The identified device(s) should then be formally evaluated in a large-scale randomised trial.

7.5   BEHAVIOURAL THERAPIES AIMED AT BEHAVIOUR MANAGEMENT

7.5.1   Introduction

Behavioural therapies based on the principles of learning theory and operant conditioning are commonly used to manage challenging behaviour and to teach adaptive skills for community living, particularly in residential and educational settings. Much of the early intensive intervention in autism is based on these behavioural principles and there is some evidence for short-term efficacy of such programmes (Matson, 2007; Matson & Smith, 2008). However, as with other types of psychosocial interventions there is less evidence with regards to the efficacy of behavioural therapies for adults with autism. From a behaviour management perspective, challenging behaviours are more common in people with autism and a learning disability than in individuals with a learning disability alone and have been found to persist into adulthood and to co-vary with the severity of autism (Matson & Rivet, 2008). However, some doubts have been expressed as to the efficacy of behavioural therapies in bringing about long-term changes in challenging behaviour. For instance, Matson and Rivet (2008) reported that 28% of their autistic sample showed challenging behaviour in all four areas of aggression/destruction, stereotypy, self-injurious behaviour and disruptive behaviour, despite having learning-based treatment plans in place aimed specifically at these behaviours. In addition to concerns regarding the longevity of treatment effects there is also very little evidence pertaining to the generalisability of effects across challenging behaviours or adaptive skill areas, or across settings. Traditionally, challenging behaviour and adaptive behaviour outcomes have been identified as a greater problem for people with autism and a coexisting learning disability, with higher levels of language and intellectual functioning generally being associated with better outcomes (Billstedt *et al.*, 2005; Howlin *et al.*, 2004; Paul & Cohen, 1984). However, recent studies have suggested that there is a gap between intellectual and adaptive functioning, even in people with 'high-functioning' (IQ > 70) autism and this discrepancy appears to widen with age (Kanne *et al.*, 2011; Klin *et al.*, 2007; Szatmari *et al.*, 2003). Thus, determining the efficacy of behavioural therapies aimed at acquiring or increasing adaptive behaviour skills is of particular importance in adults with autism. It is also important to note that the origins of challenging behaviour may have multiple causes including the environment, and underlying physical and psychological disorders, and functional analysis of challenging behaviour may be necessary to appropriately target any intervention.

7.5.2   Studies considered[54]

No RCTs, observational, quasi-experimental or case series were found that provided relevant clinical evidence in adults with autism and met the eligibility criteria for this review. Based on the rules for extrapolation, the decision was taken to extrapolate from studies of adults with a learning disability for behavioural interventions aimed at behaviour management. One RCT (N = 72) met the extrapolation eligibility criteria and was included (MATSON1981 [Matson *et al.*, 1981]). In addition, one quasi-experimental parallel group controlled study (N = 21) (HARRIS1984 [Harris & Bloom, 1984]) and two observational before-and-after studies (N = 69) (BATHAEE2001 [Bat-Haee, 2001], FELDMAN1999 [Feldman *et al.*, 1999]) were included. All of these studies were published in peer-reviewed journals between 1981 and 2001. In addition, 44 studies were excluded because they did not meet eligibility criteria. The most common reasons for exclusion were: data giving any measure of effect size could not be extracted, the mean age of the sample was below 15 years, or the sample size was fewer than ten participants per arm. Further information about included and excluded studies can be found in Appendix 14e.

The single included RCT compared an intervention called independence training with a no-treatment control group (see Table 43).

Table 43: Study information table for RCTs of behavioural therapies in adults with a learning disability

	Independence training
No. trials (total participants)	1 (72)
Study ID	MATSON1981
N/% female	26/36
Mean age	32 years
IQ	Not reported – moderate to severe learning disabilities
Axis I/II disorders	100% learning disabilities
Comparator	No-treatment control group
Length of treatment	4 months
Length of follow-up	7 months (including 3-month post-test follow-up)

---

[54]Here and elsewhere in the guideline, each study considered for review is referred to by a study ID in capital letters (primary author and date of study publication, except where a study is in press or only submitted for publication, then a date is not used).

Table 44: Study information table for quasi-experimental trials of behavioural therapies in adults with a learning disability

	Behavioural weight control programme
No. trials (total participants)	1 (21)
Study ID	HARRIS1984
N/% female	17/81
Mean age	25 years
IQ	Range not reported (mean 52.5)
Axis I/II disorders	100% learning disabilities
Comparator	No-treatment control group (study dropouts)
Length of treatment	7 weeks
Length of follow-up	26 weeks (including 19 week post-test follow-up)

The quasi-experimental study compared a behavioural weight control programme with a no-treatment control group composed of study dropouts (see Table 44).

Of the two observational studies one reported change-from-baseline scores for participants having adaptive skills training and one reported change-from-baseline scores for self-instructional pictorial manuals to teach childcare skills (see Table 45).

7.5.3   Clinical evidence for behavioural therapies aimed at behaviour management

Independence training compared with no-treatment control group
There were no RCTs or quasi-experimental or observational studies that could be included in the review of behavioural therapies aimed at behaviour management in adults with autism. Based on the expert judgement of the GDG and the rules of extrapolation, data were included for adults with a learning disability and a single RCT was found that provided relevant clinical evidence and met the inclusion criteria. MATSON1981 compared independence training with a no-treatment control group (see Table 46). The independence training was aimed at teaching showering behaviours and used behavioural therapy techniques such as modelling and prompting while also emphasising self-evaluation and social reinforcement, with participants providing prompts to each other on showering skills. The primary outcome was successful acquisition or performance of activities of daily living. The target behaviour (showering) was broken down into 27 task-analysed steps and rated using a task-specific checklist. This study found evidence for a statistically significant treatment effect (test for overall effect: $Z = 11.71$, $p < 0.00001$), with participants who received

Table 45: Study information table for observational studies of behavioural therapies in adults with a learning disability

	Adaptive skills training	Self-instructional pictorial childcare manuals
No. trials (total participants)	1 (59)	1 (10)
Study ID	BATHAEE2001*	FELDMAN1999*
N/% female	45/76	10/100
Mean age	44 years	28 years
IQ	Not reported (mental age 2 to 17 months)	71 to 76 (mean 73.8)
Axis I/II disorders	100% learning disabilities	100% learning disabilities
Comparator	No comparator	No comparator
Length of treatment	10 years	Until mothers reached training criterion of 80% or higher for two sessions
Length of follow-up	10 years	3 years
Note. *Efficacy data not extractable.		

independence training showing superior showering skills compared with the participants receiving no treatment. However, this evidence was very low quality due to downgrading based on risk of bias (conferred by non-blind ratings and lack of an attention-placebo control group), indirectness (because of extrapolating from adults with a learning disability), and imprecision (the outcome measure was designed specifically for this study and no formal assessment of reliability and validity was reported).

Observational study of adaptive skills training
One of the two included observational studies for behavioural therapies aimed at behaviour management in adults with a learning disability examined the change-from-baseline scores for activities of daily living with no control group over two consecutive 5-year periods (BATHAEE2001). Efficacy data could not be extracted for this study. However, the authors reported evidence for statistically significant change-from-baseline scores over the first 5-year period from 1987/1988 to 1992/1993 in dressing ($t = 2.26$, $p < 0.03$; $N = 59$), grooming ($t = 2.85$, $p < 0.005$; $N = 59$), eating ($t = 2.52$, $p < 0.01$; $N = 59$) and toileting ($t = 2.82$; $p < 0.005$; $N = 59$) as assessed using the Behavior Maturity Checklist II-1978; the changes in toileting

Table 46: Evidence summary table for behavioural therapies compared with no-treatment control for adults with a learning disability

	Activities of daily living	**Self-care**
Study ID	MATSON1981	HARRIS1984
Effect size	MD = 8.40 (6.99, 9.81)	SMD = 0.44 (-0.43, 1.30)
Quality of evidence (GRADE)	Very low[1,3,4]	Very low[2,3,5]
Number of studies/ participants	K = 1; N = 72	K = 1; N = 21
Forest plot	1.4.2, Appendix 15	1.4.2, Appendix 15

Note. [1]Downgraded due to risk of bias as there was no attention-placebo control group so participants did not receive same care apart from the intervention, and there was no blinding conferring a risk of performance and detection bias. [2]Downgraded due to risk of bias as the control group consisted of dropouts from the experimental group so there was high risk for selection bias. The study was also non-randomised and non-blind increasing the risk of performance and detection bias. [3]Downgraded due to indirectness because of extrapolating from adults with a learning disability. [4]Downgraded due to imprecision as the outcome measure was designed specifically for this study and lacks formal assessments of reliability and validity. [5]Downgraded due to imprecision as the sample size was small.

remained statistically significant over the second 5-year period from 1992/1993 to 1997/1998 (t = 2.18; p < 0.03; N = 51). These results are suggestive of beneficial long-term treatment effects of adaptive skills training on activities of daily living. However, this study is very low quality because efficacy data could not be extracted.

Behavioural weight control programme compared with no-treatment control group
The single included quasi-experimental study examining the effects of behavioural therapies on behaviour management in adults with a learning disability compared a behavioural weight control programme with a no-treatment control group (see Table 46). The behavioural weight control programme in HARRIS1984 included training about diet, emphasising the importance of exercise, identifying external stimuli associated with food intake, using positive reinforcement and focusing on long-term and short-term goals. The primary outcome was self-care, which in this case was reflected by weight loss. This study found no evidence for a significant treatment effect (test for overall effect: Z = 0.99, p = 0.32), with participants who received the behavioural therapy losing no more weight than participants who received treatment as usual. In addition, there were serious methodological concerns with this study as the no-treatment control group was composed of the participants who had dropped out of the behavioural weight control programme, and, therefore, control and experimental groups were not selected independently of potentially confounding factors.

This concern, together with the indirectness of the evidence, contributed to the downgrading of the evidence to very low quality.

Observational study of self-instructional pictorial childcare manuals
The other included observational study examining behavioural therapies aimed at behaviour management in adults with a learning disability involved an examination of the effects of self-instructional pictorial manuals to teach childcare skills, with no control group (FELDMAN1999). Efficacy data could not be extracted for this study. However, the authors reported evidence for significant change-from-baseline scores in percentages of correct parenting skill steps (t = 6.12; p < 0.001), suggesting that self-instruction based on behavioural principles may be beneficial for improving childcare skills in adults with a learning disability. However, this evidence is of very low quality from an indirect and small sample and efficacy data could not be extracted.

7.5.4   Clinical evidence summary for behavioural therapies aimed at behaviour management

The single included RCT provides limited evidence for the efficacy of behavioural therapies in developing activities of daily living skills for adults with a learning disability, and these findings are supported by the results of the observational study of adaptive skills training. However, the evidence reviewed above is of very low quality and in addition to concerns regarding indirectness, imprecision and risk of bias, there is also uncertainty regarding the generalisability of these findings. For three of the four included studies a task-specific outcome measure designed specifically for the study is used, and whether these beneficial effects will generalise across skill areas or across settings is uncertain.

7.5.5   Health economic evidence for behavioural therapies aimed at behaviour management

No studies assessing the cost effectiveness of behavioural therapies aimed at behaviour management in adults with autism or in populations with a learning disability were identified by the systematic search of the economic literature undertaken for this guideline. Details on the methods used for the systematic search of the economic literature are described in Chapter 3.

7.5.6   From evidence to recommendations

There is limited evidence for the efficacy of behavioural therapies in activities of daily living training for adults with a learning disability. Problems in these areas also significantly impair the day-to-day functioning of many people with autism. With this issue in mind the GDG drew on their knowledge and expertise and decided that adaptive skills training based on behavioural principles could be beneficial for adults with autism who need help with developing daily living skills. It was concluded that such programmes should be structured and predictable, in line with both the knowledge of effectiveness of behavioural therapies beyond autism and the particular importance of structure and consistency for people with autism.

There was no evidence for the use of behavioural therapies for challenging behaviour in adults with autism. However, the GDG judged that this was an important issue in autism and that these interventions may be beneficial. Thus, based on the expert knowledge and judgement of the GDG it was decided that behavioural therapies should be considered for managing challenging behaviour in the context of a comprehensive behaviour management and treatment approach (see also Chapter 8, Sections 8.2.8 and 8.2.9).

7.5.7 Recommendations

Psychosocial interventions focused on life skills

7.5.7.1   For adults with autism of all ranges of intellectual ability, who need help with activities of daily living, consider a structured and predictable training programme based on behavioural principles.

Psychosocial interventions for challenging behaviour

7.5.7.2   Psychosocial interventions for challenging behaviour should be based on behavioural principles and informed by a functional analysis of behaviour (see recommendation 5.4.7.21).

7.5.7.3   Psychosocial interventions for challenging behaviour should include:
- clearly identified target behaviour(s)
- a focus on outcomes that are linked to quality of life
- assessment and modification of environmental factors that may contribute to initiating or maintaining the behaviour
- a clearly defined intervention strategy
- a clear schedule of reinforcement, and capacity to offer reinforcement promptly and contingently on demonstration of the desired behaviour
- a specified timescale to meet intervention goals (to promote modification of intervention strategies that do not lead to change within a specified time)
- a systematic measure of the target behaviour(s) taken before and after the intervention to ascertain whether the agreed outcomes are being met.

7.6 COGNITIVE BEHAVIOURAL THERAPIES

7.6.1 Introduction

Cognitive behavioural therapy (CBT) was originally developed for the treatment of depression (Beck *et al.*, 1979) but has since been adapted for use, and found to be effective, for treating a range of mental health problems including anxiety disorders (Butler *et al.*, 2006; Salkovskis, 1999), psychosis (Tarrier *et al.*, 1998) and eating disorders (Fairburn *et al.*, 1993). Cognitive behavioural therapies are typically discrete, time-limited, structured interventions. They involve collaborative service user and therapist interaction in order to: (a) identify the types and effects of thoughts, beliefs and interpretations on current symptoms; (b) develop skills to identify, monitor and then counteract problematic thoughts, beliefs and interpretations related to the target symptoms or problems; and (c) learn a repertoire of coping skills appropriate to the target thoughts, beliefs and/or problem areas.

Several authors have recommended the use of CBT for adults with autism (Attwood, 1997, 2004 and 2006b; Cardaciotto & Herbert, 2004; Gaus, 2000 and 2007; Hare & Paine, 1997; Tsai, 2006). However, the evidence base for efficacy is essentially limited to case studies of, for instance, the use of CBT for treating coexisting depression in adults with autism (Hare, 1997; Hare & Paine, 1997) or coexisting social anxiety disorder (Cardaciotto & Herbert 2004). There are controlled studies for the use of CBT to treat coexisting conditions in children and young people with autism. However, the evidence for efficacy is generally limited (Howlin, 2010), with only a handful of positive RCTs reported (Chalfant *et al.*, 2007; Reaven *et al.*, 2009; Sofronoff *et al.*, 2005 and 2007; Wood *et al.*, 2009). In addition, concerns have been raised about the suitability of CBT approaches for people with autism given that the therapy is based on techniques such as abstraction that may require greater social and emotional understanding than may be possible for many people with autism (Howlin, 2010). In light of this it is important, when reviewing the evidence for CBT to treat coexisting conditions in adults with autism, to consider the adaptations that may need to be made to the standard treatment of coexisting conditions. For instance, a number of autism-specific adaptations to CBT have been suggested, including a greater use of written and visual material, avoidance of the use of metaphor and abstract concepts in favour of concrete examples, and where appropriate, involvement of a family member or key worker as a co-therapist in order to improve generalisation of skills (Anderson & Morris, 2006).

Traditionally, CBT was considered as unsuitable for people with a learning disability due to the heavily cognitive emphasis. However, cognitive behavioural therapies have been successfully adapted for individuals with a learning disability (Hatton, 2002; Taylor *et al.*, 2008; Willner, 2005), and there have been a number of controlled trials in adults with a learning disability in the use of CBT for anger management. Anger management programmes have been largely based on the work of Raymond Novaco (1975, 1976 and 1979) and typically involve functional analysis of anger provoking situations, psychoeducation, appraisal of hypothetical anger provoking situations and stress inoculation (Lindsay *et al.*, 2004).

The review of CBT for coexisting conditions and of anger management in adults with autism is of clinical importance given the high prevalence of coexisting conditions in people with autism (Hofvander *et al.*, 2009; Howlin, 2000) and the higher incidence of aggression towards others and objects found in people with autism and a learning disability compared with individuals with a learning disability alone (Cohen *et al.*, 2010).

CBT has also been adapted to target anti-victimisation skills in adults with a learning disability. Such interventions have been based on the Hickson and Khemka (1999 & 2001) framework for decision-making in situations involving interpersonal conflict and abuse. These CBT curricula include instruction for both cognitive decision-making aspects (focusing on problem identification and definition, alternative choice generation and consequence evaluation) and motivational aspects of decision-making (including perceptions of control and goals clarification) with the specific aim of empowering women with a learning disability to resist abuse. Anti-victimisation adaptations of CBT are clinically relevant for adults with autism given that many adults with autism experience peer victimisation (see Chapter 4, Section 4.3.4).

7.6.2   Studies considered[55]

No RCTs were found that provided relevant clinical evidence for cognitive behavioural therapies in adults with autism and met the eligibility criteria for this review. However, one quasi-experimental parallel group controlled trial in adults with autism (N = 24) was found and included (RUSSELL2009 [Russell *et al.*, 2009]). Based on the expert judgement of the GDG and the rules for extrapolation the decision was taken to extrapolate from adults with a learning disability for cognitive behavioural therapies aimed at behaviour management. Two RCTs (N = 81) (KHEMKA2000 [Khemka, 2000], KHEMKA2005 [Khemka *et al.*, 2005]), five quasi-experimental parallel group controlled trials (N = 249) (LINDSAY2004 [Lindsay *et al.*, 2004], MAZZUCCHELLI2001 [Mazzucchelli, 2001], MCGRATH2010 [McGrath *et al.*, 2010], ROSE2005 [Rose *et al.*, 2005], TAYLOR2005 [Taylor *et al.*, 2005]) and two observational studies (N = 65) (BENSON1986 [Benson *et al.*, 1986], KING1999 [King *et al.*, 1999]) in adults with a learning disability were found and included. All of these studies were published in peer-reviewed journals between 1986 and 2010. In addition, 11 studies were excluded as they did not meet eligibility criteria. The reasons for exclusion included: mean age of below 15 years, sample of fewer than ten participants per arm, descriptive paper, or data could not be extracted that could be entered into a meta-analysis or narratively reviewed. Further information about included and excluded studies can be found in Appendix 14e.

The quasi-experimental parallel group controlled trial in adults with autism compared CBT with treatment as usual (see Table 47) to treat coexisting OCD.

The two RCTs in adults with a learning disability compared anti-victimisation interventions with treatment as usual (see Table 48). Three of the five quasi-experimental parallel group controlled trials compared anger management with either treatment as usual or a waitlist control (see Table 49). The remaining two quasi-experimental

---

[55]Here and elsewhere in the guideline, each study considered for review is referred to by a study ID in capital letters (primary author and date of study publication, except where a study is in press or only submitted for publication, then a date is not used).

Table 47: Study information table for RCTs of cognitive behavioural therapies in adults with autism

	CBT for OCD
No. trials (total participants)	1 (24)
Study ID	RUSSELL2009
N/% female	3/13
Mean age	24 and 32 years
IQ	Range not reported (mean VIQ 100.3; mean PIQ 95.5)
Axis I/II disorders	100% autism; 100% OCD
Comparator	Treatment as usual control group
Length of treatment	10 to 50 (mean 27.5) treatment sessions
Length of follow-up	Mean 15.9 months

Table 48: Study information table for RCTs of cognitive behavioural therapies in adults with a learning disability

	Anti-victimisation interventions
No. trials (total participants)	2 (81)
Study IDs	(1) KHEMKA2000 (2) KHEMKA2005
N/% female	(1) 45/100 (2) 36/100
Mean age	(1) 36 years (2) 34 years
IQ	(1) Range not reported (mean 60.89) (2) Range not reported (mean 55.92)
Axis I/II disorders	(1)–(2) 100% learning disabilities
Comparator	(1)–(2) Treatment as usual control group
Length of treatment	(1) 10 training sessions spread over several weeks (2) 6 to 12 weeks
Length of follow-up	(1) 10 training sessions (2) 12 weeks

Table 49: Study information table for quasi-experimental parallel group controlled trials of cognitive behavioural therapies in adults with a learning disability

	Anti-victimisation interventions	**Anger management**
No. trials (total participants)	2 (58)	3 (169)
Study IDs	(1) MAZZUCCHELLI2001 (2) MCGRATH2010	(1) LINDSAY2004 (2) ROSE2005 (3) TAYLOR2005
N/% female	(1) 15/75 (2) 30/50	(1) 14/30 (2) 15/17 (3) 0/0
Mean age	(1) 31 and 37 years (2) 33 and 36 years	(1) 24 and 28 years (2) 35 and 39 years (3) 29 and 30 years
IQ	(1) Range not reported (means 56 and 60) (2) Not reported (borderline, mild or moderate learning disabilities)	(1) Range not reported (means 65 and 66) (2) 24 to 113 (mean 72) (3) Range not reported (means 67 and 71)
Axis I/II disorders	(1)–(2) 100% learning disabilities	(1)–(3) 100% learning disabilities
Comparator	(1)–(2) Waitlist control group	(1) Treatment as usual (2) Waitlist control group (3) Treatment as usual
Length of treatment	(1) 4 weeks (2) 10 sessions	(1) 9 months (approximately 40 sessions) (2) 16 2-hour sessions (3) 18 sessions
Length of follow-up	(1) 9 weeks (2) 3 months	(1) 9 months (2) 6 months (3) 4 months

trials compared anti-victimisation interventions with waitlist control (see Table 49). There were also two observational studies that reported change-from-baseline scores for adults with a learning disability receiving an anger management programme (see Table 50).

Table 50: Study information table for observational studies of cognitive behavioural therapies in adults with a learning disability

	Anger management
No. trials (total participants)	2 (65)
Study IDs	(1) BENSON1986* (2) KING1999*
N/% female	(1) 17/31 (2) 4/36
Mean age	(1) 32 years (2) 30 years
IQ	(1) Not reported (mild or moderate learning disabilities) (2) Not reported (mild learning disabilities)
Axis I/II disorders	(1)–(2) 100% learning disabilities
Comparator	(1)–(2) No comparator
Length of treatment	(1) 12 weekly sessions (2) 15 weekly sessions
Length of follow-up	(1) 19 weeks (2) 27 weeks
Note. *Efficacy data not extractable.	

7.6.3   Clinical evidence for cognitive behavioural therapies

Cognitive behavioural therapies compared with treatment as usual for coexisting conditions

A single quasi-experimental study was included for cognitive behavioural therapies in adults with autism (see Table 51). RUSSELL2009 compared CBT with treatment as usual in adults with autism and coexisting OCD. The intervention involved exposure and response prevention, and cognitive appraisal of OCD-related beliefs. The primary outcome was treatment effects on the coexisting OCD symptoms, as measured by the Yale-Brown Obsessive Compulsive Scale (Y-BOCS) severity scale. The authors reported that OCD symptoms were carefully distinguished from the repetitive phenomena typically seen in autism. This study failed to find evidence for significant treatment effects (test for overall effect: $Z = 0.79$, $p = 0.43$), with participants receiving CBT showing no significant difference in severity of OCD symptoms compared with participants receiving treatment as usual.

Table 51: Evidence summary table for CBT compared with treatment as usual for coexisting conditions in adults with autism

	Severity of OCD symptoms
Study ID	RUSSELL2009
Effect size	MD = 2.42 (-3.60, 8.44)
Quality of evidence (GRADE)	Very low[1,2]
Number of studies/participants	K = 1; N = 24
Forest plot	1.4.3, Appendix 15

Note. [1]Downgraded due to risk of bias as there was no attention-placebo control group so participants did not receive the same care apart from the intervention, and the trial was non-randomised and non-blind so there was a risk of selection, performance and detection bias. [2]Downgraded for imprecision as the sample size was small.

Anti-victimisation interventions compared with waitlist control

Two RCT in adults with a learning disability compared anti-victimisation interventions with waitlist control groups (see Table 52). The interventions used a cognitive-behavioural approach to attempt to teach participants to anticipate and avoid potential situations of abuse or bullying. The interventions emphasised self-directed decision-making, which combined instruction on cognitive and motivational aspects of decision-making, through the use of simulated interpersonal situations of abuse. Two quasi-experimental parallel-group controlled trials in adults with a learning disability also compared anti-victimisation interventions with waitlist control. Meta-analysis, which combined continuous measures of anti-victimisation skills, revealed a statistically significant treatment effect (test for overall effect: Z = 4.29, p < 0.0001) suggesting that participants receiving the intervention showed superior anti-victimisation skills compared with control participants. However, there is significant heterogeneity for the meta-analysis ($I^2 = 78\%$, p = 0.01) suggesting that it may not be valid to combine the results from these trials into a meta-analysis. Nevertheless, when considered individually the treatment effects remained statistically significant for the RCTs (tests for overall effect: Z = 6.18, p < 0.00001; and Z = 3.13, p = 0.002 for mean differences in KHEMKA2000 and KHEMKA2005 respectively) but not for one of the quasi-experimental studies (test for overall effect: Z = 0.65, p = 0.51 for MAZZUCCHELLI2001). The second of the included quasi-experimental studies comparing anti-victimisation intervention with waitlist control examined dichotomous data for rates of bullying in the sample following the intervention (see Table 52) and again failed to find evidence for a significant treatment effect (test for overall effect: Z = 0.91, p = 0.36).

To summarise, the evidence for the use of CBT for anti-victimisation interventions in adults with a learning disability is largely positive and suggestive of significant

Table 52: Evidence summary table for cognitive behavioural therapies compared with treatment as usual or waitlist control in adults with a learning disability

	Anti-victimisation skills training (continuous)	Anti-victimisation skills training (dichotomous)	Anger management
Study IDs	KHEMKA2000 KHEMKA2005 MAZZUCCHELLI2001	MCGRATH2010	LINDSAY2004 ROSE2005 TAYLOR2005
Effect size	SMD = 1.07 (0.58, 1.56)	RR = 0.64 (0.25, 1.67)	SMD = −0.59 (−0.90, −0.27)
Quality of evidence (GRADE)	Very low[1,2,3,4]	Very low[1,2]	Very low[1,2]
Number of studies/ participants	K = 3; N = 80	K = 1; N = 38	K = 3; N = 169
Forest plot	1.4.3, Appendix 15	1.4.3, Appendix 15	1.4.3, Appendix 15

Note. [1]Downgraded for risk of bias as there is no attention-placebo control group so participants did not receive the same care apart from the intervention and non-blinding means there is a risk of performance and detection bias. [2]Downgraded for indirectness because of extrapolating from adults with a learning disability. [3]Downgraded for imprecision as the reliability and validity of the outcome measures is unclear. [4]Two RCTs (KHEMKA2000, KHEMKA2005) and one quasi-experimental study (MAZZUCCHELLI2001) combined with high heterogeneity.

treatment effects. However, this evidence is indirect as it was extrapolated from a population of adults with a learning disability. There are also methodological limitations that necessitate caution when interpreting the results.

Anger management compared with treatment as usual or waitlist control
Three of the five included quasi-experimental studies in adults with a learning disability compared anger management programmes with treatment as usual or waitlist control groups (see Table 52). These interventions were based on the work of Novaco (1975, 1976 & 1979) and included behavioural relaxation training, stress inoculation, discussion on appropriate and inappropriate behaviour, problem-solving strategies and role play. The primary outcome was anger as measured by provocation or anger inventories (such as the Dundee Provocation Inventory [DPI], the Anger Inventory and the Provocation Inventory). These studies were combined in a meta-analysis and provide limited evidence for statistically significant beneficial effects of the use of CBT for anger management in adults with a learning disability (test for overall effect: $Z = 3.60$, $p = 0.0003$).

Observational studies of anger management

Finally two observational studies with no control groups examine the effects of anger management training in adults with a learning disability (BENSON1986, KING1999). Efficacy data could not be extracted for these studies. However, the authors reported data suggestive of positive treatment effects. BENSON1986 reported statistically significant change-from-baseline scores for aggressive gestures on the videotaped role-play test ($t = 3.71$; $p < 0.0005$). KING1999 reported statistically significant change-from-baseline for scores on the Anger Inventory ($t = 5.19$; $p < 0.05$). Thus, these two observational studies provide limited evidence for positive treatment effects of the use of CBT for anger management in adults with a learning disability, and as these results are consistent with the quasi-experimental studies they lend support to the efficacy of this intervention.

7.6.4   Clinical evidence summary for cognitive behavioural therapies

The single included study in adults with autism compared CBT with treatment as usual for the severity of coexisting OCD symptoms. However, this trial reported no evidence for significant treatment effects. The study also failed to detail any autism-specific modifications that were made to the standard CBT treatment and this may reflect the fact that no such adaptation took place and could, in part, account for the lack of efficacy. In contrast the evidence for cognitive behavioural therapies aimed at anti-victimisation skills or anger management in adults with a learning disability provided more promising results with limited evidence for positive treatment effects for CBT on both outcomes. However, it is important to bear in mind that this evidence is of low quality and is indirect. Thus, it is important to consider any adaptations that may need to be made in order to generalise results to adults with autism.

7.6.5   Health economic evidence for cognitive behavioural therapies

No studies assessing the cost effectiveness of cognitive behavioural therapies for adults with autism or populations with a learning disability were identified by the systematic search of the economic literature undertaken for this guideline. Details on the methods used for the systematic search of the economic literature are described in Chapter 3.

7.6.6   From evidence to recommendations

The evidence concerning the cognitive behavioural treatment of coexisting conditions is very limited and provides no specific evidence to support the development of adaptations to CBT to make it potentially more effective for people with autism. Effective psychological interventions, predominantly CBT, exist for depression and anxiety disorders, for which there is extensive NICE guidance. The GDG considered that these interventions could be appropriate for many adults with autism. However, the evidence reviewed in this guideline does not provide any guidance on autism-specific adaptations to psychological interventions for coexisting conditions. In the absence of such evidence, and given the high prevalence of depression and anxiety disorders in adults with autism, GDG members drew on their knowledge and expertise, both of psychological interventions and autism, to develop some recommendations on how CBT (and other psychological interventions) might be adapted in order to increase their effectiveness in autism. These included a more concrete, structured, approach with a greater use of written and visual information than might typically be the case in CBT. The GDG was of the view that an emphasis on the behavioural rather than the cognitive aspects of CBT could be beneficial as could shorter sessions or regular breaks. Careful consideration should be given to the use of group-based approaches and the excessive use of metaphors or hypothetical situations should be avoided. Consideration should also be given to the increased involvement of a family member or key worker as co-therapist to support the generalisation of benefits.

The evidence for cognitive behavioural therapies for anti-victimisation skills and anger management training in adults with a learning disability was somewhat more promising and addressed a key area of concern for people with autism and their families, partners and carers. The GDG therefore recommended the use of these interventions for adults with autism, but did not recommend that specific adaptations of the method for autism be considered. However, for interventions for coexisting disorders, and for delivery of anti-victimisation skills and anger management training, the GDG was of the view that professionals delivering such interventions should be familiar with the impact of autism on a person's psychological functioning. Where they have concerns about adapting an intervention they should consider seeking advice from a specialist in autism if they do not have particular knowledge and expertise. The GDG also expressed concern that anti-victimisation and anger management interventions may not be suitable for all ranges of intellectual ability due to their cognitive component and thus should only be considered for individuals with no or a mild learning disability. This is also consistent with the mean IQ of the samples that form the evidence base.

7.6.7 Recommendations

Psychosocial interventions focused on life skills

7.6.7.1   For adults with autism without a learning disability or with a mild learning disability, who are at risk of victimisation, consider anti-victimisation interventions based on teaching decision-making and problem-solving skills.

7.6.7.2   Anti-victimisation interventions should typically include:
- identifying and, where possible, modifying and developing decision-making skills in situations associated with abuse
- developing personal safety skills.

7.6.7.3   For adults with autism without a learning disability or with a mild to moderate learning disability, who have problems with anger and aggression, offer an anger management intervention, adjusted to the needs of adults with autism.

7.6.7.4   Anger management interventions should typically include:
- functional analysis of anger and anger-provoking situations
- coping-skills training and behaviour rehearsal
- relaxation training
- development of problem-solving skills.

Psychosocial interventions for coexisting mental disorders

7.6.7.5   For adults with autism and coexisting mental disorders, offer psychosocial interventions informed by existing NICE guidance for the specific disorder.

7.6.7.6   Staff delivering interventions for coexisting mental disorders to adults with autism should:
- have an understanding of the core symptoms of autism and their possible impact on the treatment of coexisting mental disorders
- consider seeking advice from a specialist autism team regarding delivering and adapting these interventions for people with autism.

7.6.7.7   Adaptations to the method of delivery of cognitive and behavioural interventions for adults with autism and coexisting common mental disorders should include:
- a more concrete and structured approach with a greater use of written and visual information (which may include worksheets, thought bubbles, images and 'tool boxes')
- placing greater emphasis on changing behaviour, rather than cognitions, and using the behaviour as the starting point for intervention
- making rules explicit and explaining their context
- using plain English and avoiding excessive use of metaphor, ambiguity and hypothetical situations
- involving a family member, partner, carer or professional (if the person with autism agrees) to support the implementation of an intervention
- maintaining the person's attention by offering regular breaks and incorporating their special interests into therapy if possible (such as using computers to present information).

7.6.8   Research recommendation

7.6.8.1   Facilitated self-help for anxiety and depression in adults with autism
What is the clinical and cost effectiveness of facilitated self-help for the treatment of mild anxiety and depressive disorders in adults with autism?

Why this is important
Anxiety and depressive disorders commonly coexist in people with autism and are associated with poorer health outcomes and quality of life. This may occur because of the direct impact of the anxiety or depression but also because of a negative interaction with

217

the core symptoms of autism. There is limited access and poor uptake of facilitated self-help by people with autism, largely due to limited availability but also because current systems for the delivery of such interventions are not adapted for use by people with autism. In adults without autism, facilitated self-help is an effective intervention for mild to moderate depression and anxiety. The development of novel methods for the delivery of facilitated self-help could make effective interventions available to a wider group of people.

The suggested programme of research would need to: (a) develop current methods for the delivery of self-help measures to take into account the impact of autism and possibly include developments in the nature of the materials, the methods for their delivery and the nature, duration and extent of their facilitation; (b) test the feasibility of the novel methods in a series of pilot studies; and (c) formally evaluate the outcomes (including symptoms, satisfaction and quality of life) in a large-scale randomised trial.

7.6.8.2   Cognitive behavioural therapy (CBT) for anxiety disorders in adults with autism

What is the clinical and cost effectiveness of CBT for the treatment of moderate and severe anxiety disorders in adults with autism?

Why this is important

Anxiety disorders commonly coexist in people with autism and are associated with poorer health outcomes and quality of life. This may occur because of the direct impact of the anxiety but also because of a negative interaction with the core symptoms of autism. There is limited access and poor uptake of psychological treatment services by people with autism, largely due to limited availability but also because current systems for the delivery of such interventions are not adapted for use for people with autism. In adults without autism, CBT is an effective intervention for moderate to severe anxiety disorders. The adaptation of CBT for adults with autism and a coexisting anxiety disorder could make effective interventions more widely available.

The suggested programme of research would need to: (a) develop current methods for the delivery of CBT to take into account the impact of autism and the nature and duration of the intervention; (b) test the feasibility of the novel treatments in a series of pilot studies (for the commonly experienced anxiety disorders in autism); and (c) formally evaluate the outcomes (including symptoms, satisfaction and quality of life) in a large-scale randomised controlled trial.

7.7   LEISURE PROGRAMMES

7.7.1   Introduction

For individuals with autism, leisure pursuits may well involve isolated activities such as playing video games and watching television (Jennes-Coussens *et al.*, 2006; Wagner *et al.*, 2005). However, inclusion in social, leisure and community activities is increasingly being seen as a contributor to quality of life (Baker & Palmer, 2006;

Iwasaki, 2007), and there is research suggesting a positive relationship between leisure participation, quality of life and stress reduction as described by the World Health Organization Quality of Life Assessment Working Group (The Group, WHOQOL, 1998). Previous research has found an increased prevalence of stress and associated anxiety in people with autism (Bellini, 2004; Gillot *et al.*, 2001; Green *et al.*, 2000; Kim *et al.*, 2000), and many of the challenging or problem behaviours that can be associated with autism, including aggression, self-injury and property destruction, have been seen as related in some way to stress (Groden *et al.*, 1994; Prior & Ozonoff, 1998). Thus, given the role of leisure as a means of enhancing quality of life and as a coping mechanism for dealing with acute and chronic life stressors (Hutchinson *et al.*, 2003 and 2008), it can be hypothesised that the introduction of therapeutic interventions based on developing structured leisure activities could be beneficial for people with autism. However, many individuals with autism have been denied access to the full range of recreational opportunities because of others' misconceptions about them (Coyne, 2004), and there is a need to systematically develop and evaluate programmes designed to provide opportunities for adults with autism to experience leisure (García-Villamisar & Dattilo, 2011).

7.7.2   Studies considered[56]

Two RCTs were found that provided relevant clinical evidence in adults with autism (N = 111) and met the eligibility criteria for this review (García-Villamisar & Dattilo, 2010 [GARCIAVILLAMISAR2010]; García-Villamisar & Dattilo, 2011 [GARCIAVILLAMISAR2011]). Both of these studies were published in peer-reviewed journals. There were no excluded studies for leisure programmes. Further information about included studies can be found in Appendix 14e.

The two RCTs in adults with autism (see Table 53) both compared a leisure programme intervention with a waitlist control.

7.7.3   Clinical evidence for leisure programmes

Leisure programmes compared with waitlist control
GARCIAVILLAMISAR2010 compared a leisure programme intervention with a waitlist control group (see Table 54). The leisure programme intervention consisted of a group recreation context from 17:00 to 19:00 (2 hours) each day (5 days per week) for participants to interact with media (a CD player, radio, magazines), engage in exercise (swimming, playing catch, playing Frisbee, hiking, bowling), play games and do crafts (computer games, puzzles, collections, printing, darts), attend events

---

[56]Here and elsewhere in the guideline, each study considered for review is referred to by a study ID in capital letters (primary author and date of study publication, except where a study is in press or only submitted for publication, then a date is not used).

Table 53: Study information table for included RCTs of leisure programme interventions in adults with autism

	Leisure programmes
No. trials (total participants)	2 (111)
Study IDs	(1) GARCIAVILLAMISAR2010 (2) GARCIAVILLAMISAR2011
N/% female	(1) 30/42 (2) 16/40
Mean age	(1) 31 and 30 years (2) 32 years
IQ	(1)–(2) Not reported
Axis I/II disorders	(1) 100% autism (3% Asperger's syndrome) (2) 100% autism
Comparator	(1)–(2) Waitlist
Length of treatment	(1)–(2) 1 year
Length of follow-up	(1)–(2) 1 year

Table 54: Evidence summary table for leisure programmes compared with waitlist control in adults with autism

	Quality of life	Emotion recognition
Study ID	GARCIAVILLAMISAR2010	GARCIAVILLAMISAR2011
Effect size	MD = 8.33 (5.21, 11.45)	MD = 12.77 (2.12, 23.42)
Quality of evidence (GRADE)	Moderate[1]	Low[1,2]
Number of studies/ participants	K = 1; N = 71	K = 1; N = 40
Forest plot	1.4.4, Appendix 15	1.4.4, Appendix 15

Note. [1]Downgraded for risk of performance bias due to the lack of an attention-placebo control group. [2]Downgraded for imprecision as the sample size was small.

(parties, fairs, cinema, concerts, museums) and participate in other recreational activities (socialising, youth groups). The criteria for selecting activities were that they should be understandable (flexible, structured, have a well-defined beginning and end, clear visual presentation of instructions, minimal verbal direction), reactive (provide reinforcement through sensory feedback), comfortable (commensurate with participant's skills and challenging) and active (frequent changes between activities). GARCIAVILLAMISAR2010 found evidence for a significant beneficial effect of the leisure programme on quality of life (test for overall effect: $Z = 5.23$, $p < 0.00001$), with participants receiving the leisure intervention showing superior quality of life scores compared with participants in the waitlist control group.

GARCIAVILLAMISAR2011 examined the effects of a comparable leisure programme on emotion recognition as assessed by the Facial Discrimination Battery. Again, a significant treatment effect was observed (test for overall effect: $Z = 2.35$, $p = 0.02$), with participants in the leisure programme intervention group showing significantly higher scores on a test of emotion recognition than the waitlist control group.

Thus, these two RCTs provide evidence of significant treatment effects of a leisure programme intervention on quality of life and emotion recognition in a group of adults with autism. It should, however, be noted that the lack of an attention-placebo control group increases the risk of performance bias.

7.7.4 Clinical evidence summary for leisure programmes

The results from these two trials suggest that leisure programmes can improve quality of life and emotion recognition in adults with autism. The authors concluded that participation in recreational activities positively influenced the stress and quality of life of adults with autism and had positive effects on social-emotional cognition. Given the findings that individuals with autism have higher levels of loneliness and social dissatisfaction compared with their typically developing peers (Huang & Wheeler, 2006), these results suggest that a leisure programme that is designed to encourage and support participation of adults with autism in group recreational activities may have tangible benefits.

7.7.5 Health economic evidence for leisure programmes

No studies assessing the cost effectiveness of leisure programmes for adults with autism were identified by the systematic search of the economic literature undertaken for this guideline. Details on the methods used for the systematic search of the economic literature are described in Chapter 3.

7.7.6 From evidence to recommendations

The two trials from adults with autism present limited evidence for the beneficial effects of leisure programmes that provide regular group recreation and structure and support and encourage a focus on the interests and abilities of adults with autism, but can be delivered individually. Leisure programmes were found to have a positive effect on quality of life and also impact on a core symptom of autism as reflected in improvements in social-emotional cognition. As adults with autism often experience social exclusion, and inclusion in social, community and leisure activities has been found to reduce stress, which is a significant coexisting problem in autism, the GDG was of the view that a structured leisure activity programme should be recommended for adults with autism without a learning disability or with a mild to moderate learning disability.

7.7.7   Recommendations

Psychosocial interventions focused on life skills

7.7.7.1   For adults with autism without a learning disability or with a mild to moderate learning disability, who are socially isolated or have restricted social contact, consider:
● a group-based structured leisure activity programme
● an individually delivered structured leisure activity programme for people who find group-based activities difficult.

7.7.7.2   A structured leisure activity programme should typically include:
● a focus on the interests and abilities of the participant(s)
● regular meetings for a valued leisure activity
● for group-based programmes, a facilitator with a broad understanding of autism to help integrate the participants
● the provision of structure and support.

7.8   SOCIAL LEARNING INTERVENTIONS

7.8.1   Introduction

Impairment in social interaction is one of the core symptoms of autism. The prevalence of friendships and participation in social groups is low in adults with autism. For instance, studies have found that, regardless of intellectual ability, the estimate for adults with autism who have no peer relationships, or no particular friend with whom they share activities, was around 50% (Mawhood *et al.*, 2000; Orsmond *et al.*, 2004). In addition, individuals with autism who do have friends often report atypical definitions of what a friend is and experience friendships that are based on common interests and characterised by minimal social interaction (Orsmond *et al.*, 2004). However, the low incidence of social relationships, and differences in friendships, does not necessarily reflect a lack of desire for such relationships but more likely a lack of the necessary skills for developing such relationships. For instance, adolescents with autism report wanting friends (Marks *et al.*, 2000), and higher levels of loneliness have been found for individuals with autism compared with typically-developing peers (Bauminger & Kasari, 2000; Bauminger *et al.*, 2003).

Impairments in social interaction impact upon many aspects of life for an individual with autism. For instance, social skills have been associated with employment success (Chadsey-Rusch, 1992) and individuals with autism who do not have a learning disability often find obtaining and keeping a job difficult as a consequence of their social impairments (Barnard *et al.*, 2000; Morgan, 1996). Individuals with autism and intelligence in the normal range often know the social rules and can learn the skills but do not know to apply those skills (Hillier *et al.*, 2007). Interventions based on social learning principles have used techniques including instruction, discussion, modelling (including video modelling), feedback, role play and reinforcement to teach adolescents and adults with autism the 'rules' of social interaction in the context of social skills groups, which have the additional advantage of allowing social skills to be learned and practised at the same time within the group context (Herbrecht *et al.*, 2009; Hillier *et al.*, 2007; Howlin & Yates, 1999; Laugeson *et al.*, 2009; Tse *et al.*, 2007; Webb *et al.*, 2004). Other interventions have been aimed at improving social-interaction skills in adults with autism by targeting fundamental autistic impairments such as 'theory of mind' deficits (Hadwin *et al.*, 1995; Ozonoff & Miller, 1995) and computer–based interventions have been developed to teach emotion recognition (Golan & Baron-Cohen, 2006). The social skills group interventions date back to the 1980s and were aimed at improving communication and interaction skills and at facilitating positive social experience with peers for children with autism (Mesibov, 1984; Ozonoff & Miller, 1995). Participants often value the friendships they gain more than the skills learned during the course of social skills group interventions (Hillier *et al.*, 2007). Social skills groups vary in terms of the teaching techniques, frequency and duration of group sessions, group composition, and so on, however, certain common principles have emerged, such as the teaching of social skills in concrete terms, having a predictable and structured learning environment and providing the opportunity to engage with peers in positive surroundings (Barry *et al.*, 2003; Herbrecht *et al.*, 2009; Krasny *et al.*, 2003; Williams White *et al.*, 2006). There is evidence for the efficacy of social skills group interventions in children with autism (Williams White *et al.*, 2006), however, the generalisability of effects outside of the social skills groups and to new social situations and interactions is unclear, with only limited evidence for generalisation outside the group context (Tse *et al.*, 2007).

7.8.2   Studies considered[57]

One RCT was found that provided relevant clinical evidence for social learning interventions in adults with autism (N = 41) and met the eligibility criteria for this review (GOLAN2006 [Golan & Baron-Cohen, 2006]). There were also two

---

[57]Here and elsewhere in the guideline, each study considered for review is referred to by a study ID in capital letters (primary author and date of study publication, except where a study is in press or only submitted for publication, then a date is not used).

observational studies of social learning interventions in adults with autism (N = 23) (HILLIER2007 [Hillier *et al.*, 2007], HOWLIN1999 [Howlin & Yates, 1999]). Based on the expert judgement of the GDG, the decision was taken to extrapolate from adolescents with autism (with a group mean age of at least 15 years old) for social learning interventions aimed at social interaction. On this basis, one RCT (N = 33) (LAUGESON2009 [Laugeson *et al.*, 2009]) and three observational studies (N = 73) (HERBRECHT2009 [Herbrecht *et al.*, 2009], TSE2007 [Tse *et al.*, 2007], WEBB2004 [Webb *et al.*, 2004]) in adolescents with autism were found and included. Finally, the GDG agreed, as previously mentioned, to extrapolate from adults with a learning disability for interventions aimed at behaviour management. On this basis, one RCT (N = 48) that examined the effects of a social learning intervention on challenging behaviour in adults with a learning disability was included (LEE1977 [Lee, 1977]). All of these studies were published in peer-reviewed journals between 1977 and 2009. In addition, 30 studies were excluded because they did not meet eligibility criteria. The most common reasons for exclusion were a mean age of below 15 years old or a sample of fewer than ten participants per arm. Further information about included and excluded studies can be found in Appendix 14e.

The RCT in adults with autism compared an emotion recognition computer-based intervention with treatment as usual (see Table 55). The RCT in adolescents with autism compared a social skills group with waitlist control (see Table 56).

Table 55: Study information table for RCTs of social learning interventions in adults with autism

	Emotion recognition computer software programme
No. trials (total participants)	1 (41)
Study IDs	GOLAN2006
N/% female	10/24
Mean age	31 years
IQ	80 to 140 (mean VIQ 108 and 110; mean PIQ 112 and 115)
Axis I/II disorders	100% autism (Asperger's syndrome and high-functioning autism)
Comparator	Treatment as usual
Length of treatment	10 weeks (minimum of 10 hours)
Length of follow-up	15 weeks

Table 56: Study information table for RCTs of social learning interventions in adolescents with autism

	Social skills group
No. trials (total participants)	1 (33)
Study ID	LAUGESON2009
N/% female	5/15
Mean age	15 years
IQ	Range not reported (mean VIQ 88 and 96)
Axis I/II disorders	100% autism (70% high-functioning autism, 27% Asperger's syndrome; 3% PDD-NOS)
Comparator	Waitlist control group
Length of treatment	12 weeks
Length of follow-up	24 weeks

Table 57: Study information table for RCTs of social learning interventions in adults with a learning disability

	Social skills group
No. trials (total participants)	1 (48)
Study ID	LEE1977
N/% female	26/54
Mean age	Median 37 years
IQ	12 to 87 (mean 47)
Axis I/II disorders	100% learning disabilities
Comparator	Treatment as usual
Length of treatment	10 weeks
Length of follow-up	10 weeks

The RCT in adults with a learning disability compared a social skills group with treatment as usual (see Table 57). Finally, all of the observational studies reported change-from-baseline scores for participants receiving social skills group interventions (see Table 58 for adults with autism and Table 59 for adolescents with autism).

Table 58: Study information table for observational studies of social learning interventions in adults with autism

	Social skills group
No. trials (total participants)	2 (23)
Study IDs	(1) HILLIER2007* (2) HOWLIN1999*
N/% female	(1) 2/15 (2) 0/0
Mean age	(1) 19 years (2) 28 years
IQ	(1) 81 to 141 (mean 108.08) (2) Non-verbal IQ 86 to 138 (mean 109)
Axis I/II disorders	(1) 100% autism (8% autism, 31% PDD-NOS, 62% Asperger's syndrome) (2) 100% autism
Comparator	(1)–(2) No comparator
Length of treatment	(1) 8 weeks (2) 1 year
Length of follow-up	(1) 8 weeks (2) 1 year
Note. *Efficacy data not extractable.	

7.8.3 Clinical evidence for social learning interventions

Emotion recognition training compared with treatment as usual

One RCT compared a computer-based emotion recognition software programme with treatment as usual in adults with autism (see Table 60). GOLAN2006 trained emotion recognition in adults with autism using 'Mind Reading', a computer-based interactive guide to emotions and mental states. The primary outcome was emotion recognition as assessed by the recognition of complex emotions in faces and voices measured using the Cambridge Mindreading (CAM) Face-Voice Battery. This study found no evidence for a significant treatment effect on the CAM face task (test for overall effect: $Z = 1.06$, $p = 0.29$) with no significant differences in recognising emotion in the face found in participants receiving emotion recognition training compared with participants receiving treatment as usual.

Table 59: Study information table for observational studies of social learning interventions in adolescents with autism

	Social skills group
No. trials (total participants)	3 (73)
Study IDs	(1) HERBRECHT2009* (2) TSE2007* (3) WEBB2004*
N/% female	(1) 2/12 (2) 18/39 (3) 0/0
Mean age	(1)–(3) 15 years
IQ	(1) Range not reported (mean 93.4) (2) Not reported (3) 81 to 132 (mean 100.5)
Axis I/II disorders	(1) 100% autism; 18% OCD, 12% impulsivity or aggression, 6% hyperactivity (2)–(3) 100% autism
Comparator	(1)–(3) No comparator
Length of treatment	(1) 5 months (2) 12 weeks (3) 6.5 weeks
Length of follow-up	(1) 11 months (2) 12 weeks (3) 10 weeks
Note. *Efficacy data not extractable.	

Social skills group interventions compared with waitlist control or treatment as usual
There were no included RCTs comparing social skills group interventions with treatment as usual or waitlist control in adults with autism. However, there were two observational studies of social skills group interventions in adults with autism. HILLIER2007 examined the effects of a social skills group intervention (called 'Aspirations') that aimed to foster understanding of a range of social and vocational issues, enhance insight and awareness, and provide social opportunities for group members. Similarly in HOWLIN1999 the intervention took the form of a social skills group where techniques such as role play, team activities, structured games, and feedback based on behavioural observations, were used to allow focus on major issues raised by group members and core features of conversational ability. Efficacy

Table 60: Evidence summary table for social learning interventions compared with treatment as usual in adults with autism

	Emotion recognition
Study ID	GOLAN2006
Effect size	MD = 2.70 (-2.27, 7.67)
Quality of evidence (GRADE)	Low[1,2]
Number of studies/participants	K = 1; N = 40
Forest plot	1.4.5, Appendix 15
Note. [1]Downgraded for risk of bias as there was no attention-placebo control group so participants did not receive the same care apart from the intervention, and the trial was non-blind so there is a risk of performance and detection bias. [2]Downgraded for imprecision as the sample size was small.	

data could not be extracted for these studies. However, the authors of both studies reported results suggestive of beneficial treatment effects. HILLIER2007 reported a statistically significant change-from-baseline score on the EQ (Z = 2.520; p = 0.012), suggesting that a social learning intervention may have significant positive effects on a measure of core symptoms of autism pertaining to social interaction. HOWLIN1999 reported a statistically significant treatment effect of the social skills group on the percentage of conversation maintaining or initiating observed during a video recording of simulated social activities, in this case, a 'party' scenario (Z = -2.43; p = 0.015). These two studies reported limited evidence for a positive treatment effect for social skills groups on social-interaction skills in adults with autism.

Based on the expert judgment of the GDG and the rules of extrapolation, studies from adolescents with autism were included in the analysis of social learning interventions. A single RCT (LAUGESON2009) compared a social skills group intervention called the 'PEERS' (Program for the Education and Enrichment of Relational Skills) intervention with waitlist control (see Table 61). The intervention involved parents and teenagers attending separate concurrent sessions that instructed them on key elements about making and keeping friends. This study found evidence for a statistically significant treatment effect (test for overall effect: Z = 6.24, p < 0.00001) with participants receiving the social skills group intervention showing superior scores on the Test of Adolescent Social Skills Knowledge (TASSK) compared with the waitlist control group.

There were also three observational studies examining the effects of social skills group interventions in adolescents with autism (HERBRECHT2009, TSE2007, WEBB2004). Efficacy data could not be extracted for these studies. However, the results reported by the authors provide mixed evidence for beneficial treatment

Table 61: Evidence summary table for social learning interventions compared with waitlist control in adolescents with autism

	Social interaction
Study ID	LAUGESON2009
Effect size	MD = 6.30 (4.32, 8.28)
Quality of evidence (GRADE)	Very low[1,2,3]
Number of studies/participants	K = 1; N = 33
Forest plot	1.4.5, Appendix 15

Note. [1]Downgraded for risk of bias as there was no attention-placebo control group so participants did not receive the same care apart from the intervention, and the trial was non-blind so there is risk of performance and detection bias. [2]Downgraded for indirectness due to extrapolating from adolescents with autism. [3]Downgraded for imprecision because the sample size was small.

effects of social skills groups. HERBRECHT2009 examined the effects of the Frankfurt social skills training (KONTAKT) programme, which used techniques including teaching of rules, social-interaction games, role play and group discussion, to focus on learning to initiate social overtures, conversation skills, understanding social rules and relationships, identification and interpretation of verbal and non-verbal social signals, problem solving, coping strategies and improving self-confidence. HERBRECHT2009 failed to find evidence for significant treatment effects on the only blinded measure of social interaction, a blind-expert video rating (F = 1.5; p = 0.24). WEBB2004 also failed to find evidence for a significant treatment effect of a social skills group (t = 1.287; p = 0.230) with no significant change-from-baseline score on the Social Skills Rating System following participation in the social skills group. Conversely, TSE2007 reported evidence suggestive of beneficial effects of the social skills group, which combined psychoeducational and experiential methods to teach social skills, with an emphasis on learning through role play. TSE2007 reported evidence for statistically significant change-from-baseline scores for social interaction as measured by the parent-completed SRS (effect size 0.39; p = 0.003) and challenging behaviour as measured by the Aberrant Behaviour Checklist (Community Version) Irritability Subscale (effect size = 0.72; p = 0.002).

Finally, based on the expert judgment of the GDG, a single RCT was included that compared a social skills group with treatment as usual for behaviour management in adults with a learning disability (see Table 62). LEE1977 examined the effects of social adjustment training on challenging behaviour as assessed by Part 2 of the AAMD ABS. However, this study failed to find evidence for a significant treatment effect on challenging behaviour (test for overall effect: Z = 0.41, p = 0.68).

Table 62: **Evidence summary table for social learning interventions compared with treatment as usual in adults with a learning disability**

	Maladaptive behaviour
Study ID	LEE1977
Effect size	MD = –2.03 (–11.79, 7.73)
Quality of evidence (GRADE)	Very low[1,2,3]
Number of studies/participants	K = 1; N = 44
Forest plot	1.4.5, Appendix 15

Note. [1]Downgraded for risk of bias as there was no attention-placebo control group so participants did not receive the same care apart from the intervention, and the trial was non-blind so there is risk of performance and detection bias. [2]Downgraded for indirectness due to extrapolating from adults with a learning disability. [3]Downgraded for imprecision as the sample size was small.

7.8.4   Clinical evidence summary for social learning interventions

The evidence for social learning interventions is inconsistent. There is no evidence for beneficial effects of emotion recognition training in adults with autism. The evidence for social skills groups is more mixed. The evidence from observational studies in adults with autism, and from the RCT in adolescents with autism, is positive. However, the evidence from the observational studies in adolescents with autism is more mixed with one study reporting limited evidence for significant treatment effects of a social skills group intervention on social interaction, and the other two studies failing to find evidence for significant beneficial effects.

7.8.5   Health economic evidence for social learning interventions

No studies assessing the cost effectiveness of social learning interventions for adults or adolescents with autism were identified by the systematic search of the economic literature undertaken for this guideline. Details on the methods used for the systematic search of the economic literature are described in Chapter 3.

7.8.6   From evidence to recommendations

The efficacy data for social learning interventions for social interaction is limited and variable. However, these interventions address an important area that could improve significant problems of isolation for people with autism. In adults with autism there

230

is one RCT for the rather specific area of emotion recognition training that finds no evidence for a treatment effect. However, the observational studies in adults with autism suggest positive effects associated with social skills groups. For adolescents with autism the single RCT of a social skills group intervention found evidence of significant treatment effects, while the observational studies provided a more mixed outcome.

Based on the positive evidence from the observational studies in adults and the expert knowledge of the GDG, the GDG judged that social learning programmes may help to address significant issues for adults with autism, including social isolation, which may in turn impact on other outcomes such as employment. The GDG also discussed potential problems that some individuals with autism might have with group-based interventions and felt that it was important to offer individual-based social learning programmes in such circumstances. In addition, the GDG felt that the cognitive aspects of these interventions meant that they might not be appropriate for adults with a severe or profound learning disability. This is consistent with the mean IQ of the samples that form the evidence base.

7.8.7 Recommendations

Psychosocial interventions for the core symptoms of autism
7.8.7.1   For adults with autism without a learning disability or with a mild to moderate learning disability, who have identified problems with social interaction, consider:
   ● a group-based social learning programme focused on improving social interaction
   ● an individually delivered social learning programme for people who find group-based activities difficult.
7.8.7.2   Social learning programmes to improve social interaction should typically include:
   ● modelling
   ● peer feedback (for group-based programmes) or individual feedback (for individually delivered programmes)
   ● discussion and decision-making
   ● explicit rules
   ● suggested strategies for dealing with socially difficult situations.

7.9   SUPPORTED EMPLOYMENT PROGRAMMES

7.9.1   Introduction

Adults with autism experience high unemployment—a survey by the NAS found that only 12% of adults with autism without a learning disability are in full-time employment (Barnard *et al.,* 2001). Moreover, follow-up studies have found that for those individuals in employment, the majority of jobs were unskilled and poorly paid (Howlin *et al.*, 2004). Adults with autism are also more likely to switch jobs frequently, have difficulty adjusting to new job settings and earn lower wages than their typically-developing peers (Howlin, 2000; Hurlbutt & Chalmers, 2004; Jennes-Coussens *et al.*, 2006; Müller *et al.*, 2003) or people with less severe language disorders or learning disability (Cameto *et al.*, 2004). As well as conferring financial and economic advantages, regular employment can also bring psychological and social benefits to individuals with autism, including improved self-esteem and greater social integration. People with autism may possess the technical skills required for a job, however they may not be able to convey this in interviews because of difficulties with engaging in reciprocal conversation and with thinking and responding quickly to interview questions (Berney, 2004; Romoser, 2000). Moreover, even if people with autism can successfully negotiate the interview process, there are frequently problems with maintaining employment due to atypical social communication with their employers and/or fellow employees, and sensory issues in the workplace (Hurlbutt & Chalmers, 2004). The inability to make appropriate use of their skills and training, or to find suitable work despite, for some people, many years of trying, can result in frustration, loss of self-esteem and, possibly, entry into a cycle of anxiety and depression or other psychiatric disturbance (Howlin, 1997).

Research in people with a learning disability has suggested that the outcome of supported employment programmes appear to be superior to a sheltered workshop or other day service options (facility-based pre-vocational skills training to prepare individuals for employment in the community), in terms of financial gains for employees, wider social integration, increased worker satisfaction, higher self-esteem and savings on service costs (Beyer & Kilsby, 1996; McCaughrin *et al.*, 1993; Noble *et al.*, 1991; Rhodes *et al.*, 1987; Stevens & Martin, 1999). Specialised supported employment schemes enable people with autism to secure and maintain a paid job in a regular work environment. These programmes involve: (a) emphasising the use of individual strengths and interests, identifying appropriate work experience and jobs, and ensuring the appropriate 'fit' between employment and employee; (b) preparing the person for employment using structured teaching techniques; (c) using a job coach to provide individualised training and support for the supported employee in the workplace; and (d) collaborating with families, partners, carers and employers in order to provide necessary long-term support. The key elements associated with successful schemes include careful job placement, prior job training, advocacy, follow-up monitoring and long-term support to ensure job retention (Keel *et al.*, 1997; Mawhood & Howlin, 1999; Trach & Rusch, 1989; Wehman & Kregel, 1985). The aim of supported employment programmes is to enable individuals with autism to be a contributing member of the workforce through the provision of a stable and predictable work environment, and supported employment can increase feelings of self-worth for the person with autism while also helping to increase public awareness and understanding of autism. One of the few specialised employment services for individuals with autism in the UK is 'Prospects', which was established by the NAS in 1994 and offers work-preparation programmes, job-finding, interview and in-work support tailored to the needs of job seekers with autism (NAO, 2009).

7.9.2   Studies considered[58]

No RCTs were found that provided relevant clinical evidence for supported employ-
ment interventions in adults with autism and met the eligibility criteria for this review.
However, three quasi-experimental parallel group controlled trials (N = 145) were
found (GARCIAVILLAMISAR2000 [García-Villamisar *et al.*, 2000], GARCIAVIL-
LAMISAR2002 [García-Villamisar *et al.*, 2002], GARCIAVILLAMISAR2007
[García-Villamisar & Hughes, 2007], MAWHOOD1999 [Mawhood & Howlin,
1999]). One of these trials was reported across two papers (GARCIAVIL-
LAMISAR2000/2002), with different outcomes in each; data were extracted from
both, but in terms of sample size participants (N = 51) were only counted once. One
observational before-and-after study (N = 89) was also included (HOWLIN2005
[Howlin *et al.*, 2005]). In addition to data from a new group of 89 participants, this
study reported follow-up data for one of the quasi-experimental trials. These data
were only extracted once to avoid duplication. All of these papers were published in
peer-reviewed journals between 1999 and 2007. In addition, three studies were
excluded as data could not be extracted for efficacy analysis. Further information
about included and excluded studies can be found in Appendix 14e.

Of the three included quasi-experimental parallel group controlled trials (four
papers) in an autism population (see Table 63), one compared a supported employment programme with a sheltered workshop programme; one compared a supported
employment programme with waitlist control; and one compared a supported
employment programme with treatment as usual.

The observational study (see Table 64) reported change-from-baseline scores for
participants in a supported employment programme.

7.9.3   Clinical evidence for supported employment programmes

Supported employment programmes compared with sheltered workshop programmes
GARCIAVILLAMISAR2000/2002 found that supported employment programmes
had statistically significant beneficial effects on autistic behaviours as measured by
CARS (test for overall effect: Z = 2.96, p = 0.003) and quality of life as measured by
the Quality of Life Survey (test for overall effect: Z = 4.06, p < 0.0001) compared
with sheltered workshop programmes (see Table 65). However, there were a number
of methodological concerns with this trial which suggest that caution should be exercised when interpreting the results; this is reflected in the lower grade of the evidence.
For instance, the lack of randomisation in group allocation increases the risk of bias.
However, the sample size figures reported varied throughout the papers with no explanation given regarding the changing values and no indication of which were the correct

---

[58]Here and elsewhere in the guideline, each study considered for review is referred to by a study ID in capital letters (primary author and date of study publication, except where a study is in press or only submitted for publication, then a date is not used).

Table 63: Study information table for quasi-experimental studies of supported employment programmes in adults with autism

	Supported employment
No. trials (total participants)	3 (145)
Study IDs	(1) GARCIAVILLAMISAR2000/2002* (2) GARCIAVILLAMISAR2007 (3) MAWHOOD1999
N/% female	(1) 12/24 (2) 12/27 (3) 3/6
Mean age	(1) 21 years (2) 24 and 26 years (3) 28 and 31 years
IQ	(1) Range not reported (means 56 and 57) (2) Range not reported (means 81 and 82) (3) 66 to 128 (means 98 and 99)
Axis I/II disorders	(1) 100% autism; 43% epilepsy (2)–(3) 100% autism
Comparator	(1) Sheltered workshop (2) Waitlist control (3) Treatment as usual
Length of treatment	(1)–(2) Mean 30 months (3) Mean 17 months
Length of follow-up	(1) 3 years (2) Mean 30 months (3) 24 months
Note. *Studies combined for study characteristics as these two papers report different outcomes from the same study.	

figures. The sample sizes used for analysis were selected from the demographic table based on the assumption that this was reflective of the intention-to-treat sample.

Supported employment versus waitlist control
GARCIAVILLAMISAR2007 found statistically significant effects of a supported employment programme on executive function as measured by the SOC Planning Task from the Cambridge Neuropsychological Tests: Automated Battery (CANTAB), which is a computerised version of the Tower of London Planning Task (see Table 66). This study found that the average planning time required for this task was

Table 64: Study information table for observational studies of supported employment programmes in adults with autism

	Supported employment
No. trials (total participants)	1 (89)
Study ID	HOWLIN2005*
N/% female	17/19
Mean age	31 years
IQ	60 to 139 (mean 110.7)
Axis I/II disorders	100% autism
Comparator	No comparator
Length of treatment	1 year
Length of follow-up	1 year
Note. *Efficacy data not extractable.	

Table 65: Evidence summary table for supported employment programmes compared with sheltered workshop programmes

Outcome	Autistic behaviours	Quality of life
Study IDs	GARCIAVILLAMISAR2000	GARCIAVILLAMISAR2002
Effect size	MD = −6.07 (−10.09, −2.05)	MD = 5.20 (2.69, 7.71)
Quality of evidence (GRADE)	Very low[1,2]	Very low[1,2]
Number of studies/ participants	K = 1; N = 51	K = 1; N = 51
Forest plot	1.4.6, Appendix 15	1.4.6, Appendix 15
Note. [1]Downgraded for risk of bias as group allocation was not randomised.[2]Downgraded for imprecision as sample size figures varied throughout the paper with no explanation given regarding the changing values. The sample sizes used for analysis were selected from the demographic table but it was not clear that this assumption was valid or correct.		

**Table 66: Evidence summary table for supported employment programme
compared with waitlist control group**

	Executive function
Study ID	GARCIAVILLAMISAR2007
Effect size	MD = −2.75 (−4.41, −1.09)
Quality of evidence (GRADE)	Very low[1,2,3]
Number of studies/ participants	K = 1; N = 44
Forest plot	1.4.6, Appendix 15

Note. [1]Downgraded for risk of bias as group allocation was not randomised. [2]Downgraded for imprecision as the sample size was not reported for each group and this analysis was based on the assumption of equal numbers in each group, which may be invalid. [3]Downgraded for imprecision because the sample size was small.

significantly shorter for the supported employment group compared with the waitlist control group (test for overall effect: Z = 3.26, p = 0.001). However, this study was also methodologically flawed in that the sample sizes for each group were not reported. Analysis was conducted on the assumption of equal sample sizes across the two groups; however this assumption may be invalid. As a result of this, the quality of this evidence is downgraded based on imprecision, in addition to the downgrading based on lack of randomised allocation to groups.

Supported employment compared with treatment as usual
MAWHOOD1999 also found evidence for a significant benefit of a supported employment programme compared with treatment as usual (see Table 67) in terms of the number of participants finding paid employment (test for overall effect: Z = 2.26, p = 0.02). The risk ratio indicates that the participants on the supported employment programme were over two and a half times more likely to find paid employment than the control group. Moreover, narrative results reported in HOWLIN2005 provide support for longevity of treatment effects: at 7 to 8 years' follow-up 68% of those who originally found paid employment remained in a permanent job.

Observational studies of supported employment
HOWLIN2005 compared before-and-after outcomes for 89 people with autism in a supported employment programme. This study also reported long-term follow-up data for MAWHOOD1999, as discussed above. It was not possible to extract efficacy data for this study. However, the authors reported significant change-from-baseline scores for job placements before and after the supported employment programme with 28 more people in work after joining the 'Prospects' programme ($X^2 = 17.62$, p < 0.001).

Table 67: Evidence summary table for supported employment programmes compared with treatment as usual

	Job placements
Study ID	MAWHOOD1999
Effect size	RR = 2.53 (1.13, 5.67)
Quality of evidence (GRADE)	Very low[1]
Number of studies/ participants	K = 1; N = 50
Forest plot	1.4.6, Appendix 15
Note. [1]Downgraded for risk of bias as group allocation was not randomised.	

7.9.4   Clinical evidence summary for supported employment programme

The data from supported employment programmes are consistently positive. However, a number of methodological limitations with the studies suggest that some caution should be exercised when interpreting the results and this is reflected in the very low quality of the data. However, the initial results are promising, and, crucially, follow-up results are suggestive of long-term beneficial effects with significant job retention 7 to 8 years after initiation of the supported employment programme.

7.9.5   Health economic evidence – systematic literature review

The systematic search of the economic literature undertaken for the guideline identified one eligible study on supported employment programmes for adults with autism, which was conducted in the UK (Mawhood & Howlin, 1999). Details on the methods used for the systematic review of the economic literature are described in Chapter 3; details about the study and the results can be found in Appendix 18 and the completed methodology checklist of the study is provided in Appendix 17. The economic evidence profile is presented in Appendix 19, accompanying the respective GRADE clinical evidence profile.

Mawhood and Howlin (1999) conducted an economic analysis alongside an RCT comparing supported employment programmes with treatment as usual (MAWHOOD1999). The study population was adults with high-functioning autism (IQ >70) and the primary outcome measure was the proportion of people employed in each arm at the end of the study. The time horizon of the study was 2 years, although the length of participants' involvement with the programme varied considerably, as individuals continued to register throughout the evaluation period (mean 17 months; range 5 to 24 months). Costs included intervention costs only.

According to the study findings, 63% of the supported employment programme group and 25% of the treatment as usual group were employed at the end of 2 years. In both groups, the average time to find employment was 8 months; the individuals who found employment worked 35 hours per week. The monthly cost of the employment support scheme was calculated at £672 per participant in the first year and £388 in the second year in 1994/95 prices (equivalent to a monthly cost of £1,143 and £635 in the first and second year, respectively, in 2009/10 prices). The cost per hour worked by participants who found employment was £14.64 in the first year and £5.72 in the second year in 1994/95 prices. The costs of finding a job were substantial and individuals' support needs were high at the beginning of employment, which contributed to the high cost in the first year of the programme. However, the largest part of the difference in the cost per participant, as well as in the cost per hour worked by participants who found employment between the first and the second year of the programme, is attributable to the fact that only eight people were registered with the scheme in the first year, while 18 were registered in the second year, resulting also in substantially more hours worked in the second year (14,642) compared with the first year (4,405). In fact, the changes in cost per person (and, subsequently, in cost per hour worked by study participants) between the first and the second year can be attributed to economies of scale. The control group in the study received treatment as usual. However, no cost data were reported for the control group.

Mawhood and Howlin's (1999) study is directly applicable to the guideline. However, it has potentially serious limitations as it did not report the cost of treatment as usual, and therefore it did not provide an incremental analysis between the intervention and the control. The time horizon of 2 years is also too short to fully take into account the benefits of the programme accrued after that period. Nevertheless, the study provides an indication of the costs associated with provision of a supported employment programme in the UK.

7.9.6   Health economic evidence – economic modelling

Introduction – objective of economic modelling
Provision of supported employment programmes in adults with autism is an area with potentially major resource implications. An economic model was therefore developed to assess the cost effectiveness of these programmes for adults with autism. Supported employment programmes are delivered by a range of different providers including health, social care and third sector organisations. The economic analysis considered the individual placement and support approach (IPS), according to guidance published by the Department of Health (Department of Health, 2006b), and used resource use estimates from the perspective of the NHS and personal social services (PSS), as reported in Curtis (2010). The economic analysis draws heavily on MAWHOOD1999, which compared a supported employment programme with treatment as usual in the UK and reported the number of participants who found paid employment in each group. In addition, the model considered follow-up data

(employment rates) for the supported employment group of MAWHOOD1999, which are reported in HOWLIN2005.

Interventions assessed
According to MAWHOOD1999, a supported employment programme was provided by support workers who were responsible for assessing participants (regarding their level of functioning and their past educational and job history) for finding a job and preparing for work, as well as ensuring that participants could cope with the social and occupational demands of employment. They also spent time educating and informing potential and existing employers, and advising work colleagues and supervisors on how to deal with or avoid problems. Treatment as usual is not described in MAWHOOD1999, but it was speculated to consist of day care services, which is also reported as an alternative to supported employment in Curtis (2010).

Model structure
A simple decision-tree followed by a two-state Markov model was constructed using Microsoft Excel XP in order to assess the costs and outcomes associated with provision of supported employment programmes versus treatment as usual in adults with autism actively seeking work.

According to the decision-tree, which was based on data reported in MAWHOOD1999, interventions were provided over a period of 17 months. Over this period, a number of participants in both groups found paid employment; the amount of time spent in employment was 8 months (MAWHOOD1999 reports that participants were registered with the supported employment scheme over a period of 17 months on average; the mean length of time spent in paid work during the study evaluation period was 8.1 months for those participants in the intervention group who found employment and 8.4 months for those participants in the control group who found employment). Subsequently, a Markov model was developed to estimate the number of adults remaining in employment every year, from endpoint of the decision-tree (that is, from the end of provision of the intervention) and up to 8 years, using the 8-year follow-up data reported in HOWLIN2005.

The Markov model consisted of the states of 'employed' and 'unemployed' and was run in yearly cycles. People in the 'employed' state could remain in this state or move to the 'unemployed' state. Similarly, people in the 'unemployed' state could remain in this state or move to the 'employed' state. In both arms of the Markov model, people who were in the 'unemployed' state were assumed to receive treatment as usual consisting of day care services for the duration of time they remained unemployed. It must be noted that people in the 'employed' state were assumed to spend only a proportion of each year (and not the full year) in employment. A schematic diagram of the economic model is presented in Figure 11.

Costs and outcomes considered in the analysis
The economic analysis adopted the perspective of the NHS and PSS, as recommended by NICE (2009e). In the main analysis, costs consisted of intervention costs only. In two secondary analyses, costs consisted of (a) intervention and

**Figure 11: Schematic diagram of the economic model structure constructed
for the assessment of the cost effectiveness of supported employment
programmes versus treatment as usual (day care services)**

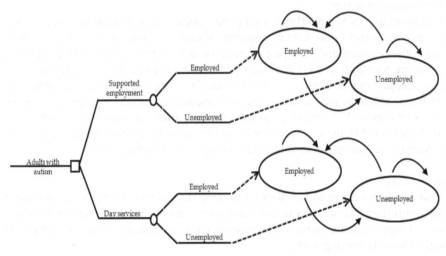

accommodation costs and (b) intervention and other NHS and PSS costs (including
mental health care, primary and secondary care, as well as local authority costs).
The measure of outcome was the quality-adjusted life year (QALY).

Clinical input parameters of the economic model
Data on employment rates following treatment as usual and the relative effect of
supported employment programmes versus treatment as usual at the end of the intervention period were taken from MAWHOOD1999. The annual transition probability
of moving from the 'employed' to the 'unemployed' health state over 8 years from the
end of the intervention period was estimated using data reported in HOWLIN2005.
The study reported that 68% of the participants in the employment support programme
described in MAWHOOD1999 who had found employment during the study period
remained in permanent employment at the 8 years' follow-up. From these data it was
possible to estimate the annual transition probability from employed to unemployed
status, assuming a constant rate of moving to unemployment over the 8 years' follow-
up period. This rate was conservatively applied to both intervention and treatment as
usual groups, although it was speculated that people attending a supported employment programme were more likely to retain their jobs after the end of the intervention
compared with those under treatment as usual. If this were the case, then the economic
analysis has underestimated the long-term relative effect (in terms of remaining in paid
employment) of supported employment programmes versus treatment as usual. The
annual transition probability of moving from the 'unemployed' to the 'employed'
health state over 8 years from the end of intervention period was estimated using data
reported in MAWHOOD1999 for the control group.

The mean time in employment of every person who remained in the 'employed' state of the Markov model each year following completion of intervention was derived from a systematic review of RCTs on IPS in people with severe mental illness (Bond *et al.*, 2008) according to which, among IPS participants who obtained competitive work, the average duration of employment was 47% within every year of employment.

Clinical input parameters of the economic analysis are provided in Table 68.

Utility data and estimation of QALYs

In order to express outcomes in the form of QALYs, the health states of the economic model needed to be linked to appropriate utility scores. Utility scores represent the health-related quality of life (HRQoL) associated with specific health states on a scale from 0 (death) to 1 (perfect health); they are estimated using preference-based measures that capture people's preferences on the HRQoL experienced in the health states under consideration.

The systematic search of the literature identified no studies reporting utility scores for adults with autism. To estimate QALYs for adults with autism being in the two health states of 'employed' and 'unemployed', data reported in the economic analysis that was undertaken to support the NICE public guidance on managing long-term sickness absence and incapacity for work (NICE, 2009f) were used. The economic analysis (Pilgrim *et al.*, 2008) used utility scores for the health states of 'being at work' and 'being on long-term sick leave' estimated based on the findings of a study aiming to predict the HRQoL of people who had been or were on long-term sick leave (Peasgood *et al.*, 2006), which utilised data from the British Household Panel Survey (Taylor *et al.*, 2003). The British Household Panel Survey is a longitudinal annual survey designed to capture information on a nationally representative sample of around 10,000–15,000 of the non-immigrant population of Great Britain that began in 1991. Utility scores were estimated from Short Form Health Survey – 36-items data, using the Short Form Health Survey – six dimensions algorithm (Brazier *et al.*, 2002). In the economic analysis (Pilgrim *et al.*, 2008), the utility scores associated with being at work or being on long-term sick leave were assumed to be the same for all individuals in each state, independent of their health status; in other words, it was assumed that the quality of life of the individual is more greatly affected by being at work or on sick leave than by the illness itself. In addition, the utility scores for people at work and those on sick leave were assumed to capture wage and benefit payments, respectively. Utility scores were reported separately for four age categories (under 35 years; 35 to 45 years; 45 to 55 years; and over 55 years).

The economic analysis undertaken for this guideline used the utility scores reported in Pilgrim and colleagues (2008) for adults aged below 35 years, which is consistent with the average age of participants in MAWHOOD1999 (31 years). The difference in utility between the states of 'being at work' and 'being on sick leave' was smaller in this age group (0.17) compared with the age group of 35 to 45 years (0.21), thus providing a more conservative estimate and potentially underestimating the benefit and the cost effectiveness of a supported employment programme. It must

Table 68: Input parameters utilised in the economic model of supported employment versus standard care for adults with autism

Input parameter	Deterministic value	Probabilistic distribution	Source of data – comments
Clinical data			
Probability of employment – standard care	0.25	Beta distribution α = 5, β = 15	MAWHOOD1999
Risk ratio of employment – supported employment programme versus treatment as usual	2.53	Log-normal distribution 95% CIs: 1.13 to 5.67	MAWHOOD1999; note that the probability of employment under supported employment was not allowed to exceed 0.90 in probabilistic analysis
Probability of employment at 8 years' follow-up	0.68	**Beta distribution** α = 13, β = 6	HOWLIN2005; data for supported employment programmes utilised in both supported employment and treatment as usual
Annual transition probability from 'employed' to 'unemployed'	0.0463	Distribution dependent on above distribution	–
Annual transition probability from 'unemployed' to 'employed'	0.184	Distribution dependent on distribution of 'probability of employment – treatment as usual'	MAWHOOD1999; annual probability estimated using the probability of employment over 17 months for treatment as usual
Proportion of time employed within 'employed' state	0.47	**Beta distribution** α = 158.39, β = 178.61	Bond and colleagues (2008); distribution determined according to method of moments
Utility scores Employed Unemployed	0.83 0.66	**Beta distribution** α = 83, β = 17 α = 66, β = 34	Pilgrim and colleagues (2008); utility scores for general population being in work or on sick leave; distribution parameters based on assumption

Cost data (2010 prices)			
Annual intervention cost Supported employment programme Treatment as usual (day care services)	£2,746 £1,632	**Gamma distribution** $\alpha = 11.11, \beta = 247.14$ $\alpha = 11.11, \beta = 146.88$	Curtis (2010); standard error of intervention cost assumed to be 30% of its mean estimate due to lack of relevant data
SECONDARY ANALYSIS **Annual accommodation cost** Private accommodation Supported accommodation Residential care	£0 £64,486 £67,449	not applicable (N/A) $\alpha = 11.11, \beta = 5,804$ $\alpha = 11.11, \beta = 6,070$	Curtis (2010); standard error of accommodation cost assumed to be 30% of its mean estimate
Percentage of unemployed in different types of accommodation Private accommodation Supported accommodation Residential care	0.79 0.05 0.16	**No distribution assigned**	Knapp and colleagues (2009)
Change in accommodation when finding employment Private accommodation Supported accommodation Residential care	+ 0.010 −0.005 −0.005	**Beta distribution** $\alpha = 0.10, \beta = 9.90$ following above distribution following above distribution	Assumption
SECONDARY ANALYSIS Weekly health and social service cost – unemployed Weekly health and social service cost – employed	£46 £35	**Gamma distribution** $\alpha = 24.72, \beta = 1.87$ $\alpha = 6.15, \beta = 5.70$	Schneider and colleagues (2009)
Discount rate	0.035	N/A	NICE (2009e)

be noted that the utility of the 'unemployed' state is likely to be lower than the utility of 'being on sick leave', and therefore the analysis is likely to have further underestimated the scope for benefit of a supported employment programme. In addition, the utility scores used in the analysis refer to the general population and are not specific to adults with autism. It is possible that adults with autism get greater utility from finding employment compared with the general population, as employment may bring them further psychological and social benefits, including improved self-esteem and greater social integration (SESAMI Research Team and Practice Partnership, 2007). Utility data used in the economic analysis are reported in Table 68.

Cost data
Intervention costs for supported employment programmes and day care services were based on Curtis (2010). The report provides unit costs for IPS for four different grades of staff, two with professional qualifications (for example, psychology, occupational therapy) and two with no particular qualifications, ranging from Band 3 to Band 6, and for different caseloads, ranging from ten to 25. Estimation of unit costs for IPS took into account the following cost components: wages, salary on-costs, superannuation, direct and indirect overheads, capital, team leaders who would supervise no more than ten staff and would be available to provide practical support, and a marketing budget. For this analysis, it was assumed that a supported employment programme was provided by specialists in Band 6 with a caseload of 20 people. The average annual cost per person under these conditions was £2,746.

Curtis (2010) also provides unit costs for the equivalent of IPS in day care. In the economic analysis, day care was conservatively assumed to be provided by unqualified staff in Band 3, also with a caseload of 20 people. Curtis (2010) reported that the number of day care sessions ranged from 34 to 131 annually. The lower number of sessions (34) was selected for the economic analysis, resulting in an annual cost of £1,632.

It should be noted that the economic model utilised a 17-month cost for both interventions for the initial period of provision of the interventions. However, after entering the Markov model, people in the 'unemployed' state were assumed to incur the annual cost of day care services in every model cycle they remained unemployed, and this applied to both arms of the model.

Secondary analysis including accommodation costs
Change in employment status may have important implications for the type of accommodation inhabited by adults with autism. Knapp and colleagues (2009) estimated that 79% of adults with autism without a learning disability live in private accommodation, 5% live in supported accommodation, and 16% live in residential care. If gaining employment shifts a percentage of people living in supported accommodation and residential care to private accommodation, this may lead to substantial savings to PSS. Therefore, a sub-analysis estimated the impact on the cost effectiveness of supported employment programmes following an increase in private accommodation by 1% (that is, reaching 80%) and a reduction in both supported accommodation and residential care by 0.5% (that is, falling at 4.5% and 15.5%, respectively) in those

adults with autism who found employment and remained employed beyond 8 months (that is, those entering the Markov model in the 'employed' state). However, the model conservatively assumed that once people moved out of employment (transitioned from 'employed' state to 'unemployed' state), they returned to their previous type of accommodation, even if they were re-employed at a later stage. The cost of private accommodation to the NHS and PSS is zero. The costs of supported accommodation and residential care comprise accommodation setting costs, as well as the costs of staff employed in such settings or supporting the residents, and were taken from Curtis (2010).

Secondary analysis including NHS and PSS costs
The impact of supported employment on health and social care service usage by adults with autism is not known. Schneider and colleagues (2009) estimated the changes in costs to mental health, primary and secondary care, local authority and voluntary day care services incurred by people with mental health problems (mainly schizophrenia, bipolar disorder, anxiety disorders or depression) associated with gaining employment following registration with supported employment programmes. The study reported baseline and 12 months' follow-up data for people remaining unemployed throughout the study (n = 77), people who found employment during the 12 months between baseline and follow-up (n = 32), and people who were already in employment at baseline and remained in employment at follow-up (n = 32). Cost data on people who found employment between baseline and follow-up were utilised in the economic analysis; cost data at baseline were used for the state of 'unemployed' and cost data at follow-up were used for the state of 'employed' in both the decision-tree and the Markov part of the model. Service costs included mental health services (contacts with psychiatrist, psychologist, community psychiatric nurse, attendance at a daycentre, counselling or therapeutic group work, and inpatient mental healthcare), primary care (contacts with GP, district nurse, community physiotherapist, dentist or optician), local authority services (day centres run by social services, home care and social work inputs), other secondary NHS care (hospital outpatient appointments and inpatient care for needs other than mental health) and a negligible amount of voluntary day care run by not-for-profit agencies that are independent of the public sector (about 0.3 to 0.5% of the total cost). This secondary analysis did not consider potential changes in accommodation type and respective changes in costs, because it already included local authority service costs and there was the risk of double counting services.

All costs were expressed in 2010 prices, uplifted, where necessary, using the Hospital and Community Health Services Pay and Prices Index (Curtis, 2010). Discounting of costs and outcomes was undertaken at an annual rate of 3.5%, as recommended by NICE (NICE, 2009e).

Data analysis and presentation of the results
In order to take into account the uncertainty characterising the model input parameters, a probabilistic analysis was undertaken, in which input parameters were assigned probability distributions, rather than being expressed as point estimates

(Briggs *et al.*, 2006). Subsequently, 1000 iterations were performed, each drawing random values out of the distributions fitted onto the model input parameters. Mean costs and QALYs for each intervention were then calculated by averaging across 1000 iterations. The incremental cost-effectiveness ratio (ICER) was then estimated for the main analysis and the two secondary analyses, expressing the additional cost per extra QALY gained associated with provision of supported employment instead of standard care.

The probability of employment for treatment as usual and the probability of employment at 8 years were given a beta distribution. Beta distributions were also assigned to utility values, the proportion of time employed within the 'employed' state, and the percentage increase in private accommodation when finding employment. The risk ratio of supported employment programmes versus treatment as usual was assigned a log-normal distribution. Costs were assigned a gamma distribution. The estimation of distribution ranges was based on available data in the published sources of evidence and further assumptions, where relevant data were not available. Table 68 provides details on the types of distributions assigned to each input parameter and the methods employed to define their range.

Results of probabilistic analysis in main and secondary analyses are also presented in the form of cost-effectiveness acceptability curves (CEACs), which demonstrate, in each of the analyses undertaken (main and two secondary analyses) the probability of supported employment programmes being cost effective relative to treatment as usual at different levels of willingness-to-pay per QALY, that is, at different cost-effectiveness thresholds the decision-maker may set (Fenwick *et al.*, 2001).

One-way sensitivity analyses (run with the point estimates rather than the distributions of the input parameters) explored the impact of the uncertainty characterising the model input parameters on the main analysis: the intervention cost for supported employment programmes and treatment as usual was changed by 50 to investigate whether the conclusions of the analysis would change. In addition, a threshold analysis explored the minimum relative effect of the supported employment programme that is required in order for the intervention to be cost effective using the NICE cost-effectiveness threshold.

Results

Main analysis
The results of the main analysis are presented in Table 69. Supported employment programmes are associated with a higher cost but also produce a higher number of QALYs compared with treatment as usual. The ICER of supported employment programmes versus treatment as usual is £1,467 per QALY gained, which is well below the NICE cost-effectiveness threshold of £20,000 to £30,000/QALY (NICE, 2009e), indicating that supported employment programmes may be a cost-effective option when compared with treatment as usual.

The cost effectiveness plane showing the incremental costs and QALYs of supported employment programmes versus treatment as usual resulting from 1000 iterations of the model are shown in Figure 12. Figure 13 provides the CEAC

Table 69: Results of main analysis – mean total costs and QALYs of each intervention assessed per adult with autism seeking employment

Intervention	Supported employment programmes	Treatment as usual	Difference
Total cost	£7,329	£7,173	£157
Total QALYs	5.43	5.32	0.11
ICER		£1,467/QALY	

Figure 12: Cost effectiveness plane showing incremental costs and QALYs of supported employment programmes versus treatment as usual per person with autism. Results of the main analysis, based on 1000 iterations.

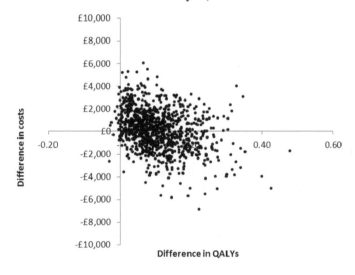

showing the probability of supported employment programmes being cost effective relative to treatment as usual for different levels of willingness-to-pay per extra QALY gained. According to the CEAC, the probability of supported employment programmes being cost effective at the NICE lower cost-effectiveness threshold of £20,000/QALY is 77.5%, while at the NICE upper cost-effectiveness threshold of £30,000/QALY it is 84.7%.

Secondary analysis including accommodation costs

The results of the secondary analysis including accommodation costs are presented in Table 70. A supported employment programme is more effective and less costly overall than treatment as usual and therefore is the dominant option.

Figure 13: CEAC of supported employment programmes versus treatment as usual. Results of the main analysis. X axis shows the level of willingness-to-pay per extra QALY gained and Y axis shows the probability of supported employment programmes being cost effective at different levels of willingness-to-pay.

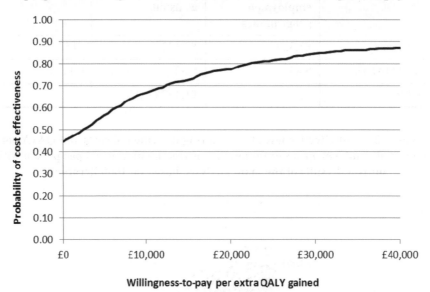

Willingness-to-pay per extra QALY gained

Table 70: Results of secondary analysis including accommodation costs – mean total costs and QALYs of each intervention assessed per adult with autism seeking employment

Intervention	Supported employment	Treatment as usual	Difference
Total cost	£102,605	£103,723	–£1,117
Total QALYs	5.43	5.32	0.11
ICER	Supported employment dominant		

The cost effectiveness plane is shown in Figure 14. Figure 15 provides the CEAC for this analysis. The probability of supported employment programmes being cost effective at the NICE lower cost-effectiveness threshold is 80.4%, while at the NICE upper cost-effectiveness threshold it is 84.5%.

Secondary analysis including NHS and PSS costs
The results of the secondary analysis including NHS and PSS costs are presented in Table 71. A supported employment programme is the dominant option in this secondary analysis as well.

Figure 14: Cost effectiveness plane showing incremental costs and QALYs of supported employment programmes versus treatment as usual per person with autism. Results of secondary analysis including accommodation costs, based on 1000 iterations.

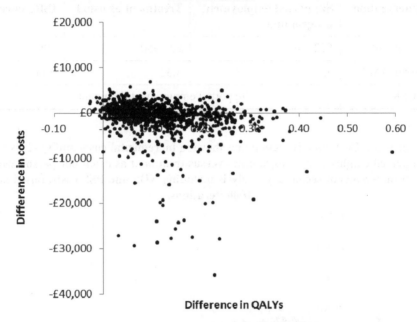

Figure 15: CEAC of supported employment programmes versus treatment as usual. Results of secondary analysis including accommodation costs.

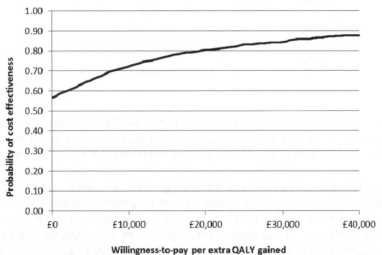

Table 71: Results of secondary analysis including NHS and PSS costs – mean total costs and QALYs of each intervention assessed per adult with autism seeking employment

Intervention	Supported employment programme	Treatment as usual	Difference
Total cost	£22,339	£22,950	–£611
Total QALYs	5.43	5.32	0.11
ICER	Supported employment dominant		

Figure 16: Cost effectiveness plane showing incremental costs and QALYs of supported employment programmes versus treatment as usual per person with autism. Results of secondary analysis including NHS and PSS costs, based on 1000 iterations.

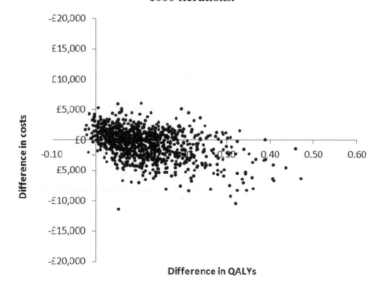

The cost-effectiveness plane is shown in Figure 16. Figure 17 presents the CEAC and shows that the probability of supported employment programmes being cost effective at £20,000/QALY is 80.8%, while at £30,000/QALY the probability rises to 85.3%.

One-way sensitivity analysis on the findings of the main analysis revealed that if the intervention cost of supported employment programmes changed by 50%, the ICER ranged from £15,190/QALY to a supported employment programme being dominant. If the cost of treatment as usual changed by 50%, then the ICER ranged from a supported employment programme being dominant to £15,452 per QALY

Figure 17: CEAC of supported employment programmes versus treatment as usual. Results of secondary analysis including NHS and PSS costs.

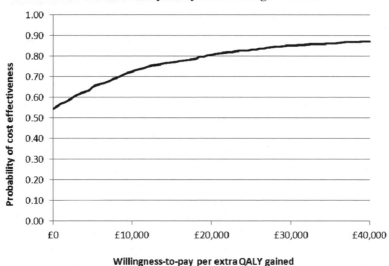

gained. Threshold analysis revealed that the minimum risk ratio of supported employment programmes versus treatment as usual required in order for the intervention to be considered cost effective according to NICE criteria was 1.45 (using the upper £30,000/QALY threshold) or 1.59 (using the lower £20,000/QALY threshold).

Discussion of findings – limitations of the analysis
The results of the economic analysis indicate that a supported employment programme is likely to be a cost-effective intervention compared with standard care. Supported employment programmes resulted in a higher number of QALYs compared with treatment as usual comprising day care services. In the main analysis, which considered intervention costs only, the ICER of supported employment programmes versus treatment as usual was £1,467/QALY. In a secondary analysis that assumed a small increase (1%) in adults with autism living in private accommodation after finding more permanent employment, supported employment was the dominant option, as it resulted in a higher number of QALYs and lower overall costs compared with standard care. Similarly, in a secondary analysis that considered a reduction in NHS and PSS costs following initiation of employment, supported employment programmes dominated treatment as usual. The probability of supported employment programmes being cost effective did not differ much across these three analyses: at the NICE lower cost-effectiveness threshold of £20,000/QALY it ranged from 77.5 to 80.8%, while at the NICE upper cost-effectiveness threshold it increased in a range from 84.5 to 85.3%.

In terms of clinical data, the economic analysis was based exclusively on one study comparing a supported employment programme with treatment as usual

(MAWHOOD1999, followed up by HOWLIN2005). The original study had a small sample size (N = 50), however, the risk ratio of a supported employment programme versus treatment as usual was significant and the follow-up data indicated the longevity of treatment effects. Another limitation of the study was that MAWHOOD1999 did not describe treatment as usual. (Based on current practice, the GDG estimated that it consisted of day care services.)

In order to develop the economic model the GDG needed to make a judgment as to whether the economic analysis could be deemed relevant only to adults with autism who do not have learning disability (IQ > 70) or to adults with autism across the range of intellectual ability. In MAWHOOD 1999 an IQ of 70 or above on either the performance or the verbal scale of the Wechsler Adult Intelligence Scale (WAIS) was a criterion for entry to the study, indicating that almost all of the population did not have a learning disability; it should be noted, however, that the range of IQ scores reported in the study indicated that a small percentage had an IQ below 70. The GDG also reviewed a study by Schaller and Yang (2005) of a database of over 800 people with autism in which 23.5% had a diagnosis of a mild or moderate learning disability (that is, an IQ below 70), which reported a significant association between an IPS model and successful retention in employment. The GDG therefore took the view that the economic model was relevant to, and should include in its study population, adults with autism across the full range of intellectual ability.

Three analyses were undertaken: the main analysis included intervention costs only, as no other cost data that could be linked to the employment status of adults with autism were identified in the literature. A secondary analysis assumed that a small proportion of adults with autism living in supported accommodation or residential care would move to private accommodation after finding permanent employment. This secondary analysis was undertaken to explore the potential impact of employment status on costs associated with accommodation, given that supported accommodation and residential care incur substantial costs to PSS; consequently employed individuals moving to private accommodation were expected to reduce significantly the total cost borne by PSS. The findings of the secondary analysis confirmed this hypothesis, as a minimal shift to private accommodation (1%) made supported employment programmes least costly, overall, than treatment as usual. If financial independence gained from finding employment leads to a more substantial shift to private accommodation, this would lead to greater savings for social services.

Another secondary analysis considered extra NHS and PSS costs associated with employment status. Cost data were taken from Schneider and colleagues (2009), who measured costs incurred by people with mental health problems including schizophrenia, bipolar disorder, anxiety disorders or depression attending employment support programmes. The study reported that study participants entering work showed a substantial decrease in mental health services costs which outweighed a slight increase in other secondary care costs, making an overall reduction in health and social care costs statistically significant. The authors' estimate was that the reduction in mental health service use was possibly an effect of getting a job, although they did not rule out the possibility that a third variable, such as cognitive impairment, might be driving both employment outcomes and reduction in service use. Following this finding, the authors concluded that mental health providers may save money if their service users obtain employment. However, it may be that adults with autism have a different pattern of health and social care service usage compared with adults with other mental health problems, and this is why cost data reported by Schneider and colleagues (2009) were considered in a secondary analysis and not in the main analysis. Moreover, the cost data reported in Schneider and colleagues were based on a small study sample (n = 32).

Where data were not available, or further estimates needed to be made, the economic analysis adopted conservative estimates that were likely to underestimate the cost effectiveness of supported employment programmes. The intervention cost of supported employment programme was estimated to be high because it was assumed that the intervention was provided by specialists in Band 6; in contrast it was assumed that day care services were provided by unqualified staff in Band 3 and that the minimum number of sessions per year, from the range reported in the literature, was attended by the treatment as usual group. The transition probability to unemployment was assumed to be the same for supported employment programmes and treatment as usual, although it was estimated that participants in a supported employment programme were more likely to retain their jobs after the end of the intervention compared with those having treatment as usual.

Utility scores, which are required for the estimation of QALYs, were not available for adults with autism. Instead, utility scores obtained from the general population for the states 'being at work' and 'being on sick leave' were used in the analysis, based on data reported in Pilgrim and colleagues (2008). It is acknowledged that these scores are not directly relevant to adults with autism in employed or unemployed status. Moreover, the utility of the 'unemployed' state is potentially lower than the utility of 'being on sick leave'. Nevertheless, the utility scores used in the economic analysis are likely to capture, if somewhat conservatively, the HRQoL of adults with autism with regard to their employment status. It is possible that adults with autism get greater utility from finding employment compared with the general population, as employment may bring further psychological and social benefits, including improved self-esteem and greater social integration (SESAMI Research Team and Practice Partnership, 2007).

The analysis adopted the NHS and PSS perspective. Other costs such as lost productivity or wages earned and the tax gains to the exchequer were not taken into account because they were beyond the perspective of the analysis. However, some of these cost categories were partially and indirectly taken into account; Pilgrim and colleagues (2008) considered that the utility scores for people at work and those on sick leave, which were used in this economic analysis, did capture wage and benefit payments, respectively, although these might be valued differently from wages and benefit payments received by adults with autism with or without employment.

In addition to the effects considered in the analysis, supported employment programmes have further qualitative effects on adults with autism who find employment, which are difficult to quantify, such as satisfaction resulting from having a better job, increased social networks due to employment, and improvement in self-esteem. In addition, such programmes have a positive effect on the HRQoL of families, partners and carers of adults with autism, which was not possible to capture in the economic analysis.

Overall, although based on limited evidence, the findings of the economic analysis indicate that a supported employment programme is likely to be a cost-effective intervention for adults with autism because it can increase the rate of employment in this population group, improve the person's wellbeing, and potentially reduce the economic burden to health and social services and the wider society.

7.9.7 From evidence to recommendations

The effect sizes for supported employment programmes are large and the data are consistently positive for the effects of these programmes on increasing the number of job placements. Moreover, positive effects for supported employment programmes appear to have an impact beyond employment, with additional improvements observed in autistic behaviours, quality of life and executive function. The economic model that was developed for this guideline suggested that a supported employment programme is likely to be a cost-effective intervention for adults with autism. On this basis the GDG judged that supported employment programmes should be recommended for adults with autism and where they are delivered should be individualised but include common core elements of prior and on-the-job training, advocacy and long-term support to ensure job retention.

7.9.8 Recommendations

Psychosocial interventions focused on life skills

7.9.8.1   For adults with autism without a learning disability or with a mild learning disability, who are having difficulty obtaining or maintaining employment, consider an individual supported employment programme.

7.9.8.2   An individual supported employment programme should typically include:
- help with writing CVs and job applications and preparing for interviews
- training for the identified work role and work-related behaviours
- carefully matching the person with autism with the job
- advice to employers about making reasonable adjustments to the workplace
- continuing support for the person after they start work
- support for the employer before and after the person starts work, including autism awareness training.

7.10 SUPPORT FOR FAMILIES, PARTNERS AND CARERS

7.10.1 Introduction

Caring for an adolescent or adult with autism can have great impact upon the psychological wellbeing of the carer (Seltzer *et al.*, 2001). An increased prevalence of stress has been found among parents of children with autism compared with parents of typically developing children (Dyson, 1993; Wolf *et al.*, 1989) or parents of children with other developmental disorders such as Down's syndrome (Boyd, 2002; Sanders & Morgan, 1997). Parents of children with autism also report more symptoms of anxiety and marital dissatisfaction than parents of children with other types of disability (Dunn *et al.*, 2001; Holroyd & McArthur, 1976; Konstantareas & Homatidis, 1989). However, although there has been an abundance of research examining the impact of caring for a young child with autism, very few studies have examined the impact of caring for an adolescent or adult with autism (Lounds *et al.*, 2007). Hare and colleagues (2004) interviewed the families of adults with autism who either lived at home or maintained close contact with their families and found that most of their sample received very little family or informal support, although levels of formal support, such as respite and day care, were quite high. In addition, this study highlighted the need for greater support of parents of older people with autism, for instance, many parents reported attending parent support groups when their child was younger but had not done so since their child had reached adulthood. Interventions aimed at supporting families, partners and carers reviewed here include direct support for families, partners and carers such as support services (including support groups) and information at the point of diagnosis and throughout the care pathway, as well as interventions that facilitate the family in supporting the delivery of interventions.

7.10.2   Studies considered[59]

No RCTs were found that provided relevant clinical evidence for support for families, partners and carers of adults with autism and met the eligibility criteria for this review. However, one quasi-experimental parallel group controlled study (N = 20) was found, which included parents of adolescents with autism with a mean age of 14 and 15 years (for control group and experimental groups respectively) and based on the expert judgement of the GDG and the extrapolation rules, this study (ERGUNERTEK-INALP2004 [Ergüner-Tekinalp & Akkök, 2004]) was included. In addition, eight studies were excluded predominantly because the mean age of the children with autism was under 15 years. Based on the judgement of the GDG and the extrapolation rules, an additional search was performed for support for families, partners and carers of adults with a learning disability. One RCT was found and included (BOTSFORD2004 [Botsford & Rule, 2004]). Both studies were published in peer-reviewed journals in 2004. In addition, 33 studies were excluded, predominantly because the mean age of the children with a learning disability was under 15 years old. Further information about included and excluded studies can be found in Appendix 14e.

The single included quasi-experimental parallel group controlled study compared a coping skills training programme with treatment as usual (see Table 72).

---

[59]Here and elsewhere in the guideline, each study considered for review is referred to by a study ID in capital letters (primary author and date of study publication, except where a study is in press or only submitted for publication, then a date is not used).

Table 72: Study information table for quasi-experimental studies of supportive interventions for mothers of adolescents with autism

	Coping skills training programme for mothers of adolescents with autism
No. trials (total participants)	1 (20)
Study ID	ERGUNERTEKINALP2004*
N/% female	20/100
Mean age	Mother: 39 and 42 years Offspring: 14 and 15 years
IQ	Not reported
Axis I/II disorders	Mothers of offspring with autism
Comparator	Treatment as usual
Length of treatment	4 weeks
Length of follow-up	4 weeks
Note. *Efficacy data not extractable.	

The single included RCT of support for families of adults with a learning disability compared a psychoeducational group permanency planning intervention with treatment as usual (see Table 73).

7.10.3   Clinical evidence for support for families, partners and carers

Coping skills training programme compared with treatment as usual
There were no RCTs for interventions to support families, partners and carers of adults with autism. The single included quasi-experimental study (ERGUNERTEK-INALP2004) in mothers of adolescents with autism compared a coping skills training programme with treatment as usual. The programme consisted of eight group sessions where techniques such as instruction, discussion, sharing and application of techniques were applied in order to provide support for understanding stress and coping, teaching general coping strategies, problem solving, relaxation training, positive thinking and social support. Efficacy data could not be extracted for this study as mean and standard deviation values were not reported. However, the authors reported statistically significant endpoint differences between experimental and control groups in social support as measured by the Coping Strategy Indicator (Mann Whitney U = 16.00, p = 0.01) and hopelessness as measured by the Beck Hopelessness Scale (Mann Whitney U = 7.50, p = 0.001). The authors concluded that participating in this group intervention helped

Table 73: Study information table for RCTs of supportive interventions for mothers of adults with a learning disability

	Psychoeducational group permanency planning
No. trials (total participants)	1 (27)
Study ID	BOTSFORD2004
N/% female	27/100
Mean age	Mother: 64 years Offspring: 34 years
IQ	Not reported
Axis I/II disorders	Mothers of offspring with a learning disability
Comparator	Treatment as usual
Length of treatment	6 weeks
Length of follow-up	6 weeks

mothers of adolescents with autism to feel socially supported and more positive about themselves and their lives. However, this study is of a very low quality due to the non-randomised group allocation, the fact that efficacy data could not be extracted, the short duration of the follow-up and the small sample size.

Psychoeducational group permanency planning programme compared with treatment as usual

Based on the extrapolation rules an additional search was conducted for interventions to support families, partners and carers of adults with a learning disability. This search resulted in one included RCT (BOTSFORD2004), which compared a psychoeducational permanency planning group intervention with treatment as usual (see Table 74).

This group intervention provided opportunities for parents to express concerns about the future of their offspring and aimed to increase participants' awareness and knowledge about options and resources, to identify obstacles to planning, to strengthen relationships with professionals, and to teach problem solving on specific planning issues and concerns. Group sessions included speakers on residential, financial and legal resources followed by group discussion, and also discussion and interaction between parents. The primary outcome of this study was mothers' awareness and knowledge of planning as measured by clustered variables that emerged from coded interviews with mothers using standardised (including Heller & Factor's [1991] Community Resources Scale) and original scales. BOTSFORD2004 found evidence for statistically significant treatment effects from their multivariate analysis of covariance on the outcome clusters of knowledge and awareness about planning

Table 74: Evidence summary table for psychoeducational group permanency planning intervention compared with treatment as usual for mothers of adults with a learning disability

	Knowledge and awareness about	Competence and confidence to plan	Appraisals of the planning process	Intermediate planning behaviours	Residential and legal planning
Study ID	BOTSFORD2004	BOTSFORD2004	BOTSFORD2004	BOTSFORD2004	BOTSFORD2004
Effect size	SMD = −0.99 (−1.79, −0.19)	SMD = −1.36 (−2.20, −0.53)	SMD = −0.61 (−1.39, 0.16)	SMD = −0.49 (−1.25, 0.28)	SMD = −1.02 (−1.82, −0.21)
Quality of evidence (GRADE)	Very low [1,2,3]	Very low [1,2,3]	Very low [1,2,3]	Very low [1,2,3]	Very low [1,2,3]
Number of studies/ participants	K = 1; N = 27	K = 1; N = 27	K = 1; N = 27	K = 1; N = 27	K = 1; N = 27
Forest plot	1.4.7, Appendix 15	1.4.7, Appendix 15	1.4.7, Appendix 15	1.4.7, Appendix 15	1.4.7, Appendix 15

Note. [1]Downgraded for risk of bias due to: non-blind allocation, administration and assessment; unclear randomisation methods; unclear whether the control group received the same care apart from the intervention; the relatively short duration of follow-up; and concerns regarding the reliability and validity of outcome measures. [2]Downgraded for indirectness as extrapolating from adults with a learning disability. [3]Downgraded for imprecision because the sample size was small and the group N is not clear (assumed N = 13 in the experimental group and N = 14 in the control group but it is not clear that this assumption is correct).

(test for overall effect: $Z = 2.43$, $p = 0.02$), competence and confidence to plan (test for overall effect: $Z = 3.19$, $p = 0.001$) and residential and legal planning (test for overall effect: $Z = 2.48$, $p = 0.01$). No significant treatment effects were observed for the outcome variables of appraisals of the planning process or intermediate planning behaviours (tests for overall effect: $Z = 1.55$, $p = 0.12$; and $Z = 1.25$, $p = 0.21$ respectively). This study was of very low quality due to downgrading on the basis of risk of bias (because of non-blind allocation, administration and assessment; unclear randomisation methods; relatively short duration of follow-up; and concerns regarding the reliability and validity of outcome measures), for indirectness (extrapolating from adults with a learning disability), and for imprecision (due to small sample size and the fact that the numbers of participants in each group were not clear).

7.10.4   Clinical evidence summary for support for families, partners and carers

There is limited evidence that for both mothers of adolescents with autism and mothers of adults with a learning disability, group interventions that incorporate discussion, teaching and social support can be beneficial in terms of increasing mothers' positive feelings about themselves and their lives and in terms of increasing awareness and knowledge about permanency planning. However, there is only a single study for each population and all the evidence is of a very low quality.

7.10.5   Health economic evidence for support for families, partners and carers

No studies assessing the cost effectiveness of support for families, partners and carers of adults or adolescents with autism were identified by the systematic search of the economic literature undertaken for this guideline. Details on the methods used for the systematic search of the economic literature are described in Chapter 3.

7.10.6   From evidence to recommendations

There was limited evidence for the efficacy of group-based interventions in the support of families, partners and carers of adolescents or adults with autism or a learning disability. Evidence from a single quasi-experimental study of a group-based coping skills training programme suggested beneficial treatment effects on maternal wellbeing for mothers of adolescents with autism. The single RCT reviewed for parents of adults with a learning disability provided limited evidence for beneficial effects of a psychoeducational group-based programme in raising awareness and increasing knowledge about permanency planning issues. On this basis the GDG concluded that for families, partners and carers of adults with autism health and social care professionals should consider offering information on, and help in accessing, support groups and should be offered an assessment of their own needs including the need for support, advice on accessing this support, and needs for future care planning.

In developing these recommendations the GDG drew on their expert knowledge and on the reviews conducted in Chapter 4 on the experience of families, partners and carers. The GDG took the view that it was important that all the interventions should provide the psychoeducational components, and any associated information, in an accessible format, for instance, in both written and verbal form. Finally, the GDG, based on their expert opinion and knowledge of services, recognised the additional support needs of adults with autism who become parents and for parents of adults with autism who do not have autism themselves but may be supporting the delivery of interventions to their sons and daughters and who will need to be supported, advised and trained in doing so.

7.10.7   Recommendations

7.10.7.1   Offer families, partners and carers of adults with autism an assessment of their own needs including:
- personal, social and emotional support
- support in their caring role, including respite care and emergency plans
- advice on and support in obtaining practical support
- planning of future care for the person with autism.

7.10.7.2   When the needs of families, partners and carers have been identified, provide information about, and facilitate contact with, a range of support groups including those specifically designed to address the needs of families, partners and carers of people with autism.

7.10.7.3   Offer information, advice, training and support to families, partners and carers if they:
- need help with the personal, social or emotional care of the family member, partner or friend, **or**
- are involved in supporting the delivery of an intervention for their family member, partner or friend (in collaboration with professionals).

8   BIOMEDICAL INTERVENTIONS

8.1   INTRODUCTION

Psychosocial interventions remain the predominant treatment approach for adults with autism. However, increasing interest is being directed towards pharmacological interventions as single agents and in combination with psychosocial interventions (Broadstock *et al.*, 2007). These interventions may be aimed at the core symptoms of autism (difficulties in social interaction and communication and repetitive behaviour), but more usually drugs are used to target coexisting behavioural problems including aggression, irritability, hyperactivity and self-injury. Autism is a risk factor for challenging behaviour (Murphy *et al.*, 2005) and children with autism tend not to 'grow out' of behavioural problems (Matson & Shoemaker, 2009). In fact, challenging behaviour becomes an issue of even greater significance in adults with autism, particularly those with a learning disability because of their physical size and the longer history of these problems (Matson *et al.*, 2011). In addition to the potential to manage behaviour and reduce harm, it has been suggested that pharmacological interventions may also improve response rates to psychological interventions aimed at core symptoms of autism (Findling, 2005; Malone *et al.*, 2005; McDougle *et al.*, 2003), and may assist people with autism to live outside institutional settings (Posey & McDougle, 2001).

Psychotropic medication such as antipsychotics, anticonvulsants and drugs affecting cognition (largely cognitive enhancers) have been used in people with autism as have other biomedical interventions including hormones (for example, oxytocin), vitamins and supplements, and different diets. Drugs aimed at coexisting conditions in autism have also been investigated, such as stimulants for coexisting hyperactivity disorder/ADHD, antidepressants for depression, and hormones (for example, melatonin) for insomnia.

Esbensen and colleagues (2009) examined medication use in 286 adolescents and adults with autism over a 4.5-year period and found evidence for increasing medication prevalence over time, both in terms of the number of psychotropic and non-psychotropic medications, and the proportion of individuals taking these medications. At the start of the study 77% of participants aged over 20 years were taking medication, and of those, 37% were taking an antidepressant, 26% an antipsychotic and 29% an anticonvulsant. These figures increased over the study period with 88% taking medication, 44% an antidepressant, 38% an antipsychotic and 31% an anticonvulsant 4.5 years later. However, despite the widespread use of medication in people with autism, very little is known about the efficacy and safety of these drugs in this population because there have been few placebo-controlled trials, particularly in adults.

The majority of the research studies investigating pharmacological interventions in autism have focused on children and young people. However, developmental differences in pharmacological response and symptomology may mean that findings from studies with children are not directly transferable to an adult population and vice versa (Broadstock *et al.*, 2007). For example, coexisting psychiatric disorders, including depression and behavioural problems, have been found to increase in adolescence and adulthood (Korkmaz, 2000; Larsen & Mouridsen, 1997; Rumsey *et al.*, 1985).

The atypical antipsychotics risperidone and aripiprazole are the only medications that have US Food and Drug Administration (FDA) approval for the treatment of behavioural problems associated with autism, specifically irritability. However, these drugs are indicated for use in children, not adults. No drug has autism as a licensing indication in the UK. This means that recommendations for specific pharmacological interventions would be for off-licence indications.

8.1.1   Clinical review protocol (biomedical interventions)

The review protocol, including the review questions, information about the databases searched, and the eligibility criteria used for this section of the guideline, can be found in Table 75 (further information about the search strategy can be found in Appendix 9).

Table 75: Clinical review protocol for the review of biomedical interventions

Component	Description
Review question	For adults with autism, what is the effectiveness of biomedical interventions (for example, dietary interventions, pharmacotherapy and physical-environmental adaptations)? (RQ – C4)
Subquestion	For adults with autism, is the effectiveness of interventions moderated by: • the nature and severity of the condition • the presence of coexisting conditions • age • the presence of sensory sensitivities (including pain thresholds) • IQ • language level? (RQ – C5) For adults with autism, what amendments, if any, need to be made to the current recommendations for psychosocial and pharmacological treatment (including the nature of drug interactions and side effects) for coexisting common mental health disorders? (RQ – C6)

Continued

Table 75: *(Continued)*

Component	Description
Objectives	To evaluate the clinical effectiveness of biomedical interventions for autism.
Criteria for considering studies for the review	
• *Population*	Adults and young people aged 18 years and older with suspected autism across the range of diagnostic groups (including atypical autism, Asperger's syndrome and pervasive developmental disorder). Consideration should be given to the specific needs of: • people with coexisting conditions • women • older people • people from black and minority ethnic groups • transgender people. Excluded groups include: • children (under 18 years). However, the GDG made a consensus-based decision to extrapolate from literature involving children and young people (under 18 years) for interventions where there was not sufficient evidence from an adult population and where the mechanisms of biomedical interventions were judged by the GDG to be equivalent in children/young people and adults. For interventions concerned with the management of behaviour, and where data from adult autism populations were not sufficient, the GDG decided that extrapolating from a learning disabilities population was valid.
• *Intervention(s)*	• Pharmacotherapy (for example, antipsychotics, antidepressants, anticonvulsants). • Vitamins and dietary supplements (for example, omega-3 fatty acid supplements, vitamin B12, vitamin A). • Hormones (for example, oxytocin, secretin, melatonin).
• *Comparison*	Placebo-controlled, other active interventions
• *Critical outcomes*	Outcomes involving core features of autism (social-interaction and communication difficulties, repetitive behaviour); overall autistic behaviour; symptom severity/improvement; management of challenging behaviour; outcomes involving treatment of coexisting conditions; side effects.

Continued

Table 75: *(Continued)*

Component	Description
• *Study design*	• RCTs The GDG agreed by consensus that where there were no RCTs found in the evidence search, or the results from the RCTs were inconclusive, that the following studies would be included in the review of evidence: • observational • quasi-experimental • case series.
• *Include unpublished data?*	Yes, but only where: • the evidence was accompanied by a trial report containing sufficient detail to properly assess the quality of the data • the evidence was submitted with the understanding that data from the study and a summary of the study's characteristics would be published in this guideline.
• *Restriction by date?*	No
• *Minimum sample size*	• RCT/observational/quasi-experimental studies: N = 10 per arm (ITT). • Case series studies: N = 10 in total. Exclude studies with more than 50% attrition from either arm of the trial (unless adequate statistical methodology has been applied to account for missing data).
• *Study setting*	• Primary, secondary, tertiary and other health and social care settings (including prisons and forensic services). • Others in which NHS services are funded or provided, or NHS professionals are working in multi-agency teams.
Electronic databases	AEI, AMED, ASSIA, BEI, CDSR, CENTRAL, CINAHL, DARE, Embase, ERIC, HMIC, MEDLINE, PsycINFO, Sociological Abstracts, SSA
Date searched	Systematic reviews: 1995 up to 09/09/2011. RCTs, quasi-experimental studies, observational studies, case series: inception of database up to 09/09/2011.
Searching other resources	Hand reference searching of retrieved literature

Continued

Table 75: *(Continued)*

Component	Description

The review strategy	• The initial aim is to conduct a meta-analysis evaluating the clinical effectiveness of the interventions. However, in the absence of adequate data, the literature will be presented via a narrative synthesis of the available evidence.
	• Narratively review literature that takes into consideration any amendments due to common mental health disorders.
	• Consider subgroup meta-analyses that take into account the effectiveness of interventions as moderated by:
	  – the nature and severity of the condition
	  – the presence of coexisting conditions
	  – age
	  – the presence of sensory sensitivities (including pain thresholds)
	  – IQ
	  – language level.

8.1.2 Outcomes

A large number of outcomes were reported by the biomedical studies. Those that reported sufficient data to be extractable and were not excluded (see Appendix 14f) are in Table 76.

Table 76: Outcomes extracted from biomedical studies

Category	Sub-category	Scale
Core symptoms of autism	Social-communication difficulties	• Clinical Global Impression (CGI) – Improvement Language (CGI-I Language) (clinician-rated) (Chez *et al.*, 2007) • DSM-IV clinical evaluation (clinician-rated) (Mousain-Bosc *et al.*, 2006)

Continued

Table 76: (*Continued*)

Category	Sub-category	Scale
		• Language Development Survey (Rescorla, 1989) (caregiver report) • Preschool Language Scale-3 (PLS-3) (clinician-rated) (Zimmerman *et al.*, 1992)
	Social-interaction difficulties	• DSM-IV clinical evaluation (clinician-rated) (Mousain-Bosc *et al.*, 2006) • Joint Attention Measure from the EScs (Early Social Communication Scales) (JAMES) (Mundy *et al.*, 2003) (clinician-rated) • Reading the Mind in the Eyes Test (Baron-Cohen *et al.*, 2001b)
	Repetitive behaviour	• Children's Y-BOCS-PDD (clinician-rated) (Scahill *et al.*, 2006) • DSM-IV clinical evaluation (clinician-rated) (Mousain-Bosc *et al.*, 2006) • YBOCS (clinician-rated) (Goodman *et al.*, 1989a and 1989b)
Autistic behaviours		• ABC (caregiver report) (Krug *et al.*, 1993) • CARS (clinician-rated) (Schopler *et al.*, 1980) • Children's Psychiatric Rating Scale (CPRS) Autism Factor (clinician-rated) (Fish, 1985) • Diagnose of Psykotisk Adferd hos Børn (Diagnosis of Psychotic Behaviour in Children; Haracopos & Kelstrup, 1975) (clinician-rated)

Continued

Table 76: (***Continued***)

Category	Sub-category	Scale
		• Ritvo-Freeman Real-life Rating Scale (clinician-rated) (Freeman *et al.*, 1986)
Symptom severity/ improvement		• BSE (clinician-rated) (Barthelemy *et al.*, 1990) • CGI Severity (CGI-S) and CGI-I (clinician-rated) (Guy, 1976a) • CGI-I Behaviour (clinician-rated) (Chez *et al.*, 2007)
Challenging behaviour	Total score	• Aberrant Behaviour Checklist (Community Version) (caregiver report) (Aman *et al.*, 1995a) • General Assessment Parents Scale (GAP) (caregiver report) (Buitelaar *et al.*, 1992) • Global Behaviour Rating Scale (GBRS) (caregiver report) (Levy *et al.*, 2003)
	Aggression	• Conners' Parent Scale (CPS) Conduct Subscale (caregiver report) (Goyette *et al.*, 1978) • GAP (Buitelaar *et al.*, 1992) • MOAS (clinician-rated) (Sorgi *et al.*, 1991) • Overt Aggression Scale (caregiver report) (Yudofsky *et al.*, 1986) • Self-Injurious Behaviour Questionnaire (SIB-Q) (clinician-rated) (Gualtieri, 2002)
	Irritability	• Aberrant Behaviour Checklist (Community Version) Irritability Subscale (caregiver report) (Aman *et al.*, 1985) • CGI Irritability (clinician-rated) (Hollander *et al.*, 2010)

Continued

Table 76: (*Continued*)

Category	Sub-category	Scale
		• Nurse's Observation Scale for In-patient Evaluation (NOSIE-30) Irritability Subscale (clinician-rated) (Honigfeld *et al.*, 1966)
	Hyperactivity	• Aberrant Behaviour Checklist (Community Version) Hyperactivity Subscale (caregiver report) (Aman *et al.*, 1985)
Quality of life	–	• Composite Autonomic Symptom Scale: Home Life, Activity and Skills Checklist Subscales (caregiver report) (Suarez *et al.*, 1999)
Side effects	Global	• Checklist derived from *Physicians' Desk Reference* (Physician's Desk Reference Staff, 1997) (clinician-rated) • Clinical Global Assessment (CGA) derived from CGI (clinician-rated) (Singh & Owino, 1992) • CGI scale (clinician-rated) (Guy, 1976a) • Dosage Treatment Emergent Symptom Scale (DOTES) (clinician-rated) (Guy, 1976b)
Coexisting conditions	Insomnia	• Actigraph • Sleep Disturbance Scale for Children (caregiver report) (Bruni *et al.*, 1996)
	Gastrointestinal symptoms	• Additional Rating Scale (ARS) – Gastrointestinal Symptoms Subscale (caregiver report) (Munasinghe *et al.*, 2010)

8.2   ANTIPSYCHOTICS FOR BEHAVIOUR MANAGEMENT

8.2.1   Introduction

Antipsychotic drugs, whose primary mode of action is to block receptors in the brain's dopamine pathways, have been used to treat challenging behaviour in autism, and are generally used in combination with, or as an adjunct to, psychological and psychosocial interventions aimed at the treatment of the core symptoms of autism. Antipsychotic drugs have been classified as 'typical' (haloperidol, chlorpromazine, fluphenazine and sulpiride) and 'atypical' (aripiprazole, olanzapine and risperidone), although that distinction is increasingly called into question (Kendall, 2011). Some atypical antipsychotics differ from the typical antipsychotics in that they exhibit antagonism of serotonin (5-hydroxytryptamine [5-HT]) type 2A receptors in addition to blocking dopamine (Posey *et al.,* 2008).

For this guideline, the GDG followed rules developed for extrapolation, judging that the primary data concerning antipsychotics for behaviour management in adults with autism could be supplemented, if necessary, by evidence from a learning disabilities population (see Chapter 3, Section 3.5.8 for further explanation of the rationale and rules for extrapolation). A learning disability, like autism, is a risk factor for challenging behaviour (Murphy *et al.,* 2005). In addition, in the management of people with a learning disability, antipsychotics are often used to treat challenging behaviour (Matson & Neal, 2009).

Reviewing the use of antipsychotics in autism (and learning disabilities populations where primary data are lacking) is important because antipsychotics are widely prescribed for challenging behaviour in people with autism. However, there appears to be limited evidence with regards to their efficacy and safety. Moreover, little is known about the potential for atypical response to medications in people with autism. Antipsychotics have been associated with a number of adverse effects, for instance, weight gain, diabetes, increased prolactin levels, involuntary repetitive body movements (tardive dyskinesia), extrapyramidal side effects, and lowering of seizure threshold (see Matson & Hess, 2011).

There is controversy surrounding the use of antipsychotics for managing challenging behaviour in people with autism and/or a learning disability, for instance Spreat and Conroy (1998) noted that over 90% of antipsychotic drug prescriptions for people with a learning disability in residential settings were for 'behavioural control'.

Current practice

Antipsychotic drugs have been widely used in people with autism; for instance, a longitudinal study of 286 adolescents and adults in the US found that they were the second most commonly taken drug among people aged over 20 years (38%), after antidepressants (44%) (Esbensen *et al.*, 2009). In a UK audit of drug use for challenging behaviour in a learning disabilities sample (in which the commonest coexisting diagnosis was autism), 96% were prescribed antipsychotic medication (Marshall, 2004). In another community sample of people with a learning difficulty, Dhumad and Markar (2007) reported that autism was the reason for prescribing antipsychotic medication in 20% of people.

8.2.2   Studies considered[60]

Three RCTs (N = 107) providing relevant clinical evidence in adults with autism met the eligibility criteria for this review. All three were published in peer-reviewed journals between 1998 and 2006. Due to the lack of primary data, and based on the GDG's consensus decision, a separate search was conducted for antipsychotics for behaviour management in people with a learning disability. Nine RCTs (N = 564) provided relevant clinical evidence, met eligibility criteria and were included. All nine were published in peer-reviewed journals between 1966 and 2008. However, data could not be extracted for the calculation of effect sizes for four of these and, therefore, analysis was restricted to a narrative synthesis for these studies. Five RCTs (N = 308) in a learning disabilities population did allow for extraction of efficacy data. Two observational studies in a learning disabilities population (N = 40) were considered in a narrative synthesis. These studies were published in peer-reviewed journals between 2006 and 2007. In addition, 19 studies were excluded from the analysis. The most common reasons for exclusion were that the papers did not have efficacy data that could be entered into a meta-analysis or be included in a narrative synthesis, or participants had a comorbid psychotic disorder. Further information about both included and excluded studies can be found in Appendix 14f.

Of the three included trials in an autism population (see Table 77), two compared risperidone with placebo (HELLINGS2006 [Hellings *et al.*, 2006], MCDOUGLE1998A [McDougle *et al.*, 1998a]), and one compared haloperidol with placebo (REMINGTON2001 [Remington *et al.*, 2001]).

Of the two included observational trials in a learning disabilities population (see Table 78), one involved open-label olanzapine (HANDEN2006 [Handen & Hardan, 2006]) and one open-label risperidone (READ2007 [Read & Rendall, 2007]).

Of the nine included RCTs in a learning disabilities population (see Table 79), three compared risperidone with placebo (GAGIANO2005 [Gagiano *et al.*, 2005], TYRER2008 [Tyrer *et al.*, 2008], VANDENBORRE1993 [Vanden Borre *et al.*, 1993]); TYRER2008 was a three-armed trial and also compared haloperidol with placebo and with risperidone. Three studies compared zuclopenthixol with placebo (HAESSLER2007 [Haessler *et al.*, 2007], IZMETH1988 [Izmeth *et al.*, 1988], SINGH1992 [Singh & Owino, 1992]), one study compared prothipendyl with placebo (MCKENZIE1966 [McKenzie & Roswell-Harris, 1966]), one study compared pipamperone with placebo (VANHEMERT1975 [van Hemert, 1975]), and one study compared two antipsychotics: cis(z)-clopenthixol with haloperidol (KARSTEN1981 [Karsten *et al.*, 1981]).

---

[60]Here and elsewhere in the guideline, each study considered for review is referred to by a study ID in capital letters (primary author and date of study publication, except where a study is in press or only submitted for publication, then a date is not used).

Table 77: Study information table of placebo-controlled trials of antipsychotics for behaviour management in adults with autism

	Risperidone	**Haloperidol**
No. trials (total participants)	2 RCTs (71)	1 RCT (36)
Study IDs	(1) HELLINGS2006 (2) MCDOUGLE1998A	REMINGTON2001
N/% female	(1) 17/43 (2) 9/29	6/17
Mean age	(1) 22 years (2) 28 years	16 years
IQ	(1) Not reported (27.5% mild learning disability, 22.5% moderate learning disability, 27.5% severe learning disability and 22.5% profound learning disability) (2) Mean 54.6	Not reported
Axis I/II disorders	(1) 90% autism (70% autistic disorder; 20% PDD-NOS); 100% learning disability (2) 100% autism (55% autism; 45% PDD-NOS)	100% autism
Dose	(1) 1 mg per day for children and adolescents; 2 mg per day for adults (2) Mean dose 2.9 mg per day	Final dose 1 to 1.5 mg per day
Comparator	(1)–(2) Placebo	Placebo
Length of treatment	(1) 3 to 5 weeks per intervention (2) 12 weeks	6 weeks per intervention
Length of follow-up	(1) 22 weeks (open-label continuation) (2) 24 weeks (open-label continuation)	21 weeks

Table 78: Study information table of open-label observational trials of antipsychotics for behaviour management in adults with a learning disability

	Olanzapine	Risperidone
No. trials (total participants)	1 Observational (16)	1 Observational (24)
Study IDs	HANDEN2006*	READ2007*
N/% female	6/38	5/21
Mean age	15 years	27 years
IQ	36 to 79 (mean 55)	Not reported (75% with a severe or profound learning disability)
Axis I/II disorders	100% disruptive behaviour disorder (disruptive behaviour disorder; ADHD; oppositional defiant disorder; conduct disorder); 100% learning disability	33% autism, 54% epilepsy, 46% organic behaviour disorder; 100% learning disability
Dose	2.5 to 20 mg per day (mean dose 13.7 mg per day)	Final dose 0.5 to 6 mg per day (mean final dose 2.92 mg per day)
Comparator	No comparator	No comparator
Length of treatment	8 weeks	4 to 103 days (mean duration of treatment: 76.4 days)
Length of follow-up	8 weeks	Mean follow-up 76.4 days
Note. *Efficacy data not extractable.		

8.2.3   Clinical evidence for antipsychotics

Risperidone compared with placebo for behaviour management
Two of the three included RCTs for adults with autism compared risperidone with placebo (see Table 80). Meta-analysis, which combined results from HELLINGS2006 and MCDOUGLE1998A, revealed statistically significant beneficial treatment effects of risperidone on challenging behaviour (test for overall effect: Z = 3.06, p = 0.002).

Table 79: Study information table of placebo-controlled and alternative treatment-controlled trials of antipsychotics for behaviour management in adults with a learning disability

	Risperidone	Risperidone or haloperidol	Zuclopenthixol	Prothipendyl	Pipamperone	Cis(z)-clopenthixol
No. trials (*total participants*)	2 RCTs (114)	1 RCT (86)	3 RCTs (204)	1 RCT (40)	1 RCT (20)	1 RCT (100)
Study IDs	(1) GAGIANO2005 (2) VANDENBORRE1993*	TYRER2008*	(1) HAESSLER2007 (2) IZMETH1988 (3) SINGH1992	MCKENZIE1966	VANHEMERT1975*	KARSTEN1981
N/% female	(1) 30/39 (2) Not reported	33/38	(1) Not reported (2) 45/40 (3) 24/46	20/50	20/100	44/44
Mean age	(1) Not reported (18 to 59 years) (2) 31 years	38 to 43 years	(1) Not reported (18 to 50 years) (2) 30 to 32 years (3) 34 to 38 years	21 to 26 years	Median 33 years	25 to 27 years
IQ	(1) 35 to 83 (mean not reported) (2) Not reported (severe or profound learning disability)	Not reported (1% borderline learning disability; 35% mild learning disability; 48% moderate learning disability; 16% severe or profound learning disability)	(1) 30 to 70 (mean not reported) (2) 20 to 80 (means 48 and 51) (3) Not reported (2% mild learning disability; 33% moderate learning disability; 65% severe learning disability)	19 to 58 (means 25 and 34)	Not reported (45% moderate learning disability; 50% severe learning disability; and 5% profound learning disability)	Not reported

Continued

Table 79: (*Continued*)

	Risperidone	Risperidone or haloperidol	Zuclopenthixol	Prothipendyl	Pipamperone	Cis(z)-clopenthixol
Axis I/II disorders	(1) 100% disruptive behaviour disorders (antisocial personality disorder; conduct disorder; disruptive behaviour disorder; intermittent explosive disorder; oppositional defiant disorder); 100% learning disability (2) 100% learning disability	16% autism; 100% learning disability	(1) 100% learning disability (2) 21% psychiatric disorder, 26% epilepsy; 100% learning disability (3) 40% physical disorders, 29% epilepsy, 17% psychiatric disorders; 100% learning disability	100% learning disability	100% learning disability	100% learning disability
Dose	(1) 1 to 4 mg per day (mean dose 1.45 mg per day) (2) 4 to 12 mg per day (mean final dose 8.3 mg per day)	Risperidone: 1 to 2 mg per day Haloperidol: 2.5 to 5 mg per day	(1) 2 to 20 mg per day (mean 11.4 mg per day) (2) 119 mg per week (intramuscular injection) (3) 10 to 150 mg per day (modal dose 20 mg per day)	80 mg (one tablet) to 320 mg (four tablets) 6-hourly	40 to 80 mg day	Cis(z)-clopenthixol: available as 5 and 25 mg tablets Haloperidol: available as 1 and 4 mg tablets

Comparator	(1)–(2) Placebo	Risperidone, haloperidol, or placebo	(1)–(3) Placebo	Placebo	Placebo	Haloperidol
Length of treatment	(1) 4 weeks (2) 3 weeks per intervention	12 weeks	(1) Up to 12 weeks (discontinuation period) (2)–(3) 12 weeks	16 weeks	3 weeks per intervention	12 weeks
Length of follow-up	(1) 52 weeks (open-label continuation) (2) 8 weeks	26 weeks (optional continuation)	(1) 18 weeks (6 week open-label phase followed by discontinuation) (2) 12 weeks (3) 18 weeks (open-label continuation)	16 weeks	4 months (open-label continuation)	12 weeks

Note. *Efficacy data not extractable.

Table 80: Evidence summary table for risperidone compared with placebo in adults with autism

	Challenging behaviour (irritability and aggression)	Core symptom of autism: repetitive behaviour	Autistic behaviours	Symptom severity or improvement
Study IDs	HELLINGS2006 MCDOUGLE1998A	MCDOUGLE1998A	MCDOUGLE1998A	MCDOUGLE1998A
Effect size	SMD = −0.79 (−1.29, −0.28)	SMD = −0.94 (−1.68, −0.19)	SMD = −0.72 (−1.45, 0.01)	SMD = −1.40 (−2.18, −0.61)
Quality of evidence (GRADE)	Moderate[1]	Moderate[1]	Moderate[1]	Moderate[1]
Number of studies/participants	K = 2; N = 66	K = 1; N = 31	K = 1; N = 31	K = 1; N = 31
Forest plot	1.5.1, Appendix 15	1.5.1, Appendix 15	1.5.1, Appendix 15	1.5.1, Appendix 15

Note. [1]Downgraded for imprecision as sample size was small.

In addition, MCDOUGLE1998A examined the effects of risperidone on autistic behaviours (as measured by the Ritvo-Freeman Real-life Rating Scale), the core autism symptom of repetitive behaviours (as measured by the YBOCS) and symptom severity or improvement (as measured by the CGI-I subscale) and found significant treatment effects for all outcomes (test for overall effect: $Z = 1.95$, $p = 0.05$; $Z = 2.47$, $p = 0.01$; and $Z = 3.48$, $p = 0.0005$ respectively).

MCDOUGLE1998A reported observational data for adverse events and found some evidence for mild, transient sedation but concluded that risperidone was well-tolerated with no evidence of extrapyramidal side effects, cardiac events or seizures. HELLINGS2006 also presented only observational data with regards to adverse events. However, in HELLINGS2006 results were suggestive of side effects of increased appetite and weight gain. For instance, weight gain greater than 3 kg occurred in 70% of the participants, and mean weight gain over the 46 weeks was 7.9 kg for children, 8.3 kg for adolescents and 6.0 kg for adults.

In summary, the evidence from adults with autism suggests that risperidone may have a modest effect in the treatment and management of challenging behaviour. However, it is important to bear in mind the methodological limitations of the studies, notably the small sample sizes, as reflected by their moderate GRADE rating for quality. It is also important to note that although results are suggestive of adverse events associated with risperidone, the studies only examined short-term side effects and only reported observational data for side-effect profiles. However, existing NICE guidance on the use of antipsychotics in schizophrenia in adults (NICE, 2009c) provides evidence on adverse events associated with antipsychotics and this evidence may be extrapolated to adults with autism.

Based on the expert judgement of the GDG data from adults with a learning disability were included in order to extrapolate to adults with autism. Three of the nine included RCTs from a learning disabilities population compared risperidone with placebo; one of these studies also included a haloperidol comparison group. Efficacy data could only be extracted for two of these studies (see Table 81).

Both studies that allowed extraction of efficacy data (GAGIANO2005, TYRER2008) examined the effects of risperidone on symptom severity or improvement. Meta-analysis revealed a trend for a statistically significant positive treatment effect of risperidone on symptom severity or improvement (test for overall effect: $Z = 1.71$, $p = 0.09$). However, the evidence was inconsistent, with GAGIANO2005 reporting a statistically significant difference between participants receiving risperidone and those receiving placebo (test for overall effect: $Z = 1.95$, $p = 0.05$) and TYRER2008 reporting no significant difference between the two groups (test for overall effect: $Z = 0.38$, $p = 0.70$). However, it should be noted that the quality of the data from GAGIANO2005 was downgraded on the basis of indirectness as in addition to participants having a learning disability and not autism, the participants also had coexisting psychiatric conditions including conduct disorder, disruptive behaviour disorder, intermittent explosive disorder, oppositional defiant disorder and antisocial personality disorder. It is also important to note that the addition of the TYRER2008 data to the meta-analysis is problematic given that the data are skewed, and although medians and interquartile ranges were reported, the mean and

Table 81: Evidence summary table for risperidone compared with placebo in adults with a learning disability

	Challenging behaviour	Aggression	Symptom severity or improvement	Quality of life
Study IDs	TYRER2008	TYRER2008	GAGIANO2005 TYRER2008	TYRER2008
Effect size	MD = −4.77 (−18.38, 8.84)	MD = 0.58 (−4.90, 6.06)	SMD = −0.30 (−0.64, 0.04)	MD = 2.88 (−2.56, 8.32)
Quality of evidence (GRADE)	Low[1,2]	Low[1,2]	Very low[1,2,3,4]	Low[1,2]
Number of studies/participants	K = 1; N = 58	K = 1; N = 58	K = 2; N = 132	K = 1; N = 58
Forest plot	1.5.1, Appendix 15	1.5.1, Appendix 15	1.5.1, Appendix 15	1.5.1, Appendix 15

Note. [1]Data are skewed in TYRER2008 and medians and interquartile ranges were reported. However, means and standard deviation values were requested in order to be entered into the meta-analysis and extract efficacy data. However, because the data were skewed this analysis is flawed. [2]Downgraded for indirectness because of extrapolation from adults with a learning disability. [3]Downgraded for indirectness because in GAGIANO2005 adults with a learning disability also had coexisting psychiatric conditions including conduct disorder, disruptive behaviour disorder, intermittent explosive disorder, oppositional defiant disorder and antisocial personality disorder. [4]Downgraded for inconsistency because GAGIANO2005 found significant differences whereas TYRER2008 did not.

standard deviation scores were requested in order to be entered into the current meta-analysis.

TYRER2008 also examined the effects of risperidone on challenging behaviour, aggression and quality of life and found no evidence for any significant differences between participants receiving risperidone and those receiving placebo for any of these outcomes (test for overall effect: $Z = 0.69$, $p = 0.49$; $Z = 0.21$, $p = 0.84$; and $Z = 1.04$, $p = 0.30$ respectively). TYRER2008 concluded that antipsychotic drugs should no longer be regarded as an acceptable routine treatment for aggressive challenging behaviour in people with a learning disability. However, GAGIANO2005 concluded that risperidone is effective in managing disruptive behaviour disorders in adults with a learning disability.

Side effect outcomes were not reported in TYRER2008, and GAGIANO2005 concluded that risperidone was well tolerated. It is important to note, however, that although side effects were reported equally by both the risperidone and placebo groups in GAGIANO2005 during the double-blind phase, observational data for the open-label continuation phase suggested a high incidence of somnolence and statistically significant weight gain with an overall mean change in weight of 3.8 kg ($p \leq 0.001$) over the 48 weeks.

Efficacy data could not be extracted for the remaining included RCT in adults with a learning disability. VANDENBORRE1993 did not report mean and standard deviation scores. However, the authors reported statistically significant ($p = 0.01$) differences in challenging behaviour (as measured by the Aberrant Behaviour Checklist [Community Version] total score) with a larger change-from-baseline score in the risperidone group compared with the control group. The paper also reported a significant difference between the risperidone and placebo groups for endpoint scores in symptom severity or improvement ($p < 0.01$). Thus, these results are suggestive of efficacy. However, the authors also reported that adverse reactions were more numerous under risperidone treatment with ten times more reporting of sedation and six times more reporting of drowsiness as a treatment-emergent side effect.

In summary, the evidence from RCTs in adults with a learning disability for the efficacy and tolerability of risperidone for treating and managing challenging behaviour is limited. The results from GAGIANO2005 when entered into the meta-analysis, and the narratively described results of VANDENBORRE1993, corroborate the results found in an autism population and suggest that risperidone may have a positive treatment effect on symptom severity or improvement and challenging behaviour, but a negative treatment effect in terms of adverse events, in this case increasing incidence of sedation in addition to the weight gain reported in the autism studies. However, TYRER2008 found no significant differences between participants receiving risperidone and those receiving placebo for any of the outcomes examined including challenging behaviour, aggression, symptom severity or improvement, or quality of life. This inconsistency is reflected in the downgrading of the quality of the evidence to very low.

Open-label risperidone for behaviour management
One open-label observational study examined the effects of risperidone in adults with a learning disability without a control group (READ2007). Efficacy data could not be

extracted. However, the authors reported significant change-from-baseline scores with risperidone for challenging behaviour (as measured by the Aberrant Behaviour Checklist [Community Version] total score), symptom severity ($p < 0.001$) and quality of life (for the Home Life, Activity and Skills Checklist Subscales: range $p < 0.001$ to $p = 0.014$). The authors concluded that risperidone was efficacious and well tolerated for managing violent and self-injurious behaviour and improving quality of life in adults with a learning disability. However, there was a trend for statistically significant weight gain ($p = 0.061$) with a mean of 1.74 kg increase in body weight over the 12-week trial. Thus, this study provides some support for the findings of GAGIANO2005 and VANDENBORRE1993 reported above.

Haloperidol compared with placebo for behaviour management
One of the three included RCTs for adults with autism compared haloperidol with placebo (see Table 82). REMINGTON2001 was a three-armed trial comparing haloperidol with clomipramine and placebo. Data were not extracted for clomipramine here as these are reported in Section 8.11. REMINGTON2001 found no significant treatment effect for haloperidol compared with placebo for autistic behaviours (test for overall effect: $Z = 1.18$, $p = 0.24$) or for global side effects (test for overall effect: $Z = 1.66$, $p = 0.10$). However, although statistically significant differences were not observed on the side-effect scales, there was a notable attrition rate for the study with 21% dropout during the haloperidol phase as a result of identified side effects ($N = 5$ fatigue; $N = 1$ dystonia; and $N = 1$ depression), compared with 3% dropout in the placebo phase due to side effects (in this case, nosebleeds).

Table 82: Evidence summary table for haloperidol compared with placebo in adults with autism

	Autistic behaviours	Side effects (global)
Study IDs	REMINGTON2001	REMINGTON2001
Effect size	MD = −2.70 (−7.19, 1.79)	MD = 1.50 (−0.28, 3.28)
Quality of evidence (GRADE)	Very low[1,2,3]	Very low[1,2,3]
Number of studies/ participants	K = 1; N = 33	K = 1; N = 33
Forest plot	1.5.1, Appendix 15	1.5.1, Appendix 15

Note. [1]Downgraded for risk of bias because of a high risk of attrition bias due to higher dropout as a consequence of side effects in the haloperidol group. [2]Downgraded for indirectness because this was an adolescent sample with autism. [3]Downgraded for imprecision because sample size was small.

One of the included RCTs in adults with a learning disability also examined treatment effects of haloperidol in a three-armed comparison of haloperidol, risperidone and placebo (TYRER2008; see above). The results of the comparison of haloperidol with placebo are presented in Table 83. TYRER2008 found no evidence for significant treatment effects of haloperidol on challenging behaviour or quality of life (test for overall effect: Z = 0.56, p = 0.57; Z = 0.67, p = 0.51 respectively). However, there was a trend for a statistically significant difference between participants receiving haloperidol and participants receiving placebo for aggression (test for overall effect: Z = 1.83, p = 0.07), and a statistically significant group difference for symptom severity or improvement (test for overall effect: Z = 2.50, p = 0.01) with participants receiving haloperidol showing superior scores. In addition, consistent results were found when haloperidol was compared with risperidone with a trend for positive treatment effects in favour of haloperidol for aggression (test for overall effect: Z = 1.90, p = 0.06) and a statistically significant difference between the two antipsychotics for symptom severity or improvement (test for overall effect: Z = 2.08, p = 0.04), with superior scores for participants receiving haloperidol compared with participants receiving risperidone. In summary, TYRER2008 found some evidence for positive treatment effects of haloperidol (compared with placebo or risperidone) on aggression and symptom severity or improvement. However, it should be noted that there is uncertainty about this analysis because the data were skewed and medians and interquartile ranges were reported in the original trial report and may better represent the likely effects of the trial. The quality of this evidence was also downgraded on the basis of indirectness.

Table 83: Evidence summary table for haloperidol compared with placebo in adults with a learning disability

	Challenging behaviour	Aggression	Symptom severity or improvement	Quality of life
Study IDs	TYRER2008	TYRER2008	TYRER2008	TYRER2008
Effect size	MD = −4.30 (−19.30, 10.70)	MD = −4.12 (−8.53, 0.29)	MD = −0.88 (−1.57, −0.19)	MD = −1.87 (−7.38, 3.64)
Quality of evidence (GRADE)	Low[1,2]	Low[1,2]	Low[1,2]	Low[1,2]
Number of studies/ participants	K = 1; N = 57	K = 1; N = 57	K = 1; N = 57	K = 1; N = 57
Forest plot	1.5.1, Appendix 15	1.5.1, Appendix 15	1.5.1, Appendix 15	1.5.1, Appendix 15

Note. [1]Data are skewed in TYRER2008 and medians and interquartile ranges were reported. However, means and standard deviation values were requested in order to be entered into the meta-analysis and to extract efficacy data. However, because the data were skewed this analysis is flawed. [2]Downgraded for indirectness due to extrapolation from adults with a learning disability.

Zuclopenthixol compared with placebo for behaviour management

There were no RCTs or quasi-experimental or observational studies comparing zuclopenthixol with placebo in adults with autism. Based on the expert judgement of the GDG, data were included from adults with a learning disability. Of the nine included RCTs examining antipsychotics for behaviour management in adults with a learning disability, three compared zuclopenthixol with placebo (see Table 84). HAESSLER2007 compared participants who discontinued zuclopenthixol and switched to placebo after a 6-week open-label trial with participants who continued with zuclopenthixol for a further 12 weeks in a double-blind phase. Dichotomous outcome data were reported with participants showing a deterioration of at least three points on the MOAS at two subsequent visits designated as non-responders and participants without deterioration considered to be responders. A significant difference was observed between zuclopenthixol and placebo (test for overall effect: Z = 1.96, p = 0.05), with the risk ratio indicating that participants who received zuclopenthixol were more than seven times more likely to respond to treatment for aggressive challenging behaviour than participants receiving placebo. The authors concluded that discontinuation of zuclopenthixol in adults with a learning disability led to an increase in aggressive behaviour.

SINGH1992 also examined the effects of discontinuing zuclopenthixol treatment (following a 6-week open-label phase) in adults with a learning disability. Dichotomous data were extracted for 'severity of behavioural disorder' as measured by the Clinical Global Assessment (CGA), which was derived from the CGI. Participants 'causing fewer problems in management' were rated as 'responders'

Table 84: Evidence summary table for zuclopenthixol compared with placebo in adults with a learning disability

	Challenging behaviour: aggression (endpoint data)	Challenging behaviour: irritability (change from baseline)	Symptom severity or improvement (endpoint comparison)	Symptom severity or improvement (change from baseline)
Study IDs	HAESSLER2007	IZMETH1988	SINGH1992	IZMETH1988
Effect size	RR = 7.37 (1.00, 54.39)	MD = −2.20 (−3.86, −0.54)	RR = 3.96 (0.50, 31.09)	MD = 0.70 (0.25, 1.15)
Quality of evidence (GRADE)	Low[1, 2]	Very low[1,3,4]	Very low[1,2,3,4]	Very low[1,3,4]
Number of studies/participants	K = 1; N = 39	K = 1; N = 85	K = 1; N = 43	K = 1; N = 85
Forest plot	1.5.1, Appendix 15	1.5.1, Appendix 15	1.5.1, Appendix 15	1.5.1, Appendix 15

Note. [1]Downgraded for indirectness due to extrapolating from adults with a learning disability. [2]Downgraded for imprecision because the sample size was small. [3]Downgraded for risk of bias due to a high risk of attrition bias because of a greater dropout rate in the placebo group. [4]Downgraded for indirectness because the study is very old.

and the number of participants remaining unchanged or 'causing more problems' combined to produce a 'non-responder' total. The risk ratio indicated that adults with a learning disability who continued with zuclopenthixol were nearly four times more likely to respond to treatment in reducing the severity of the behavioural disorder than participants who discontinued and switched to placebo. However, this treatment effect was not statistically significant (test for overall effect: $Z = 1.31$, $p = 0.19$).

Finally, IZMETH1988 examined the effects of discontinuing zuclopenthixol decanoate injection following a 4-week open-label trial. Data could not be extracted for endpoint comparison. However, data extracted and analysed for change-from-baseline scores for symptom severity (of the behavioural disorder) found evidence for a significant treatment effect (test for overall effect: $Z = 3.04$, $p = 0.002$), with significantly greater reduction in severity of illness observed for the zuclopenthixol decanoate group compared with the placebo group at week 12 (endpoint). Statistically significant differences in change-from-baseline scores for irritability (as measured by the Nurse's Observation Scale for In-patient Evaluation [NOSIE-30]) were also observed (test for overall effect: $Z = 2.60$, $p = 0.009$), with people who continued treatment with zuclopenthixol decanoate showing greater clinical improvement than participants who discontinued and switched to placebo.

Prothipendyl compared with placebo for behaviour management
There were no RCTs or quasi-experimental or observational studies comparing prothipendyl with placebo in adults with autism. As described above, extrapolation data were considered from an adult learning disabilities population. Of the nine included RCTs examining antipsychotics for behaviour management in adults with a learning disability, one compared prothipendyl with placebo (see Table 85).

Table 85: Evidence summary table for prothipendyl compared with placebo in adults with a learning disability

	Symptom severity or improvement
Study ID	MCKENZIE1966
Effect size	RR = 1.69 (1.00, 2.85)
Quality of evidence (GRADE)	Very low[1,2,3,4]
Number of studies/participants	K = 1; N = 39
Forest plot	1.5.1, Appendix 15

[1]Downgraded for risk of bias due to a high risk of selection bias because of pre-trial group differences in IQ. [2]Downgraded for indirectness due to extrapolating from adults with a learning disability. [3]Downgraded for indirectness because the study is very old.

Dichotomous outcome data were extracted from MCKENZIE1966 for clinical assessment of symptom severity or improvement with participants showing slight improvement, good improvement, very good improvement, or excellent improvement combined to produce a 'responders' category and participants showing no change or deterioration combined to produce a 'non-responders' group. A significant treatment effect was observed (test for overall effect: $Z = 1.97$, $p = 0.05$), with the risk ratio indicating that participants receiving prothipendyl were over one and a half times more likely to respond to treatment for behavioural disorders than participants receiving placebo. However, it is important to bear in mind the modest size of this effect, and the very low quality of this evidence due to indirectness, pre-trial group differences in IQ, the age of the study, and the small sample size. It should also be noted that prothipendyl has no licence for any indication in the UK.

Pipamperone compared with placebo for behaviour management
There were no RCTs or quasi-experimental or observational studies comparing pipamperone with placebo in adults with autism. As described above, extrapolation data were considered from an adult learning disabilities population. Of the nine included RCTs examining antipsychotics for behaviour management in adults with a learning disability, one compared pipamperone with placebo (VANHEMERT1975). The data reported in VANHEMERT1975 could not be entered into a meta-analysis as neither continuous (mean and standard deviation values) nor dichotomous data were presented. As a result it was not possible to extract efficacy data. However, the authors reported that for six of the ten challenging behaviour checklist items (fits of anger, actual aggressiveness, fussiness, impulsiveness, sleep disorders and manageability), participants who received pipamperone showed a better response than participants treated with placebo ($p < 0.05$; range from $p = 0.004$ to $p = 0.041$). However, without efficacy data it is difficult to quantify these findings. Moreover, the indirectness, small sample size, and age of the study seriously limit the conclusions that can be drawn. It should also be noted that pipamperone has no licence for any indication in the UK.

Cis(z)-clopenthixol compared with haloperidol for behaviour management
The final included RCT, which examined antipsychotics in an extrapolation population of adults with a learning disability, compared two active antipsychotic drugs, cis(z)-clopenthixol and haloperidol (see Table 86). Dichotomous data were extracted (as reported) with participants showing improved symptoms rated as 'responders' and participants showing unchanged or deteriorated symptoms rated as 'non-responders'. KARSTEN1981 found a statistically significant difference for symptom severity or improvement (test for overall effect: $Z = 3.25$, $p = 0.001$), with the risk ratio indicating that participants receiving treatment with cis(z)-clopenthixol were over three times more likely to respond to treatment than participants receiving haloperidol. Dichotomous data were also calculated from the data reported in KARSTEN1981 for side effects (measured by the CGI), with no side effect rated as 'event' and all side-effect categories (side effects interfering slightly with functioning, side effects

Table 86: Evidence summary table for cis(z)-clopenthixol compared with haloperidol in adults with a learning disability

	Symptom severity or improvement	**Side effects**
Study IDs	KARSTEN1981	KARSTEN1981
Effect size	RR = 3.43 (1.63, 7.21)	RR = 0.85 (0.66, 1.08)
Quality of evidence (GRADE)	Low[1, 2]	Low[1, 2]
Number of studies/ participants	K = 1; N = 98	K = 1; N = 98
Forest plot	1.5.1, Appendix 15	1.5.1, Appendix 15

Note. [1]Downgraded for indirectness due to extrapolating from adults with a learning disability. [2]Downgraded for indirectness because the study is very old.

interfering moderately with functioning, and side effects interfering markedly with functioning) combined to produce a 'no event' total score. Marginal but non-statistically significant differences were observed for side effects (test for overall effect: $Z = 1.36$, $p = 0.17$) with the risk ratio indicating that participants receiving cis(z)-clopenthixol were 15% more likely to exhibit side effects than participants receiving haloperidol.

In summary this comparison of two antipsychotic drug treatments suggested that cis(z)-clopenthixol may be superior to haloperidol in improving the severity of illness. It is important to note that for these data, as for much of the antipsychotic literature, the evidence is only low quality due to downgrading for indirectness and the age of the study.

Open-label olanzapine for behaviour management
Finally, one open-label observational study examined the effects of olanzapine in adolescents with a learning disability without a control group (HANDEN2006). Efficacy data could not be extracted. However, the authors reported statistically significant changes from baseline for irritability and hyperactivity, and for symptom severity or improvement ($p \leq 0.002$). The authors concluded that olanzapine may be useful in treating disruptive behaviour in adolescents with a learning disability. However, the authors also suggested that side effects, especially weight gain, were a significant issue, with an average weight gain of 12.7 lb over the 8-week trial and 67% of participants gaining 10 lb and more.

In summary, the results from this study suggest there are positive treatment effects on challenging behaviour, but also with the negative side effect of increased weight gain.

8.2.4   Clinical evidence summary for antipsychotics

The majority of the evidence on the use of antipsychotics for behaviour management in adults with autism compared risperidone with placebo, and there is limited evidence for a modest treatment effect of risperidone on irritability and aggression. In addition, there is some evidence that autistic behaviours, the core autistic symptom of repetitive behaviour, and global symptom severity may respond favourably to treatment with risperidone. However, the data from placebo-controlled and observational studies of risperidone in adults with a learning disability is inconsistent. In addition, most of the studies in autism and learning disabilities populations report data suggestive of adverse events associated with risperidone, in particular, sedation and weight gain. (Note, this is consistent with the evidence of adverse effects associated with the use of these drugs for schizophrenia.) It is also important to note that these trials were run over short time periods and very little is known about the long-term effects of antipsychotics in adults with autism.

The evidence for haloperidol was very limited and inconsistent, with no evidence for significant treatment effects in adults with autism. The results for clopenthixol provided limited evidence (low quality [GRADE]) for a beneficial effect on the management of challenging behaviour in adults with a learning disability. The evidence for olanzapine for behaviour management is extremely limited (very low quality [GRADE]) with just one open-label study.

8.2.5   Health economic evidence for antipsychotics

No studies assessing the cost effectiveness of antipsychotics in adults with autism were identified by the systematic search of the economic literature undertaken for this guideline. Details on the methods used for the systematic search of the economic literature are described in Chapter 3.

8.2.6   From evidence to recommendations

The GDG considered the evidence for antipsychotic medication to be of low quality, with two drugs (risperidone and zuclopenthixol) having the most evidence, and with more limited evidence for the use of haloperidol. The limited evidence suggested that the effects of these drugs were more likely to be seen on the management of challenging behaviour rather than on the core symptoms of autism. The mechanisms by which these drugs exerted any beneficial effect was unclear from the data reviewed and it was also unclear whether the effects were mediated by a change in any psychotic symptoms, reduced levels of anxiety or more general sedation.

Therefore, the GDG's judgement was that antipsychotics should not be used to manage core symptoms of autism but may be considered for the treatment and management of challenging behaviour, including irritability, aggression and self-harm, in adults with autism. The GDG recognised that antipsychotics were often used for the management of challenging behaviour without review of the underlying causes of that behaviour and agreed that a functional analysis of behaviour should be a core component of treatment. This analysis, along with a consideration of any coexisting mental and physical disorders and the wider social and physical environment, should help determine whether an antipsychotic should be used. The GDG did not think it appropriate to recommend any specific antipsychotic but considered that the choice of antipsychotic medication should be influenced by a consideration of the side-effect profile, the service user's personal preferences and any past experience of taking the drug.

The GDG felt that an integrated approach to treating challenging behaviour in adults with autism was important and consequently judged that antipsychotics should normally be used in conjunction with psychological or other interventions (which are targeted at the challenging behaviour) except where the behaviour is very severe. In addition, due to the concerns regarding side effects associated with antipsychotic use, and the lack of data about long-term effects, the GDG concluded that where antipsychotics are used for the treatment of challenging behaviour in adults with autism there should be regular review of the benefits of the drug, any side effects, adherence and physical health, with particular emphasis on monitoring weight gain. Monitoring of the benefits of treatment should also be undertaken and the GDG was of the view that treatment should not be continued after 6 weeks in the absence of clear evidence of important clinical benefit. The recommendations for the monitoring of side effects are true for all biomedical interventions and therefore form general principles. The GDG drew on the *Schizophrenia* guideline (NICE, 2009c) when formulating advice on the monitoring and management of side effects and other adverse effects because they did not consider that there would be significant differences in the effects on the population covered by this guideline, save for a potentially greater sensitivity to side effects in people with autism.

8.2.7 Recommendations for general principles for biomedical interventions

8.2.7.1   When deciding on options for pharmacological interventions for challenging behaviour or coexisting mental disorders in adults with autism:
- be aware of the potential for greater sensitivity to side effects and idiosyncratic responses in people with autism **and**
- consider starting with a low dose.

8.2.7.2   For any intervention[61] used in adults with autism, there should be a regular review of:
- the benefits of the intervention, where feasible using a formal rating of the target behaviour(s)
- any adverse events
- specific monitoring requirements of pharmacological interventions as highlighted by the summary of product characteristics
- adherence to the intervention.

---

[61]This also applies to psychosocial interventions.

8.2.8 Recommendations for antipsychotics

8.2.8.1 Do not use antipsychotic medication for the management of core symptoms of autism in adults.

8.2.8.2 Consider antipsychotic medication[62] in conjunction with a psychosocial intervention for challenging behaviour when there has been no or limited response to psychosocial or other interventions (such as environmental adaptations). Antipsychotic medication should be prescribed by a specialist and quality of life outcomes monitored carefully. Review the effects of the medication after 3–4 weeks and discontinue it if there is no indication of a clinically important response at 6 weeks.

8.2.9 Recommendations for challenging behaviour

Pharmacological interventions for challenging behaviour

8.2.9.1 Consider antipsychotic medication[63] for challenging behaviour on its own when psychosocial or other interventions could not be delivered because of the severity of the challenging behaviour. Antipsychotic medication should be prescribed by a specialist and quality of life outcomes monitored carefully. Review the effects of the medication after 3–4 weeks and discontinue it if there is no indication of a clinically important response at 6 weeks.

8.3 ANTICONVULSANTS FOR BEHAVIOUR MANAGEMENT

8.3.1 Introduction

Anticonvulsants are routinely used for the treatment of epilepsy and are licensed for the treatment of bipolar disorder. They have also been used off-label to treat challenging behaviour in people with autism who do not have coexisting epilepsy. It has been suggested that anticonvulsant medication may assist in the treatment and management of challenging behaviour in autism due to the potential anti-aggressive and anti-impulsive effects of the drugs (Hollander *et al.*, 2003a). However, the literature on the use of anticonvulsants for treating agitated or aggressive behaviour in people without bipolar disorder has mostly come from single case reports or small retrospective case series (Ruedrich *et al.*, 1999). These reports have concerned a number of anticonvulsants including carbamazepine, lamotrigine, levetiracetam, sodium valproate and topiramate. Anticonvulsants have diverse mechanisms of action including blockage of voltage-gated ion channels (Na and Ca), reduction of glutamatergic excitation and enhancement of

---

[62] At the time of publication (2012), no antipsychotic medication had a UK marketing authorisation for this indication in adults with autism. Informed consent should be obtained and documented.

[63] At the time of publication (2012), no antipsychotic medication had a UK marketing authorisation for this indication in adults with autism. Informed consent should be obtained and documented.

GABA-ergic inhibition (Munshi *et al.*, 2010). It has been suggested that the latter mechanism may be relevant to the treatment of challenging behaviour in people with autism given theories of decreased inhibitory control in autism (Casanova *et al.*, 2003). Anticonvulsants have been associated with adverse events, including weight gain, sedation, gastrointestinal upset, alopecia, tremor and a higher incidence of certain birth defects when used in pregnancy (Lubetsky & Handen, 2008). It should be noted that there is a higher incidence of epilepsy in people with autism, perhaps up to 20 to 25% (Canitano, 2007), and they may well require treatment with anticonvulsants for coexisting epilepsy.

Current practice

In a longitudinal study of young people and adults with autism in the US, Esbensen and colleagues (2009) found that 31% of those aged 20 years and older with autism were taking anticonvulsant medication at the end of the longitudinal study. However, due to the high rate of coexisting epilepsy in this study it is not possible to ascertain the prevalence rate of anticonvulsants targeted at behaviour management from that of medication aimed at symptoms of epilepsy. Tsakanikos and colleagues (2007) examined patterns of change in referral trends for adults with a learning disability and autism to specialist mental health services in south London from 1983 to 2000 (N = 137) and found that 6% of the participants were taking anticonvulsant medication. However, this study does not describe the target of anticonvulsant medication in this population, namely whether these drugs were prescribed for behaviour management or coexisting epilepsy. If it is the latter, then this might represent an under-prescription of anticonvulsants given the prevalence estimates of coexisting epilepsy of 20 to 25% (Canitano, 2007).

8.3.2   Studies considered[64]

There were no RCTs or quasi-experimental, observational or case series studies providing relevant clinical evidence for anticonvulsants in adults with autism. Due to the lack of primary data, and based on the expert judgement of the GDG, a separate search was conducted for anticonvulsants for behaviour management in people with a learning disability. Five studies were found but all were excluded, predominantly on the basis of coexisting epilepsy. Based on the expert judgement of the GDG the decision was then taken to extrapolate from evidence for children with autism for the use of anticonvulsants in behaviour management. Three RCTs (N = 92) provided relevant clinical evidence, met extrapolation eligibility criteria, and were therefore included. All three studies were published in peer-reviewed journals between 2001 and 2010. However, data could not be extracted for the calculation of effect sizes for one of the studies and so analysis is restricted to a narrative review for that study. One observational study in children with autism (N = 15) is also considered in a narrative

---

[64]Here and elsewhere in the guideline, each study considered for review is referred to by a study ID in capital letters (primary author and date of study publication, except where a study is in press or only submitted for publication, then a date is not used).

review. This study was published in a peer-reviewed journal in 2004. In total, seven studies were excluded from the analysis, predominantly because the sample had coexisting epilepsy. Further information about both included and excluded studies can be found in Appendix 14f.

Of the three included RCTs in children with autism (see Table 87), two compared valproate with placebo (HELLINGS2005 [Hellings *et al.*, 2005], HOLLANDER2010

Table 87: Study information table of placebo-controlled trials of anticonvulsants for behaviour management in children with autism

	Valproate	**Lamotrigine**
No. trials (total participants)	2 (57)	1 (35)
Study IDs	(1) HELLINGS2005 (2) HOLLANDER2010	BELSITO2001*
N/% female	(1) 10/33 (2) 4/15	2/6
Mean age	(1) 11 years (2) 9 years	6 years
IQ	(1) 20 to 137 (mean 54) (2) 30 to 126 (mean 63.3)	Not reported
Axis I/II disorders	(1) 100% autism (N = 27 autistic disorder; N = 1 PDD-NOS; N = 2 'Asperger's disorder') (2) 100% autism (N = 23 autistic disorder; N = 4 Asperger's syndrome)	100% autism
Dose	(1) 20 mg per kg per day (2) Not reported	Mean dose 5 mg per kg per day
Comparator	(1)–(2) Placebo	Placebo
Length of treatment	(1) 8 weeks (2) 12 weeks	12 weeks
Length of follow-up	(1) 8 weeks (2) 12 weeks	18 weeks
Note. *Efficacy data not extractable.		

Table 88: Study information table of observational open-label trials of anticonvulsants for behaviour management in children with autism

	Topiramate
No. trials (total participants)	1 (15)
Study ID	HARDAN2004*
N/% female	3/20
Mean age	15 years
IQ	Not reported
Axis I/II disorders	100% autism (N = 11 autistic disorder; N = 2 'Asperger's disorder'; N = 2 PDD-NOS)
Dose	Mean dose 235 mg ± 88 mg per day
Comparator	No comparator
Length of treatment	8 to 56 weeks (mean 25 weeks)
Length of follow-up	8 to 56 weeks (mean 25 weeks)
Note. *Efficacy data not extractable.	

[Hollander *et al.*, 2010]) and one compared lamotrigine with placebo (BELSITO2001 [Belsito *et al.*, 2001]).

The one included observational trial in children with autism (see Table 88) involved open-label topiramate (HARDAN2004 [Hardan *et al.*, 2004]).

8.3.3   Clinical evidence for anticonvulsants

Valproate compared with placebo for behaviour management
There were no RCTs or quasi-experimental or observational studies comparing valproate with placebo in adults with autism or in adults with a learning disability. Based on the GDG's consideration of the rules for extrapolation, data were included from a population of children with autism. Of the three included RCTs examining anticonvulsants for behaviour management in children with autism, two compared valproate with placebo (see Table 89).

HELLINGS2005 failed to find a significant difference between participants receiving valproate and those taking placebo for aggression, symptom severity or improvement, or side effects (tests for overall effect: Z = 0.09, p = 0.93; Z = 1.20,

Table 89: Evidence summary table for valproate compared with placebo in children with autism

	Challenging behaviour – irritability (continuous data)	Challenging behaviour – irritability (dichotomous data)	Challenging behaviour – aggression	Symptom severity or improvement	Side effects
Study IDs	HELLINGS2005 HOLLANDER2010	HOLLANDER2010	HELLINGS2005	HELLINGS2005	HELLINGS2005
Effect size	SMD = −0.05 (−0.58, 0.48)	RR = 6.87 (1.02, 46.28)	MD = 0.14 (−2.93, 3.21)	MD = −0.37 (−0.97, 0.23)	RR = 1.19 (0.88, 1.61)
Quality of evidence (GRADE)	Very low[1,2,3]	Low[2,3]	Low[2,3]	Low[2,3]	Low[2,3]
Number of studies/ participants	K = 2; N = 57	K = 1; N = 27	K = 1; N = 30	K = 1; N = 30	K = 1; N = 30
Forest plot	1.5.2, Appendix 15	1.5.2, Appendix 15	1.5.2, Appendix 15	1.5.2, Appendix 15	1.5.2, Appendix 15

Note. [1]Downgraded for inconsistency as HELLINGS2005 found no significant treatment response and HOLLANDER2010 found a positive response for valproate on Aberrant Behaviour Checklist (Community Version) Irritability Subscale scores. [2]Downgraded for indirectness due to extrapolating from children with autism. [3]Downgraded for imprecision because the sample size was small.

p = 0.23; and Z = 1.15, p = 0.25 respectively). HELLINGS2005 also examined the treatment effects of valproate on irritability, as did HOLLANDER2010. However, meta-analysis again failed to find a statistically significant treatment effect for valproate (test for overall effect: Z = 0.19, p = 0.85). However, HELLINGS2005 concluded that the null result cannot be viewed as conclusive, partly owing to the large placebo response, the small sample size and the heterogeneity of the sample (with large differences in aggression frequency and severity for different weeks during the 8-week period and large standard deviations reported for each measure).

HOLLANDER2010 did, however, find a significant positive treatment effect for valproate on irritability as measured by dichotomous outcome data from the CGI Irritability scale (test for overall effect: Z = 1.98, p = 0.05). The risk ratio indicates that participants receiving treatment with valproate were nearly two times more likely to respond than those taking placebo. However, even within HOLLAN-DER2010 the results were not consistent, with no statistically significant treatment effects observed on the continuous outcome measure of irritability as assessed by the Aberrant Behaviour Checklist (Community Version) (test for overall effect: Z = 1.09, p = 0.28).

To sum up, the data on valproate for behaviour management in children with autism is inconsistent both between studies and within studies, with HELLINGS2006 reporting no effect of valproate on challenging behaviour and HOLLANDER2010 reporting mixed treatment effects on irritability. Moreover, the quality of this evidence is very low to low, with the GRADE rating reflecting downgrading due to inconsistency, imprecision (small sample sizes) and indirectness (extrapolating from children with autism).

Lamotrigine compared with placebo for behaviour management
There were no RCTs or quasi-experimental or observational studies comparing lamotrigine with placebo in adults with autism or in adults with a learning disability. Based on the expert judgement of the GDG, data were included from a population of children with autism. Of the three included RCTs examining anticonvulsants for behaviour management in children with autism, one compared lamotrigine with placebo (BELSITO2001). However, efficacy data could not be extracted for BELSITO2001 because no measure of variability was reported. The authors found no evidence for statistically significant treatment effects, with negligible differences observed in change-from-baseline scores between participants receiving lamotrigine and those taking placebo on irritability (p = 0.3751) or autistic behaviours (p = 0.7941). In summary, narrative review of this single RCT comparing lamotrigine with placebo provides no evidence for beneficial treatment effects for this anticonvulsant for behaviour management in children with autism.

Open-label topiramate for behaviour management
Finally, one open-label observational study examined the effects of topiramate in children and young people with autism without a control group (HARDAN2004). Efficacy data could not be extracted. Narrative review of the results suggests a significant change-from-baseline score on the CPS Conduct Subscale as a measure

of challenging behaviour (t = 3.04, p = 0.009). Significant change-from-baseline differences were also observed on the CPS Inattention (t = 3.11, p = 0.008) and Hyperactivity (t = 4.30, p = 0.001) Subscales. However, 20% of the sample (N = 3) discontinued the study because of side effects, with two participants experiencing cognitive difficulties (such as disorientation and speech problems including word-finding difficulties) and one developing a skin rash. The authors concluded that topiramate may be beneficial for treating secondary symptoms of autism. However, double-blind placebo-controlled studies are needed to assess the efficacy and safety of this drug.

8.3.4   Clinical evidence summary for anticonvulsants

No evidence was identified for the use of anticonvulsants for behaviour management in adults with autism or in adults with a learning disability. All of the available evidence comes from children with autism and thus is indirect. This evidence was also downgraded on the basis of inconsistency. The majority of the placebo-controlled trials of anticonvulsants for behaviour management in children with autism compared valproate with placebo. However, no clear conclusions can be drawn because mixed results were found both between studies and within studies. For instance, HELLINGS2005 found no evidence for significant treatment effects on challenging behaviour, whereas HOLLANDER2010 found evidence for a positive treatment effect on irritability. However, while HOLLANDER2010 found significant treatment effects of valproate on a dichotomous measure of irritability (as assessed by the CGI Irritability scale), significant treatment effects were not replicated on the continuous outcome measure (Aberrant Behaviour Checklist [Community Version] Irritability Subscale) in the same study. As with all other biomedical interventions it is also important to bear in mind that the evidence is concerned with the use of medication as an adjunctive therapeutic intervention aimed at behaviour management and not the core symptoms of autism.

8.3.5   Health economic evidence for anticonvulsants

No studies assessing the cost effectiveness of anticonvulsants in adults with autism were identified by the systematic search of the economic literature undertaken for this guideline. Details on the methods used for the systematic search of the economic literature are described in Chapter 3.

8.3.6   From evidence to recommendations

The evidence for the use of anticonvulsants for behaviour management in autism is indirect (extrapolating from data from studies in children), of only very low to low quality, and is inconsistent with mixed results reported. On this basis, the GDG concluded that there is no good evidence to recommend the use of anticonvulsants for either core symptoms of autism or for managing challenging behaviour in adults with autism.

8.3.7   Recommendations for anticonvulsants

8.3.7.1   Do not use anticonvulsants for the management of core symptoms of autism in adults.

8.3.7.2   Do not routinely use anticonvulsants for the management of challenging behaviour in adults with autism.

8.4   DRUGS AFFECTING COGNITION FOR BEHAVIOUR MANAGEMENT

8.4.1   Introduction

Post-mortem analysis of the brains of individuals with pervasive developmental disorders have revealed limbic system abnormalities, including decreased neuronal size and increased cell packing density of the hippocampus, amygdala, mammillary bodies, septum and anterior cingulate cortex (Kemper & Bauman, 1993). These interrelated structures are known to be involved in memory processes and the neuropathological findings suggest neurodevelopmental immaturity in these brain regions in autism. Another disease process in which memory processes are affected and related structures are involved is Alzheimer's disease. There are several competing hypotheses concerning the neurochemical mechanisms underpinning the changes in memory function observed in Alzheimer's disease. The oldest of these theories is the cholinergic hypothesis (Francis *et al.*, 1999), which proposes that the memory problems seen in Alzheimer's disease are caused by reduced synthesis of the neurotransmitter acetylcholine. Based on this hypothesis, drugs used to treat dementia include acetylcholinesterase inhibitors (donepezil, galantamine and rivastigmine), which reduce the rate at which acetylcholine is broken down and consequently increase its concentration in the brain to combat the loss caused by the death of cholinergic neurons (Stahl, 2000). There is some evidence for the efficacy of these drugs in treating Alzheimer's disease (Birk, 2006; Birks & Harvey, 2006; Birks *et al.*, 2009). For instance, donepezil hydrochloride, which belongs to this class of drugs, has been found to improve executive function deficits in dementia. On this basis it has been hypothesised that acetylcholinesterase inhibitors have a role in treating executive function deficits in autism (Yoo *et al.*, 2007), however they have also been associated with adverse events including common side effects (occurring in approximately 10 to 20% of cases) such as nausea and vomiting (linked to cholinergic excess) and less common side effects such as muscle cramps, decreased heart rate (bradycardia), decreased appetite and weight, and increased gastric acid production.

Another class of drugs used in the treatment of Alzheimer's disease is the N-methyl-D-aspartate (NMDA) blocker. NMDA blockers are thought to be effective by preventing a phenomenon called 'excitotoxicity' (Kemp & McKernan, 2002), which may account for the changes observed in Alzheimer's disease whereby persistent activation of NMDA receptors by the excitatory amino acid glutamate leads to excessive calcium entry and subsequent neuronal death (Lipton, 2006). There is evidence for the efficacy of the NMDA blocker memantine in treating moderate to severe Alzheimer's disease (Reisberg *et al.*, 2003). In addition, there is some evidence for glutamatergic abnormalities in autism (Fatemi *et al.*, 2002; Jamain *et al.*, 2002; Shuang *et al.*, 2004), and it has been proposed that NMDA blockers may enhance frontal lobe function and translate to a population of people with autism (Chez *et al.*, 2007). Reported evidence (based on prescribing information) for side effects of memantine in Alzheimer's disease are infrequent and mild, but include hallucinations, confusion, dizziness, headache and fatigue.

Finally, amantadine, a compound structurally similar to memantine which has known non-competitive glutamate NMDA antagonist activity (Kornhuber *et al.*, 1994), has been used to treat influenza, herpes zoster and Parkinson's disease, and has also been identified as having a possible role in the treatment of autism due to reports of its efficacy in treating behavioural disturbance in traumatic brain injury (Gualtieri *et al.*, 1989) and hyperactivity and irritability in ADHD (Masters, 1997).

8.4.2   Studies considered[65]

There were no RCTs or quasi-experimental, observational or case series studies providing relevant clinical evidence for drugs affecting cognition for behaviour management in adults with autism. Due to the lack of primary data, and based on the expert judgement of the GDG, a decision was made to extrapolate from children with autism. Two RCTs (N = 82) were found that provided relevant clinical evidence, met extrapolation eligibility criteria and were included. In addition, four observational studies were included in a narrative synthesis (N = 196). All of these studies were published in peer-reviewed journals between 2001 and 2007. No studies on drugs affecting cognition considered for full text review were subsequently excluded. Further information about included studies can be found in Appendix 14f.

Of the two included RCTs in children with autism (see Table 90), one involved a comparison of donepezil hydrochloride with placebo (CHEZ2003 [Chez *et al.*, 2003]) and one involved a comparison of amantadine hydrochloride with placebo (KING2001 [King *et al.*, 2001]).

Of the four observational studies (see Table 91), three examined the effects of memantine (CHEZ2007 [Chez *et al.*, 2007], ERICKSON2007 [Erickson *et al.*, 2007], OWLEY1996 [Owley *et al.*, 2006]) and one of galantamine (NICOLSON2006 [Nicolson *et al.*, 2006]).

---

[65]Here and elsewhere in the guideline, each study considered for review is referred to by a study ID in capital letters (primary author and date of study publication, except where a study is in press or only submitted for publication, then a date is not used)

Table 90: Study information table of placebo-controlled trials of drugs affecting cognition for behaviour management in children with autism

	Donepezil hydrochloride	Amantadine hydrochloride
No. trials (total participants)	1 (43)	1 (39)
Study IDs	CHEZ2003	KING2001
N/% female	8/19	5/13
Mean age	7 years	7 years
IQ	Not reported	Not reported
Axis I/II disorders	100% autism	100% autism
Dose	1.25 to 2.5 mg per day	5 mg per kg per day
Comparator	Placebo	Placebo
Length of treatment	6 weeks	4 weeks
Length of follow-up	6 weeks	5 weeks

Table 91: Study information table of observational studies of drugs affecting cognition for behaviour management in children with autism

	Memantine	Galantamine
No. trials (total participants)	3 (183)	1 (13)
Study IDs	(1) CHEZ2007* (2) ERICKSON2007* (3) OWLEY2006*	NICOLSON2006*
N/% female	(1) 22/15 (2) Not reported (3) 0/0	3/23
Mean age	(1) 9 years (2) 11 years (3) 8 years	9 years
IQ	(1)–(2) Not reported (3) Non-verbal IQ mean 96.8	Not reported

Continued

Table 91: *(Continued)*

	Memantine	**Galantamine**
Axis I/II disorders	(1) 100% autism (70% autism; 30% PDD-NOS) (2) 100% autism (72% autistic disorder; 17% Asperger's syndrome; 11% PDD-NOS); 61% learning disability (3) 100% autism (71% autistic disorder; 14% Asperger's syndrome; 14% PDD-NOS)	100% autism; 54% learning disability
Dose	(1) Final dose 2.5 to 30 mg per day, mean dose 12.67 mg per day (2) 2.5 to 20 mg per day, mean 10.1 mg per day (3) 5 to 20 mg per day	2 to 24 mg per day, mean final dose 18.4 mg per day
Comparator	(1)–(3) No comparator	No comparator
Length of treatment	(1) 1 to 20 months (mean 9.27 months) (2) 1.5 to 56 weeks (mean 19.3 weeks) (3) 8 weeks	12 weeks
Length of follow-up	(1) 1 to 20 months (mean 9.27 months) (2) 1.5 to 56 weeks (mean 19.3 weeks) (3) 8 weeks	12 weeks
Note. *Efficacy data not extractable.		

8.4.3 Clinical evidence for drugs affecting cognition

Donepezil hydrochloride compared with placebo for autistic behaviours
There were no RCTs or quasi-experimental or observational studies comparing donepezil hydrochloride with placebo in adults with autism. Based on the rules for extrapolation, data were included from a population of children with autism. Of the two included RCTs examining drugs affecting cognition for behaviour management in children with autism, one compared donepezil hydrochloride with placebo (see Table 92).

Table 92: Evidence summary table for donepezil hydrochloride compared with placebo in children with autism

	Autistic behaviours
Study ID	CHEZ2003
Effect size	MD = 0.40 (–4.88, 5.68)
Quality of evidence (GRADE)	Low[1,2]
Number of studies/participants	1 (34)
Forest plot	1.5.3, Appendix 15
Note. [1]Downgraded for indirectness due to extrapolating from children with autism. [2]Downgraded for imprecision because the sample size was small.	

CHEZ2003 found no evidence for a significant treatment effect on autistic behaviours (test for overall effect: $Z = 0.15$, $p = 0.88$), with no statistically significant difference in scores on the CARS between children receiving donepezil hydrochloride and those taking placebo. To conclude, this single trial failed to find evidence for a significant treatment effect of donepezil hydrochloride on autistic behaviours.

Amantadine hydrochloride compared with placebo for behaviour management
The second included RCT of drugs affecting cognition in children with autism, compared amantadine hydrochloride with placebo (see Table 93). KING2001 examined the effects of amantadine hydrochloride on behaviour management as assessed by the parent-rated Aberrant Behaviour Checklist (Community Version). Dichotomous data were extracted for this scale, with responders categorised on the basis of a reduction of at least 25% in Irritability and/or Hyperactivity Subscale scores

Table 93: Evidence summary table for amantadine hydrochloride compared with placebo in children with autism

	Challenging behaviour
Study ID	KING2001
Effect size	RR = 1.29 (0.60, 2.74)
Quality of evidence (GRADE)	Low[1,2]
Number of studies/participants	1 (38)
Forest plot	1.5.3, Appendix 15
Note. [1]Downgraded for indirectness due to extrapolating from children with autism. [2]Downgraded for imprecision because the sample size was small.	

at the end of treatment. This trial failed to find evidence for a significant treatment effect (test for overall effect: Z = 0.65, p = 0.51), suggesting that participants receiving amantadine hydrochloride were no more likely to show a treatment response for challenging behaviour than participants receiving placebo.

Open-label memantine for behaviour management
There were no RCTs or quasi-experimental or observational studies comparing memantine with placebo in adults with autism. Based on the rules for extrapolation, data were included from a population of children with autism. However, there were no RCTs comparing memantine with placebo that met extrapolation eligibility criteria in children with autism. There were, however, three observational studies (of the four included) that examined the effects of memantine on behaviour management in children with autism without a control group (CHEZ2007, ERICKSON2007, OWLEY2006). Efficacy data could not be extracted for these studies, however they are considered in a narrative synthesis.

Both CHEZ2007 and OWLEY2006 examined the effects of memantine on challenging behaviour in children with autism and both studies reported statistically significant change-from-baseline scores on the CGI Behaviour scale (71% improvement, p < 0.001 [CHEZ2007]) and for the Aberrant Behaviour Checklist (Community Version) Irritability Subscale (p = 0.027 [OWLEY2006]).

CHEZ2007 also examined the effects of memantine on the core autistic symptom of social-communication difficulties as measured by the CGI-I based on both receptive language skills and expressive utterances (70% improvement, p < 0.001 [CHEZ2007]). However, there are some concerns with regards to the precision of the outcome measurement because the CGI scale is more commonly used to rate global symptom severity or improvement, and it is not clear whether it is precise enough to evaluate and differentiate language and behaviour scores as used in this study.

Both ERICKSON2007 and OWLEY2006 used the CGI to rate symptom severity (as it is more commonly used). However, there is inconsistent evidence for the effects of memantine in children with autism, with ERICKSON2007 reporting significant change-from-baseline scores on the CGI Severity (CGI-S) scale (p = 0.008) and OWLEY2006 failing to find a statistically significant pre- to post-test difference in symptom severity (p = 0.165).

CHEZ2007 found no evidence for serious side effects and this is the largest study considered in this review. However, ERICKSON2007 and OWLEY2006 narratively reported results suggestive of adverse events with memantine. For instance, in ERICKSON2007 there was a high attrition rate, with 39% of participants experiencing adverse events including irritability, rash, emesis, increased seizure frequency, and excessive sedation; 22% of participants dropped out of the trial because of these adverse events. While in OWLEY2006, 36% of participants experienced hyperactivity associated with memantine, and for 14% the hyperactivity was severe enough for parents to withdraw their children from the study.

To summarise, these observational trials provide suggestive evidence for beneficial effects of memantine on challenging behaviour and the core autistic symptom of social-communication difficulties in children with autism. However, the evidence for treatment effects on symptom severity is inconsistent. In addition, there are concerns regarding side effects, imprecision of outcome measures and indirectness; because efficacy data cannot be extracted, further placebo-controlled trials of memantine are needed.

Open-label galantamine for behaviour management
Finally, one open-label observational study examined the effects of galantamine in children with autism without a control group (NICOLSON2006). Efficacy data could not be extracted. Narrative review of the results suggests significant change-from-baseline scores for irritability (t = 2.5, p = 0.03), autistic behaviours (t = 4.3, p = 0.001) as measured by the autism factor of the Children's Psychiatric Rating Scale (CPRS), and symptom severity or improvement (t = 2.3, p = 0.04). To conclude, this single observational study reports evidence suggestive of a treatment effect for galantamine in children with autism. However, due to the small sample size and low grade of the evidence caution should be exercised when interpreting these results.

8.4.4 Clinical evidence summary for drugs affecting cognition

There were no RCTs examining the effects of drugs affecting cognition on behaviour management in adults with autism. Based on the rules for extrapolation the GDG extrapolated from data on children with autism. However, even with these data only two RCTs were included. These placebo-controlled trials failed to find evidence for statistically significant treatment effects of donepezil hydrochloride on autistic behaviours or for amantadine hydrochloride on challenging behaviour. Conversely, the open-label observational trials on memantine and galantamine in children with autism provide some evidence suggestive of beneficial effects on challenging behaviour, core symptoms of autism, autistic behaviours and symptom severity or improvement.

8.4.5 Health economic evidence for drugs affecting cognition

No studies assessing the cost effectiveness of drugs affecting cognition in adults with autism were identified by the systematic search of the economic literature undertaken for this guideline. Details on the methods used for the systematic search of the economic literature are described in Chapter 3.

8.4.6 From evidence to recommendations

The evidence for drugs affecting cognition is of very low quality, indirect, inconclusive, and includes a number of studies with small sample sizes. There were only two placebo-controlled trials, both of which failed to find evidence for significant treatment effects for donepezil hydrochloride or amantadine hydrochloride in children with autism. The observational studies report more positive results, however it is not possible to extract efficacy data from these studies, the methodology has an inherent risk of bias, and the results reported are far from conclusive. In light of this evidence, the GDG decided not to recommend the use of drugs to improve cognitive functioning for adults with autism.

8.4.7 Recommendations

8.4.7.1 Do not use drugs specifically designed to improve cognitive functioning (for example, cholinesterase inhibitors) for the management of core symptoms of autism or routinely for associated cognitive or behavioural problems in adults.

8.5 HORMONAL INTERVENTIONS: ADRENOCORTICOTROPHIC HORMONE FOR BEHAVIOUR MANAGEMENT

8.5.1 Introduction

Animal models have associated adrenocorticotrophic hormone (ACTH) with a number of functions including, of most relevance to autism, social behaviour. For example, the synthetic ACTH (4-9) analogue ORG 2766 was found to normalise environmentally-induced disturbances of social behaviour in rats (Niesink & van Ree, 1983). ORG 2766 is a neuropeptide that has lost its peripheral activity on the adrenal cortex and exclusively affects the functioning of the brain. Neuropeptides may exert their effects on the nervous system by acting as a neurotransmitter, as a neurohormone, or as a neuromodulator, that is, by modulating the activity of the classic neurotransmitter systems (Gispen, 1980; Versteeg, 1980).

8.5.2 Studies considered[66]

There were no RCTs or quasi-experimental, observational or case series studies providing relevant clinical evidence for ACTH for behaviour management in adults with autism. Due to the lack of primary data, and based on the expert judgement of the GDG, a decision was made to extrapolate from children with autism. Two RCTs (N = 68) were found providing relevant clinical evidence, met extrapolation eligibility criteria and were included. Both of these studies were published in peer-reviewed

---

[66]Here and elsewhere in the guideline, each study considered for review is referred to by a study ID in capital letters (primary author and date of study publication, except where a study is in press or only submitted for publication, then a date is not used).

Table 94: Study information table of placebo-controlled trials of ORG 2766 for behaviour management in children with autism

	ORG 2766
No. trials (total participants)	2 (68)
Study IDs	(1) BUITELAAR1992 (2) BUITELAAR1996
N/% female	(1) 4/19 (2) 15/32
Mean age	(1) 10 years (2) 10 to 11 years
IQ	(1) Range and mean not reported (19% in IQ range 22 to 40; 19% in IQ range 40 to 55; 15% in IQ range 55 to 70; and 48% in IQ range 70 to 85) (2) Range not reported (means 77 and 80)
Axis I/II disorders	(1)–(2) 100% autism (autistic disorder)
Dose	(1)–(2) 40 mg per day
Comparator	(1)–(2) Placebo
Length of treatment	(1) 8 weeks per intervention (2) 6 weeks
Length of follow-up	(1) 36 weeks (2) 6 weeks

journals between 1992 and 1996. In addition, one study was excluded because there were fewer than ten participants per arm for analysis due to the crossover design. Further information about both included and excluded studies can be found in Appendix 14f.

Both of the included RCTs in children with autism (see Table 94) involved a comparison of ORG 2766 with placebo (BUITELAAR1992 [Buitelaar *et al.*, 1992], BUITELAAR1996 [Buitelaar *et al.*, 1996]).

8.5.3   Clinical evidence for adrenocorticotrophic hormone

ORG 2766 compared with placebo for behaviour management
There were no RCTs or quasi-experimental or observational studies comparing ORG 2766 with placebo in adults with autism. Based on the rules for extrapolation, data

303

Table 95: Evidence summary table for ORG 2766 compared with placebo in children with autism

	Challenging behaviour (social withdrawal)	Challenging behaviour (social isolation)	Symptom severity or improvement
Study ID	BUITELAAR1996	BUITELAAR1992	BUITELAAR1992 BUITELAAR1996
Effect size	RR = 1.55 (0.57, 4.22)	SMD = -0.92 (−1.82, −0.02)	SMD = −0.97 (−1.48, -0.45)
Quality of evidence (GRADE)	Very low[1,2,3,4]	Very low[2,3,4]	Low[1,3]
Number of studies/ participants	K = 1; N = 47	K = 1; N = 21	K = 2; N = 68
Forest plot	1.5.4, Appendix 15	1.5.4, Appendix 15	1.5.4, Appendix 15

Note. [1]Downgraded for risk of bias because the randomisation methods were unclear in BUITELAAR1996 (authors state 'randomised in principle') and there was a trend for group differences in age and CARS score at baseline. [2] Downgraded for inconsistency as BUITELAAR1992 found statistically significant treatment effects for challenging behaviour as measured by social isolation on the GAP, whereas BUITELAAR1996 found no significant differences for social withdrawal as measured by the Aberrant Behaviour Checklist (Community Version). [3]Downgraded for indirectness due to extrapolating from children with autism. [4]Downgraded for imprecision because the sample size was small.

were included from a population of children with autism. Of the two included RCTs examining adrenocorticotrophic hormone for behaviour management in children with autism, both compared ORG 2766 with placebo (see Table 95).

Inconsistent results were found for the effects of ORG 2766 on challenging behaviour. For instance, BUITELAAR1992 found modest treatment effects on the General Assessment Parents Scale (GAP) Social Isolation Subscale, which was designed for this study (test for overall effect: $Z = 2.01$, $p = 0.04$) with superior ratings observed for participants in the ORG 2766 phase relative to the placebo phase. Whereas BUITELAAR1996 analysed dichotomous data for the Aberrant Behaviour Checklist (Community Version), with responders classified as participants showing reliable improvement on the Social Withdrawal Subscale either at home, at school or in both contexts, and no significant difference in treatment response was observed between participants receiving ORG 2766 and participants receiving placebo (test for overall effect: $Z = 0.86$, $p = 0.39$).

Conversely, more consistent evidence was found for the effects of ORG 2766 on symptom severity or improvement as measured by the CGI. Combining data from BUITELAAR1992 and BUITELAAR1996 in a meta-analysis found a statistically significant treatment effect for ORG2766 on symptom severity or improvement (test for overall effect: $Z = 3.69$, $p = 0.0002$) with superior ratings for participants receiving ORG 2766 compared with those taking placebo.

8.5.4   Clinical evidence summary for adrenocorticotrophic hormone

To summarise, the two included placebo-controlled trials provide some evidence for the efficacy of ACTH on symptom severity in children with autism. However, the results are inconsistent with regards to treatment effects for challenging behaviour, and the modest effect sizes in BUITELAAR1992 and small samples contribute to the downgrading of the quality of the evidence to low or very low. The evidence was also downgraded on the basis of methodological concerns with BUITE-LAAR1996 regarding the method of randomisation. It is also possible that there may be an overlap of participants across the two studies leading to double counting because both studies were conducted by the same first author and in the same setting. Finally, the data from the studies are indirect as they come from children with autism.

8.5.5   Health economic evidence for adrenocorticotrophic hormone

No studies assessing the cost effectiveness of ACTH in adults with autism were identified by the systematic search of the economic literature undertaken for this guideline. Details on the methods used for the systematic search of the economic literature are described in Chapter 3.

8.5.6   From evidence to recommendations

The GDG reached the decision that there is insufficient evidence on which to make a recommendation about the use of adrenocorticotrophic hormones for behaviour management in adults with autism.

8.6   HORMONAL INTERVENTIONS: SECRETIN FOR AUTISTIC BEHAVIOURS

8.6.1   Introduction

Secretin is a gastrointestinal polypeptide that helps digestion and has been used to treat peptic ulcers and evaluate pancreatic function (Tulassay *et al.*, 1992; Watanabe *et al.*, 1991). Results from mammalian studies have suggested that secretin affects the central nervous system and may function as a neurotransmitter (Charlton *et al.*, 1983; Fremeau *et al.*, 1983). The use of secretin for the treatment of autistic behaviours has gained interest in recent years for several reasons (Parikh *et al.*, 2008) including the increased incidence of gastrointestinal problems in children with autism (Horvath & Perman, 2002). In addition, a non-blinded, uncontrolled case series of children with autism reported improvements in social, cognitive and communication domains following synthetic intravenous secretin during a routine endoscopy evaluation for gastrointestinal problems (Horvath *et al.*, 1998).

8.6.2   Studies considered[67]

There were no RCTs or quasi-experimental, observational or case series studies providing relevant clinical evidence for secretin for autistic behaviours in adults with autism. Due to the lack of primary data, and based on the expert judgement of the GDG, a decision was made to extrapolate from children with autism. Three RCTs (N = 182) were found providing relevant clinical evidence, met extrapolation eligibility criteria and were included. All of these studies were published in peer-reviewed journals between 2000 and 2003. In addition, ten studies were excluded from the analysis. These studies were excluded on the basis that efficacy data could not be extracted for use in either a meta-analysis or narrative review, or the sample had fewer than ten participants per arm. Further information about both included and excluded studies can be found in Appendix 14f.

There were three included RCTs in children with autism (see Table 96) which involved a comparison of secretin with placebo (CHEZ2000 [Chez *et al.*, 2000], DUNNGEIER2000 [Dunn-Geier *et al.*, 2000], LEVY2003 [Levy *et al.*, 2003]).

8.6.3   Clinical evidence for secretin

Secretin compared with placebo for autistic behaviours
There were no RCTs or quasi-experimental or observational studies comparing secretin with placebo in adults with autism. Based on the rules for extrapolation, data were included from a population of children with autism. Three RCTs compared secretin with placebo in children with autism and met extrapolation eligibility criteria (see Table 97).

LEVY2003 and DUNNGEIER2000 both examined treatment effects of single-dose secretin on the core autistic symptom of social-communication difficulties in children with autism. However, neither trial found evidence for a statistically significant treatment effect on communication (test for overall effect: $Z = 1.15$, $p = 0.25$), and the non-significant treatment effects across the two studies were also in opposite directions.

CHEZ2000 and LEVY2003 also examined the effects of secretin on autistic behaviour as measured by the CARS or the Real Life Ritvo Behaviour Scale. However, the meta-analysis revealed no evidence for a significant treatment effect of secretin (test for overall effect: $Z = 1.13$, $p = 0.26$).

---

[67]Here and elsewhere in the guideline, each study considered for review is referred to by a study ID in capital letters (primary author and date of study publication, except where a study is in press or only submitted for publication, then a date is not used).

Table 96: Study information table for placebo-controlled trials of secretin for autistic behaviours in children with autism

	Secretin
No. trials (total participants)	3 (182)
Study IDs	(1) CHEZ2000 (2) DUNNGEIER2000 (3) LEVY2003
N/% female	(1) 3/12 (2) 7/7 (3) 12/19
Mean age	(1) 6 years (2) 5 years (3) 6 years
IQ	(1)–(3) Not reported
Axis I/II disorders	(1)–(3) 100% autism
Dose	(1) Single dose 2 imperial units (IU) per kg (2) Single dose injection of 2 clinical units (CU) per kg to a maximum of 75 CU (3) Single dose injection of 2 CU per kg to a maximum of 75 CU
Comparator	(1)–(3) Placebo
Length of treatment	(1)–(3) Single dose
Length of follow-up	(1) 8 weeks (2) 3 weeks (3) 8 weeks

Finally, LEVY2003 examined the effects of secretin on challenging behaviour as measured by the parent-rated Global Behaviour Rating Scales (GBRS) developed for this study. As for the other outcome measures there was no statistically significant difference between participants receiving secretin and those taking placebo (test for overall effect: $Z = 0.54$, $p = 0.59$).

8.6.4　Clinical evidence summary for secretin

All three included RCTs in children with autism failed to find significant treatment effects for single-dose secretin on autistic behaviours, the core autism symptom of social-communication difficulties or challenging behaviour. Moreover, the data were

Table 97: Evidence summary table for secretin compared with placebo in children with autism

	Core symptoms of autism (social-communication difficulties)	Autistic behaviours	Challenging behaviour
Study IDs	LEVY2003 DUNNGEIER2000	CHEZ2000 LEVY2003	LEVY2003
Effect size	SMD = −0.29 (−0.77, 0.20)	SMD = −0.24 (−0.67, 0.18)	SMD = −0.14 (−0.64, 0.36)
Quality of evidence (GRADE)	Very low[1,2,3]	Low[1,3]	Low[1,3]
Number of studies/ participants	K = 2; N = 157	K = 2; N = 86	K = 1; N = 62
Forest plot	1.5.5, Appendix 15	1.5.5, Appendix 15	1.5.5, Appendix 15

Note. [1]Downgraded for risk of bias because in LEVY2003 there was a significant difference between the groups in baseline CARS total score. [2]Downgraded for inconsistency because the studies found modest (but non-significant) effect sizes in different directions. [3]Downgraded for indirectness due to extrapolating from children with autism.

indirect due to extrapolation, and there is some risk of bias conferred by baseline differences between groups, small sample sizes and short follow-up periods.

8.6.5   Health economic evidence for secretin

No studies assessing the cost effectiveness of secretin in adults with autism were identified by the systematic search of the economic literature undertaken for this guideline. Details on the methods used for the systematic search of the economic literature are described in Chapter 3.

8.6.6   From evidence to recommendations

There was no evidence for secretin in adults with autism, and all three of the included RCTs from an extrapolation population of children with autism failed to find positive beneficial effects of this gastrointestinal hormone and neurotransmitter on autistic behaviours. Consequently, the GDG judged that secretin should not be recommended for the treatment of the core symptoms of autism.

8.6.7   Recommendations

8.6.7.1   Do not use secretin for the management of core symptoms of autism in adults.

8.7 HORMONAL INTERVENTIONS: OXYTOCIN FOR CORE SYMPTOMS OF AUTISM

8.7.1 Introduction

Oxytocin is a hormone synthesised in the hypothalamus, and has a role in female reproduction. Synthetic oxytocin, also known as 'pitocin' and 'syntocinon', has been widely used for inducing labour, in postpartum care and for enhancing lactation (Gimpl, 2008). In addition to peripheral effects, oxytocin also acts as a neurotransmitter in the brain and appears to play a key role in social behaviour and social understanding with receptors distributed in various brain regions including the limbic system and amygdala (Andari *et al.*, 2010). Mammalian research suggests that oxytocin reduces anxiety through amygdala-dependent mechanisms and enhances reward via dopamine-dependent mesolimbic reward pathways (Donaldson & Young, 2008). In addition, research in humans is consistent with an anxiolytic effect of oxytocin. Oxytocin has been found to reduce levels of anxiety (Heinrichs *et al.*, 2003) and amygdala activation to social stimuli (Domes *et al.*, 2007; Kirsch *et al.*, 2005), and increase levels of trust (Kosfeld *et al.*, 2005), gaze to the eyes (Guastella *et al.*, 2008) and accurate emotion processing (Di Simplicio *et al.*, 2009; Fischer-Shofty *et al.*, 2010). It is postulated that oxytocin may have a role in treating autism because the amygdala and face-processing regions have been implicated in emotion recognition deficits in autism (Baron-Cohen *et al.*, 2000). In addition, Gregory and colleagues (2009) found genomic and epigenetic evidence for a reduced function of the oxytocin receptor in autism. Modahl and colleagues (1998) found evidence for significantly lower levels of plasma oxytocin in children with autism and a significant correlation between levels of the hormone and social impairment in a subgroup with severe social cognition impairments. In addition to the social domain, some evidence from animals has been found for significant effects of oxytocin on repetitive behaviours. For instance, intravenous oxytocin has been found to induce stereotypic behaviours in mice (Drago *et al.*, 1986; Insel & Winslow, 1991; Meisenberg & Simmons, 1983; Nelson & Alberts, 1997), and to inhibit extinction and promote perseverative behaviours (De Wied *et al.*, 1993). However, it is important to be cautious when making analogies between animal and human behaviour.

Current safety information regarding the use of intranasal oxytocin in humans largely comes from research into its use by mothers to promote lactation and not in clinical trials where it is used to target psychological problems. However, MacDonald and colleagues (2011) systematically reviewed 38 RCTs conducted between 1990 and 2010 that investigated the central effects of intranasal oxytocin in mostly typically developing samples and found no evidence for reliable side effects or adverse outcomes when oxytocin was delivered in doses of 18 to 40 IU for short-term use in controlled research settings. However, comprehensive product information describing possible side effects associated with the use of oxytocin for promoting lactation[68]

---

[68]Novartis Medical Information: 1800 671 203, under 'Oxytocin'. Available at: www.novartis.com.au/products_healthcare.html [accessed September 2011].

reports that cardiovascular changes, including tachycardia and bradycardia, can be common. With intravenous infusion, nausea, vomiting and headaches have also been reported to occur; less frequent reactions include water intoxication and associated neonatal hyponatraemia, skin rashes and anaphylactoid reactions[69]. Safety information regarding the use of intranasal oxytocin is available from European countries such as the Netherlands, where it is marketed for improving lactation (MacDonald *et al.*, 2011); it lists headaches, nausea and allergic dermatitis occurring rarely, and abnormal uterine contractions occurring sometimes.

It is important to note—assuming it proved to be efficacious and safe—that there are potential practical problems with delivering oxytocin as a routine treatment for the core symptoms of autism. It is destroyed in the gastrointestinal tract and therefore must be administered as an injection or intranasal spray. However, oxytocin has a half-life of about 3 minutes in the blood when administered intravenously (MacDonald *et al.*, 2011).

8.7.2 Studies considered[70]

Four placebo-controlled trials of oxytocin were found for review. All four were published in peer-reviewed journals between 2003 and 2010, and were in an adult population with autism. However, all four studies were excluded because they failed to meet sample size eligibility criteria (in each study the sample had fewer than ten participants per arm for analysis due to the crossover design). These studies (ANDARI2010 [Andari *et al.*, 2010]; GUASTELLA2010 [Guastella *et al.*, 2010]; HOLLANDER2003 [Hollander *et al.*, 2003b]; HOLLANDER2007 [Hollander *et al.*, 2007]) are, however, narratively reviewed below in order to provide background for the GDG when considering the use of oxytocin in adults with autism. Further information about these excluded studies can be found in Appendix 14f.

8.7.3 Clinical evidence for oxytocin

All of the placebo-controlled studies examining oxytocin in adults with autism were excluded on the basis that the sample sizes were insufficient to be entered into meta-analysis because they were crossover studies and failed to meet the eligibility criteria of at least ten participants per arm. The results of these studies will, however, be described because the GDG felt that a recommendation should be made with regards to the use of oxytocin in adults with autism due to the recent interest in this intervention. Four

---

[69]Novartis Medical Information: 1800 671 203, under 'Oxytocin'. Available at: www.novartis.com.au/products_healthcare.html [accessed September 2011].

[70]Here and elsewhere in the guideline, each study considered for review is referred to by a study ID in capital letters (primary author and date of study publication, except where a study is in press or only submitted for publication, then a date is not used).

crossover RCTs examined the effects of oxytocin on core symptoms of autism in adults; three of these trials examined the effects of oxytocin on social behaviour and one examined treatment effects on repetitive behaviour.

The studies examining the effects of oxytocin on social cognition in adults with autism reported results suggestive of potential benefits. For instance, ANDARI2010 found that oxytocin inhalation produced more appropriate social behaviour in the context of a computer-based social ball tossing game ($z = 1.99$, $p < 0.047$). GUASTELLA2010 found that oxytocin inhalation improved performance on the Reading the Mind in the Eyes Test with 60% of participants demonstrating improvement ($t = 2.43$, $p = 0.03$). In addition, HOLLANDER2007 found that intravenous oxytocin increased the retention of affective speech comprehension in autism, but not for participants who received placebo first, as demonstrated by the statistically significant three-way interaction of time by treatment by order (in which drug or placebo was administered) ($z = 2.134$, $p = 0.033$).

The single trial examining the effects of oxytocin on repetitive behaviours in adults with autism also suggested potential benefits. HOLLANDER2003 found a significant reduction in repetitive behaviour following oxytocin infusion compared with placebo infusion as demonstrated by the statistically significant time by treatment interaction ($F = 3.487$, $p = 0.027$).

However, it was not possible to extract efficacy data for these studies due to the small sample sizes. The statistical analysis reported by the authors implies that the treatment effects, although statistically significant, were modest in size. The results also imply that the response to oxytocin may be inconsistent. For instance, ANDARI2010 states that some participants responded strongly to oxytocin, others more weakly, and some not at all. The results from GUASTELLA2010 suggest that oxytocin did not improve performance on a measure of social cognition for 40% of participants, and HOLLANDER2007 found that the order of administration affected the treatment response to oxytocin.

8.7.4   Clinical evidence summary for oxytocin

Although the review identified and described a number of placebo-controlled trials for oxytocin in adults with autism, efficacy data could not be extracted from these studies due to insufficient sample sizes. Moreover, these studies could be described as 'proof of concept' studies rather than standard placebo-controlled RCTs and as a result the ecological validity and generalisability of results is unknown. Moreover, the results are suggestive of only modest treatment effects and inconsistent responses and the studies have methodological limitations.

8.7.5   Health economic evidence for oxytocin

No studies assessing the cost effectiveness of oxytocin in adults with autism were identified by the systematic search of the economic literature undertaken for this guideline. Details on the methods used for the systematic search of the economic literature are described in Chapter 3.

8.7.6   From evidence to recommendations

The studies reviewed above suggest that oxytocin may be beneficial in helping to reduce repetitive behaviours and to improve some aspects of communication in some adults with autism. Based on the absence of any included RCTs, and the practical issues regarding the half-life of oxytocin and the barriers that this might present to routine administration, the GDG judged that it is unlikely to be beneficial for people with autism and further evidence would be needed in order for oxytocin to be recommended for the treatment of core symptoms of autism in adults.

8.7.7   Recommendations

8.7.7.1   Do not use oxytocin for the management of core symptoms of autism in adults.

8.8   HORMONAL INTERVENTIONS: MELATONIN FOR COEXISTING CONDITIONS

8.8.1   Introduction

Melatonin is a hormone and neurotransmitter that induces sleep by inhibiting the wakefulness-generating system (Arendt, 2003; Cajochen *et al.*, 2003; Sachs *et al.*, 1997) and has been used to treat insomnia. It has been used successfully to promote sleep in children with neurodevelopmental conditions (Miyamoto *et al.*, 1999; Wheeler *et al.*, 2005; Zhdanova *et al.*, 1999). Most studies have not found evidence for serious adverse events or development of tolerance (Jan *et al.*, 1999; Saebra *et al.*, 2000). A few studies have reported side effects of tiredness, dizziness and headache associated with melatonin treatment (for example, Paavonen *et al.*, 2003; Palm *et al.*, 1997), however these immediately disappeared after discontinuation (Arendt, 1997; Jan & O'Donnel, 1996).

Sleep problems are common in people with autism with prevalence rates ranging from 43 to 83% in children (Miano & Ferri, 2010; Richdale & Schreck, 2009). It has been proposed that because prefrontal cortex functions are particularly prone to the deficits induced by sleep deprivation, and individuals with autism may already have compromised function of the prefrontal cortex, poor sleep may impair the daytime functioning of people with autism more than their neurotypical peers (Tani *et al.*, 2003). Sleep problems in people with autism may be caused by a circadian rhythm disturbance (Guénolé *et al.*, 2011), and melatonin regulation has been found to be abnormal in children with autism, with reports of a daytime elevation in melatonin, as well as decreased amplitude and lack of night-time elevation (Jan *et al.*, 1999; Nir *et al.*, 1995; Richdale *et al.*, 1999; Ritvo *et al.*, 1993). Rossignol and Frye (2011) reviewed nine studies reporting melatonin or melatonin-metabolite concentrations in people with autism and all but one of these found evidence of abnormal melatonin levels. Moreover, correlations have been found between levels of melatonin or melatonin metabolites and autistic symptoms or clinical findings (Leu *et al.*, 2010; Melke *et al.*, 2008; Nir *et al.*, 1995; Tordjman *et al.*, 2005). There is also evidence for abnormalities in genes that code for melatonin receptors or enzymes involved in melatonin synthesis in people with autism. For instance, the acetylserotonin methyltranserase gene, which codes for the last enzyme involved in melatonin synthesis, has been found to be abnormal in people with autism (Cai *et al.*, 2008; Jonsson *et al.*, 2010; Melke *et al.*, 2008; Toma *et al.*, 2007).

In evaluating the treatment of coexisting conditions, like insomnia, in people with autism it is important to consider the extent to which modifications need to be made to the routine treatment of these conditions as a consequence of the autism.

Current practice
Rossignol and Frye (2011) reviewed studies reporting the prevalence of melatonin usage in people with autism; three survey studies (Aman *et al.*, 2003; Green *et al.*, 2006; Polimeni *et al.*, 2005) reported by Rossignol and Frye (2011) estimated a mean prevalence of 7.2% (95% CI, 5.6 to 8.7%).

8.8.2   Studies considered[71]

There were no RCTs or quasi-experimental, observational or case series studies providing relevant clinical evidence for melatonin for the coexisting condition of sleep disorder in adults with autism. Due to the lack of primary data, and following the rules for extrapolation, a decision was made to extrapolate from data from a population of children with autism. No RCTs meeting the extrapolation eligibility criteria were found for children with autism. One open-label observational before-and-after trial (N = 15) was found. This study was published in a peer-reviewed journal in 2003. In addition, two observational studies were excluded from the analysis because no data were reported for the statistical analysis of treatment effects. Further information about both included and excluded studies can be found in Appendix 14f.

The included open-label observational before-and-after trial in children with autism (PAAVONEN2003 [Paavonen *et al.*, 2003]) examined the effects of melatonin on sleep in children with autism with no control group (see Table 98).

---

[71]Here and elsewhere in the guideline, each study considered for review is referred to by a study ID in capital letters (primary author and date of study publication, except where a study is in press or only submitted for publication, then a date is not used).

Table 98: Study information table of observational open-label trials of melatonin for coexisting conditions in children with autism

	Melatonin
No. trials (total participants)	1 (15)
Study ID	PAAVONEN2003*
N/% female	2/13
Mean age	10 years
IQ	Not reported
Axis I/II disorders	100% autism (Asperger's syndrome); 7% ADHD
Dose	3 mg per day 30 minutes before bedtime
Comparator	No comparator
Length of treatment	2 weeks
Length of follow-up	5 weeks
Note. *Efficacy data not extractable.	

8.8.3   Clinical evidence for melatonin

Open-label melatonin for coexisting sleep disorders
There were no included RCTs or quasi-experimental or observational studies comparing melatonin with placebo, or examining open-label melatonin with no control group, in adults with autism. Based on the rules for extrapolation, data were included from a population of children with autism. There were also no included RCTs of melatonin in children with autism. However, one open-label observational before-and-after trial was included (PAAVONEN2003). Efficacy data could not be extracted for this study. However, PAAVONEN2003 reported results suggestive of a statistically significant change from baseline after melatonin treatment in the form of decreased mean nocturnal activity ($p = 0.041$) and sleep onset latency ($p = 0.002$) as measured by an actigraph. However, the authors also reported a significantly greater number of awakenings ($p = 0.048$) post-melatonin treatment, which suggests that the effects of melatonin on sleep patterns in children with autism were inconsistent.

8.8.4   Clinical evidence summary for melatonin

This single open-label observational before-and-after trial provides some suggestion that melatonin may help with insomnia in children with autism. However, the lack of efficacy data, and the indirectness and inconsistency of the evidence, contributed to the GDG judging that there was insufficient evidence to make a recommendation about the use of melatonin for insomnia in adults with autism.

8.8.5   Health economic evidence for melatonin

No studies assessing the cost effectiveness of melatonin in adults with autism were identified by the systematic search of the economic literature undertaken for this guideline. Details on the methods used for the systematic search of the economic literature are described in Chapter 3.

8.8.6   From evidence to recommendations

No recommendation is made due to lack of evidence for melatonin in people with autism and sleep-related problems.

8.9   STIMULANTS FOR COEXISTING CONDITIONS

8.9.1   Introduction

Stimulants (also known as psychostimulants) are psychoactive drugs that affect the action of certain chemicals in the brain and can bring about improvements in attention and behaviour organisation. Stimulants are predominantly used as a first-line treatment for hyperactivity and inattention in people diagnosed with ADHD. Prevalence estimates suggest that 11 to 14% of individuals with autism are treated for ADHD symptoms with stimulant medication (Aman *et al.*, 1995b and 2003; Langworthy-Lam *et al.*, 2002; Martin *et al.*, 1999). The most prescribed and studied stimulant medication in children without a learning disability is methylphenidate, which is a central nervous system stimulant. Its action has been linked to inhibition of the dopamine transporter, with consequent increases in dopamine available for synaptic transmission (Volkow *et al.*, 1998). There is some evidence suggesting significant reduction of overactivity and inattention with methylphenidate in children with autism (Lubetsky & Handen, 2008), however side effects have been found with higher doses (Handen *et al.*, 2000; Quintana *et al.*, 1995). In addition, response rates for children with autism are significantly lower than the 77% response rate reported for children with ADHD (Greenhill *et al.*, 2001). It is also important to consider whether individuals with autism may be at higher risk of experiencing the side effects associated with stimulant medication including motor tics, social withdrawal, irritability and appetite loss (Handen *et al.*, 1991; Posey *et al.*, 2004). The review of evidence for the use of stimulants to treat hyperactivity in individuals with autism will consider whether any modifications need to be made to the recommendations for the treatment of hyperactivity symptoms and ADHD (NICE, 2009d) as a result of the autism.

Current practice

In the UK, methylphenidate is a Schedule 2 controlled drug and is currently licensed for the management of ADHD in children and young people over 6 years old, but not for the treatment of ADHD in adults (although it is used off-label). Both immediate-release and modified-release formulations are available in the UK. Methylphenidate is used in the treatment of ADHD and associated symptoms in children with autism; this is unsurprising given the extent of comorbidity between the disorders but the GDG was unable to identify any data on the extent of its use in adults with autism.

8.9.2   Studies considered[72]

There were no RCTs or quasi-experimental, observational or case series studies providing relevant clinical evidence for the effects of stimulants on hyperactivity or ADHD symptoms in adults with autism. Due to the lack of primary data, and following the rules on extrapolation, the GDG decided to include evidence from children with autism. One RCT (N = 66) was found that met the extrapolation eligibility criteria; this was supplemented by two papers reporting a secondary analysis of the same dataset. All were published in peer-reviewed journals between 2005 and 2009. In addition, five studies were excluded from the analysis. Two were not included because data could not be extracted due to the lack of a control group, a naturalistic retrospective chart review design, and no reported statistics that could be used in a meta-analysis or narrative synthesis (NICKELS2008 [Nickels *et al.*, 2008], STIGLER2004 [Stigler *et al.*, 2004]). Three studies were excluded due to insufficient samples of fewer than ten participants per arm. Further information about both included and excluded studies can be found in Appendix 14f.

The single included RCT of stimulants (see Table 99) compared methylphenidate with placebo to target coexisting hyperactivity in children with autism (RUPP2005 [Research Units on Pediatric Psychopharmacology (RUPP) Autism Network, 2005]). In the secondary analysis papers also reporting data from this trial, methylphenidate was compared with placebo for core symptoms of autism (social-interaction difficulties and repetitive behaviour) and those data are extracted here too (JAHROMI2009 [Jahromi *et al.*, 2009], POSEY2007 [Posey *et al.*, 2007]).

8.9.3   Clinical evidence for stimulants

Methylphenidate compared with placebo for coexisting hyperactivity

There were no included RCTs or quasi-experimental or observational studies comparing methylphenidate with placebo, or examining open-label

---

[72]Here and elsewhere in the guideline, each study considered for review is referred to by a study ID in capital letters (primary author and date of study publication, except where a study is in press or only submitted for publication, then a date is not used).

**Table 99: Study information table for placebo-controlled trials of stimulants
for coexisting conditions in children with autism**

	Methylphenidate
No. trials (total participants)	1 (66)
Study IDs	RUPP2005 (secondary analysis: JAHROMI2009; POSEY2007)
N/% female	7/11
Mean age	8 years
IQ	16 to 135 (mean 62.6)
Axis I/II disorders	100% autism; 100% hyperactivity/impulsivity (CGI-S; Special Needs and Autism Project – IV)
Dose	Low, medium and high dosage levels of 0.125, 0.250 and 0.5 mg per kg three times a day
Comparator	Placebo
Length of treatment	1 week for each phase (placebo, low dose, medium dose, high dose)
Length of follow-up	12 weeks (including open-label continuation)

methylphenidate with no control group, in adults with autism. Based on the rules
for extrapolation, data were included from a population of children with autism.
There was a single included crossover RCT (RUPP2005) with secondary analysis
(JAHROMI2009, POSEY2007) for methylphenidate in children with autism
(see Table 100).

RUPP2005 found evidence for significant treatment effects of methylphenidate on
the Aberrant Behaviour Checklist (Community Version) Hyperactivity Subscale (test
for overall effect: $Z = 3.50$, $p = 0.0005$) with participants receiving optimal-dose
methylphenidate in the active drug phase exhibiting fewer hyperactive behaviours
than participants in the placebo phase.

However, the secondary analysis papers found no evidence for significant treatment effects of methylphenidate on core symptoms of autism. JAHROMI2009 found
no statistically significant differences between scores in the methylphenidate phase
and scores in the placebo phase for the social-communication measure of joint attention initiation as assessed by observational ratings (test for overall effect: $Z = 1.36$,
$p = 0.17$). POSEY2007 also failed to find statistically significant treatment effects
for methylphenidate on repetitive behaviour as assessed by the Children's Y-BOCS-
PDD (test for overall effect: $Z = 0.95$, $p = 0.34$). Thus, there is some evidence for

Table 100: Evidence summary table for methylphenidate compared with placebo in children with autism

	Hyperactivity	Core symptoms of autism (social interaction difficulties)	Core symptoms of autism (repetitive behaviour)
Study ID	RUPP2005	JAHROMI2009	POSEY2007
Effect size	MD = −8.80 (−13.72, −3.88)	MD = 6.50 (−2.85, 15.85)	MD = −0.92 (−2.82, 0.98)
Quality of evidence (GRADE)	Moderate[1]	Low[1,2]	Moderate[1]
Number of studies/ participants	K = 1; N = 62	K = 1; N = 34	K = 1; N = 63
Forest plot	1.5.6, Appendix 15	1.5.6, Appendix 15	1.5.6, Appendix 15

Note. [1]Downgraded for indirectness due to extrapolating from children with autism. [2]Downgraded for imprecision due to small sample size.

the efficacy of methylphenidate in treating hyperactive symptoms but not core symptoms of autism.

There are also safety concerns based on the high rate of discontinuation owing to adverse events in the RUPP2005 trial. Of the original participants, 18% dropped out owing to intolerable side effects, reporting irritability as the primary reason for discontinuation (accounting for 46% of the dropouts). This is of particular concern because the rate of adverse events may be underestimated in this trial given the short duration for each dosage level of methylphenidate (1 week each), and the fact that previous adverse response to methylphenidate was an exclusion criterion.

8.9.4   Clinical evidence summary for stimulants

This single placebo-controlled crossover trial and secondary analyses provide some evidence for the efficacy of methylphenidate in treating hyperactive behaviour in children with autism. However, no evidence was found for significant treatment effects of methylphenidate on core symptoms of autism and the high discontinuation rate owing to adverse events provides cause for concern with regards to safety.

8.9.5 Health economic evidence for stimulants

No studies assessing the cost effectiveness of stimulants in adults with autism were identified by the systematic search of the economic literature undertaken for this guideline. Details on the methods used for the systematic search of the economic literature are described in Chapter 3.

8.9.6 From evidence to recommendations

There is evidence from one trial, of moderate quality, for the efficacy of methylphenidate in treating hyperactivity in children with autism. However, the evidence for treatment effects on core symptoms of autism was not statistically significant. The authors concluded that clinicians could feel more confident that methylphenidate targeting hyperactivity will not exacerbate core symptoms of autism. However, further research is needed in order to justify targeting these outcomes for treatment. It is also important to note that this evidence is indirect (due to extrapolating from children) and there are concerns about adverse event given the high attrition rate during methylphenidate treatment in the RUPP2005 study. On this basis the GDG concluded that the treatment of coexisting problems, including hyperactivity, in people with autism should be in line with existing NICE guidance (see, for example, NICE, 2009d).

8.9.7 Recommendations

8.9.7.1 For adults with autism and coexisting mental disorders, offer pharmacological interventions informed by existing NICE guidance for the specific disorder.

8.10 ANXIOLYTICS FOR COEXISTING CONDITIONS

8.10.1 Introduction

There is considerable evidence that autism coexists with anxiety disorders (Bellini, 2004; Gillott *et al.*, 2001; Green *et al.*, 2000; Kim *et al.*, 2000). Tantam (2000) stated that anxiety is almost universally comorbid with Asperger's syndrome and that high trait anxiety is a common feature in individuals across the autism spectrum, with social anxiety, panic and obsessive–compulsive rituals being the most common symptoms of anxiety shown by individuals with autism. The review of the evidence for the use of anxiolytics to treat anxiety in people with autism considers if any autism-specific modifications need to be made to the existing NICE guidance for anxiety disorders (NICE, 2005a, 2005b and 2011c).

8.10.2   Studies considered

Three studies examining the effects of buspirone in the treatment of individuals with autism were found in the initial search (Buitelaar *et al.*, 1998; Edwards *et al.*, 2006; Realmuto *et al.*, 1989). However, all of these studies were excluded at the first sift (on the basis of the abstract) due to a mean sample age of below 15 years or a sample of fewer than ten participants per arm.

8.10.3   Clinical evidence for anxiolytics

As discussed above, there was no clinical evidence for anxiolytics in adults with autism that met the eligibility criteria.

8.10.4   Clinical evidence summary for anxiolytics

There was no clinical evidence for anxiolytics in adults with autism. The GDG was of the view that future placebo-controlled trials of anxiolytics in adults with autism would be required in order to determine whether any adjustment to the usual treatment of anxiety disorders may be needed for individuals with autism. The safety and efficacy of anxiolytics targeted at behaviour management in autism also needs to be studied in future placebo-controlled trials.

8.10.5   Health economic evidence for anxiolytics

No studies assessing the cost effectiveness of anxiolytics in adults with autism were identified by the systematic search of the economic literature undertaken for this guideline. Details on the methods used for the systematic search of the economic literature are described in Chapter 3.

8.10.6   From evidence to recommendations

There was no clinical evidence for the use of anxiolytics in adults with autism. However, given the high prevalence of anxiety disorders in people with autism the GDG considered that anxiolytics may be used to treat coexisting anxiety disorders in adults with autism. Based on an understanding that the likely mechanisms of action of anxiolytics may well be the same in people with and without autism, the GDG decided to recommend the use of anxiolytics as set out in existing NICE guidelines (NICE, 2005a, 2005b and 2011c). Some adjustment in the dosing of the drugs may be required (for example starting at a lower dose and gradually increasing it if necessary), to take account of the increased sensitivity to drugs found in some people with autism.

8.10.7   Recommendations

8.10.7.1   For adults with autism and coexisting mental disorders, offer pharmacological interventions informed by existing NICE guidance for the specific disorder.

8.11   ANTIDEPRESSANTS FOR AUTISTIC BEHAVIOURS

8.11.1   Introduction

Psychiatric disorders, especially anxiety and depression, are common in people with autism (Gillberg & Billsteadt, 2000; Howlin, 2000). There are a number of antidepressants available, including monoamine-oxidase inhibitors, tricyclic antidepressants, selective serotonin reuptake inhibitors (SSRIs) and serotonin-norepinephrine reuptake inhibitors. Results from surveys suggest that 22% of individuals with autism are prescribed antidepressants (Aman *et al.*, 2003). As well as being used to treat depressive symptoms in individuals with autism, antidepressant medication has also been targeted at ritualistic and stereotypic behaviours (Hollander *et al.*, 1998). There has only been limited systematic evaluation of interventions for depression in children with autism, however results are suggestive of the efficacy of antidepressants (Ghaziuddin *et al.*, 2002; Stewart *et al.*, 2006). There is less evidence for the role of antidepressants in treating core symptoms of autism or autistic behaviours. However, these are the target symptoms in the antidepressant trials reviewed here.

Tricyclic antidepressants (including amitriptyline, clomipramine, doxepin, imipramine and trimipramine) belong to the oldest class of antidepressant drug. They were thought to exert their therapeutic effect by inhibiting the reuptake of monoamine neurotransmitters into the presynaptic neurone, thus enhancing noradrenergic and serotonergic neurotransmission, but as with other antidepressants, this is no longer accepted as an explanation of their efficacy (Hyman & Nestler, 1996). All tricyclic antidepressants cause, to varying degrees, anticholinergic side effects (dry mouth, blurred vision, constipation, urinary retention and sweating), sedation and postural hypotension. They are also toxic in overdose, with seizures and arrhythmias being a particular concern. This, and the perceived poor tolerability of tricyclic antidepressants in general, has led to a decline in their use in the UK over the last decade.

SSRIs are more widely used because they are better tolerated, and they are the antidepressant drug group most often used in people with autism (Antochi *et al.*, 2003). SSRIs inhibit the reuptake of serotonin into the presynaptic neurone thus increasing neurotransmission. SSRIs are associated with fewer anticholinergic side effects and are less likely to cause postural hypotension or sedation. They are also less cardiotoxic and much safer in overdose than tricyclic antidepressants. The most problematic side effects of SSRIs are nausea, diarrhoea and headache.

As serotonin has been linked to the mediation of psychological processes that are altered in autism (for instance, mood, social interaction, sleep, obsessive–compulsive behaviours and aggression) (Saxena, 1995), it has been suggested that inhibition of serotonin reuptake may result in improvement of symptoms of autism (Williams *et al.*, 2010). In addition, the aggregation of depressive symptoms in certain families affected by autism has suggested possible overlap in genetic influences underlying the two conditions (Bailey *et al.*, 1995; Daniels *et al.*, 2008; Ghaziuddin & Greden, 1998; Sullivan *et al.*, 2000). However, there is also evidence for substantial independence of their respective genetic origins (Constantino *et al.*, 2003; Hallett *et al.*, 2009).

Prevalence rates for depression in people with autism vary widely, with estimates ranging from 1.4% (Simonoff *et al.*, 2008) to 38% (Lainhart & Folstein, 1994). The reasons for this inconsistency are thought to lie in the phenotypic overlap between the two conditions, for instance, the tendency for autistic symptomatology to mask key features of depression and the fact that symptoms of depression in children with autism may be atypical (Magnuson & Constantino, 2011). Research has suggested that 'higher-functioning' or more socially adjusted individuals with autism may show a heightened risk for depression (Ghaziuddin *et al.*, 2002; Simonoff *et al.*, 2008). For instance, Vickerstaff and colleagues (2007) found that superior cognitive abilities and greater condition insight were associated with lower self-perceived social competence and subsequently higher rates of depression in children with autism. Similarly, Sterling and colleagues (2008) found that depression in adults with autism was associated with higher cognitive ability, less social impairment and older age. The review of the evidence for the use of antidepressants to treat depression in people with autism considers whether any autism-specific modifications need to be made to existing NICE guidance (NICE, 2009a)

8.11.2   Studies considered[73]

Two RCTs (N = 66) examining the effects of antidepressants in people with autism were found. One of these studies included an adolescent sample, however, the GDG decided to include it following the rules for extrapolation because the mean age was 16 years. Two open-label observational studies with no control group (N = 65) were also included, one of which also had an adolescent sample with a mean age of 16 years, which the GDG decided to include. All of these studies were published in peer-reviewed journals between 1992 in 2001. In addition, eight studies were excluded from the analysis, predominantly due to the mean age of the sample being below 15 years. Further information about both included and excluded studies can be found in Appendix 14f.

Of the two RCTs (see Table 101), one compared clomipramine with placebo (REMINGTON2001 [Remington *et al.*, 2001]) and one compared fluvoxamine with placebo (MCDOUGLE1996 [McDougle *et al.*, 1996]).

Of the two observational before-and-after studies (see Table 102), one examined the effects of fluoxetine with no control group (COOK1992 [Cook *et al.*, 1992]) and

---

[73]Here and elsewhere in the guideline, each study considered for review is referred to by a study ID in capital letters (primary author and date of study publication, except where a study is in press or only submitted for publication, then a date is not used).

Table 101: Study information table of placebo-controlled trials of antidepressants in adolescents and adults with autism

	Clomipramine	Fluvoxamine
No. trials (total participants)	1 (36)	1 (30)
Study IDs	REMINGTON2001	MCDOUGLE1996
N/% female	6/17	3/10
Mean age	16 years	30 years
IQ	Not reported	25 to 115 (mean 79.9)
Axis I/II disorders	100% autism	100% autism (autistic disorder); 3% Fragile X syndrome
Dose	Final dose 100 to 150 mg per day (mean 123 mg per day)	200 to 300 mg per day (mean dose 276.7 mg per day)
Comparator	Placebo	Placebo
Length of treatment	6 weeks per intervention	12 weeks
Length of follow-up	21 weeks	12 weeks

one examined the effects of sertraline with no control group (MCDOUGLE1998B [McDougle *et al.*, 1998b]).

8.11.3   Clinical evidence for antidepressants

Clomipramine compared with placebo for autistic behaviours
Of the two RCTs examining antidepressants in adolescents and adults with autism, one involved a comparison of clomipramine with placebo (see Table 103). REMING-TON2001 found no evidence for a statistically significant treatment effect of clomipramine on autistic behaviours as measured by the CARS (test for overall effect: $Z = 0.57$, $p = 0.57$). This trial also found no statistically significant difference between participants receiving clomipramine and those taking placebo in global side effects as measured by the Dosage Treatment Emergent Symptom Scale (DOTES) (test for overall effect: $Z = 1.43$, $p = 0.15$). However, the attrition rate in this study does give cause for concern regarding adverse events associated with clomipramine. For instance, 34% of the clomipramine group dropped out due to side effects of

Table 102: Study information table of open-label observational studies of antidepressants in adolescents and adults with autism

	Fluoxetine	Sertraline
No. trials (total participants)	1 (23)	1 (42)
Study IDs	COOK1992*	MCDOUGLE1998B*
N/% female	5/22	15/36
Mean age	16 years	26 years
IQ	Not reported but had a learning disability	25 to 114 (mean 60.5)
Axis I/II disorders	100% autism (autistic disorder); 96% learning disability; 13% OCD; 26% impulse control disorder no other symptoms with self-injurious behaviour; 22% impulse control disorder no other symptoms without self-injurious behaviour; 4% cyclothymia; 4% bipolar disorder no other symptoms; 4% eating disorder	100% autism (52% autistic disorder; 14% 'Asperger's disorder'; 33% PDD-NOS); 67% learning disability
Dose	Dose ranged from 20 mg every other day to 80 mg per day	50 to 200 mg per day
Comparator	No comparator	No comparator
Length of treatment	11 to 426 days (mean 189 days)	12 weeks
Length of follow-up	11 to 426 days (mean 189 days)	12 weeks
Note. *Efficacy data not extractable.		

fatigue or lethargy, tremors, tachycardia, insomnia, diaphoresis, nausea or vomiting, or decreased appetite, whereas only 3% of the placebo group dropped out due to side effects (in this case, nosebleeds). To summarise, this single trial provides no evidence for significant beneficial effects of clomipramine on autistic behaviours and the attrition rate suggests that there are grounds for concerns about safety.

Fluvoxamine compared with placebo for autistic behaviours
The remaining included RCT for antidepressants in adults and adolescents with autism compared fluvoxamine with placebo (see Table 104). MCDOUGLE1996 found evidence for statistically significant treatment effects on the core autistic symptom of

Table 103: Evidence summary table for clomipramine compared with placebo in adolescents with autism

	Autistic behaviours	**Global side effects**
Study IDs	REMINGTON2001	REMINGTON2001
Effect size	MD = –1.60 (–7.07, 3.87)	MD = 1.20 (–0.45, 2.85)
Quality of evidence (GRADE)	Very low[1,2,3]	Very low[1,2,3]
Number of studies/ participants	K = 1; N = 32	K = 1; N = 32
Forest plot	1.5.7, Appendix 15	1.5.7, Appendix 15

Note. [1]Downgraded for risk of attrition bias due to high dropout in the clomipramine group. [2]Downgraded for indirectness because the sample includes children and adolescents with autism and mean age is 16 years. [3]Downgraded for imprecision because the sample size was small.

repetitive behaviour (test for overall effect: Z = 2.81, p = 0.005), autistic behaviours (test for overall effect: Z = 2.15, p = 0.03), reduction in aggression and maladaptive behaviour (test for overall effect: Z = 2.40, p = 0.02, and Z = 3.83, p = 0.0001, respectively) and symptom severity or improvement (test for overall effect: Z = 2.01, p = 0.04 for dichotomous measure; Z = 4.37, p <0.0001 for continuous measure). In summary, this study found evidence for significant treatment effects, with participants receiving fluvoxamine showing superior scores to those taking placebo. Moreover, fluvoxamine was well tolerated and all participants completed the trial. However, the quality of this study was downgraded due to the small sample size and there may be reliability and validity issues with the measure of repetitive behaviour using the Y-BOCS; although this scale is valid and reliable for assessing the severity of obsessive–compulsive symptoms in individuals with OCD, its validity and reliability for assessing repetitive thoughts in autism is unknown.

Open-label fluoxetine for behaviour management
Of the two open-label observational before-and-after studies with no control group, one examined the effects of fluoxetine on behaviour management in adolescents with autism (COOK1992). It was not possible to extract efficacy data from this study. However, the authors reported statistically significant change-from-baseline scores for CGI ratings of overall clinical severity (t = 4.03, p <0.002) and of severity of perseverative or compulsive behaviour (t = 3.13, p <0.005). However, 26% of participants had side effects that significantly interfered with function or outweighed therapeutic effects, including hyperactivity, insomnia, elated affect, decreased appetite,

Table 104: Evidence summary table for fluvoxamine compared with placebo in adults with autism

	Core symptom of autism (repetitive behaviour)	Autistic behaviour	Challenging behaviour (aggression; change-from-baseline)	Maladaptive behaviour (change-from-baseline)	Symptom severity behaviour or improvement (dichotomous)	Symptom severity or improvement (continuous)
Study IDs	MCDOUGLE1996	MCDOUGLE1996	MCDOUGLE1996	MCDOUGLE1996	MCDOUGLE1996	MCDOUGLE1996
Effect size	MD = -8.20 (-13.92, -2.48)	SMD = -0.82 (-1.56, -0.07)	SMD = -0.92 (-1.68, -0.17)	SMD = -1.61 (-2.43, -0.79)	RR = 17.00 (1.07, 270.41)	SMD = -1.94 (-2.80, -1.07)
Quality of evidence (GRADE)	Low[1,2]	Moderate[1]	Moderate[1]	Moderate[1]	Moderate[1]	Moderate[1]
Number of studies/ participants	K = 1; N = 30	K = 1; N = 30	K = 1; N = 30	K = 1; N = 30	K = 1; N = 30	K = 1; N = 30
Forest plot	1.5.7, Appendix 15	1.5.7, Appendix 15	1.5.7, Appendix 15	1.5.7, Appendix 15	1.5.7, Appendix 15	1.5.7, Appendix 15

Note. [1]Downgraded for imprecision because the sample size was small. [2]Downgraded for imprecision as Y-BOCS valid and reliable for assessing severity of obsessive–compulsive symptoms in individuals with OCD but reliability and validity for assessing repetitive thoughts in autism is unknown.

behavioural problems and maculopapular rash. These results provide limited evidence of possible beneficial treatment effects of fluoxetine for behaviour management in adolescents with autism. However, there is some evidence for adverse events. In addition, the efficacy and safety evidence is of very low quality having been downgraded on the basis of very serious risk of bias (due to no control and lack of extractable efficacy data), indirectness (because of coexisting psychiatric diagnoses and age of the sample) and imprecision (as a result of the small sample size).

Open-label sertraline for autistic behaviours
Finally, the remaining open-label observational before-and-after study with no control group examined the change-from-baseline effects of sertraline on autistic behaviours in adults with autism (MCDOUGLE1998B). It was not possible to extract efficacy data for this study. However, the authors reported statistically significant main effects of time in their one-way ANOVA analysis for the core autistic symptom of repetitive behaviour as measured by the Y-BOCS ($F = 4.78$, $p = 0.000$), autistic behaviours as measured by the Ritvo-Freeman Real-Life Rating Scale ($F = 10.74$, $p = 0.0001$), maladaptive behaviour as measured by the Vineland Adaptive Behaviour Scale ($F = 18.52$, $p = 0.0001$), and symptom severity or improvement as measured by the CGI ($F = 15.78$, $p = 0.0001$) with participants showing superior scores following sertraline treatment. This study provides evidence suggestive of beneficial treatment effects of sertraline on autistic behaviours in adults with autism, however the evidence is of a very low quality due to the lack of a control group, the very small sample size and the fact that efficacy data could not be extracted. In addition, there are concerns with the Y-BOCS scale as a measure for repetitive thoughts in autism.

8.11.4   Clinical evidence summary for antidepressants

The two placebo-controlled trials examining the use of antidepressants for autistic behaviours in adolescents and adults with autism provide inconsistent results, with the single trial of clomipramine providing no evidence for efficacy and the attrition rate raising safety concerns, and the single trial of fluvoxamine providing evidence for tolerability and significant beneficial treatment effects. Thus, there is some evidence to suggest that fluvoxamine may be effective for treating the core autistic symptom of repetitive behaviour and autistic behaviours and for reducing challenging and maladaptive behaviour. However, this evidence is only of a low to moderate quality due to concerns about the reliability and validity of the Y-BOCS as a measure of repetitive behaviour in autism and the small sample size.

8.11.5   Health economic evidence for antidepressants

No studies assessing the cost effectiveness of antidepressants in adults with autism were identified by the systematic search of the economic literature undertaken for this guideline. Details on the methods used for the systematic search of the economic literature are described in Chapter 3.

8.11.6   From evidence to recommendations

There is evidence from one trial, of moderate quality, for the efficacy of fluvoxamine in treating autistic behaviours in adults with autism. This study also found fluvoxamine to be well tolerated, with all participants completing the trial. However, the GDG concluded that further research examining the efficacy and safety of fluvoxamine and other SSRIs was necessary in order to provide evidence for clinically important treatment effects. At present the GDG concluded that there was not sufficient evidence to recommend antidepressants targeted at core symptoms of autism in adults. There was also no evidence for autism-specific modifications to antidepressant treatment of coexisting depression and consequently the GDG concluded that treatment of coexisting depression should be in accordance with existing NICE guidance (NICE, 2009a) with some account taken of the increased sensitivity to drugs in some people with autism.

8.11.7   Recommendations

8.11.7.1   Do not use antidepressant medication for the routine management of core symptoms of autism in adults.

8.11.7.2   For adults with autism and coexisting mental disorders, offer pharmacological interventions informed by existing NICE guidance for the specific disorder.

8.11.8   Research recommendation

8.11.8.1   Pharmacological treatments for depression in adults with autism
What is the clinical and cost effectiveness of selective serotonin reuptake inhibitors (SSRIs) for the treatment of moderate and severe depression in adults with autism?

Why this is important
Depression commonly coexists with autism and is associated with poorer health outcomes and quality of life. This may occur because of the direct impact of the depression but also because of a negative interaction with the core symptoms of autism. There is poor recognition and consequently suboptimal treatment for depression in adults with autism. However, it is probable that when depression is recognised the most commonly used treatment is antidepressant medication as it is an effective intervention for moderate to severe depression. Little is known about the extent of the use of antidepressant medication, adherence to prescribed medication and its effectiveness in adults with autism. Moreover, concerns have also been raised about the

increased sensitivity of people with autism to the side effects of SSRIs and other anti-depressant drugs.

The suggested programme of research would need to: (a) describe the current use of SSRIs in adults with depression and autism; (b) review the potential impact of increased sensitivity of adults with autism to the side effects of medication; and (c) formally evaluate the outcomes (including symptoms, satisfaction and quality of life) of SSRIs in a series of randomised controlled trials.

8.12   EXCLUSION DIETS, VITAMINS, MINERALS AND SUPPLEMENTS FOR AUTISTIC BEHAVIOURS

8.12.1   Introduction

There has been increasing interest in dietary interventions for people with autism, which has been motivated by findings of increased incidence of gastrointestinal problems in children with autism (Horvath & Perman, 2002; White, 2003). For instance, a gluten- and casein-free diet has been proposed as a therapeutic intervention for autism. This exclusion diet eliminates the dietary intake of gluten (found most often in wheat, barley and rye) and casein (found most often in milk). Such a diet is based on the hypothesis that the intestinal barrier is abnormally permeable in people with autism and as a result gluten or casein are able to enter the blood through a 'leaky' small intestinal mucosa and induce antigenic responses that directly affect the central nervous system (White, 2003). There is some evidence for increased intestinal permeability in children with autism (D'Eufemia *et al.*, 1996). It has been proposed that peptides from gluten and casein may have an aetiological role in the pathogenesis of autism (Reichelt *et al.*, 1981), and that the physiology and psychology of autism may be explained by excessive opioid activity linked to these peptides (Israngkun *et al.*, 1986). The 'opioid excess' theory postulates that autistic behaviours mimic the influence of opioids on human brain function (White, 2003). Anecdotal reports and limited single-blind studies have claimed to demonstrate improvements in social-communication and cognitive skills in people with autism using a gluten- and casein-free diet (White, 2003). However, a Cochrane review of this diet for people with autism found that the evidence for efficacy was poor, and that larger-scale good quality RCTs were needed (Millward *et al.*, 2008).

The ketogenic diet is another exclusion diet that has been proposed as a treatment for autism. It is a high-fat, adequate-protein, low-carbohydrate diet that was originally introduced as a therapeutic intervention for epileptic seizures (Wilder, 1921). The low carbohydrate mimics a state of starvation and leads the liver to convert fats into fatty acids and ketone bodies. The ketone bodies pass into the brain and replace the glucose (which would normally be extracted from carbohydrates) as an energy source. An elevated level of ketone bodies in the blood, a state known as ketosis, leads to a reduction in the frequency of epileptic seizures (Freeman *et al.*, 2007). This diet lost popularity as a standard treatment for epilepsy with the advent of modern anticonvulsant drugs, but it has seen a slight resurgence in recent years in epilepsy treatment, and it has been suggested that it may be beneficial for behaviour and hyperactivity when applied to control seizures in Rett syndrome (Haas *et al.*, 1986). More recently the ketogenic diet has been proposed as a potential therapeutic intervention for autism based on the hypothesis that people with autism may have deficient glucose oxidation, which a ketogenic diet would address by allowing ketone bodies to be used as an alternative energy source in the brain (Evangeliou *et al.*, 2003). Evidence has been found for deficient glucose oxidation in autism (Siegel *et al.*, 1995). However, the question of how this diet works and how it might specifically impact on autistic behaviours remains to be answered.

Dietary supplements including vitamins and minerals, such as magnesium–vitamin B6, have also been proposed for people with autism based on the hypothesis that they have nutritional deficiencies that may be the cause of some of the symptoms of autism. Dietary supplements as an adjunct or alternative to exclusion diets have also been put forward as a treatment for autism. For instance, digestive enzyme supplementation has been suggested as an alternative or addition to a gluten- and casein-free diet. It uses peptidase enzymes to break down exorphins into smaller peptides that do not have opioid activity, and there are pilot data from a non-controlled study suggesting improvements in autistic symptoms following such supplementation (Brudnak *et al.*, 2002).

Other supplements have targeted brain regions of dysfunction in autism, for instance, the amino acid L-carnosine, which accumulates in the enterorhinal subfrontal cortex and is believed to act on the frontal lobe system. The theory that frontal lobe abnormalities may play a role in autism is not a new idea (Damasio & Maurer, 1978; Mundy, 2003) and is based on findings for the role of the frontal regions in higher-order cognitive, language, social and emotional functions (Stuss & Knight, 2002), which are known to be deficient in autism (Baron-Cohen, 1991; Kanner, 1943; Ozonoff *et al.*, 1991). However, the mechanism of action of L-carnosine is not well understood. For instance, an alternative mode of action of L-carnosine is related to the chelation properties of the dipeptide. Zinc and copper are endogenous transition metals that can be synaptically released during neuronal activity, and are required for normal functioning in the nervous system. However, they can also be neurotoxic and L-carnosine may act as an endogenous neuroprotective agent by modulating the neurotoxic effects of zinc and copper (Horning *et al.*, 2000). These hypotheses are speculative and there has been very little research into the use of L-carnosine as an intervention in autism. Finally, dietary supplements have also been proposed to target coexisting conditions in people with autism, for instance, iron supplementation targeted at sleep problems. There is some evidence for low serum ferritin concentration levels in children with autism (Dosman *et al.*, 2006; Latif *et al.*, 2002), which suggests iron deficiency because ferritin is an intracellular protein that stores iron and releases it in a controlled fashion, and thus the amount of ferritin stored reflects the amount of iron stored. Research has suggested a relationship between low ferritin and restless legs syndrome (Connor *et al.*, 2003; Earley, 2003; Earley *et al.*, 2000), the symptoms of which are relieved by activity and worsen at night resulting in delayed onset of sleep (Walters, 1995). The sleep problems experienced by children with autism, such as longer sleep latency, muscle twitches, and increased muscle activity during rapid eye movement sleep (Elia *et al.*, 2000; Patzold *et al.*, 1998; Thirumalai *et al.*, 2002), along with the finding of low ferritin levels, may suggest an association between sleep disturbance in autism and restless legs syndrome and, thus, iron supplementation may be hypothesised to have beneficial effects for sleep problems in people with autism.

In summary, there is very little evidence regarding safety and efficacy for exclusion diets, vitamins, minerals or supplements for the treatment of autism. Moreover, it is important to bear in mind that, unlike drugs, dietary supplements do not go through rigorous safety and efficacy testing by bodies such as the Medicines and Healthcare products Regulatory Agency (MHRA), and some dietary supplements can be associated with adverse side effects and/or interact and perhaps interfere with the action of other supplements or prescribed drugs.

8.12.2   Studies considered[74]

There were no RCTs or quasi-experimental, observational or case series studies providing relevant clinical evidence and meeting eligibility criteria for diets, vitamins, minerals or supplements in adults with autism. Due to the lack of primary data, and in line with the rules for extrapolation, a decision was made to extrapolate from data from children with autism. Three RCTs (N = 94), which met the extrapolation eligibility criteria, were found for children with autism. Five observational studies (N = 195), including one case-control study, were also found. All of these studies were published in peer-reviewed journals between 1988 in 2010. In addition, 15 studies were excluded, predominantly due to small samples of fewer than ten participants per arm, or because data to enter into meta-analysis or include in a narrative synthesis could not be extracted. Further information about both included and excluded studies can be found in Appendix 14f.

Of the three RCTs (see Table 105), one compared a gluten- and casein-free diet with treatment as usual (KNIVSBERG2003 [Knivsberg *et al.*, 2003]), one compared a digestive enzyme supplementation with placebo (MUNASINGHE2010 [Munasinghe *et al.*, 2010]) and one compared L-carnosine with placebo (CHEZ2002 [Chez *et al.*, 2002]).

Of the five observational studies (see Table 106), the case-control study compared micronutrients with standard medication (MEHLMADRONA2010 [Mehl-Madrona *et al.*, 2010]) and of the four observational before-and-after studies, two examined the effects of magnesium–vitamin B6 supplement (MARTINEAU1988 [Martineau *et al.*, 1988], MOUSAINBOSC2006 [Mousain-Bosc *et al.*, 2006]), one examined the effects of iron supplementation (DOSMAN2007 [Dosman *et al.*, 2007]) and one examined the effects of a ketogenic diet (EVANGELIOU2003 [Evangeliou *et al.*, 2003]).

---

[74]Here and elsewhere in the guideline, each study considered for review is referred to by a study ID in capital letters (primary author and date of study publication, except where a study is in press or only submitted for publication, then a date is not used).

**Table 105: Study information table of placebo-controlled or
treatment-as-usual controlled trials of diet, vitamins or supplements
in children with autism**

	Gluten- and casein-free diet	Digestive enzyme supplementation	L-carnosine
No. trials (total participants)	1 (20)	1 (43)	1 (31)
Study IDs	KNIVSBERG2003	MUNASINGHE2010	CHEZ2002
N/% female	Not reported	7/16	10/32
Mean age	7 years	6 years	7 years
IQ	Range not reported (means 81 and 85)	Not reported	Not reported
Axis I/II disorders	100% autism	100% autism (88% autistic disorder; 12% PDD-NOS)	100% autism
Dose	Not reported	½ to 9 capsules per day according to manufacturer's recommended dose	400 mg twice daily
Comparator	Treatment as usual	Placebo	Placebo
Length of treatment	1 year	3 months	8 weeks
Length of follow-up	1 year	6 months	8 weeks

8.12.3 Clinical evidence for exclusion diets, vitamins, minerals and supplements

Exclusion diets for autistic behaviours

There were no included RCTs or quasi-experimental or observational studies comparing exclusion diets with treatment as usual, or examining exclusion diets with no control group, in adults with autism. Based on the expert judgement of the GDG, data were included from a population of children with autism. One RCT compared a gluten- and casein-free diet with treatment as usual (see Table 107); one observational before-and-after study examined the effects of a ketogenic diet on autistic behaviours (EVANGELIOU2003) and this is narratively described below.

KNIVSBERG2003 found evidence for a significant treatment effect of a gluten- and casein-free diet compared with treatment as usual (test for overall effect: Z = 3.19, p = 0.001), with fewer autistic behaviours (as assessed by the

Table 106: Study information table of included observational trials of diet, vitamins or supplements in children with autism

	Micronutrients	Magnesium–vitamin B6	Iron supplement	Ketogenic diet
No. trials (total participants)	1 (88)	2 (44)	1 (33)	1 (30)
Study IDs	MEHLMADRONA2010	(1) MARTINEAU1988* (2) MOUSAINBOSC2006*	DOSMAN2007*	EVANGELIOU2003*
N/% female	20/23	(1) 6/55 (2) 12/36	6/18	14/47
Mean age	8 to 9 years	(1) 6 years (2) 4 years	7 years	Median 7 years
IQ	Range not reported (means 89 and 91)	(1) 30 to 80 (mean 50) (2) Not reported	Not reported	Not reported
Axis I/II disorders	100% autism	(1)–(2) 100% autism	100% autism	100% autism
Dose	Not reported	(1) 30 mg per kg per day pyridoxine hydrochloride and 10 mg per kg per day magnesium lactate (2) 6 mg per kg per day magnesium; 0.6 mg per kg per day vitamin B6	Oral preparation 6 mg elemental iron per kg per day N = 23; 2 sachets of sprinkles, total of 60 mg per day N = 10	John Radcliffe diet, which distributes daily energy intake as follows: 30% of energy as medium chain triglyceride oil, 30% as fresh cream, 11% as saturated fat, 19% as carbohydrates and 10% as protein
Comparator	Standard medication management	(1)–(2) No comparator	No comparator	No comparator
Length of treatment	3 to 98 months (experimental group mean: 24 months; control group mean: 18 months)	(1) 8 weeks (2) Mean 8 months	8 weeks	6 months (with continuous administration for 4 weeks at a time, interrupted by 2-week intervals that were diet free)
Length of follow-up	3 to 98 months (experimental group mean: 24 months; control group mean: 18 months)	(1) 14 weeks (2) 24 months	8 weeks	6 months

Note. *Efficacy data not extractable.

**Table 107: Evidence summary table for a gluten- and casein-free diet
compared with treatment as usual control in children with autism**

	Autistic behaviours
Study ID	KNIVSBERG2003
Effect size	MD = −5.60 (-9.04, −2.16)
Quality of evidence (GRADE)	Very low[1,2,3]
Number of studies/participants	K = 1; N = 20
Forest plot	1.5.8, Appendix 15

Note. [1]Downgraded for risk of performance bias because it was unclear whether the intervention groups received the same care apart from treatment, and the study was non-blinded. [2]Downgraded for indirectness due to extrapolating from children with autism. [3]Downgraded for imprecision because the sample size was small.

Diagnose of Psykotisk Adferd hos Børn [Diagnosis of Psychotic Behaviour in Children] Social Isolation and Bizarre Behaviour Subscale) observed in children following a gluten- and casein-free diet relative to the control group. However, there was a high risk of performance bias in this study as it is unclear if the control group received the same care apart from the intervention, and participants receiving care and individuals administering care were not blind to group allocation.

EVANGELIOU2003 examined the effects of a ketogenic diet on autistic behaviours in an observational before-and-after study. However, there was no control group and efficacy data could not be extracted for this study. The authors reported evidence suggestive of an overall improvement in autistic behaviour as measured by the CARS following a ketogenic diet intervention (t = 5.347, p <0.001).

In summary these studies provide data suggestive of significant positive treatment effects of exclusion diets on autistic behaviours. However, this evidence is of very low quality and the addition of attention-placebo control groups would be important in order to reduce the risk of bias in these studies.

Vitamins, minerals and supplements for autistic behaviours
There were no included RCTs or quasi-experimental or observational studies comparing vitamins, minerals or supplements with treatment as usual or placebo, or examining dietary supplements with no control group, in adults with autism. Based on the rules for extrapolation, data were included from a population of children with autism. A range of supplements have been examined in children with autism. One RCT examined the effects of a digestive enzyme supplementation compared with placebo (see Table 108). One placebo-controlled study compared L-carnosine supplementation with placebo (see Table 109). Of the observational studies, which

Table 108: Evidence summary table for digestive enzyme supplementation compared with placebo in children with autism

	Core symptom of autism (social-communication difficulties)	Challenging behaviour	Gastrointestinal symptoms
Study IDs	MUNASINGHE2010	MUNASINGHE2010	MUNASINGHE2010
Effect size	MD = 1.36 (–15.74, 18.46)	MD = 0.18 (–0.27, 0.63)	MD = 0.14 (–0.19, 0.47)
Quality of evidence (GRADE)	Low[1,2]	Low[1,2]	Low[1,2]
Number of studies/ participants	K = 1; N = 43	K = 1; N = 43	K = 1; N = 43
Forest plot	1.5.8, Appendix 15	1.5.8, Appendix 15	1.5.8, Appendix 15

Note. [1]Downgraded for indirectness due to extrapolating from children with autism. [2]Downgraded for imprecision because the sample size was small.

Table 109: Evidence summary table for L-carnosine compared with placebo in children with autism

	Autistic behaviours	Symptom severity or improvement
Study IDs	CHEZ2002	CHEZ2002
Effect size	MD = –4.01 (-9.03, 1.01)	MD = 2.14 (–0.99, 5.27)
Quality of evidence (GRADE)	Very low[1,2,3]	Very low[1,2,3]
Number of studies/ participants	K = 1; N = 31	K = 1; N = 31
Forest plot	1.5.8, Appendix 15	1.5.8, Appendix 15

Note. [1]Downgraded for risk of bias due to baseline group differences in autistic behaviours as measured by the GARS. [2]Downgraded for indirectness due to extrapolating from children with autism. [3]Downgraded for imprecision because the sample size was small.

will be narratively reviewed below, one open-label before-and-after study with no control group examined the effects of iron supplementation (DOSMAN2007); two open-label before-and-after studies examined the effects of a magnesium–vitamin B6 supplement (MARTINEAU1988, MOUSAINBOSC2006); and one observational case-control study compared a vitamin and mineral supplementation (micronutrient) with standard medication management in children with autism (MEHLMADRONA2010).

MUNASINGHE2010 compared a digestive enzyme supplement (Peptizyde™) with placebo in children with autism. Peptizyde™ is a combination of three plant-derived proteolytic enzymes (peptidase, protease 4.5 and papain) and is designed as a supplement or alternative to the gluten- and casein-free diet. This study failed to find evidence for significant treatment effects of Peptizyde™ on the core autistic symptom of social-communication difficulties as assessed by the parent-completed Language Development Survey – Vocabulary Scale (test for overall effect: $Z = 0.16$, $p = 0.88$), challenging behaviour as measured by the parent-rated GBRS (test for overall effect: $Z = 0.78$, $p = 0.44$), or for parent-rated gastrointestinal symptoms (test for overall effect: $Z = 0.84$, $p = 0.40$).

CHEZ2002 compared L-carnosine supplementation with placebo. This study failed to find evidence for a statistically significant treatment effect of L-carnosine supplementation on autistic behaviours over placebo as measured by the CARS (test for overall effect: $Z = 1.56$, $p = 0.12$) or on symptom severity or improvement of autism as assessed by the CGI (test for overall effect: $Z = 1.34$, $p = 0.18$). In addition, this study is downgraded for risk of bias due to baseline group differences in autistic behaviours as measured by the GARS.

One open-label observational study with no control group examined the effects of iron supplementation on coexisting sleep problems in children with autism (DOSMAN2007). However, efficacy data could not be extracted for this study. The authors reported evidence suggestive of a statistically significant treatment effect of iron supplementation on coexisting sleep problems with the restless sleep score showing improvement following iron supplementation ($p = 0.04$). However, no significant change-from-baseline treatment effect was found for challenging behaviour (as measured by CGI ratings of irritability; $p = 0.11$).

Two observational open-label studies with no comparators (MARTINEAU1988; MOUSAINBOSC2006) examined the effects of a magnesium–vitamin B6 supplement on autistic behaviours and, although efficacy data could not be extracted, both studies reported results suggestive of statistically significant change-from-baseline scores after magnesium–vitamin B6 supplementation. MARTINEAU1988 reported a significant change-from-baseline score for symptom severity ($t = 3.28$, $p < 0.01$). MOUSAINBOSC2006 found improved post-treatment scores on core autistic symptoms of social-communication difficulties, social-interaction difficulties and repetitive behaviour ($p < 0.0001$) as assessed by DSM-IV clinical evaluation. However, although these data are suggestive of significant positive treatment effects of magnesium–vitamin B6 supplementation, this evidence is of very low quality having been downgraded for risk of bias (due to the lack of a control group and because efficacy data cannot be extracted), for indirectness (extrapolating from children with autism), and for imprecision (due to small sample sizes). In addition MARTINEAU1988 was also downgraded for risk of bias because the sample was selected for previous sensitivity to the treatment and the age of the study calls the generalisability of findings into question.

Finally, an observational case-control study compared micronutrients with standard medication management in children with autism (see Table 110). The experimental group was given a broad-based micronutrient supplement, EMPowerplus, which consisted of all 14 of the known vitamins, 16 dietary minerals, three amino acids and three antioxidants. MEHLMADRONA2010 found no evidence for a statistically significant treatment effect on autistic behaviours as measured by the CARS (test for overall effect: $Z = 0.16$, $p = 0.87$). However, there was evidence for statistically significant treatment effects on challenging behaviour as measured by the Aberrant Behaviour Checklist (Community Version) Irritability Subscale (test for overall effect: $Z = 5.77$, $p < 0.00001$) and for symptom severity for improvement as measured by the CGI (test for overall effect: $Z = 4.11$, $p < 0.0001$). Thus, the evidence from this study suggests that the children with autism receiving micronutrients showed less challenging behaviour, and less severe symptoms than participants receiving standard medication. However, this study was downgraded to very low quality based on the indirectness of the evidence and the high risk of bias as a result of the lack of randomisation and blinding.

Table 110: Evidence summary table for micronutrients compared with standard medication in children with autism

	Autistic behaviours	**Challenging behaviour (irritability)**	**Symptom severity**
Study IDs	MEHLMADRONA2010	MEHLMADRONA2010	MEHLMADRONA2010
Effect size	MD = 0.50 (–5.62, 6.62)	MD = –7.40 (–9.91, –4.89)	MD = –1.38 (–2.04, –0.72)
Quality of evidence (GRADE)	Very low[1,2]	Very low[1,2]	Very low[1,2]
Number of studies/ participants	K = 1; N = 88	K = 1; N = 88	K = 1; N = 88
Forest plot	1.5.8, Appendix 15	1.5.8, Appendix 15	1.5.8, Appendix 15

Note. [1]Downgraded for risk of bias because this is a non-randomised and non-blinded study. [2]Downgraded for indirectness due to extrapolating from children with autism.

8.12.4 Clinical evidence summary for exclusion diets, vitamins, minerals and supplements

No studies examining exclusion diets, vitamins, minerals or supplements in adults with autism could be included, therefore all the data reviewed are indirect involving extrapolation from studies of children with autism. The single RCT examining the effects of exclusion diets in children with autism found limited evidence for a positive effect of a gluten- and casein-free diet on autistic behaviours. In addition, an observational before-and-after study examining the effects of a ketogenic diet on autistic behaviours in children with autism reported limited evidence also suggestive of beneficial effects. However, the quality of this evidence was downgraded due to high risk of bias as a consequence of the lack of blinding. The addition of an attention-placebo control group would be important in order to reduce the risk of bias in these studies.

The evidence for vitamins, minerals and supplements is more mixed. The two RCTs examining the effects of supplements in children with autism, one of which compared L-carnosine with placebo and the other digestive enzyme supplementation with placebo, both failed to find evidence for statistically significant treatment effects on autistic behaviours. The observational studies of vitamins, minerals and supplements were, on the whole, more positive. For instance, the only case-controlled observational study compared micronutrients with standard medication for children with autism and found evidence for significant treatment effects on challenging behaviour and symptom severity or improvement although no significant treatment effects were observed for autistic behaviours as assessed by the CARS. The observational before-and-after studies (with no control group) present results suggestive of improvements in coexisting sleep problems as a result of iron supplementation, and for symptom severity and core symptoms of autism following magnesium–vitamin B6 supplementation.

To summarise, the evidence for exclusion diets in children with autism suggests there may be some potential benefits. However, the risk of bias and indirectness of the data result in a very low quality evidence base. The evidence for vitamins, minerals and supplements is inconsistent with some suggestion of beneficial effects of micronutrients for challenging behaviour, iron supplementation for coexisting sleep problems and magnesium–vitamin B6 supplementation for autistic behaviours. However, further randomised placebo-controlled studies are required to corroborate the existing low to very low quality evidence for diets, vitamins, minerals and supplements in people with autism.

8.12.5 Health economic evidence for restrictive diets, vitamins, minerals and supplements

No studies assessing the cost effectiveness of restrictive diets, vitamins, minerals or supplements in adults with autism were identified by the systematic search of the economic literature undertaken for this guideline. Details on the methods used for the systematic search of the economic literature are described in Chapter 3.

8.12.6   From evidence to recommendations

The evidence for the use of exclusion diets, vitamins, minerals and supplements in autism is indirect (extrapolated from data from children) and of only low to very low quality. Of the four trials from which efficacy data could be extracted, two suggested positive treatment effects: one for a gluten- and casein-free diet and one for a dietary supplement (micronutrients). However, two trials failed to find significant treatment effects of supplements for either L-carnosine or for a digestive enzyme supplementation, and the latter of these studies is of a higher quality compared with the other studies and is the only blinded trial (although it is important to note that it is still low quality). On the basis of this evidence the GDG concluded that there was insufficient evidence for the safety and efficacy of exclusion diets or vitamins, minerals or supplements and that further randomised and blinded placebo-controlled trials would be required before the use of such interventions could be recommended to treat autistic behaviours in adults.

8.12.7   Recommendations

8.12.7.1   Do not use the following interventions for the management of core symptoms of autism in adults:
- exclusion diets (such as gluten- or casein-free and ketogenic diets)
- vitamins, minerals and dietary supplements (such as vitamin B6 or iron supplementation).

8.13   CHELATION FOR AUTISTIC BEHAVIOURS

8.13.1   Introduction

Chelation, also known colloquially as detoxification, involves using one or more substances (chelating agents) to remove materials that are toxic, including heavy metals such as mercury, from the body. There are a wide range of chelating agents associated with different efficacy and side effects. These include alpha lipoic acid, cysteine, dimercaptosuccinic acid, sodium dimercaptopropane sulfonate, ethylene-dinitrilotetraacetic acid, nanocolloidal detox factors, thiamine tetrahydrofurfuryl disulfide and zeolite. There is currently no clinical evidence that chelation is an effective treatment for individuals with autism (Research Autism, 2011b) and there are safety concerns associated with it (Fombonne, 2008).

8.13.2   Studies considered

Three studies examining the effects of chelating agents (meso-2, 3-dimercapto-succinic acid or thiamine tetrahydrofurfuryl disulfide) in the treatment of people with autism were found in the initial search (Adams *et al.*, 2009a and 2009b; Geier &

Geier, 2006; Lonsdale *et al.*, 2002). However, all of these studies were excluded at the first sift (on the basis of the abstract) due to a mean sample age of below 15 years.

8.13.3   Clinical evidence for chelation

As discussed above, there was no clinical evidence for chelation in adults with autism that met the eligibility criteria.

8.13.4   Clinical evidence summary for chelation

There was no clinical evidence for chelation in adults with autism.

8.13.5   Health economic evidence for chelation

No studies assessing the cost effectiveness of chelation in adults with autism were identified by the systematic search of the economic literature undertaken for this guideline. Details on the methods used for the systematic search of the economic literature are described in Chapter 3.

8.13.6   From evidence to recommendations

There was no clinical evidence for the use of chelation in adults with autism. However, the GDG, mindful that chelation was actively sought out by people with autism and their families, judged that it was highly controversial and posed a potential serious risk to health. On the basis of these safety concerns, the GDG decided that chelation should not be recommended for the treatment of autism.

8.13.7   Recommendations

8.13.7.1   Do not use chelation for the management of core symptoms of autism in adults.

8.14   TESTOSTERONE REGULATION FOR AUTISTIC BEHAVIOURS

8.14.1   Introduction

Testosterone regulation involves using a drug, such as leuprolide, to reduce the amount of testosterone and oestrogen in the body. Geier and Geier (2005) suggested that this drug may be effective for the treatment of autism, with the proposed mode of action being that excess testosterone may increase the toxicity of mercury. However, the links between autism and testosterone, and between autism and vaccines containing the mercury-based preservative thimerosal that were hypothesised to cause autism, have been discredited (Allen, 2007; Parker *et al.*, 2004). There is no evidence for the efficacy of testosterone regulation as a treatment for autism (Research Autism, 2011c). In addition, if used in children or young people, leuprolide could cause significant and irreversible damage to sexual development and functioning.

8.14.2   Studies considered

One study examining the effects of testosterone regulation, using anti-androgen therapy, in the treatment of people with autism was found in the initial search (Geier & Geier, 2006). However, his study was excluded at the first sift (on the basis of the abstract) due to a mean sample age of below 15 years.

8.14.3   Clinical evidence for testosterone regulation

As discussed above, there was no clinical evidence for testosterone regulation in adults with autism that met the eligibility criteria.

8.14.4   Clinical evidence summary for testosterone regulation

There was no clinical evidence for testosterone regulation in adults with autism.

8.14.5   Health economic evidence for testosterone regulation

No studies assessing the cost effectiveness of testosterone regulation in adults with autism were identified by the systematic search of the economic literature undertaken for this guideline. Details on the methods used for the systematic search of the economic literature are described in Chapter 3.

8.14.6   From evidence to recommendations

There was no clinical evidence for the use of testosterone regulation in adults with autism. However, the GDG was mindful that testosterone regulation was highly controversial and might be offered to adults with autism. In view of the serious risk to health and the lack of any evidence of benefit, the decision was taken that testosterone regulation should not be recommended for the treatment of autism.

8.14.7   Recommendations

8.14.7.1   Do not use testosterone regulation for the management of core symptoms of autism in adults.

8.15   HYPERBARIC OXYGEN THERAPY FOR AUTISTIC BEHAVIOURS

8.15.1   Introduction

Hyperbaric oxygen therapy is the medical use of oxygen at a level higher than atmospheric pressure administered in a pressurised chamber. The aim of the therapy is to increase oxygen absorption in bodily tissue. It has been used at high pressures (over 2.0 atmospheres absolute) for the treatment of conditions such as decompression sickness, arterial gas embolism, carbon monoxide poisoning (Leach *et al.*, 1998), amyotrophic lateral sclerosis (Steele *et al.*, 2004) and complex regional pain syndrome (Kiralp *et al.*, 2004). The therapy has also been used at lower pressures (1.5 atmospheres absolute or less) to treat fetal alcohol syndrome (Stoller, 2005) and ischemic brain injury (Neubauer *et al.*, 1992). When used to treat standard medical conditions, hyperbaric oxygen therapy is generally safe provided there is proper installation, trained administration, and expert advice available (Research Autism, 2011d). But there are risks, which can include damage to the ears, sinuses, lungs and teeth due to pressure in the chamber, and too much oxygen can cause seizures and lung problems. It has been proposed as a treatment for autism on the basis that neuroimaging results have suggested that there may be hypoperfusion to several areas of the brain, in particular to temporal regions, in people with autism and hyperbaric oxygen therapy can compensate for decreased blood flow by increasing the oxygen content of plasma and body tissues (Rossignol & Rossignol, 2006).

8.15.2   Studies considered

Six studies examining the effects of hyperbaric oxygen therapy for people with autism were found in the initial search (Bent *et al.*, 2011; Chungpaibulpatana *et al.*, 2008; Granpeesheh, *et al.*, 2010; Jepson *et al.*, 2011; Rossignol *et al.*, 2007 and 2009). However, these studies were excluded at the first sift (on the basis of the abstract) due to a mean sample age of below 15 years.

8.15.3   Clinical evidence for hyperbaric oxygen therapy

As discussed above, there was no clinical evidence for hyperbaric oxygen therapy in adults with autism that met the eligibility criteria.

8.15.4   Clinical evidence summary for hyperbaric oxygen therapy

There was no clinical evidence for hyperbaric oxygen therapy in adults with autism.

8.15.5   Health economic evidence for hyperbaric oxygen therapy

No studies assessing the cost effectiveness of hyperbaric oxygen therapy in adults with autism were identified by the systematic search of the economic literature undertaken for this guideline. Details on the methods used for the systematic search of the economic literature are described in Chapter 3.

8.15.6   From evidence to recommendations

There was no clinical evidence for the use of hyperbaric oxygen therapy in adults with autism. Moreover, the GDG was mindful of the risks and judged that they might not be justified in the treatment of core symptoms of autism. The GDG therefore decided that hyperbaric oxygen therapy should not be recommended for the treatment of autism.

8.15.7   Recommendations

8.15.7.1   Do not use hyperbaric oxygen therapy for the management of core symptoms of autism in adults.

9. SUMMARY OF RECOMMENDATIONS

9.1 GENERAL PRINCIPLES OF CARE

Principles for working with adults with autism and their families, partners and carers

9.1.1.1   All staff working with adults with autism should:
- work in partnership with adults with autism and, where appropriate, with their families, partners and carers
- offer support and care respectfully
- take time to build a trusting, supportive, empathic and non-judgemental relationship as an essential part of care.

9.1.1.2   All staff working with adults with autism should have an understanding of the:
- nature, development and course of autism
- impact on personal, social, educational and occupational functioning
- impact of the social and physical environment.

9.1.1.3   All health and social care professionals providing care and support for adults with autism should have a broad understanding of the:
- nature, development and course of autism
- impact on personal, social, educational and occupational functioning
- impact of and interaction with the social and physical environment
- impact on and interaction with other coexisting mental and physical disorders and their management
- potential discrepancy between intellectual functioning as measured by IQ and adaptive functioning as reflected, for example, by difficulties in planning and performing activities of daily living including education or employment.

9.1.1.4   All health and social care professionals providing care and support for adults with autism should:
- aim to foster the person's autonomy, promote active participation in decisions about care and support self-management
- maintain continuity of individual relationships wherever possible
- ensure that comprehensive information about the nature of, and interventions and services for, their difficulties is available in an appropriate language or format (including various visual, verbal and aural, easy-read, and different colour and font formats)
- consider whether the person may benefit from access to a trained advocate.

9.1.1.5   All health and social care professionals providing care and support for adults with autism and their families, partners and carers should:
- ensure that they are easily identifiable (for example, by producing or wearing appropriate identification) and approachable
- clearly communicate their role and function

- address the person using the name and title they prefer
- clearly explain any clinical language and check that the person with autism understands what is being said
- take into account communication needs, including those arising from a learning disability, sight or hearing problems or language difficulties, and provide communication aids or independent interpreters (someone who does not have a personal relationship with the person with autism) if required.

9.1.1.6   All health and social care professionals providing care and support for adults with autism and their families, partners and carers should ensure that they are:
- familiar with recognised local and national sources (organisations and websites) of information and/or support for people with autism
- able to discuss and advise on how to access and engage with these resources.

9.1.1.7   Encourage adults with autism to participate in self-help or support groups or access one-to-one support, and provide support so that they can attend meetings and engage in the activities.

9.1.1.8   In all settings, take into account the physical environment in which adults with autism are assessed, supported and cared for, including any factors that may trigger challenging behaviour. If necessary make adjustments or adaptations to the:
- amount of personal space given (at least an arm's length)
- setting using visual supports (for example, use labels with words or symbols to provide visual cues about expected behaviour)
- colour of walls and furnishings (avoid patterns and use low-arousal colours such as cream)
- lighting (reduce fluorescent lighting, use blackout curtains or advise use of dark glasses or increase natural light)
- noise levels (reduce external sounds or advise use of earplugs or ear defenders).

Where it is not possible to adjust or adapt the environment, consider varying the duration or nature of any assessment or intervention (including taking regular breaks) to limit the negative impact of the environment.

9.1.1.9   All health and social care professionals providing care and support for adults with autism should:
- be aware of under-reporting and under-recognition of physical disorders in people with autism
- be vigilant for unusual likes and dislikes about food and/or lack of physical activity
- offer advice about the beneficial effects of a healthy diet and exercise, taking into account any hyper- and/or hypo-sensory sensitivities; if necessary, support referral to a GP or dietician.

9.1.1.10   All staff working with adults with autism should be sensitive to issues of sexuality, including asexuality and the need to develop personal and sexual relationships. In particular, be aware that problems in social interaction and communication may lead to the person with autism misunderstanding another person's behaviour or to their possible exploitation by others.

9.1.1.11   Ensure that adults with autism who have caring responsibilities receive support to access the full range of mental and physical health and social care services, including:

- specific information, advice and support to parents about their parenting role, including parent training if needed, by professionals experienced in the care of adults and children with autism
- social support, such as childcare, to enable them to attend appointments, groups and therapy sessions, and to access education and employment.

Structures for the organisation and delivery of care and interventions

9.1.1.12   In order to effectively provide care and support for adults with autism, the local autism multi-agency strategy group[75] should include representation from managers, commissioners and clinicians from adult services, including mental health, learning disability, primary healthcare, social care, housing, educational and employment services, the criminal justice system and the third sector. There should be meaningful representation from people with autism and their families, partners and carers.

9.1.1.13   In each area a specialist community-based multidisciplinary team for adults with autism (the specialist autism team) should be established. The membership should include:

- clinical psychologists
- nurses
- occupational therapists
- psychiatrists
- social workers
- speech and language therapists
- support staff (for example, staff supporting access to housing, educational and employment services, financial advice, and personal and community safety skills).

9.1.1.14   The specialist autism team should have a key role in the delivery and coordination of:

- specialist diagnostic and assessment services
- specialist care and interventions
- advice and training to other health and social care professionals on the diagnosis, assessment, care and interventions for adults with autism (as not all may be in the care of a specialist team)
- support in accessing, and maintaining contact with, housing, educational and employment services

---

[75]See recommendation 1.1.1 in *Autism: Recognition, Referral and Diagnosis of Children and Young People on the Autism Spectrum* (NICE, 2011a).

346

- support to families, partners and carers where appropriate
- care and interventions for adults with autism living in specialist residential accommodation
- training, support and consultation for staff who care for adults with autism in residential and community settings.

Involving families, partners and carers

9.1.1.15   Discuss with adults with autism if and how they want their families, partners or carers to be involved in their care. During discussions, take into account any implications of the Mental Capacity Act (HMSO, 2005) and any communication needs the person may have (see recommendation 9.1.1.5).

9.1.1.16   If the person with autism wants their family, partner or carer(s) to be involved, encourage this involvement and:
- negotiate between the person with autism and their family, partner or carer(s) about confidentiality and sharing of information on an ongoing basis
- explain how families, partners and carers can help support the person with autism and help with care plans
- make sure that no services are withdrawn because of involvement of the family, partner or carer(s), unless this has been clearly agreed with both the person with autism and their family, partner or carer(s).

9.1.1.17   Give all families, partners and carer(s) (whether or not the person wants them to be involved in their care) verbal and written information about:
- autism and its management
- local support groups and services specifically for families, partners and carers
- their right to a formal carer's assessment of their own physical and mental health needs, and how to access this.

9.1.1.18   If a person with autism does not want their family, partners or carer(s) to be involved in their care:
- give the family, partner or carer(s) verbal and written information about who they can contact if they are concerned about the person's care
- bear in mind that people with autism may be ambivalent or negative towards their family or partner. This may be for many different reasons, including a coexisting mental disorder or prior experience of violence or abuse.

9.2   IDENTIFICATION AND ASSESSMENT

Principles for the effective assessment of autism

9.2.1.1   Staff who have responsibility for the identification or assessment of adults with autism should adapt these procedures, if necessary, to ensure their effective delivery, including modifications to the setting in which assessment is delivered (see recommendation 9.1.1.8) and the duration and pacing of the assessment.

Identification and initial assessment of possible autism

9.2.1.2   Consider assessment for possible autism when a person has:
- one or more of the following:
    - persistent difficulties in social interaction
    - persistent difficulties in social communication
    - stereotypic (rigid and repetitive) behaviours, resistance to change or restricted interests, **and**
- one or more of the following:
    - problems in obtaining or sustaining employment or education
    - difficulties in initiating or sustaining social relationships
    - previous or current contact with mental health or learning disability services
    - a history of a neurodevelopmental condition (including learning disabilities and attention deficit hyperactivity disorder) or mental disorder.

9.2.1.3   For adults with possible autism who do not have a moderate or severe learning disability, consider using the Autism-Spectrum Quotient – 10 items (AQ-10)[76]. (If a person has reading difficulties, read out the AQ-10.) If a person scores above six on the AQ-10, or autism is suspected based on clinical judgement (taking into account any past history provided by an informant), offer a comprehensive assessment for autism.

9.2.1.4   For adults with possible autism who have a moderate or severe learning disability, consider a brief assessment to ascertain whether the following behaviours are present (if necessary using information from a family member, partner or carer):
- difficulties in reciprocal social interaction including:
    - limited interaction with others (for example, being aloof, indifferent or unusual)
    - interaction to fulfil needs only
    - interaction that is naive or one-sided
- lack of responsiveness to others
- little or no change in behaviour in response to different social situations
- limited social demonstration of empathy
- rigid routines and resistance to change
- marked repetitive activities (for example, rocking and hand or finger flapping), especially when under stress or expressing emotion.

If two or more of the above categories of behaviour are present, offer a comprehensive assessment for autism.

---

[76]Allison and colleagues (2012).

Comprehensive (diagnostic, needs and risks) assessment of suspected autism

9.2.1.5   A comprehensive assessment should:
- be undertaken by professionals who are trained and competent
- be team-based and draw on a range of professions and skills
- where possible involve a family member, partner, carer or other informant or use documentary evidence (such as school reports) of current and past behaviour and early development.

9.2.1.6   At the beginning of a comprehensive assessment, discuss with the person the purpose of the assessment and how the outcome of the assessment will be fed back to them. Feedback should be individualised, and consider involving a family member, partner, carer or advocate, where appropriate, to support the person and help explain the feedback.

9.2.1.7   During a comprehensive assessment, enquire about and assess the following:
- core autism signs and symptoms (difficulties in social interaction and communication and the presence of stereotypic behaviour, resistance to change or restricted interests) that have been present in childhood and continuing into adulthood
- early developmental history, where possible
- behavioural problems
- functioning at home, in education or in employment
- past and current physical and mental disorders
- other neurodevelopmental conditions
- hyper- and/or hypo-sensory sensitivities and attention to detail.

Carry out direct observation of core autism signs and symptoms especially in social situations.

9.2.1.8   To aid more complex diagnosis and assessment for adults, consider using a formal assessment tool, such as:
- the following tools for people who do not have a learning disability:
  – the Adult Asperger Assessment (AAA; includes the Autism-Spectrum Quotient [AQ] and the Empathy Quotient [EQ])[77]
  – the Autism Diagnostic Interview – Revised (ADI-R)[78]
  – the Autism Diagnostic Observation Schedule – Generic (ADOS-G)[79]
  – the Asperger Syndrome (and high-functioning autism) Diagnostic Interview (ASDI)[80]
  – the Ritvo Autism Asperger Diagnostic Scale – Revised (RAADS-R)[81]
- the following tools in particular for people with a learning disability:
  – the ADOS-G
  – the ADI-R.

---

[77]Baron-Cohen and colleagues (2005).
[78]Lord and colleagues (1997).
[79]Lord and colleagues (2000).
[80]Gillberg and colleagues (2001).
[81]Ritvo and colleagues (2011).

9.2.1.9   To organise and structure the process of a more complex assessment, consider using a formal assessment tool, such as the Diagnostic Interview for Social and Communication Disorders (DISCO)[82], the ADOS-G or the ADI-R.

9.2.1.10   During a comprehensive assessment, take into account and assess for possible differential diagnoses and coexisting disorders or conditions, such as:

- other neurodevelopmental conditions (use formal assessment tools for learning disabilities)
- mental disorders (for example, schizophrenia, depression or other mood disorders, and anxiety disorders, in particular, social anxiety disorder and obsessive–compulsive disorder)
- neurological disorders (for example, epilepsy)
- physical disorders
- communication difficulties (for example, speech and language problems, and selective mutism)
- hyper- and/or hypo-sensory sensitivities.

9.2.1.11   Do not use biological tests, genetic tests or neuroimaging for diagnostic purposes routinely as part of a comprehensive assessment.

9.2.1.12   During a comprehensive assessment, assess the following risks:

- self-harm (in particular in people with depression or a moderate or severe learning disability)
- rapid escalation of problems
- harm to others
- self-neglect
- breakdown of family or residential support
- exploitation or abuse by others.

Develop a risk management plan if needed.

9.2.1.13   Develop a care plan based on the comprehensive assessment, incorporating the risk management plan and including any particular needs (such as adaptations to the social or physical environment), and also taking into account the needs of the family, partner or carer(s).

9.2.1.14   Provide a 'health passport' (for example, a laminated card) for adults with autism, which includes information for all staff about the person's care and support needs. Advise the person to carry the health passport at all times.

9.2.1.15   As part of a comprehensive assessment consider developing a 24-hour crisis management plan, where necessary in conjunction with specialist mental health services, which should detail:

- the likely trigger(s) for a crisis
- the nature and speed of the reaction to any trigger(s), including details about the way in which autism may impact on a person's behaviour leading up to and during a crisis
- the role of the specialist team and other services (including outreach and out-of-hours services) in responding to a crisis

---

[82]Wing and colleagues (2002).

- advice to primary care professionals and other services on their responsibilities and appropriate management in a crisis
- advice for families, partners and carers about their role in a crisis
- the nature of any changes or adaptations to the social or physical environment (see recommendation 9.1.1.8) needed to manage a crisis.

9.2.1.16 Consider obtaining a second opinion (including referral to another specialist autism team if necessary), if there is uncertainty about the diagnosis or if any of the following apply after diagnostic assessment:
- disagreement about the diagnosis within the autism team
- disagreement with the person, their family, partner, carer(s) or advocate about the diagnosis
- a lack of local expertise in the skills and competencies needed to reach diagnosis in adults with autism
- the person has a complex coexisting condition, such as a severe learning disability, a severe behavioural, visual, hearing or motor problem, or a severe mental disorder[83].

9.2.1.17 On an individual basis, and using information from the comprehensive assessment and physical examination, and clinical judgement, consider further investigations, including:
- genetic tests, as recommended by the regional genetics centre, if there are specific dysmorphic features, congenital anomalies and/or evidence of a learning disability
- electroencephalography if there is suspicion of epilepsy
- hearing or sight tests, if there is suspicion of hearing or visual impairment
- other medical tests depending on individual signs and symptoms (for example, sudden onset of challenging behaviour, change in usual patterns of behaviour, sudden change in weight, or suspicion that the person might be in pain and is unable to communicate this).

9.2.1.18 Offer all adults who have received a diagnosis of autism (irrespective of whether they need or have refused further care and support) a follow-up appointment to discuss the implications of the diagnosis, any concerns they have about the diagnosis, and any future care and support they may require.

Assessment of challenging behaviour

9.2.1.19 Assessment of challenging behaviour should be integrated into a comprehensive assessment for adults with autism.

9.2.1.20 When assessing challenging behaviour carry out a functional analysis (see recommendation 9.4.1.3) including identifying and evaluating any factors that may trigger or maintain the behaviour, such as:
- physical disorders
- the social environment (including relationships with family members, partners, carers and friends)

---

[83]Adapted from *Autism: Recognition, Referral and Diagnosis of Children and Young People on the Autism Spectrum* (NICE, 2011a).

- the physical environment, including sensory factors
- coexisting mental disorders (including depression, anxiety disorders and psychosis)
- communication problems
- changes to routines or personal circumstances.

Identifying the correct interventions and monitoring their use

9.2.1.21 When discussing and deciding on interventions with adults with autism, consider:
- their experience of, and response to, previous interventions
- the nature and severity of their autism
- the extent of any associated functional impairment arising from the autism, a learning disability or a mental or physical disorder
- the presence of any social or personal factors that may have a role in the development or maintenance of any identified problem(s)
- the presence, nature, severity and duration of any coexisting disorders
- the identification of predisposing and possible precipitating factors that could lead to crises if not addressed[84].

9.2.1.22 When discussing and deciding on care and interventions with adults with autism, take into account the:
- increased propensity for elevated anxiety about decision-making in people with autism
- greater risk of altered sensitivity and unpredictable responses to medication
- environment, for example whether it is suitably adapted for people with autism, in particular those with hyper- and/or hypo-sensory sensitivities (see recommendation 9.1.1.8)
- presence and nature of hyper- and/or hypo-sensory sensitivities and how these might impact on the delivery of the intervention
- importance of predictability, clarity, structure and routine for people with autism
- nature of support needed to access interventions.

9.2.1.23 When discussing and deciding on interventions with adults with autism, provide information about:
- the nature, content and duration of any proposed intervention
- the acceptability and tolerability of any proposed intervention
- possible interactions with any current interventions and possible side effects
- the implications for the continuing provision of any current interventions[85].

---

[84]Adapted from *Common Mental Health Disorders: Identification and Pathways to Care* (NICE, 2011b).
[85]Adapted from *Common Mental Health Disorders: Identification and Pathways to Care* (NICE, 2011b).

9.2.1.24 When deciding on options for pharmacological interventions for challenging behaviour or coexisting mental disorders in adults with autism:
- be aware of the potential for greater sensitivity to side effects and idio-syncratic responses in people with autism **and**
- consider starting with a low dose.

9.2.1.25 For any intervention used in adults with autism, there should be a regular review of:
- the benefits of the intervention, where feasible using a formal rating of the target behaviour(s)
- any adverse events
- specific monitoring requirements of pharmacological interventions as highlighted by the summary of product characteristics
- adherence to the intervention.

9.3   INTERVENTIONS FOR AUTISM

Psychosocial interventions for the core symptoms of autism

9.3.1.1 For adults with autism without a learning disability or with a mild to moderate learning disability, who have identified problems with social interaction, consider:
- a group-based social learning programme focused on improving social interaction
- an individually delivered social learning programme for people who find group-based activities difficult.

9.3.1.2 Social learning programmes to improve social interaction should typically include:
- modelling
- peer feedback (for group-based programmes) or individual feedback (for individually delivered programmes)
- discussion and decision-making
- explicit rules
- suggested strategies for dealing with socially difficult situations.

9.3.1.3 Do not provide 'facilitated communication' for adults with autism.

Psychosocial interventions focused on life skills

9.3.1.4 For adults with autism of all ranges of intellectual ability, who need help with activities of daily living, consider a structured and predictable train-ing programme based on behavioural principles.

9.3.1.5 For adults with autism without a learning disability or with a mild to moderate learning disability, who are socially isolated or have restricted social contact, consider:
- a group-based structured leisure activity programme

> - an individually delivered structured leisure activity programme for people who find group-based activities difficult.

9.3.1.6   A structured leisure activity programme should typically include:
- a focus on the interests and abilities of the participant(s)
- regular meetings for a valued leisure activity
- for group-based programmes, a facilitator with a broad understanding of autism to help integrate the participants
- the provision of structure and support.

9.3.1.7   For adults with autism without a learning disability or with a mild to moderate learning disability, who have problems with anger and aggression, offer an anger management intervention, adjusted to the needs of adults with autism.

9.3.1.8   Anger management interventions should typically include:
- functional analysis of anger and anger-provoking situations
- coping-skills training and behaviour rehearsal
- relaxation training
- development of problem-solving skills.

9.3.1.9   For adults with autism without a learning disability or with a mild learning disability, who are at risk of victimisation, consider anti-victimisation interventions based on teaching decision-making and problem-solving skills.

9.3.1.10   Anti-victimisation interventions should typically include:
- identifying and, where possible, modifying and developing decision-making skills in situations associated with abuse
- developing personal safety skills.

9.3.1.11   For adults with autism without a learning disability or with a mild learning disability, who are having difficulty obtaining or maintaining employment, consider an individual supported employment programme.

9.3.1.12   An individual supported employment programme should typically include:
- help with writing CVs and job applications and preparing for interviews
- training for the identified work role and work-related behaviours
- carefully matching the person with autism with the job
- advice to employers about making reasonable adjustments to the workplace
- continuing support for the person after they start work
- support for the employer before and after the person starts work, including autism awareness training.

Biomedical (pharmacological, physical and dietary) interventions and the core symptoms of autism

9.3.1.13   Do not use anticonvulsants for the management of core symptoms of autism in adults.

9.3.1.14   Do not use chelation for the management of core symptoms of autism in adults.

9.3.1.15   Do not use the following interventions for the management of core symptoms of autism in adults:
- exclusion diets (such as gluten- or casein-free and ketogenic diets)
- vitamins, minerals and dietary supplements (such as vitamin B6 or iron supplementation).

9.3.1.16   Do not use drugs specifically designed to improve cognitive functioning (for example, cholinesterase inhibitors) for the management of core symptoms of autism or routinely for associated cognitive or behavioural problems in adults.

9.3.1.17   Do not use oxytocin for the management of core symptoms of autism in adults.

9.3.1.18   Do not use secretin for the management of core symptoms of autism in adults.

9.3.1.19   Do not use testosterone regulation for the management of core symptoms of autism in adults.

9.3.1.20   Do not use hyperbaric oxygen therapy for the management of core symptoms of autism in adults.

9.3.1.21   Do not use antipsychotic medication for the management of core symptoms of autism in adults.

9.3.1.22   Do not use antidepressant medication for the routine management of core symptoms of autism in adults.

9.4   INTERVENTIONS FOR CHALLENGING BEHAVIOUR

9.4.1.1   Before initiating other interventions for challenging behaviour, address any identified factors that may trigger or maintain the behaviour (see recommendation 9.2.1.20) by offering:
- the appropriate care for physical disorders (for example, gastrointestinal problems or chronic pain)
- treatment for any coexisting mental disorders, including psychological and pharmacological interventions (for example, anxiolytic, antidepressant or antipsychotic medication), informed by existing NICE guidance
- interventions aimed at changing the physical or social environment (for example, who the person lives with) when problems are identified, such as:
  - advice to the family, partner or carer(s)
  - changes or accommodations to the physical environment (see recommendation 9.1.1.8).

9.4.1.2   Offer a psychosocial intervention for the challenging behaviour first if no coexisting mental or physical disorder, or problem related to the physical or social environment, has been identified as triggering or maintaining challenging behaviour.

9.4.1.3   When deciding on the nature and content of a psychosocial intervention to address challenging behaviour, use a functional analysis. The functional analysis should facilitate the targeting of interventions that address the function(s) of problem behaviour(s) by:

- providing information, from a range of environments, on:
  - factors that appear to trigger the behaviour
  - the consequences of the behaviour (that is, the reinforcement received as a result of their behaviour[86])
- identifying trends in behaviour occurrence, factors that may be evoking that behaviour, and the needs that the person is attempting to meet by performing the behaviour.

9.4.1.4   In addition to the functional analysis, base the choice of intervention(s) on:

- the nature and severity of the behaviour
- the person's physical needs and capabilities
- the physical and social environment
- the capacity of staff and families, partners or carers to provide support
- the preferences of the person with autism and, where appropriate, their family, partner or carer(s)
- past history of care and support.

Psychosocial interventions for challenging behaviour

9.4.1.5   Psychosocial interventions for challenging behaviour should be based on behavioural principles and informed by a functional analysis of behaviour (see recommendation 9.4.1.3).

9.4.1.6   Psychosocial interventions for challenging behaviour should include:

- clearly identified target behaviour(s)
- a focus on outcomes that are linked to quality of life
- assessment and modification of environmental factors that may contribute to initiating or maintaining the behaviour
- a clearly defined intervention strategy
- a clear schedule of reinforcement, and capacity to offer reinforcement promptly and contingently on demonstration of the desired behaviour
- a specified timescale to meet intervention goals (to promote modification of intervention strategies that do not lead to change within a specified time)
- a systematic measure of the target behaviour(s) taken before and after the intervention to ascertain whether the agreed outcomes are being met.

Combined interventions for challenging behaviour

9.4.1.7   Consider antipsychotic medication[87] in conjunction with a psychosocial intervention for challenging behaviour when there has been no or limited response to psychosocial or other interventions (such as environmental adaptations). Antipsychotic medication should be prescribed by a specialist

---

[86]Reinforcement may be by the person with autism or those working with or caring for them.

[87]At the time of publication (June 2012), no antipsychotic medication had a UK marketing authorisation for this indication in adults with autism. Informed consent should be obtained and documented.

and quality of life outcomes monitored carefully. Review the effects of the medication after 3–4 weeks and discontinue it if there is no indication of a clinically important response at 6 weeks.

Pharmacological interventions for challenging behaviour

9.4.1.8   Consider antipsychotic medication[15] for challenging behaviour on its own when psychosocial or other interventions could not be delivered because of the severity of the challenging behaviour. Antipsychotic medication should be prescribed by a specialist and quality of life outcomes monitored carefully. Review the effects of the medication after 3–4 weeks and discontinue it if there is no indication of a clinically important response at 6 weeks.

9.4.1.9   Do not routinely use anticonvulsants for the management of challenging behaviour in adults with autism.

9.5   INTERVENTIONS FOR COEXISTING MENTAL DISORDERS

9.5.1.1   Staff delivering interventions for coexisting mental disorders to adults with autism should:
- have an understanding of the core symptoms of autism and their possible impact on the treatment of coexisting mental disorders
- consider seeking advice from a specialist autism team regarding delivering and adapting these interventions for people with autism.

Psychosocial interventions for coexisting mental disorders

9.5.1.2   For adults with autism and coexisting mental disorders, offer psychosocial interventions informed by existing NICE guidance for the specific disorder.

9.5.1.3   Adaptations to the method of delivery of cognitive and behavioural interventions for adults with autism and coexisting common mental disorders should include:
- a more concrete and structured approach with a greater use of written and visual information (which may include worksheets, thought bubbles, images and 'tool boxes')
- placing greater emphasis on changing behaviour, rather than cognitions, and using the behaviour as the starting point for intervention
- making rules explicit and explaining their context
- using plain English and avoiding excessive use of metaphor, ambiguity and hypothetical situations
- involving a family member, partner, carer or professional (if the person with autism agrees) to support the implementation of an intervention
- maintaining the person's attention by offering regular breaks and incorporating their special interests into therapy if possible (such as using computers to present information).

Pharmacological interventions for coexisting mental disorders

9.5.1.4   For adults with autism and coexisting mental disorders, offer pharmacological interventions informed by existing NICE guidance for the specific disorder.

9.6   ASSESSMENT AND INTERVENTIONS FOR FAMILIES, PARTNERS AND CARERS

9.6.1.1   Offer families, partners and carers of adults with autism an assessment of their own needs including:
- personal, social and emotional support
- support in their caring role, including respite care and emergency plans
- advice on and support in obtaining practical support
- planning of future care for the person with autism.

9.6.1.2   When the needs of families, partners and carers have been identified, provide information about, and facilitate contact with, a range of support groups including those specifically designed to address the needs of families, partners and carers of people with autism.

9.6.1.3   Offer information, advice, training and support to families, partners and carers if they:
- need help with the personal, social or emotional care of the family member, partner or friend, **or**
- are involved in supporting the delivery of an intervention for their family member, partner or friend (in collaboration with professionals).

9.7   ORGANISATION AND DELIVERY OF CARE

Developing local care pathways

9.7.1.1   Local care pathways should be developed to promote implementation of key principles of good care. Pathways should be:
- negotiable, workable and understandable for adults with autism, their families, partners and carers, and professionals
- accessible and acceptable to all people in need of the services served by the pathway
- responsive to the needs of adults with autism and their families, partners and carers
- integrated so that there are no barriers to movement between different levels of the pathway
- outcome focused (including measures of quality, service user experience and harm)[88].

---

[88]Adapted from *Common Mental Health Disorders: Identification and Pathways to Care* (NICE, 2011b).

9.7.1.2   Autism strategy groups should be responsible for developing, managing and evaluating local care pathways. The group should appoint a lead professional responsible for the local autism care pathway. The aims of the strategy group should include:
- developing clear policy and protocols for the operation of the pathway
- ensuring the provision of multi-agency training about signs and symptoms of autism, and training and support on the operation of the pathway
- making sure the relevant professionals (health, social care, housing, educational and employment services and the third sector) are aware of the local autism pathway and how to access services
- supporting the integrated delivery of services across all care settings
- supporting the smooth transition to adult services for young people going through the pathway
- auditing and reviewing the performance of the pathway[89].

9.7.1.3   The autism strategy group should develop local care pathways that promote access to services for all adults with autism, including:
- people with coexisting physical and mental disorders (including substance misuse)
- women
- people with learning disabilities
- older people
- people from black and minority ethnic groups
- transgender people
- homeless people
- people from the traveller community
- people in the criminal justice system
- parents with autism.

9.7.1.4   When providing information about local care pathways to adults with autism and their families, partners and carers, all professionals should:
- take into account the person's knowledge and understanding of autism and its care and management
- ensure that such information is appropriate to the communities using the pathway[90].

9.7.1.5   The autism strategy group should design local care pathways that promote a range of evidence-based interventions at each step in the pathway and support adults with autism in their choice of interventions[91].

9.7.1.6   The autism strategy group should design local care pathways that respond promptly and effectively to the changing needs of all populations served by the pathways. Pathways should have in place:
- clear and agreed goals for the services offered to adults with autism

---

[89]Adapted from *Common Mental Health Disorders: Identification and Pathways to Care* (NICE, 2011b).
[90]Adapted from *Common Mental Health Disorders: Identification and Pathways to Care* (NICE, 2011b).
[91]Adapted from *Common Mental Health Disorders: Identification and Pathways to Care* (NICE, 2011b).

- robust and effective means for measuring and evaluating the outcomes associated with the agreed goals
- clear and agreed mechanisms for responding promptly to identified changes to people's needs[92].

9.7.1.7   The autism strategy group should design local care pathways that provide an integrated programme of care across all care settings. Pathways should:

- minimise the need for transition between different services or providers
- allow services to be built around the pathway and not the pathway around the services
- establish clear links (including access and entry points) to other care pathways (including those for physical healthcare needs)
- have designated staff who are responsible for the coordination of people's engagement with the pathway[93].

Improving access to care

9.7.1.8   There should be a single point of referral (including self-referral) to specialist services for adults with autism.

9.7.1.9   Support access to services and increase the uptake of interventions by:

- delivering assessment and interventions in a physical environment that is appropriate for people with hyper- and/or hypo-sensory sensitivities (see recommendation 9.1.1.8)
- changing the professional responsible for the person's care if a supportive and caring relationship cannot be established.

9.7.1.10   Support access to services and increase the uptake of interventions by:

- ensuring systems (for example, care coordination or case management) are in place to provide for the overall coordination and continuity of care for adults with autism
- designating a professional to oversee the whole period of care (usually a member of the primary healthcare team for those not in the care of a specialist autism team or mental health or learning disability service)[94].

9.8   RESIDENTIAL CARE

9.8.1.1   If residential care is needed for adults with autism it should usually be provided in small, local community-based units (of no more than six people and with well-supported single person accommodation). The environment should be structured to support and maintain a collaborative

---

[92]Adapted from *Common Mental Health Disorders: Identification and Pathways to Care* (NICE, 2011b).
[93]Adapted from *Common Mental Health Disorders: Identification and Pathways to Care* (NICE, 2011b).
[94]Adapted from *Common Mental Health Disorders: Identification and Pathways to Care* (NICE, 2011b).

approach between the person with autism and their family, partner or carer(s) for the development and maintenance of interpersonal and community living skills.

9.8.1.2   Residential care environments should include activities that are:
- structured and purposeful
- designed to promote integration with the local community and use of local amenities
- clearly timetabled with daily, weekly and sequential programmes that promote choice and autonomy.

9.8.1.3   Residential care environments should have:
- designated areas for different activities that provide visual cues about expected behaviour
- adaptations to the physical environment for people with hyper- and/or hypo-sensory sensitivities (see recommendation 9.1.1.8)
- inside and outside spaces where the person with autism can be alone (for example, if they are over-stimulated).

9.8.1.4   Residential care staff should:
- understand the principles and attitudes underpinning the effective delivery of residential care for adults with autism
- work in collaboration with health and community care staff from a range of specialist services to support the delivery of a comprehensive care plan
- be trained in assessing and supporting the needs of adults with autism
- be consistent and predictable, but with some flexibility to allow change and choice
- be committed to involving families, partners and carers.

9.9   RESEARCH RECOMMENDATIONS

9.9.1   Facilitated self-help for anxiety and depression in adults with autism

What is the clinical and cost effectiveness of facilitated self-help for the treatment of mild anxiety and depressive disorders in adults with autism?

Why this is important
Anxiety and depressive disorders commonly coexist in people with autism and are associated with poorer health outcomes and quality of life. This may occur because of the direct impact of the anxiety or depression but also because of a negative interaction with the core symptoms of autism. There is limited access and poor uptake of facilitated self-help by people with autism, largely due to limited availability but also because current systems for the delivery of such interventions are not adapted for use by people with autism. In adults without autism, facilitated self-help is an effective intervention for mild to moderate depression and anxiety. The development of novel methods for the delivery of facilitated self-help could make effective interventions available to a wider group of people.

The suggested programme of research would need to: (a) develop current methods for the delivery of self-help measures to take into account the impact of autism and possibly include developments in the nature of the materials, the methods for their delivery and the nature, duration and extent of their facilitation; (b) test the feasibility of the novel methods in a series of pilot studies; and (c) formally evaluate the outcomes (including symptoms, satisfaction and quality of life) in a large-scale randomised trial.

9.9.2 Cognitive behavioural therapy (CBT) for anxiety disorders in adults with autism

What is the clinical and cost effectiveness of CBT for the treatment of moderate and severe anxiety disorders in adults with autism?

Why this is important
Anxiety disorders commonly coexist in people with autism and are associated with poorer health outcomes and quality of life. This may occur because of the direct impact of the anxiety but also because of a negative interaction with the core symptoms of autism. There is limited access and poor uptake of psychological treatment services by people with autism, largely due to limited availability but also because current systems for the delivery of such interventions are not adapted for use for people with autism. In adults without autism, CBT is an effective intervention for moderate to severe anxiety disorders. The adaptation of CBT for adults with autism and a coexisting anxiety disorder could make effective interventions more widely available.

The suggested programme of research would need to: (a) develop current methods for the delivery of CBT to take into account the impact of autism and the nature and duration of the intervention; (b) test the feasibility of the novel treatments in a series of pilot studies (for the commonly experienced anxiety disorders in autism); and (c) formally evaluate the outcomes (including symptoms, satisfaction and quality of life) in a large-scale randomised controlled trial.

9.9.3 Pharmacological treatments for depression in adults with autism

What is the clinical and cost effectiveness of selective serotonin reuptake inhibitors (SSRIs) for the treatment of moderate and severe depression in adults with autism?

Why this is important
Depression commonly coexists with autism and is associated with poorer health outcomes and quality of life. This may occur because of the direct impact of the depression but also because of a negative interaction with the core symptoms of autism. There is poor recognition and consequently suboptimal treatment for depression in adults with autism. However, it is probable that when depression is recognised the most commonly used treatment is antidepressant medication as it is an effective intervention for

moderate to severe depression. Little is known about the extent of the use of antidepressant medication, adherence to prescribed medication and its effectiveness in adults with autism. Moreover, concerns have also been raised about the increased sensitivity of people with autism to the side effects of SSRIs and other antidepressant drugs.

The suggested programme of research would need to: (a) describe the current use of SSRIs in adults with depression and autism; (b) review the potential impact of increased sensitivity of adults with autism to the side effects of medication; and (c) formally evaluate the outcomes (including symptoms, satisfaction and quality of life) of SSRIs in a series of randomised controlled trials.

9.9.4   The structure and organisation of specialist teams

What structure and organisation of specialist autism teams are associated with improvements in care for people with autism?

Why this is important
The Department of Health's autism strategy (2010)[95] proposes the introduction of a range of specialist services for people with autism; these will usually be built around specialist autism teams. However, there is little evidence to guide the establishment and development of these teams. There is uncertainty about the precise nature of the population to be served (all people with autism or only those who have an IQ of 70 or above), the composition of the team, the extent of the team's role (for example, diagnosis and assessment only, a primarily advisory role or a substantial care coordination role), the interventions provided by the team, and the team's role and relationship with regard to non-statutory care providers. Therefore it is likely that in the near future a number of different models will be developed, which are likely to have varying degrees of success in meeting the needs of people with autism. Given the significant expansion of services, this presents an opportunity for a large-scale observational study, which should provide important information on the characteristics of teams associated with positive outcomes for people with autism in terms of access to services and effective coordination of care.

9.9.5   Augmentative communication devices for adults with autism

What is the clinical and cost effectiveness of augmentative communication devices for adults with autism?

Why this is important
Many people with autism experience significant communication problems (for example, the absence of any spoken language or significant deficits in interpersonal skills),

---

[95]Department of Health (2010) *Fulfilling and Rewarding Lives: the Strategy for Adults with Autism in England.*

which have a profound effect on their ability to lead a full and rewarding life. It is probable that these problems are related to the core symptoms of autism and are likely to persist for most people given the life-long course of autism and the lack of effective interventions for these core symptoms. A number of communication devices have been developed for autism but few, if any, have been subjected to a proper evaluation in adults. Despite this lack of formal evaluation, individual services have made considerable investments in augmentative communication devices. Research that provides high-quality evidence on the acceptability and the clinical and cost effectiveness of augmentative communication devices could bring about significant improvements in the lives of adults with autism.

The suggested programme of research would need to identify current devices for which there is: (a) some evidence of benefit (for example, case series and small-scale pilot studies); (b) some evidence that it meets a key communication need for people with autism (based on reviews of people's need in this area); and (c) indication that the device is feasible for routine use. The identified device(s) should then be formally evaluated in a large-scale randomised trial.

10   APPENDICES

APPENDIX 1:
SCOPE FOR THE DEVELOPMENT OF THE CLINICAL GUIDELINE

1   GUIDELINE TITLE

Autistic spectrum conditions: diagnosis and management of autistic spectrum conditions in adults[96]

1.1   SHORT TITLE

Autistic spectrum conditions in adults[97]

2   THE REMIT

The Department of Health has asked NICE: 'To produce a clinical guideline on the management of autistic spectrum disorders in adults'[98]

3   CLINICAL NEED FOR THE GUIDELINE

3.1   EPIDEMIOLOGY

Autistic spectrum conditions are lifelong neurological conditions. The way that they are expressed in individual people will differ at different stages of their lives, in response to interventions, and if they have coexisting conditions such as learning or language difficulties. A recent study conducted by Leicester University shows that the prevalence for all autistic spectrum conditions in adults in England is approximately 1%.

---

[96]During development of the guideline the title was changed to 'Autism: Recognition, Referral, Diagnosis and Management of Adults on the Autism Spectrum'.

[97]During development of the guideline the short title of the guideline was changed to 'Autism'.

[98]The original scope noted 'We are using the term "autistic spectrum conditions" rather than "autistic spectrum disorders" because this is the terminology more recently used in the Department of Health's Autism Strategy, and is preferred by many (but not all) adults on the autistic spectrum'. But during development of the guideline, the GDG opted to use the term 'autism' rather than autism spectrum condition or disorder.

In the past 30 years there has been a 25-fold increase in the prevalence of autistic spectrum conditions. This is probably a result of widening diagnostic categories, including the relatively recent subgroup of Asperger's syndrome, and the growth of services, better awareness and improved detection. This increase has had a significant impact on referrals to diagnostic services.

People with autistic spectrum conditions commonly experience difficulty with cognitive and behavioural flexibility, altered sensory sensitivity (which can have both advantages and disadvantages), sensory processing difficulties, stereotyped mannerisms, emotional regulation difficulties, and a narrow and often highly focused range of interests and activities.

These features may be along a continuum from mild to severe. For a diagnosis of autistic spectrum conditions to be made there must be both the presence of impairments (as defined by the World Health Organization) and an impact on the person's functioning.

The two major diagnostic classification systems (DSM-IV and ICD-10) use similar but not identical criteria to diagnose autistic spectrum conditions. In the guideline we use ICD-10. Where we have included disorders not clearly specified in ICD-10 we have used the relevant DSM-IV criteria.

Both DSM-IV and ICD-10 use the term pervasive developmental disorder, which encompasses autism, Asperger's syndrome and atypical autism (or pervasive developmental disorder not otherwise specified). For the purposes of this clinical guideline the term autistic spectrum conditions is used instead of pervasive developmental disorder because it is more widely understood.

The June 2009 National Audit Office report 'Supporting people with autism through adulthood' reported that a significant proportion of adults with autism across the whole autistic spectrum are excluded both socially and economically. Their conditions are often overlooked by health, education and social care professionals, which creates barriers to accessing the support and services they need to live independently. In addition, people with autistic spectrum conditions are more likely to have coexisting mental health and medical health problems, other developmental conditions and adaptive impairments. 'Diagnostic overshadowing' means there may be a tendency to overlook symptoms of autistic spectrum conditions in these groups and attribute them to being part of an intellectual disability. While this is an important issue, the signs and symptoms of autism can also lead to the misdiagnosis of co-occurring disorders.

3.2   Current practice

There is wide variation in rates of identification and referral for diagnostic assessment, waiting times for diagnosis, models of multi-professional working, assessment criteria, diagnostic practice, biomedical investigation and genetic counselling for adults with features of autistic spectrum conditions. These factors contribute to delays in reaching a diagnosis and subsequent access to appropriate services.

When the diagnostic assessment process works well, professionals and carers communicate right from the start and the adults with autism are involved in the decisions relating to their care. This lays the foundation for a long-term understanding between adults with autism, carers and the professionals supporting their needs. However, many adults or their carers who suspect they have an autistic spectrum condition have had difficulties accessing a diagnostic assessment, particularly if they are not in contact with a specialist service for the assessment or treatment of another disorder. Even if they have managed to obtain a diagnosis they may receive no follow-up support because of the absence of appropriate services or of an agreed care pathway.

The use of biomedical investigations to rule out other conditions, and thresholds for referral for genetic counselling vary markedly. Opinion also varies on the value of biomedical investigations in the diagnostic assessment of autistic and coexisting conditions.

People with other existing conditions featuring intellectual, physical or sensory disability and/or mental health problems may not be recognised as having symptoms of an autistic spectrum condition. Some adults may be misdiagnosed as having personality disorders, eating disorders, or depression and their autistic spectrum condition may be overlooked.

Some of the behaviours that define autistic spectrum conditions may also feature in other disabilities (such as learning disabilities), or be the result of other conditions (such as epilepsy). People may be wrongly diagnosed as having a mental illness when they have features of an autistic spectrum condition, or they may be misdiagnosed with autism when they have another condition. Misdiagnosis can lead to delays in receiving the necessary care and support.

The process and content of information-sharing varies widely, for instance in the provision of information and support for the person and their family while awaiting diagnosis and immediately after.

Current awareness and understanding of autism in adults among front-line health, education and social care professionals leaves room for improvement. In line with the Department of Health's Autism Strategy, a better understanding of the condition may enable better service delivery.

Current treatment and management for autistic spectrum conditions is often focused on children and adolescence. Transition from child and adolescent mental health services to adult services can often be challenging and requires significant collaboration between several government organisations.

Due to the qualitative impairments in communication and social-interaction skills, adults with autistic spectrum conditions often have difficulty in engaging in long-term employment or other purposeful/meaningful activity, especially if the person has a learning disability.

There are variations in practice of diagnosis and appropriate referral for adults with autistic spectrum conditions. Adults at the higher end of the autistic spectrum often may not get a diagnosis because of beliefs that, for example, if a person is in a settled relationship or can talk fluently they cannot have an autistic spectrum condition. This may lead to inappropriate crisis admissions to services as a result of mental health problems, physical illness, homelessness or coming into contact with the criminal justice system.

People with autistic spectrum conditions are at risk of exclusion and inequalities in service provision, particularly people from black or minority ethnic groups, older people, women and people with gender identity problems.

The Department of Health published *Fulfilling and Rewarding Lives: the Strategy for Adults with Autism in England* (2010) on designing services to improve care and support from all public services. The National Audit Office is currently undertaking a study, 'Supporting people with autism through adulthood', focusing particularly on the transition from adolescence to adulthood.

Clinical guidance for diagnosis has been published for the NHS in Scotland: *Assessment, Diagnosis and Clinical Interventions for Children and Young People with Autism Spectrum Disorders* (Scottish Intercollegiate Guidelines Network, 2007). *The Autistic Spectrum Disorder (ASD) Strategic Action Plan for Wales* (2009) focused on the role of strategic health plans to develop services and interagency cooperation between health and education for children and young people with autistic spectrum conditions. *The Autistic Spectrum Disorder (ASD) Strategic Action Plan for Wales* (2009) focused on diagnosis, access to services, community support, employment and housing. This NICE guideline, along with the NICE guideline on autistic spectrum disorders in children and young people that is currently in development[99], will provide guidance for the NHS in England.

4   THE GUIDELINE

The guideline development process is described in detail on the NICE website (see Section 6, 'Further information').

This scope defines what the guideline will (and will not) examine, and what the guideline developers will consider. The scope is based on the referral from the Department of Health.

The areas that will be addressed by the guideline are described in the following sections.

4.1   POPULATION

4.1.1   Groups that will be covered

a) Adults (18 or older), with suspected or diagnosed high functioning (for example, above average cognitive functioning) or low functioning (for example, profound communication problems) autistic spectrum conditions.
b) People with autistic spectrum conditions across the range of diagnostic groups, including atypical autism, Asperger's syndrome, pervasive developmental disorder and Rett's syndrome.

---

[99]The NICE guideline on children and young people was published in 2011.

c) Consideration will be given to the specific needs of:
- people with coexisting conditions (such as dyslexia, dyspraxia, sensory sensitivity, depression, ADHD, OCD, personality disorders, eating disorders and anxiety disorders)
- women
- older people
- people from black or minority ethnic groups
- transgender people.

4.1.2 Groups that will not be covered

a) Children from birth up to 18 years old.

4.2 HEALTHCARE SETTING

a) Primary, secondary, tertiary, health and social care and healthcare settings (including prisons and forensic services).
b) Other settings in which NHS services are funded or provided, or where NHS professionals are working in multi-agency teams.
c) The guideline will also comment on and include recommendations about the interface with other services, such as social services, education services and the voluntary sector.

4.3 CLINICAL MANAGEMENT

4.3.1 Key clinical issues that will be covered

a) Signs and symptoms that should prompt health, education and social care professionals working with adults and/or their carers to consider the presence of an autistic spectrum condition. These will include signs and symptoms that should trigger referral for specialist assessment.
b) Validity, specificity and reliability of the components of diagnostic assessment after referral, including:
- structure for assessment, including strengths and skills
- diagnostic thresholds
- assessment tools, including imaging, genetic and biomedical techniques
- assessment of risk
- the impact of coexisting developmental, mental and physical conditions on the assessment.
c) Psychosocial interventions, including: applied behavioural analysis, cognitive behavioural therapies, social groups, befriending schemes, mentoring and supported employment programmes.

d) Pharmacological interventions, including: anticonvulsants, antidepressants, and antipsychotics for the treatment of symptoms that may arise from coexisting conditions.
e) Physical interventions, such as diet.
f) Information and day-to-day support (such as a telephone helpline or advocates) for adults with a suspected autistic spectrum condition, and their families and carers, during the process of referral, assessment, diagnosis and the delivery of any interventions.
g) The organisation and delivery of care, and care pathways for the components of treatment and management (including transition planning), based on an ethos of multi-professional working.

4.3.2   Clinical issues that will not be covered

a)   Coexisting conditions if an autistic spectrum condition is not a primary diagnosis.

4.4   Main outcomes

a) Diagnostic accuracy and the identification of coexisting conditions.
b) Health-related quality of life.
c) Functioning in social/occupational/educational settings.
d) Outcomes for coexisting conditions, such as depression, anxiety and substance misuse.
e) Continuity of care.

4.5   Economic aspects

Developers will take into account both clinical and cost effectiveness when making recommendations involving a choice between alternative interventions. A review of the economic evidence will be conducted and analyses will be carried out as appropriate. The preferred unit of effectiveness is the quality-adjusted life year (QALY), but a different unit of effectiveness may be used depending on the availability of appropriate clinical and utility data for adults with autistic spectrum conditions. Costs considered will be from an NHS and personal social services (PSS) perspective in the main analyses. In addition, further analyses may be conducted that will consider wider social costs associated with the care of adults with autistic spectrum conditions. Such costs may include, for example, special education and training costs, voluntary sector respite care costs and costs of housing services. Further detail on the methods can be found in *The Guidelines Manual* (NICE, 2009e) (see 'Further information').

4.6   STATUS

4.6.1   Scope

This is the final scope.

4.6.2   Timing

The development of the guideline recommendations will begin in July 2010.

5   RELATED NICE GUIDANCE

5.1   GUIDANCE UNDER DEVELOPMENT

NICE is currently developing the following related guidance (details available from the NICE website):

'Autism spectrum disorders in children and young people. NICE clinical guideline'. Publication expected September 2011.

6   FURTHER INFORMATION

Information on the guideline development process is provided in:
● 'How NICE clinical guidelines are developed: an overview for stakeholders the public and the NHS'.
● *The Guidelines Manual* (NICE, 2009e).
● These are available from the NICE website (www.nice.org.uk/ GuidelinesManual).
● Information on the progress of the guideline will also be available from the NICE website (www.nice.org.uk).

APPENDIX 2:

DECLARATIONS OF INTERESTS BY GUIDELINE

DEVELOPMENT GROUP MEMBERS

With a range of practical experience relevant to autism in the GDG, members were appointed because of their understanding and expertise in healthcare for people with autism and support for their families, partners and carers, including: scientific issues; health research; the delivery and receipt of healthcare, along with the work of the healthcare industry; and the role of professional organisations and organisations for people with autism and their families, partners or carers.

To minimise and manage any potential conflicts of interest, and to avoid any public concern that commercial or other financial interests have affected the work of the GDG and influenced guidance, members of the GDG must declare as a matter of public record any interests held by themselves or their families which fall under specified categories (see below). These categories include any relationships they have with the healthcare industries, professional organisations and organisations for people with autism and their families/carers.

Individuals invited to join the GDG were asked to declare their interests before being appointed. To allow the management of any potential conflicts of interest that might arise during the development of the guideline, GDG members were also asked to declare their interests at each GDG meeting throughout the guideline development process. The interests of all the members of the GDG are listed below, including interests declared prior to appointment and during the guideline development process.

Categories of interest
Paid employment

Personal pecuniary interest: financial payments or other benefits from either the manufacturer or the owner of the product or service under consideration in this guideline, or the industry or sector from which the product or service comes. This includes: holding a directorship or other paid position; carrying out consultancy or fee paid work; having shareholdings or other beneficial interests; and receiving expenses and hospitality over and above what would be reasonably expected to attend meetings and conferences.

Personal family interest: financial payments or other benefits from the healthcare industry that were received by a family member.

Non-personal pecuniary interest: financial payments or other benefits received by the GDG member's organisation or department, but where the GDG member has not personally received payment, including fellowships and other support provided by the healthcare industry. This includes a grant, fellowship or other payment to sponsor a post or contribute to the running costs of the department; commissioning of research or other work; contracts with, or grants from, NICE.

Personal non-pecuniary interest: these include, but are not limited to, clear opinions or public statements the GDG member has made about autism, holding office in a professional organisation or advocacy group with a direct interest in autism, other reputational risks relevant to autism.

GDG – declarations of interest	
Professor Simon Baron-Cohen (chair)	
Employment	Director, Autism Research Centre, Cambridge University
Personal pecuniary interest	Has NHS funding for an Asperger's clinic
Personal family interest	None
Non-personal pecuniary interest	None
Personal non-pecuniary interest	Developer of the AQ-10 (Allison *et al.,* 2012)
Non-personal non-pecuniary interest	Cambridge University are conducting a trial on oxytocin. Conducts medico-legal assessments in relation to autism.
Action taken	Did not participate in discussions regarding case identification tools, specifically the AQ-10.
Professor Gillian Baird	
Employment	Consultant Paediatrician and Professor of Paediatric Neurodisability, Guy's and St Thomas' NHS Foundation trust and King's Health partners
Personal pecuniary interest	None
Personal family interest	None
Non-personal pecuniary interest	None
Personal non-pecuniary interest	Chair of the NICE guideline, *Autism: Recognition, Referral and Diagnosis of Children and Young People on the Autism Spectrum.*

	Member of DSM-5 working party. Member of ICD-11 working party. Author or co-author of several papers relevant to recognition, diagnosis, coexisting conditions and management of children and young people with autism.
Action taken	None
Dr Carole Buckley	
Employment	GP
Personal pecuniary interest	None
Personal family interest	None
Non-personal pecuniary interest	None
Personal non-pecuniary interest	None
Action taken	None
Dr Peter Carpenter	
Employment	Consultant Psychiatrist (Learning Disabilities), Associate Medical Lead Learning Disabilities and Specialist Adult Services. Avon and Wiltshire Mental Health Partnership NHS Trust.
Personal pecuniary interest	Has been employed by the National Autistic Society as a clinician Receives payments for clinical work, some of which includes work in autism, from Priory Healthcare and Castlebeck Receives payments for medico-legal reports relating to people with autism
Personal family interest	None
Non-personal pecuniary interest	Received payment from a drug company for participating in a conference.
Personal non-pecuniary interest	None
Action taken	None
Dr Juli Crocombe	
Employment	Consultant Psychiatrist, St George's Hospital, Stafford

Personal pecuniary interest	None
Personal family interest	None
Non-personal pecuniary interest	Received payment from a drug company for participating in a Continuing Professional Development event.
Personal non-pecuniary interest	Supports the National Autistic Society in its quest for the provision of appropriate and adequate health and social services for adults with autism in the UK.
Action taken	None
Ms Jackie Dziewanowska	
Employment	Autism Spectrum Disorder Nurse Consultant. Clinical Lead, Nottingham City Asperger Service.
Personal pecuniary interest	None
Personal family interest	None
Non-personal pecuniary interest	None
Personal non-pecuniary interest	None
Action taken	None
Ms Annie Foster-Jones	
Employment	Autism Specialist Nurse, Cheshire & Wirral Partnership. NHS Foundation Trust, Learning Disabilities Clinical Service Unit.
Personal pecuniary interest	None
Personal family interest	None
Non-personal pecuniary interest	None
Personal non-pecuniary interest	None
Action taken	None
Dr Marga Hogenboom	
Employment	GP, Camphill Medical Practice Bieldside, Scotland. Medical Adviser, Camphill, Aberdeen.

Personal pecuniary interest	None
Personal family interest	None
Non-personal pecuniary interest	None
Personal non-pecuniary interest	Director, Camphill Wellbeing Trust
Action taken	None
Professor Patricia Howlin	
Employment	Professor of Clinical Child Psychology, King's College London. Consultant Clinical Psychologist.
Personal pecuniary interest	Expert advisor/paid consultant to Dr Richard Solomon's National Institute of Health funded PLAY (Play and Language for Autistic Youngsters) project. Paid consultant to the Rand Corporation Review of Evidence of Psychosocial and Related Interventions for Children with Autism.
Personal family interest	None
Non-personal pecuniary interest	Consultation to NHS services in Cornwall and Mid Glamorgan. Consultation to the University of Oslo, for which my Trust is paid.
Personal non-pecuniary interest	Co-chair of the Scientific and Advisory committee of Research Autism Chair of Scientific Advisory Group, Autistica. Chair of Mental Health Research Network's Autism Clinical Research group.
Action taken	None
Mr Campbell Main	
Employment	Representing service user and carer concerns
Personal pecuniary interest	None
Personal family interest	None
Non-personal pecuniary interest	None

Personal non-pecuniary interest	None
Action taken	None
Ms Melissa McAuliffe	
Employment	Asperger Specialist – Social Care, Rehabilitation and Recovery Team
Personal pecuniary interest	None
Personal family interest	None
Non-personal pecuniary interest	None
Personal non-pecuniary interest	Employed by the London Borough of Newham and seconded to the East London NHS Foundation Trust to work in the Asperger Service. The NICE guidelines will have a direct impact on how this service runs. Member of the British Association of Social Workers.
Action taken	None
Mr Richard Mills	
Employment	Director of Research, the National Autistic Society. Honorary Secretary and Research Director, Research Autism.
Personal pecuniary interest	None
Personal family interest	None
Non-personal pecuniary interest	None
Personal non-pecuniary interest	Employed by the National Autistic Society and Research Autism
Action taken	None
Ms Joan Panton	
Employment concerns	Representing service user and carer
Personal pecuniary interest	None
Personal family interest	None
Non-personal pecuniary interest	None

Personal non-pecuniary interest	None
Action taken	None
Ms Maggi Rigg	
Employment	Cambian Group Advisory Board
Personal pecuniary interest	None
Personal family interest	None
Non-personal pecuniary interest	None
Personal non-pecuniary interest	None
Action taken	None
Ms Anya Ustaszewski	
Employment	Autism and Disability Awareness Trainer and Rights Advocate. Musician and Composer (freelance). Representing service user and carer concerns.
Personal pecuniary interest	None
Personal family interest	None
Non-personal pecuniary interest	None
Personal non-pecuniary interest	Steering Committee Member of London Autistic Rights Movement. Trustee of ASSERT Brighton and Hove Trustee of AutreachIT.
Action taken	None
NCCMH staff	
Professor Stephen Pilling	
Employment	Director, NCCMH. Professor of Clinical Psychology and Clinical Effectiveness. Director, Centre for Outcomes Research and Effectiveness, University College London.
Personal pecuniary interest	Funding of £1,200,000 per annum from NICE to develop clinical guidelines. Funding from British Psychological

	Society (2005 to 2011) of £6,000,000 to establish the Clinical Effectiveness Programme at the Centre for Outcomes Research and Effectiveness, University College London with Professors P. Fonagy and S. Michie. Funding for the Dynamic Interpersonal Therapy Competences Framework.
Personal family interest	None
Non-personal pecuniary interest	RCT to evaluate multisystemic therapy with Professor P. Fonagy; Department of Health funding of £1,000,000 (2008 to 2012). RCT to evaluate collaborative care for depression with Professor D. Richards; Medical Research Council Funding of £2,200,000 (2008 to 2012). Developing a UK Evidence Base for Contingency Management in Addiction with Professor J. Strang; National Institute of Health Research Grant of £2,035,042 (2009 to 2013).
Personal non-pecuniary interest	None
Mr Nadir Cheema	
Employment	Health Economist, NCCMH
Personal pecuniary interest	None
Personal family interest	None
Non-personal pecuniary interest	None
Personal non-pecuniary interest	None
Ms Naomi Glover	
Employment	Research Assistant, NCCMH
Personal pecuniary interest	None
Personal family interest	None
Non-personal pecuniary interest	None
Personal non-pecuniary interest	None
Action taken	None

Ms Flora Kaminski	
Employment	Research Assistant, NCCMH
Personal pecuniary interest	None
Personal family interest	None
Non-personal pecuniary interest	None
Personal non-pecuniary interest	None
Action taken	None
Ms Rachael Lee	
Employment	Research Assistant, NCCMH (from September 2011)
Personal pecuniary interest	None
Personal family interest	None
Non-personal pecuniary interest	None
Personal non-pecuniary interest	None
Action taken	None
Ms Katherine Leggett	
Employment	Project Manager, NCCMH
Personal pecuniary interest	None
Personal family interest	None
Non-personal pecuniary interest	None
Personal non-pecuniary interest	None
Action taken	None
Dr Odette Megnin-Viggars	
Employment	Systematic Reviewer, NCCMH (from March 2010)
Personal pecuniary interest	None
Personal family interest	None
Non-personal pecuniary interest	None
Personal non-pecuniary interest	None
Action taken	None

Ms Sarah Stockton	
Employment	Senior Information Scientist, NCCMH
Personal pecuniary interest	None
Personal family interest	None
Non-personal pecuniary interest	None
Personal non-pecuniary interest	None
Action taken	None
Dr Clare Taylor	
Employment	Senior Editor, NCCMH
Personal pecuniary interest	None
Personal family interest	None
Non-personal pecuniary interest	None
Personal non-pecuniary interest	None
Action taken	None
Dr Amina Udechuku	
Employment	Systematic Reviewer, NCCMH (March 2010 to June 2011)
Personal pecuniary interest	None
Personal family interest	None
Non-personal pecuniary interest	None
Personal non-pecuniary interest	None
Action taken	None

APPENDIX 3:
SPECIAL ADVISORS TO THE GUIDELINE DEVELOPMENT GROUP

None

APPENDIX 4: STAKEHOLDERS WHO RESPONDED TO EARLY REQUESTS FOR EVIDENCE

None

APPENDIX 5: STAKEHOLDERS AND EXPERTS WHO SUBMITTED COMMENTS IN RESPONSE TO THE CONSULTATION DRAFT OF THE GUIDELINE

Stakeholders

ADRC (Autism Diagnostic Research Centre – Southampton)
Ambitious about Autism
Association Directors of Adult Social Services
Association for Family Therapy and Systemic Practice
Autism Alliance UK
Autism Cymru
Autism NI
Autism Rights Group Highland
Autism West Midlands
Berkshire Autistic Society
Brain-in-Hand Ltd
Brighton and Hove City Council
British Dietetic Association
British Psychological Society
Calderstones Partnership NHS Foundation Trust
Cochrane Collaboration Developmental, Psychosocial and Learning Problems Group
College of Social Work
Craegmoor
Dorset Healthcare University Foundation NHS Trust
European Association for Behaviour Analysis
Hampshire Autistic Society
Hartlepool Borough Council (Tees Valley ASD Group, Middlesbrough Council Stockton Borough Council, and Redcar and Cleveland Council)
Hertfordshire Partnership NHS Foundation Trust
Institute of Psychiatry, King's College London
London Borough of Tower Hamlets
National Autistic Society
NHS Direct
Northumberland, Tyne and Wear NHS Trust
Nottinghamshire Healthcare NHS Trust
Optical Confederation, and the Local Optical Committee Support Unit
Prison Reform Trust
Pyramid Educational Consultants
Queen's University Belfast

Royal College of Nursing
Royal College of Psychiatrists
Royal College of Psychiatrists, Learning Disability Faculty
Royal College of Speech and Language Therapists
Sheffield Asperger Syndrome Service
Social Care Institute for Excellence
Somerset County Council
Somerset Partnership NHS
South London and Maudsley NHS Trust
Specialist Autism Services
Sussex Partnership NHS Foundation Trust
Tees, Esk and Wear Valleys NHS Foundation Trust
WaASP (Worcestershire adult Asperger Syndrome Parents)
Welsh Government
Welsh Health Boards ASD Assessment and Diagnosis (Adults) Network
Worcestershire Health and Care NHS Trust

Experts

Stefan Gleeson
Dr Iain McClure

APPENDIX 6:

RESEARCHERS CONTACTED TO REQUEST INFORMATION ABOUT UNPUBLISHED OR SOON-TO-BE PUBLISHED STUDIES

Dr Marco Bertelli
Professor Terry Brugha
Dr Adam Guastella
Professor Christopher McDougle
Dr Gary Remington
Professor Peter Tyrer

APPENDIX 7:
ANALYTIC FRAMEWORK AND REVIEW QUESTIONS

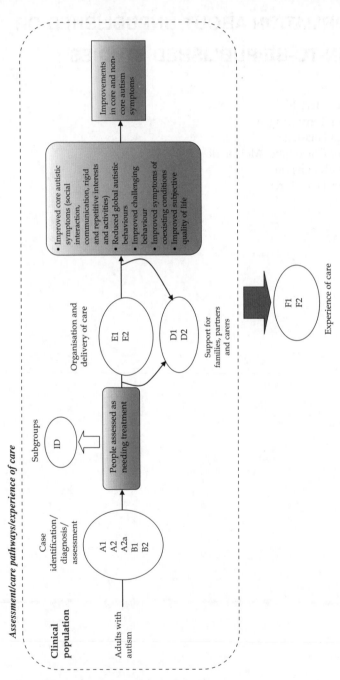

Chapter 4: experience of care

No.	Primary review questions
F1	For adults with autism, what are their experiences of having autism, of access to services, and of treatment?
F2	For families, partners and carers of adults with autism, what are their experiences of caring for people with autism, and what support is available for families, partners and carers?

Chapter 5: case identification

No.	Primary review questions
A1	What signs or symptoms should prompt any professional who comes into contact with an adult with possible autism to consider assessment?
A2 and A2a	What are the most effective methods/tools for case identification in autism in adults? a. What amendments, if any, need to be made to the agreed methods for case identification to take into account individual variation (for example, gender, age, intellectual abilities, including cognitive strengths as well as difficulties, communication problems, developmental disorders, coexisting mental disorders and physical problems including hyper/hyposensitivities, motor impairments, and visual and hearing impairments)?

Chapter 5: diagnosis and assessment

No.	Primary review questions
B1	In adults with possible autism, what are the key components of, and the most effective structure for, a diagnostic assessment? To answer this question, consideration should be given to: • the nature and content of the clinical interview and observation (including an early developmental history where possible) • formal diagnostic methods/ psychological instruments (including risk assessment) • biological measures • the setting(s) in which the assessment takes place • who the informant needs to be (to provide a developmental history).
B2	• When making a differential diagnosis of autism in adults, what amendments, if any, need to be made to the usual methods to make an assessment of autism itself in light of potential coexisting conditions

	(for example, common mental health disorders, ADHD, personality disorders, gender/identity disorders, eating disorders, Tourette's syndrome, and drug or alcohol misuse)?
B3	What are the most effective methods for assessing an individual's needs (for example, their personal, social, occupational, educational and housing needs) for adults with autism?

Chapter 6: organisation and delivery of care

No.	Primary review questions
E1	What are the effective models for the delivery of care to people with autism including: • the structure and design of care pathways • systems for the delivery of care (for example, case management) • advocacy services?
E2	For adults with autism, what are the essential elements in the effective provision of: • support services for the individual (including accessing and using services) • day care • residential care?

Treatment of autism in adults

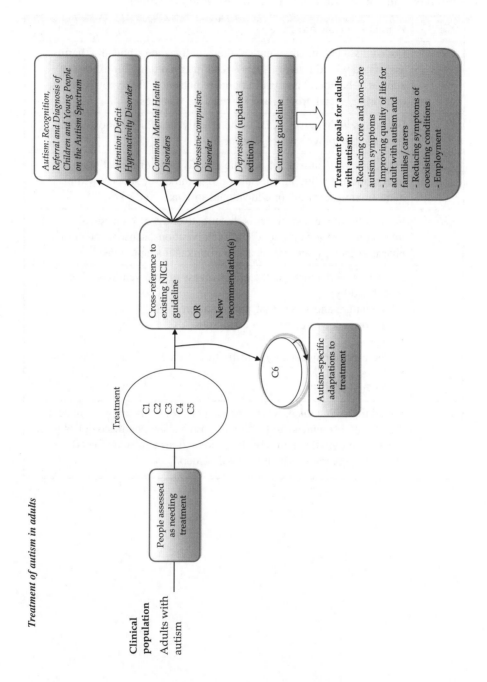

Chapters 7 and 8: psychosocial and biomedical interventions

No.	Primary review question
C1	For adults with autism, what are the benefits and/or potential harms associated with different psychosocial interventions (for example, applied behavioural analysis, cognitive behavioural therapy [CBT], mentoring, social groups, and befriending schemes)?
C2	For adults with autism, what is the effectiveness of vocational and supported employment programmes?
C3	For adults with autism, what is the effectiveness of educational interventions (including specialist programmes, or support within mainstream education, or educational software, and so on)?
C4	For adults with autism, what is the effectiveness of biomedical interventions (for example, dietary interventions, sensory integration, pharmacotherapy, and physical-environmental adaptations)?
C5	For adults with autism, is the effectiveness of interventions moderated by: • the nature and severity of the condition • the presence of coexisting conditions • age • the presence of sensory sensitivities (including pain thresholds) • IQ • language level?
C6	For adults with autism, what amendments, if any, need to be made to the current recommendations for psychosocial and pharmacological treatment (including the nature of drug interactions and side effects) for coexisting common mental health disorders?

APPENDIX 8:

REVIEW PROTOCOLS

Experience of care review protocol

Component	Description
Review question(s)	For adults with autism, what are their experiences of having autism, of access to services, and of treatment? (RQ–F1) For families, partners and carers of adults with autism, what are their experiences of caring for people with autism, and what support is available for families, partners and carers? (RQ–F2)
Subquestion	None
Chapter	4
Topic group	Experience of care
Objectives	To identify the emerging themes for the experiences of adults with autism and their families, partners and carers in terms of the experience of autism and in terms of experiences of accessing services and of treatment.
Criteria for considering studies for the review	
• *Population*	Adults and young people aged 18 years and older with suspected autism across the range of diagnostic groups (including atypical autism, Asperger's syndrome and pervasive developmental disorder), and their families, partners and carers.
• *Intervention*	None
• *Comparison*	None
• *Critical outcomes*	None specified – any narrative description of service user or carer experience of autism
• *Study design*	Systematic reviews of qualitative studies, qualitative studies, surveys
• *Include unpublished data?*	No

• *Restriction by date?*	No
• *Minimum sample size*	No minimum sample size
• *Study setting*	Any setting
Electronic databases	ASSIA, CINAHL, Embase, HMIC, IBSS, MEDLINE, PsycBOOKS, PsycEXTRA, PsycINFO, Sociological Abstracts, SSA
Date searched	CINAHL, Embase, HMIC, MEDLINE, PsycBOOKS, PsycEXTRA, PsycINFO: 01.01.1996 to 09.09.2011 ASSIA, IBSS, Sociological Abstracts, SSA: 01.01.1996 to 10.10.2011
Searching other resources	Hand reference searching of retrieved literature
The review strategy	Thematic analysis of primary qualitative studies reporting experiences of adults with autism and/or their families, partners and carers.

Signs and symptoms that should prompt assessment of autism in adults review protocol

Component	Description
Review question(s)	What signs or symptoms should prompt any professional who comes into contact with an adult with possible autism to consider assessment? (RQ–A1)
Chapter	5
Subsection	5.2
Topic group	Assessment and case identification
Objectives	• To identify the signs and symptoms that would prompt referral for further diagnostic assessment of autism in adult • To suggest how recognition of autism can be improved
Criteria for considering studies for the review	
• *Population*	Adults and young people aged 18 years and older with suspected autism across the range of diagnostic groups (including atypical autism, Asperger's syndrome and pervasive developmental disorder)

	Consideration should be given to the specific needs of: • people with coexisting conditions • women • older people • people from black and minority ethnic groups • transgender people.
• *Comparison*	People with or without diagnosed autism
• *Critical outcomes*	Sensitivity, specificity, positive predictive value, negative predictive value, AUC
• *Study design*	Cross-sectional, systematic reviews
Electronic databases	AEI, ASSIA, BEI, CDSR, CENTRAL, CINAHL, DARE, Embase, ERIC, HMIC, MEDLINE, PsycINFO, Sociological Abstracts, SSA
Date searched	Systematic reviews: 1995 up to 09/09/2011 RCTs, quasi-experimental studies, observational studies, case series: inception of database up to 09/09/2011.
The review strategy	To provide a GDG consensus-based narrative of signs and symptoms that should prompt assessment as well as identify any amendments that need to be made to take into account individual variation

Case identification tools review protocol

Component	Description
Review question(s)	What are the most effective methods/tools for case identification in autism in adults? (RQ–A2)
Subquestion	What amendments, if any, need to be made to the agreed methods for case identification to take into account individual variation (for example, gender, age, intellectual abilities, including cognitive strengths as well as difficulties, communication problems, developmental disorders, coexisting mental disorders and physical health problems including hyper/hyposensitivities, motor impairments, and visual and hearing impairments)? (RQ–A2a)
Chapter	5
Subsection	5.3
Topic group	Assessment and case identification

Objectives	• To identify and evaluate case identification tools used in the recognition of autism. • To suggest how recognition of autism can be improved.

Criteria for considering studies for the review	
• *Population*	Adults and young people aged 18 years and older with suspected autism across the range of diagnostic groups (including atypical autism, Asperger's syndrome and pervasive developmental disorder). Consideration should be given to the specific needs of: • people with coexisting conditions • women • older people • people from black and minority ethnic groups • transgender people.
• *Intervention*	Case identification instruments (for example, the AQ, SCQ, ABC)
• *Index test*	Case identification instruments
• *Comparison*	DSM or ICD diagnosis of autism
• *Critical outcomes*	**Sensitivity**: the proportion of true positives of all cases diagnosed with autism in the population. **Specificity**: the proportion of true negatives of all cases not diagnosed with autism in the population.
• *Important, but not critical outcomes*	**Positive predictive value**: the proportion of people with positive test results who are correctly diagnosed. **Negative predictive value**: the proportion of people with negative test results who are correctly diagnosed. **AUC:** are constructed by plotting the true positive rate as a function of the false positive rate for each threshold.
• *Other outcomes*	**Reliability** (for example, inter-rater, test-retest) **Validity** (for example, construct, content)
• *Study design*	Cohort and case-control
• *Include unpublished data?*	No
• *Restriction by date?*	No
• *Minimum sample size*	N = 10 per arm Exclude studies with >50% attrition from either arm of trial (unless adequate statistical methodology has been applied to account for missing data).

Study setting	• Primary, secondary, tertiary, and other health and social care and healthcare settings (including prisons and forensic services). • Others in which NHS services are funded or provided, or NHS professionals are working in multi-agency teams.
Electronic databases	AEI, ASSIA, BEI, CDSR, CENTRAL, CINAHL, DARE, Embase, ERIC, HMIC, MEDLINE, PsycINFO, Sociological Abstracts, SSA
Date searched	Systematic reviews: 1995 up to 09/09/2011 RCTs, quasi-experimental studies, observational studies, case series: inception of database up to 09/09/2011.
Searching other resources	Hand reference searching of retrieved literature
The review strategy	To conduct diagnostic accuracy meta-analyses on the sensitivity and specificity of case identification tools. This is dependent on available data from the literature. In the absence of this, a narrative review of case identification tools will be conducted and guided by a pre-defined list of consensus-based criteria (for example, the clinical utility of the tool, administrative characteristics, and psychometric data evaluating its sensitivity and specificity).

Assessment and diagnosis review protocol

Component	Description
Review question(s)	In adults with possible autism, what are the key components of, and the most effective structure for, a diagnostic assessment? To answer this question, consideration should be given to: • the nature and content of the clinical interview and observation (including an early developmental history where possible) • formal diagnostic methods/ psychological instruments (including risk assessment) • biological measures • the setting(s) in which the assessment takes place • who the informant needs to be (to provide a developmental history). (RQ–B1)

	What are the most effective methods for assessing an individual's needs (for example, their personal, social, occupational, educational, and housing needs) for adults with autism? (RQ–B3)
Subquestion	When making a differential diagnosis of autism in adults, what amendments, if any, need to be made to the usual methods to make an assessment of autism itself in light of potential coexisting conditions (for example, common mental health disorders, ADHD, personality disorders, gender/identity disorders, eating disorders, Tourette's syndrome, and drug or alcohol misuse)? (RQ–B2)
Chapter	5
Subsection	5.4
Topic group	Assessment and case identification
Objectives	• To identify the key components of an effective clinical interview to diagnose the presence and severity of autism in adults • To evaluate the diagnostic accuracy of assessment tools that aid the diagnosis of autism in adults • To identify what amendments, if any, need to be made to take into account individual differences (for example, coexisting conditions) • To identify the most effective methods for assessing an individual's needs • To evaluate an individual's quality of life • To suggest how diagnosis of autism in adults can be improved
Criteria for considering studies for the review	
• *Population*	Adults and young people aged 18 years and older with suspected autism across the range of diagnostic groups (including atypical autism, Asperger's syndrome and pervasive developmental disorder) Consideration should be given to the specific needs of: • people with coexisting conditions • women • older people • people from black and minority ethnic groups • transgender people.

• *Intervention*	Formal assessments of the nature and severity of autism (including problem specification or diagnosis).
• *Index test*	Formal assessments of the nature and severity of autism (including problem specification or diagnosis).
• *Comparison*	DSM or ICD clinical diagnosis of autism (or equivalent)
• *Critical outcomes*	**Sensitivity**: the proportion of true positives of all cases diagnosed with autism in the population **Specificity**: the proportion of true negatives of all cases not diagnosed with autism in the population
• *Important, but not critical outcomes*	**Positive predictive value**: the proportion of people with positive test results who are correctly diagnosed. **Negative predictive value**: the proportion of people with negative test results who are correctly diagnosed. **AUC:** are constructed by plotting the true positive rate as a function of the false positive rate for each threshold.
• *Other outcomes*	**Reliability** (for example, inter-rater, test-retest) **Validity** (for example, construct, content)
• *Study design*	Case-control and cohort
• *Include unpublished data?*	No
• *Restriction by date?*	No
• *Minimum sample size*	N = 10 per arm Exclude studies with >50% attrition from either arm of trial (unless adequate statistical methodology has been applied to account for missing data).
• *Study setting*	• Primary, secondary, tertiary, health and other health and social care settings (including prisons and forensic services). • Others in which NHS services are funded or provided, or NHS professionals are working in multi-agency teams.
Electronic databases	AEI, ASSIA, BEI, BIOSIS previews, CDSR, CENTRAL, CINAHL, DARE, Embase, ERIC, HMIC, MEDLINE, PsycINFO, Sociological Abstracts
Date searched	Generic, RCTs, quasi-experimental studies, observational studies: inception of database up to 09/09/2011. Generic, systematic reviews: 1995 up to 09/09/2011.

Searching other resources	Hand reference searching of retrieved literature
The review strategy	• To provide a GDG-consensus based narrative identifying the key components of an effective clinical diagnostic interview (considering possible amendments due to individual variation). • To conduct diagnostic accuracy meta-analyses on the sensitivity, specificity, reliability and validity of assessment tools. This is dependent on available data from the literature. In the absence of this, a narrative review of assessment tools will be conducted and guided by a pre-defined list of consensus-based criteria (for example, the clinical utility of the tool, administrative characteristics, and psychometric data evaluating its sensitivity, specificity, reliability and validity).

Organisation and delivery of care review protocol

Component	Description
Review question(s)	What are the effective models for the delivery of care to people with autism including: • the structure and design of care pathways • systems for the delivery of care (for example, case management) • advocacy services? (RQ–E1) For adults with autism, what are the essential elements in the effective provision of: • support services for the individual (including accessing and using services) • day care • residential care? (RQ–E2)
Subquestion	None
Chapter	6
Topic group	None
Objectives	To evaluate the components and effectiveness of different models for the organisation and delivery of care.

Criteria for considering studies for the review	
• *Population*	Adults and young people aged 18 years and older with suspected autism across the range of diagnostic groups (including atypical autism, Asperger's syndrome and pervasive developmental disorder) Consideration should be given to the specific needs of: • people with coexisting conditions • women • older people • people from black and minority ethnic groups • transgender people. Excluded groups include: • children (under 18 years) Where data from adult autism populations were not sufficient, the GDG decided that extrapolating from intellectual learning disabilities population was valid.
• *Intervention(s)*	• Case co-ordination models (for example, case management, collaborative care, key worker systems) • Advocacy and support services • Multidisciplinary team models (for example, specialist assessment teams, specialist community teams, assertive community treatment teams) • Models of care delivery (for example, stepped care, clinical care pathways) • Day care services (including the model and content of services) • Residential care (including the model and content of services
• *Comparison*	Treatment as usual, standard care or other interventions
• *Critical outcomes*	Outcomes involving core features of autism (social interaction, communication, repetitive interests/activities); overall autistic behaviour; management of challenging behaviour; continuity of care, satisfaction with treatment, engagement, and healthcare utilisation (including access to treatment).
• *Study design*	• RCTs The GDG agreed by consensus that where there were no RCTs found in the evidence search, or the results from the RCTs were inconclusive, that the following studies would be included in the review of evidence: • observational • quasi-experimental • case series.

• *Minimum sample size*	• RCT/observational/quasi-experimental studies: N = 10 per arm (ITT) • Case series studies: N = 10 in total Exclude studies with >50% attrition from either arm of trial (unless adequate statistical methodology has been applied to account for missing data).
• *Study setting*	• Primary, secondary, tertiary, and other health and social care settings (including prisons and forensic services) • Others in which NHS services are funded or provided, or NHS professionals are working in multi-agency teams
Electronic databases	AEI, AMED, ASSIA, BEI, CDSR, CENTRAL, CINAHL, DARE, Embase, MEDLINE, PsycINFO, Sociological Abstracts, SSA
Date searched	Systematic reviews: 1995 up to 09/09/2011 RCTs, quasi-experimental, observational studies, case series: inception of database up to 09/09/2011
Searching other resources	Hand reference searching of retrieved literature
The review strategy	• The initial aim is to conduct a meta-analysis evaluating the clinical effectiveness of the interventions. However, in the absence of adequate data, the literature will be presented via a narrative synthesis of the available evidence. • Narratively review literature that takes into consideration any amendments due to common mental health disorders. • Consider subgroup meta-analyses that take into account the effectiveness of interventions as moderated by: – the nature and severity of the condition – the presence of co-existing conditions? – age – the presence of sensory sensitivities (including pain thresholds) – IQ – language level.

Psychosocial interventions review protocol

Component	Description
Review question(s)	For adults with autism, what are the benefits and/or potential harms associated with different psychosocial interventions (for example, applied behavioural analysis, cognitive behavioural therapy [CBT], mentoring, social groups, and befriending schemes)? (RQ–C1)
	For adults with autism, what is the effectiveness of vocational and supported employment programmes? (RQ–C2)
	For adults with autism, what is the effectiveness of educational interventions (including specialist programmes, or support within mainstream education, or educational software, and so on)? (RQ–C3)
	What information and day-to-day support do families, partners and carers need: • during the initial period of assessment and diagnosis • when interventions and care are provided (for example, telephone helpline, information packs, advocates or respite care, interpreters and other language tools) • during periods of crisis? (RQ–D1)
	What role can families, partners and carers play in supporting the delivery of interventions for adults with autism? (RQ–D2)
Subquestion	For adults with autism, is the effectiveness of interventions moderated by: • the nature and severity of the condition • the presence of coexisting conditions • age • the presence of sensory sensitivities (including pain thresholds) • IQ • language level? (RQ–C5)
	For adults with autism, what amendments, if any, need to be made to the current recommendations for psychosocial and pharmacological treatment (including the nature of drug interactions and side effects) for coexisting common mental health disorders? (RQ–C6)
Chapter	7
Topic group	Psychological/educational/social interventions
Objectives	To evaluate the clinical effectiveness of psychosocial interventions for autism.

Criteria for considering studies for the review	
• *Population*	Adults and young people aged 18 years and older with suspected autism across the range of diagnostic groups (including atypical autism, Asperger's syndrome and pervasive developmental disorder)
	Consideration should be given to the specific needs of: • people with coexisting conditions • women • older people • people from black and minority ethnic groups • transgender people. Excluded groups include: • children (under 18 years)
	However, it was decided, based on GDG consensus, that where primary data from an adult population were absent it might be valid to extrapolate from an autism population with a mean age of 15 years or above.
	For interventions concerned with the management of behaviour, and where data from adult autism populations were not sufficient, the GDG decided that extrapolating from a learning disabilities population was valid.
• *Intervention(s)*	• Psychosocial interventions aimed at behaviour management (for example, applied behaviour analysis, behavioural therapies, CBT, social learning) • Communication (for example, augmentative and alternative communication, facilitated communication, picture exchange system) • Vocational/employment interventions (for example, vocational rehabilitation programmes, individual supported employment)
• *Comparison*	Treatment as usual, waitlist control, other active interventions
• *Critical outcomes*	Outcomes involving core features of autism (social interaction, communication, repetitive interests/activities); overall autistic behaviour; management of challenging behaviour; outcomes involving treatment of coexisting conditions
• *Study design*	• RCTs The GDG agreed by consensus that where there were no RCTs found in the evidence search, or the results from the RCTs were inconclusive, that the following studies would be included in the review of evidence: • observational • quasi-experimental • case series.

• *Include unpublished data?*	Yes, but only where the evidence was: • accompanied by a trial report containing sufficient detail to properly assess the quality of the data • submitted with the understanding that data from the study and a summary of the study's characteristics will be published in the full guideline.
• *Restriction by date?*	No
• *Minimum sample size*	• RCT/observational/quasi-experimental studies: N = 10 per arm (ITT) • Case series studies: N = 10 in total Exclude studies with >50% attrition from either arm of trial (unless adequate statistical methodology has been applied to account for missing data).
• *Study setting*	• Primary, secondary, tertiary, and other health and social care settings (including prisons and forensic services) • Others in which NHS services are funded or provided, or NHS professionals are working in multi-agency teams
Electronic databases	AEI, AMED, ASSIA, BEI, CDSR, CENTRAL, CINAHL, DARE, Embase, ERIC, HMIC, MEDLINE, PsycINFO, Sociological Abstracts, SSA
Date searched	Systematic reviews: 1995 to 09.09.2011. RCT, quasi-experimental, observational studies, case series: inception of database to 09.09.2011.
Searching other resources	Hand reference searching of retrieved literature

The review strategy	• The initial aim is to conduct a meta-analysis evaluating the clinical effectiveness of the interventions. However, in the absence of adequate data, the literature will be presented via a narrative synthesis of the available evidence.
	• Narratively review literature that takes into consideration any amendments due to common mental health disorders.
	• Consider subgroup meta-analyses that take into account the effectiveness of interventions as moderated by:
	  – the nature and severity of the condition
	  – the presence of coexisting conditions?
	  – age
	  – the presence of sensory sensitivities (including pain thresholds)
	  – IQ
	  – language level.

Biomedical interventions review protocol
Clinical review protocol for the review of biomedical interventions

Component	Description
Review question	For adults with autism, what is the effectiveness of biomedical interventions (for example, dietary interventions, pharmacotherapy, and physical-environmental adaptations)? (RQ–C4)
Subquestion	For adults with autism, is the effectiveness of interventions moderated by: • the nature and severity of the condition • the presence of coexisting conditions • age • the presence of sensory sensitivities (including pain thresholds) • IQ • language level? (RQ–C5) For adults with autism, what amendments, if any, need to be made to the current recommendations for psychosocial and pharmacological treatment (including the nature of drug interactions and side effects) for coexisting common mental health disorders? (RQ–C6)
Chapter	8
Topic group	Biomedical interventions
Objectives	To evaluate the clinical effectiveness of biomedical interventions for autism.
Criteria for considering studies for the review	
• *Population*	Adults and young people aged 18 years and older with suspected autism across the range of diagnostic groups (including atypical autism, Asperger's syndrome and pervasive developmental disorder). Consideration should be given to the specific needs of: • people with coexisting conditions • women • older people • people from black and minority ethnic groups • transgender people. Excluded groups include: • children (under 18 years). However, the GDG made a consensus-based decision to extrapolate from literature involving children (under 18 years) for interventions where there was not sufficient

	evidence from an adult population and where the mechanisms of biomedical interventions were judged by the GDG to be equivalent in children/young people and adults. For interventions concerned with the management of behaviour, and where data from adult autism populations were not sufficient, the GDG decided that extrapolating from a learning disabilities population was valid.
• *Intervention(s)*	• Pharmacotherapy (for example, antipsychotics, antidepressants, anticonvulsants) • Vitamins and dietary supplements (for example, omega-3 fatty acid supplements, vitamin B12, vitamin A) • Hormones (for example, oxytocin, secretin, melatonin)
• *Comparison*	Placebo-controlled, other active interventions
• *Critical outcomes*	Outcomes involving core features of autism (social interaction and communication, repetitive interests/activities); overall autistic behaviour; symptom severity/improvement; management of challenging behaviour; outcomes involving treatment of coexisting conditions; side effects
• *Study design*	• RCTs The GDG agreed by consensus that where there were no RCTs found in the evidence search, or the results from the RCTs were inconclusive, that the following studies would be included in the review of evidence: • observational • quasi-experimental • case series.
• *Include unpublished data?*	Yes, but only where: • the evidence was accompanied by a trial report containing sufficient detail to properly assess the quality of the data • the evidence was submitted with the understanding that data from the study and a summary of the study's characteristics will be published in the full guideline. Therefore, the GDG should not accept evidence submitted as commercial in confidence. However, the GDG should recognise that unpublished evidence submitted by investigators, might later be retracted by those investigators if the inclusion of such data would jeopardise publication of their research.

• *Restriction by date?*	No
• *Minimum sample size*	• RCT/observational/quasi-experimental studies: N = 10 per arm (ITT) • Case series studies: N = 10 in total Exclude studies with >50% attrition from either arm of trial (unless adequate statistical methodology has been applied to account for missing data).
• *Study setting*	• Primary, secondary, tertiary, health and social care and healthcare settings (including prisons and forensic services) • Others in which NHS services are funded or provided, or NHS professionals are working in multi-agency teams
Electronic databases	AEI, AMED, ASSIA, BEI, CDSR, CENTRAL, CINAHL, DARE, Embase, ERIC, HMIC, MEDLINE, PsycINFO, Sociological Abstracts, SSA
Date searched	Systematic reviews: 1995 to 09/09/2011. RCTs, quasi-experimental studies, observational studies, case series: inception of database to 09/09/2011.
Searching other resources	Hand-reference searching of retrieved literature

The review strategy	• The initial aim is to conduct a meta-analysis evaluating the clinical effectiveness of the interventions. However, in the absence of adequate data, the literature will be presented via a narrative synthesis of the available evidence.
	• Narratively review of the literature that takes into consideration any amendments due to common mental health disorders.
	• Consider subgroup meta-analyses that take into account the effectiveness of interventions as moderated by:
	  – the nature and severity of the condition
	  – the presence of coexisting conditions
	  – age
	  – the presence of sensory sensitivities (including pain thresholds)
	  – IQ
	  – language level.

APPENDIX 9:
SEARCH STRATEGIES FOR THE IDENTIFICATION
OF CLINICAL STUDIES

The search strategies can be found on the CD accompanying this guideline.

APPENDIX 10:

QUALITY CHECKLIST TEMPLATES FOR CLINICAL STUDIES AND REVIEWS

The methodological quality of each study was evaluated using NICE checklists (NICE, 2009e). The checklists for systematic reviews and for RCTs are reproduced below (for other checklists and further information about how to complete each checklist, see *The Guidelines Manual* [NICE, 2009e]). The completed checklists can be found in Appendix 16.

Methodology checklist template: systematic reviews and meta-analyses

Study identification *Include author, title, reference, year of publication*			
Guideline topic:	Review question no:		
Checklist completed by:			
SCREENING QUESTIONS			
In a well-conducted, relevant systematic review:	*Circle one option for each question*		
The review addresses an appropriate and clearly focused question that is relevant to the guideline review question	Yes	No	Unclear
The review collects the type of studies you consider relevant to the guideline review question	Yes	No	Unclear
The literature search is sufficiently rigorous to identify all the relevant studies	Yes	No	Unclear
Study quality is assessed and reported	Yes	No	Unclear
An adequate description of the methodology used is included, and the methods used are appropriate to the question	Yes	No	Unclear

Methodology checklist template: randomised controlled trials

Study identification *Include author, title, reference, year of publication*	
Guideline topic:	Review question no:
Checklist completed by:	
	Circle one option for each question

A. Selection bias (systematic differences between the comparison groups)

A1	An appropriate method of randomisation was used to allocate participants to treatment groups (which would have balanced any confounding factors equally across groups)	Yes	No	Unclear	N/A
A2	There was adequate concealment of allocation (such that investigators, clinicians and participants cannot influence enrolment or treatment allocation)	Yes	No	Unclear	N/A
A3	The groups were comparable at baseline, including all major confounding and prognostic factors	Yes	No	Unclear	N/A

Based on your answers to the above, in your opinion was selection bias present? If so, what is the likely direction of its effect?

Low risk of bias	Unclear/unknown risk	High risk of bias

Likely direction of effect:

B. Performance bias (systematic differences between groups in the care provided, apart from the intervention under investigation)

B1	The comparison groups received the same care apart from the intervention(s) studied	Yes	No	Unclear	N/A
B2	Participants receiving care were kept 'blind' to treatment allocation	Yes	No	Unclear	N/A
B3	Individuals administering care were kept 'blind' to treatment allocation	Yes	No	Unclear	N/A

Based on your answers to the above, in your opinion was performance bias present? If so, what is the likely direction of its effect?

Low risk of bias	Unclear/unknown risk	High risk of bias		

Likely direction of effect:				

C. Attrition bias (systematic differences between the comparison groups with respect to loss of participants)				
C1	All groups were followed up for an equal length of time (or analysis was adjusted to allow for differences in length of follow-up)	Yes	No	Unclear	N/A
C2	a. How many participants did not complete treatment in each group?				
	b. The groups were comparable for treatment completion (that is, there were no important or systematic differences between groups in terms of those who did not complete treatment)	Yes	No	Unclear	N/A
C3	a. For how many participants in each group were no outcome data available?				
	b. The groups were comparable with respect to the availability of outcome data (that is, there were no important or systematic differences between groups in terms of those for whom outcome data were not available).	Yes	No	Unclear	N/A

Based on your answers to the above, in your opinion was attrition bias present? If so, what is the likely direction of its effect?				

Low risk of bias	Unclear/unknown risk	High risk of bias		

Likely direction of effect:				

D. Detection bias (bias in how outcomes are ascertained, diagnosed or verified)				
D1	The study had an appropriate length of follow-up	Yes	No	Unclear	N/A
D2	The study used a precise definition of outcome	Yes	No	Unclear	N/A
D3	A valid and reliable method was used to determine the outcome	Yes	No	Unclear	N/A

D4	Investigators were kept 'blind' to participants' exposure to the intervention	Yes	No	Unclear	N/A
D5	Investigators were kept 'blind' to other important confounding and prognostic factors	Yes	No	Unclear	N/A

Based on your answers to the above, in your opinion was detection bias present? If so, what is the likely direction of its effect?

Low risk of bias	Unclear/unknown risk	High risk of bias

Likely direction of effect:

APPENDIX 11:
SEARCH STRATEGIES FOR THE IDENTIFICATION
OF HEALTH ECONOMIC EVIDENCE

The search strategies can be found on the CD accompanying this guideline.

APPENDIX 12:
METHODOLOGY CHECKLIST TEMPLATE FOR ECONOMIC STUDIES

This checklist is designed to determine whether an economic evaluation provides evidence that is useful to inform the decision-making of the GDG. It is not intended to judge the quality of the study per se or the quality of reporting. For further information about how to complete the checklist, see *The Guidelines Manual* (NICE, 2009e).

Study identification *Including author, title, reference, year of publication*			
Guideline topic:		**Question no:**	
Checklist completed by:			
Section 1: Applicability (relevance to specific guideline review question(s) and the NICE reference case). This checklist should be used first to filter out irrelevant studies.	**Yes/Partly/ No/Unclear/N/A**	**Comments**	
1.1	Is the study population appropriate for the guideline?		
1.2	Are the interventions appropriate for the guideline?		
1.3	Is the healthcare system in which the study was conducted sufficiently similar to the current UK NHS context?		
1.4	Are costs measured from the NHS and personal social services (PSS) perspective?		
1.5	Are all direct health effects on individuals included?		
1.6	Are both costs and health effects discounted at an annual rate of 3.5%?		

1.7	Is the value of health effects expressed in terms of quality-adjusted life years (QALYs)?		
1.8	Are changes in health-related quality of life (HRQoL) reported directly from patients and/or carers?		
1.9	Is the valuation of changes in HRQoL (utilities) obtained from a representative sample of the general public?		
1.10	Overall judgement: Directly applicable/Partially applicable/N/A There is no need to use section 2 of the checklist if the study is considered 'not applicable'.		
Other comments:			

Section 2: Study limitations (the level of methodological quality). This checklist should be used once it has been decided that the study is sufficiently applicable to the context of the clinical guideline.	Yes/Partly/ No/Unclear/N/A	Comments
2.1 Does the model structure adequately reflect the nature of the health condition under evaluation?		
2.2 Is the time horizon sufficiently long to reflect all important differences in costs and outcomes?		
2.3 Are all important and relevant health outcomes included?		
2.4 Are the estimates of baseline health outcomes from the best available source?		

2.5	Are the estimates of relative treatment effects from the best available source?		
2.6	Are all important and relevant costs included?		
2.7	Are the estimates of resource use from the best available source?		
2.8	Are the unit costs of resources from the best available source?		
2.9	Is an appropriate incremental analysis presented or can it be calculated from the data?		
2.10	Are all important parameters whose values are uncertain subjected to appropriate sensitivity analysis?		
2.11	Is there no potential conflict of interest?		
2.12	Overall assessment: Minor limitations/Potentially serious limitations/Very serious limitations		
Other comments:			

APPENDIX 13:
RESEARCH RECOMMENDATIONS

The GDG has made the following recommendations for research, based on its review of the evidence, to improve NICE guidance and care for people with autism in the future.

13.1   GUIDED SELF-INSTRUCTION FOR ANXIETY AND DEPRESSION IN AUTISM

What is the clinical and cost effectiveness of facilitated self-help for the treatment of mild anxiety and depressive disorders in adults with autism?

Why this is important
Anxiety and depressive disorders are commonly coexisting disorders in people with autism and are associated with poorer health outcomes and quality of life. This may occur because of the direct impact of the anxiety or depression but also because of a negative interaction with the core symptoms of autism. There is limited access and poor uptake of such interventions by people with autism in significant part due to limited availability, but also because current systems for the delivery of facilitated self-help are not adapted for use by people with autism. In adults without autism facilitated self-help is an effective intervention for mild to moderate depression and anxiety. The development of novel methods for the delivery of facilitated self-help could make effective interventions available to a wider group of people than is currently the case.

The suggested programme of research would need to: (a) develop current methods for the delivery of self-help measures to take into account the impact of the autism and possibly include developments in the nature of the materials, the methods for their delivery and the nature, duration and extent of their facilitation; (b) test the feasibility of the novel methods in a series of pilot studies; and (c) formally evaluate the outcome (including symptoms, satisfaction and quality of life) in a large-scale randomised trial.

13.2   The structure and organisation of specialist teams

What structure and organisation for specialist autism teams are associated with improvements in care for people with autism?

Why this is important

The Department of Health's (2010) autism strategy proposes the introduction of a range of specialist services for people with autism; these will usually be built around specialist autism teams. However, there is little evidence to guide the establishment and development of these teams including uncertainty about the precise nature of the population to be served (all people with autism or only those who are 'high functioning'), the composition of the team, the extent of the team's role (for example, diagnosis and assessment only, a primarily advisory role or a substantial care coordination role), the interventions provided by the team and the team's role and relationship with regard to non-statutory care providers. Therefore it is likely that in the near future a number of different models will be developed, which are likely to have varying degrees of success in meeting the needs of people with autism. Given the significant expansion of services, this presents an opportunity for a large-scale observational study, which should provide important information on the characteristics of teams associated with positive outcomes for people with autism in terms of access to services, effective coordination of care and outcomes for service users and their families.

13.3   Augmented communication devices for adults with autism

What is the clinical and cost effectiveness of augmented communication devices for adults with autism?

Why this is important

Many people with autism experience very significant communication problems (for example, the absence of any spoken language or significant deficits in interpersonal skills), which have a profound effect on their ability to lead a full and rewarding life. It is probable that these problems are related to the core symptoms of autism and are likely to persist for most people given the life-long course of autism and the lack of effective interventions for these core symptoms. A number of communication devices have been developed for autism but few, if any, have been subject to a proper evaluation in adults. Despite this lack of formal evaluation, individual services have made considerable investments in augmented communication devices. Research that provides high-quality evidence on the acceptability and the clinical and cost effectiveness of augmented communication devices could bring about significant improvements in the lives of adults with autism.

The suggested programme of research would need to identify current devices for which there is: (a) some evidence of benefit (for example, case series and small scale pilot studies); (b) some evidence that it meets a key communication need for people with autism (based on reviews of people's need in this area); and (c) indication that the device is feasible for routine use. The identified device(s) should then be formally evaluated in a large-scale randomised trial.

11.   REFERENCES

Adams, J. B., Baral, M., Geis, E., *et al.* (2009a) Safety and efficacy of oral DMSA therapy for children with autism spectrum disorders: Part A – Medical results. *BMC Clinical Pharmacology*, *9*, 16.

Adams, J. B., Baral, M., Geis, E., *et al.* (2009b) Safety and efficacy of oral DMSA therapy for children with autism spectrum disorders: Part B – Behavioral results. *BMC Clinical Pharmacology*, *9*, 17.

Adult Task and Finish Group (2009) *The Autistic Spectrum Disorder (ASD) Strategic Action Plan for Wales*. Cardiff: Welsh Assembly Government. Available at: www.wales.nhs.uk/documents/ASD-strategy.pdf [accessed 20 May 2012].

AGREE Collaboration (2003) Development and validation of an international appraisal instrument for assessing the quality of clinical practice guidelines: the AGREE project. *Quality and Safety in Health Care*, *12*, 18–23.

Allen, A. (2007) Thiomersal on trial: the theory that vaccines cause autism goes to court. *Slate* online magazine, 28 May. Available at: www.slate.com/articles/health_and_science/medical_examiner/2007/05/thimerosal_on_trial.html [accessed 20 May 2012].

Allison, C., Auyeung, B., Baron-Cohen, S. (2012) Towards brief 'red flags' for autism screening: the short Autism Spectrum Quotient and the short Quantitative Checklist for Autism in toddlers in 1,000 cases and 3,000 controls. *Journal of the American Academy of Child and Adolescent Psychiatry*, *51*, 202–212.

Altheide, D. L. (1996) *Qualitative Media Analysis*. Thousand Oaks, CA: Sage Publications.

Altman, D. G. & Bland, J. M. (1994a) Diagnostic tests 2: predictive values. *British Medical Journal*, *309*, 102.

Altman, D. G. & Bland, J. M. (1994b) Diagnostic tests 1: sensitivity and specificity. *British Medical Journal*, *308*, 1552.

Aman, M. G., Singh, N. N., Stewart, A. W., *et al.* (1985) The Aberrant Behavior Checklist. *American Journal of Mental Deficiency*, *89*, 492–502.

Aman, M. G., Burrow, W. H. & Wolford, P. L. (1995a) The Aberrant Behavior Checklist-Community: factor validity and effect of subject variables for adults in group homes. *American Journal of Mental Retardation*, *100*, 283–292.

Aman, M. G., van Bourgondien, M. E., Wolford, P. L., *et al.* (1995b) Psychotropic and anticonvulsant drugs in subjects with autism: prevalence and patterns of use. *Journal of the American Academy of Child and Adolescent Psychiatry*, *34*, 1672–1681.

Aman, M. G., Lam, K. S. & Collier-Crespin, A. (2003) Prevalence and patterns of use of psychoactive medicines among individuals with autism in the Autism Society of Ohio. *Journal of Autism and Developmental Disorders*, *33*, 527–534.

American Psychological Association (1980) *Diagnostic and Statistical Manual of Mental Disorders* (3rd edn) (DSM-III). Washington, DC: APA.

American Psychological Association (1994) *Diagnostic and Statistical Manual of Mental Disorders* (4th edn) (DSM-IV). Washington, DC: APA.

American Psychological Association (forthcoming in 2013) *Diagnostic and Statistical Manual of Mental Disorders* (5th edn) (DSM-5). Washington, DC: APA.

Amirkhan, J. H. (1990) A factor analytically derived measure of coping: the Coping Strategy Indicator. *Journal of Personality and Social Psychology, 59*, 1066–1074.

Andari, E., Duhamel, J-R., Zalla, T., *et al.* (2010) Promoting social behavior with oxytocin in high-functioning autism spectrum disorders. *Proceedings of the National Academy of Sciences of the United States of America, 107*, 4389–4394.

Anderson, S. & Morris, J. (2006) Cognitive behaviour therapy for people with Asperger syndrome. *Behavioural and Cognitive Psychotherapy, 34*, 293–303.

Andrews, G., Peters, L. & Teeson, M. (1994) *The Measurement of Consumer Outcomes in Mental Health*. Canberra, Australia: Australian Government Publishing Services.

Antochi, R., Stavrakaki, C. & Emery, P. C. (2003) Psychopharmacological treatments in persons with dual diagnosis of psychiatric disorders and developmental disabilities. *Postgraduate Medicine Journal, 9*, 139–146.

Arendt, J. (1997) Safety of melatonin in long-term use(?). *Journal of Biological Rhythms, 12*, 673–681.

Arendt, J. (2003) Importance and relevance of melatonin to human biological rhythms. *Journal of Neuroendocrinology, 15*, 427–431.

Asperger, H. (1944). Die 'Autistischen Psychopathen' im Kindesalter. [The 'autistic psychopaths' in childhood]. *Archiv für Psychiatrie und Nervenkrankheiten, 117*, 76–136.

Attwood, T. (1997). *Asperger's Syndrome: a Guide for Parents and Professionals*. London: Jessica Kingsley Publishers.

Attwood, T. (2004) Cognitive behaviour therapy for children and adults with Asperger's syndrome. *Behaviour Change, 21*, 147–162.

Attwood, T. (2006a) The pattern of abilities and development of girls with Asperger's syndrome. In *Asperger's and Girls* (T. Attwood), pp. 1–7. Arlington, TX: Future Horizons.

Attwood, T. (2006b) *The Complete Guide to Asperger's Syndrome*. London: Jessica Kingsley Publishers.

Auyeung, B., Baron-Cohen, S., Ashwin, E., *et al.* (2009). Fetal testosterone and autistic traits. *British Journal of Psychology, 100*, 1–22.

Bailey, A., Le Couteur, A., Gottesman, I., *et al.* (1995) Autism as a strongly genetic disorder: evidence from a British twin study. *Psychological Medicine, 25*, 63–77.

Baird, G., Simonoff, E., Pickles, A., *et al.* (2006) Prevalence of disorders of the autism spectrum in a population cohort of children in South Thames: the Special Needs and Autism Project (SNAP). *The Lancet, 368*, 210–215.

Baker, D. A. & Palmer, R. J. (2006) Examining the effects of perceptions of community and recreation participation on quality of life. *Social Indicators Research, 75*, 395–418.

Barlow, J. & Kirby, N. (1991) Residential satisfaction of persons with an intellectual disability living in an institution or in the community. *Australia and New Zealand Journal of Developmental Disabilities, 17*, 7–23.

References

Barnard, J., Prior, A. & Potter, D. (2000) *Inclusion and Autism: Is it Working? 1,000 Examples of Inclusion in Education and Adult Life from the National Autistic Society's Members.* London: NAS.

Barnard, J., Harvey, V., Potter, D. & Prior, A. (2001) *Ignored or Ineligible? The Reality for Adults with Autism Spectrum Disorders.* London: NAS.

Barnhill, G. P. (2007) Outcomes in adults with Asperger syndrome. *Focus on Autism and Other Developmental Disabilities, 22,* 116–126.

Baron-Cohen, S. (1991) The development of a theory of mind in autism: deviance and delay? *Psychiatric Clinics of North America, 14,* 33–51.

Baron-Cohen, S. (2000) Is Asperger's syndrome/high-functioning autism necessarily a disability? *Development and Psychopathology, 12,* 489–500.

Baron-Cohen, S. (2008) *Autism and Asperger Syndrome.* Oxford: Oxford University Press.

Baron-Cohen, S. & Wheelwright, S. (2004) The Empathy Quotient (EQ): an investigation of adults with Asperger syndrome or high functioning autism, and normal sex differences. *Journal of Autism and Developmental Disorders, 34,* 163–175.

Baron-Cohen, S., Ring, H. A., Bullmore, E. T., *et al.* (2000) The amygdala theory of autism. *Neuroscience Biobehavioral Reviews, 24,* 355–364.

Baron-Cohen, S., Wheelwright, S., Skinner, R., *et al.* (2001a) The Autism-Spectrum Quotient (AQ): evidence from Asperger Syndrome/high functioning autism, males and females, scientists and mathematicians. *Journal of Autism and Developmental Disorders, 31,* 5–17.

Baron-Cohen, S., Wheelwright, S., Hill, J., *et al.* (2001b) The 'Reading the Mind in the Eyes' Test, revised version: a study with normal adults, and adults with Asperger syndrome or high-functioning autism. *Journal of Child Psychology and Psychiatry, 42,* 241–251.

Baron-Cohen, S., Wheelwright, S., Robinson, J., *et al.* (2005) The Adult Asperger Assessment (AAA): a diagnostic method. *Journal of Autism and Developmental Disorders, 35,* 807–819.

Baron-Cohen, S., Scott, F. J., Allison, C., *et al.* (2009) Prevalence of autism-spectrum conditions: UK school-based population study. *British Journal of Psychiatry, 194,* 500–509.

Barry, T., Klinger, L. G., Lee, J. M., *et al.* (2003) Examining the effectiveness of an outpatient clinic-based social skills group for high-functioning children with autism. *Journal of Autism and Developmental Disorders, 33,* 685–701.

Barthelemy, C., Adrien, J. L., Tanguay, P., *et al.* (1990) The Behavioral Summarized Evaluation: validity and reliability of a scale for the assessment of autistic behaviours. *Journal of Autism and Developmental Disorders, 20,* 189–203.

Bashe, P. M., Kirby, B. L. & Attwood, T. (2005) *The OASIS Guide to Asperger Syndrome: Advice, Support, Insight, and Inspiration.* New York, NY: Crown Publishers.

Bass, M. & Drewett, R. (1996) *Supported Employment for People with Learning Disabilities.* Social Care Research 86. May. York: Joseph Rowntree Foundation.

Available at: www.jrf.org.uk/publications/supported-employment-people-with-learning-difficulties [accessed 11 September 2012].

Bat-haee, M. A. (2001) A longitudinal study of active treatment of adaptive skills of individuals with profound mental retardation. *Psychological Reports*, *89*, 345–354.

Bates, E., Bretherton, I., Snyder, L., *et al.* (1988) *From First Words to Grammar: Individual Differences and Dissociable Mechanisms*. New York, NY: Cambridge University Press.

Bauminger, N. & Kasari, C. (2000) Loneliness and friendship in high-functioning children with autism. *Child Development*, *71*, 447–456.

Bauminger, N., Shulman, C. & Agam, G. (2003) Peer interaction and loneliness in high-functioning children with autism. *Journal of Autism and Developmental Disorders*, *33*, 489–507.

Bebko, J. M., Perry, A. & Bryson, S. E. (1996) Multiple method validation study of facilitated communication: individual differences and subgroup results. *Journal of Autism and Developmental Disorders*, *26*, 19–42.

Beck, A. R. & Pirovano, C. M. (1996) Facilitated communicator's performance on a task of receptive language. *Journal of Autism and Developmental Disorders*, *26*, 497–512.

Beck, A. T., Lester, L. & Trexler, L. (1974) The Hopelessness Scale. *Journal of Consulting and Clinical Psychology*, *42*, 861–874.

Beck, A. T., Rush, A. J., Shaw, B. F., *et al.* (1979) *Cognitive Therapy of Depression*. New York, NY: Guilford Press.

Begeer, S., El Bouk, S., Boussaid, W., *et al.* (2009) Underdiagnosis and referral bias of autism in ethnic minorities. *Journal of Autism and Developmental Disorders*, *39*, 142–148.

Bellini, S. (2004) Social skill deficits and anxiety in high-functioning adolescents with autism spectrum disorders. *Focus on Autism and Other Developmental Disabilities*, *19*, 78–86.

Belmonte, M. K., Allen, G., Beckel-Mitchener, A., *et al.* (2004) Autism and abnormal development of brain connectivity. *The Journal of Neuroscience*, *24*, 9228–9231.

Belsito, K. M., Law, P. A., Kirk, K. S., *et al.* (2001) Lamotrigine therapy for autistic disorder: a randomized, double-blind, placebo-controlled trial. *Journal of Autism and Developmental Disorders*, *31*, 175–181.

Bemporad, J. R. (1979) Adult recollections of a formerly autistic child. *Journal of Autism and Developmental Disorders*, *9*, 179–197.

Benson, B. (1992) *Teaching Anger Management to Persons with Mental Retardation*. Champaign, IL: International Diagnostic System, Inc.

Benson, B. (1994) Anger management training: a self-control program for people with mild mental retardation. In *Mental Health in Mental Retardation* (ed. N. Bouras), pp. 224–232. Cambridge: Cambridge University Press.

Benson, B. & Ivins, J. (1992) Anger, depression and self-concept in adults with mental retardation. *Journal of Intellectual Disability Research*, *36*, 169–175.

Benson, B. A., Rice, C. J. & Miranti, S. V. (1986) Effects of anger management training with mentally retarded adults in group treatment. *Journal of Consulting and Clinical Psychology*, *54*, 728–729.

Bent, S., Bertoglio, K., Ashwood, P., *et al.* (2011) Brief report: hyperbaric oxygen therapy (HBOT) in children with autism spectrum disorder: a clinical trial. *Journal of Autism and Developmental Disorders, 42*, 1127–1132.

Berlin, J. A. (2001) Does blinding of readers affect the results of meta-analyses? *Lancet, 350*, 185–186.

Berney, T. (2004) Asperger syndrome from childhood into adulthood. *Advances in Psychiatric Treatment, 10*, 341–351.

Berument, S. K., Rutter, M., Lord, C., *et al.* (1999) Autism screening questionnaire: diagnostic validity. *British Journal of Psychiatry, 175*, 444–451.

Bettelheim, B. (1967) *The Empty Fortress: Infantile Autism and the Birth of the Self.* New York, NY: The Free Press.

Beyer, S. & Kilsby, M. (1996) The future of employment for people with learning disabilities: a keynote review. *British Journal of Learning Disabilities, 24*, 134–137.

Bhaumik, S., Watson, J. M., Devapriam, J., *et al.* (2009) Aggressive challenging behaviour in adults with intellectual disability following community resettlement. *Journal of Intellectual Disability Research, 53*, 298–302.

Bhaumik, S., Tyrer, F., Barrett, M., *et al.* (2010) The relationship between carers' report of autistic traits and clinical diagnoses of autism spectrum disorders in adults with intellectual disability. *Research in Developmental Disabilities, 31*, 705–712.

Biklen, D. (1990) Communication unbound: autism and praxis. *Harvard Educational Review, 60*, 291–314.

Biklen, D. & Schubert, A. (1991) New words: the communication of students with autism. *Remedial and Special Education, 12*, 46–57.

Biklen, D., Morton, M. W., Saha, S. N., *et al.* (1991) 'I AMN NOT A UTISTIVC OH THJE TYP' ('I'm not autistic on the type writer'). *Disability, Handicap and Society, 6*, 161–180.

Biklen, D., Morton, M. W., Gold, D., *et al.* (1992) Facilitated communication: implications for individuals with autism. *Topics in Language Disorders, 12*, 1–28.

Biklen, D., Saha, N. & Kliewer, C. (1995) How teachers confirm the authorship of facilitated communication: a portfolio approach. *Journal of the Association for Persons with Severe Handicaps, 20*, 45–56.

Billstedt, E., Gillberg, C. & Gillberg, C. (2005) Autism after adolescence: population-based 13- to 22-year follow-up study of 120 individuals with autism diagnosed in childhood. *Journal of Autism and Developmental Disorders, 35*, 351–360.

Birks, J. & Harvey, R. J. (2006) Donepezil for dementia due to Alzheimer's disease. *Cochrane Database of Systematic Reviews, 1*, Art. No.: CD001190. DOI: 10.1002/14651858.CD001190.pub2.

Birks, J., Grimley Evans, J., Iakovidou, V., *et al.* (2009) Rivastigmine for Alzheimer's disease. *Cochrane Database of Systematic Reviews, 2*, Art. No.: CD001191. DOI: 10.1002/14651858.CD001191.pub2.

Bishop, D., Whitehouse, A., Watt, H., *et al.* (2008) Autism and diagnostic substitution: evidence from a study of adults with a history of developmental language disorder. *Developmental Medicine and Child Neurology, 50*, 1–5.

Blacher, J., Kraemer, B. R. & Howell, E. J. (2010) Family expectations and transition experiences for young adults with severe disabilities. *Advances in Mental Health and Learning Disabilities*, 4, 3–16.

Bloeman, O. J. N, Deeley, Q., Sundram, F., *et al.* (2010) White matter integrity in Asperger syndrome: a preliminary diffusion tensor magnetic resonance imaging study in adults. *Autism Research*, 3, 203–213.

Bolton, P., Macdonald, H., Pickles, A., *et al.* (1994) A case-control family history of autism. *Journal of Child Psychology and Psychiatry*, 35, 877–900.

Bomba, C., O'Donnell, L., Markowitz, C., *et al.* (1996) Evaluating the impact of facilitated communication on the communicative competence of fourteen students with autism. *Journal of Autism and Developmental Disorders*, 26, 43–58.

Bond, G. R., Drake, R. E. & Becker, D. R. (2008) An update on randomized controlled trials of evidence-based supported employment. *Psychiatric Rehabilitation Journal*, 31, 280–290.

Botsford, A. L. & Rule, D. (2004) Evaluation of a group intervention to assist aging parents with permanency planning for an adult offspring with special needs. *Social Work*, 49, 423–431.

Bouras, N. & Drummond, C. (1992) Behaviour and psychiatric disorders of people with a mental handicap living in the community. *Journal of Intellectual Disability Research*, 36, 349–357.

Bouras, N., Kon, Y. & Drummond, C. (1993) Medical and psychiatric needs of adults with a mental handicap. *Journal of Intellectual Disability Research*, 37, 177–182.

Bower, P., Gilbody, S., Richards, D., *et al.* (2006) Collaborative care for depression in primary care: making sense of a complex intervention: systematic review and meta-regression. *British Journal of Psychiatry*, 189, 484–493.

Boyatzis, R. E. (1998). *Transforming Qualitative Information: Thematic Analysis and Code Development*. Thousand Oaks, CA: Sage Publications.

Boyd, B. A. (2002) Examining the relationship between stress and lack of social support in mothers of children with autism. *Focus on Autism and Other Developmental Disabilities*, 17, 208–215.

Braman, B. J. & Brady, M. P. (1995) Facilitated communication for children with autism: an examination of face validity. *Behavioral Disorders*, 21, 110–119.

Brand, D., Green, L. & Statham, D. (2010a) *Facts about FACS 2010: a Guide to Fair Access to Care Services. SCIE Adult Services Guide 33*. London: SCIE. Available at: www.scie.org.uk/publications/guides/guide33/files/guide33.pdf

Brand, D., Green, L. & Statham, D. (2010b) *Facts about FACS 2010: Your Questions Answered*. Leaflet. London: SCIE. Available at: www.scie.org.uk/publications/guides/guide33/files/facs-leaflet.pdf

Braun, V. & Clarke, V. (2006) Using thematic analysis in psychology. *Qualitative Research in Psychology*, 3, 77–101.

Brazier, J., Roberts, J. & Deverill, M. (2002) The estimation of a preference-based measure of health from the SF-36. *Journal of Health Economics*, 21, 271–292.

Briggs, A., Sculpher, M. & Claxton, K. (2006*) Decision Modelling for Health Economic Evaluation*. Oxford: Oxford University Press.

Brim, O. G., Ryff, C. D. & Kessler, R. C. (2004) The MIDUS national survey: an overview. In *How Healthy Are We? A National Study of Well-being at Midlife* (eds O. G. Brim, C. D. Ryff & R. C. Kessler), pp. 1–36. Chicago, IL: University of Chicago Press.

Broadstock, M., Doughty, C. & Eggleston, M. (2007) Systematic review of the effectiveness of pharmacological treatments for adolescents and adults with autism spectrum disorder. *Autism, 11*, 335–348.

Bromley, J., Hare, D. J., Davison, K., *et al.* (2004) Mothers supporting children with autistic spectrum disorders: social support, mental health status and satisfaction with services. *Autism, 8*, 409–423.

Brotherson, M. J. (1994) Interactive focus group interviewing: a qualitative research method in early intervention. *Topics in Early Childhood Special Education, 14*, 101–118.

Brown, G. L., Goodwin, F. K., Ballenger, J. C., *et al.* (1979) Aggression in humans correlates with cerebrospinal fluid amine metabolites. *Psychiatric Research, 1*, 131–139.

Brudnak, M. A., Rimland, B., Kerry, R. E., *et al.* (2002) Enzyme-based therapy for autism spectrum disorders – is it worth another look? *Medical Hypotheses, 58*, 422–428.

Brugha, S. T., McManus, S., Bankart, J., *et al.* (2011) Epidemiology of autism spectrum disorders in adults in the community in England. *Archives of General Psychiatry, 65*, 459–465.

Brugha, T., Cooper, S. A., McManus, S., *et al.* (2012) *Estimating the Prevalence of Autism Spectrum Conditions in Adults: Extending the 2007 Adult Psychiatric Morbidity Survey.* London: NHS, The Health and Social Care Information Centre.

Bruni, O., Ottaviano, S., Guidetti, V., *et al.* (1996) The Sleep Disturbance Scale for Children (SDSC). Construction and validation of an instrument to evaluate sleep disturbances in childhood and adolescence. *Journal of Sleep Research, 5*, 251–261.

Buitelaar, J. K., van Engeland, H., de Kogel, K., *et al.* (1992) The adrenocorticotrophic hormone (4–9) analog ORG 2766 benefits autistic children: report on a second controlled clinical trial. *Journal of the American Academy of Child and Adolescent Psychiatry, 31*, 1149–1156.

Buitelaar, J. K., Dekker, M. E. M., van Ree, J. M., *et al.* (1996) A controlled trial with ORG 2766, an ACTH-(4–9) analog, in 50 relatively able children with autism. *European Neuropsychopharmacology, 6*, 13–19.

Buitelaar, J. K., van der Gaag, R. J. & van der Hoeven, J. (1998) Buspirone in the management of anxiety and irritability in children with pervasive developmental disorders: results of an open-label study. *Journal of Clinical Psychiatry, 59*, 56–59.

Burlingame, G. M., Lambert, M. J., Reisinger, C. W., *et al.* (1995) Pragmatics of tracking mental health outcomes in a managed care setting. *Journal of Mental Health Administration, 22*, 226–236.

Butler, A. C., Chapman, J. E., Forman, E. M., *et al.* (2006) The empirical status of cognitive-behavior therapy: a review of meta-analyses. *Psychology Review, 26*, 17–31.

Caballo, C., Crespo, C., Jenaro, C., *et al.* (2005) Factor structure for the Schalock and Keith Quality of Life Questionnaire: validation on Mexican and Spanish samples. *Journal of Intellectual Disability Research*, *49*, 773–776.

Cai, G., Edelmann, L., Goldsmith, J. E., *et al.* (2008) Multiplex ligation-dependent probe amplification for genetic screening in autism spectrum disorders: efficient identification of known microduplications and identification of a novel microduplication in ASMT. *BMC Medical Genomics*, *1*, 50.

Cajochen, C., Krauchi, K. & Wirz-Justice, A. (2003) Role of melatonin in the regulation of human circadian rhythms and sleep. *Journal of Neuroendocrinology*, *15*, 432–437.

Cambridge Cognition (2002) *Cambridge Neuropsychological Tests: Automated Battery (CANTAB)*. Cambridge: Cambridge Cognition.

Cameto, R., Levine, P. & Wagner, M. (2004) *Transition Planning for Students with Disabilities: a Special Topic Report from the National Longitudinal Transition Study-2 (NLTS-2)*. Menlo Park, CA: SRI International.

Canitano, R. (2007) Epilepsy in autism spectrum disorders. *European Child and Adolescent Psychiatry*, *16*, 61–66.

Cardaciotto, L. & Herbert, J. D. (2004) Cognitive behavior therapy for social anxiety disorder in the context of Asperger's syndrome: a single subject report. *Cognitive and Behavioral Practice*, *11*, 75–81.

Casanova, M. F., Buxhoeveden, D. & Gomez, J. (2003) Disruption in the inhibitory architecture of the cell minicolumn: implications for ASD. *Neuroscientist*, *9*, 496–507.

Cederlund, M., Hagberg, B. & Gillberg, C. (2010) Asperger syndrome in adolescent and young adult males. Interview, self- and parent assessment of social, emotional, and cognitive problems. *Research in Development Disabilities*, *31*, 287–298.

Cesaroni, L. & Garber, M. (1991) Exploring the experience of autism through firsthand accounts. *Journal of Autism and Developmental Disorders*, *21*, 303–313.

Chadsey-Rusch, J. (1992) Toward defining and measuring social skills in employment settings. *American Journal of Mental Retardation*, *96*, 405–418.

Chalfant, A. M., Rapee, R. & Caroll, L. (2007) Treating anxiety disorders in children with high functioning autism spectrum disorders. A controlled trial. *Journal of Autism and Developmental Disorders*, *37*, 1842–1857.

Charlton, C. G., Miller, R. L., Crawley, J. N., *et al.* (1983) Secretin modulation of behavioural and physiological functions in the rat. *Peptides*, *4*, 739–742.

Charmaz, K. (2001). Grounded theory. In *Contemporary Field Research: Perspectives and Formulations* (2nd edn) (ed. R. Emerson), pp. 335– 352. Prospect Heights, IL: Waveland Press.

Chervin, R. D. & Hedger, K. M. (2001) Clinical prediction of periodic leg movements during sleep in children. *Sleep Medicine, 2*, 501–510.

Chez, M. G., Buchanan, C. P., Bagan, B. T., *et al.* (2000) Secretin and autism: a two-part clinical investigation. *Journal of Autism and Developmental Disorders*, *30*, 87–94.

Chez, M. G., Buchanan, C. P., Aimonovitch, M. C., *et al.* (2002) Micronutrients versus standard medication management in autism: a naturalistic case-control study. *Journal of Child and Adolescent Psychopharmacology*, *17*, 833–837.

References

Chez, M. G., Buchanan, T. M., Becker, M., *et al.* (2003) Donepezil hydrochloride: a double-blind study in autistic children. *Journal of Pediatric Neurology, 1,* 83–88.

Chez, M. G., Burton, Q., Dowling, T., *et al.* (2007) Memantine as adjunctive therapy in children diagnosed with autistic spectrum disorders: an observation of initial clinical response and maintenance tolerability. *Journal of Child Neurology, 22,* 574–579.

Chou, Y.-C., Lin, L-C., Pu, C-Y., *et al.* (2008) Outcomes and costs of residential services for adults with intellectual disabilities in Taiwan: a comparative evaluation. *Journal of Applied Research in Intellectual Disabilities, 21,* 114–125.

Chou, Y.-C., Pu, C., Kröger, T., *et al.* (2011) Outcomes of a new residential scheme for adults with intellectual disabilities in Taiwan: a 2-year follow-up. *Journal of Intellectual Disability Research, 55,* 823–831.

Chungpaibulpatana, J., Sumpatanarax, T., Thadakul, N., *et al.* (2008) Hyperbaric oxygen therapy in Thai autistic children. *Journal of the Medical Association of Thailand, 91,* 1232–1238.

Clandinin, D. J. & Conelly, F. M. (1999) *Narrative Inquiry: Experience and Story in Qualitative Research.* San Francisco, CA: Jossey-Bass.

Clarke, J. & van Amerom, G. (2008) Asperger's syndrome: differences between parents' understanding and those diagnosed. *Social Work in Health Care, 46,* 85–106.

Clarkson, G. (1994) Creative music therapy and facilitated communication: new ways of reaching students with autism. *Preventing School Failure, 28,* 31–33.

Clifford, P. I. (1987) *Problems Questionnaire.* London: National Unit for Psychiatric Research and Development.

Cochrane Collaboration (2011) *Review Manager (RevMan)* [Computer program]. Version 5.1 for Windows. Copenhagen: The Nordic Cochrane Centre, The Cochrane Collaboration.

Cohen, I. L., Tsiouris, J. A., Flory, M. J., *et al.* (2010) A large scale study of the psychometric characteristics of the IBR Modified Overt Aggression scale: findings and evidence for increased self-destructive behaviors in adult females with autism spectrum disorder. *Journal of Autism and Developmental Disorders, 40,* 599–609.

Conelly, F. M., & Clandinin, D. J. (1990) Stories of experience and narrative inquiry. *Educational Researcher, 19,* 2–14.

Conners, C., Sitarenios, G., Parker, J. D., *et al.* (1998) The revised Conners' Parent Rating Scale (CPRS-R): factor structure, reliability, and criterion validity. *Journal of Abnormal Child Psychology, 26,* 257–268.

Connor, J. R., Boyer, P. J., Menzies, B. S., *et al.* (2003) Neuropathological examination suggests impaired brain iron acquisition in restless legs syndrome. *Neurology, 61,* 304–309.

Constantino, J. N. (2002) *The Social Responsiveness Scale.* Los Angeles, CA: Western Psychological Services.

Constantino, J. N., Hudziak, J. J. & Todd, R. D. (2003) Deficits in reciprocal social behaviour in male twins: evidence for a genetically independent domain of psychopharmacology. *Journal of the American Academy of Child and Adolescent Psychiatry*, *42*, 458–467.

Cook, E. H., Jr, Rowlett, R., Jselskis, C., *et al.* (1992) Fluoxetine treatment of children and adults with autistic disorder and mental retardation. *Journal of the American Academy of Child and Adolescent Psychiatry, 31*, 739–745.

Courchesne, E., C. Karns, M., Davis, H. R., *et al.* (2001) Unusual brain growth patterns in early life of patients with autistic disorder. *Neurology*, *57*, 245–254.

Coyne, I. (1997) Sampling in qualitative research. Purposeful and theoretical sampling: merging or clear boundaries? *Journal of Advanced Nursing, 26*, 623–630.

Coyne, P. (2004) Introduction. In *Supporting Individuals with Autism Spectrum Disorder in Recreation* (eds P. Coyne & A. Fullerton), pp. 1–11. Champaign, IL: Sagamore Publishing.

Crane, L., Goddard, L. & Pring, L. (2009) Sensory processing in adults with autism spectrum disorders. *Autism*, 13, 215–228.

Crews, W. D., Sanders, E. C., Hensley, L. G., *et al.* (1995) An evaluation of facilitated communication in a group of nonverbal individuals with mental retardation. *Journal of Autism and Developmental Disorders*, *25*, 205–213.

Crossley, R. (1992) Who said that? In *Facilitated Communication Training* (ed. DEAL Communication Centre), pp. 42–54. Melbourne, Australia: DEAL Communication Centre.

Crossley, R. & Remington-Gurley, J. (1992) Getting the words out: facilitated communication training. *Topics in Language Disorders*, *12*, 29–45.

CSIP Choice and Access Team (2007) *Improving Access to Psychological Therapies: Positive Practice Guide.* London: Department of Health.

Cuccaro, M. L., Wright, H. H., Rownd, C. V., *et al.* (1996) Brief report: professional perceptions of children with developmental difficulties: the influence of race and socioeconomic status. *Journal of Autism and Developmental Disorders*, *26*, 461–469.

Cullen, C., Whoriskey, M., Mackenzie, K., *et al.* (1995) The effects of deinstitutionalization on adults with learning disabilities. *Journal of Intellectual Disability Research*, *39*, 484–494.

Curtis, L. (2010) *Unit Costs of Health and Social Care 2010.* Canterbury: Personal Social Services Research Unit, University of Kent.

Dagnan, D., Howard, B. & Drewett, R. F. (1994a) A move from hospital to community-based homes for people with learning disabilities: activities outside the home. *Journal of Intellectual Disability Research*, *38*, 567–576.

Dagnan, D., Ruddick, L. & Jones, J. (1998) A longitudinal study of the quality of life of older people with intellectual disability after leaving hospital. *Journal of Intellectual Disability Research*, *42*, 112–121.

Damasio, A. R. & Maurer, R. G. (1978) A neurological model for childhood autism. *Archives of Neurology*, *35*, 777–786.

Daniels, J. L., Forssen, U., Hultman, C. M., *et al.* (2008) Parental psychiatric disorders associated with autism spectrum disorders in the offspring. *Pediatrics*, *121*, e1357–e1362.

Danielsson, S., Gillberg, I. C., Billstedt, E., *et al.* (2005) Epilepsy in young adults with autism: a prospective population-based follow-up study of 120 individuals diagnosed in childhood. *Epilepsia, 46*, 918–23.

Deeks, J. J. (2002) Issues in the selection of a summary statistic for meta-analysis of clinical trials with binary outcomes. *Statistics in Medicine, 21*, 1575–1600.

Department of Health (1999) *National Service Framework for Mental Health: Modern Standards and Service Models*. London: Department of Health.

Department of Health (2004) *Quality and Outcomes Framework: Guidance*. London: Department of Health.

Department of Health (2006a) *Models of Care for Alcohol Misusers (MoCAM)*. London: The Stationery Office.

Department of Health (2006b) *Vocational Services for People with Severe Mental Health Problems: Commissioning Guidance*. London: CSIP for Department of Work and Pensions and Department of Health.

Department of Health (2010) *Fulfilling and Rewarding Lives: the Strategy for Adults with Autism in England*. London: Department of Health. Available at: www.dh.gov.uk/en/PublicationsandstatisticsPublications/PublicationsPolicyAnd Guidance/DH_113369

D'Eufemia, P., Celli, M., Finocchiaro, R., *et al.* (1996) Abnormal intestinal permeability in children with autism. *Acta Paediatrica, 85*, 1076–1079.

De Vries, A. L. C., Noens, I. L. J., Cohen-Kettenis, P. T., *et al.* (2010) Autism spectrum disorders in gender dysphoric children and adolescents. *Journal of Autism and Developmental Disorders, 40*, 930–936.

De Wied, D., Diamant, M. & Fodor, M. (1993) Central nervous system effects of the neurohypophyseal hormones and related peptides. *Frontiers in Neuroendocrinology, 14*, 251–302.

Dhumad, S. & Markar, D. (2007) Audit on the use of antipsychotic medication in a community sample of people with learning disability. *The British Journal of Developmental Disabilities, 53*, 47–51.

DiLavore, P. C., Lord, C. & Rutter, M. (1995) The pre-linguistic autism diagnostic observation schedule. *Journal of Autism and Developmental Disorders, 25*, 355–379.

Di Simplicio, M., Massey-Chase, R., Cowen, P. J., *et al.* (2009) Oxytocin enhances processing of positive versus negative emotional information in healthy male volunteers. *Journal of Psychopharmacology, 23*, 241–248.

Domes, G., Heinrichs, M., Gläscherb, J., *et al.* (2007) Oxytocin attenuates amygdala responses to emotional faces regardless of valence. *Biological Psychiatry, 62*, 1187–1190.

Donaldson, Z. R. & Young, L. J. (2008) Oxytocin, vasopressin, and the neurogenetics of sociality. *Science, 322*, 900–904.

Donnelly, M., McGilloway, S., Mays, N., *et al.* (1996) One and two year outcomes for adults with learning disabilities discharged to the community. *British Journal of Psychiatry, 168*, 598–606.

Dosman, C., Drmic, I., Brian, J., *et al.* (2006) Ferritin as an indicator of suspected iron deficiency in children with autism spectrum disorder: prevalence of low serum ferritin concentration. *Developmental Medicine and Child Neurology*, *48*, 1008–1009.

Dosman, C. F., Brian, J. A., Drmic, I. E., *et al.* (2007) Children with autism: effect of iron supplementation on sleep and ferritin. *Pediatric Neurology*, *36*, 152–158.

Drago, F., Pedersen, C. A., Caldwell, J. D., *et al.* (1986) Oxytocin potently enhances novelty-induced grooming behaviour in the rat. *Brain Research*, *368*, 287–295.

Dunn, M. E., Burbine, T., Bowers, C. A., *et al.* (2001) Moderators of stress in parents of children with autism. *Community Mental Health Journal*, *37*, 39–52.

Dunn-Geier, J., Ho, H. H., Auersperg, E., *et al.* (2000) Effect of secretin on children with autism: a randomized controlled trial. *Developmental Medicine and Child Neurology*, *42*, 796–802.

Dy, S. M., Garg, P., Nyberg, D., *et al.* (2005) Critical pathway effectiveness: assessing the impact of patient, hospital care, and pathway characteristics using qualitative comparative analysis. *Health Services Research*, *40*, 499–516.

Dyson, L. L. (1993) Response to the presence of a child with disabilities: parental stress and family functioning over the time. *American Journal on Mental Retardation*, *98*, 207–218.

Dziobek, I., Fleck, S., Kalbe, E., *et al.* (2006) Introducing MASC: a movie for the assessment of social cognition. *Journal of Autism and Developmental Disorders*, *36*, 623–636.

Earley, C. J. (2003) Restless legs syndrome. *New England Journal of Medicine*, *348*, 2103–2109.

Earley, C. J., Connor, J. R., Beard, J. L., *et al.* (2000) Abnormalities in CSF concentrations of ferritin and transferring in restless legs syndrome. *Neurology*, *54*, 1698–1700.

Eberlin, M., McConnachie, G., Ibel, S., *et al.* (1993) Facilitated communication: a failure to replicate the phenomenon. *Journal of Autism and Developmental Disorders*, *23*, 507–530.

Eccles, M., Freemantle, N. & Mason, J. (1998) North of England evidence based guideline development project: methods of developing guidelines for efficient drug use in primary care. *British Medical Journal*, *316*, 1232–1235.

Ecker, C., Marquand, A., Mourão-Miranda, J., *et al.* (2010) Describing the brain in autism in five dimensions: magnetic resonance imaging-assisted diagnosis of autism spectrum disorder using a multiparameter classification approach. *Journal of Neuroscience*, *30*, 10612–10623.

Edelson, S. M., Rimland, B., Berger, C. L., *et al.* (1998) Evaluation of a mechanical hand-support for facilitated communication. *Journal of Autism and Developmental Disorders*, *28*, 153–157.

Editors of *The Lancet* (2010) Retraction – Ileal-lymphoid-nodular hyperplasia, non-specific colitis, and pervasive developmental disorder in children. *The Lancet, 375*, 445.

Edwards, D. J., Chugani, D. C., Chugani, H. T., *et al.* (2006) Pharmacokinetics of buspirone in autistic children. *Journal of Clinical Pharmacology*, *46*, 508–514.

Ehlers, S. & Gillberg, C. (1993) The epidemiology of Asperger syndrome: a total population study. *Journal of Child Psychology and Psychiatry*, *34*, 1327–1350.

References

Elia, M., Ferri, R., Musumeci, S. A., *et al.* (2000) Sleep in subjects with autistic disorder: a neurophysiological and psychological study. *Brain Development*, *22*, 88–92.

Elliott, R. O., Jr., Hall, K. L. & Soper, H. V. (1991) Analog language teaching versus natural language teaching: generalization and retention of language learning for adults with autism and mental retardation. *Journal of Autism and Developmental Disorders*, *21*, 433–447.

Emmerson, B., Frost, A., Fawcett, L., *et al.* (2006) Do clinical pathways really improve clinical performance in mental health settings? *Australasian Psychiatry*, *14*, 395–398.

Ergüner-Tekinalp, B. & Akkök, F. (2004) The effects of a coping skills training programme on the coping skills, hopelessness, and stress levels of mothers of children with autism. *International Journal for the Advancement of Counselling*, *26*, 257–269.

Erickson, C. A., Posey, D. J., Stigler, K. A., *et al.* (2007) A retrospective study of memantine in children and adolescents with pervasive developmental disorders. *Psychopharmacology*, *191*, 141–147.

Esbensen, A. J., Greenberg, J. S., Seltzer, M. M., *et al.* (2009) A longitudinal investigation of psychotropic and non-psychotropic medication use among adolescents and adults with autism spectrum disorders. *Journal of Autism and Developmental Disorders*, *39*, 1339–1349.

Evangeliou, A., Vlachonikolis, I., Mihailidou, H., *et al.* (2003) Application of a ketogenic diet in children with autistic behavior: pilot study. *Journal of Child Neurology*, *18*, 113–118.

Evans-Lacko, S. E., Jarrett, M., McCrone, P., *et al.* (2008) Clinical pathways in psychiatry. *The British Journal of Psychiatry*, *193*, 4–5.

Fairburn, C. G., Marcus, M. D. & Wilson, G. T. (1993) Cognitive behaviour therapy for binge eating and bulimia nervosa: a treatment manual. In *Binge Eating: Nature, Assessment and Treatment* (eds C. G. Fairburn & G. T. Wilson), pp. 361–404. New York, NY: Guilford Press.

Fatemi, S. H., Halt, A. R., Stary, J. M., *et al.* (2002) Glutamic acid decarboxylase 65 and 67 kDa proteins are reduced in the autistic parietal and cerebellar cortices. *Biological Psychiatry*, *52*, 805–810.

Feldman, M. A., Ducharme, J. M. & Case, L. (1999) Using self-instructional pictorial manuals to teach child-care skills to mothers with intellectual disabilities. *Behavior Modification*, *23*, 480–497.

Fenwick, E., Claxton, K. & Sculpher, M. (2001) Representing uncertainty: the role of cost-effectiveness acceptability curves. *Health Economics*, *10*, 779–787.

Findling, R. L. (2005) Pharmacological treatment of behavioural symptoms in autism and pervasive developmental disorders. *Journal of Clinical Psychiatry*, *66*, 26–31.

Fischer, J. E., Bachmann, L. M. & Jaeschke, R. (2003) A readers' guide to the interpretation of diagnostic test properties: clinical example of sepsis. *Intensive Care Medicine*, *29*, 1043–1051.

Fischer-Shofty, M., Shamay-Tsoory, S. G., Harari, H., *et al.* (2010) The effect of intranasal administration of oxytocin on fear recognition. *Neuropsychologia*, *48*, 179–184.

Fish, B. (1985) Children's Psychiatric Rating Scale. *Psychopharmacology Bulletin*, *21*, 753–770.

Folstein, S. & Rutter, M. (1977) Infantile autism: a genetic study of 21 twin pairs. *Journal of Child Psycholology and Psychiatry*, *18*, 297–321.

Fombonne, E. (2008) Thimerosal disappears but autism remains. *Archives of General Psychiatry*, *65*, 15–16.

Francis, P. T., Palmer, A. M., Snape, M., *et al.* (1999) The cholinergic hypothesis of Alzheimer's disease: a review of progress. *Journal of Neurology, Neurosurgery and Psychiatry*, *66*, 137–147.

Freeman, B. J., Ritvo, E. R., Yokota, A., *et al.* (1986) A scale for rating symptoms of patients with the syndrome of autism in real life settings. *Journal of the American Academy of Child Psychiatry*, *25*, 130–136.

Freeman, J. M., Kossoff, E. H. & Hartman, A. L. (2007) The ketogenic diet: one decade later. *Pediatrics*, *119*, 535–543.

Fremeau, R. T., Jr., Jensen, R. T., Charlton, C. G., *et al.* (1983) Secretin: specific binding to rat brain membranes. *Journal of Neuroscience*, *3*, 1620–1625.

Frith, U. (1989) *Autism: Explaining the Enigma*. Oxford: Basil Blackwell.

Frith, U. (1991) *Autism and Asperger's Syndrome*. Cambridge: Cambridge University Press.

Furukawa, T. A., Barbui, C., Cipriani, A., *et al.* (2006) Imputing missing standard deviations in meta-analyses can provide accurate results. *Journal of Clinical Epidemiology*, *59*, 7–10.

Fyson, R. & Kitson, D. (2007) Independence or protection – does it have to be a choice? Reflections on the abuse of people with learning disabilities in Cornwall. *Critical Social Policy*, *27*, 426–436.

Gadow, K. D., DeVincent, C. J., Pomeroy, J., *et al.* (2004) Psychiatric symptoms in preschool children with PDD and clinic and comparison samples. *Journal of Autism and Developmental Disorders*, *34*, 379–393.

Gadow, K. D., DeVincent, C. J., Pomeroy, J., *et al.* (2005) Comparison of DSM-IV symptoms in elementary school-age children with PDD versus clinic and community samples. *Autism*, *9*, 392–415.

Gagiano, C., Read, S., Thorpe, L., *et al.* (2005) Short- and long-term efficacy and safety of risperidone in adults with disruptive behaviour disorders. *Psychopharmacology*, *179*, 629–636.

Galli-Carminetti, G., Chauvet, I. & Deriaz, N. (2006) Prevalence of gastrointestinal disorders in adult clients with pervasive developmental disorders. *Journal of Intellectual Disability Research*, *50*, 711–718.

Ganz, M. L. (2006) The cost of autism. In *Understanding Autism: From Basic Neuroscience to Treatment* (eds J. Rubenstein & S. Moldin), pp. 1–23. Boca Raton, FL: CRC Press.

Ganz, M. L. (2007) The lifetime distribution of the incremental societal costs of autism. *Archives of Paediatrics and Adolescent Medicine*, *161*, 343–349.

García-Villamsiar, D. A. & Dattilo, J. (2010) Effects of a leisure programme on quality of life and stress of individuals with ASD. *Journal of Intellectual Disability Research*, *54*, 611–619.

García-Villamisar, D. & Dattilo, J. (2011) Social and clinical effects of a leisure programme on adults with autism spectrum disorder. *Research in Autism Spectrum Disorders, 5*, 246–253.

García-Villamisar, D. & Hughes, C. (2007) Supported employment improves cognitive performance in adults with autism. *Journal of Intellectual Disability Research, 51*, 142–150.

García-Villamisar, D., Ross, D. & Wehman, P. (2000) Clinical differential analysis of persons with autism in a work setting: a follow-up study. *Journal of Vocational Rehabilitation, 14*, 183–185.

García-Villamisar, D., Wehman, P. & Diaz Navarro, M. (2002) Changes in the quality of autistic people's life that work in supported and sheltered employment. A 5-year follow-up study. *Journal of Vocational Rehabilitation, 17*, 309–312.

García-Villamisar, D., Rojahn, J., Zaja, R. H., *et al.* (2010) Facial emotion processing and social adaptation in adults with and without autism spectrum disorder. *Research in Autism Spectrum Disorders, 4*, 755–762.

Gask, L., Usherwood, T., Thompson, H., *et al.* (1998) Evaluation of a training package in the assessment and management of depression in primary care. *Medical Education, 32*, 190–198.

Gaskell, G., Dockrell, J. & Rehman, H. (1995) Community care for people with challenging behaviours and mild learning disability: an evaluation of an assessment and treatment unit. *British Journal of Clinical Psychology, 34*, 383–395.

Gaus, V. (2000) "I feel like an alien": individual psychotherapy for adults with Asperger's disorder using a cognitive behavioral approach. *NADD Bulletin, 3*, 62–65.

Gaus, V. L. (2007) *Cognitive-Behavioral Therapy for Adult Asperger Syndrome.* New York, NY: Guilford Press.

Geier, M. & Geier, D. (2005) The potential importance of steroids in the treatment of autistic spectrum disorders and other disorders involving mercury toxicity. *Medical Hypotheses, 64*, 946–54.

Geier, D. A. & Geier, M. R. (2006) A clinical trial of combined anti-androgen and anti-heavy metal therapy in autistic disorders. *Neuroendocrinology Letters, 27*, 833–838.

Geschwind, D. H. (2008). Autism: many genes, common pathways? *Cell, 135*, 391–395.

Ghaziuddin, M. & Greden, J. (1998) Depression in children with autism/pervasive developmental disorders: a case-control family history study. *Journal of Autism and Developmental Disorders, 28*, 111–115.

Ghaziuddin, M., Ghaziuddin, N. & Greden, J. (2002) Depression in persons with autism: implications for research and clinical care. *Journal of Autism and Developmental Disorders, 32*, 299–306.

Gilbody, S., Bower, P., Fletcher, J., *et al.* (2006) Collaborative care for depression: a cumulative meta-analysis and review of longer term outcomes. *Archives of Internal Medicine, 166*, 2314–2321.

Gillberg, C. (1991) Clinical and neurobiological aspects of Asperger's syndrome in six family studies. In *Autism and Asperger's Syndrome* (ed. U. Frith), pp. 122–46. Cambridge: Cambridge University Press.

Gillberg, C. & Billstedt, E. (2000) Autism and Asperger syndrome: co-existence with other clinical disorders. *Acta Psychiatrica Scandinavica*, *102*, 321–330.

Gillberg, C. & Coleman, M. (2000) *The Biology of Autistic Syndromes* (3rd edn). London: Cambridge University Press.

Gillberg, C., Rastam, M. & Wentz, E. (2001) The Asperger Syndrome (and high functioning autism) Diagnostic Interview (ASDI): a preliminary study of a new structured clinical interview. *Autism*, *5*, 57–66.

Gillberg, I. C. & Gillberg, C. (1989) Asperger syndrome – some epidemiological considerations: a research note. *Journal of Child Psychology and Psychiatry*, *30*, 631–638.

Gillot, A., Furniss, F. & Walter, A. (2001) Anxiety in high-functioning children with autism. *Autism*, *5*, 277–286.

Gimpl, G. (2008) Oxytocin receptor ligands: a survey of the patent literature. *Expert Opinion*, *18*, 1239–1251.

Gispen, W. H. (1980) On the neurochemical mechanism of action of ACTH. *Progress in Brain Research*, *53*, 193–206.

Glaser, B. & Strauss, A. (1967). *The Discovery of Grounded Theory: Strategies for Qualitative Research*. New York: Aldine.

Goetz, J. P. & Lecompte, M. D. (1984) *Ethnography and Qualitative Design in Educational Research*. New York: Academic.

Golan, O. & Baron-Cohen, S. (2006) Systemizing empathy: teaching adults with Asperger syndrome or high-functioning autism to recognize complex emotions using interactive multimedia. *Development and Psychopathology*, *18*, 591–617.

Golan, O., Baron-Cohen, S. & Hill, J. (2006) The Cambridge Mindreading (CAM) face-voice battery: testing complex emotion recognition in adults with and without Asperger syndrome. *Journal of Autism and Developmental Disorders*, *36*, 169–183.

Goodman, W. K., Price, L. H., Rasmussen, S. A., *et al.* (1989a) The Yale-Brown Obsessive Compulsive Scale. I: development, use, and reliability. *Archives of General Psychiatry*, *46*, 1006–1011.

Goodman, W. K., Price, L. H., Rasmussen, S. A., *et al.* (1989b) The Yale-Brown Obsessive Compulsive Scale. II: validity. *Archives of General Psychiatry*, *46*, 1012–1016.

Goyette, C. H., Conners, C. K. & Ulrich, R. F. (1978) Normative data on revised Conners Parent and Teacher Rating Scales. *Journal of Abnormal Child Psychology*, *6*, 221–236.

Graetz, J. E. (2010) Autism grows up: opportunities for adults with autism. *Disability and Society*, *25*, 33–47.

Granpeesheh, D., Tarboxa, J., Dixon, D. R., *et al.* (2010) Randomized trial of hyperbaric oxygen therapy for children with autism. *Research in Autism Spectrum Disorders*, *4*, 268–275.

Gray, D. E. (1998) *Autism and the Family*. Springfield, IL: Charles C. Thomas.

Green, J., Gilchrist, A., Burton, D., *et al.* (2000) Social and psychiatric functioning in adolescents with Asperger syndrome compared with conduct disorder. *Journal of Autism and Developmental Disorders*, *30*, 279–293.

References

Green, V. A., Pituch, K. A., Itchon, J., *et al.* (2006) Internet survey of treatments used by parents of children with autism. *Research in Developmental Disabilities*, *27*, 70–84.

Greenhill, L. L., Swanson, J. M., Vitiello, B., *et al.* (2001) Impairment and deportment responses to different methylphenidate doses in children with ADHD: the MTA titration trial. *Journal of the American Academy of Child and Adolescent Psychiatry*, *40*, 180–187.

Gregory, S. G., Connelly, J. J., Towers, A., *et al.* (2009) Genomic and epigenetic evidence for OXTR deficiency in autism. *BMC Medicine*, *7*, 62.

Gresham, F. M. & Elliot, S. N. (1990) *Social Skills Rating System Manual*. Circle Pines, MN: American Guidance Service.

Groden, J., Cautela, J. R., Prince, S., *et al.* (1994) The impact of stress and anxiety on individuals with autism and developmental disabilities. In: *Behavioural Issues in Autism* (eds E. Schopler & G. B. Mesibov), pp. 177–194. New York, NY: Plenum.

Gruenewald, T. L., Mroczek, D. K., Ryff, C. D., *et al.* (2008). Diverse pathways to positive and negative affect in adulthood and later life: an integrative approach using recursive partitioning. *Developmental Psychology*, *44*, 330–343.

Gualtieri, C. T. (2002) *Psychopharmacology of Brain Injured and Mentally Retarded Patients*. Philadelphia, PA: Lippincott Williams and Wilkins.

Gualtieri, T., Chandler, M., Coons, T. B., *et al.* (1989) Amantadine: a new clinical profile for traumatic brain injury. *Clinical Neuropharmacology*, *12*, 258–270.

Guastella, A. J., Mitchell, P. B. & Dadds, M. R. (2008) Oxytocin increases gaze to the eye region of human faces. *Biological Psychiatry*, *63*, 3–5.

Guastella, A. J., Einfeld, S. L., Gray, K. M., *et al.* (2010) Intranasal oxytocin improves emotion recognition for youth with autism spectrum disorders. *Biological Psychiatry*, *67*, 692–694.

Guénolé, F., Godbout, R., Nicolautism, A., *et al.* (2011) Melatonin for disordered sleep in individuals with autism spectrum disorders: systematic review and discussion. *Sleep Medicine Reviews*, *15*, 379–387.

Guy, W. (1976a) Clinical Global Impressions. In *ECDEU Assessment Manual for Psychopharmacology, Revised* (DHEW Publication No. ADM 76-338), pp. 218–222. Rockville, MD: National Institute of Mental Health (NIMH).

Guy, W. (1976b) Dosage Record and Treatment Emergent Symptoms scale (DOTES). In *ECDEU Assessment Manual for Psychopharmacology, Revised* (DHEW Publication No. ADM 76-338), pp. 223–244. Rockville, MD: NIMH.

Haas, R. H., Rice, M. A., Trauner, D. A., *et al.* (1986) Therapeutic effects of a ketogenic diet in Rett syndrome. *American Journal of Medical Genetics*, Suppl. 1, 225–246.

Hadwin, J., Baron-Cohen, S., Howlin, P., *et al.* (1995) Can we teach children with autism concepts of emotions, belief and pretence? *Development and Psychopathology*, *8*, 345–365.

Haessler, F., Glaser, T., Beneke, M., *et al.* (2007) Zuclopenthixol in adults with intellectual disabilities and aggressive behaviours: discontinuation study. *The British Journal of Psychiatry*, *190*, 447–448.

Hallett, V., Ronald, A. & Happe, F. (2009) Investigating the association between autistic-like and internalizing traits in a community-based twin sample. *Journal of the American Academy of Child and Adolescent Psychiatry*, *48*, 618–627.

Hallmayer, J., Cleveland, S., Torres, A., *et al.* (2011) Genetic heritability and shared environmental factors among twin pairs with autism. *Archives of General Psychiatry*, *68*, 1095–1102.

Handen, B. L. & Hardan, A. Y. (2006) Open-label, prospective trial of olanzapine in adolescents with subaverage intelligence and disruptive behavioral disorders. *Journal of the American Academy of Child and Adolescent Psychiatry*, *45*, 928–935.

Handen, B. L., Feldman, H., Gosling, A., *et al.* (1991) Adverse side effects of Ritalin among mentally retarded children with ADHD. *Journal of the American Academy of Child and Adolescent Psychiatry*, *30*, 241–245.

Handen, B. J., Johnson, C. R. & Lubetsky, M. (2000) Efficacy of methylphenidate among children with autism and symptoms of attention-deficit hyperactivity disorder. *Journal of Autism and Developmental Disorders*, *30*, 245–255.

Haracopos, D. & Kelstrup, A. (1975) *Psykotisk Adfærd [Psychotic Behaviour]*. Copenhagen: Så-materialer.

Hardan, A. Y., Jou, R. J. & Handen, B. L. (2004) A retrospective assessment of topiramate in children and adolescents with pervasive developmental disorders. *Journal of Child and Adolescent Psychopharmacology*, *14*, 426–432.

Hare, D. J. (1997) The use of cognitive-behaviour therapy with people with Asperger's syndrome. *Autism*, *1*, 215–225.

Hare, D. J. & Paine, C. (1997) Developing cognitive behavioural treatments for people with Asperger's syndrome. *Clinical Psychology Forum*, *110*, 5–8.

Hare, D. J., Gould, J., Mills, R., *et al.* (2000) *A Preliminary Study of Autistic Disorders in the Three Special Hospitals of England*. London: NAS.

Hare, D. J., Pratt, C., Burton, M., *et al.* (2004) The health and social care needs of family carers supporting adults with autistic spectrum disorders. *Autism*, *8*, 425–444.

Harris, M. B. & Bloom, S. R. (1984) A pilot investigation of a behavioral weight control program with mentally retarded adolescents and adults: effects on weight, fitness, and knowledge of nutritional and behavioral principles. *Rehabilitation Psychology*, *29*, 177–182.

Hassiotis, A., Robotham, D., Canagasabey, A., *et al.* (2009) Randomized, single-blind, controlled trial of a specialist behaviour therapy team for challenging behaviour in adults with intellectual disabilities. *American Journal of Psychiatry*, *166*, 1278–1285.

Hatton, C. (2002) Psychosocial interventions for adults with intellectual disabilities and mental health problems: a review. *Journal of Mental Health*, *11*, 357–373.

Heckler, S. (1994) Facilitated communication: a response by child protection. *Child Abuse and Neglect*, *18*, 495–503.

Heidgerken, A. D., Geffken, G., Modi, A., *et al.* (2005) A survey of autism knowledge in a health care setting. *Journal of Autism and Developmental Disorders*, *35*, 323–330.

Heinrichs, M., Baumgartner, T., Kirschbaum, C., *et al.* (2003) Social support and oxytocin interact to suppress cortisol and subjective responses to psychological stress. *Biological Psychiatry*, *54*, 1389–1398.

Heller, T. & Factor, A. (1991) Permanency planning for adults with mental retardation living with family caregivers. *American Journal on Mental Retardation, 96,* 163–176.

Hellings, J. A., Weckbaugh, M., Nickel, E. J., *et al.* (2005) A double-blind, placebo-controlled study of valproate for aggression in youth with pervasive developmental disorders. *Journal of Child and Adolescent Psychopharmacology, 15,* 682–692.

Hellings, J. A., Zarcone, J. R., Reese, R. M., *et al.* (2006) A crossover study of risperidone in children, adolescents and adults with mental retardation. *Journal of Autism and Developmental Disorders, 36,* 401–411.

Hemming, H. (1983) The Swansea relocation study of mentally handicapped adults. *International Journal of Rehabilitation Research, 6,* 494–495.

Herbrecht, E., Poustka, F., Birnkammer, S., *et al.* (2009) Pilot evaluation of the Frankfurt Social Skills Training for children and adolescents with autism spectrum disorder. *European Child and Adolescent Psychiatry, 18,* 327–335.

Hickson, L. & Khemka, I. (1999) Decision-making and mental retardation. In *International Review of Research in Mental Retardation,* Volume 22 (ed. L. M. Glidden), pp. 227–265. San Diego, CA: Academic Press.

Hickson, L. & Khemka, I. (2001) The role of motivation in the interpersonal decision making of people with mental retardation. In *Personality and Motivational Differences in Persons with Mental Retardation* (ed. H. N. Switzky), pp. 199–255. Mahwah, NJ: Erlbaum.

Higgins, J. P. T. & Green, S. (eds) (2011) *Cochrane Handbook for Systematic Reviews of Interventions.* Version 5.1.0 [updated March 2011]. The Cochrane Collaboration. Available at: www.cochrane-handbook.org

Higgins, J. P. T. & Thompson, S. G. (2002) Quantifying heterogeneity in a meta-analysis. *Statistics in Medicine, 21,* 1539–1558.

Hillier, A., Fish, T., Cloppert, P., *et al.* (2007) Outcomes of a social and vocational skills support group for adolescents and young adults on the autism spectrum. *Focus on Autism and Other Developmental Disabilities, 22,* 107–115.

Hirshoren, A. & Gregory, J. (1995) Further negative findings of facilitated communication. *Psychology in the Schools, 32,* 109–113.

HMSO (2005) *Mental Capacity Act 2005.* London: The Stationery Office. Available at www.legislation.gov.uk/ukpga/2005/9/contents

HMSO (2009) *Autism Act 2009.* London: The Stationery Office. Available at www.legislation.gov.uk/ukpga/2009/15/contents

Hofvander, B., Delorme, R., Chaste, P., *et al.* (2009) Psychiatric and psychosocial problems in adults with normal-intelligence autism spectrum disorders. *BMC Psychiatry, 9,* 35.

Holburn, S., Pfadt, A., Vietze, P.M., *et al.* (1996) *Person-centered Planning Quality of Life Indicators.* Albany, NY: New York State Office of Mental Retardation and Developmental Disabilities.

Holburn, S., Jacobson, J. W., Schwartz, A. A., *et al.* (2004) The Willowbrook Futures Project: a longitudinal analysis of person-centered planning. *American Journal on Mental Retardation, 109,* 63–76.

Hollander, E., Cartwright, C., Wong, C. M., *et al.* (1998) A dimensional approach to the autism spectrum. *CNS Spectrum, 3*, 22–39.

Hollander, E., Tracy, K., Swann, A. C., *et al.* (2003a) Divalproex in the treatment of impulsive aggression: efficacy in cluster B personality disorders. *Neuropsychopharmacology, 28*, 1186–1197.

Hollander, E., Novotny, S., Hanratty, M., *et al.* (2003b) Oxytocin infusion reduces repetitive behaviors in adults with autistic and Asperger's disorders. *Neuropsychopharmacology, 28*, 193–198.

Hollander, E., Bartz, J., Chaplin, W., *et al.* (2007) Oxytocin increases retention of social cognition in autism. *Biological Psychiatry, 61*, 498–503.

Hollander, E., Chaplin, W., Soorya, L., *et al.* (2010) Divalproex sodium vs placebo for the treatment of irritability in children and adolescents with autism spectrum disorders. *Neuropsychopharmacology, 35*, 990–998.

Holmes, N., Shah, A. & Wing, L. (1982) The Disability Assessment Schedule: a brief device for use with the mentally retarded. *Psychological Medicine, 12*, 879–890.

Holroyd, J. (1987) The questionnaire on resources and stress: an instrument to measure family response to a handicapped family member. *Journal of Community Psychology, 2*, 92–94.

Holroyd, J. & McArthur, D. (1976) Mental retardation and stress on the parents: a contrast between Down's syndrome and childhood autism. *American Journal of Mental Deficiency, 80*, 431–436.

Honigfeld, G., Gillis, R. D. & Klett, C. J. (1966) NOSIE-30: a treatment-sensitive ward behavior scale. *Psychological Reports, 19*, 180–182.

Horning, M. S., Blakemore, L. J. & Trombly, P. Q. (2000) Endogenous mechanisms of neuroprotection: role of zinc, copper, and carnosine. *Brain Research, 852*, 56–61.

Horvath, K. & Perman, J. A. (2002) Autism and gastrointestinal symptoms. *Current Gastroenterology Reports, 4*, 251–258.

Horvath, K., Stefanatos, G., Sokolski, K. N., *et al.* (1998) Improved social and language skills after secretin administration in patients with autistic spectrum disorders. *Journal of the Association for Academic Minority Physicians, 9*, 9–15.

Howlin, P. (1997) *Autism and Asperger Syndrome: Preparing for Adulthood.* London: Routledge.

Howlin, P. (1998) *Children with Autism and Asperger Syndrome: a Guide for Practitioners and Carers.* Chichester: Wiley.

Howlin, P. (2000) Outcome in adult life for more able individuals with autism or Asperger syndrome. *Autism, 4*, 63–83.

Howlin, P. (2010) Evaluating psychological treatments for children with autism-spectrum disorders. *Advances in Psychiatric Treatment, 16*, 133–140.

Howlin, P. & Yates, P. (1999) The potential effectiveness of social skills groups for adults with autism. *Autism, 3*, 299–307.

Howlin, P., Goode, S., Hutton, J., *et al.* (2004) Adult outcomes for children with autism. *Journal of Child Psychology and Psychiatry, 45*, 212–229.

Howlin, P., Alcock, J. & Burkin, C. (2005) An 8 year follow-up of a specialist supported employment service for high-ability adults with autism or Asperger syndrome. *Autism, 9*, 533–549.

Huang, A. X. & Wheeler, J. J. (2006) High-functional autism: an overview of characteristics and related issues. *International Journal of Special Education, 21,* 109–122.

Hudson, A., Melita B. & Arnold, N. (1993) Brief report: a case study assessing the validity of facilitated communication. *Journal of Autism and Developmental Disorders, 23,* 165–173.

Hurlbutt, K. & Chalmers, L. (2002) Adults with autism speak out: perceptions of their life experiences. *Focus on Autism and other Developmental Disabilities, 17,* 103–111.

Hurlbutt, K. & Chalmers, L. (2004) Employment and adults with Asperger syndrome. *Focus on Autism and Other Developmental Disabilities, 19,* 215–222.

Hutchinson, S. L., Loy, D. P., Kleiber, D. A., *et al.* (2003) Leisure as a coping resource: variations in coping with traumatic injury or illness. *Leisure Sciences, 25,* 143–162.

Hutchinson, S. L., Bland, A. D. & Kleiber, D. A. (2008) Leisure and stress-coping: implications for therapeutic recreation practice. *Therapeutic Recreation Journal, 42,* 9–23.

Huws, J. C. & Jones, R. S. P. (2008) Diagnosis, disclosure, and having autism: an interpretive phenomenological analysis of the perceptions of young people with autism. *Journal of Intellectual and Developmental Disability, 33,* 99–107.

Hyman, S. E. & Nestler, E. J. (1996) Initiation and adaptation: a paradigm for understanding psychotropic drug action. *American Journal of Psychiatry, 153,* 151–162.

Ingersoll, B. & Schreibman, L. (2006) Teaching reciprocal imitation skills to young children with autism using a naturalistic behavioral approach: effects on language, pretend play, and joint attention. *Journal of Autism and Developmental Disorders, 36,* 487–505.

Insel, T. R. & Winslow, J. T. (1991) Central administration of oxytocin modulates the infant rat's response to social isolation. *European Journal of Pharmacology, 203,* 149–152.

Israngkun, P. P., Newman, H. A. I., Patel, S. T., *et al.* (1986) Potential biochemical markers for infantile autism. *Neurochemical Pathology, 5,* 51–70.

Iwasaki, Y. (2007) Leisure and quality of life in an international and multicultural context: what are major pathways linking leisure to quality of life? *Social Indicators Research, 82,* 233–264.

Izmeth, M. G. A., Khan, S. Y., Kumarajeewa, D. I. S. C., *et al.* (1988) Zuclopenthixol decanoate in the management of behavioural disorders in mentally handicapped patients. *Pharmatherapeutica, 5,* 217–227.

Jacobson, N. S. & Truax, P. (1991) Clinical significance: a statistical approach to defining meaningful change in psychotherapy research. *Journal of Consulting and Clinical Psychology, 59,* 12–19.

Jadad, A. R., Moore, R. A., Carroll, D., *et al.* (1996) Assessing the quality of reports of randomised clinical trials: is blinding necessary? *Controlled Clinical Trials, 17,* 1–12.

Jahromi, L. B., Kasari, C. L., McCracken, J. T., *et al.* (2009) Positive effects of methylphenidate on social communication and self-regulation in children with pervasive developmental disorders and hyperactivity. *Journal of Autism and Developmental Disorders, 39*, 395–404.

Jamain, S., Betancur, C., Quach, H., *et al.* (2002) Linkage and association of the glutamate receptor 6 gene with autism. *Molecular Psychiatry, 7*, 302–310.

James, I. A., Mukaetova-Ladinska, E., Reichelt, K., *et al.* (2006) Diagnosing Aspergers syndrome in the elderly: a series of case presentations. *International Journal of Geriatric Psychiatry, 21*, 951–960.

Jan, J. E. & O'Donnel, M. E. (1996) Use of melatonin in the treatment of pediatric sleep disorders. *Journal of Pineal Research, 21*, 193–199.

Jan, J. E., Freeman, R. D. & Fast, D. K. (1999) Melatonin treatment of sleep/wake cycle disorders in children and adolescents. *Developmental Medicine and Child Neurology, 41*, 491–500.

Janzen-Wilde, M. L., Duchan, J. F. & Higginbotham, D. J. (1995) Successful use of facilitated communication with an oral child. *Journal of Speech and Hearing Research, 38*, 658–676.

Järbrink, K. & Knapp, M. (2001) The economic impact of autism in Britain, *Autism, 5*, 7–22.

Jennes-Coussens, M., Magill-Evans, J. & Koning, C. (2006) The quality of life of young men with Asperger syndrome: a brief report. *Autism, 10*, 403–414.

Jepson, B., Granpeesheh, D., Tarbox, J., *et al.* (2011) Controlled evaluation of the effects of hyperbaric oxygen therapy on the behavior of 16 children with autism spectrum disorders. *Journal of Autism and Developmental Disorders, 41*, 575–588.

Johnston, C. & Mash, E. (1989) A measure of parenting satisfaction and efficacy. *Journal of Clinical Child Psychology, 18*, 167–176.

Jones, R. S. P., Zahl, A. & Huws, J. C. (2001) First-hand accounts of emotional experiences in autism: a qualitative analysis. *Disability and Society, 16*, 393–401.

Jones, R., Wheelwright, S., Farrell, K., *et al.* (2011) Brief report: female-to-male transsexual people and autistic traits. *Journal of Autism and Developmental Disorders*, DOI: 10.1007/s10803-011-1227-8. Available at: docs. autismresearchcentre. com/papers/2011_Jones_transsexualautism_JADD.pdf/ [accessed August 2012].

Jonsson, L., Ljunggren, E., Bremer, A., *et al.* (2010) Mutation screening of melatonin-related genes in patients with autism spectrum disorders. *BMC Medical Genomics, 3*, 10.

Kanne, S. M., Gerber, A. J., Quirmbach, L. M., *et al.* (2011) The role of adaptive behavior in autism spectrum disorders: implications for functional outcome. *Journal of Autism and Developmental Disorders, 41*, 1007–1018.

Kanner, L. (1943) Autistic disturbance of affective contact. *Nervous Child, 2*, 217–250.

Karsten, D., Kivimäki, T., Linna, S-L., *et al.* (1981) Neuroleptic treatment of oligophrenic patients. A double-blind clinical multicentre trial of cis(Z)-clopenthixol and haloperidol. *Acta Psychiatrica Scandinavica Supplement, 294*, 39–45.

Kearney, C. A., Durand, V. M. & Mindell, J. A. (1995) It's not where but how you live: choice and adaptive/maladaptive behavior in persons with severe handicaps. *Journal of Developmental and Physical Disabilities, 7*, 11–24.

References

Keel, J. H., Mesibov, G. B. & Woods, A. V. (1997) TEACCH – Supported employment programme. *Journal of Autism and Developmental Disorders*, *27*, 3–9.

Kemp, J. A. & McKernan, R. M. (2002) NMDA receptor pathways as drug targets. *Nature Neuroscience*, *5*, 1039–1042.

Kemper, T. & Bauman, M. (1993) The contribution of neuropathologic studies to the understanding of autism. *Neurologic Clinics*, *11*, 175–187.

Kendall, T. (2011) The rise and fall of the atypical antipsychotics. *The British Journal of Psychiatry*, *199*, 266–268.

Khemka, I. (1997) Increased independent interpersonal decision-making skills of women with mental retardation in response to social-interpersonal situations involving abuse. Unpublished doctoral dissertation, Teachers College, Columbia University, New York, NY.

Khemka, I. (2000) Increasing independent decision-making skills of women with mental retardation in simulated interpersonal situations of abuse. *American Journal on Mental Retardation*, *105*, 387–401.

Khemka, I., Hickson, L. & Reynolds, G. (2005) Evaluation of a decision-making curriculum designed to empower women with mental retardation to resist abuse. *American Journal of Mental Retardation*, *110*, 193–204.

Kim, J. A., Szatmari, P., Bryson, S. E., *et al.* (2000) The prevalence of anxiety and mood problems among children with autism and Asperger syndrome. *Autism*, *4*, 117–132.

King, B. H., Wright, D. M., Handen, B. L., *et al.* (2001) Double-blind, placebo-controlled study of amantadine hydrochloride in the treatment of children with autistic disorder. *Journal of the American Academy of Child and Adolescent Psychiatry*, *40*, 658–665.

King, N., Lancaster, N., Wynne, G., *et al.* (1999) Cognitive-behavioural anger management training for adults with mild intellectual disability. *Scandinavian Journal of Behaviour Therapy*, *28*, 19–22.

Kiralp, M. Z., Yildiz, S., Vural, D., *et al.* (2004) Effectiveness of hyperbaric oxygen therapy in the treatment of complex regional pain syndrome. *Journal of International Medical Research*, *32*, 258–262.

Kirsch, P., Esslinger, C., Chen, Q., *et al.* (2005) Oxytocin modulates neural circuitry for social cognition and fear in humans. *Journal of Neuroscience*, *25*, 11489–11493.

Klewe, L. (1993) An empirical evaluation of spelling boards as means of communication for the multihandicapped. *Journal of Autism and Developmental Disorders*, *23*, 559–566.

Klin, A., Saulnier, C. A., Sparrow, S. S., *et al.* (2007) Social and communication abilities and disabilities in higher functioning individuals with autism spectrum disorders: the Vineland and the ADOS. *Journal of Autism and Developmental Disorders*, *37*, 748–759.

Knapp, M., Romeo, R. & Beecham, J. (2007) *The Economic Consequences of Autism in the UK*. London: Foundation for People with Learning Disabilities.

Knapp, M., Romeo, R. & Beecham, J. (2009) Economic cost of autism in the UK. *Autism*, *13*, 317–336.

Knivsberg, A-M., Reichelt, K-L., Høien, T., *et al.* (2003) Effect of dietary intervention on autistic behavior. *Focus on Autism and Other Developmental Disabilities*, *18*, 247–256.

Koegel, B. L. & Johnson, J. (1989) Motivating language use in autistic children. In *Autism: Nature, Diagnosis, and Treatment* (ed. G. Dawson), pp. 310–325. New York, NY: Guilford Press.

Koegel, R. L., O'Dell, M. C. & Koegel, L. K. (1987) A natural language teaching paradigm for nonverbal autistic children. *Journal of Autism and Developmental Disorders*, *17*, 187–200.

Konstantareas, M. M. & Gravelle, G. (1998) Facilitated communication: the contribution of physical, emotional and mental support. *Autism*, *2*, 389–414.

Konstantareas, M. M. & Homatidis, S. (1989) Assessing child symptom severity and stress in parents of autistic children. *Journal of Child Psychology and Psychiatry*, *30*, 459–470.

Korkmaz, B. (2000) Infantile autism: adult outcome. *Seminars in Clinical Neuropsychiatry*, *5*, 164–170.

Kornhuber, J., Weller, M., Schoppmeyer, K., *et al.* (1994) Amantadine and memantine are NMDA receptor antagonists with neuroprotective properties. *Journal of Neural Transmission*, *43*, 91–104.

Kosfeld, M., Heinrichs, M., Zak, P. J., *et al.* (2005) Oxytocin increases trust in humans. *Nature*, *435*, 673–676.

Kraijer, D. W. (1997a) *Autism and Autistic-like Conditions in Mental Retardation*. Andover: Taylor & Francis.

Kraijer, D. W. (1997b) *PDD-MRS: Pervasive Developmental Disorder in Mental Retardation Scale*. Andover: Taylor & Francis.

Kraijer, D. & de Bildt, A. (2005) The PDD-MRS: an instrument for identification of autism spectrum disorders in persons with mental retardation. *Journal of Autism and Developmental Disorders*, *35*, 499–513.

Krasny, L., Williams, B., Provencal, S., *et al.* (2003) Social skills interventions for the autism spectrum: essential ingredients and a model curriculum. *Child and Adolescent Psychiatric Clinics of North America*, *12*, 107–122.

Krauss M. W. & Seltzer M. M. (1999) An unanticipated life: the impact of lifelong caregiving. In *Responding to the Challenge: Current Trends and International Issues in Developmental Disabilities* (ed. J. H. Bersani), pp. 173–87. Cambridge, MA: Brookline Books.

Krauss, M. W., Seltzer, M. M. & Jacobson, H. T. (2005) Adults with autism living at home or in non-family settings: positive and negative aspects of residential status. *Journal of Intellectual Disability Research*, *49*, 111–124.

Krausz, M. & Meszaros, J. (2005) The retrospective experiences of a mother of a child with autism. *International Journal of Special Education*, *20*, 36–46.

Krueger, R. (1988) *Focus Groups: A Practical Guide for Applied Research*. Newbury Park, CA: Sage Publications.

Krug, D. A., Arick, J. R. & Almond, P. G. (1979) Autism screening instrument for educational planning background and development. In *Autism: Diagnosis,*

Instruction, Management and Research (ed. J. Oilliam). Austin, TX: University of Texas at Austin Press.

Krug, D. A., Arick, J. R. & Almond, P. G. (1980) Behavior checklist for identifying severely handicapped individuals with high levels of autistic behavior. *Journal of Child Psychology and Psychiatry, 21*, 221–229.

Krug, D. A., Arick, J. & Almond, P. (1993). *Autism Screening Instrument for Educational Planning.* Austin, TX: Pro-Ed.

Kurita, H., Koyama, T. & Osada H. (2005) Autism-spectrum Quotient-Japanese version and its short forms for screening normally intelligent persons with pervasive developmental disorders. *Psychiatry and Clinical Neurosciences, 59*, 490–496.

Lainhart, J. E. & Folstein, S. E. (1994) Affective disorders in people with autism: a review of published cases. *Journal of Autism and Developmental Disorders, 24*, 587–601.

Lange, N., DuBray, M. B., Lee, J. E., *et al.* (2010) Atypical diffusion tensor hemispheric asymmetry in autism. *Autism Research, 3*, 350–358.

Langworthy-Lam, K. S., Aman, M. G. & van Bourgondien, M. E. (2002) Prevalence and patterns of use of psychoactive medicines in individuals with autism in the Autism Society of North Carolina. *Journal of Child and Adolescent Psychopharmacology, 12*, 311–322.

Larsen, F. W. & Mouridsen, S. E. (1997) The outcome in children with childhood autism and Asperger syndrome originally diagnosed as psychotic: a 30-year follow-up study of subjects hospitalized as children. *European Child and Adolescent Psychiatry, 6*, 181–190.

Latif, A., Heinz, P. & Cook, R. (2002) Iron deficiency in autism and Asperger syndrome. *Autism, 6*, 103–114.

Lau, W. & Peterson, C. C. (2011) Adults and children with Asperger syndrome: exploring adult attachment style, marital satisfaction and satisfaction with parenthood. *Research in Autism Spectrum Disorders, 5*, 392–399.

Laugeson, E. A. & Frankel, F. (2006) *Test of Adolescent Social Skills Knowledge.* Available from: UCLA Parenting and Children's Friendship Program, 300 Medical Plaza, Los Angeles, CA 90095–6967. Reproduced in Laugeson *et al.* (2009).

Laugeson, E. A., Frankel, F., Mogil, C., *et al.* (2009) Parent-assisted social skills training to improve friendships in teens with autism spectrum disorders. *Journal of Autism and Developmental Disorders, 39*, 596–606.

Leach, R. M., Rees, P. J. & Wilmshurst, P. (1998) ABC of oxygen: hyperbaric oxygen therapy. *British Medical Journal, 317*, 1140–1143.

Lee, D. Y. (1977) Evaluation of a group counseling program designed to enhance social adjustment of mentally retarded adults. *Journal of Counseling Psychology, 24*, 318–323.

Leu, R. M., Beyderman, L., Botzolakis, E. J., *et al.* (2010) Relation of melatonin to sleep architecture in children with autism. *Journal of Autism and Developmental Disorders, 41*, 427–433.

Levy, S. E., Souders, M. C., Wray, J., *et al.* (2003) Children with autistic spectrum disorders. I: comparison of placebo and single dose of human synthetic secretin. *Archives of Disease in Childhood, 88*, 731–736.

Lindsay, W. R. (2000) *The Dundee Provocation Inventory.* NHS Tayside: Unpublished.

Lindsay, W. R., Allan, R., Parry, C., *et al.* (2004) Anger and aggression in people with intellectual disabilities: treatment and follow-up of consecutive referrals and a waiting list comparison. *Clinical Psychology and Psychotherapy, 11*, 255–264.

Lingjaerde, O., Ahlfors, U. G., Bech, P., *et al.* (1987) The UKU side effect rating scale: a new comprehensive rating scale for psychotropic drugs, and a cross-sectional study of side effects in neuroleptic treated patients. *Acta Psychiatrica Scandinavica, 76* (Suppl. 334), 1–100.

Lipton, S. A. (2006) Paradigm shift in neuroprotection by NMDA receptor blockade: memantine and beyond. *Nature Reviews Drug Discovery, 5*, 160–170.

Lombardo, M., Baron-Cohen, S., Belmonte, M., *et al.* (2011) Neural endophenotypes for social behaviour in autism spectrum conditions. In *The Handbook of Social Neuroscience* (eds J. Decety & J. Cacioppo). Oxford: Oxford University Press.

Lonsdale, D., Shamberger, R. J. & Audhya, T. (2002) Treatment of autism spectrum children with thiamine tetrahydrofurfuryl disulfide: a pilot study. *Neuroendocrinology Letters, 23*, 303–308.

Lord, C., Pickles, A., McLennan, J., *et al.* (1997) Diagnosing autism: analyses of data from the Autism Diagnostic Interview. *Journal of Autism and Developmental Disorders, 27*, 501–517.

Lord, C., Risi, S., Lambrecht, L., *et al.* (2000) The Autism Diagnostic Observation Schedule-Generic: a standard measure of social and communication deficits associated with the spectrum of autism. *Journal of Autism and Developmental Disorders, 30*, 205–223.

Lord, C., Rutter, M., DiLavore, P. C., *et al.* (2001) *Autism Diagnostic Observation Schedule.* Los Angeles, CA: Western Psychological Services.

Lounds, J., Seltzer, M. M., Greenberg, J. S., *et al.* (2007) Transition and change in adolescents and young adults with autism: longitudinal effects on maternal well-being. *American Journal on Mental Retardation, 112*, 401–417.

Lovaas, O. & T. Smith (1988) Intensive behavioural treatment for young autistic children. In *Advances in Clinical Child Psychology* (eds B. Lahey, A. Kazdin), pp. 285–324. New York, NY: Plenum Publishing.

Lubetsky, M. J. & Handen, B. L. (2008) Medication treatment in autism spectrum disorder. *Speaker's Journal, 8*, 97–107.

MacDonald, E., Dadds, M. R., Brennan, J. L., *et al.* (2011) A review of safety, side-effects and subjective reactions to intranasal oxytocin in human research. *Psychoneuroendocrinology, 36*, 1114–1126.

MacLeod, A. & Johnston, P. (2007) Standing out and fitting in: a report on a support group for individuals with Asperger syndrome using a personal account. *British Journal of Special Education, 34*, 83–88.

Magana, S. & Smith, M. J. (2006) Psychological distress and well-being of Latina and non-Latina white mothers of youth and adults with an autism spectrum disorder: cultural attitudes towards coresidence status. *American Journal of Orthopsychiatry, 76*, 346–357.

Magnuson, K. M. & Constantino, J. N. (2011) Characterization of depression in children with autism spectrum disorders. *Journal of Developmental and Behavioral Pediatrics, 32*, 332–340.

References

Malone, R. P., Gratz, S. S., Delaney, M. A., *et al.* (2005) Advances in drug treatments for children and adolescents with autism and other pervasive developmental disorders. *CNS Drugs, 19*, 923–934.

Mandell, D. S., Wiggins, L. D., Arnstein Carpenter, L., *et al.* (2009) Racial/ethnic disparities in the identification of children with autism spectrum disorders. *American Journal of Public Health, 99*, 493–498.

Mann, T. (1996) *Clinical Guidelines: Using Clinical Guidelines to Improve Patient Care Within the NHS.* London: NHS Executive.

Marks, S. U., Schrader, C., Longaker, T., *et al.* (2000) Portraits of three adolescent students with Asperger's syndrome: personal stories and how they can inform practice. *The Journal of the Association for Persons with Severe Handicaps, 25,* 3–17.

Marshall, A. (1994) Discourse analysis in an occupational context. In *Qualitative Research Methods in Organizational Research* (ed. C. Cassel & G. Syinon). Thousand Oaks, California: SEGA.

Marshall, T. (2004) Audit of the use of psychotropic medication for challenging behaviour in a community learning disability service. *The Psychiatrist, 28*, 447–450.

Martin, A., Scahill, L., Klin, A., *et al.* (1999) Higher-functioning pervasive developmental disorders: rates and patterns of psychotropic drug use. *Journal of the American Academy of Child and Adolescent Psychiatry, 38*, 923–931.

Martineau, J., Barthelemy, C., Cheliakine, C., *et al.* (1988) Brief report: an open middle-term study of combined vitamin B6-magnesium in a subgroup of autistic children selected on their sensitivity to this treatment. *Journal of Autism and Developmental Disorders, 18*, 435–447.

Masters, K. J. (1997) Alternative medications for ADHD. [Letter] *Journal of the American Academy of Child and Adolescent Psychiatry, 36*, 301.

Matson, J. L. (2007) Determining treatment outcome in early intervention programmes for autism spectrum disorders: a critical analysis of measurement issues in learning based interventions. *Research in Developmental Disabilities, 28*, 207–218.

Matson, J. L. & Hess, J. A. (2011) Psychotropic drug efficacy and side effects for persons with autism spectrum disorders. *Research in Autism Spectrum Disorders, 5*, 230–236.

Matson, J. L. & Neal, D. (2009) Psychotropic medication use for challenging behaviours in persons with intellectual disabilities: an overview. *Research in Developmental Disabilities, 30*, 572–586.

Matson, J. L. & Rivet, T. T. (2008) Characteristics of challenging behaviours in adults with autistic disorder, PDD-NOS, and intellectual disability. *Journal of Intellectual and Developmental Disability, 33*, 323–329.

Matson, J. L. & Shoemaker, M. (2009) Intellectual disability and its relationship to autism spectrum disorders. *Research in Developmental Disabilities, 30*, 1107–1114.

Matson, J. L. & Smith, K. R. M. (2008) Current status of intensive behavioral interventions for young children with autism and PDD-NOS. *Research in Autism Spectrum Disorders, 2*, 60–74.

Matson, J. L., DiLorenzo, T. M. & Esveldt-Dawson, K. (1981) Independence training as a method of enhancing self-help skills acquisition of the mentally retarded. *Behaviour Research and Therapy*, *19*, 399–405.

Matson, J. L., Wilkins, J. & Gonzalez, M. (2007a) Reliability and factor structure of the Autism Spectrum Disorders – Diagnosis Scale for Intellectually Disabled Adults (ASD-DA). *Journal of Developmental and Physical Disabilities*, *19*, 565–577.

Matson, J. L., Boisjoli, J. A., Gonzalez, M. L., *et al.* (2007b) Norms and cut off scores for the Autism Spectrum Disorders Diagnosis for Adults (ASD-DA) with intellectual disability. *Research in Autism Spectrum Disorders*, *1*, 330–338.

Matson, J. L., Wilkins, J., Boisjoli, J. A., *et al.* (2008) The validity of the Autism Spectrum Disorders Diagnosis for Intellectually Disabled Adults (ASD-DA). *Research in Developmental Disabilities*, *29*, 537–546.

Matson, J. L., Sipes, M., Fodstad, J. C., *et al.* (2011) Issues in the management of challenging behaviour of adults with autism spectrum disorder. *CNS Drugs*, *25*, 597–606.

Mawhood, L. & Howlin, P. (1999) The outcome of a supported employment scheme for high-functioning adults with autism or Asperger syndrome. *Autism*, *3*, 229–254.

Mawhood, L., Howlin, P. & Rutter, M. (2000) Autism and developmental receptive language disorder – a comparative follow-up in early adult life. I: cognitive and language outcomes. *Journal of Child Psychology and Psychiatry*, *41*, 547–559.

Mazzucchelli, T. G. (unpublished) Protective Behaviours Skills Evaluation. [Unpublished questionnaire]

Mazzucchelli, T. G. (2001) Feel safe: a pilot study of a protective behaviours programme for people with intellectual disability. *Journal of Intellectual and Developmental Disability*, *26*, 115–126.

McCaughrin, W. B., Ellis, W., Rusch, F., *et al.* (1993) Cost effectiveness of supported employment. *Mental Retardation*, *31*, 41–48.

McConkey, R., Abbott, S., Walsh, P. N., *et al.* (2007) Variations in the social inclusion of people with intellectual disabilities in supported living schemes and residential settings. *Journal of Intellectual Disability Research*, *51*, 207–217.

McDougle, C. J., Naylor, S. T., Cohen, D. J., *et al.* (1996) A double-blind, placebo-controlled study of fluvoxamine in adults with autistic disorder. *Archives of General Psychiatry*, *53*, 1001–1008.

McDougle, C. J., Holmes, J. P., Carlson, D. C., *et al.* (1998a) A double-blind, placebo-controlled study of risperidone in adults with autistic disorder and other pervasive developmental disorders. *Archives of General Psychiatry*, *55*, 633–641.

McDougle, C. J., Brodkin, E. S., Naylor, S. T., *et al.* (1998b) Sertraline in adults with pervasive developmental disorders: a prospective open-label investigation. *Journal of Clinical Psychopharmacology*, *18*, 62–66.

McDougle, C. J., Stigler, K. A. & Posey, D. J. (2003) Treatment of aggression in children and adolescents with autism and conduct disorder. *Journal of Clinical Psychiatry*, *64*, 16–25.

McGrath, L., Jones, R. S. P. & Hastings, R. P. (2010) Outcomes of anti-bullying intervention for adults with intellectual disabilities. *Research in Developmental Disabilities*, *31*, 376–380.

McGrew, K., Gilman, C. J. & Johnson, S. D. (1989) *Family Needs Survey Results: Responses From Parents of Young Children with Disabilities.* Minneapolis, MN: Institute on Community Integration.

McKenzie, M. E. & Roswell-Harris, D. (1966) A controlled trial of prothipendyl (tolnate) in mentally subnormal patients. *The British Journal of Psychiatry, 112*, 95–100.

Mehl-Madrona, L., Leung, B., Kennedy, C., *et al.* (2010) Micronutrients versus standard medication management in autism: a naturalistic case-control study. *Journal of Child and Adolescent Psychopharmacology, 20*, 95–103.

Meisenberg, G. & Simmons, W. H. (1983) Centrally mediated effects of neurohypophyseal hormones. *Neuroscience Biobehavioral Reviews, 7*, 263–280.

Melke, J., Goubran Botros, H., Chaste, P., *et al.* (2008) Abnormal melatonin synthesis in autism spectrum disorders. *Molecular Psychiatry, 13*, 90–98.

Meltzoff, A. N. & Gopnik, A. (1994) The role of imitation in understanding persons and developing a theory of mind. In *Understanding Other Minds: Perspectives from Autism* (eds S. Baron-Cohen, H. Tager-Flusberg & D. Cohen), pp. 335–366. Oxford: Oxford University Press.

MENCAP (1999) *Living in Fear: The Need to Combat Bullying of People with a Learning Disability.* London: MENCAP.

Mesibov, G. B. (1984) Social skills training with verbal autistic adolescents and adults: a program model. *Journal of Autism and Developmental Disorders, 14*, 395–404.

Miano, S. & Ferri, R. (2010) Epidemiology and management of insomnia in children with autistic spectrum disorders. *Pediatric Drugs, 12*, 75–84.

Millward, C., Ferriter, M., Calver, S. J., *et al.* (2008) Gluten- and casein-free diets for autistic spectrum disorder. *Cochrane Database of Systematic Reviews, 2*, Art. No.: CD003498. DOI: 10.1002/14651858.CD003498.pub3

Miyamoto, A., Junichi, O., Takahashi, S., *et al.* (1999) Serum melatonin kinetics and long-term melatonin treatment for sleep disorders in Rett syndrome. *Brain Development, 21*, 59–62.

Modahl, C., Green, L., Fein, D., *et al.* (1998) Plasma oxytocin levels in autistic children. *Biological Psychiatry, 43*, 270–277.

Molony, H. & Taplin, J. E. (1990) The deinstitutionalization of people with developmental disability under the Richmond program. I: changes in adaptive behavior. *Australia and New Zealand Journal of Developmental Disabilities, 16*, 149–159.

Montee, B. B., Miltenberger, R. G. & Wittrock, D. (1995) An experimental analysis of facilitated communication. *Journal of Applied Behavior Analysis, 2*, 189–200.

Morgan, D. (1988) *Focus Groups as Qualitative Research.* Newbury Park, CA: Sage Publications.

Morgan, D. (1993) Qualitative content analysis: a guide to paths not taken. *Qualitative Health Research, 3*, 112–121.

Morgan, H. (1996) Underpinning philosophy in the provision of services for adults with autism: a critique of global values related to specific practice. In *Adults with*

Autism: A Guide to Theory and Practice (ed. H. Morgan), pp. 31–52. Cambridge: Cambridge University Press.

Mount, B. (1992) *Person-centered Planning: Finding Directions for Change. A Sourcebook of Values, Ideas, and Methods to Encourage Person-centered Development.* New York, NY: Graphic Futures.

Mount, B. (1994) Benefits and limitations of personal futures planning. In *Creating Individual Supports for People with Developmental Disabilities: a Mandate for Change at Many Levels* (eds V. J. Bradley, J. W. Ashbaugh & B. C. Blaney), pp. 97–108. Baltimore, MD: Brookes.

Mousain-Bosc, M., Roche, M., Polge, A., *et al.* (2006) Improvement of neurobehavioral disorders in children supplemented with magnesium-vitamin B6. II: pervasive developmental disorder-autism. *Magnesium Research, 19*, 53–62.

Müller, E., Schuler, A., Burton, B. A., *et al.* (2003) Meeting the vocational support needs of individuals with Asperger syndrome and other autism spectrum disabilities. *Journal of Vocational Rehabilitation, 18*, 163–175.

Munasinghe, S. A., Oliff, C., Finn, J., *et al.* (2010) Digestive enzyme supplementation for autism spectrum disorders: a double-blind randomized controlled trial. *Journal of Autism and Developmental Disorders, 40*, 1131–1138.

Mundy, P. (2003) Annotation: the neural basis of social impairments in autism: the role of the dorsal medial-frontal cortex and anterior cingulate system. *Journal of Child Psychology and Psychiatry, 44*, 793–809.

Mundy, P., Delgado, C., Block, J., *et al.* (2003) *A Manual for the Abridged Early Social Communication Scales (ESCS).* Coral Gables, FL: University of Miami.

Munshi, K. R., Oken, T., Guild, D. J., *et al.* (2010) The use of antiepileptic drugs (AEDs) for the treatment of pediatric aggression and mood disorders. *Pharmaceuticals, 3*, 2986–3004.

Murphy, G. H., Beadle-Brown, J., Wing, L., *et al.* (2005) Chronicity of challenging behaviours in people with severe intellectual disabilities and/or autism: a total population sample. *Journal of Autism and Developmental Disorders, 35*, 405–418.

Myles, B. S. & Simpson, R. L. (1994) Facilitated communication with children diagnosed as autistic in public school settings. *Psychology in the Schools, 31*, 208–220.

Myles, B. S., Simpson, R. L. & Smith, S. M. (1996a) Collateral behavioral and social effects of using facilitated communication with individuals with autism. *Focus on Autism and Other Developmental Disabilities, 11*, 163–169.

Myles, B. S., Simpson, R. L. & Smith, S. M. (1996b) Impact of facilitated communication combined with direct instruction on academic performance of individuals with autism. *Focus on Autism and Other Developmental Disabilities, 11*, 37–44.

NAO (2009) *Supporting People with Autism Through Adulthood: Report by the Comptroller and Auditor General.* HC 556 Session 2008–2009. 5 June. London: The Stationery Office.

NCCMH (2006) *Obsessive-compulsive Disorder: Core Interventions in the Treatment of Obsessive-compulsive Disorder and Body Dysmorphic Disorder.* Leicester and

London: The British Psychological Society and the Royal College of Psychiatrists. [Full guideline]

NCCMH (2010a) *Depression: the Treatment and Management of Depression in Adults (Update).* Leicester and London: The British Psychological Society and the Royal College of Psychiatrists. [Full guideline]

NCCMH (2010b) *Depression in Adults with a Chronic Physical Health Problem: Treatment and Management.* Leicester and London: The British Psychological Society and the Royal College of Psychiatrists. [Full guideline]

NCCMH (2010c) *Schizophrenia: Core Interventions in the Treatment and Management of Schizophrenia in Adults in Primary and Secondary Care (Update).* Leicester and London: The British Psychological Society and the Royal College of Psychiatrists. [Full guideline]

NCCMH (2011) *Common Mental Health Disorders: Identification and Pathways to Care.* Leicester and London: The British Psychological Society and the Royal College of Psychiatrists. [Full guideline]

NCCMH (2012) *Service User Experience in Adult Mental Health: Improving the Experience of Care for People Using Adult NHS Mental Health Services.* Leicester and London: The British Psychological Society and the Royal College of Psychiatrists. [Full guideline]

Nelson, E. & Alberts, J. R. (1997) Oxytocin-induced paw sucking in infant rats. *Annals of the New York Academy of Sciences, 807*, 543–545.

Neubauer, R. A., Gottlieb, S. F. & Miale, A. (1992) Identification of hypometabolic areas in the brain using brain imaging and hyperbaric oxygen. *Clinical Nuclear Medicine, 17*, 477–481.

NICE (2005a) *Obsessive-compulsive Disorder (OCD): Core Interventions in the Treatment of Obsessive-compulsive Disorder and Body Dysmorphic Disorder.* Clinical guideline 31. Available at: guidance.nice.org.uk/CG31 [NICE guideline]

NICE (2005b) *Post-traumatic Stress Disorder (PTSD): the Management of PTSD in Adults and Children in Primary and Secondary Care.* Clinical guideline 26. Available at: guidance.nice.org.uk/CG26 [NICE guideline]

NICE (2006) *Dementia: Supporting People with Dementia and their Carers in Health and Social Care.* Clinical guideline 42. Available at: guidance.nice.org.uk/CG42 [NICE guideline]

NICE (2009a) *Depression: The Treatment and Management of Depression in Adults (Update).* Clinical guideline 90. Available at: guidance.nice.org.uk/CG90 [NICE guideline]

NICE (2009b) *Depression in Adults with a Chronic Physical Health Problem: Treatment and Management.* Clinical guideline 91. Available at: guidance.nice.org.uk/CG91 [NICE guideline]

NICE (2009c) *Schizophrenia: Core Interventions in the Treatment and Management of Schizophrenia in Adults in Primary and Secondary Care.* Clinical guideline 82. Available at: guidance.nice.org.uk/CG82 [NICE guideline]

NICE (2009d) *Attention Deficit Hyperactivity Disorder: Diagnosis and Management of ADHD in Children, Young People and Adults.* Clinical guideline 72. Available at: guidance.nice.org.uk/CG72 [NICE guideline]

NICE (2009e) *The Guidelines Manual.* Available at: www.nice.org.uk

NICE (2009f) *Managing Long-term Sickness Absence and Incapacity for Work.* NICE public health guidance 19. Available at: guidance.nice.org.uk/PH19

NICE (2011a) *Autism: Recognition, Referral and Diagnosis of Children and Young People on the Autism Spectrum.* Clinical guideline 128. Available at: www.nice.org.uk/ CG128 [NICE guideline]

NICE (2011b) *Common Mental Health Disorders: Identification and Pathways to Care.* Clinical guideline 123. Available at: www.nice.org.uk/CG123 [NICE guideline]

NICE (2011c) *Generalised Anxiety Disorder and Panic Disorder (With or Without Agoraphobia) in Adults: Management in Primary, Secondary and Community Care.* Clinical guideline 113. Available at: guidance.nice.org.uk/CG113 [NICE guideline]

Nickels, K. C., Katusic, S. K., Colligan, R. C., *et al.* (2008) Stimulant medication treatment of target behaviors in children with autism: a population-based study. *Journal of Developmental and Behavioral Pediatrics, 29*, 75–81.

Nicolson, R., Craven-Thuss, B. & Smith, J. (2006) A prospective, open-label trial of galantamine in autistic disorder. *Journal of Child and Adolescent Psychopharmacology, 16*, 621–629.

Niesink, R. J. M. & van Ree, J. M. (1983) Normalizing effects of an ACTH 4-9 analog (ORG 2766) on 'disturbed' social behaviour of rats: implication of endogeneous opioid systems. *Science, 221*, 960–962.

Nihira, K., Foster, R., Shelhaas, M., *et al.* (1974) *AAMD Adaptive Behavior Scale.* Revised edition. Washington, DC: American Association of Mental Deficiency.

NIMH (1985) CGI (Clinical Global Impression) scale. *Psychopharmacology Bulletin, 21*, 839–842.

Nir, I., Meier, D., Zilber, N., *et al.* (1995) Brief report: circadian melatonin, thyroid-stimulating hormone, prolactin and cortisol levels in serum of young adults with autism. *Journal of Autism and Developmental Disorders, 25*, 641–654.

Noble, J., Conley, R. W., Banerjee, S., *et al.* (1991) Supported employment in New York State: a comparison of benefits and costs. *Journal of Disability Policy Studies, 2*, 39–73.

Norton, R. (1983) Measuring marital quality: a critical look at the dependent variable. *Journal of Marriage and the Family, 45*, 141–151.

Novaco, R. W. (1975) *Anger Control: the Development and Evaluation of an Experimental Treatment.* Lexington, MA: Health.

Novaco, R. W. (1976) The functions and regulations of the arousal of anger. *American Journal of Psychiatry, 133*, 1124–1128.

Novaco, R. W. (1979) The cognitive regulation of anger and stress. In *Cognitive-Behavioural Interventions: Theory Research and Procedures* (eds P. Kendall & C. Hollon), pp. 241–285. New York, NY: Academic Press.

Novaco, R. W. (2003) *The Novaco Anger Scale and Provocation Inventory (NAS-PI).* Los Angeles, CA: Western Psychological Services.

Nunnally, J. C. & Bernstein, I. H. (1994) *Psychometric Theory* (3rd edn). New York, NY: McGraw-Hill, Inc.

Olney, M. (1995) Reading between the lines: a case study on facilitated communication. *Journal of the Association for Persons with Severe Handicaps*, *20*, 57–65.

Olsson, G. & von Knorring, A. L. (1997) Depression among Swedish adolescents measured by the self-rating scale Center for Epidemiology Studies-Depression Child (CES-DC). *European Child and Adolescent Psychiatry*, *6*, 81–87.

Orritt, E. J., Paul, S. C. & Behrman, J. A. (1985) The Perceived Support Network Inventory. *American Journal of Community Psychology*, *13*, 565–583.

Orsmond, G. I. & Seltzer, M. M. (2007) Siblings of individuals with autism or Down syndrome: effects on adult lives. *Journal of Intellectual Disability Research*, *51*, 682–696.

Orsmond, G. I., Krauss, M. W. & Seltzer, M. M. (2004) Peer relationships and social and recreational activities among adolescents and adults with autism. *Journal of Autism and Developmental Disorders*, *34*, 245–256.

Orsmond, G. I., Kuo, H. & Seltzer, M. M. (2009) Siblings of individuals with an autism spectrum disorder: sibling relationships and wellbeing in adolescence and adulthood. *Autism*, *13*, 59–80.

Ospina, M. B., Krebs Seida, J., Clark, B., *et al.* (2008) Behavioural and developmental interventions for autism spectrum disorder: a clinical systematic review. *Public Library of Science (PLOS) ONE*, *3*, e3755. Available at: www.plosone.org/article/info%3Adoi%2F10.1371%2Fjournal.pone.0003755 [accessed October 2011].

Oswald, D. P. (1994) Facilitator influence in facilitated communication. *Journal of Behavioral Education*, *4*, 191–199.

Owens, J. A., Spirito, A., McGuinn, M., *et al.* (2000) Sleep habits and sleep disturbance in elementary school-aged children. *Journal of Developmental and Behavioral Pediatrics*, *21*, 27–36.

Owley, T., Salt, J., Guter, S., *et al.* (2006) A prospective, open-label trial of memantine in the treatment of cognitive, behavioral, and memory dysfunction in pervasive developmental disorders. *Journal of Child and Adolescent Psychopharmacology*, *16*, 517–524.

Ozonoff, S. & Miller, J. N. (1995) Teaching theory of mind: a new approach to social skills training for individuals with autism. *Journal of Autism and Developmental Disorders*, *25*, 415–434.

Ozonoff, S., Pennington, B. F. & Rogers, S. J. (1991) Executive function deficits in high-functioning autistic individuals: relationship to theory of mind. *Journal of Child Psychology and Psychiatry*, *32*, 1081–1105.

Paavonen, E. J., Nieminen-von Wendt, T., Vanhala, R., *et al.* (2003) Effectiveness of melatonin in the treatment of sleep disturbances in children with Asperger disorder. *Journal of Child and Adolescent Psychopharmacology*, *13*, 83–95.

Palm, L., Blennow, G. & Wetterberg, L. (1997) Long-term melatonin treatment in blind children and young adults with circadian sleep-wake disturbances. *Developmental Medicine and Child Neurology*, *39*, 319–325.

Panella, M., Demarchi, M. L., Carnevale, L., *et al.* (2006) The management of schizophrenia through clinical pathways. In *Contributed Presentation Abstracts – ISPOR 9th Annual European Congress*, Copenhagen, 28–31 October: A318.

Parikh, M. S., Kolevzon, A. & Hollander, E. (2008) Psychopharmacology of aggression in children and adolescents with autism: a critical review of efficacy and tolerability. *Journal of Child and Adolescent Psychopharmacology, 18,* 157–178.

Parker, S. K., Schwartz, B., Todd, J., *et al.* (2004) Thimerosal-containing vaccines and autistic spectrum disorder: a critical review of published data. *Pediatrics, 114,* 793–804.

Patzold, L. M., Richdale, A. L. & Tonge, B. J. (1998) An investigation into sleep characteristics of children with autism and Asperger's disorder. *Journal of Paediatric Child Health, 34,* 528–533.

Paul, R. & Cohen, D. J. (1984) Outcomes of severe disorders of language acquisition. *Journal of Autism and Developmental Disorders, 14,* 405–421.

Peasgood, T., Roberts, J. & Tsuchiya, A. (2006) *Incapacity Benefit: a Health or Labour Market Phenomenon?* SERP No. 2006011. Sheffield: Sheffield Economic Research Paper Series.

Physician's Desk Reference Staff (1997) *Physicians' Desk Reference.* Montvale, NJ: Medical Economics Company.

Pilgrim, H., Carroll, C., Rick, J., *et al.* (2008) *Modelling the Cost Effectiveness of Interventions, Strategies, Programmes and Policies to Reduce the Number of Employees on Sickness Absence.* Revised report. Project ID No. 00345-0955. Brighton: Institute for Employment Studies. Available at: www.employment-studies.co.uk/pdflibrary/ltsi10b.pdf [accessed May 2012].

Polimeni, M. A., Richdale, A. L. & Francis, A. J. (2005) A survey of sleep problems in autism, Asperger's disorder and typically developing children. *Journal of Intellectual Disability Research, 49,* 260–268.

Polirstok, S. R., Dana, L., Buono, S., *et al.* (2003) Improving functional communication skills in adolescents and young adults with severe autism using gentle teaching and positive approaches. *Topics in Language Disorders, 23,* 146–153.

Polkinghorne, D. E. (1988) *Narrative Knowing and the Human Sciences.* Albany, NY: State University of New York Press.

Pope, A. (1998) Developing days. In *Developing and Managing High Quality Services for People with Learning Disabilities: Manchester's Joint Service* (eds M. Burton & M. Kellaway). Aldershot: Ashgate.

Posey, D. J. & McDougle, C. J. (2001) Pharmacotherapeutic management of autism. *Expert Opinion on Pharmacotherapy, 2,* 587–600.

Posey, D. J., Puntney, J. I., Sasher, T. M., *et al.* (2004) Guanfacine treatment of hyperactivity and inattention in pervasive developmental disorders: a retrospective analysis of 80 cases. *Journal of Child and Adolescent Psychopharmacology, 14,* 233–242.

Posey, D. J., Aman, M. G., McCracken, J. T., *et al.* (2007) Positive effects of methylphenidate on inattention and hyperactivity in pervasive developmental disorders: an analysis of secondary measures. *Biological Psychiatry, 61,* 538–544.

Posey, D. J., Stigler, K. A., Erickson, C. A., *et al.* (2008) Antipsychotics in the treatment of autism. *The Journal of Clinical Investigation, 118,* 6–14.

Prior, M. & Ozonoff, S. (1998) Psychological factors in autism. In: *Autism and Pervasive Developmental Disorders* (ed. F. R. Volkmar), pp. 64–98. New York, NY: Cambridge University Press.

Pruchno, R. (1990) The effects of help patterns on the mental health of spouse caregivers. *Research on Aging, 12,* 57–71.

Punshon, C., Skirrow, P. & Murphy, G. (2009) The 'not guilty verdict': psychological reactions to a diagnosis of Asperger syndrome in adulthood. *Autism, 13,* 265–283.

Quintana, H., Birmaher, B., Stedge, D., *et al.* (1995) Use of methylphenidate in the treatment of children with autistic disorder. *Journal of Autism and Developmental Disorders, 25,* 283–294.

Raghavan, R., Newell, R., Waseem, F., *et al.* (2009) A randomized controlled trial of a specialist liaison worker model for young people with intellectual disabilities with challenging behaviour and mental health needs. *Journal of Applied Research in Intellectual Disabilities, 22,* 256–263.

Read, S. G. & Rendall, M. (2007) An open-label study of risperidone in the improvement of quality of life and treatment of symptoms of violent and self-injurious behaviour in adults with intellectual disability. *Journal of Applied Research in Intellectual Disabilities, 20,* 256–264.

Realmuto, G. M., August, G. J. & Garfinkel, B. D. (1989) Clinical effect of buspirone in autistic children. *Journal of Clinical Psychopharmacology, 9,* 122–125.

Reaven, J. A., Blakeley-Smith, A., Nichols, S., *et al.* (2009) Cognitive-behavioral group treatment for anxiety symptoms in children with high-functioning autism spectrum disorders. *Focus on Autism and Other Developmental Disabilities, 24,* 27–37.

Regal, R. A., Rooney, J. R. & Wandas, T. (1994) Facilitated communication: an experimental evaluation. *Journal of Autism and Developmental Disorders, 24,* 345–355.

Reichelt, K. L., Hole, K., Hamberfer, A., *et al.* (1981) Biologically active peptide containing fractions in schizophrenia and childhood autism. *Advances in Biochemical Psychopharmacology, 28,* 627–643.

Reisberg, B., Doody, R., Stoffler, A., *et al.* (2003) Memantine in moderate-to-severe Alzheimer's disease. *New England Journal of Medicine, 348,* 1333–1341.

Remington, G., Sloman, L., Konstantareas, M., *et al.* (2001) Clomipramine versus haloperidol in the treatment of autistic disorder: a double-blind, placebo-controlled, crossover study. *Journal of Clinical Psychopharmacology, 21,* 440–444.

Rescorla, L. (1989) The Language Development Survey: a screening tool for delayed language in toddlers. *Journal of Speech and Hearing Disorders, 54,* 587–599.

Research Autism (2011a) *Facilitated Communication and Autism.* London: Research Autism. Available at: www.researchautism.net/autism_treatments_therapies_intervention.ikml? print&ra=16&infolevel=4 [accessed September 2011; last updated 11 April 2012].

Research Autism (2011b) *Chelation and Autism.* London: Research Autism. Available at: www.researchautism.net/autism_treatments_therapies_intervention.ikml? print&ra=25 [accessed September 2011; last updated 7 November 2011].

Research Autism (2011c) *Testosterone Regulation and Autism.* London: Research Autism. Available at: www.researchautism.net/autism_treatments_therapies_intervention.ikml?print&ra=24&infolevel=4 [accessed September 2011; last updated 7 November 2011].

Research Autism (2011d) *Hyperbaric Therapy and Autism.* London: Research Autism. Available at: www.researchautism.net/autism_treatments_therapies_intervention.ikml?print&ra=67&infolevel=4 [accessed September 2011; last updated 15 May 2012].

Research Units on Pediatric Psychopharmacology (RUPP) Autism Network (2005) Randomized, controlled, crossover trial of methylphenidate in pervasive developmental disorders with hyperactivity. *Archives of General Psychiatry, 62,* 1266–1274.

Rhodes, L., Ramsing, K. & Hill, M. (1987) Economic evaluation of employment services: a review of applications. *Journal of the Association of Persons with Severe Handicaps, 12,* 175–181.

Richdale, A. L. & Schreck, K. A. (2009) Sleep problems in autism spectrum disorders: prevalence, nature, and possible biopsychosocial aetiologies. *Sleep Medicine Reviews, 13,* 403–411.

Richdale, A. L., Francis, A., Gavidia, S. G., *et al.* (1999) Stress, behaviour and sleep problems in children with an intellectual disability. *Journal of Intellectual and Developmental Disabilities, 25,* 147–161.

Rimland, B. (1992) Facilitated communication: problems, puzzles and paradoxes: six challenges for researchers. *Autism Research Review, 5,* 3.

Ritvo, E. R., Ritvo, R., Yuwiller, A., *et al.* (1993) Elevated daytime melatonin concentrations in autism: a pilot study. *European Child and Adolescent Psychiatry, 2,* 75–78.

Ritvo, R. A., Ritvo, E. R., Guthrie, D., *et al.* (2008) A scale to assist the diagnosis of autism and Asperger's disorder in adults (RAADS): a pilot study. *Journal of Autism and Developmental Disorders, 38,* 213–223.

Ritvo, R. A., Ritvo, E. R. & Guthrie, D. (2011) The Ritvo Autism Asperger Diagnostic Scale-Revised (RAADS-R): a scale to assist the diagnosis of autism spectrum disorders in adults: an international validation study. *Journal of Autism and Developmental Disorders, 41,* 1076–1089.

Robledo, J. A. & Donnellan, A. M. (2008) Properties of supportive relationships from the perspective of academically successful individuals with autism. *Intellectual and Developmental Disabilities, 46,* 299–310.

Rogers, S. (1999) An examination of the imitation deficit in autism. In *Imitation in Infancy* (eds J. Nadel & G. Butterworth), pp. 254–279. Cambridge: Cambridge University Press.

Rogers, S. & Pennington, B. (1991) A theoretical approach to the deficits in infantile autism. *Developmental Psychology, 3,* 137–162.

Romoser, M. (2000) Malemployment in autism. *Focus on Autism and Other Developmental Disabilities, 15,* 246–247.

Rose, J., Loftus, M., Flint, B., *et al.* (2005) Factors associated with the efficacy of a group intervention for anger in people with intellectual disabilities. *British Journal of Clinical Psychology*, *44*, 305–317.

Rossignol, D. A. & Frye, R. E. (2011) Melatonin in autism spectrum disorders: a systematic review and meta-analysis. *Developmental Medicine and Child Neurology*, *53*, 783–792.

Rossignol, D. A. & Rossignol, L. W. (2006) Hyperbaric oxygen therapy may improve symptoms in autistic children. *Medical Hypotheses*, *67*, 216–228.

Rossignol, D. A., Rossignol, L. W., James, S. J., *et al.* (2007) The effects of hyperbaric oxygen therapy on oxidative stress, inflammation, and symptoms in children with autism: an open-label pilot study. *BMC Pediatrics*, *7*, 36.

Rossignol, D. A., Rossignol, L. W., Smith, S., *et al.* (2009) Hyperbaric treatment for children with autism: a multicenter, randomized, double-blind, controlled trial. *BMC Pediatrics*, *9*, 21.

Ruedrich, S., Swales, T. P., Fossaceca, C., *et al.* (1999) Effect of divalproex sodium on aggression and self-injurious behaviour in adults with intellectual disability: a retrospective review. *Journal of Intellectual Disability Research*, *43*, 105–111.

Rumsey, J. M., Rapoport, J. L. & Sceery, W. R. (1985) Autistic children as adults: psychiatric, social, and behavioural outcomes. *Journal of the American Academy of Child Psychiatry*, *24*, 465–473.

Russell, A. J., Mataix-Cols, D., Anson, M. A. W., *et al.* (2009) Psychological treatment for obsessive-compulsive disorder in people with autism spectrum disorders: a pilot study. *Psychotherapy and Psychosomatics*, *78*, 59–61.

Rutter, M. (1978) Diagnosis and definition. In *Autism: a Reappraisal of Concepts and Treatment* (eds M. Rutter & E. Schopler.), pp. 1–26. New York, NY: Plenum Press.

Rutter, M., Bailey, A. & Lord, C. (2003) *Social Communication Questionnaire (SCQ)*. Los Angeles, CA: Western Psychological Services.

Ryan, S. (2010) 'Meltdowns', surveillance and managing emotions; going out with children with autism. *Health and Place*, *16*, 868–875.

Ryan, S. & Cole, K. R. (2009) From advocate to activist? Mapping the experiences of mothers of children on the autism spectrum. *Journal of Applied Research in Intellectual Disabilities*, *22*, 43–53.

Sabin, L. A. & Donnellan, A. M. (1993) A qualitative study of the process of facilitated communication. *Journal of the Association for Persons with Severe Handicaps*, *18*, 200–211.

Sachs, R. L., Hughes, R. J., Edgar, D. M., *et al.* (1997) Sleep promoting effects of melatonin: at what doses, in whom, under what conditions and by what mechanisms. *Sleep*, *20*, 192–197.

Saebra, M. L. V., Bignotto, M., Pinto, L., *et al.* (2000) Randomized double-blind clinical trial, controlled with placebo, of the toxicology of chronic melatonin treatment. *Journal of Pineal Research*, *29*, 193–200.

Salkovskis, P. M. (1999) Understanding and treating obsessive-compulsive disorder. *Behaviour Research and Therapy*, *37*, S29–S52.

Sanders, J. L. & Morgan, S. B. (1997) Family stress and adjustment as perceived by parents of children with autism or Down syndrome: for intervention. *Child and Family Behavior Therapy*, *19*, 15–32.

Sattler, J. M. (2001) *Assessment of Children: Cognitive Applications* (4th edn). San Diego, CA: Jerome M. Sattler Publisher Inc.

Saxena, P. R. (1995) Serotonin receptors: subtypes, functional responses and therapeutic relevance. *Pharmacology and Therapeutics*, *66*, 339–368.

Scahill, L., McDougle, C. J., Williams, S. K., *et al.* (2006) Children's Yale-Brown Obsessive Compulsive Scale modified for Pervasive Developmental Disorders. *Journal of the American Academy of Child and Adolescent Psychiatry*, *45*, 1114–1123.

Schaller, J. & Yang, N. (2005) Competitive employment for people with autism: correlates of successful closures in competitive employment and supported employment. *Rehabilitation Counseling Bulletin*, *49*, 4–16.

Schalock, R. L. & Keith, K. D. (1993) *Quality of Life Questionnaire*. Worthington, OH: IDS Publishers.

Schalock, R. L., Gadwood, L. S. & Perry, P. B. (1984) Effects of different training environments on the acquisition of community living skills. *Applied Research in Mental Retardation*, *5*, 425–438.

Schneider, J., Boyce M., Johnson R., *et al.* (2009) Impact of supported employment on service costs and income of people. *Journal of Mental Health*, 18, 533–542.

Schopler, E. & Reichler, J. (1971) *Individualized Assessment and Treatment for Autistic and Developmentally Delayed Children. Vol. I. Psychoeducational Profile*. Baltimore, MD: University Park Press.

Schopler, E., Reichler, R. J., DeVellis, R. F., *et al.* (1980) Toward objective classification of childhood autism: Childhood Autism Rating Scale (CARS). *Journal of Autism and Developmental Disorders*, *10*, 91–103.

Schopler, E., Reichler, R. & Renner, B. (1988) *Childhood Autism Rating Scale (CARS)*. Los Angeles, CA: Western Psychological Services.

Schunemann, H. J., Best, D., Vist, G. *et al.* for the GRADE Working Group (2003) Letters, numbers, symbols and words: how to communicate grades of evidence and recommendations. *Canadian Medical Association Journal*, *169*, 677–680.

Schwartz, C. (2003) Self-appraised lifestyle satisfaction of persons with intellectual disability: the impact of personal characteristics and community residential facilities. *Journal of Intellectual and Developmental Disability*, *28*, 227–240.

Scottish Intercollegiate Guidelines Network (2007*) Assessment, Diagnosis and Clinical Interventions for Children and Young People with Autism Spectrum Disorders: A National Clinical Guideline*. Edinburgh: SIGN.

Seale, C. (1999) *The Quality of Qualitative Research*. London: Sage Publications.

Seltzer, G. B. & Seltzer, M. M. (1978) *The Community Adjustment Scale*. Cambridge, MA: Educational Projects.

Seltzer, M. M. & Krauss, M. W. (1989) Aging parents with mentally retarded children: family risk factors and sources of support. *American Journal on Mental Retardation*, *94*, 303–312.

Seltzer, M. M. & Krauss, M. W. (1994) Aging parents with co-resident adult children: the impact of lifelong caregiving. In *Life Course Perspectives on Adulthood and Old Age* (eds M. M. Seltzer, M. W. Krauss & M. P. Janicki), pp. 3–18. Washington, DC: The American Association on Mental Retardation Monograph Series.

Seltzer, M. M., Krauss, M. W., Orsmond, G. I., *et al.* (2001) Families of adolescents and adults with autism: uncharted territory. *International Review of Research in Mental Retardation, 23,* 267–294.

Seltzer, M. M., Krauss, M. W., Shattuck, P. T., *et al.* (2003) The symptoms of autism spectrum disorders in adolescence and adulthood. *Journal of Autism and Developmental Disorders, 33,* 565–581.

SESAMI Research Team and Practice Partnership (2007) The SESAMI evaluation of employment support in the UK: background and baseline data. *Journal of Mental Health, 16,* 375–388.

Shattuck, P. T., Seltzer, M. M., Greenberg, J. S., *et al.* (2007) Change in autism symptoms and maladaptive behaviors in adolescents and adults with an autism spectrum disorder. *Journal of Autism and Developmental Disorders, 13,* 129–135.

Sheehan, C. & Matuozzi, R. (1996) Investigation of the validity of facilitated communication through the disclosure of unknown information. *Mental Retardation, 34,* 94–107.

Shtayermman, O. (2007) Peer victimisation in adolescents and young adults diagnosed with Asperger's syndrome: a link to depressive symptomatology, anxiety symptomology and suicidal ideation. *Issues in Comprehensive Pediatric Nursing, 30,* 87–107.

Shtayermman, O. (2009) An exploratory study of the stigma associated with a diagnosis of Asperger's syndrome: the mental health impact on the adolescents and young adults diagnosed with a disability with a social nature. *Journal of Human Behaviour in the Social Environment, 19,* 298–313.

Shu, B., Lin, L., Hsieh, S., *et al.* (2006) Process of self-identity transformation in women with autistic adolescent. *Journal of Nursing Research, 14,* 55–63.

Shuang, M., Liu, J., Jia, M. X., *et al.* (2004) Family-based association study between autism and glutamate receptor 6 gene in Chinese Han trios. *American Journal of Medical Genetics, 131B,* 48–50.

Siaperas, P. & Beadle-Brown, J. (2006) A case study of the use of a structured teaching approach in adults with autism in a residential home in Greece. *Autism, 10,* 330–343.

Siegel, B. V., Jr., Nuechterlein, K. H., Abel, L., *et al.* (1995) Glucose metabolic correlates of continuous test performance in adults with a history of infantile autism, schizophrenics, and controls. *Schizophrenia Research, 17,* 85–94.

Simon, E. W., Whitehair, P. M. & Toll, D. M. (1996) A case study: follow up assessment of facilitated communication. *Journal of Autism and Developmental Disorders, 26,* 9–18.

Simonoff, E., Pickles, A., Charman, T., *et al.* (2008) Psychiatric disorders in children with autism spectrum disorders: prevalence, comorbidity, and associated factors in a population-derived sample. *Journal of the American Academy of Child and Adolescent Psychiatry, 47,* 921–929.

Simpson, R. L. & Myles B. S. (1995a) Effectiveness of facilitated communication with children and youth with autism. *Journal of Autism and Developmental Disorders*, *23*, 175–183.

Simpson, R. L. & Myles, B. S. (1995b) Facilitated communication and children with disabilities: an enigma in search of a perspective. *Focus on Exceptional Children*, *27*, 1–16.

Singh, I. & Owino, J. E. (1992) A double-blind comparison of zuclopenthixol tablets with placebo in the treatment of mentally handicapped in-patients with associated behavioural disorders. *Journal of Intellectual Disability Research*, *36*, 541–549.

Sinnot-Oswald, M., Gliner, J. A. & Spencer, K. C. (1991) Supported and sheltered employment: quality of life issues. *Education and Training in Mental Retardation*, *26*, 388–397.

Skinner, B. F. (1953) *Science and Human Behavior*. Oxford: Macmillan.

Skinner, D., Rodriquez, P. & Bailey, D. B. (1999) Qualitative analysis of Latino parents' religious interpretations of their child's disability. *Journal of Early Intervention, 22*, 271–285.

Smith, I. & Bryson, S. (1994) Imitation and action in autism: a critical review. *Psychological Bulletin*, *116*, 259–273.

Smith, J. A. (1996) Beyond the divide between cognition and discourse: using interpretative phenomenological analysis in health psychology. *Psychology and Health*, *11*, 261–271.

Smith, J. A., Jarman, M. & Osborn, M. (1999) Doing interpretative phenomenological analysis. In *Qualitative Health Psychology: Theories and Methods* (eds M. Murray & K. Chamberlain), pp. 219–240. London: Sage Publications.

Smith, L. E., Hong, J., Seltzer, M. M., *et al.* (2010) Daily experiences among mothers of adolescents and adults with autism spectrum disorder. *Journal of Autism and Developmental Disorders*, *40*, 167–178.

Smith, M. D. & Belcher, R. G. (1993) Facilitated communication with adults with autism. *Journal of Autism and Developmental Disorders*, *23*, 175–183.

Smith, M. D., Haas, P. J. & Belcher, R. G. (1994) Facilitated communication; the effects of facilitator knowledge and level of assistance on output. *Journal of Autism and Developmental Disorders*, *24*, 357–367.

Sofronoff, K., Attwood, T. & Hinton, S. (2005) A randomized controlled trial of a CBT intervention for anxiety in children with Asperger syndrome. *Journal of Child Psychology and Psychiatry*, *46*, 1152–1160.

Sofronoff, K., Attwood, T., Hinton, S., *et al.* (2007). A randomized controlled trial of a cognitive behavioural intervention for anger management in children diagnosed with Asperger syndrome. *Journal of Autism and Developmental Disorders*, *37*, 1203–1214.

Sorgi, P., Ratey, J., Knoedler, D. W., *et al.* (1991) Rating aggression in the clinical setting, a retrospective adaptation of the overt aggression scale: preliminary results. *Journal of Neuropsychiatry*, *3*, 52–56.

Soule, D., Bell, J. & Smith, D. (1978) *Behavior Maturity Checklist II (BMCL-II)*. Goldsboro, NC: O'Berry Center.

Sparrow, S. S., Balla, D. A. & Cichetti, D. V. (1984) *Vineland Adaptive Behavior Scale: Interview Edition, Survey Form Manual.* Circle Pines, MN: American Guidance Service.

Sperry, L. A. & Mesibov, G. B. (2005) Perceptions of social challenges of adults with autism spectrum disorder. *Autism, 9,* 362–376.

Spreat, S. & Conroy, J. (1998) Use of psychotropic medications for persons with mental retardation who live in Oklahoma nursing homes. *Psychiatric Services, 49,* 510–512.

Spreat, S. & Conroy, J. W. (2002) The impact of deinstitutionalization on family contact. *Research in Developmental Disabilities, 23,* 202–210.

Spreat, S., Conroy, J. W. & Rice, D. M. (1998) Improve quality in nursing homes or institute community placement? Implementation of OBRA for individuals with mental retardation. *Research in Developmental Disabilities, 19,* 507–518.

Stahl, S. M. (2000) The new cholinesterase inhibitors for Alzheimer's disease, part 2: illustrating their mechanisms of action. *Journal of Clinical Psychiatry, 61,* 813–814.

Steele, J., Matos, L. A., Lopez, E. A., *et al.* (2004) A phase 1 safety study of hyperbaric oxygen therapy for amyotrophic lateral sclerosis. *Amyotrophic Lateral Sclerosis, 5,* 250–254.

Sterling, L., Dawson, G., Estes, A., *et al.* (2008) Characteristics associated with presence of depressive symptoms in adults with autism spectrum disorder. *Journal of Autism and Developmental Disorders, 38,* 1011–1018.

Stevens, P. & Martin, N. (1999) Supporting individuals with intellectual disability and challenging behaviour in integrated work settings: an overview and model for service provision. *Journal of Intellectual Disability Research, 43,* 19–29.

Stewart, M. E., Barnard, L., Pearson, J., *et al.* (2006) Presentation of depression in autism and Asperger syndrome: a review. *Autism, 10,* 103–116.

Stigler, K. A., Desmond, L. A., Posey, D. J., *et al.* (2004) A naturalistic retrospective analysis of psychostimulants in pervasive developmental disorders. *Journal of Child and Adolescent Psychopharmacology, 14,* 49–56.

Stoller, K. P. (2005) Quantification of neurocognitive changes before, during, and after hyperbaric oxygen therapy in a case of fetal alcohol syndrome. *Pediatrics, 116,* 586–591.

Stone, W., Ousley, O. & Littleford, C. (1997) Motor imitation in young children with autism: what's the object? *Journal of Abnormal Child Psychology, 25,* 475–485.

Strauss, A. (1987) *Qualitative Analysis for Social Scientists.* New York, NY: Cambridge University Press.

Stuefen, R.M. (2001) *A Collaborative Survey of Families with Children Who Have Disabilities.* Sioux Falls, SD: University of South Dakota Children's Care Hospital and School.

Stuss, D. & Knight, R. (2002) *Principles of Frontal Lobe Function.* New York, NY: Oxford University Press.

Suarez, G. A., Opfer-Gehrking, T. L., Offord, K. P., *et al.* (1999) The Autonomic Symptom Profile: a new instrument to assess autonomic symptoms. *Neurology, 52,* 523–528.

Sullivan, P. F., Neale, M. C. & Kendler, K. S. (2000) Genetic epidemiology of major depression: review and meta-analysis. *American Journal of Psychiatry, 157,* 1552–1562.

Swanson, J. M. (2000) *The SNAP-IV Teacher and Parent Rating Scale.* Irvine, CA: University of California. Available at: www.adhd.net\\snap-iv-form.pdf [accessed May 2011].

Szatmari, P., Bryson, S. E., Boyle, M. H., *et al.* (2003) Predictors of outcome among high functioning children with autism and Asperger syndrome. *Journal of Child Psychology and Psychiatry, 44,* 520–528.

Szempruch, J. & Jacobson, J. (1993) Evaluating facilitated communication skills of people with developmental disabilities. *Research in Developmental Disabilities, 14,* 253–264.

Tani, P., Lindberg, N., Nieminen-von Wendt, T., *et al.* (2003) Insomnia is a frequent finding in adults with Asperger syndrome. *BMC Psychiatry, 3,* 12.

Tantam, D. (2000) Psychological disorder in adolescents and adults with Asperger syndrome. *Autism, 4,* 47–62.

Tarrier, N., Yusupoff, I., Kinney, C., *et al.* (1998) Randomised controlled trial of intensive cognitive behaviour therapy for patients with chronic schizophrenia. *British Medical Journal, 317,* 303–307.

Taylor, B., Miller, E., Farrington, C. P., *et al.* (1999) Autism and measles, mumps, and rubella vaccine: no epidemiological evidence for a causal association. *The Lancet, 353,* 2026–2029.

Taylor, I. & Marrable, T. (2011) Access to social care for adults with autistic spectrum conditions. London: Social Care Institute for Excellence and University of Sussex.

Taylor, J. L., Novaco, R. W., Gillmer, B. T., *et al.* (2005) Individual cognitive-behavioural anger treatment for people with mild-borderline intellectual disabilities and histories of aggression: a controlled trial. *British Journal of Clinical Psychology, 44,* 367–382.

Taylor, J. L., Lindsay, W. R. & Willner, P. (2008) CBT for people with intellectual disabilities: emerging evidence, cognitive ability and IQ effects. *Behavioural and Cognitive Psychotherapy, 36,* 723–734.

Taylor, M. F. (ed.) with Brice, J., Buck, N. & Prentice-Lane, E. (2003) *British Household Panel Survey User Manual Volumes A and B.* Colchester: University of Essex.

The Group, WHOQOL (1998) The World Health Organization Quality of Life Assessment (WHOQOL): development and general psychometric properties. *Social Science and Medicine, 46,* 1569–1585.

Thirumalai, S. S., Shubin, R. A. & Robinson, R. (2002) Rapid eye movement sleep behaviour disorder in children with autism. *Journal of Child Neurology, 17,* 173–178.

Thomas, K., Ellis, R. & McLaurin, C. (2007) Access to care for autism-related services. *Journal of Autism and Developmental Disorders, 37,* 1902–1912.

Toma, C., Rossi, M., Sousa, I., *et al.* (2007) Is ASMT a susceptibility gene for autism spectrum disorders? A replication study in European populations. *Molecular Psychiatry, 12,* 977–979.

Tordjman, S., Anderson, G. M., Pichard, N., *et al.* (2005) Nocturnal excretion of 6-sulphatoxymelatonin in children and adolescents with autistic disorder. *Journal of Biological Psychiatry*, *57*, 134–138.

Trach, J. R. & Rusch, F. R. (1989) Supported employment programme evaluation: evaluating degree of implementation and selected outcomes. *American Journal on Mental Retardation*, *94*, 134–140.

Tsai, L. (2006) Diagnosis and treatment of anxiety disorders in individuals with autism spectrum disorder. In *Stress and Coping in Autism* (eds M. G. Baron, J. Groden, G. Groden, *et al.*), pp. 388–440. New York, NY: Oxford University Press.

Tsakanikos, E., Sturmey, P., Costello, H., *et al.* (2007) Referral trends in mental health services for adults with intellectual disability and autism spectrum disorders. A*utism*, *11*, 9–17.

Tse, J., Strulovitch, J., Tagalakis, V., *et al.* (2007) Social skills training for adolescents with Asperger syndrome and high-functioning autism. *Journal of Autism and Developmental Disorders*, *37*, 1960–1968.

Tulassay, Z., Bodnar, A., Farkas, I., *et al.* (1992) Somatostatin versus secretin in the treatment of actively bleeding gastric erosions. *Digestion*, *51*, 211–216.

Tyrer, P., Oliver-Africano, P. C., Ahmed, Z., *et al.* (2008) Risperidone, haloperidol, and placebo in the treatment of aggressive challenging behaviour in patients with intellectual disability: a randomised controlled trial. *The Lancet*, *371*, 57–63.

Vanden Borre, R., Vermote, R., Buttiëns, M., *et al.* (1993) Risperidone as add-on therapy in behavioural disturbances in mental retardation: a double-blind placebo-controlled cross-over study. *Acta Psychiatrica Scandinavica*, *87*, 167–171.

Vanhaecht, K., Bollmann, M., Bower, K., *et al.* (2007) Prevalence and use of clinical pathways in 23 countries: an international survey by the European Pathway Association. *Journal of Integrated Care Pathways*, *10*, 28–34.

Van Hemert, J. C. J. (1975) Pipamperone (Dipiperon, R3345) in troublesome mental retardates: a double-blind placebo controlled cross-over study with long-term follow-up. *Acta Psychiatrica Scandinavica*, *52*, 237–245.

Vázquez, C. A. (1994) Brief report: a multitask controlled evaluation of facilitated communication. *Journal of Autism and Developmental Disorders*, *24*, 369–379.

Versteeg, D. H. G. (1980) Interaction of peptides related to ACTH, MSH and β–LPH with neurotransmitters in the brain. *Pharmacology and Therapeutics*, *11*, 535–557.

Vickerstaff, S., Heriot, S., Wong, M., *et al.* (2007) Intellectual ability, self-perceived social competence, and depressive symptomatology in children with high-functioning autistic spectrum disorders. *Journal of Autism and Developmental Disorders*, *37*, 1647–1664.

Volkmar, F. R., Cicchetti, D. V., Dykens, E., *et al.* (1988) An evaluation of the Autism Behavior Checklist. *Journal of Autism and Developmental Disorders*, *8*, 81–97.

Volkow, N. D., Wang, G. J., Fowler, J. S., *et al.* (1998) Dopamine transporter occupancies in the human brain induced by therapeutic doses of oral methylphenidate. *American Journal of Psychiatry*, *155*, 1325–1331.

Wagner, M., Newman, L., Cameto, R., *et al.* (2005) *After High School: a First Look at the Postschool Experiences of Youth with Disabilities. A Report from the*

National Longitudinal Transition Study-2 (NLTS-2). Menlo Park, CA: SRI International.

Wagner, S. (2006) Educating the female student with Asperger's. In *Asperger's and Girls: World-renowned Experts Join Those with Asperger's Syndrome to Resolve Issues that Girls and Women Face Every Day!* (eds T. Attwood, T. Grandin, C. Faherty, *et al.*), pp. 15–32. Arlington, TX: Future Horizons.

Wakabayashi, A., Baron-Cohen, S., Wheelwright, S., *et al.* (2006) The Autism-spectrum Quotient (AQ) in Japan: a cross-cultural comparison. *Journal of Autism and Developmental Disorders*, *36*, 263–270.

Walters, A. S. (1995) Toward a better definition of the restless legs syndrome. *Movement Disorders*, *10*, 634–642.

Watanabe, Y., Tsumura, H. & Sasaki, H. (1991) Effect of continuous intravenous infusion of secretin preparation (secrepan) in patients with hemorrhage from chronic peptic ulcer and acute gastric mucosal lesion (AGML). *Gastroenterology Japan*, *26* (Suppl. 3), 86–89.

Webb, B. J., Miller, S. P., Pierce, T. B., *et al.* (2004) Effects of social skill instruction for high-functioning adolescents with autism spectrum disorders. *Focus on Autism and Other Developmental Disabilities*, *19*, 53–62.

Wehman, P. & Kregel, J. (1985) A supported work approach to competitive employment for individuals with moderate and severe handicaps. *The Journal of the Association for Persons with Severe Handicaps*, *10*, 3–11.

Wehman, P., McLaughlin, P. J. & Wehman, T. (2005) *Intellectual and Developmental Disabilities: Toward Full Community Inclusion* (3rd edn). Austin, TX: PRO-ED.

Wehmeyer, M. L. & Bolding, N. (2001) Enhanced self-determination of adults with intellectual disability as an outcome of moving to community-based work or living environments. *Journal of Intellectual Disability Research*, *45*, 371–383.

Weiss, M. J., Wagner, S. & Bauman, M. L. (1996) A validated case study of facilitated communication. *Mental Retardation*, *34*, 220–230.

Wheeler, B., Taylor, B., Simonsen, K., *et al.* (2005) Melatonin treatment in Smith-Magenis syndrome. *Sleep*, *28*, 1609–1610.

Wheeler, D. L., Jacobson, J. W., Paglieri, R. A., *et al.* (1993) An experimental assessment of facilitated communication. *Mental Retardation*, *31*, 49–60.

White, J. F. (2003) Intestinal psychopathology in autism. *Experimental Biology and Medicine*, *228*, 639–649.

Whiting, P. F., Rutjes, A. W. S., Westwood, M. E., *et al.* (2011) QUADAS-2: a revised tool for the quality assessment of diagnostic accuracy studies. *Annals of Internal Medicine*, *155*, 529–536.

Whittle, C. & Hewison, A. (2007) Integrated care pathways: pathways to change in health care? *Journal of Health Organization and Management*, *21*, 297–306.

Wilder, R. M. (1921) The effects of ketonemia on the course of epilepsy. *Mayo Clinic Proceedings*, *2*, 307–308.

Wilkinson, L. A. (2008) The gender gap in Asperger syndrome: where are the girls? *TEACHING Exceptional Children Plus*, *4*, Art. 3. Available at: escholarship.bc.edu/education/tecplus/vol4/iss4/art3 [accessed April 2011].

Williams, K., Wheeler, D. M., Silove, N., *et al.* (2010) Selective serotonin reuptake inhibitors (SSRIs) for autism spectrum disorders (ASD). *Cochrane Database of Systematic Reviews, 8*, Art. No.: CD004677. DOI: 10.1002/14651858.CD004677. pub2

Williams White, S., Keonig, K. & Scahill, L. (2006) Social skills development in children with autism spectrum disorders: a review of the intervention research. *Journal of Autism and Developmental Disorders, 37*, 1858–1868.

Willner, P. (2005) Readiness for cognitive therapy in people with intellectual disabilities. *Journal of Applied Research in Intellectual Disabilities, 19*, 5–16.

Wilson, A., Tobin, M., Ponzio, V., *et al.* (1997) Developing a clinical pathway in depression: sharing our experience. *Australasian Psychiatry, 7*, 17–19.

Wing, L. (1976) *Early Childhood Autism: Clinical, Educational and Social Aspects.* Oxford: Pergamon Press.

Wing, L. (1981) Asperger Syndrome: a clinical account. *Psychological Medicine, 11*, 115–130.

Wing, L. (1988) The autistic continuum. In *Aspects of Autism: Biological Research* (ed. L. Wing). London: Gaskell, Royal College of Psychiatrists and The National Autistic Society.

Wing, L. (2003) *Diagnostic Interview for Social and Communication Disorders* (11th edn). London: National Autistic Society.

Wing, L., Leekam, L., Libby, S., *et al.* (2002) The Diagnostic Interview for Social and Communication Disorders: background, inter-rater reliability and clinical use. *Journal of Child Psychology and Psychiatry, 43*, 307–325.

Wolf, L. C., Noh, S., Fisman, S. N., *et al.* (1989) Brief report: psychological effects of parenting stress on parents of autistic children. *Journal of Autism and Developmental Disorders, 19*, 157–166.

Wood, J. J., Drahota, A., Sze, K., *et al.* (2009) Cognitive behavioral therapy for anxiety in children with autism spectrum disorders: a randomized, controlled trial. *Journal of Child Psychology and Psychiatry, 50*, 224–234.

Woodbury-Smith, M. R., Robinson, J., Wheelwright, S., *et al.* (2005) Screening adults for Asperger syndrome using the AQ: a preliminary study of its diagnostic validity in clinical practice. *Journal of Autism and Developmental Disorders, 35*, 331–335.

World Health Organization (1992) *The ICD-10 Classification of Mental Behavioural Disorders: Clinical Descriptions and Diagnostic Guidelines.* Geneva, Switzerland: WHO.

Yoo, J. H., Valdovinos, M. G. & Williams, D. C. (2007) Relevance of donepezil in enhancing learning and memory in special populations: a review of the literature. *Journal of Autism and Developmental Disorders, 37*, 1883–1901.

Yudofsky, S. C., Silver, J. M., Jackson, W., *et al.* (1986) The overt aggression scale for the objective rating of verbal and physical aggression. *American Journal of Psychiatry, 143*, 35–39.

Zhdanova, I. V., Wurtman, R. J. & Wagstaff, J. (1999) Effects of a low dose of melatonin on sleep in children with Angelman syndrome. *Journal of Pediatric Endocrinology and Metabolism, 12*, 57–67.

Zimmerman, I. L., Steiner, V. G. & Pond, R. E. (1992) *PLS-3: Preschool Language Scale-3*. San Antonio, TX : The Psychological Corporation.

Zucker, N. L., Losh, M., Bulik, C. M., *et al.* (2007) Anorexia nervosa and autism spectrum disorders: guided investigation of social cognitive endophenotypes. *Psychological Bulletin, 133*, 976–1006.

12.   ABBREVIATIONS

3di	Developmental, Dimensional and Diagnostic Interview
5-HT	5-hydroxytryptamine
AAA	Adult Asperger Assessment
AAMD	American Association on Mental Deficiency (now the American Association on Intellectual and Developmental Disability)
ABC	Autism Behavior Checklist
ABS	Adaptive Behavior Scale
ACTH	adrenocorticotrophic hormone
ADHD	attention deficit hyperactivity disorder
ADI (-R)	Autism Diagnostic Interview (Revised)
ADOS (-4, -G)	Autism Diagnostic Observation Schedule (Module 4, Generic)
AEI	Australian Education Index
AGREE	Appraisal of Guidelines for Research and Evaluation Instrument
AMED	Allied and Complementary Medicine Database
AQ (-J, -10, -20, 21, 50)	Autism-spectrum Quotient (Japanese-language, 10-item, 21-item, 50-item full)
ASD	autism spectrum disorders
ASD-DA	Autism Spectrum Disorders Diagnosis Scale for Intellectually Disabled Adults
ASDI	Asperger Syndrome (and high-functioning autism) Diagnostic Interview
ASQ	Autism Screening Questionnaire
ASSIA	Applied Social Services Index and Abstracts
AUC	area under the curve
BEI	British Education Index
BMJ	*British Medical Journal*
BSE (-R)	Behavior Summarized Evaluation (Revised)
CAM	Cambridge Mindreading
CANTAB	Cambridge Neuropsychological Tests: Automated Battery
CARS	Childhood Autism Rating Scale
CBT	cognitive behavioural therapy
CDSR	Cochrane Database of Systematic Reviews
CEAC	cost-effectiveness acceptability curve
CENTRAL	Cochrane Central Register of Controlled Trials

CGA	Clinical Global Assessment
CGI (-I, -S)	Clinical Global Impression (Improvement, Severity) scale
CI	confidence interval
CINAHL	Cumulative Index to Nursing and Allied Health Literature
CPRS	Children's Psychiatric Rating Scale
CPS	Conners' Parent Scale
CSIP	Care Services Improvement Partnership
CU	clinical unit
CY-BOCS	Children's Yale-Brown Obsessive Compulsive Scale
DARE	Database of Abstracts and Reviews of Effectiveness
df	degrees of freedom
DISCO	Diagnostic Interview for Social and Communication Disorders
DOTES	Dosage Treatment Emergent Symptom Scale
DPI	Dundee Provocation Inventory
DSM (-III, -IV, -5, R, -TR)	*Diagnostic and Statistical Manual of Mental Disorders* (3rd edition, 4th edition, 5th edition, revised, text revision)
EconLit	American Economic Association's electronic bibliography
EED	Economic Evaluation Database
Embase	Excerpta Medica database
EQ	Empathy Quotient
ERIC	Education Resources in Curriculum
FACS	Fair Access to Care Services
FN	false negative
FP	false positive
GABA	*gamma*-Aminobutyric acid
GAP	General Assessment Parents Scale
GARS	Gilliam Autistic Rating Scale
GBRS	Global Behaviour Rating Scales
GDG	Guideline Development Group
GP	general practitioner
GRADE	Grading of Recommendations: Assessment, Development and Evaluation
GRP	Guideline Review Panel
HMIC	Health Management Information Consortium
HMSO	Her Majesty's Stationery Office
HoNOS-PbR	Health of the Nation Outcome Scales, Payment by Results
HRQoL	health-related quality of life
HTA	Health Technology Assessment
IBSS	International Bibliography of the Social Sciences

ICD (-10, -11)	*International Classification of Diseases* (10th revision, 11th revision)
ICER	incremental cost-effectiveness ratio
IHP	Intensive Habilitation Programme
IPS	individual placement and support
IQ	intelligence quotient
ITT	intention-to-treat
IU	imperial unit
IV	inverse variance
JAMES	Joint Attention Measure from the EScs (Early Social Communication Scales)
KONTAKT	Frankfurt Social Skills Training programme
LR+	positive likelihood ratio
LR-	negative likelihood ratio
MASC	Movie for the Assessment of Social Cognition
MD	mean difference
MEDLINE	Medical Literature Analysis and Retrieval System Online
M–H	Mantel–Haenszel
MOAS	Modified Overt Aggression Scale
MRC	Medical Research Council
n or N	number of participants
N/A	not applicable
NAO	National Audit Office
NAS	National Autistic Society
NCCMH	National Collaborating Centre for Mental Health
NHS	National Health Service
NICE	National Institute for Health and Clinical Excellence
NIHR	National Institute for Health Research
NIMH	National Institute of Mental Health
NMDA	N-methyl-D-aspartate
NOSIE-30	Nurse's Observation Scale for Inpatient Evaluation
NOS	not otherwise specified
OCD	obsessive–compulsive disorder
OR	odds ratio
ORG 2766	synthetic ACTH (4–9) analogue
PDD (-NOS)	pervasive developmental disorder (not otherwise specified)
PDD-MRS	Pervasive Developmental Disorder in Mental Retardation Scale

PDDRS	Pervasive Developmental Disorders Rating Scale
PEERS	Program for the Education and Enrichment of Relational Skills
PICO	population, intervention, comparison and outcome
PIQ	performance IQ
PLS-3	Preschool Language Scale-3
PSS	personal social services
PsycBOOKS	A full-text database of books and chapters in the American Psychological Association's electronic databases
PsycEXTRA	A grey literature database, which is a companion to PsycINFO
PsycINFO	Psychological Information Database. An abstract (not full text) database of psychological literature from the 1800s to the present
QALY	quality-adjusted life year
QoL-Q	Quality of Life Questionnaire
RAADS (-R)	Ritvo Autism and Asperger's Diagnostic Scale (–Revised)
RCT	randomised controlled trial
ROC	receiver operating characteristics
RQ	review question
RR	relative risk/risk ratio
RUPP	Research Units on Pediatric Psychopharmacology
SBS	Sensory Behavior Schedule
SCIE	Social Care Institute for Excellence
SCQ	Social Communication Questionnaire
SD	standard deviation
SE	standard error
SIB-Q	Self-Injurious Behaviour Questionnaire
SMD	standardised mean difference
SOC	Stockings of Cambridge
SPSS (-PS)	Statistical Package for the Social Sciences (Propensity Score)
SRS	Social Responsiveness Scale
SSA	Social Services Abstracts
SSRI	selective serotonin reuptake inhibitor
TASSK	Test of Adolescent Social Skills Knowledge
TEACCH	Treatment and Education of Autistic and related Communication-Handicapped Children
TN	true negative
TP	true positive
VABS	Vineland Adaptive Behaviour Scale

Abbreviations

VIQ   verbal IQ

X   no data available

WAIS (-III, -R)   Wechsler Adult Intelligence Scale (3rd version, Revised)
WHOQOL   World Health Organization Quality of Life Assessment
WISC (-III, -R)   Wechsler Intelligence Scale for Children (3rd version, Revised)

Y-BOCS   Yale-Brown Obsessive Compulsive Scale